Sport in the Sociocultural Process

Sport in the Sociocultural Process
Third Edition

Marie Hart   *Suite Five Productions*
Greensboro, North Carolina

Susan Birrell   *University of Iowa*

wcb
Wm. C. Brown Company Publishers
Dubuque, Iowa

PHYSICAL EDUCATION

Consulting Editor
  Aileene Lockhart
  Texas Woman's University

HEALTH

Consulting Editor
  Robert Kaplan
  The Ohio State University

PARKS AND RECREATION

Consulting Editor
  David Gray
  California State University, Long Beach

Copyright © 1972, 1976, 1981, by Wm. C. Brown Company Publishers

Library of Congress Catalog Card Number: 80–68191

ISBN 0–697–07099–9

Printed in the United States of America

Contents

Preface

In the past fifteen or twenty years, a growing number of social scientists have been intrigued with the question, What is the meaning of sport in society? That is, what is the signficance that sport comes to have for those individuals or groups who are involved in it? To appreciate the fact that sport provides personal meaning to individuals, we can consult the numerous biographies of sport figures, in which we find ample evidence that sport is indeed important, often serving as the organizing principle around which a person's life is structured. Moreover, through thoughtful and often provocative research, sport psychologists provide more formal data pertinent to an understanding of the personal meaning of sport.

But what is the meaning of sport in *society*? Why is sport endorsed, even sponsored, by such disparate social groupings as a family, a church, a gang; by groups of pool hustlers, prisoners, or friends; by countries engaged in cold war tactics or good will delegations? To all these groupings, or social systems, sport is an important activity not only for the personal enjoyment that those involved derive from it but because of the special meaning sport takes on for the group. In these cases, we can talk about the social significance of sport and investigate the symbolic meaning sport comes to have. These concerns guide the sociologist's investigation of sport as a social activity.

Sociologists explore sport as both a social process and a social product. As a stylized form of the social processes of competition and cooperation and as an activity which generally requires a high degree of coordinated interaction, sport is naturally of interest to many social scientists who study social processes. And yet sport is clearly a social product as well: a cultural artifact so deeply embedded in society that it must be understood in terms of the social context in which it occurs. Our co-operative adherence to a set of mutually agreeable rules reflects our loyalty to the social heritage of each game. It is this social legacy of sport and games that we stress when we refer to "sport in the sociocultural process." And it is these elements of sport that we must analyze if we are to begin to understand the meaning of sport in society.

The meaning of the term *sport* and the meaning sport has in society are two very different things. In terms of definition, sport has some inherent qualities that distinguish it from other activities. While no consensus exists as to the precise definition of sport, most agree that the essence of sport in its purest form can best be denoted with reference to certain characteristics: the voluntary nature of our involvement, the separation from the real world in terms of time and space, the autotelic nature of the activity, the element of self-imposed physical challenge. But qualities or characteristics of sport as an activity do not instill sport with any social meaning. Social meanings are assigned, not inherent. And that is the dominant theme and organizing principle of this anthology.

Many observers fail to understand that sport is devoid of inherent social meanings. When individuals assume that the value system of sport necessarily reflects the status quo, they fail to realize that sport is often adopted by delinquent, deviant, or minority groups who feel that the values represented in sport are not inconsistent with their own somewhat unique ones. Likewise, when commentators bemoan what they perceive as the implicit political bias of sport toward elitism and conservatism, a conception of sport particularly prevalent in the late 1960's, they go beyond essential depictions of sport and make the erroneous assumption that social qualities are inherent in sport. Taken as a whole, the selections included in this anthlogy support a different approach: in order to understand the significance of sport in the variety of contexts in which it occurs, sport must be understood as a symbolic system, as an activity capable of representing and expressing a variety of meanings. Any society or social grouping can project its own meaning on to sport and use sport as a symbol to carry its messages concerning appropriate values, norms and attitudes. Sport then serves as a medium for the expression of normative messages, but not necessarily only those of the dominant or mainstream society.

Using this scheme of interpretation one can easily understand why it is possible that a hundred different nations, representing a wide range of political systems and ideological orientations, can come together at the

Olympic Games, participate in the same activities, and go home confident that sport has helped demonstrate the strength of their own particular system. Without compromise, sport can reflect capitalistic, communistic, fascist, or socialist values because it is what is emphasized using sport as context that is meaningful, not any quality of sport itself.

When sport is conceptualized as a symbolic system, we come to realize that virtually any group or society can use sport as a purveyor of its own ideology, regardless of the content of that ideology. Sport can be examined, then, with reference to its use by either the dominant value system of a society or the conflicting values of a subgroup, subculture, or countercultural group. Moreover, in a very important sense, those groups or individuals who control sport also control a significant message system. Thus, they are in a position to exert considerable power by arranging for their own value system to be transmitted through the innocent activities of play and sport. Subtle as the process can be, the messages get through. Even if these groups never realize the extent to which their control of the symbolic system, sport, has empowered them, their influence is widely felt.

This anthology is based upon the major theme of sport as a system of symbols. The selections in this book are organized around the many related minor themes introduced above. Part I begins with a collection of articles concerned with defining sport, games and play. This is followed by articles reflecting several sociological approaches to the study of sport: an interactionist approach, a structural functionalist approach and a neo-Marxist approach, as well as an article reviewing a series of related empirical cross-cultural studies.

Part II provides a lengthy analysis of the relationship of sport to dominant institutional structures, focusing on North American society. In the last few years, guided perhaps by the academic interest in sport, people have come to understand that sport is more than a few hours fun. It is bigger and more enduring than the individuals who participate in it. The rules to most of our major sports were codified before most of us were born, and the championships which mark the epitome of successful performance—the Stanley Cup, the World Series, Wimbledon—have traditions many generations long. Children learn the game and enjoy it, grow up following it, grow old, die, yet the game remains. Thus we say that sport is an institution: a recognizable, enduring pattern of social life.

It is as an institution that sport has received the recent increase in scholarly attention. The boom of professional sport, the economic overtone to our childhood games, the steady increase of sport as a media product have raised the profile of sport in North American society and made it virtually impossible for people to ignore the salience of sport.

As a high profile institution, sport must be investigated in terms of its interface with other major institutions: the family, the educational system, economics, politics, the media, and religion. In the study of sport's relationship to these institutions, we see sport clearly being used as a symbolic system, as a flexible entity adopted or sponsored by other institutions whenever sport is believed to represent and sustain their values. For example, we see the family endorsing sport only when sport is judged to aid in the attainment of family goals—integration ("the family that plays together stays together") and, more important, moral education. To that end, the family endorses, sponsors, and financially supports youth sport in the community.

Similar patterns are obvious in the financial and moral support furnished sport by other institutions. The sum of money spent to stage an Olympic contest or to send a team to any international contest furnishes one example. If sport were not judged to have a positive relationship to the goals of the nation, could such a thing ever take place? Another example is the presence of sport in the school. If sport were not judged to be consistent with educational goals, would football teams continue to be sponsored, and would school grounds include expensive tracks, playing fields, or swimming pools? Would professional sport exist if it were not deemed economically feasible? Would the church sponsor youth sports if they believed that the values taught through sport were profane or morally unsound? All these systems or institutions work on the assumption that their message, philosophy, or values can be promoted through sport. And this is the major emphasis of Part II of the reader.

Part III presents a variation on that theme. The fact that sport is often used to demonstrate the values of society's dominant institutions does not mean that sport is solely the product of these groups or that the sporting experience is the same for all members of society. Many people are excluded from the mainstreams of society and sport because of some social property, such as social class, sex, or racial or ethnic origin. Not only do financial barriers serve to preserve the class-bound nature of some sports (e.g., yachting or polo) but coventional beliefs about which groups should have access to opportunities and facilities have created more subtle but just as powerful limits to participation. For example, when the *nouveau riche* began to adopt the upper class fad of roller skating in the late 1800's, the old rich abandoned the sport to them, suddently finding it too common. And the conventional beliefs about women's participation in sport have undoubtedly hindered women's pursuit of physical excellence.

Yet, regardless of their exclusion from the mainstream of sport, these groups of individuals continue to embrace sport and to interpret it according to their own needs, with their own style of involvement. The exclusion of Blacks from professional baseball did not kill their love of the game. Instead, they established their own league, separate in opportunity yet equal in skill. Moreover, it is not unusual for immigrants to bring the sports of their old land to a new country and to continue to identify and feel at home with those activities, sometimes using them as a symbol of the retention of their strong nationalistic identity. Thus one focus of Part III is on the significance sport holds for members of the social categories of class, sex, and ethnic origin.

Another focus is upon sport as a subcultural phenomenon, for it sometimes happens that sport, or the practice of certain sports or certain styles of sport, is rejected by the dominant institutional systems of a society and has to rely on subgroup or subcultural sponsorship to survive. King Edward III banned sport in 1365 because it interfered with archery practice and thus the defense of the nation; the Puritans condemned sport as an ungodly form of idleness; legislation has been passed to ban the seemingly vulgar blood sports; and parents sometimes refuse to allow their children to participate in certain dangerous sports. Yet these practices often live on as significant elements of other "deviant" social groups. Often we find sport serving as a platform for statements of countercultural values, as in the Black power salute of the 1968 Olympic Games or the invention of "non-competitive" games for children. For other groups, such as pool hustlers or surf bums, involvement in a particular sport labels them as antisocial or subcultural, and their involvement serves as a badge of their rejection of more dominant, acceptable, societal values.

Part IV turns our attention toward the use of sport as a cultural clue providing important insight into cross-cultural comparisons. Here the issue of sport as a mirror of society is raised. To say "sport is a mirror of society" is in many cases to make so general a statement as to say nothing of sociological significance. As the previous discussion has argued, sport can mirror not only the dominant values of a society but the values of divergent, even deviant, groups within that society as well. However, from another perspective, it does make sense to discuss sport in this way. The dominant and most highly legitimated focus of sport (for example, the national sport of a country) can be used as representative of the structure of sport in a society and thus examined for the purpose of cross-cultural comparisons. Through such a cross-cultural investigation of sport we gain added insight into the process of sport as a meaning creating system. Different cultures adopt or invent different sporting activities, and those differences tell us much about the expressive systems of those cultures. Other seemingly diverse cultures will adopt the same sport, slightly modifying its meaning to conform to their own societal values and meaning systems.

For example, Japan has fanatically adopted the American pastime of baseball. Is there something similar in the American and Japanese value systems and ways of life which is somehow exemplified by the game of baseball? Would an understanding of the structure of baseball somehow furnish new insight into a comparative study of those two cultures? Or is the significance of a comparison of Japanese and American baseball to be found not in the similarities but in the differences between two styles of playing the same game? Further investigation would show that in Libya and among the Pueblo Indians of the American southwest the game of baseball takes on even different meanings while the structure remains essentially unchanged. Part IV discusses sport in cross-cultural contexts and addresses these issues.

Sport in the Sociocultural Process is intended for those interested in the study of sport in society, regardless of whether they are physical educators, sociologists, anthropologists, or other members of the social science community. The book should serve the interests of those who are new to the field and those who already have some understanding of sport in the sociocultural process.

In the eight years which have elapsed since the publication of the first edition of this anthology, the study of sport as a serious social activity has intensified and our body of knowledge about sport has increased significantly. With so much new material available, it is necessary to limit the scope of an anthology in some way. In keeping with the plan of the earlier editions of this anthology, this third edition focuses upon one aspect of our sociological understanding of sport—the sociocultural aspect. Material relevant to the psychology or social psychology of sport has not been included.

The selections have been chosen with an eye to continuity. The themes stated here in the preface recur in each section and serve as a unifying structure for the collection. In this way, an attempt has been made to provide an anthology that can serve as a skeleton text as well.

Appreciation is extended to the authors whose work is reprinted in this anthology, particularly those who contributed original articles. We also wish to thank Rick Gruneau and John Loy for their comments during preparation of the book, and Janie Palmer and Liz Reeves for technical help during manuscript preparation.

Susan Birrell
Hamilton, Ontario

Part I

Play, Games, Sport and Culture

Section A

Definitions

Before one can investigate an important social phenomenon such as sport it is wise to delineate the topic of concern. In this section two scholars—a historian, and a sociologist—present their own ideas about the definition of sport.

The Dutch historian Huizinga considers play not only as precultural and pervading all of life, but also as the recreating and dynamic force which brings about new cultural forms. Huizinga was the first prominent scholar to turn attention to the significance of play in society. By focusing on the element of contest which he found at the root of play, he developed the thesis of play as a culture creating activity, arguing that "in its earliest phases culture has the play-character, . . . it proceeds in the shape and the mood of play."[1]

Loy defines sport with reference to the work of Huizinga and Roger Caillois, but he also extends the definition into a more sociological discussion of the meaning of sport. Loy takes a more systematic and categorical approach than Huizinga, and he describes the social structure of which sport is a part. He pursues the definition from sport as a game occurence to sport as an institutional pattern. In so doing, he provides a useful framework for analyzing the kind and degree of sport involvement of both producers and consumers of sport.

1. Johan Huizinga, *Homo Ludens: A Study of the Play Element in Culture* (Boston: Beacon Press, 1950), p. 46.

The Play-Element in Contemporary Civilization

Johan Huizinga

Let us not waste time arguing about what is meant by "contemporary." It goes without saying that any time we speak of has already become an historical past, a past that seems to crumble away at the hinder end the further we recede from it. Phenomena which a younger generation is constantly relegating to "former days" are, for their elders, part of "our own day," not merely because their elders have a personal recollection of them but because their culture still participates in them. This different time-sense is not so much dependent on the generation to which one happens to belong as on the knowledge one has of things old and new. A mind historically focussed will embody in its idea of what is "modern" and "contemporary" a far larger section of the past than a mind living in the myopia of the moment. "Contemporary civilization" in our sense, therefore, goes deep into the nineteeth century.

The question to which we address ourselves is this: To what extent does the civilization we live in still develop in play-forms? How far does the play-spirit dominate the lives of those who share that civilization? The nineteenth century, we observed, had lost many of the play-elements so characteristic of former ages. Has this leeway been made up or has it increased?

It might seem at first sight that certain phenomena in modern social life have more than compensated for the loss of play-forms. Sport and athletics, as social functions, have steadily increased in scope and conquered ever fresh fields both nationally and internationally.

Contests in skill, strength and perseverence have, as we have shown, always occupied an important place in every culture either in connection with ritual or simply for fun and festivity. Feudal society was only really interested in the tournament; the rest was just popular recreation and nothing more. Now the tournament, with its highly dramatic staging and aristocratic embellishments, can hardly be called a sport. It fulfilled one of the functions of the theatre. Only a numerically small upper class took active part in it. This one-sidedness of medieval sporting life was due in large measure to the influence of the Church. The Christian ideal left but little room for the organized practice of sport and the cultivation of bodily exercise, except insofar as the latter contributed to gentle education. Similarly, the Renaissance affords fairly numerous examples of body-training cultivated for the sake of perfection, but only on the part of individuals, never groups or classes. If anything, the emphasis laid by the Humanists on learning and erudition tended to perpetuate the old under-estimation of the body, likewise the moral zeal and severe intellectuality of the Reformation and Counter-Reformation. The recognition of games and bodily exercises as important cultural values was withheld right up to the end of the eighteenth century.

The basic forms of sportive competition are, of course, constant through the ages. In some the trial of strength and speed is the whole essence of the contest, as in running and skating matches, chariot and horse races, weight-lifting, swimming, diving, marksmanship, etc.[1] Though human beings have indulged in such activities since the dawn of time, these only take on the character of organized games to a very slight degree. Yet nobody, bearing in mind the agonistic principle which animates them, would hesitate to call them games in the sense of play—which, as we have seen, can be very serious indeed. There are, however, other forms of contest which develop of their own accord into "sports." These are the ball-games.

What we are concerned with here is the transition from occasional amusement to the system of organized clubs and matches. Dutch pictures of the seventeenth century show us burghers and peasants intent upon their game of *kolf;* but, so far as I know, nothing is heard of games being organized in clubs or played as matches. It is obvious that a fixed organization of this kind will most readily occur when two groups play against one another. The great ball-games in particular require the existence of permanent teams, and herein lies the starting-point of modern sport. The process arises quite spontaneously in the meeting of village against village, school against school, one part of a town against the rest, etc. That the process started in nineteenth century England is understandable up to a point, though how far the specifically Anglo-Saxon bent of mind can be deemed an efficient cause is less certain. But it cannot be doubted that the structure of English social life had much to do with it. Local self-government encouraged the spirit of association and solidarity. The absence of obligatory military training favoured the occasion for, and the need of, physical exercise. The peculiar form of education tended to work in the same direction, and finally the geography of the country and the nature of the terrain, on the whole flat and, in the ubiquitous commons, offering the most perfect playing-fields that could be desired, were of the greatest importance. Thus England became the cradle and focus of modern sporting life.

Ever since the last quarter of the nineteenth century games, in the guise of sport,[2] have been taken more and more seriously. The rules have become increasingly strict and elaborate. Records are established at a higher, or faster, or longer level than was ever conceivable before. Everybody knows the delightful prints from the first half of the nineteenth century, showing the cricketers in tophats. This speaks for itself.

Now, with the increasing systematization and regimentation of sport, something of the pure play-quality is inevitably lost. We see this very clearly in the official distinction between amateurs and professionals (or "gentlemen and players" as used pointedly to be said). It means that the play-group marks out those for whom playing is no longer play, ranking them inferior to the true players in standing but superior in capacity. The spirit of the professional is no longer the true play-spirit; it is lacking in spontaneity and carelessness.[3] This affects the amateur too, who begins to suffer from an inferiority complex. Between them they push sport further and further away from the play-sphere proper until it becomes a thing *sui generis*: neither play nor earnest. In modern social life sport occupies a place alongside and apart from the cultural process. The great competitions in archaic cultures had always formed part of the sacred festivals and were indispensable as health and happiness-bringing activities. This ritual tie has now been completely severed; sport has become profane, "unholy" in every way and has no organic connection whatever with the structure of society, least of all when prescribed by the government. The ability of modern social techniques to stage mass demonstrations with the maximum of outward show in the field of athletics does not alter the fact that neither the Olympiads nor the organized sports of American Universities nor the loudly trumpeted international contests have, in the smallest degree, raised sport to the level of a culture-creating activity. However important it may be for the players or spectators, it remains sterile. The old play-factor has undergone almost complete atrophy.

This view will probably run counter to the popular feeling of today, according to which sport is the apotheosis of the play-element in our civilization. Nevertheless popular feeling is wrong. By way of emphasizing the fatal shift towards over-seriousness we would point out that it has also infected the non-athletic games where calculation is everything, such as chess and some card-games.

A great many board-games have been known since the earliest times, some even in primitive society, which attached great importance to them largely on account of their chanceful character. Whether they are games of chance or skill they all contain an element of seriousness. The merry play-mood has little scope here, particularly where chance is at a minimum as in chess, draughts, backgammon, halma, etc. Even so all these games remain within the definition of play as given in our first chapter. Only recently has publicity seized on them and annexed them to athletics by mean of public championships, world tournaments, registered records and press reportage in a literary style of its own, highly ridiculous to the innocent outsider.

Card-games differ from board-games in that they never succeed in eliminating chance completely. To the extent that chance predominates they fall into the category of gambling and, as such, are little suited to club life and public competition. The more intellectual card-games, on the other hand, leave plenty of room for associative tendencies. It is in this field that the shift towards seriousness and over-seriousness is so striking. From the day of *ombre* and *quadrille* to whist and bridge, card-games have undergone a process of increasing refinement, but only with bridge have the modern social techniques made themselves master of the game. The paraphernalia of handbooks and systems and professional training has made bridge a deadly earnest business. A recent newspaper article estimated the yearly winnings of the Culbertson couple at more than two hundred thousand dollars. An enormous amount of mental energy is expended in this universal craze for bridge with no more tangible result than the exchange of relatively unimportant sums of money. Society as a whole is neither benefited nor damaged by this futile activity. It seems difficult to speak of it as an elevating recreation in the sense of Aristotle's *diagoge*. Proficiency at bridge is a sterile excellence, sharpening the mental faculties very one-sidedly without enriching the soul in any way, fixing and consuming a quantity of intellectual energy that might have been better applied. The most we can say, I think, is that it might have been applied worse. The status of bridge in modern society would indicate, to all appearances, an immense increase in the play-element today. But appearances are deceptive. Really to play, a man must play like a child. Can we assert that this is so in the case of such an ingenious game as bridge? If not, the virtue has gone out of the game.

The attempt to assess the play-content in the confusion of modern life is bound to lead us to contradictory conclusions. In the case of sport we have an activity nominally known as play but raised to such a pitch of technical organization and scientific thoroughness that the real play-spirit is threatened with extinction. Over against this tendency to over-seriousness, however, there are other phenomena pointing in the opposite direction. Certain activities whose whole *raison d'être* lies in the field of material interest, and which had nothing of play about them in their initial stages, develop what we can only call play-forms as a secondary characteristic. Sport and athletics showed us play stiffening into seriousness but still being felt as play; now we come to serious business degenerating into play but still being called serious. The two phenomena are linked by the strong agonistic habit which still holds universal sway, though in other forms than before.

The impetus given to this agonistic principle which seems to be carrying the world back in the direction of play derives, in the main, from external factors independent of culture proper—in a word, communications, which have made intercourse of every sort so extraordinarily easy for mankind as a whole. Technology, publicity and propaganda everywhere promote the competitive spirit and afford means of satisfying it on an unprecedented scale. Commercial competition does not, of course, belong to the immemorial sacred play-forms. It only appears when trade begins to create fields of activity within which each must try to surpass and outwit his neighbour. Commercial rivalry soon makes limiting rules imperative, namely the trading customs. It remained primitive in essence until quite late, only becoming really intensive with the advent of modern communications, propaganda and statistics. Naturally a certain play-element had entered into business competition at an early stage. Statistics stimulated it with an idea that had originally arisen in sporting life, the idea, namely, of trading records. A record, as the word shows, was once simply a memorandum, a note which the inn-keeper scrawled on the walls of his inn to say that such and such a rider or traveller had been the first to arrive after covering so and so many miles. The statistics of trade and production could not fail to introduce a sporting element into economic life. In consequence, there is now a sporting side to almost every triumph of commerce or technology: the highest turnover, the biggest tonnage, the fastest crossing, the greatest altitude, etc. Here a purely ludic element has, for once, got the better of utilitarian considerations, since the experts inform us that smaller units—less monstrous steamers and aircraft, etc.—are more efficient in the long run. Business becomes play. This process goes so far that some of the great business concerns deliberately instill the play-spirit into their workers so as to step up production. The trend is now reversed: play becomes business. A captain of industry, on whom the Rotterdam Academy of Commerce had conferred an honorary degree, spoke as follows:

> "Ever since I first entered the business it has been a race between the technicians and the sales department. One tried to produce so much that the sales department would never be able to sell it, while the other tried to sell so much that the technicians would never be able to keep pace. This race has always continued: sometimes one is ahead, sometimes the other. Neither my brother nor myself has regarded the business as a task, but always as a game, the spirit of which it has been our constant endeavour to implant into the younger staff."

These words must, of course, be taken with a grain of salt. Nevertheless there are numerous instances of big concerns forming their own Sports Societies and even engaging workers with a view not so much to their professional capacities as to their fitness for the football eleven. Once more the wheel turns.

It is less simple to fix the play-element in contemporary art than in contemporary trade. As we tried to make clear in our tenth chapter, a certain playfulness is by no means lacking in the process of creating and "producing" a work of art. This was obvious enough in the arts of the Muses or "music" arts, where a strong play-element may be called fundamental, indeed, essential to them. In the plastic arts we found that a play-sense was bound up with all forms of decoration; in other words, that the play-function is especially operative where mind and hand move most freely. Over and above this it asserted itself in the master-piece or show-piece expressly commissioned, *the tour de force,* the wager in skill or ability. The question that now arises is whether the play-element in art has grown stronger or weaker since the end of the eighteenth century.

A gradual process extending over many centuries has succeeded in de-functionalizing art and making it more and more a free and independent occupation for individuals called artists. One of the land-marks of this emancipation was the victory of framed canvases over panels and murals, likewise of prints over miniatures and illuminations. A similar shift from the social to the individual took place when the Renaissance saw the main task of the architect no longer in the building of churches and palaces but of dwelling-houses; not in splendid galleries but in drawing-rooms and bed-rooms. Art became more intimate, but also more isolated; it became an affair of the individual and his taste. In the same way chamber music and songs expressly designed for the satisfaction of personal aestheticisms began to surpass the more public forms of art both in importance and often in intensity of expresssion.

Along with these changes in form there went another, even more profound, in the function and appreciation of art. More and more it was recognized as an independent and extremely high cultural value. Right into the eighteenth century art had occupied a subordinate place in the scale of such values. Art was a superior ornament in the live of the privileged. Aesthetic enjoyment may have been as high as now, but it was interpreted in terms of religious exaltation or as a sort of curiosity whose purpose was to divert and distract. The artist was an artisan and in many cases a menial, whereas the scientist or scholar had the status at least of a member of the leisured classes.

The great shift began in the middle of the eighteenth century as a result of new aesthetic impulses which took both romantic and classical form, though the romantic current was the more powerful. Together they brought about an unparalleled rise in aesthetic enjoyment all the more fervent for having to act as a substitute for religion. This is one of the most important phases in the history of civilization. We must leap over the full story of this apotheosis of art and can only point out that the line of art-hierophants runs unbroken from Winckelmann to Ruskin and beyond. All the time, art-worship and connoisseurship remained the privilege of the few. Only towards the end of the nineteenth century did the appreciation of art, thanks largely to photographic reproduction, reach the broad mass of the simply educated. Art becomes public property, love of art *bon ton*. The idea of the artist as a superior species of being gains acceptance, and the public at large is washed by the mighty waves of snobbery. At the same time a convulsive craving for originality distorts the creative impulse. This constant striving after new and unheard-of forms impels art down the steep slope of Impressionism into the turgidities and excrescences of the twentieth century. Art is far more susceptible to the deleterious influences of modern techniques of production than is science. Mechanization, advertising, sensation-mongering have a much greater hold upon art because as a rule it works directly for a market and has a free choice of all the techniques available.

None of these conditions entitles us to speak of a play-element in contemporary art. Since the eighteenth century art, precisely because recognized as a cultural factor, has to all appearances lost rather than gained in playfulness. But is the net result a gain or loss? One is tempted to feel, as we felt about music, that it was a blessing for art to be largely unconscious of its high purport and the beauty it creates. When art becomes self-conscious, that is, conscious of its own grace, it is apt to lose something of its eternal child-like innocence.

From another angle, of course, we might say that the play-element in art has been fortified by the very fact that the artist is held to be above the common run of mortals. As a superior being he claims a certain amount of veneration for his due. In order to savour his superiority to the full he will require a reverential public or a circle of kindred spirits, who will pour forth the requisite veneration more understandingly than the public at large with its empty phrases. A certain esotericism is as necessary for art today as it was of old. Now all esoterics presuppose a convention: we, the initiates, agree to take such and such a thing thus and thus, so we will understsand it, so admire it. In other words, esoterics requires a play-community which shall steep itself in its own mystery. Wherever there is a catch-word ending in -ism we are hot on the tracks of a play-community. The modern apparatus of publicity with its puffy art-criticism, exhibitions and lectures is calculated to heighten the play-character of art.

It is a very different thing to try to determine the play-content of modern science, for it brings us up against a fundamental difficulty. In the case of art we took play as a primary datum of experience, a generally accepted quantity; but when it comes to science we are constantly being driven back on our definition of that quantity and having to question it afresh. If we apply to science our definition of play as an activity occurring within certain limits of space, time and meaning, according to fixed rules, we might arrive at the amazing and horrifying conclusion that all branches of science and learning are so many forms of play because each of them is isolated within its own field and bounded by the strict rules of its own methodolgy. But if we stick to the full terms of our definition we can see at once that, for an activity to be called play, more is needed than limitations and rules. A game is time-bound, we said; it has no contact with any reality outside itself, and its performance is its own end. Further, it is sustained by the consciousness of being a pleasurable, even mirthful, relaxation from the strains of ordinary life. None of this is applicable to science. Science is not only perpetually seeking contact with reality by its usefulness, i.e., in the sense that it is *applied*, it is perpetually trying to establish a universally valid pattern of reality, i.e., as *pure* science. Its rules, unlike those of play, are not unchallengeable for all time. They are constantly being belied by experience and undergoing modification, whereas the rules of a game cannot be altered without spoiling the game itself.

The conclusion, therefore, that all science is merely a game can be discarded as a piece of wisdom too easily come by. But it is legitimate to enquire whether a science is not liable to indulge in play within the closed precincts of its own method. Thus, for instance, the scientist's continued penchant for systems tends in the direction of play. Ancient science, lacking adequate foundation in empiricism, lost itself in a sterile systematization of all conceivable concepts and properties. Though observation and calculation act as a brake in this respect they do not altogether exclude a certain capriciousness in scientific activities. Even the most delicate experimental analysis can be, not indeed manipulated while actually in progress, but played in the interests of subsequent theory. True, the margin of play is always detected in the end, but this detection proves that it exists. Jurists have of old been reproached with similar manoeuvres. Philologists too are not altogether blameless in this respect, seeing that ever since the Old Testament and the Vedas they have delighted in perilous etymologies, a favourite game to this day for those whose curiosity outstrips their knowledge. And is it so certain that the new schools of psychology are not being led astray by the frivolous and facile use of Freudian terminology at the hands of competents and incompetents alike?

Apart from the possibility of the scientific worker or amateur juggling with his own method he may also be seduced into the paths of play by the competitive impulse proper. Though competition in science is less directly conditioned by economic factors than in art, the logical development of civilization which we call science is more inextricably bound up with dialectics than is the aesthetic. In an earlier chapter we discussed the origins of science and philosophy and found that they lay in the agonistic sphere. Science, as some one has not unjustly said, is polemical. But it is a bad sign when the urge to forestall the other fellow in discovery or to annihilate him with a demonstration, looms too large in the work done. The genuine seeker after truth sets little store by triumphing over a rival.

By way of tentative conclusion we might say that modern science, so long as it adheres to the strict demands of accuracy and veracity, is far less liable to fall into play as we have defined it, than was the case in earlier times and right up to the Renaissance, when scientific thought and method showed unmistakable play-characteristics.

These few observations on the play-factor in modern art and science must suffice here, though much has been left unsaid. We are hastening to an end, and it only remains to consider the play-element in contemporary social life at large and especially in politics. But let us be on our guard against two misunderstandings from the start. Firstly, certain play-forms may be used consciously or unconsciously to cover up some social or political design. In this case we are not dealing with the eternal play-element that has been the theme of this book, but with false play. Secondly, and quite independently of this, it is always possible to come upon phenomena which, to a superficial eye, have all the appearance of play and might be taken for permanent play-tendencies, but are, in point of fact, nothing of the sort. Modern social life is being dominated to an ever-increasing extent by a quality that has something in common with play and yields the illusion of a strongly developed play-factor. This quality I have ventured to call by the name of Puerilism,[4] as being the most appropriate appellation for that blend of adolescence and barbarity which has been rampant all over the world for the last two or three decades.

It would seem as if the mentality and conduct of the adolescent now reigned supreme over large areas of civilized life which had formerly been the province of responsible adults. The habits I have in mind are, in themselves, as old as the world; the difference lies in the place they now occupy in our civilization and the brutality with which they manifest themselves. Of these habits that of gregariousness is perhaps the strongest and most alarming. It results in puerilism of the lowest order: yells or other signs of greeting, the wearing of badges and sundry items of political haberdashery, walking in marching order or at a special pace and the whole rigmarole of collective voodoo and mumbo-jumbo. Closely akin to this, if at a slightly deeper psychological level, is the insatiable thirst for trivial recreation and crude sensationalism, the delight in mass-meetings, mass-demonstrations, parades, etc. The club is a very ancient institution, but it is a disaster when whole nations turn into clubs, for these, besides promoting the precious qualities of friendship and loyalty, are also hotbeds of sectarianism, intolerance, suspicion, superciliousness and quick to defend any illusion that flatters self-love or group-consciousness. We have seen great nations losing every shred of honour, all sense of humour, the very idea of decency and fair play. This is not the place to investigate the causes, growth and extent of this world-wide bastardization of culture; the entry of half-educated masses into the international traffic of the mind, the relaxation of morals and the hypertrophy of technics undoubtedly play a large part.

One example of official puerilism must suffice here. It is, as we know from history, a sign of revolutionary enthusiasm when governments play at nine-pins with names, the venerable names of cities, persons, institutions, the calendar, etc. *Pravda*[5] reported that as a result of their arrears in grain deliveries three *kolkhozy* in the district of Kursk, already christened Budenny, Krupskaya and the equivalent of Red Cornfield, has been re-christened Sluggard, Saboteur and Do-Nothing by the local soviet. Though this *trop de zèle* received an official rebuff from the Central Committee and the offensive soubriquets were withdrawn, the puerilistic attiude could not have been more clearly expressed.

Very different is the great innovation of the late Lord Baden-Powell. His aim was to organize the social force of boyhood as such and turn it to good account. This is not puerilism, for it rests on a deep understanding of the mind and aptitudes of the immature; also the Scout Movement expressly styles itself a game. Here, if anywhere, we have an example of a game that comes as close to the culture-creating play of archaic times as our age allows. But when Boy-Scoutism in degraded form seeps through into politics we may well ask whether the puerilism that flourishes in present-day society is a play-function or not. At first sight the answer appears to be a definite yes, and such has been my interpretation of the phenomenon in other studies.[6] I have now come to a different conclusion. According to our definition of play, puerilism is to be distinguished from playfulness. A child playing is not puerile in the pejorative sense we mean here. And if our modern puerilism were genuine play we ought to see civilization returning to the great archaic forms of recreation where ritual, style and dignity are in perfect unison. The spectacle of a society rapidly goose-stepping into helotry is, for some, the dawn of the millennium. We believe them to be in error.

More and more the sad conclusion forces itself upon us that the play-element in culture has been on the wane ever since the eighteenth century, when it was in full flower. Civilization today is no longer played, and even where it still seems to play it is false play—I had almost said, it plays false, so that it becomes increasingly difficult to tell where play ends and non-play begins. This is particularly true of politics. Not very long ago political life in parliamentary democratic form was full of unmistakable play-features. One of my pupils has recently worked up my observations on this subject into a thesis on parliamentary eloquence in France and England, showing how, ever since the end of the eighteenth century, debates in the House of Commons have been conducted according to the rules of a game and in the true play-spirit. Personal rivalries are always at work, keeping up a continual match between the players whose object is to checkmate one another, but without prejudice to the interests of the country which they serve with all seriousness. The mood and manners of parliamentary democracy were, until recently, those of fair play both in England and in the countries that had adopted the English model with some felicity. The spirit of fellowship would allow the bitterest opponents a friendly chat even after the most virulent debate.

It was in this style that the "Gentleman's Agreement" arose. Unhappily certain parties to it were not always aware of the duties implicit in the word gentleman. There can be no doubt that it is just this play-element that keeps parliamentary life healthy, at least in Great Britain, despite the abuse that has lately been heaped upon it. The elasticity of human relationships underlying the political machinery permits it to "play," thus easing tensions which would otherwise be unendurable or dangerous—for it is the decay of humour that kills. We need hardly add that this play-factor is present in the whole apparatus of elections.

In American politics it is even more evident. Long before the two-party system had reduced itself to two gigantic teams whose political differences were hardly discernible to an outsider, electioneering in America had developed into a kind of national sport. The presidential election of 1840 set the pace for all subsequent elections. The party then calling itself Whig had an excellent candidate, General Harrison of 1812 fame, but not platform. Fortune gave them something infinitely better, a symbol on which they rode to triumph: the log cabin which was the old warrior's modest abode during his retirement. Nomination by majority vote, i.e., by the loudest clamour, was inaugurated in the election of 1860 which brought Lincoln to power. The emotionality of American politics lies deep in the origins of the American nation itself: Americans have ever remained true to the rough and tumble of pioneer life. There is a great deal that is endearing in American politics, something naive and spontaneous for which we look in vain in the dragoonings and drillings, or worse, of the contemporary European scene.

Though there may be abundant traces of play in domestic politics there would seem, at first sight, to be little opportunity for it in the field of international relationships. The fact, however, that these have touched the nadir of violence and precariousness does not in itself exclude the possibility of play. As we have seen from numerous examples, play can be cruel and bloody and, in addition, can often be false play. Any law-abiding community or community of States will have charteristics linking it in one way or another to a play-community. International law between States is maintained by the mutual recognition of certain principles which, in effect, operate like play-rules despite the fact that they may be founded in metaphysics. Were it otherwise there would be no need to lay down the *pacta sunt servanda* principle, which explicitly recognizes that the integrity of the system rests on a general willingness to keep to the rules. The moment that one or the other party withdraws from this tacit agreement the whole system of international law must, if only temporarily, collapse unless the remaining parties are strong enough to outlaw the "spoilsport."

The maintenance of international law has, at all stages, depended very largely on principles lying outside the strict domain of law, such an honour, decency, and good form. It is not altogether in vain that the European rules of warfare developed out of the code of honour proper to chivalry. International law tacitly assumed that a beaten Power would behave like a gentleman and a good loser, which unhappily it seldom did. It was a point of international decorum to declare your war officially before entering upon it, though the aggressor often neglected to comply with this awkward convention and began by seizing some outlying colony or the like. But it is true to say that until quite recently war was conceived as a noble game—the sport of kings—and that the absolutely binding character of its rules rested on, and still retained, some of the formal play-elements we found in full flower in archaic warfare.

A cant phrase in current German political literature speaks of the change from peace to war as "das Eintreten des Ernstfalles"—roughly, "the serious development of an emergency." In strictly military parlance, of course, the term is correct. Compared with the sham fighting of manoeuvres and drilling and training, real war is undoubtedly what seriousness is to play. But German political theorists mean something more. The term "Ernstfall" avows quite openly that foreign policy has not attained its full degree of seriousness, has not achieved its object or proved its efficiency, until the stage of actual hostilities is reached. The true relation between States is one of war. All diplomatic intercourse, insofar as it moves in the paths of negotiation and agreement, is only a prelude to war or an interlude between two wars. This horrible creed is accepted and indeed professed by many. It is only logical that its adherents, who regard war and the preparations for it as the sole form of serious politics, should deny that war has any connection with the contest and hence with play. The agonistic factor, they tell us, may have been operative in the primitive stages of civilization, it was all very well then, but war nowadays is far above the competitiveness of mere savages. It is based on the "friend-foe principle." All "real" relationships between nations and States, so they say, are dominated by this ineluctable principle.[7] Any "other" group is always either your friend or your enemy. Enemy, of course, is not to be understood as *inimicus* or $\epsilon\chi\theta\rho o\varsigma$, i.e., a person you hate, let alone a wicked person, but purely and simply as *hostis* or $\pi o\lambda\epsilon\mu\iota o\varsigma$, i.e., the stranger or foreigner who is in your group's way. The theory refuses to regard the enemy even as a rival or adversary. He is merely in your way and is thus to be made away with. If ever anything in history has corresponded to this gross over-simplification of the idea of enmity, which reduces it to an almost mechanical relationship, it is precisely that primitive antagonism between phratries, clans or tribes where, as we saw, the play-element was hypertrophied and distorted. Civilization is supposed to have carried us beyond this stage. I know of no sadder or deeper fall from human reason than Schmitt's barbarous and pathetic delusion about the friend-foe principle. His inhuman cerebrations do not even hold water as a piece of formal logic. For it is not war that is serious, but peace. War and everything to do with it remains fast in the daemonic and magical bonds of play. Only by transcending that pitiable friend-foe relationship will mankind enter into the dignity of man's estate. Schmitt's brand of "seriousness" merely takes us back to the savage level.

Here the bewildering antithesis of play and seriousness presents itself once more. We have gradually become convinced that civilization is rooted in noble play and that, if it is to unfold in full dignity and style, it cannot afford to neglect the play-element. The observance of play-rules is nowhere more imperative than in the relations between countries and States. Once they are broken, society falls into barbarism and chaos. On the other hand we cannot deny that modern warfare has lapsed into the old agonistic attitude of playing at war for the sake of prestige and glory.

Now this is our difficulty: modern warfare has, on the face of it, lost all contact with play. States of the highest cultural pretensions withdraw from the comity of nations and shamelessly announce that "pacta non sunt servanda." By so doing they break the play-rules inherent in any system of international law. To that extent their playing at war, as we have called it, for the sake of prestige is not true play; it, so to speak, plays the play-concept of war false. In contemporary politics, based as they are on the utmost preparedness if not actual preparation for war, there would seem to be hardly any trace of the old play-attitude. The code of honour is flouted, the rules of the game are set aside, international law is broken, and all the ancient associations of war with ritual and religion are gone. Nevertheless the methods by which war-policies are conducted and war-preparations carried out still show abundant traces of the agonistic attitude as found in primitive society. Politics are and have always been something of a game of chance; we have only to think of the challenges, the provocations, the threats and denunciations to realize that war and the policies leading up to it are always, in the nature of things, a gamble, as Neville Chamberlain said in the first days of September 1939. Despite appearances to the contrary, therefore, war has not freed itself from the magic circle of play.

Does this mean that war is still a game, even for the aggressed, the persecuted, those who fight for their rights and their liberty? Here our gnawing doubt whether war is really play or earnest finds unequivocal answer. It is the *moral* content of an action that makes it serious. When the combat has an ethical value it ceases to be play. The way out of this vexing dilemma is only closed to those who deny the objective value and validity of ethical standards. Carl Schmitt's acceptance of the formula that war is the "serious development of an emergency" is therefore correct—but in a very different sense from that which he intended. His point of view is that of the aggressor who is not bound by ethical considerations. The fact remains that politics and war are deeply rooted in the primitive soil of culture played in and as contest. Only through an ethos that transcends the friend-foe relationship and recognizes a higher goal than the gratification of the self, the group or the nation will a political society pass beyond the "play" of war to true seriousness.

So that by a devious route we have reached the following conclusion: real civilization cannot exist in the absence of a certain play-element, for civilization presupposes limitation and mastery of the self, the ability not to confuse its own tendencies with the ultimate and highest goal, but to understand that it is enclosed within certain bounds freely accepted. Civilization will, in a sense, always be played according to certain rules, and true civilization will always demand fair play. Fair play is nothing less than good faith expressed in play terms. Hence the cheat or the spoil-sport shatters civilization itself. To be a sound culture-creating force this play-element must be pure. It must not consist in the darkening or debasing of standards set up by reason, faith or humanity. It must not be a false seeming, a masking of political purposes behind the illusion of genuine play-forms. True play knows no propaganda; its aim is in itself, and its familiar spirit is happy inspiration.

In treating of our theme so far we have tried to keep to a play-concept which starts from the positive and generally recognized characteristics of play. We took play in its immediate everyday sense and tried to avoid the philosophical short-circuit that would assert all human action to be play. Now, at the end of our argument, this point of view awaits us and demands to be taken into account.

"Child's play was what he called all human opinions," says late Greek tradition of Heraclitus.[8] As a pendant to this lapidary saying let us quote at greater length the profound words of Plato which we introduced into our first chapter: "Though human affairs are not worthy of great seriousness it is yet necessary to be serious; happiness is another thing. . . . I say that a man must be serious with the serious, and not the other way about. God alone is worthy of supreme seriousness, but man is made God's plaything, and that is the best part of him. Therefore every man and woman should live life accordingly, and play the noblest games, and be of another mind from what they are at present. For they deem war a serious thing, though in war there is neither play nor culture worthy the name, which are the things *we* deem most serious. Hence all must live in peace as well as they possibly can. What, then, is the right way of living? Life must be lived as play, playing certain games, making sacrifices, singing and dancing, and then a man will be able to propitiate the gods, and defend himself against his enemies, and win in the contest." Thus "men will live according to Nature since in most respects they are puppets, yet having a small part in truth." To which Plato's companion rejoins: "You make humanity wholly bad for us, friend, if you say that." And Plato answers: "Forgive me. It was with my eyes on God and moved by Him that I spoke so. If you like, then, humanity is not wholly bad, but worthy of some consideration."[9]

The human mind can only disengage itself from the magic circle of play by turning towards the ultimate. Logical thinking does not go far enough. Surveying all the treasures of the mind and all the splendours of its achievements we shall still find, at the bottom of every serious judgement, something problematical left. In our heart of hearts we know that none of our pronouncements is absolutely conclusive. At that point, where our judgment begins to waver, the feeling that the world is serious after all wavers with it. Instead of the old saw: "All is vanity," the more positive conclusion forces itself upon us that "all is play." A cheap metaphor, no doubt, mere impotence of the mind; yet it is the wisdom Plato arrived at when he called man the plaything of the gods. In singular imagery the thought comes back again in the *Book of Proverbs*, where Wisdom says: "The Lord possessed me in the beginning of his ways, before he made any thing from the beginning. I was set up from eternity, and of old before the earth was made. . . . I was with him forming all things: and was delighted every day, playing before him at all times; playing in the world. And my delights were to be with children of men."[10]

Whenever we are seized with vertigo at the ceaseless shuttlings and spinnings in our mind of the thought: What is play? What is serious? we shall find the fixed, unmoving point that logic denies us, once more in the sphere of ethics. Play, we began by saying, lies outside morals. In itself it is neither good nor bad. But if we have to decide whether an action to which our will impels us is a serious duty or is licit as play, our moral conscience will at once provide the touchstone. As soon as truth and justice, compassion and forgiveness have part in our resolve to act, our anxious question loses all meaning. One drop of pity is enough to lift our doing beyond intellectual distinctions. Springing as it does from a belief in justice and divine grace, conscience, which is moral awareness, will always whelm the question that eludes and deludes us to the end, in a lasting silence.

NOTES

1. A happy variation of the natatorial contest is found in *Beowulf*, where the aim is to hold your opponent under water until he is drowned.
2. It is probably significant that we no longer speak of "games" but of "sport." Our author may not have been sufficiently familiar with the development of "sport" in the last ten or twenty years, here and in America, to stress the all-important point that sport has become a business, or, to put it bluntly, a commercial racket. Trans.
3. Note G. K. Chesterton's dictum: If a thing is worth doing at all it is worth doing badly! Trans.
4. Cf. *In the Shadow of To-morrow*, Heinemann, 1936, chapter 16.
5. January 9th, 1935.
6. *Over de grenzen van spel en ernst in de cultuur*, p. 25, and *In the Shadow of To-morrow*, ch. 16.
7. Carl Schmitt, *Der Begriff des Politischen*, Hamburg, 1933.
8. *Fragments*, 70.
9. *Laws*, 803-4; cf. also 685. Plato's words echo sombrely in Luther's mouth when he says: "All creatures are God's masks and mummeries" (Erlanger Ausgabe, xi, p. 115).
10. viii, 22-3, 30-1. This is the Douay translation, based on the Vulgate. The text of the English A.V. and R.V. does not bring out the idea of "play."

The Nature of Sport: A Definitional Effort

John W. Loy, Jr.

Sport is a highly ambiguous term having different meanings for various people. Its ambiguity is attested to by the range of topics treated in the sport sections of daily newspapers. Here one can find accounts of various sport competitions, advertisements for the latest sport fashions, advice on how to improve one's skills in certain games, and essays on the state of given organized sports, including such matters as recruitment, financial success, and scandal. The broad yet loose encompass of sport reflected in the mass media suggests that sport can and perhaps should be dealt with on different planes of discourse if a better understanding of its nature is to be acquired. As a step in this direction we shall discuss sport as a game occurrence, as an institutional game, as a social institution, and as a social situation or social system.

I. SPORT AS A GAME OCCURRENCE

Perhaps most often when we think of the meaning of sport, we think of sports. In our perspective sports are considered as a specialized type of game. That is, a sport as one of the many "sports" is viewed as an actual game occurence or event. Thus in succeeding paragraphs we shall briefly outline what we consider to be the basic characteristics of games in general. In describing these characteristics we shall continually make reference to sports in particular as a special type of game. A game we define as any form of playful competition whose outcome is determined by physical skill, strategy, or chance employed singly or in combination.[1]

IA. "Playful." By "playful competition" we mean that any given contest has one or more elements of play. We purposely have not considered game as a subclass of play,[2] for if we had done so, sport would logically become a subset of play and thus preclude the subsumption of professional forms of sport under our definition of the term. However, we wish to

From *Quest,* Monograph X (May, 1968): 1-15.

recognize that one or more aspects of play constitute basic components of games and that even the most highly organized forms of sport are not completely devoid of play characteristics.

The Dutch historian Johan Huizinga has made probably the most thorough effort to delineate the fundamental qualities of play. He defines play as follows:

> Summing up the formal characteristics of play we might call it a free activity standing quite consciously outside "ordinary" life as being "not serious," but at the same time absorbing the player intensely and utterly. It is an activity connected with no material interest, and no profit can be gained by it. It proceeds within its own proper boundaries of time and space according to fixed rules and in an orderly manner. It promotes the formation of social groupings which tend to surround themselves with secrecy and to stress their differences from the common world by disguise or other means (Huizinga, 1955, p. 13).

Caillois has subjected Huizinga's definition to critical analysis (Caillois, 1961, pp. 3-10) and has redefined play as an activity which is free, separate, uncertain, unproductive, and governed by rules and make-believe (*Ibid.*, pp. 9-10). We shall briefly discuss these qualities ascribed to play by Huizinga and Caillois and suggest how they relate to games in general and to sports in particular.

IA1. "Free." By free is meant that play is a voluntary activity. That is, no one is ever strictly forced to play, playing is done in one's free time, and playing can be initiated and terminated at will. This characteristic of play is no doubt common to many games, including some forms of amateur sport. It is not, however, a distinguishing feature of all games, especially those classified as professional sport.

IA2. "Separate." By separate Huizinga and Caillois mean that play is spatially and temporally limited. This feature of play is certainly relevant to sports. For many, if not most, forms of sport are conducted in spatially circumscribed environments, examples being the bullring, football stadium, golf course, race track, and swimming pool. And with few exceptions every form of sport has rules which precisely determine the duration of a given contest.

IA3. "Uncertain." The course or end result of play cannot be determined beforehand. Similarly, a chief characteristic of all games is that they are marked by an uncertain outcome. Perhaps it is this factor more than any other which lends excitement and tension to any contest. Strikingly uneven competition is routine for the contestants and boring for the spectators; hence efforts to insure a semblance of equality between opposing sides are a notable feature of sport. These efforts typically focus on the matters of size, skill, and experience. Examples of attempts to establish equality based on size are the formation of athletic leagues and conferences composed of social organizations of similar size and the designation of weight class for boxers and wrestlers. Illustrations of efforts to insure equality among contestants on the basis of skill and experience are the establishment of handicaps for bowlers and golfers, the designation of various levels of competition within a given organization as evidenced by freshman, junior varsity, and varsity teams in scholastic athletics, and the drafting of players from established teams when adding a new team to a league as done in professional football and basketball.

IA4. "Unproductive." Playing does not in itself result in the creation of new material goods. It is true that in certain games such as poker there may occur an exchange of money or property among players. And it is a truism that in professional sports victory may result in substantial increases of wealth for given individuals. But the case can be made, nevertheless, that a game *per se* is non-utilitarian.[3] For what is produced during any sport competition is a game, and the production of the game is generally carried out in a prescribed setting and conducted according to specific rules.

IA5. "Governed by rules." All types of games have agreed-upon rules, be they formal or informal. It is suggested that sports can be distinguished from games in general by the fact that they usually have a greater variety of norms and a larger absolute number of formal norms (i.e., written prescribed and proscribed rules.[4] Similarly, there is a larger number of sanctions and more stringent ones in sports than in games. For example, a basketball player must leave the game after he has committed a fixed number of fouls; a hockey player must spend a certain amount of time in the penalty box after committing a foul; and a football player may be asked to leave the game if he shows unsportsmanlike conduct.

With respect to the normative order of games and sports, one explicit feature is that they usually have definite criteria for determining the winner. Although it is true that some end in a tie, most contests do not permit such an ambivalent termination by providing a means of breaking a deadlock and ascertaining the "final" victor. The various means of determining the winner in sportive endeavors are too numerous to enumerate. But it is relevant to observe that in many sport competitions where "stakes are high," a series of contests are held between opponents in an effort to rule out the element of chance and decide the winner on the basis of merit. A team may be called "lucky" if it beats an opponent once by a narrow margin; but if it does so repeatedly, then the appelations of "better" or "superior" are generally applied.

IA6. "Make-believe." By the term make-believe Huizinga and Caillois wish to signify that play stands outside "ordinary" or "real" life and is distinguished by an "only pretending quality." While some would deny this characteristic of play as being applicable to sport, it is interesting to note that Veblen at the turn of the century stated:

> Sports share this characteristic of make-believe with the games and exploits to which children, especially boys, are habitually inclined. Make-believe does not enter in the same proportion into all sports, but it is present in a very appreciable degree in all (Veblen, 1934, p. 256).

Huizinga observes that the " 'only pretending' quality of play betrays a consciousness of the inferiority of play compared with 'seriousness' " (Huizinga, 1955, p. 8). We note here that occasionally one reads of a retiring professional athlete who remarks that he is "giving up the game to take a real job"[5] and that several writers have commented on the essential shallowness of sport.[6] Roger Kahn, for example, has written that:

> The most fascinating and least reported aspect of American sports is the silent and enduring search for a rationale. Stacked against the atomic bomb or even against a patrol in Algeria, the most exciting rally in history may not seem very important, and for the serious and semi-serious people who make their living through sports, triviality is a nagging, damnable thing. Their drive for self-justification has contributed much to the development of sports (Kahn, 1957, p. 10).

On the other hand, Huizinga is careful to point out that "the consciousness of play being 'only pretend' does not by any means prevent it from proceeding with the utmost seriousness" (Huizinga, 1955, p. 8). As examples, need we mention the seriousness with which duffers treat their game of golf, the seriousness which fans accord discussions of their home team, or the seriousness that national governments give to Olympic Games and university alumni to collegiate football?[7,8]

Accepting the fact that the make-believe quality of play has some relevance for sport, it nevertheless remains difficult to empirically ground the "not-ordinary-or-real-life" characteristic of play. However, the "outside-of-real-life" dimension of a game is perhaps best seen in its "as-if" quality, its artificial obstacles, and its potential resources for actualization or production.

IA6(a). In a game the contestants act as if all were equal, and numerous aspects of "external reality" such as race, education, occupation, and financial status are excluded as relevant attributes for the duration of a given contest.[9]

IA6(b). The obstacles individuals encounter in their workaday lives are not usually predetermined by them and are "real" in the sense that they must be adequately coped with if certain inherent and socially conditioned needs are to be met; on the other hand, in games obstacles are artificially created to be overcome. Although these predetermined obstacles set up to be conquered can sometimes attain "life-and-death" significance, as in a difficult Alpine climb, they are not usually essentially related to an individual's daily toil for existence.[10]

IA6(c). Similarly, it is observed that in many "real" life situations the structures and processes needed to cope with a given obstacle are often not at hand; however, in a play or game situation all the structures and processes necessary to deal with any deliberately created obstacle and to realize any possible alternative in course of action are potentially available.[11]

In sum, then, games are playful in that they typically have one or more elements of play: freedom, separateness, uncertainty, unproductiveness, order, and make-believe. In addition to having elements of play, games have components of competition.

IB. "Competition." Competition is defined as a struggle for supremacy between two or more opposing sides. We interpret the phrase "between two or more opposing sides" rather broadly to encompass the competitive relationships between man and other objects of nature, both animate and inanimate. Thus competitive relationships include:

1. competition between one individual and another, e.g., a boxing match or a 100-yard dash;
2. competition between one team and another, e.g., a hockey game or a yacht race;
3. competition between an individual or a team and an animate object of nature, e.g., a bullfight or a deer-hunting party;
4. competition between an individual or a team and an inanimate object of nature, e.g., a canoeist running a set of rapids or a mountain climbing expedition; and finally,
5. competition between an individual or team and an "ideal" standard e.g., an individual attempting to establish a world land-speed record on the Bonneville salt flats or a basketball team trying to set an all-time scoring record. Competition against an "ideal" standard might also be conceptualized as man against time or space, or as man against himself.[12]

The preceding classification has been set forth to illustrate what we understand by the phrase "two or more opposing sides" and is not intended to be a classification of competition *per se*. While the scheme may have some relevance for such a purpose, its value is limited by the fact that its categories are neither mutually exclusive nor inclusive. For instance, an athlete competing in a cross-country race may be competitively involved in all of the following ways: as an individual against another individual; as a team member against members of an opposing team; and as an individual or team member against an "ideal" standard (e.g., an attempt to set an individual and/or team record for the course).[13]

IC. "Physical skill, strategy, and chance." Roberts and Sutton-Smith suggest that the various games of the world can be classified:

> . . . on the basis of outcome attributes: (1) games of *physical skill,* in which the outcome is determined by the players' motor activities; (2) games of *strategy,* in which the outcome is determined by rational choices among possible courses of action; and (3) games of *chance,* in which the outcome is determined by guesses or by some uncontrolled artifact such as a die or wheel (Roberts and Sutton-Smith, 1962, p. 166).

Examples of relatively pure forms of competitive activities in each of these categories are weight-lifting contests, chess matches, and crap games, respectively. Many, if not most, games are, however, of a mixed nature. Card and board games, for instance, generally illustrate a combination of strategy and chance. Whereas most sports reflect a combination of strategy and physical skill. Although chance is also associated with sport, its role in determining the outcome of a contest is generally held to a minimum in order that the winning side can attribute its victory to merit rather than to a fluke of nature. Rather interestingly it appears that a major role of chance in sport is to insure equality. For example, the official's flip of a coin before the start of a football game randomly determines what team will receive the kickoff and from what respective side of the field; and similarly the drawing of numbers by competitors in track and swimming is an attempt to assure them equal opportunity of getting assigned a given lane.

ID. "Physical prowess." Having discussed the characteristics which sports share in common with games in general, let us turn to an account of the major attribute which distinguishes sports in particular from games in general. We observe that sports can be distinguished from games by the fact that they demand the demonstration of physical prowess. By the phrase "the demonstration of physical prowess" we mean the employment of developed physical skills and abilities within the context of gross physical activity to conquer an opposing object of nature. Although many games require a minimum of physical skill, they do not usually demand the degree of physical skill required by sports. The idea of "developed physical skills" implies much practice and learning and suggests the attainment of a high level of proficiency in one or more general physical abilities relevant to sport competition, e.g., strength, speed, endurance, or accuracy.

Although the concept of physical prowess permits sports to be generally differentiated from games, numerous borderline areas exist. For example, can a dart game among friends, a horseshoe pitching contest between husband and wife, or a fishing contest between father and son be considered sport? One way to arrive at an answer to these questions is to define a sport as any highly organized game requiring physical prowess. Thus a dart game with friends, a horseshoe pitching contest between spouses, or a fishing contest between a father and son would not be considered sport; but formally sponsored dart, horseshoe, or fishing tournaments would be legitimately labelled sport. An alternative approach to answering the aforementioned questions, however, is to define a sport as an institutionalized game demanding the demonstration of physical prowess. If one accepts the latter approach, then he will arrive at a different set of answers to the above questions. For this approach views a game as a unique event and sport as an institutional pattern. As Weiss has rather nicely put it:

> A game is an occurrence; a sport is a pattern. The one is in the present, the other primarily past, but instantiated in the present. A sport defines the conditions to which the participants must submit if there is to be a game; a game gives rootage to a set of rules and thereby enables a sport to be exhibited (1967, p. 82).

II.   SPORT AS AN INSTITUTIONALIZED GAME

To treat sport as an institutionalized game is to consider sport as an abstract entity. For example, the organization of a football team as described in a rule book can be discussed without reference to the members of any particular team; and the relationships among team members can be characterized without reference to unique personalities or to particular times and places. In treating sport as an institutionalized game we conceive of it as distinctive, enduring patterns of culture and social structure combined into a single complex, the elements of which include values, norms, sanctions, knowledge, and social positions (i.e., roles and statuses).[14] A firm grasp of the meaning of "institutionalization" is necessary for understanding the idea of sport as an institutional pattern, or blueprint if you will, guiding the organization and conduct of given games and sportive endeavors.

The formulation of a set of rules for a game or even their enactment on a particular occasion does not constitute a sport as we have conceptualized it here. The institutionalization of a game implies that it has a tradition of past exemplifications and definite guidelines for future realizations. Moreover, in a concrete game situation the form of a particular sport need not reflect all the characteristics represented in its institutional pattern. The more organized a sport contest in a concrete setting, however, the more likely it will illustrate the institutionalized nature of a given sport. A professional baseball game, for example, is a better illustration of the institutionalized nature of baseball than is a sandlot baseball game; but both games are based on the same institutional pattern and thus may both be considered forms of sport. In brief, a sport may be treated analytically in terms of its degree of institutionalization and dealt with empirically in terms of its degree of organization. The latter is an empirical instance of the former.

In order to illustrate the institutionalized nature of sport more adequately, we contrast the organizational, technological, symbolic, and educational spheres of sports with those of games. In doing so we consider both games and sports in their most formalized and organized state. We are aware that there are institutionalized games other than sports which possess characteristics similar to the ones we ascribe to sports, as for example chess and bridge; but we contend that such games are in the minority and in any case are excluded as sports because they do not demand the demonstration of physical prowess.

IIA. "Organizational sphere." For present purposes we rather arbitrarily discuss the organizational aspects of sports in terms of teams, sponsorship, and government.

IIAI. "Teams." Competing sides for most games are usually selected rather spontaneously and typically disband following a given contest. In sports, however, competing groups are generally selected with care and, once membership is established, maintain a stable social organization. Although individual persons may withdraw from such organizations after they are developed, their social positions are taken up by others, and the group endures.[15]

Another differentiating feature is that as a rule sports show a greater degree of role differentiation than games do. Although games often involve several contestants (e.g., poker), the contestants often perform identical activities and thus may be considered to have the same roles and statuses. By contrast, in sports involving a similar number of participants (e.g., basketball), each individual or combination of just a few individuals performs specialized activities within the group and may be said to possess a distinct role. Moreover, to the extent that such specialized and differentiated activities can be ranked in terms of some criteria, they also possess different statuses.

IIA2. "Sponsorship." In addition to there being permanent social groups established for purposes of sport competition, there is usually found in the sport realm social groups which act as sponsoring bodies for sport teams. These sponsoring bodies may be characterized as being direct or indirect. Direct sponsoring groups include municipalities which sponsor Little League baseball teams, universities which support collegiate teams, and business corporations which sponsor AAU teams. Indirect sponsoring groups include sporting goods manufacturers, booster clubs, and sport magazines.

IIA3. "Government." While all types of games have at least a modicum of norms and sanctions associated with them, the various forms of sport are set apart from any games by the fact that they have more—and more formal and more institutionalized—sets of these cultural elements. In games rules are often passed down by oral tradition or spontaneously established for a given contest and forgotten afterwards; or, even where codified, they are often simple and few. In sports rules are usually many, and they are formally codified and typically enforced by a regulatory body. There are international organizations governing most sports, and in America there are relatively large social organizations governing both amateur and professional sports. For example, amateur sports in America are controlled by such groups as the NCAA, AAU, and AIAW; and the major professional sports have national commissioners with enforcing officials to police competition.

IIB. "Technological sphere." In a sport, technology denotes the material equipment, physical skills, and body of knowledge which are necessary for the conduct of competition and potentially available for technical improvements in competition. While all types of games require a minimum of knowledge and often a minimum of physical skill and material equipment, the various sports are set apart from many games by the fact that they typically require greater knowledge and involve higher levels of physical skill and necessitate more material equipment. The technological aspects of a sport may be dichotomized into those which are intrinsic and those which are extrinsic. Intrinsic technological aspects of a sport consist of the physical skills, knowledge, and equipment which are required for the conduct of a given contest *per se*. For example, the intrinsic technology of football includes: (a) the equipment necessary for the game—field, ball, uniform, etc.; (b) the repertoire of physical skills necessary for the game—running, passing, kicking, blocking, tack-ling, etc.; and (c) the knowledge necessary for the game—rules, strategy, etc. Examples of extrinsic technological elements associated with foot-ball include: (a) physical equipment such as stadiums, press facilities, dressing rooms, etc.; (b) physical skills such as possessed by coaches, cheer leaders, and ground crews; and (c) knowledge such as possessed by coaches, team physicians, and spectators.

IIC. "Symbolic sphere." The symbolic dimension of a sport includes elements of secrecy, display, and ritual. Huizinga contends that play "pro-motes the formation of social groupings which tend to surround them-selves with secrecy and to stress their difference from the common world by disguise or other means" (1955, p. 13). Caillois criticizes his conten-tion and states to the contrary that "play tends to remove the very nature of the mysterious." He further observes that "when the secret, the mask or the costume fulfills a sacramental function one can be sure that not play, but an institution is involved" (1961, p. 4).

Somewhat ambivalently we agree with both writers. On the one hand, to the extent that Huizinga means by "secrecy" the act of making distinctions between "play life" and "ordinary life," we accept his prop-osition that groups engaged in playful competition surround themselves with secrecy. On the other hand, to the extent that he means by "secrecy" something hidden from others, we accept Caillois's edict that an insti-tution and not play is involved.

IIC1. The latter type of secrecy might well be called "sanctioned secrecy" in sports, for there is associated with many forms of sport com-petition rather clear norms regarding approved clandestine behavior. For example, football teams are permitted to set up enclosed practice fields, send out scouts to spy on opposing teams, and exchange a limited num-ber of game films revealing the strategies of future opponents. Other kinds of clandestine action such as slush funds established for coaches and gambling on games by players are not always looked upon with such favor.[16]

IIC2. A thorough reading of Huizinga leads one to conclude that what he means by secrecy is best discussed in terms of display and ritual. He points out, for example, that "the 'differentness' and secrecy of play are most vividly expressed in 'dressing up'" and states that the higher forms of play are "a contest *for* something or a representation *of* some-thing"—adding that "representation means display" (1955, p. 13). The "dressing-up" element of play noted by Huizinga is certainly characteristic of most sports. Perhaps it is carried to its greatest height in bullfighting, but it is not absent in some of the less overt forms of sport. Veblen writes:

> It is noticeable, for instance, that even very mild-mannered and matter-of-fact men who go out shooting are apt to carry an excess of arms and accoutrements in order to impress upon their own imagination the seriousness of their undertaking. These huntsmen are also prone to a histrionic, prancing gait and to an elaborate exaggeration of the motions, whether of stealth or of onslaught, involved in their deeds of exploit (1934, p. 256).

A more recent account of "dressing-up" and display in sports has been given by Stone (1955), who treats display as spectacle and as a counterforce to play. Stone asserts that the tension between the forces of play and display constitute an essential component of sport. The following quotation gives the essence of his account:

> Play and dis-play are precariously balanced in sport, and, once that balance is upset, the whole character of sport in society may be affected. Furthermore, the spectacular element of sport, may, as in the case of American professional wrestling, destroy the game. The rules cease to apply, and the "cheat" and the "spoilsport" replace the players.
>
> The point may be made in another way. The spectacle is predictable and certain; the game, unpredictable and uncertain. Thus spectacular display may be reckoned from the outset of the performance. It is announced by the appearance of the performers—their physiques, costumes, and gestures. On the other hand, the spectacular play is solely a function of the uncertainty of the game (pp. 261-62 in Larrabee and Meyershon). (Stone, 1955, p. 98).

In a somewhat different manner another sociologist, Erving Goffman, has analyzed the factors of the uncertainty of a game and display. Concerning the basis of "fun in games" he states that "mere uncertainty of outcome is not enough to engross the players" (1961, p. 68) and suggests that a successful game must combine "sanctioned display" with problematic outcome. By display Goffman means that "games give the players an opportunity to exhibit attributes valued in the wider social world, such as dexterity, strength, knowledge, intelligence, courage, and self-control" (*Ibid.*). Thus for Goffman display represents spectacular play involving externally relevant attributes, while for Stone display signifies spectacular exhibition involving externally non-relevant attributes with respect to the game situation.

IIC3. Another concept related to display and spectacle and relevant to sports is that of ritual. According to Leach, "ritual denotes those aspects of prescribed formal behavior which have no direct technological consequences" (1964, p. 607). Ritual may be distinguished from spectacle by the fact that it generally has a greater element of drama and is less ostentatious and more serious. "Ritual actions are 'symbolic' in that they assert something about the state of affairs, but they are not necessarily purposive: i.e., the performer of ritual does not necessarily seek to alter the state of affairs" (*Ibid.*). Empirically ritual can be distinguished from spectacle by the fact that those engaged in ritual express an attitude of solemnity toward it, an attitude which they do not direct toward spectacle.

Examples of rituals in sport are the shaking of hands between team captains before a game, the shaking of hands between coaches after a game, the singing of the national anthem before a game, and the singing of the school song at the conclusion of a game.[17]

IID. "Educational sphere." The educational sphere focuses on those activities related to the transmission of skills and knowledge to those who lack them. Many if not most people learn to play the majority of socially preferred games in an informal manner. That is, they acquire the required skills and knowledge associated with a given game through the casual instruction of friends or associates. On the other hand, in sports, skills and knowledge are often obtained by means of formal instruction. In short, the educational sphere of sports is institutionalized, whereas in most games it is not. One reason for this situation is the fact that sports require highly developed physical skills which games often do not; to achieve proficiency requires long hours of practice and qualified instruction, i.e., systematized training. Finally, it should be pointed out that associated with the instructional personnel of sport programs are a number of auxiliary personnel such as managers, physicians, and trainers—a situation not commonly found in games.

III. SPORT AS A SOCIAL INSTITUTION

Extending our notion of sport as an institutional pattern still further, we note that in its broadest sense, the term sport supposes a social institution. Schneider writes that the term institution:

> . . . denotes an aspect of social life in which distinctive value-orientations and interests, centering upon large and important social concern . . . generate or are accompanied by distinctive modes of social interaction. Its use emphasizes "important" social phenomena; relationships of "strategic structural significance" (1964, p. 338).

We argue that the magnitude of sport in the Western world justifies its consideration as a social institution. As Boyle succinctly states:

Sport permeates any number of levels of contemporary society, and it touches upon and deeply influences such disparate elements as status, race relations, business life, automotive design, clothing styles, the concept of the hero, language, and ethical values. For better or worse it gives form and substance to much in American life (1963, pp. 3-4).

When speaking of sport as a social institution, we refer to the sport order. The sport order is composed of all organizations in society which organize, facilitate, and regulate human action in sport situations. Hence, such organizations as sporting goods manufacturers, sport clubs, athletic teams, national governing bodies for amateur and professional sports, publishers of sport magazines, etc., are part of the sport order. For analytical purposes four levels of social organization within the sport order may be distinguished: namely, the primary, technical, managerial, and corporate levels.[18] Organizations at the primary level permit face-to-face relationships among all members and are characterized by the fact that administrative leadership is not formally delegated to one or more persons or positions. An example of a social organization associated with sport at the primary level is an informally organized team in a sandlot baseball game.

Organizations at the technical level are too large to permit simultaneous face-to-face relationships among their members but small enough so that every member knows of every other member. Moreover, unlike organizations at the primary level, organizations at the technical level officially designate administrative leadership positions and allocate individuals to them. Most scholastic and collegiate athletic teams, for example, would be classified as technical organizations with coaches and athletic directors functioning as administrative leaders.

At the managerial level organizations are too large for every member to know every other member but small enough so that all members know one or more of the administrative leaders of the organization. Some of the large professional ball clubs represent social organizations related to sport at the managerial level.

Organizations at the corporate level are charatcerized by bureaucracy: they have centralized authority, a hierarchy of personnel, and protocol) and procedural emphases; and they stress the rationalization of operations and impersonal relationships. A number of the major governing bodies of amateur and professional sport at the national and international levels illustrate sport organizations of the corporate type.

In summary, the sport order is composed of the congeries of primary, technical, managerial, and corporate social organizations which arrange, facilitate, and regulate human action in sport situations. The value of the concept lies in its use in macro-analyses of the social significance of sport. We can make reference to the sport order in a historical and/or comparative perspective. For example, we can speak of the sport order of nineteenth-century America or contrast the sport order of Russia with that of England.

IV. SPORT AS A SOCIAL SITUATION

As was just noted, the sport order is composed of all social organizations which organize, facilitate, and regulate human action in sport situations. Human "action consists of the structures and processes by which human beings form meaningful intentions and, more or less successfully, implement them in concrete situations" (Parsons, 1966, p. 5). A sport situation consists of any social context wherein individuals are involved with sport. And the term situation denotes "the total set of objects, whether persons, collectivities, culture objects, or himself to which an actor responds" (Friedsam, 1964, p. 667). The set of objects related to a specific sport situation may be quite diverse, ranging from the elements of the social and physical environments of a football game to those associated with two sportniks[19] in a neighborhood bar arguing the pros and cons of the manager of their local baseball team.

Although there are many kinds of sport situations, most if not all must be conceptualized as social systems. A social system may be simply defined as "a set of persons with an identifying characteristic plus a set of relationships established among these persons by interaction" (Caplow, 1964, p. 1). Thus the situation represented by two teams contesting within the confines of a football field, the situation presented by father and son fishing from a boat, and the situation created by a golf pro giving a lesson to a novice each constitutes a social system.

Social systems of prime concern to the sport sociologist are those which directly or indirectly relate to a game occurrence. That is to say, a sport sociologist is often concerned with why man gets involved in sport and what effect his involvement has on other aspects of his social environment. Involvement in a social system related to a game occurence can be analyzed in terms of degree and kind of involvement.

Degree of involvement can be assessed in terms of frequency, duration, and intensity of involvement. The combination of frequency and duration of involvement may be taken as an index of an individual's "investment" in a sport situation, while intensity of involvement may be considered an index of an individual's "personal commitment" to a given sport situation.[20]

Kind of involvement can be assessed in terms of an individual's relationship to the "means of production" of a game. Those having direct or indirect access to the means of production are considered "actually involved" and are categorized as "producers." Those lacking access to the means of production are considered "vicariously involved" and are categorized as "consumers." We have tentatively identified three categories of producers and three classes of consumers.

Producers may be characterized as being primary, secondary, or tertiary with respect to the production of a game. "Primary producers" are the contestants who play the primary roles in the production of a game, not unlike the roles of actors in the production of a play. "Secondary producers" consist of those individuals, who while not actually competing in a sport contest, perform tasks which have direct technological consequences for the outcome of a game. Secondary producers include club owners, coaches, officials, trainers, and the like. It may be possible to categorize secondary producers as entrepreneurs, managers, and technicians. "Tertiary producers" consist of those who are actively involved in a sport situation but whose activities have no direct technological consequences for the outcome of a game. Examples of tertiary producers are cheerleaders, band members, and concession workers. Tertiary producers may be classified as service personnel.

Consumers, like producers, are designated as being primary, secondary, or tertiary. "Primary consumers" are those individuals who become vicariously involved in a sport through "live" attendance at a sport competition. Primary consumers may be thought of as "active spectators." "Secondary consumers" consist of those who vicariously involve themseslves in a sport as spectators via some form of the mass media, such as radio or television. Secondary consumers may be thought of as "passive spectators." "Tertiary consumers" are those who become vicariously involved with sport other than as spectators. Thus an individual who engages in conversation related to sport or a person who reads the sport section of the newspaper would be classified as a tertiary consumer.

In concluding our discussion of the nature of sport we note that a special type of consumer is the *fan.* A fan is defined as an individual who has both a high personal investment in and a high personal commitment to a given sport.

NOTES

1. This definition is based largely on the work of Caillois (1961) and Roberts and others (1959). Other definitions and classifications of games having social import are given in Berne (1964) and Piaget (1951).
2. As have done Huizinga (1955), Stone (1955), and Caillois (1961).
3. Cf. Goffman's discussion of "rules of irrelevance" as applied to games and social encounters in general (1961, pp. 19-26).
4. E.g., compare the rules given for games in any edition of Hoyle's *Book of Games* with the NCAA rule books for various collegiate sports.
5. There is, of course, the amateur who gives up the "game" to become a professional.
6. For an early discussion of the problem of legitimation in sport, see Veblen, 1934, pp. 268-270.
7. An excellent philosophical account of play and seriousness is given by Kurt Riezler (1941, pp. 505-517).
8. A sociological treatment of how an individual engaged in an activity can become "caught up" in it is given by Goffman in his analysis of the concept of "spontaneous involvement" (1961, pp. 37-45).
9. For a discussion of how certain aspects of "reality" are excluded from a game situation, see Goffman's treatment of "rules of irrelevance." Contrawise see his treatment of "rules of transformation" for a discussion of how certain aspects of "reality" are permitted to enter a game situation (1961, pp. 29-34).
10. Professional sports provide an exception, of course, especially such a sport as professional bullfighting.
11. Our use of the term "structures and processes" at this point is similar to Goffman's concept of "realized resources" (1961, pp. 16-19).
12. Other possible categories of competition are, of course, animals against animals as seen in horse racing or animals against an artificial animal as seen in dog racing. As noted by Weiss: "When animals or machines race, the speed offers indirect testimony to men's excellence as trainers, coaches, riders, drivers and the like—and thus primarily to an excellence in human leadership, judgment, strategy, and tactics" (1967, p. 22).
13. The interested reader can find examples of sport classifications in Schiffer (1965), McIntosh (1963), and Sapora and Mitchell (1961).
14. This definition is patterned after one given by Smelser (1963, p. 28).
15. Huizinga states that the existence of permanent teams is, in fact, the starting-point of modern sport (1955, p. 196).
16. Our discussion of "sanctioned secrecy" closely parallels Johnson's discussion of "official secrecy" in bureaucracies (1960, pp. 295-296).
17. For an early sociological treatment of sport, spectacle, exhibition, and drama, see Sumner (1960, pp. 467-501). We note in passing that some writers consider the totality of sport as a ritual; see especially Fromm (1955, p. 132) and Beisser (1967, pp. 148-151 and pp. 214-225).
18. Our discussion of these four levels is similar to Caplow's treatment of small, medium, large, and giant organizations (Caplow, 1964, pp. 26-27).
19. The term sportnik refers to an avid fan or sport addict.
20. Cf. McCall and Simmons (1966, pp. 171-172).

REFERENCES

Berne, Eric. *Games People Play*. New York: Grove Press, 1964.

Beisser, Arnold R. *The Madness in Sports*. New York: Appleton-Century-Crofts, 1967.

Boyle, Robert H. *Sport—Mirror of American Life*. Boston: Little, Brown, 1963.

Caillois, Roger. *Man, Play and Games*, tr. Meyer Barash. New York: Free Press, 1961.

Caplow, Theodore. *Principles of Organization*. New York: Harcourt, Brace and World, 1964.

Friedsam, H. J. "Social Situation," in *A Dictionary of the Social Sciences*, edited by Julius Gould and William L. Kolb, p. 667. New York: Free Press, 1964.

Fromm, Eric. *The Sane Society*. New York: Fawcett, 1955.

Goffman, Erving. *Encounters*. Indianapolis: Bobbs-Merrill, 1961.

Huizinga, Johan. *Homo Ludens—A Study of the Play-Element in Culture*. Boston: Beacon Press, 1955.

Johnson, Harry M. *Sociology: A Systematic Introduction*. New York: Harcourt, Brace, 1960.

Kahn, Roger. "Money, Muscles—and Myths," *Nation*, CLXXXV (July 6, 1957), 9-11.

Leach, E. R. "Ritual," in *A Dictionary of the Social Sciences*, ed. Julius Gould and William L. Kolb. New York: Free Press, 1964.

Lüschen, Günther. "The Interdependence of Sport and Culture." Paper presented at the National Convention of the American Association for Health, Physical Education and Recreation, Las Vegas, 1967.

McCall, George J., and J. L. Simmons, *Identities and Interactions*. New York: Free Press, 1966.

McIntosh, Peter C. *Sports in Society*. London: C. A. Watts, 1963.

Piaget, Jean. *Play, Dreams and Imitation in Childhood*, tr. C. Gattegno and F. M. Hodgson. New York: W. W. Norton, 1951.

Riezler, Kurt. "Play and Seriousness," *The Journal of Philosophy*, XXXVIII (1941), 505-517.

Roberts, John M., and others. "Games in Culture," *American Anthropologist*, LXI (1959), 597-605.

————, and Brian Sutton-Smith. "Child Training and Game Involvement," *Ethnology*, I (1962), 166-185.

Sapora, Allen V., and Elmer D. Mitchell. *The Theory of Play and Recreation*. New York: Ronald Press, 1961.

Schiffer, Donald. "Sports," *Colliers Encyclopedia* 21 (1965): 449-460.

Schneider, Louis. "Institution," in *A Dictionary of the Social Sciences*, ed. Julius Gould and William L. Kolb. New York: Free Press, 1964.

Smelser, Neil J. *The Sociology of Economic Life*. Englewood Cliffs, N. J.: Prentice-Hall, 1963.

Stone, Gregory P. "American Sports: Play and Display," *Chicago Review*, IX (Fall 1955), 83-100.

Sumner, William Graham. *Folkways*. New York: Mentor, 1960.

Torkildsen, George E. "Sport and Culture." M. S. thesis, University of Wisconsin, 1957.

Veblen, Thorstein. *The Theory of the Leisure Class*. New York: Modern Library, 1934.

Weiss, Paul. "Sport: A Philosophical Study." Unpublished manuscript, 1967.

Section B

Models for Understanding Sport
in the Sociocultural Process

Scholars from many of the social sciences have turned their attention to the search for a deeper understanding of sport in society. And while they may all concur that sport is indeed a significant aspect of social life, they differ in their opinions as to the most productive manner in which to study it. The selections featured in this section were chosen to represent several diverse approaches to the study of sport as a social phenomenon.

Goffman is a highly regarded social psychologist whose special genius is his remarkable insight into the workings of everyday life. Goffman's writing often reflects his interest in the game-like qualities that typify many aspects of day to day human interaction. In "Fun in Games," Goffman explores in depth the social aspects of games and the social conditions under which game playing can occur. He presents insight into what is fun about fun (a balance between boredom and tension) and he goes on to apply his observations to the understanding of all social interactions.

Goffman's approach may be considered an example of analysis from an interactionist perspective. As the label implies, interactionists—closely allied to symbolic interactionists, phenomenologists, and ethnomethodologists—focus upon the process of interaction and study how individuals interact with one another to create and communicate the meaning of social acts.

In contrast, Luschen's article is written from a structural functionalist perspective. Social scientists sympathetic to that perspective tend to concentrate upon the function that social phenomena—sport, for example—serve in the social system. The title of Luschen's essay, "The Interdependence of Sport and Culture" nicely illustrates the structural functionalist's assumption that social phenomena are systematically interelated so that changes in one part of the system necessarily create changes in other parts of the system.

Luschen first investigates the relationship of the appearance of sport forms in culture to the salience of other cultural values such as technology, Protentantism, and achievement orientation. He then turns his attention to a discussion of the possible functions and dysfunctions of sport. He concludes with the suggestion that the function of sport in society may change as the culture evolves from a primitive one to a modern state.

Brohm's work is a programmatic statement from the neo-Marxist perspective, a perspective which has become a highly visible force in the study of sport. That perspective, as interpreted by Brohm, views sport as a political entity controlled by the state and thus, in capitalist nations, a tool of elitism and imperialism. As Brohm states it: "Sport is a concentrated form, an officially promoted microcosm, of all the ideological prejudices of bureaucratic, bourgeois society."

The final selection in this section is not as self-conscious a statement of a theoretical perspective. Instead it represents an example of a significant research tradition based upon cross-cultural studies. Brian Sutton-Smith is a developmental psychologist whose long collaboration with anthropologist John Roberts and others has resulted in twenty years of fruitful research studies on games in culture. In the article included here, Sutton-Smith summarizes research findings related to the conflict-enculturation model, a model which attempts to explain the relationship between societal factors, child-rearing practices, and game forms.

Fun in Games

Erving Goffman

> MIRABELL and FAINALL [*rising from cards*]
>
> MIRABELL: *You are a fortunate man, Mr. Fainall.*
> FAINALL: *Have we done?*
> MIRABELL: *What you please. I'll play on to entertain you.*
> FAINALL: *No, I'll give you your revenge another time, when you are not so indifferent; you are thinking of something else now, and play too negligently; the coldness of a losing gamester lessens the pleasure of the winner. I'd no more play with a man that slighted his ill fortune, than I'd make love to a woman who undervalued the loss of her reputation.*
>
> —William Congreve, *The Way of the World*

INTRODUCTION

1. *Play and Seriousness.* In daily life, games are seen as part of recreation and "in principle devoid of important repercussions upon the solidity and continuity of collective and institutional life."[2] Games can be fun to play, and fun alone is the approved reason for playing them. The individual, in contrast to his treatment of "serious" activity, claims a right to complain about a game that does not pay its way in immediate pleasure and, whether the game is pleasurable or not, to plead a slight excuse, such as an indisposition of mood, for not participating. Of course, those who are tactful, ambitious, or lonely participate in recreation that is not fun for them, but their later private remarks testify that it should have been. Similarly, children, mental patients, and prisoners may not

have an effective option when officials declare game-time, but it is precisely in being thus constrained that these unfortunates seem something less than persons.

Because serious activity need not justify itself in terms of the fun it provides, we have neglected to develop an analytical view of fun and an appreciation of the light that fun throws on interaction in general. This paper attempts to see how far one can go by treating fun seriously. It begins as if addressing itself to a general consideration of social interaction, drawing on games for some illustrations. Only later will the question of fun in games be raised, and only at the end will any kind of answer be attempted.

2. *Encounters.* I limit myself to one type of social arrangement that occurs when persons are in one another's immediate physical presence, to be called here an *encounter* or a *focused gathering*. For the participants, this involves: a single visual and cognitive focus of attention; a mutual and preferential openness to verbal communication; a heightened mutual relevance of acts; an eye-to-eye cological huddle that maximizes each participant's opportunity to perceive the other participants' monitoring of him.[3] Given these communication arrangements, their presence tends to be acknowledged or ratified through expressive signs, and a "we rationale" is likely to emerge, that is, a sense of the single thing that *we* are doing together at the time. Ceremonies of entrance and departure are also likely to be employed, as are signs acknowledging the initiation and termination of the encounter or focused gathering as a unit. Whether bracketed by ritual or not, encounters provide the communication base for a circular flow of feeling among the participants as well as corrective compensations for deviant acts.

Examples of focused gatherings are: a tete-à-tete; a jury deliberation; a game of cards; a couple dancing; a task jointly pursued by persons physically close to one another; love-making; boxing. Obviously, taking turns at talking is not the only kind of activity upon which focused gatherings are built. Where a jointly sustained physical task is featured, the terms encounter and focused gathering may seem inappropriate, and a more abstract term, such as "situated activity system," may be used. It should also be added: that persons present to each other need not be engaged in any encounter, constituting, therefore, an "unfocused gathering"; that persons immediately present to each other can be parceled out into different encounters, as all partygoers know—a "multi-focused gathering"; and that persons ostensibly engaged in one encounter can simultaneously sustain an additional "subordinated" one. In the last instance the "subordinated" encounter is sustained through covert expressions or by deferential restriction of the second encounter so that it does not get in the way of the officially dominating one.

FORMALIZATIONS

1. *Rules of Irrelevance.* Encounters are everywhere, but it is difficult to describe sociologically the stuff that they are made of. I fall back on the assumption that, like any other element of social life, an encounter exhibits sanctioned orderliness arising from obligations fulfilled and expectations realized, and that therein lies its structure. Presumably, we could learn about the structure of focused gatherings by examining what happens when their orderliness breaks down. Another method recommends itself, however. It seems characteristic of encounters, as distinguished from other elements of social organization, that their order pertains largely to what shall be attended and disattended, and through this, to what shall be accepted as the definition of the situation. (Of course, *what* definition of the situation the encounter will be obliged to maintain is often determined by the social occasion or affair in whose domain the encounter takes place.) Instead of beginning by asking what happens when this definition of the situation breaks down, we can begin by asking what perspectives this definition of the situation excludes when it is being satisfactorily sustained.[4]

Here, games can serve as a starting point. They clearly illustrate how participants are willing to forswear for the duration of the play any apparent interest in the esthetic, sentimental, or monetary value of the equipment employed, adhering to what might be called *rules of irrelevance.* For example, it appears that whether checkers are played with bottle tops on a piece of squared linoleum, with gold figurines on inlaid marble, or with uniformed men standing on colored flagstones in a specially arranged court square, the pairs of players can start with the "same" positions, employ the same sequence of strategic moves and countermoves, and generate the same contour of excitement.

The elegance and strength of this structure of inattention to most things of the world is a great tribute to the social organization of human propensities. Witness the fugue-like manner in which deeply engrossed chess players are willing to help each other reposition a piece that has been brushed aside by a sleeve, dissociating this event from relevant reality and providing us with a clear example of a fundamental process, the sustaining of a subordinate side-encounter simultaneously with a main one that has been accorded the accent of reality. Another example of this is seen in "wall games," wherein school children, convicts, prisoners of war, or mental patients are ready to redefine an imprisoning wall as a part of the board that the game is played on, a board constituted of special rules of play, not bricks and mortar.[5] In Bateson's apt term, games place a "frame" around a spate of immediate events, determining the type of "sense" that will be accorded everything within the frame.[6] Rules of irrelevance are strictly applied, but, of course, only for the duration of the playing. At other times, the player will be fully alive to the game equipment as something to be cherished as an heirloom, given as an expensive gift, or stowed away in an unlocked drawer along with other cheap and easily replaceable possessions. These meanings are part of other frames in which game equipment can be handled; they cause confusion only when the individual "breaks frame" and tries disrespectfully to assert one perspective when another was expected to hold sway.

Just as properties of the material context are held at bay and not allowed to penetrate the mutual activity of an encounter, so also certain properties of the participants will be treated as if they were not present. For this let us move from games to social parties. Simmel's famous description of the encounters of "pure sociability" provides examples:

> The fact is that whatever the participants in the gathering may possess in terms of objective attributes—attributes that are centered outside the particular gathering in question—must not enter it. Wealth, social position, erudition, fame, exceptional capabilities and merits, may not play any part in sociability. At most they may perform the role of mere nuances of that immaterial character with which reality alone, in general, is allowed to enter the social work of art called sociability.[7]

> ✿   ✿   ✿   ✿

> Sociability is the game in which one "does as if" all were equal, and at the same time, as if one honored each of them in particular.[8]

> ✿   ✿   ✿   ✿

> This reduction of the personal character which homogenous interaction with others imposes on the individual may even make him lean over backward, if we may say so: a characteristically sociable behavior trait is the courtesy with which the strong and extraordinary individual not only makes himself the equal of the weaker, but even acts as if the weaker were the more valuable and superior.[9]

Simmel's embarrassing effort to treat sociability as a type of "mere" play, sharply cut off from the entanglements of serious life, may be partly responsible for sociologists having failed to identfy the rules of irrelevance in sociability with similar rules in serious areas of life. A good example of these rules in the latter areas is found in the impersonal calculable aspects of Western bureaucratic administration. Here, Weber supplies an obvious text, providing only that, as in the case of Simmel, we accept as a tendency what is stated as a fact:

> The "objective" discharge of business primarily means a discharge of business according to *calculable rules* and "without regard for persons."

> "Without regard for persons" is also the watchword of the "market" and, in general, of all pursuits of naked economic interests. A consistent execution of bureaucratic domination means the leveling of status "honor." . . .

> The second element mentioned, "calculable rules," also is of paramount importance for modern bureaucracy. The peculiarity of modern culture, and specifically of its technical and economic basis, demands this very "calculability" of results. When fully developed, bureaucracy also stands, in a specific sense, under the principle of *sine ira ac studio*. Its specific nature, which is welcomed by capitalism, develops the more perfectly the more the bureaucracy is "dehumanized," the more completely it succeeds in eliminating from official business love, hatred, and all purely personal irrational, and emotional elements which escape calculation.[10]

○   ○   ○   ○

> . . . the characteristic principle of bureaucracy [is] the abstract regularity of the execution of authority, which is a result of the demand for "equality before the law" in the personal and functional sense—hence, of the horror of "privilege," and the principle rejection of doing business "from case to case."[11]

While the explicit content of these statements is directed to administrative organization, not to focused gatherings, we must appreciate that a crucial part of the conduct of business, government, and the law has to do with the way in which an official handles clients or customers in direct face-to-face dealings. Parson's reworking of Weber presents this aspect of bureaucracy more clearly, especially in the concepts of "universalism" and "affective neutrality" as illustrated in professional-client relationships in medicine:

> Affective neutrality is also involved in the physician's role as an applied scientist. The physician is expected to treat an objective problem in objective, scientifically justifiable terms. For example whether he likes or dislikes the particular patient as a person is supposed to be irrelevant, as indeed it is to most purely objective problems of how to handle a particular disease.[12]

In his initial work, Parsons was primarily concerned with distinctive features of the high professions, but, interestingly, any well-established business in Western society would have done almost as well. Salespersons in large, well-known stores have an ethic leading them to treat all customers with equal courtesy, whatever the customer's status or the probable value of his purchase. The phrase "courteous service" points to the common expectation that an employee will show invariable good humor and consideration regardless of obvious social differences among customers.

Just as we find that certain social attributes are excluded from significance in wide ranges of encounters, so also we find that participants will hold in check certain psychological states and attitudes, for, after all, the very general rule that one enter into the prevailing mood in the encounter carries the understanding that contradictory feelings will be held in abeyance. Simmel states this theme in his discussion of the management of affect during social parties:

> It is tactless, because it militates against *inter*action which monopolizes sociability, to display merely personal moods of depression, excitement, despondency—in brief, the light and the darkness of one's most intimate life.[13]

So generally, in fact, does one suppress unsuitable affect, that we need to look at offenses to this rule to be reminded of its usual operation. Here, of course, Freud's ideas are central, for whether Freud deals with "faulty, chance, and symptomatic actions," or dreams, or wit of the "overdetermined" kind, or serious manifestations of neurosis, he deals with the kinds of feelings that the offender's fellow-participants in the encounter are suppressing. Freud deals directly with the whole range of feelings, thoughts, and attitudes that fail to be successfully held back and hence, only less directly, with rules regarding what is allowed expression:

> . . . the peculiar mode of operation, whose most striking function we recognize in the dream content, should not be attributed only to the sleeping state of the psychic life, when we possess abundant proof of its activity during the waking state in faulty actions. The same connection also forbids us from assuming that these psychic processes which impress us as abnormal and strange, are determined by deep-seated decay of psychic activity or by morbid state of function.

> The correct understanding of this strange psychic work, which allows the faulty actions to originate like the dream pictures, will only be possible after we have discovered that the psychoneurotic symptoms, particularly the psychic formations of hysteria and compulsion neurosis, repeat in their mechanisms all the essential features of this mode of operation. The continuation of our investigation would therefore have to begin at this point.

    ✧   ✧   ✧   ✧

> But the common character of the mildest, as well as the severest cases, to which the faulty and chance actions contribute, *lies in the ability to refer the phenomena to unwelcome, repressed, psychic material, which, though pushed away from consciousness, is nevertheless not robbed of all capacity to express itself.*[14]

Cruder instances can be found in any mental hospital during those moments when the patient behaves in such a way as to make the psychiatrist feel that affect "inappropriate in the situation" is being shown (as when, for example, a patient at mealtime asks for the salt in a voice that covers the whole table with misery and gloom), for what will later be seen as a "symptom" first comes to attention because it is an infraction of a rule regarding affect restraint during daily encounters.

An interesting aspect of this affective discipline has to do with the amount of open self-reference a participant employs during informal conversational encounters. In fact, socialization in our society can be measured by the rate at which a child foregoes frank demands to "look at me" or "watch me do this,"[15] just as "desocialization" is felt to be measurable by an increasing openness and persistence of self-reference.

Just as certain desires and feelings are held in abeyance for the duration of the encounter, so also we often find that the participant disengages himself from undertakings that cut across the duration and personnel of the current encounter. Patent involvement in what has happened before the encounter or what is scheduled to occur after it can be seen as preoccupation, restlessness, or impatience; and unless special legitimating circumstances are present, disrespect for the others present and undesirable qualities of personality are conveyed.

I have suggested that the character of an encounter is based in part upon rulings as to properties of the situation that should be considered irrelevant, out of frame, or not happening. To adhere to these rules is to play fair. Irrelevant visible events will be disattended; irrelevant private concerns will be kept out of mind. An effortless unawareness will be involved, and if this is not possible then an active turning-away or suppression will occur. Heroic examples of this quite fundamental process—the operation of rules of irrelevance in social interaction—can be discovered in mental hospitals, where patients can be found immersed in a game of bridge (or affecting this immersion) while one or two of the players engage in occult manneristic movements and the whole table is surrounded by the clamor of manic patients. Here it can be clearly seen that an engaging activity acts as a boundary around the participants, sealing them off from many potential worlds of meaning and action. Without this encircling barricade, presumably, participants would be immobilized by an inundation of bases of action.

2. *Realized Resources.* The social organization exhibited in a focused gathering is, then, a consequence of the effective operation of rules of irrelevance. But, although this describes what is excluded from the reality of the encounter, it tells us nothing about what is included, and it is of this that we must now try to get a systematic view.

Again, games can provide a beginning. The set of rules which tells us what should not be given relevance tells us also what we are to treat as real. There can be an event only because a game is in progress, generating the possibility of an array of game-meaningful happenings. A "schema of expression and interpretation" is involved:

> To illustrate, bridge players do not respond to each other's actions as behavioral events. They do not treat the fact that the other player withdraws a card from his hand and places it on the table as the event "putting down a pasteboard" or "effecting a translation of position of a card," but rather through the translation of the card's position the player signalizes that "he has played the ace of spades as the first card of the trick." From the player's point of view the question "What can happen?" is for him correctly decided in terms of these rules.[16]

In addition to these game-meaningful events, we find game-generated roles or identities. When a capture occurs in chess, something happens relative to the lore and culture of the game, not merely to the board positions, for a piece of given power and status is the captor and another with a character of its own is the captive. It is only in baseball that the event "grounding out to third" can occur. It is also only in baseball, however, that we can find the position of third baseman, along with the range of difficult situations this player is likely to have to face and the qualities of mind and body he will need to meet these situations well.

A matrix of possible events and a cast of roles through whose enactment the events occur constitute together a field for fateful dramatic action, a plane of being, an engine of meaning, a world in itself, different from all other worlds except the ones generated when the same game is played at other times. Riezler provides a statement of this theme in his fine paper on play and seriousness:

> I begin with the most simple case. We play games such as chess or bridge. They have rules the players agree to observe. These rules are not the rules of the "real" world or of "ordinary" life. Chess has its king and queen, knights and pawns, its space, its geometry, its laws of motion, its demands, and its goal. The queen is not a real queen, nor is she a piece of wood or ivory. She is an entity in the game defined by the movements the game allows her. The game is the context within which the queen is what she is. This context is not the context of the real world or of ordinary life. The game is a little cosmos of its own.[17]

Games, then, are world-building activities. I want to suggest that serious activities have this quality too. We are ready to see that there is no world outside the various playings of a game that quite corresponds to the game-generated reality, but we have been less willing to see that the various instances of a serious encounter generate a world of meanings that is exclusive to it. It is only around a small table that one can show coolness in poker or the capacity to be bluffed out of a pair of aces; but, similarly, it is only on the road that the roles of motorist and pedestrian take on full meaning, and it is only among persons avowedly joined in a state of talk that we can learn something of the meaning of half-concealed inattentiveness or relative frequency of times each individual talks. (Of course, the equipment employed in some serious encounters is not as well adapted for cosmos buildings as are game materials, for wider reality is rarely as well designed to be psychologically real as is a game designed just for this purpose; full-fledged identities may not emerge and, as will be considered later, a full mutual fatefulness may not arise from the moves taken by the players.)

How can we characterize these worlds of face-to-face interaction? We cannot say they belong to fantasy, at least not if we are going to argue that serious, as well as unserious, encounters generate these involvements. We cannot say the worlds are created on the spot, because, whether we refer to a game of cards or to teamwork during surgery, use is usually made of traditional equipment having a social history of its own in the wider society and a wide consensus of understanding regarding the meanings that are to be generated from it. It is only in certain interactional settings that there can arise what is said through a loving kiss; but to generate this type of event is not to invent it. Nor can we say that the encounter world includes everything that happens on the spot. In every encounter, for example, there will be locally generated sounds and locally performed body movements that are disattended, whether automatically or studiously, being barred from reality by rules of irrelevance. We can, however, say this about the worlds of focused gatherings: the material for realizing the full range of events and roles of these worlds is locally available to the participants.

I propose to try to analyze focused gatherings on the assumption that each can be viewed as having carved everything needed from the stuffs at hand; the elements of each encounter will be treated as if they constituted a full deck. There is no combination of bids and hands that any deck of cards might not bring to any table of bridge, providing the players sit long enough; in the same way, a customer, a clerk, and a floor manager can among themselves play out the drama that is possible in shops. I shall refer to these locally realizable events and roles as *realized resources.*[18]

Just as every encounter will sustain events that are part of a world that can be fully realized within the encounter, so many of the matters that are given no concern or attention will have an organizational base and a relevant world of meaning beyond the confines of the type of encounter in question. When the boss comes to dinner and is treated "the same as any other guest," the matter that is shown no consideration, whether automatically or carefully, is one that requires us to move from the employee's house to the business establishment for its full realization. When a man does not give way to preoccupation with his child ill at home but participates fully in the spirit of a golf game with his cronies, it is again an externally grounded matter that is being kept from the field of attention. Such externally grounded matters, not realized within the engagement, have a continuing significance outside the current encounters of that type.

3. *Transformation Rules.* Given the presence of realized resources, it is apparent that in each focused gathering the problem of how to allocate these resources among the participants must be solved.[19] Whatever the various solutions, it is apparent that attributes of participants will have to be employed as means for deciding on allocation. Some of these allocative attributes can be fully generated by means of a special preliminary encounter, as when bridge partners are selected according to a little game of highs and lows in a draw of cards, or when numbered cards are given out in a bakery shop to mark priority of appearance. In other cases the allocative attributes may derive directly from the realized world of the encounter, as when prizes are distributed according to game score.

Now it is possible to imagine a focused gathering where almost all externally based matters (including externally based attributes of participants) are treated as officially irrelevant. Thus, a game of checkers played between two strangers in a hospital admissions ward may constitute orderly interaction that is officially independent of sex, age, language, socioeconomic status, physical and mental condition, religion, staff-patient hierarchy, and so forth. But, in actual fact, externally realized matters are given some official place and weight in most encounters, figuring as avowed elements in the situation, even if only as determinants of the terms of address employed, as when two customers are treated alike except that one is called Sir and the other Miss. In the classic phrase of England's gentry, "Anyone for tennis?" did not quite mean *anyone;*

it is not recorded that a servant has ever been allowed to define himself as an *anyone*, although such doubtful types as tutors have occasionally been permitted to do so.[20] The role of chairman of the meeting is a locally realized resource, but the discussion may deal with matters that are not wholly at hand, just as the question of who fills the chair may be settled by externally based factors, such as stock ownership. The solid barrier by which participants in an encounter cut themselves off from externally based matters now seems to be not quite solid; like a sieve, it allows a few externally based matters to seep through into the encounter.

These externally realized but officially accredited matters seem more frequently to decide who is allowed or required to participate in the encounter than how resources are distributed once the participants have been selected, but the latter is possible. Thus, in sociable bridge games, which could well be arranged by drawing for partner and deal, husband and wife often are required either to play opposite each other, or not to, in either case introducing in a formal way the matter of marriage. The issue here, however, is that an externally realized property that is given official relevance as an allocative attribute still functions as a way of excluding *other* such attributes.[21] A clear example is a state dinner, where precedence at table is given according to governmental rank; for this externally based attribute to function locally, ranks of nobility have to be specifically excluded as a determinant of precedence, and quite explicitly are.[22]

We have now arrived at the following formulation of the order sustained in an encounter: a locally realized world of roles and events cuts the participants off from many externally based matters that might have been given relevance, but allows a few of these external matters to enter the interaction world as an official part of it. Of special importance are those properties in the wider world that constitute attributes of the encounter's participants, for these attributes are potential determinants of the way in which locally realized resources are distributed.

We must next go on to see that it is not simply a question of some potentially determinative attributes being allowed an allocative function and others not. Little understanding of the realm of social interaction can be obtained unless we recognize that in most cases the resources fully realized within an encounter cannot be allocated in a pattern that corresponds completely with the pattern in which the attribute is distributed in the wider world. We are in the habit of speaking of certain externally based attributes as being "expressed" within the mutual activity of a focused gathering, as when the boss is given the seat of honor at dinner or the eldest person present is allowed to determine when work will begin or end. With certain exceptions, however, the means of giving expression to these external matters are not refined enough to express all the externally based nuances. Thus, the locally generated and realized honor shown a boss at table may have to be used on another occasion for a visitor from out of town, a family member back from the hospital, a child recently graduated from primary to secondary school, or our first-mentioned boss's boss. And the seat of second honor at table may go to the second-ranking person, regardless of how close or distant his social position is to that of the guest of honor. The seat of honor can show precedence only, and this ordering is only a rough reflection of the infinitely different sets of relationships that can exist among those present by virtue of their socio-economic and membership characteristics. In general, then, the "regard" or "respect" that events in an encounter can be made to show for the externally based attributes of participants can be only a gesture in the right direction, accurately "expressing" only a very abstract aspect of structures in the wider world.

The question of what happens to an externally based attribute when it passes through the boundary of an encounter is even more complicated, however: it is possible not only to block (or randomize) externally based properties, or to allow them some rough expression, but also to introduce them in a partially reversed way—the negative ordering illustrated in our Biblical belief that "the last shall be first and the first last." Thus, many of the minor courtesies that men display to children or women in our society have this inverted character, with honor going to the youngest or weakest, not because youth and frailness are honored, but as a ceremonial reversal of ordinary practice. More extreme instances of this can be found during certain ceremonials and festivities. As Gluckman suggests:

> In certain armed services at Christmas, and at Christmas only, the officers wait at table on the men. This kind of reversal of role is well known in ceremonial and ritual.[23]
>
>   °   °   °   °
>
> Similarly, in the Polish ghettos, where the rabbis were powerful, once a year a sermon attacking them was preached in the synagogue by a wastrel. . . .[24]

An institutional version of this can be found in many "total institutions," where annual skits and plays are produced in which students play the roles of professors, patients, the role of psychiatrists, a prisoner the role of warden.[25] So, too, when a West Indian voodoo performance occurs, those who feel driven to come forward and play a leading role may be those to whom the community at large has accorded a low position.[26]

Let us now take stock once again. We have been focusing our attention on the boundary between the wider world and the mutual activity embedded in a focused gathering, and we have asked how properties from the outside world are selectively handled within the encounter. We found that the barrier to externally realized properties was more like a screen than like a solid wall, and we then came to see that the screen not only selects but also transforms and modifies what is passed through it. Speaking more strictly, we can think of inhibitory rules that tell participants what they must not attend to and of facilitating rules that tell them what they may recognize. (Together these rules represent one of the great themes of social organization, being one basic way in which every encounter is embedded in society.) We find, then, *transformation rules,* in the geometrical sense of that term, these being rules, both inhibitory and facilitating, that tell us what modification in shape will occur when an external pattern of properties is given expression inside the encounter.

The transformation rules of an encounter describe the fate of any property as a constituent of internal order. I have given special attention to externally based social attributes because these are of central interest in traditional sociological analysis. A consideration of these attributes in relation to the transformation rules of encounters allows us to deal directly and analytically with face-to-face instances of what are ordinarily called "deference patterns," defining deference here as interpersonal ritual.[27] These patterns establish the manner in which social attributes crucial in the wider society are dealt with during concrete occasions of face-to-face interaction.

DYNAMICS OF ENCOUNTERS

1. *Games, Play, and Gaming.* Until now in this paper, it has been useful to draw informally on games for illustrations of face-to-face interaction. There certainly are precedents for this. Students of social activity are increasingly using traditional and experimental games as working models. Games seem to display in a simple way the structure of real-life situations. They cut us off from serious life by immersing us in a demonstration of its possibilities. We return to the world as gamesmen, prepared to see what is structural about reality and ready to reduce life to its liveliest elements.

A game-theoretical approach also involves, however, important limitations in the study of face-to-face interaction. Before these limitations can be perceived and dealt with, we must look more carefully at the perspective from which they derive, introducing such defintions as seem necessary.

The game model has very serious implications for the accepted language of social psychology, especially for three key concepts, the individual, communication, and interaction.[28] The concept of the "individual" is properly split in two. We now have an "interest-identity," "team," or "side," this being something without flesh or blood that profits or loses by the outcome of the game according to a known utility function; and we have a "player," an agent-of-play, not a principal, who thinks and acts but does this for the side on which he is playing. The concept of "communicative activity" is similarly altered: the basic activity in a game is a *move*, and moves are neither communicated like messages nor performed like tasks and deeds; they are *made* or *taken*. To make a move requires some social arrangement by which a principal, acting through his agent, can commit himself to a position. To communicate that this position has been taken up is another move, quite distinct from the first, as is demonstrated by the fact that often in games our object is to make a move without informing the opposing team that we have made it. Finally, as regards interaction, we see that a game perspective reduces the situation to teams, each acting rationally to press a single type of interest or pay-off while accepting very special conditions of action. Each move must be selected from a small number of possibilities, these being largely determined by the previous move of the opposing team, just as each move largely determines the possibilities next open to the opponent. Each team is aware of this mutual determination and oriented to the control of it, the entire outcome for each team being dependent on how it fares in this outmaneuvering. The concept of interaction is thus transformed: instead of referring to mutual influence that might be peripheral and trivial, it now refers to a highly structured form of mutual fatefulness.

In the literature on games, a distinction is made between a *game*, defined as a body of rules associated with a lore regarding good strategies, and a *play*, defined as any particular instance of a given game being played from beginning to end.[29] *Playing* could then be defined as the process of move-taking through which a given play is initiated and eventually completed; action is involved, but only the strictly game-relevant aspects of action.

There are games, such as poker and bridge, which seem to require the players to sit facing each other around a small table. There are other games, such as hide-and-go-seek and war exercises, which fix the playing organically to a time and space but nevertheless require opposing teams to be out of each other's sight. There are still other games, such as chess, that ordinarily bring the players together but sometimes are played through the mails by enthusiasts without restriction to a time and space.

The varieties of interaction that occur among persons who are face to face for the avowed purpose of carrying on a game, I shall call *gaming*, including here, in addition to playing, activity that is not strictly relevant to the outcome of the play and cannot be defined in terms of the game. I shall call a focused gathering that ostensibly features plays of a game a *gaming encounter*. A play of a game has players; a gaming encounter has participants.[30] A play is a special abstraction from the more concrete unit, gaming encounter, just as the concept of player is an abstraction from that of participant.

By this time, it can be seen that a gaming encounter will be differently analyzed depending on whether it is seen as the occasion for plays of a game or as the occasion of gaming. The first kind of subject matter is codifiable and clean, the second is very sticky. Between the time when four persons sit down to bridge and the time when all four leave the table, an organic system of interaction has come into being. Whether there occur many plays of the game or an incomplete single play may be of secondary importance, marking only slight shifts and turns in the contour of feeling. (An incomplete play can provide the joint activity of a fairly well-terminated encounter.) When one player takes time out to answer the telephone, the play may be stopped in mid-air, being transfixable for any period of time, but not the social affair, the gaming encounter, for this can be threatened and even destroyed if the absent player is held too long on the telephone or must return with tragic news. Similarly, players may tacitly agree to begin to toy with the play or to shift their interest away from it, yet this very threat to play may come from a strengthening of the participants' engrossment in the side-encounter that is a standard part of some gaming encounters. Further, although kibitzers may be officially tolerated on the assumption that they will conduct themselves so as to have no real effect upon the outcome of the play, they are likely to be an integral part of the social-psychological reality of the gaming encounter; they are participants, not players, and can have a leading role in the gaming encounter while having no role in the play. In any case we must note that while it is as players that we can win a play, it is only as participants that we can get fun out of this winning.

2. *Spontaneous Involvement.* What I have said about interaction in the section on formalizations holds for focused gatherings, including the chief example used, gaming encounters, but what was said there also

holds for activity systems that are not realized within the boundaries of a face-to-face setting. For example, games played at a distance involve rules of irrelevance, a schema of interpretation, and resources realized fully within the possibilities of the game. Multi-situated game-like activities, such as the "newspaper game" or the "banking game,"[31] which involve an occupational community, with motives and positions generated and realizable within the community, can also be analyzed in these terms. This breadth of application of what has so far been considered about encounters is underlined in codes of conduct, such as government protocol, which provide a single body of formalized rules for dealing with face-to-face encounters and negotiation at a distance.

Focused gatherings do, however, have unique and significant properties which a formalistic game-theoretical view of interaction tends to overlook. The most crucial of these properties, it seems to me, is the organismic psychobiological nature of spontaneous involvement.[32] To give proper weight to this component of face-to-face behavior, some psychological imputations are necessary.

When an individual becomes engaged in an activity, whether shared or not, it is possible for him to become caught up by it, carried away by it, engrossed in it—to be, as we say, spontaneously involved in it. He finds it psychologically unnecessary to refrain from dwelling on it and psychologically unnecessary to dwell on anything else. A visual and cognitive engrossment occurs, with an honest unawareness of matters other than the activity;[33] what Harry Stack Sullivan called "selective inattention" occurs, with an effortless dissociation from all other events, distinguishing this type of unawareness both from suppression and repression.[34] When an individual engages in an encounter, his conscious awareness can bring certain shared things to life and deaden all other matters. By this spontaneous involvement in the joint activity, the individual becomes an integral part of the situation, lodged in it and exposed to it, infusing himself into the encounter in a manner quite different from the way an ideally rational player commits his side to a position in an ideally abstract game. As already considered, a game move is one thing; self-mobilization through which this move is executed during a gaming encounter is quite another. Game rules govern the one, the structure of gaming encounters governs the others.[35] I want to note here that while a player's current position on a board often can be adequately conveyed by brief signals through the mails, evidence of his spontaneous involvement in the gaming encounter can be adequately conveyed only to those in his immediate presence.

Gaming encounters provide us with fine examples of how a mutual activity can utterly engross its participants, transforming them into worthy antagonists in spite of the triviality of the game, great differences in social status, and the patent claims of other realities. Of this, the daughter of a Britsh Edwardian beauty reminds us in her autobiography:

> Sometimes, King Edward (Kingy) came to tea with Mamma, and was there when I appeared at six o'clock. On such occasions he and I devised a fascinating game. With a fine disregard for the good conditions of his trouser, he would lend me his leg, on which I used to start two bits of bread and butter (butter side down), side by side. Then, bets of a penny each were made (my bet provided by Mamma) and the winning piece of bread and butter depended, of course, on which was the more buttery. The excitement was intense while the contest was on. Sometimes he won, sometimes I did. Although the owner of a Derby winner, Kingy's enthusiasm seemed delightfully unaffected by the quality of his bets.[36]

And even when a gaming encounter begins with self-consciousness and reserve on the part of the players, we often find that the ice is soon broken and all players are being called by a familiar term of address.

It is not only possible for participants to become involved in the encounter in progress, but it is also defined as obligatory that they sustain this involvement in given measure; too much is one kind of delict; too little, another. There is no equivalent to this crucial interaction obligation in the formal logic of games, but here is a basic similarity between gaming encounters and other types of focused gatherings: both can be taken too seriously, both not seriously enough.

Why should the factor of spontaneous involvement carry so much weight in the organization of encounters? Some suggestions can be made. A participant's spontaneous involvement in the official focus of attention of an encounter tells others what he is and what his intentions are, adding to the security of the others in his presence. Further, shared spontaneous involvement in a mutual activity often brings the sharers into some kind of exclusive solidarity and permits them to express relatedness, psychic closeness, and mutual respect; failure to participate with good heart can therefore express rejection of those present or of the setting. Finally, spontaneous involvement in the prescribed focus of attention confirms the reality of the world prescribed by the transformation rules and the unreality of other potential worlds—and it is upon these confirmations that the stability of immediate definitions of the situation depends.

Assessment of spontaneous co-involvement may be particularly important during encounters with only two participants, for here the success or failure of the interaction in engrossing the participants may be perceived by them as having diagnostic significance for their relationship. Here love-making provides us with some extremely useful data, for the engrossing power of such encounters can become a crucial test of the relationship, while local physical happenings are very likely to distract at least one of the partners.[37] And we know that the relation between two persons can become such that, on whatever occasion they meet, they must—like two ex-husbands of the same woman—suppress considerations that they are not capable of banishing from mind, and thus spoil all occasions of interaction with one another.

The question of spontaneous co-involvement goes, then, to the heart of things and helps us isolate the special characteristics of face-to-face interaction. Multi-situated games and game-like activities can define the situation for their participants and create a world for them. But this is a loose world for the individual, allowing for periods of lack of interest and for wide variation in attitude and feelings, even though such multi-situated games, when institutionalized, can provide a kind of reality market—a world available whenever the individual decides to dip into it. The world of a multi-situated game can be lightly invested in, so that while the game defines the situation it does not bring the situation into lively existence. "Mere games" cannot easily be played at a distance because the chance of involving the participants may be too small; it is only devotees who play chess through the mails, a devotee by definition being someone who can become caught up in a sportive reality when rain, prolonged play, or play at a distance kills the game for others.

Face-to-face games, on the other hand, bear differently on one's sense of reality. That activity is going on before one's eyes ensures that a mere definition of the situation is experienced as having the thickness of reality. That other persons are involved ensures that engrossment must be steadily sustained in spite of the flickering of one's actual interest. Further, there seems to be no agent more effective than another person in bringing a world for oneself alive or, by a glance, a gesture, or a remark, shriveling up the reality in which one is lodged. It is only in face-to-face encounters that almost anything (even the game of buttered toast on King Edward's trousers) can become the basis of a perspective and a definition of the situation; it is only here that a definition of the situation has a favored chance of taking on the vivid character of sensed reality.

3. *Ease and Tension.* We come now to a crucial consideration. The world made up of the objects of our spontaneous involvement and the world carved out by the encounter's transformation rules can be congruent, one coinciding perfectly with the other. In such circumstances,

what the individual is obliged to attend to, and the way in which he is obliged to perceive what is around him, will coincide with what can and what does become real to him through the natural inclination of his spontaneous attention. Where this kind of agreement exists, I assume—as an empirical hypothesis—that the participants will feel *at ease* or natural, in short, that the interaction will be *euphoric* for them.

But it is conceivable that the participant's two possible worlds—the one in which he is obligated to dwell and the one his spontaneous involvement actually does or could bring alive to him—may not coincide, so that he finds himself spontaneously engrossed in matters declared irrelevant and unreal by the transformation rules. I make a second empirical assumption, that a person who finds himself in this conflict will feel uneasy, bored, or unnatural in the situation, experiencing this to the degree that he feels committed to maintaining the transformation rules. Under such circumstances, we can say that a *state of tension or dysphoria* exists for him in the encounter; he feels *uneasy*. Note that two main situations are possible for the uneasy participant: he can find himself strongly drawn to matters officially excluded (this being the case we will mainly consider); or he can find himself strongly repelled by the official focus of attention, as when issues are raised that he has suppressed, causing him to feel self-conscious, overinvolved, and acutely uncomfortable.

The perception that one participant is not spontaneously involved in the mutual activity can discredit the identity imputed to him as someone who is able and ready to immerse himself in an encounter and can weaken for the others their own involvement in the encounter and their own belief in the reality of the world it prescribes. A perceived deviation from the norm can thus have a "multiplier" effect, infecting the whole encounter.[38] In the same way, a model of appropriate involvement can shift the effect in the other direction and make for ease throughout. We must therefore allot a special place to the kind of uneasiness that can be managed unobtrusively and noncontagiously and to the kind of poise that equips the individual to do so. It is on this margin between being out of touch with the encounter and showing it that drinkers, addicts, and the emotionally bereaved concentrate, being greatly concerned to conceal their dereliction from interaction duties.

Although ease tends to be defined by persons as the "normal" state of affairs, in actuality it seems to be rarely achieved for any length of time in ordinary life. It is here, of course, that recreational games shine, for in gaming encounters euphoric interaction is relatively often achieved: gaming is often fun. Again we can claim, then, that to understand how games can be "fun" and what fun is, is to learn something important about all encounters.

It should be clearly understood that I have been using the term tension (and its opposite, lack of tension, or ease), in a restricted and special sense. A man losing money at poker and waiting with tenseness for the next card need not be in a state of tension as here defined. The gaming encounter, as a source of shared, obligatory, spontaneous involvement, can still be fun for him. The same man winning what are for him insignificant sums from players he considers too unskilled to be worth beating might have little tenseness in the occasion, although sticking out an evening of the game might be a matter of considerable tension for him. As used here, tension refers, I repeat, to a sensed discrepency between the world that spontaneously becomes real to the individual, or the one he is able to accept as the current reality, and the one in which he is obliged to dwell. This concept of tension is crucial to my argument, for I will try to show that just as the coherence and persistence of a focused gathering depends on maintaining a boundary, so the integrity of this barrier seems to depend upon the management of tension.

Under certain circumstances, persons can be so engrossed in an encounter that it is practically impossible to distract their attention; in such cases they can hardly feel ill at ease. Since we have this capacity to become engrossed, how is it we do not more often use it to avoid dysphoria?

One answer, of course, is that participants often feel alienated from the context of the interaction or from their fellow participants, and exploit any untoward event as a means of feeling and expressing disaffection. Another answer has to do with identity. The organization of an encounter and the definition of the situation it provides turn upon the conceptions the participants have concerning the identity of the participants and the identity of the social occasion of which the encounter is seen as a part. These identities are the organizational hub of the encounter. Events which cause trouble do not merely add disruptive noise but often convey information that threatens to discredit or supplant the organizing identities of the interaction. Hence, such events, however small in themselves, can weaken the whole design of the encounter, leaving the participants bewildered about what next to do, or what next to try to be.[39] In any case, of all our capacities, the one for spontaneous involvement seems to be least subject to conscious control—for to be concerned about being spontaneously involved in some activity is necessarily to be spontaneously involved in the concern, not the activity.

I have suggested that in any encounter there is likely to be some tension or dysphoria, some discrepancy between obligatory involvements and spontaneous ones. None the less, for any given encounter, it is of analytical interest to imagine those circumstances which would maximize ease or euphoria, bringing actual involvements and obligatory ones into perfect congruence. These circumstances we may refer to as the encounter's *euphoria function*. It will be apparent that a maximum of euphoria can be achieved in theory in two different ways: one, by granting the character of the activity and going on from there to obtain the most suitable recruits (in terms of the maintenance of euphoria); and, the other, by granting the recruits and, given their social attributes, determining the most effective allocation of internally-generated resources. For example, given the fact that it is the boss who is the guest at dinner, we can imagine that special combination of equality and deference that would best carry off the occasion; and given any particular allocation of locally realized resources, we can search out that dinner guest whose externally based social properties will be exactly the ones to make the occasion come off successfully.

Of course, we are unlikely to be able to manage social affairs so as to realize the euphoria function of a particular encounter, but it is useful to have this as a structural ideal, the end of a continuum along which actual events can be placed. Those who make up invitation lists for small social gatherings and table arrangements for large ones do in fact have a euphoria function in mind (although typically there will be other conditions that they must attempt to satisfy also).

Interestingly enough, the issue of a *dysphoria function* is worth considering too, and not only because of the fantasy persons sometimes have of giving a party with a maximally unsuitable combination of guests. Thus, it is reported that in order to keep resistance and morale low, those in charge of Chinese prisoner-of-war camps shifted "natural" leaders from one group to another, and gave officially sponsored positions of power to those prisoners whose externally based attributes might make them least eligible as far as their fellow prisoners were concerned.[40]

4. *Incidents.* Two key concepts, transformation rules and interaction tension, have now been introduced, and suggestions have been made concerning their relationship; for example, while it is characteristic of focused gatherings that a set of transformation rules can be adhered to through wide alterations in tension, any alteration in transformation rules is likely to lead to a marked increase or decrease in tension. Now, if we grant that tension and transformation rules are two members of the same family of terms, we must try to see what the other members look like.

During an encounter events may occur, whether intended or not, that suddenly increase the level of tension. Following everyday usage, I will refer to such events as *incidents*.

Perhaps the most common type of incident, one to which Freud gave much attention in his *Psychopathology of Everyday Life*,[41] consists of what we ordinarily call slips, boners, gaffes, or malapropisms, which unintentionally introduce information that places a sudden burden on the suppressive work being done in the encounter.

While slips are felt to be unintentional, the person who makes them is none the less held somewhat responsible. A parallel type of incident results from what might be called "leaky words": a term or phrase is used that has an appropriate and innocent meaning but also a sound that suddenly increases the difficulty of holding back official irrelevancies. In a high-school classroom, for example, sexual issues and sexual statuses may be effectively suppressed until a word is introduced whose homonymous alternate is frankly sexual, thus momentarily inundating the interaction with distracting considerations.

Another common type of incident is what might be called a "sign situation," namely, the unintended and undesired occurrence of a configuration of environmental events which all too aptly express a recognition of identities theretofore easefully disattended. For example, two persons can carry on a conversation with effective unconcern for their difference in occupational status until the unplanned-for necessity of having to pass single file through a doorway causes both participants to consider how to manage the problem of priority without giving offense. The very need to conceal this concern may constitute a painful distraction from the conversation at hand.

It may be noted here that it is the special fate of handicapped persons, such as the blind or the lame, to create contexts in which leaky words and sign situations are likely to occur. Encounters that adhere to the tactful and standard rule of "not noticing" the defects[42] are likely to have a precarious easefulness, since almost any physical movement can set the stage for a sign situation and many common phrases can similarly inundate the encounter with previously suppressed or spontaneously unattended matters. Persons with a social stigma of a racial or ethnic kind, and those with a moral stigma, such as ex-mental patients, ex-convicts, and homosexuals, also share this predicament. Such individuals must learn to deal with the unhappy property of being inimical to almost every encounter in which they find themselves. The central issue in such an individual's life situation is not that he is going to be discriminated against but that when he interacts with an ordinary member of the community both attempt to suppress matters that are embarrassingly more fundamental than the ones being explicitly considered—and make this attempt even while both ready themselves for the possibility of a breakdown in tact. Cooley provides an accurate state-ment of the consequence of this interaction predicament, with special reference to the mentally ill:

> The peculiar relations to other persons attending any marked personal deficiency or peculiarity are likely to aggravate, if not to produce, abnormal manifestations of self-feeling. Any such trait sufficiently noticeable to interrupt easy and familiar intercourse with others, and make people talk and think *about* a person or *to* him rather than *with* him, can hardly fail to have this effect. If he is naturally inclined to pride or irritability, these tendenices, which depend for correction upon the flow of sympathy, are likely to be increased. One who shows signs of mental aberration is, inevitably perhaps, but cruelly, shut off from familiar, thoughtless intercourse, partly excommunicated; his isolation is unwittingly proclaimed to him on every countenance by curiosity, indifference, aversion, or pity, and in so far as he is human enough to need free and equal communication and feel the lack of it, he suffers pain and loss of a kind and degree which others can only faintly imagine, and for the most part ignore. He finds himself apart, "not in it," and feels chilled, fearful, and suspicious. Thus "queerness" is no sooner perceived than it is multiplied by reflection from other minds. The same is true in some degree of dwarfs, deformed or disfigured persons, even the deaf and those suffering from the infirmities of old age.[43]

The incidents I have cited are instances of the intrusion of matters which have not been properly "worked up" or transformed for orderly and easeful use within the encounter. When an encounter is thoroughly and officially permeated by particular externally based social attributes, as in the interaction between a private and an officer, or between a com-moner and royalty, it is possible for the activity of the encounter to be pursued without distracting consideration being given to the social dis-tinctions. In such a context, however, an unanticipated event which could be taken to imply status equality can function as a sign situation, sud-denly throwing into doubt a ranking that has been unthinkingly taken for granted. This is part of the problem of *lèse-maiesté*, which character-istically arises when royalty indulges in games of skill, but is not a prob-lem for royalty alone. For example, we have the engaging description by W. F. Whyte of bowling among the Nortons, who were members of the street-corner society that Mr. Whyte made famous.[44] Here we are told of the various social pressures that players introduce so that their relative skill rank as bowlers will not be too inconsistent with their so-cial rank in the clique at large.

  5. *Integrations.* As suggested, in any focused gathering there are likely to be officially irrelevant matters that actively draw the concern and attention of the participants, giving rise to tension. In addition, there

are likely to be matters that are currently held back by selective inattention but would cause tension were they introduced pointedly. By contributing especially apt words and deeds, it is possible for a participant to blend these embarrassing matters smoothly into the encounter in an officially accepted way, even while giving support to the prevailing order. Such acts are the structural correlates of charm, tact, or presence of mind. These acts provide a formula through which a troublesome event can be redefined and its reconstituted meaning integrated into the prevailing definition of the situation, or a means of partially redefining the prevailing encounter, or various combinations of both.

In any case, by these means dysphoria can be intentionally reduced. I shall refer here to the integration or blending-in of tension-producing materials. What is involved is a kind of grounding of disruptive forces, an alteration of a frame for the benefit of those who are farmed by it. For example: when a pigeon flew in the window of Beatrice Lillie's New York apartment, she is said to have interrupted her conversation long enough to glance up and inquire, "Any messages?"[45] Another example may be cited from the predicament of a housemother engaged in looking after acting-out institutionalized children, one aspect of her job being to keep the participants contained in their encounters, in part by preventing sign situations from releasing into the encounter feelings of sibling rivalry theretofore held in uneasy check:

> Most activities involving our Housemother were extremely loaded with special risks. This was due to violent sibling rivalry tensions which exploded around her with much greater volatility than around other female staff, because of the obvious impact of her mother role. Any situation in which she was the central figure in the group activity had, therefore, to be handled with hair trigger sensitivity on her part. On one occasion, for example, she started to read a story to the group while they were munching their "treat" upon return from school. She was sitting on the couch and the group was ranged on either side of her when suddenly bickering broke out about who had the right "to sit right next to Emmy"—Larry, who was on her right, was viciously slapped by Danny, who in turn began to draw fire from Mike, Andy, and Bill. Group riot looked imminent when Emmy suddenly broke in with "Hey, wait a minute—I've got an idea. I'll read campfire style." "Campfire style—what's that?" Danny asked as they temporarily stopped their milling and mauling of each other. "Oh, I'll be in the center and you'll make a circle around me—that'll make me the campfire and each of you will be the same distance away." This worked out to divert them from their feuding for that afternoon's story anyway.[46]

Here we can note a very curious aspect of social interaction: desire to do the right thing and an appreciation of what should be done run well ahead of participants' capacity to do it. Individuals are always making an effort to assimilate matters through techniques that are not effective; it is after the occasion, at a time of recollection in tranquility, that they hit upon the phrase or action that would have been completely effective in the situation. Furthermore, an effort at integration that does not succeed ordinarily leaves matters in a worse state than before the task was attempted. Such failure means either that the definition of the situation is altered in a way that increases its unacceptability to participants, or that the participants must now try to disattend something to which their attention has been explicitly directed. Interestingly enough, because such an unsuccessful act is damaging, the actor is in a position of guilt; to be considerate of his now delicate position, others in the encounter usually make some effort to affect a little sign that the act has been successful, and this need to protect the offender can further alienate them from spontaneous involvement in the prescribed situation.

Again the situation of the physically handicapped provides important data, illustrating that when a very evident basis of re-identification must be treated as irrelevant (adherence to the transformation rules being under great strain) then either a failure to integrate the suppressed issue or an effort to do so may equally lead to intense uneasiness, a situation for which there is no solution. Wanting to reject an image of self as abnormal and wanting to keep others at a distance from his problem, the handicapped person may none the less feel that the tension will be intolerable unless he openly alludes to his condition and "breaks the ice."[47]

Minor integrations, or an attempt to perform them, occur constantly during conversational encounters, as when participants attempt to shift from a topic that has dried up or become dangerous to a new one that is calculated to provide safe supplies for a moment; in fact, etiquette books give explicit attention to the art of changing topics. Similarly, in order to get away with obtruding the self upon the interaction, either as speaker or as subject matter, the individual employs countless assimilating ruses to disguise the intrusion. Thus, we have a set of standard opening phrases—"The way I see it . . . ," "In my opinion . . . ," "Well, I don't know anything about that sort of thing, but I've always felt that . . . ," "Well, if you ask me . . .," The same thing happened to me, I was . . ."—whereby the willing talker provides what he takes to be a smooth connection between the established content of the encounter and a tale involving self.

Often, during an encounter, a participant will sense that a discrepancy has arisen between the image of himself that is part of the official definition of the situation and the image of himself that seems to have just been expressed by minor untoward events in the interaction. He then senses that the participants in the encounter are having to suppress awareness of the new version of him, with consequent tension. (While ordinarily this new image of him is less favorable than the initial official one, the opposite can easily occur.) At such times, the individual is likely to try to integrate the incongruous events by means of apologies, little excuses for self, and disclaimers; through the same acts, incidentally, he also tries to save his face. This may easily be observed by examining situations in which minor failures are constantly generated, for example, in games such as bowling. After making a bad shot, and while turning from the alley to face the others, the player is likely to display a facial gesture expressing that the shot was not a fair or serious measure of the player's skill and that the others, therefore, need not alter or doubt their prior evaluation of him.

During encounters, the individual is obliged to try to cope with incidents by spontaneously treating them as if they had not occurred, or by integrating them as best he can into the official definition of the situation, or by merely sustaining tension without departing physically from the situation. Once an individual is ready to be governed by this morality of interaction, others can exploit matters by intentionally tampering with the frame, introducing at his expense references and acts which are difficult to manage.[48] An apt identification of this process is provided in a novel by Chandler Brossard. A girl called Grace is leaving after a visit to the summer cottage of a friend, Harry. There are two other guests, Max and Blake. Grace has just terminated a relationship with one man, who has already departed, and has initiated a new one with Blake, who is the narrator:

> "Thanks for a fine time, Harry," Grace said, taking his hand.
> "I'm sorry you're leaving so soon," he said. "Come again next week end."
> "So long, Max."
> "So long, baby. Stay out of trouble."
>
> I carried her bag to the taxi, and the driver put it in the back of the car. She got in and closed the door. She put her face to the open window and I kissed her.
>
> "Call me tonight," I said.
> "I will."
>
> The cab drove off and I walked back to the house. Max was lying on the couch listening to a ball game.

"That was a very sweet scene, Blake," he said, talking as though he knew I had kissed Grace good-by.

"Glad you liked it."

"Good old Max," said Harry. "Always on the make for a situation. He feels frustrated if he doesn't lay at least one situation a day."[49]

The phenomenon of "making" a situation, is not, of course, restricted to New York hipsters. Jane Austen provides a contrast, illustrating at the same time how the structure of a focused gathering itself can be introduced conversationally as a means of attacking the frame and discomfiting participants:

They stood for some time without speaking a word; and then she began to imagine that their silence was to last through the two dances, and at first was resolved not to break it; till suddenly fancying that it would be the greater punishment to her partner to oblige him to talk, she made some slight observation on the dance. He replied, and was again silent. After a pause of some minutes, she addressed him a second time with—"It is *your* turn to say something now, Mr. Darcy. *I* talked about the dance, and *you* ought to make some kind of remark on the size of the room, or the number of couples."

He smiled, and assured her that whatever she wished him to say should be said.

"Very well. That reply will do for the present. Perhaps by and by I may observe that private balls are much pleasanter than public ones. But *now* we may be silent."

"Do you talk by rule, then, while you are dancing?"

"Sometimes. One must speak a little, you know. It would look odd to be entirely silent for half an hour together; and yet for the advantage of *some*, conversation ought to be so arranged, as that they may have the trouble of saying as little as possible."[50]

It may be added that "making" the situation can become culturally elaborated: the exemplary tales by which members of disadvantaged groups sustain themselves usually contain a few mots, squelches, or ripostes made under circumstances that leave their targets no satisfactory comeback.[51]

Perhaps the situations most likely to be "made" by someone present are those where there is a special reason why a participant's nonrelevant identity should be very much on everyone's mind, and where the excluded identity does not particularly threaten the possessor. For example, in our society, newly engaged couples attending small social parties are often the object of "well-meaning" quips and sallies by which references to their on-coming change in status are jokingly woven into the conversation. The female member of the couple may offer those present further reasons for raillery. She is about to enjoy a relatively full change in status in what can be defined as a favorable direction, and her past non-married status therefore ceases to be one about which others are obliged to suppress concern.[52] Furthermore, since this is the time when males present could least be suspected of attempting to initiate a sexual relationship with her, they can bestow mock sexual advances on her, using her as an object through which to vent concern that must be suppressed about other females present. (The host's wife may also be employed in this manner.)

There are, of course, other situations where an individual is lightly caught in the cross-fire between two of his statuses. In some rural communities in Western Europe, a boy confirms the seriousness of his relationship with a girl by escorting her to weddings to which either or both have been invited. At the same time, there is the rule that immediate members of the bride's and groom's families should act together during the occasion, being seated somewhat apart from other guests. The girl friend or boy friend of any youthful member of this weding group must therefore be found an escort who "stands in" for the real thing, although at a time when everyone is taking careful note of who came with whom. The stand-in is often a "safe" friend of the family, selected to ensure no misunderstanding on the part of others. It is understandable then that he (or she) will be fair game for quips and jokes: the implicit definition of oneself as the affianced of the other is established by the nature of the social occasion, and yet this definition is exactly what the various parties concerned must show they set no store by and believe no one else does either.

There are many settings in which an unstable division between officially relevant and non-relevant worlds leads someone present to attempt to make the situation. Workers are often required to sustain a task-oriented mutual activity in a context that is thoroughly imbued with claims on their identity which they must disavow, so that everywhere they turn a world that must be suppressed is thrust upon them. For example, a crew of carpenters called in after school hours to work amongst seats that can no longer hold them are likely to pass jokes about teachers; work in a church or cathedral may be "made" in the same way. In a rural community, I have observed the same kind of joking on the part of three men helping to unload lumber for the local coffin-maker, and on the part of a large work crew of shepherds engaged in the annual task of castrating young rams, the standard joke here being to grab the youngest member of the crew and make as if to place his body in the appropriate position for receiving the shears.

Obviously, in some cases, these redefining acts reduce the general level of tension, even if at the cost of someone's discomfort, and therefore become difficult to distinguish from well-intentioned efforts to integrate distracting considerations.

5. *Flooding Out.* I have considered incidents, their integration, and the making of situations; a further concept can now be mentioned. It has so far been argued that the transformation rules of an encounter oblige the participant to withhold his attention and concern from many potential matters of consideration, and that he is likely to feign such inattention when he cannot spontaneously manifest it. Evidence of this actual or feigned conformity comes to us from his manner, especially his facial expression, for manner provides the fluid field upon which the collective affective style of the encounter is intimately impressed. The participant's visible emotional state, then, will have to be in tune and tempo with the melody sustained in the interaction.

It is apparent, however, that under certain circumstances the individual may allow his manner to be inundated by a flow of affect that he no longer makes a show of concealing. The matter in which he has been affecting disinvolvement suddenly becomes too much for him, and he collapses, if only momentarily, into a person not mobilized to sustain an appropriate expressive role in the current interaction; he *floods out*. Whether the individual bursts out crying or laughing, whether he erupts into open anger, shame, impatience, boredom, or anguish, he radically alters his general support of the interaction; he is momentarily "out of play."[53] Since the individual has been active in some social role up to this time, sustaining the frame around the encounter, his flooding out constitutes one type of "breaking frame." A common example of flooding out occurs when an individual finds he can no longer "keep a straight face" and bursts out laughing.[54]

It is commonly thought that a sharp explosive expression—a flooding out—on the part of a participant will clear the air and reduce tension, but this is by no means always so. When an individual floods out, his defection is often studiously overlooked by the remaining participants and even, a moment later, by the offender himself. And when this suppression, this effortful non-perception occurs, a new distractive element has been added to the context of the encounter, increasing the amount of attended-to-material that must be treated as if not attended, and hence, by definition, increasing the tension level. Contrary to first impressions, then, a flooding out is often likely to constitute an incident.

It should be apparent that persons will differ greatly in their capacity to sustain tension without exhibiting it and without flooding out. This difference in degree of poise is to be accounted for at least in part by differences in group affiliation: middle-class American four-year-olds will sometimes blush and wriggle away when they are merely looked at, whereas Victorian *grandes dames* are reported to have been able to maintain poise under quite disastrous conditions.

It seems characteristic of teams that perform specialized work under pressure that the members develop a capacity to keep from mind, or to appear unmindful of, happenings which would cause those with less experience to flood out. Surgical teams in action provide nice illustrations, since they are obliged to maintain a single frame or perspective, a medical definition of the situation, that applies in a detailed way to a great number of minor events occurring during the task encounter; and yet the tasks performed in surgery can easily introduce lively reminders that other definitions of the situation are possible. Thus, when a small artery is accidentally cut and the blood shoots up into the face of an assistant, describing a pretty arc in doing so, attention may in fact not shift from the work that is being done except to tie off the "bleeder."[55] Similarly, when a small group of confirmed lovers of modern chamber music gather to listen to an informal, live, first performance of a local composer's quartet, everyone present can be counted on not to smile, giggle, or look quizzically about for definitional cues. An unschooled audience, however, would find great difficulty in drawing a line between the end of the tuning up and the beginning of the first movement, that is, between the tuning frame and the performing frame; its members would also feel less secure in taking the music seriously than in expressing disbelief. Unschooled audiences would, therefore, be unlikely to contain themselves on such an occasion.

Under what circumstances is flooding out likely, and when is it unlikely?

Common sense leads us to imagine that as the tension level increases, so the likelihood of flooding out increases, until the breaking point is reached and flooding out is inevitable. The work required of the transformation rules becomes intolerable, and there follows either disorder or a new, more manageable definition of the situation. The imagery here is hydraulic and not entirely adequate, for common sense neglects some important social determinants of how much tension can be withstood before a flooding out occurs.

During occasions when the reputation of large organizations or persons of high station are at stake, any open admission that things are not what they seem may carry externally relevant consequences that no one wants to face, and so a great deal of tension may be doggedly contained. It is no accident that the fable of the invisible new clothes concerns an emperor; so much difficult disregard of nakedness—so much resistance to re-identification—could hardly be sustained for a less consequential figure. Similarly, where one person is another's mentor, flooding out may be felt to be out of the question, as when an officer trainee learns that officers never break ranks and fall out because of illness or exhaustion,[56] or when a father in a burning theater restrains himself from joining the general panic flight to the exits because he does not want his small son to see him lose self-control.[57] So, too, when large numbers of participants are involved, there may be difficulty in obtaining agreement on a concerted change in the definition of the situation. On the other hand, informality can be partly defined as a license to flood out on minor pretexts; in fact, during informal encounters of a few people, small amounts of tension may be purposely engineered just for the fun of being capsized by them. Such encounters seem to have hardly any boundary, and almost anything of an extraneous nature can penetrate into the interaction. Because of this, we tend to think of such encounters as being easy, natural, and relaxed.

Instead of simply following commonsense notions, then, we must drastically limit our generalizations: we can only say that given a focused gathering which includes a given number of participants of given social statuses interacting with a given level of formality and seriousness, then the stability of role performance will vary inversely with the tension level.

I have suggested that when an individual floods out, other participants may contagiously flood out, too, or treat the incident (whether spontaneously or self-consciously) as if it had not occurred. There is also a third way in which participants respond to an offender. Seeking a tolerable level of tension, they can openly alter the rules, redefining the situation around the plight of the offender, but treating him now *not as a participant but as a mere focus of attention*—in fact, as an involuntary performer. Examples are to be found in situations where individuals are purposely teased until they flood out or at least become trapped in a "rise," thereby ensuring momentary easy involvement for the others, albeit in an encounter with new boundaries.[58] Thus, in the Shetlandic community studied by the writer, women of almost any age seemed to find it difficult to sustain an explicit compliment with equanimity and perhaps were not expected to do so. When complimented, they would often cast their heads down modestly, or, in cases where the complimenting was meant to tease, would rush at their tormentors with arms flailing, in a joking and cooperative effort to disrupt the exchange.[59]

An individual may mildly flood out, for example, by blushing, and half-induce others to reconstitute the mutual activity but now with himself temporarily in the role of mere object of attention. His willingness to withdraw in this way is presumably compensated for by the briefness with which the others require him to be outside the encounter.

There is a special kind of "free" flooding out that should be mentioned. When an alteration in official rules of irrelevance occurs, we can, perhaps, say, as Freud argued, that the "energy" previously employed to "bind" the suppressions can be set "free."[60] Further, the new rules of irrelevance—the new frame of reference—often provide a context in which it is especially difficult to maintain the previous suppressions. And so the participants flood out in regard to a definition of the situation that has just been displaced, it being safe to offend something no longer credited as reality. Typically, in such cases, we get a special-sounding "safe laughter."[61] This kind of laughter can often be distinguished by sound and gesture from the explosive, escaped, or blurted-out kind which can represent a personal failure to contain oneself, and which others present try to overlook. Interestingly enough, a laugh can start out as an involuntary failure at suppression, receive confirmation from others present, contagiously leading to a general (although usually temporary) abandonment of the previous definition of the situation, and then end with a sound that is unguilty and free. The whole encounter can thus flood out. Further, a "tipping" phenomenon can occur, with guilt for what they are about to do to the encounter for a time inhibiting those who are first to flood out, and freedom from responsibility facilitating the frame-break of those who flood out a moment later.

6. *Structure and Process.* We now may examine how the dynamics of interaction tie into its structure. During any encounter it is possible for a sub-set of participants to form a communicative byplay and, without ratifying their new mutual activity except among themselves, withdraw spontaneous involvement from the more inclusive encounter.[62] It is even possible for *all* the participants in a given encounter to join together to sustain a single, all-inclusive byplay, as when a team of workers momentarily slow up their work because of a particularly interesting bit of gossip. (It is also possible for "self collusion" to occur, as when a discomfited person finds it necessary to swear to himself and utter a brief comment to himself, in the face of needing the release but having no one present with whom to share it.) Sometimes these byplays are carried on quite furtively; always the gestures through which they are sustained will be modulated so as to show a continued respect for the official or dominant encounter.

If an individual finds himself flooding out of an officially binding encounter, one way in which he can handle his predicament is to enter into a more or less furtive byplay with one or two other participants. In this collusive encounter, a kind of ratification can be given to feelings and issues which have had to be suppressed in the dominant encounter. Unusable elements in the larger encounter can thus be removed by placing them at the center of a subordinate one. The byplay that results can realize among a small coalition of participants a congruence between official and spontaneous matters of concern that cannot be sustained by all of the participants.[63] Such draining action, while a threat to the official encounter, also provides a safety valve for it, for through the congenial world found in the byplay, the alienated participant can reassert control over himself.

As we might expect, upon the termination of an encounter in which much suppression has been needed, the ex-participants may immediately form into smaller groupings in which open expression of these tabooed matters becomes possible, giving rise not to byplays but rather to "postplays."[64]

While the affective bases of flooding out—joy, sorrow, fear, and so on—can vary, one emotion seems to have a special importance in the formation of tension-reducing byplays, namely, the moral shock that is evoked by witnessing improper acts. An example of such flooding out can often be observed when a well-meaning institutional psychiatrist attempts in the presence of a nurse to interview a mental patient who is, say, senile, mute, or paranoid. The psychiatrist's apparent sympathetic offer of a joint conversational world with the patient is at some point likely to fail to call forth "appropriate" participant activity from the patient, and at such a point there is a strong tendency indeed for the psychiatrist to glance at the nurse in a conclusive gesture of despair or derision. This sort of thing is found wherever one person tries in the presence of another to "get to" a third person who is a recalcitrant or incompetent participant.

Since a collusive byplay provides a tempting means of reducing tension, certain additional patterns of behavior are likely to be associated with it. One of these is eye-avoidance. When a person is just able to restrain himself from flooding out in laughter or tears, his "catching the eye" of another may lead to involuntary byplay, especially when the other is known to be in the same predicament and to be someone with whom the individual can safely engage in the intimacies of a collusive exchange. A minor release by one member of the coalition can form a basis for the other to give way a little more, and this in turn can be fed back into the system until both parties have lost control of themselves, while neither feels he is quite responsible for what has happened. Thus, persons may avoid each other's eyes to avoid starting a process that might finish them as participants.

Another pattern takes the form of a kind of flooding in, instead of flooding out. There will often be persons in close proximity to a conversational encounter who, while not ratified as official paritcipants, are none the less within easy hearing range of the talk and respond to this by maintaining a tactful look of inattention. When an incident occurs in this half-overheard encounter, especially a funny incident, the outsiders may find it impossible to sustain an appearance of involvement in their own official activity. During such moments, they may find themselves entering into collusive byplay with one or more participants, the resulting encounter cutting across the boundaries of the dominant one. For example, when a bus conductor finds that a passenger insists on disputing the fare or is too intoxicated to handle change properly, the conductor may in wry moral indignation collude with the next passenger in line, breaking down a barrier to do so. Similarly, when a number of persons find themselves in the same elevator, and are silent except for two or three who are openly carrying on a conversation, an appropriate remark on the part of one of the nonparticipants may collapse the boundary separating the participants from the nonparticipants.

I have suggested that tension generated in an encounter can be dealt with through actions involving the structure of the encounter: momentary reduction of a participant into a mere performer, collusive byplays, postplays. An important additional possibility must be mentioned.

When all the participants in an encounter together flood out, say, into laughter, very commonly the prior definition of the situation is resurrected after the outburst has passed. What seems to be involved is not an alteration of the transformation rules, followed by a realteration, a return to the initial formula, but rather a momentary abeyance of the dominant encounter while a subordinate one is allowed fleetingly to hold sway. The collusive byplay which results is as temporary as most but includes all the participants in the encounter. The possibility of maintaining a subordinate encounter, even while maintaining a dominant one, is pressed to its limits and burdened with a sudden task. Thus, individuals can collectively collapse as participants in a focused gathering but the next moment can set their collapse aside and dissociate themselves from it, returning to the prior world but with less tension. It is this dissociable collapse that typically occurs when situations are "made" or tension-reducing integrations are attempted. And this, too, is what is usually involved when "free" flooding out occurs.

Since the introduction of a tactful or hostile joke is likely to lead all the participants into a temporary new engagement if successful and into greater dysphoria if unsuccessful, we can understand that the right to make such efforts will not be randomly distributed among the participants of the encounter but that role differentiation will occur which places this venturesome function in special hands. This is especially true when the participants spend time together in a series of similar encounters. Thus, the right to "make a joke of something" is often restricted to the ranking person present,[65] or to a subordinate playing the part of a fool[66]—a part that allows him to take liberties during interaction in exchange for his character. In either case, this redirecting influence can be accomplished without threatening to alter the sensed distribution of influence and power within the encounter. Where material is introduced that permanently alters the transformation rules, an even closer fit between manipulation and rank may be expected.

7. *Interaction Membrane.* It should now be evident that the concept of transformation rules does not cover all the facts. When the wider world passes through the boundary of an encounter and is worked into the interaction activity, more than a re-ordering or transformation of pattern occurs. Something of an organic psychobiological nature takes place. Some of the potentially determinative wider world is easefully disattended; some is repressed; and some is suppressed self-consciously at the price of felt distraction. Where easeful disattention occurs, there will be no tendency to modify the transformation rules; where felt distraction occurs there will be pressure on the rulings. An incident endangers the transformation rules, not directly but by altering the psychic work that is being done by those who must interact in accordance with these rules.

In order to think more easily in these organic terms, an organic metaphore might be attempted. A living cell usually has a cell wall, a membrane, which cuts the cell off from components in its external milieu, ensuring a selective relation between them and the internal composition of the cell. The resilience and health of the cell is expressed in the capacity of its membrane to maintain a particular selective function. But unlike a set of transformation rules, a membrane does the actual work of filtering and does not merely designate that a selection from the external milieu is being maintained. Further, the membrane is subject to many threats, for it can sustain its work and its function over only a small range of changes in the external system.

If we think of an encounter as having a metaphorical membrane around it, we can bring our concerns into focus. We can see that the dynamics of an encounter will be tied to the functioning of the boundary-maintaining mechanisms that cut the encounter off selectively from wider worlds.[67] And we can begin to ask about the kinds of components in the encounter's external milieu that will expand or contract the range of events with which the encounter deals, and the kinds of components that will make the encounter resilient or destroy it.

BASES OF FUN

In this paper, we have come by stages to focus on the question of euphoria in encounters, arguing that euphoria arises when persons can spontaneously maintain the authorized transformation rules. We assume that participants will judge past encounters according to whether they were or were not easy to be in and will be much concerned to maximize euphoria, through, for example, integrative acts, topic selection, and avoidance of encounters likely to be dysphoric.

But of course this tells us only in a very general way what people do to ensure easeful interaction, for in pointing to the requirement that spontaneous involvement must coincide with obligatory involvement, we are merely pushing the problem back one step. We still must go on to consider what will produce this congruence for any given encounter.

In concluding this paper, then, I would like to take a speculative look at some of the conditions, once removed, that seem to ensure easeful interaction. Again, there seems to be no better starting point than what I labeled gaming encounters. Not only are games selected and discarded on the basis of their ensuring euphoric interaction, but, to ensure engrossment, they are also sometimes modified in a manner provided for within their rules, thus giving us a delicate tracer of what is needed to ensure euphoria. Instead of having to generate an allocation of spontaneous involvement that coincides with the transformation rules, it is possible to modify the transformation rules to fit the distribution and possibilities of spontaneous involvement. The practices of "balancing" teams, handicapping, limiting participation to skill classes, or adjusting the betting limits, all introduce sufficient malleability into the materials of the game to allow the game to be molded and fashioned into a shape best suited to hold the participants entranced. We can at last return, therefore, to our original theme: fun in games.

There is a common-sense view that games are fun to play when the outcome or pay-off has a good chance of remaining unsettled until the end of play (even though it is also necessary that play come to a final settlement within a reasonable period of time). The practices of balancing teams and of handicapping unmatched ones, and the practice of judiciously interposing a randomizing element, "pure luck" (especially to the degree that perfect matching or handicapping is not possible), all work to ensure that a prior knowledge of the attributes of the players will not render the outcome a foregone conclusion. On similar grounds, should the final score come to be predictable, as often happens near the end of the play, concession by the loser is likely, terminating the action in the interests of both the play and the gaming encounter.

To speak of the outcome as problematic, however, is, in effect, to say that one must look to the play itself in order to discover how things will turn out. The developing line built up by the alternating, interlocking moves of the players can thus maintain sole claim upon the attention of the participants, thereby facilitating the game's power to constitute the current reality of its players and to engross them. We can thus understand one of the social reasons why cheaters are resented; by locating the power of determining the outcome of the play in the arrangements made by one player, cheating, like mismatching, destroys the reality-generating power of the game[68] (Of course, whereas the mismatching of teams prevents a play world from developing, the discovery that someone is cheating punctures and deflates a world that has already developed.)

But this analysis is surely not enough. In games of pure chance, such as flipping coins, there would never be a problem of balancing sides, yet, unless such other factors as money bets are carefully added, mere uncertainty of outcome is not enough to engross the players.

Another possibility is that games give the players an opportunity to exhibit attributes valued in the wider social world, such as dexterity, strength, knowledge, intelligence, courage, and self-control. Externally relevant attributes thus obtain official expression within the milieu of an encounter. These attributes could even be earned within the encounter, to be claimed later outside it.

Again, this alone is not enough, for mismatched teams allow the better player to exhibit all kinds of capacities. He, at least, should be satisfied. Still, we know that, whatever his actual feelings, he is not likely to admit to getting much satisfaction out of this kind of gaming and is, in fact, quite likely to find himself bored and unengrossed in the play.

But if we combine our two principles—problematic outcome and sanctioned display—we may have something more valid. A successful game would then be one which, first, had a problematic outcome and then, within these limits, allowed for a maximum possible display of externally relevant attributes.

This dual theme makes some sense. A good player who is unopposed in displaying his powers may give the impression of too openly making claims; he would be acting contrary to the rules of irrelevance which require him to forego attending to many of his externally relevant social attributes. But as long as his efforts are called forth in the heat of close competition, they are called forth by the interaction itself and not merely for show. Uncertainty of outcome gives the player a shield behind which he can work into the interaction attributes that would threaten the membrane surrounding the encounter if openly introduced.

How far can we generalize this explanation? First we must see that this conception of a dual principle leads us back to a consideration of betting games and the efforts of those around a table to locate a euphoria function. If the participants perceive that the betting is very low relative to their financial capacities, then interest in money itself cannot penetrate the encounter and enliven it. Interest in the game may flag; participants may fail to "take it seriously." On the other hand, if the players feel that the betting is high in relation to their income and resources, then interest may be strangled, a participant in a play flooding out of the gaming encounter into an anxious private concern for his general economic welfare.[69] A player in these circumstances is forced to take the game "too seriously."

When players at the beginning of play give thought to an appropriate scale of stakes, they are seeking for that kind of screen behind which an interest in money can seep into the game. This is one reason for restricting the game to persons who, it is felt, can afford to lose roughly the same amount. We can similarly understand the tendency for the level of bets to be raised part way through the gaming, since by then the game itself has had a chance to grasp the players and inure them against what they previously considered too worrisome a loss.

We also see that the notion of taking a game too seriously or not seriously enough does not quite fit our notions of the contrast between recreational "unserious" activity and workaday "serious" activity. The issue apparently is not whether the activity belongs to the recreational sphere or the work sphere, but whether external pulls upon one's interest can be selectively held in check so that one can become absorbed in the encounter as a world in itself. The problem of too-serious or not-serious-enough arises in gaming encounters not because a game is involved but because an encounter is involved.

Financial status is not the only fundamental aspect of a person's life which can enter through the membrane of an encounter and enliven or spoil the proceedings. Physical safety, for example, seems to be another. In children's play activities, risk to the physical integrity of the body is often introduced, again on a carefully graded not-too-much-not-too-little basis. For example, slides must be steep enough to be a challenge, yet not so steep as to make an accident too likely: a little more risk than can be easily handled seems to do the trick. (Adult sports such as skiing seem to be based on the same principle—a means of creating tension in regard to physical safety is here integrated into the play activity, giving rise to merriment.)[70] All of this has been stated by Fritz Redl in his discussion of the "ego-supporting" functions of successful games:

> I would like to list a few of the things that must happen for a "game" to "break down." It breaks down if it is not fun any more; that means if certain gratification guarantees, for the sake of which individuals were lured into it, stop being gratifying. There are many reasons why that may happen. It breaks down, too, if it is not safe any more, that is, when the risks or the dangers an individual exposes himself to in the game outweigh whatever gratification he may derive from it. By safe, I mean internally and externally. The actual risks and the physical strain or the fear of hurt may become too great or the fear of one's own passivity may become too great. This is why, by choice, children sometimes do not allow themselves to play certain games, because they are afraid of their own excitation or they know that the danger of loss of self-control in this activity is so seductive and so great that they would rather not play. In fact, some of the mechanisms of games seem to be built to guarantee gratification, but they also guarantee security against one's own superego pressures or against the outside dangers. Again, a game breaks down when the "as if" character cannot be maintained, or when the reality proximity is too great, and this may vary from game to game. There are some games that stop being fun when they get too fantastic and there is not enough similarity to a real competitive situation; there are other games which stop being fun the other way around. If one comes too close to reality, then the activity may lose its game character, as do some games that are too far from reality. Where is too far away or too close? This is the question for which I do not know the answer.[71]

It is possible to go on and see in games a means of infusing or integrating into gaming encounters many different socially significant externally based matters. This seems to be one reason why different cultural milieux favor different kinds of games, and some historical changes in the equipment of a game appear to respond to social changes in the milieu in which the game is played.[72] And apart from the equipment itself, there is the issue of the wider social position of the contending players. Thus, for example, the clash of football teams on a playing field can provide a means by which the antagonism between the two groups represented by the teams may be allowed to enter an encounter in a controlled manner and to be given expression.[73] We can then predict that, at least as far as spectators are concerned, two teams drawn from the same social grouping may produce a conflict that falls flat, and two teams drawn from groupings openly opposed to each other may provide incidents during which so much externally based hostility flows into the mutual activity of the sporting encounter as to burst the membrane surrounding it, leading to riots, fights, and other signs of a breakdown in order. All this is suggested by Max Gluckman in his discussion of British football, where he attempts to explain why league teams can represent different schools, towns, and regions but with much more difficulty different religious groupings and different social classes:

> A similar situation might be found in school matches. We know that the unity and internal loyalty of schools is largely built up by formalized competition in games with other schools—and I should expect this system to work well as long as each school mainly played other schools of the same type as itself. What would happen if public schools became involved in contests with secondary modern schools? Would the whole national background of divergence in opportunity, prospects, and privilege, embitter the game till they ceased to serve their purpose of friendly rivalry? Is it only because Oxford and Cambridge can produce better teams than the provincial universities that they confine their rivalry in the main to contests between themselves?[74]

The social differences, then, between the two supporting audiences for the teams must be of the kind that can be tapped without breaking the barrel. It may be, however, that the same can be said about any major externally based experience common to members of an audience. A stage play that does not touch on issues relevant to the audience is likely to fall flat, and yet staged materials can be pressed to a point where they insufficiently disguise the realities on which they dwell, causing the audience to be moved too much. Thus, realistic plays put on for unsophisticated audiences are felt by some to be in bad taste, to "go too far," or to "come too close to home"—as was the feelings, so I was informed, when *Riders to the Sea* was staged for a Shetland audience. What has been called "symbolic distance" must be assured. A membrane must be maintained that will control the flow of externally relevant sentiments into the interaction. Interestingly enough, the same effect can be seen in the judgment adult audiences make in watching their children use sacred materials for purposes of play, as Caillois points out in discussing the fact that games are not merely current residues of past realities:

> These remarks are no less valid for the sacred than for the profane. The katcinas are semidivinities, the principal objects of worship among the Pueblo Indians of New Mexico; this does not prevent the same adults who worship them and incarnate them in their masked dances

from making dolls resembling them for the amusement of their sons. Similarly, in Catholic countries, children currently play at going to Mass, at being confirmed, at marriage and funerals. Parents permit this at least as long as the imitation remains a respectful one. In black Africa the children make masks and rhombs in the same way and are punished for the same reasons, if the imitation goes too far and becomes too much of a parody or a sacrilege.[75]

It seems, then, that in games and similar activities disguises must be provided which check, but do not stop, the flow of socially significant matters into the encounter. All this goes beyond my earlier statement that the material character of game equipment is not relevant. The game-relevant meanings of the various pieces of the game equipment are in themselves a useful disguise, for behind these meanings the sentimental, material, and esthetic value of the pieces can steal into the interaction, infusing it with tones of meaning that have nothing to do with the logic of the game but something to do with the pleasure of the gaming encounter; the traditional concern in Japan about the quality of equipment used to play *Go* is an extreme example. In this way, too, perhaps, the conversation and cuisine in a restaurant can, if good enough, not only blot out a humble setting, but also, in elegant establishments, allow us a deepened identification with the cost of the *décor*, the command in the service, and the social status of groups at the other tables—an identification we would not allow ourselves were the process not disguised. And it seems that the malleability of game arrangements—choice of games, sides, handicaps, bets—allows for the fabrication of exactly the right amount of disguise.

But here we have a theme that echoes the doctrine that has been built around projective testing, namely, that the ambiguity and malleability of test material allows subjects to structure it according to their own propensity, to express quite personal "loaded" themes because the materials are sufficiently removed from reality to allow the subject to avoid seeing what he is doing with them. A discontinuity with the world is achieved even while a connection with it is established. Of course, these tests are usually directed to one subject and his world, as opposed to an encounter with many individuals in it, but the presence of the tester focusing his attention on the subject's response does in a way supply the conditions of a two-person encounter.

A glance at the literature on projective devices encourages us to continue along this tack. Take for example the beautiful work of Erikson on play therapy published in 1937.[76] He describes children who cannot bring themselves to talk about their troubles—in fact, may even be too young to do so. The affect attached to the suppressed and repressed materials would rupture any membrane around any mutual or individual activity that alluded to this material. In some cases these constraints block any verbal communication. But by allowing the child to construct play configurations out of doll-like objects that are somewhat removed from the reality projected on them, the child feels some relief, some ease; and he does so through the process of infusing his painful concerns into the local situation in a safely transformed manner.

Once the special relevance of projective testing is granted, we need not be bound by formal test materials, but can include any situation where an individual can permit himself to interact by virtue of a disguise, in fact, transformation rules that he is allowed to create. Fromm-Reichmann provides an example:

> Perhaps my interest began with the young catatonic woman who broke through a period of completely blocked communication and obvious anxiety by responding when I asked her a question about her feeling miserable: She raised her hand with her thumb lifted, the other four fingers bent toward her palm, so that I could see only the thumb, isolated from the four hidden fingers. I interpreted the signal with, "That lonely?" in a sympathetic tone of voice. At this, her facial expression loosened up as though in great relief and gratitude, and her fingers opened. Then she began to tell me about herself by means of her fingers, and she asked me by gestures to respond in kind. We continued with this finger conversation for one or two weeks, and as we did so, her anxious tension began to decrease and she began to break through her noncommunicative isolation; and subsequently she emerged altogether from her loneliness.[77]

In both these cases what we see is an individual himself determining the kind of veil that will be drawn over his feelings while in communication with another. The system of etiquette and reserve that members of every group employ in social intercourse would seem to function in the same way, but in this case the disguise is socially standardized; it is applied by the individual but not tailored by himself to his own particular needs.

In psychotherapeutic intervention with greatly withdrawn patients, the therapist may have to agree to the patient's using a very heavy disguise, but in psychotherapy with "neurotics," we may see something of the opposiste extreme. In the psychoanalytical doctrine of transference and the psychoanalytical rule of free association, we meet the notion that a membrane can be established that is so diaphanous and yet so tough that any externally related feeling on the part of the patient can be activated and infused into the encounter without destroying the doctor-patient encounter. This is facilitated, of course, by the professional arrangement that separates the analytical couch from home life and home authorities.[78] The extension of this tell-all doctrine to group psychotherapy merely moves matters more in the direction of the kind of encounter considered in this paper.

This view of the function of disguise allows us to consider the phenomenon of "subversive ironies." One of the most appealing ways in which situations are "made" can be found in times and places of stress where matters that are extremely difficult to bear and typically excluded by the official transformation rules are introduced lightly and ironically. The classic case is "gallows humor." In concentration camps, for example, turnips were sometimes called "German pineapple,"[79] fatigue drill, "geography."[80] In a mental hospital, a patient may express to other patients his feelings about the place by referring to the medical and surgical building with conscious irony as the "hospital," thereby establishing the rest of the institution as a different kind of place.[81] In general, these subversive ironies would seem to "come off" when they open the way for some expression of feeling that is generated in the institutional situation at large but disguise what is being expressed sufficiently to ensure the orderliness of the particular encounter.

Within the same perspective, we can consider the functions of indirection in informal social control. For example, when a member of a work group begins to threaten informal work quotas by producing too much, we can follow the actions of his fellow workers who, perhaps unwilling to express directly their resentment and their desire for control, may employ a game of "binging" or "piling" through which the nonconformist is brought back into line under the guise of being the butt of a joke.[82]

Whatever the interaction, then, there is this dual theme: the wider world must be introduced, but in a controlled and disguised manner. Individuals can deal with one another face to face because they are ready to abide by rules of irrelevance, but the rules seem to exist to let something difficult be quietly expressed as much as to exclude it entirely from the scene. Given the dangers of expression, a disguise may function not so much as a way of concealing something as a way of revealing as much of it as can be tolerated in an encounter. We fence our encounters in with gates; the very means by which we hold off a part of reality can be the means by which we can bear introducing it.

As a final step, I would like to trace the same dual theme in sociability, in occasions such as parties, which form a structured setting for many comings-together during an evening.

It can be argued that informal social participation is an ultimate validation of relationships of intimacy and equality with those with whom one shares this activity.[83] A party, then, is by way of being a status blood bath, a leveling up and leveling down of all present, a mutual contamination and sacralization. Concretely phrased, a party is an opportunity to engage in encounters that will widen one's social horizons through, for example, sexual bond-formation, informality with those of high rank, or extending one's invitation circle. Where boundaries have already been tentatively widened, parties can function to confirm and consolidate work begun elsewhere.

Thus defined, a party presents us with a double set of requirements and, behind these, another illustration of our double theme. On one hand, we can look to the common rationalizations and causes of social endogamy, the rule that only equals be invited to a sociable gathering. When we ask persons about their exclusiveness, they tend to claim that they would not have "anything in common" with those not invited and that mixing different classes of persons makes everyone "uncomfortable." Presumably, what they mean here is that officially irrelevant attributes would obtrude upon the occasion, destroying the identities upon which the sociability was organized and killing spontaneous involvement in the recreation at hand.

But precisely the opposite concern will be felt, too. Often, sociable conversations and games fail not because the participants are insufficiently close socially but because they are not far enough apart. A feeling of boredom, that nothing is likely to happen, can arise when the same persons spend all their sociable moments together. Social horizons cannot be extended. One hears the phrases: "The same old people," "the same old thing, let's not go." The speakers, in fact, usually go, but not hopefully.

So we find that the euphoria function for a sociable occasion resides somewhere between little social difference and much social difference. A dissolution of some externally based social distance must be achieved, a penetration of ego-boundaries, but not to an extent that renders the participants fearful, threatened, or self-consciously concerned with what is happening socially. Too much potential loss and gain must be guarded against, as well as too little.

Too much or too little of this "working through" will force participants to look directly at the kind of work that parties are expected to do and at the impulses that cause persons to attend or stay away—impulses that ought to be concealed in what is done at parties even while providing the energy for doing it. Sociologically speaking, a very decorous party, as well as an indecorous one, can become obscene, exposing desires out of the context in which they can be clothed by locally realized events.

From this, it follows, of course, that what is a successful and happy occasion for one participant may not be such for another. Further, it follows that if the many are to be pleased, then the few may have to sacrifice themselves to the occasion, allowing their bodies to be cast into the blend to make the bell sound sweet. Perhaps they rely at such times on other kinds of pleasures.

CONCLUSIONS

I have argued in this paper that any social encounter, any focused gathering, is to be understood, in the first instance, in terms of the functioning of the "membrane" that encloses it, cutting it off from a field of properties that could be given weight. There is a set of transformation rules that officially lays down what sorts of properties are to be given what kind of influence in the allocation of locally realized resources. If a participant can become spontaneously involved in the focus of attention prescribed by these transformation rules, he will feel natural, at ease, sure about the reality in which he and the others are sustained. An encounter provides a world for its participants, but the character and stability of this world is intimately related to its selective relationship to the wider one. The naturalistic study of encounters, then, is more closely tied to studies of social structure on one hand, and more separate from them, than one might at first imagine.

I have attempted to show the effects of standard socio-economic attributes on the workings of an encounter. In this, a course has been followed that is customary in sociological analysis, but one important difference must be noted. Empirically, the effect of externally based social attributes on social encounters is very great. But the analysis and theory of this effect must give equal weight to matters such as noise, fatigue, or facial disfigurations. The race-group status of one participant in a focused gathering can have something of the same effect as the harelip of another; the route through which socio-economic factors enter an encounter is one that is equally open to a strange and undignified set of vehicles.

As far as gaming encounters and other focused gatherings are concerned, the most serious thing to consider is the fun in them. Something in which the individual can become unselfconsciously engrossed is something that can become real to him. Events that occur in his immediate physical presence are ones in which he can become easily engrossed. *Joint* engrossment in something with others reinforces the reality carved out by the individual's attention, even while subjecting this entrancement to the destructive distractions that the others are now in a position to cause.

The process of mutually sustaining a definition of the situation in face-to-face interaction is socially organized through rules of relevance and irrelevance. These rules for the management of engrossment appear to be an insubstantial element of social life, a matter of courtesy, manners, and etiquette. But it is to these flimsy rules, and not to the unshaking character of the external world, that we owe our unshaking sense of realities. To be at ease in a situation is to be properly subject to these rules, entranced by the meanings they generate and stabilize; to be ill at ease means that one is ungrasped by immediate reality and that one loosens the grasp that others have of it. To be awkward or unkempt, to talk or move wrongly, is to be a dangerous giant, a destroyer of worlds. As every psychotic and comic ought to know, any accurately improper move can poke through the thin sleeve of immediate reality.

Notes

1. I am grateful to the Center for the Integration of Social Science Theory of the University of California, Berkeley, and to the Society for the Study of Human Ecology, New York, for support during the preparation of this paper.
2. Roger Caillois, in his very useful paper, "Unity of Play: Diversity of Games," *Diogenes*, No. 19 (1957), p. 99. See also Johan Huizinga, *Homo Ludens* (Boston: Beacon Press, 1950), p. 28.
3. The term "encounter" has a range of everyday meaning that reduces its value as a general term. Sometimes it is used to refer to face-to-face meetings with another that were unexpected or in which trouble occurred; sometimes it refers to meeting another at a social occasion, the frequency of comings-together during the occasion not being the issue. All these meanings, I have to exclude.
4. I draw my orientation here from Harold Garfinkel, especially his "Some Conceptions of and Experiments With 'Trust' as a Condition of Stable Concerted Action," unpublished paper. A recent application of this paper may be found in A. K. Cohen, "The Study of Social Disorganization and Deviant Behavior," in R. K. Merton, L. Broom, and L. S. Cottrell, Jr., *Sociology Today* (New York: Basic Books, 1959), pp. 461-484, especially p. 474 ff.
5. See, for example, P. R. Reid, *Escape from Colditz* (New York: Berkley Publishing Corp., 1952), p. 63.
6. Gregory Bateson, "A Theory of Play and Fantasy," in *Psychiatric Research Reports 2*, American Psychiatric Association, 1955, p. 44.
7. Georg Simmel, *The Sociology of Georg Simmel*, trans. by K. H. Wolff (Glencoe: The Free Press, 1950), pp. 45-46.
8. *Ibid.*, p. 49.
9. *Ibid.*, pp. 48-49.

10. Max Weber, *From Max Weber: Essays in Sociology*, trans. and ed. by H. H. Gerth and C. W. Mills (New York: Oxford University Press, 1946), pp. 215-216. The stress appears in the original.
11. *Ibid.*, p. 224.
12. Talcott Parsons, *The Social System* (Glencoe: The Free Press, 1951), p. 435. For an additional treatment of universalism and affective neutrality, see the essay in which Parsons first employed the terms extensively, "The Professions and Social Structure," reprinted as Chap. 8, pp. 185-199, in his *Essays in Sociological Theory Pure and Applied* (Glencoe: The Free Press, 1949). A formal definition of "universalism" may also be found in T. Parsons and E. Shils, eds., *Toward a General Theory of Action* (Cambridge: Harvard University Press, 1952), p. 82.
13. Simmel, *op. cit.*, p. 46.
14. Sigmund Freud, *The Basic Writings of Sigmund Freud* (New York: Modern Library, 1938), pp. 177-178. The passage occurs as the ending to his monograph, *Psychopathology of Everyday Life;* the stress is in the original.
15. In Catholic nunneries, apparently, this training is elaborated in a remarkable discipline that forbids all possible "singularization," all ways of putting oneself forward or apart from the rest.
16. Garfinkel, *op. cit.*, p. 7.
17. Kurt Riezler, "Play and Seriousness," *The Journal of Philosophy*, 38 (1941), pp. 505-517, p. 505.
18. R. F. Bales, *Interaction Process Analysis* (Cambridge: Addison-Wesley, 1950), pp. 73-84, employs the term resources but defines it as merely one item for distribution, the others being authority, honor, and group solidarity.
19. Interest in allocative processes has recently been stimulated by the work of Talcott Parsons, especially T. Parsons and N. J. Smelser, *Economy and Society* (Glencoe: The Free Press, 1956), pp. 51-100.
20. It should be noted that two types of exclusion can be involved here, one determining who will participate with whom in a given type of encounter, and a second, less obvious, determining who will be allowed to participate in this type of encounter under any circumstances. In the sociologist's Golden Age of England, servants would have been considered above themselves to play tennis even amongst themselves. Similarly, there have been times when chess was restricted to court circles, and there are records of punishment given to those who bootlegged the game. (For this and other aspects of the "royal game," see the interesting paper by Norman Reider, "Chess, Oedipus and the Mater Dolorosa," *The International Journal of Psyco-Analysis*, 40 [1959], reprinted in *Psychoanalysis and the Psychoanalytic Review*, 47 [1960].) In our own society we have an array of state laws specifying that females below a given age cannot participate in sexual encounters with anyone and that females above this age can participate only with certain categories of others.
21. Often, of course, by employing externally based attributes that are either taken for granted or trivial (such as length of diplomatic residence), other externally based attributes that might be in dispute can be excluded from the situation.
22. Emily Post, *Etiquette* (New York: Funk and Wagnalls, 1937), p. 681: Rank is always official. This means that plain Mr. Smith, who has become "His Excellency the Ambassador," ranks a Prince or a Duke who is officially a Secretary of Embassy.
23. Max Gluckman, *Custom and Conflict in Africa* (Glencoe: The Free Press, 1955), p. 109.
24. *Ibid.*, p. 132.
25. E. Goffman, "The Characteristics of Total Institutions," in *Symposium on Preventive and Social Psychiatry* (Washington, D. C.: Walter Reed Army Institute of Research, April 15-17, 1957), pp. 77-78.

26. Alfred Metraux, "Dramatic Elements in Ritual Possession," *Diogenes*, No. 11 (1955), p. 29.
27. See E. Goffman, "The Nature of Deference and Demeanor," *American Anthropologist*, 58 (1956), pp. 473-502. Recent interest in comparing the character of large-scale societies, partly deriving from a re-reading of travel accounts, such as that of de Tocqueville, has led to describing the character of a society by the equalitarian or inequalitarian character of the personal encounters occurring in it, especially those occurring in public and semi-public places. While the transformation rules for public conduct are an important element of a society, they certainly do not provide us with a description of its social structure. There is a large difference between the distribution of substantive rights and power in a society and the distribution of conversational courtesies.
28. Here I draw on the work of T. C. Schelling, now available in his *The Strategy of Conflict* (Cambridge: Harvard University Press, 1960).
29. John von Neumann and Oskar Morgenstern, *Theory of Games and Economic Behavior* (Princeton: Princeton University Press, 1944), p. 49.
30. Compare here the helpful discussion of the difference between official game and spectacle in K. L. Pike, *Language in Relation to a Unified Theory of the Structure of Human Behavior* (Glendale, Calif.: Summer Institute of Linguistics, 1954), Part I, pp. 44-45.
31. See, for example, Norton Long, "The Local Community as an Ecology of Games," *American Journal of Sociology*, 64 (1958), pp. 251-256, especially p. 253. Kurt Riezler in *Man Mutable and Immutable* (Chicago: Regnery, 1950), p. 64, provides a succinct statement:

    When we speak of the world of the theatre, of politics, of journalism or high finance, we indicate a kind of unity of a way of thinking and living in a universe of response in which man aims at reputation, status, a weighty voice.
32. Among social psychologists, an explicit consideration of this element is given by T. R. Sarbin in "Role Theory," section "Organismic Dimension," pp. 233-235 in Gardner Lindzey, ed., *Handbook of Social Psychology* (Cambridge: Addison-Wesley, 1954). See also E. F. Borgatta and L. S. Cottrell, Jr., "On the Classification of Groups," *Sociometry*, 18 (1955), pp. 416-418.
33. E. Goffman, "Alienation from Interaction," *Human Relations*, 10 (1957), p. 47.
34. H. S. Sullivan, *Clinical Studies in Psychiatry* (New York: Norton, 1956), pp. 38-76, especially pp. 63-64.
35. This is not to say that formally relevant strategies for playing games will not be required to take the world of concrete face-to-face interaction into consideration. Assessing a possible bluff is a formal part of the game of poker, the player being advised to examine his opponent's minor and presumably uncalculated expressive behavior. Games vary greatly in the use the player is obliged to make of apparently non-game aspects of the local concrete situation; in checkers, little attention need be given to such matters, in poker, much. Further, formal rules in some games are expressly concerned with the social-psychological character of gaming, so that, for example, when time out is permitted, a time limit to the rest period may be stipulated.
36. Sonia Keppel, *Edwardian Daughter* (New York: British Book Centre, 1959), pp. 22-23.
37. An excellent example may be found in a short story by William Sansom, "The Kiss," in his *Something Terrible, Something Lovely* (New York: Harcourt, Brace, n.d.), pp. 54-57. This kind of encounter, if formalized in game-theoretical terms, would clearly have some distinctive ungame-like features: once started, time out cannot easily be declared, kibitzers are usually lethal, and substitutes ordinarily cannot be brought in.
38. Goffman, "Alienation," pp. 53-54.

39. E. Goffman, "Embarrassment and Social Organization," *American Journal of Sociology*, 62 (1956), p. 268.
40. See E. H. Schein, "The Chinese Indoctrination Program for Prisoners of War," *Psychiatry*, 19 (1956), p. 153.
41. Especially the section "Mistakes in Speech," *op. cit.*, pp. 69-86. In this monograph, Freud is mainly concerned with the meaning of unexpected phrasings as an expression of the speaker's unconscious or merely suppressed wishes and concerns. Later, in his *Wit and Its Relation to the Unconscious*, he gives more weight to what is our prime concern here, the relation of the incident to the encounter in which it occurs.
42. The rules of irrelevance for encounters in public life, through which physical handicaps are often officially treated as if they did not exist, are neatly described by Nigel Dennis in his brilliant story, "A Bicycle Built for Two," *Encounter*, 15 (1960), pp. 12-22, especially pp. 14-15.
43. C. H. Cooley, *Human Nature and the Social Order* (New York: Scribner's, 1922), pp. 259-260.
44. W. F. Whyte, *Street Corner Society* (revised ed.; Chicago: University of Chicago Press, 1955), "Bowling and Social Ranking," pp. 14-25.
45. Cited in *The Observer*, Sunday, Sept. 21, 1958, p. 15.
46. Fritz Redl and David Wineman, *Controls from Within* (Glencoe: The Free Press, 1952), p. 104.
47. See, for example, R. K. White, B. A. Wright, and T. Dembo, "Studies in Adjustment to Visible Injuries: Evaluation of Curiosity by the Injured," *Journal of Abnormal and Social Psychology*, 43 (1948), pp. 13-28, especially pp. 25-27. I would like to add that an interesting difference in class culture is seen here. In the urban working class, a boy with a physical or social peculiarity may have constant recognition of this shortcoming built into the nickname by which he is addressed; certain kinds of tension are therefore unlikely to build up. A middle-class youth with the same stigma is likely to be greeted more tactfully, but sometimes with more tension.
48. Such acts are difficult to sanction harshly without further increasing the difficulty caused to the encounter.
49. Chandler Brossard, *Who Walk in Darkness* (New York: New Directions, 1952), p. 184.
50. *Pride and Prejudice*, Chap. 18. I am indebted to an unpublished paper by Stephanie Rothman for this quotation.
51. See E. Goffman, "On Face-Work," *Psychiatry*, 18 (1955), pp. 213-231, "Making Points—The Aggressive Use of Face-Work," pp. 221-222. A useful statement, presented in terms of destroying another's possibility of control, may be found in Tom Burns, "The Forms of Conduct," *American Journal of Sociology*, 64 (1958), pp. 142-143.
52. A somewhat similar analysis can be made of all forms of "hazing." See E. Goffman, *The Presentation of Self in Everyday Life* (New York: Anchor, 1959), pp. 174-175.
53. Goffman, "Embarrassment," p. 267. This paper deals with one chief form of flooding out, embarrassment.
54. As a reminder that encounters involve psychobiological processes, there is the often-noted fact that under conditions of fatigue individuals seem likely to find almost anything funny enough to cause them to flood out of the frame in which they have been. See, for example, G. Bateson, "The Position of Humor in Human Communication," p. 18, in H. von Foerster, ed., *Cybernetics*, Transactions of The Ninth (1952) Conference (New York: Josiah Macy, Jr. Foundation, 1953).
55. Writer's unpublished study of two surgery wards.
56. Simon Raven, "Perish by the Sword: A Memoir of the Military Establishment," *Encounter*, 12 (1959), p. 38.

57. Cited by E. L. Quarantelli in "A Study of Panic: Its Nature, Types, and Conditions" (unpublished Master's thesis, Department of Sociology, University of Chicago, 1953), p. 75, from a published account by C. B. Kelland.
58. An excellent general statement may be found in John Dollard, "The Dozens: Dialect of Insult," *American Imago*, I (1939), pp. 3-25. A prison version is reported by Alfred Hassler, *Dairy of a Self-Made Convict* (Chicago: Regnery, 1954), pp. 126-127.

There is a "game" some of the boys "play" in here called "playing the dozens." I have no idea what the origin of the name can be, but the idea is that the participants try to make each other mad by hurling epithets. The first one to lose his temper loses the game. I listened in on one, and it stood my hair on end. The "players" vie with each other in combining the most obscene and insulting accusations against not only the opponent himself, but anyone for whose reputation he might conceivably have some regard. Mothers, sisters, wives, children all come under the ban, and the players explore possibilities of degraded behavior, generally sexual, of the most revolting nature.

Quite frequently, both players lose their tempers, and actual fights are not unknown. Occasionally, a man will "play the dozens" with someone who has not experienced it before, and in such case the consequence can be serious. One man was knifed not long ago in just such an affair.

See also Bateson and Mead, *Balinese Character* (New York: New York Academy of Sciences, 1942), discussion of teasing, pp. 148-149. A variation of the game of the "dozens," the Italian game called *La Passatella*, played by male adults in cafes, is presented in detail in Roger Vailland's novel, *The Law*, trans. by Peter Wiles (New York: Bantam Books, 1959), pp. 30-40, pp. 46-52, p. 63. For a comment on cursing contests in India, see Robert Graves, *The Future of Swearing* (London: Kegan Paul, 1936), pp. 35-40.

59. E. Goffman, "Communication Conduct in an Island Community" (unpublished Ph.D. dissertation, Department of Sociology, University of Chicago, 1953), p. 254.
60. See, for example, his analysis in *Wit and Its Relation to the Unconscious*. His argument, of course, is that once someone else has introduced the taboo material it becomes inessential to cathect its suppression, and this energy, now freed, is drained off in laughter and elation:

Following our understanding of the mechanism of laughter we should be more likely to say that the cathexis utilized in the inhibition has now suddenly become superflous and neutralized because a forbidden idea came into existence by way of auditory perception, and is, therefore, ready to be discharged through laughter.

The Basic Writings of Sigmund Freud, p. 735. Freud, of course, saw the suppressive function as associated often with sexually tinged matters, instead of merely socially irrelevant properties that disrupt identity-images, one instance of which is the sexual.

61. R. F. Bales ("The Equilibrium Problem in Small Groups," p. 143, in T. Parsons, R. F. Bales and E. A. Shils, *Working Papers in the Theory of Action* [Glencoe: The Free Press, n.d.]) suggests:

We note joking and laughter so frequently at the end of meetings that they might almost be taken as a signal that the group has completed what it considers to be a task effort, and is ready for disbandment or a new problem. This last-minute activity completes a cycle of operations involving a successful solution both of the task problems and social-emotional problems confronting the group.

If we assume that the experimental subjects Bales employed felt obliged to disattend considerations that might throw doubt on what they were being asked to do, then we can interpret their terminal flooding out as a form of safe laughter.

62. See Goffman, *The Presentation of Self*, "Team Collusion," pp. 176-190.
63. A collusive byplay is not, however, inevitably euphoric for all its participants. An individual may feel obliged to engage in a byplay because of not wanting to reject the person who signals a desire to initiate one. The importuned person may then find himself under double tension, on the one hand in regard to the dominant encounter toward which he feels disloyal, and on the other in regard to the byplay in which he must appear to be spontaneously involved, although he is actually involved in his concern over the conflicting demands upon him.
64. This phenomenon is described, under the title "Postconference Reactions," in a paper that provides a very thorough case history of the process of selective inattention and suppression, especially in regard to the management of tension during formal meetings. See S. E. Perry and G. N. Shea, "Social Controls and Psychiatric Theory in a Ward Setting," *Psychiatry*, 20 (1957), pp. 221-247, especially pp. 243-244. Terminal laughter, desribed by Bales, is a related possibility.
65. Rose Coser, "Laughter Among Colleagues," *Psychiatry*, 23 (1960), pp. 81-95.
66. O. E. Klapp, "The Fool as a Social Type," *American Journal of Sociology*, 55 (1949), pp. 157-162.
67. A clear statement of this issue in terms of an "external system," an "internal system," and a boundary can be found in G. C. Homans, *The Human Group* (New York: Harcourt, Brace, 1950), pp. 86-94.
68. Harvey Sacks has suggested to me that game etiquette may oblige those who discover a cheater to warn him secretly so that he is enabled to desist or withdraw without totally breaking up the play. Presumably, an open accusation of cheating would be even more destructive of the play than the knowledge on the part of some of the players that cheating is occurring. That which is threatened by cheating is that which determines the form that control of cheating can take.
69. It is interesting that in daily life when individuals personally convey or receive what is for them large amounts of money they often make a little joke about money matters. Presumably, the integrity of the exchange encounter is threatened by concern about the funds, and the joke is an effort to assimilate this source of distraction to the interaction in progress, thereby (hopefully) reducing tension. In any case, to demonstrate that the money is not being treated "seriously" is presumably to imply that the encounter itself is the important thing.
70. Roger Caillois, *op. cit.*, p. 107, speaks here of "games based on the pursuit of vertigo." He says, "The question is less one of overcoming fear than of voluptuously experiencing fear, a shudder, a state of stupor that momentarily causes one to lose self-control." See also his *Les Jeux et les Hommes* (Paris: Gaillimard, 1958), pp. 45-51, where he elaborates his discussion of games based on "*ilinx*."
71. Fritz Redl, discussing Gregory Bateson's "The Message 'This is Play.'" in Bertram Schaffner, ed., *Group Processes*, Transactions of the Second (1955) Conference (New York: The Josiah Macy, Jr. Foundation, 1956), pp. 212-213. See also Redl's "The Impact of Game-Ingredients on Children's Play Behavior," in Bertram Schaffner, ed., *Group Processes*, Transactions of the Fourth (1957) Conference (New York: The Josiah Macy, Jr. Foundation, 1959), pp. 33-81.
72. See, for example, K. M. Colby's treatment of the changing character of chessmen in "Gentlemen, The Queen!" *Psychoanalytic Review*, 40 (1953), pp. 144-148.
73. In this connection, see the functional interpretation of North Andamanese peacemaking ceremonies in A. R. Radcliffe-Brown, *The Andaman Islanders* (Glencoe: The Free Press, 1948), pp. 134-135, 238 ff.
74. Max Gluckman, "How Foreign Are You?," *The Listener*, Jan. 15, 1959, p. 102. Of course, the Olympic games bring teams of different nationalities against each other, but the heavy institutionalization of these competitions seems to be ex-

actly what is needed to strengthen the membrane within which these games are played; and, in spite of the dire implication, opposing Olympic teams do occasionally fight. P. R. Reid (*op. cit.*, p. 64), suggests a similar argument in his discussion of the wall games played by British prisoners of war at Colditz:

> The Poles, and later the French when they arrived, were always interested spectators. Although we had no monopoly of the courtyard, they naturally took to their rooms and watched the game from the windows. They eventually put up sides against the British and games were played against them, but these were not a success. Tempers were lost and the score became a matter of importance, which it never did in an "all-British" game.

See also George Orwell, "The Sporting Spirit," in *Shooting an Elephant* (New York: Harcourt, Brace, 1950), pp. 151-155.

75. Caillois, "Unity of Play," p. 97.
76. Erik Homburger [Erikson], "Configurations in Play—Clinical Notes," *The Psychoanalytic Quarterly*, 6 (1937), pp. 139-214.
77. Frieda Fromm-Reichmann, "Loneliness," *Psychiatry*, 22 (1959), p. 1.
78. See Melanie Klein, "The Psycho-Analytic Play Technique: its history and significance," in Klein, *et al.*, *New Directions in Psycho-Analysis* (London: Tavistock, 1955), p. 6:

> More important still, I found that the transference situation—the backbone of the psycho-analytic procedure—can only be established and maintained if the patient is able to feel that the consulting-room or the play-room, indeed the whole analysis, is something separate from his ordinary home life. For only under such conditions can he overcome his resistances against experiencing and expressing thoughts, feelings, and desires, which are incompatible with convention, and in the case of children felt to be in contrast to much of what they have been taught.

> Perhaps, then, an ocean voyage is fun not because it cuts us off from ordinary life but because in being apparently cut off from ordinary life, we can afford to experience certain aspects of it.

79. Eugen Kogon, *The Theory and Practice of Hell* (New York: Berkley Publishing Corp., n.d.), p. 108.
80. *Ibid.*, p. 103.
81. Writer's study of a mental hospital. A systematic treatment of patient joking in mental hospitals can be found in Rose Coser, "Some Social Functions of Laughter," *Human Relations*, 12 (1959), pp. 171-182. Somewhat similar practices are reported at length in a study of brain-damage cases held for surgery in a medical hospital: Edwin Weinstein and Robert Kahn, *Denial of Illiness* (Springfield: Charles Thomas, 1955), Chap. 16, "The Language of Denial."
82. See F. J. Roethlisberger and W. J. Dickson, *Management and the Worker* (Cambridge: Harvard University Press, 1950), p. 420, and the interesting paper by Lloyd Street, "Game Forms in the Factory Group," *Berkeley Publications in Society and Institutions*, 4 (1958), esp. pp. 48-50:

> Piling consisted of passing to the "speed artist" or "ratebuster" a greater number of units than he could possibly assemble. The rules of the game were to embarrass and ridicule the fast worker without hurting any of the members of the line. Typically it was necessary to pile the "rate-buster" but once or twice in order to bring him into line with the production norm (p. 48).

83. This view of sociability derives from W. L. Warner. He seems to have been the first American sociologist to have appreciated and studied this structural role of informal social life. For a recent treatment of sociability that deals with many of the themes discussed in this paper, see D. Riesman, R. J. Potter, and J. Watson, "Sociability, Permissiveness, and Equality," *Psychiatry*, 23 (1960), pp. 323-340.

The Interdependence of Sport and Culture

Günther Lüschen

INTRODUCTION

Sport is a rational, playful activity in interaction, which is extrinsically rewarded. The more it is rewarded, the more it tends to be work; the less, the more it tends to be play. If we describe it in an action system frame of reference, this activity depends on the organic, personality, social, and cultural systems. By tradition, physical education has tried to explain this action system largely on the grounds of the organic system, and sometimes making reference to the personality system. Only on rare occasions has it been approached systematically from the social and cultural systems as well. Yet it seems obvious that any action going on in this system ought to be explained with reference to all of the subsystems of the action system.

Even such a simple motor activity as walking is more than a matter of organic processes initiated by the personality system. It is determined by the social and cultural systems as well, as is most evident in the way the Israelians from the Yemen walk. Since in their former society in the Yemen, the Jews were the outcasts, and every Yemenite could feel free to hit a Jew (whenever he could get hold of one), the Yemenitic Jew would always run in order to escape this oppression. This way of walking finally became an integrated pattern of his culture. And though the environment in Israel no longer is hostile to him, the Yemenitic Israelite still carries this pattern with him as part of his culture and walks in a shy and hasty way. This example shows in addition that the different subsystems of action are not independent from one another; they are structurally related. Thus, in dealing with the cultural system of sport and its interdependence with general culture, we will not always be

From *International Review of Sport Sociology* 2 (1967): 27-41. Reprinted by permission.

able to explain the culture of sport and that of its environment in terms of the cultural system, and therefore should refer as well to the social and personality system to describe and explain what we call culture. It was Radcliffe-Brown who stressed the point that culture should be explained through its social structure. Furthermore, one should discuss the function of a unit within general culture, as well as cultural process and change (1952).

CONCEPTS OF CULTURE AND REVIEW OF RESULTS

Culture as a concept does not refer to behavior itself. It deals with those patterns and abstractions that underlie behavior or are the result of it. Thus culture exists of cognitive elements which grow out of everyday or scientific experience. It consists of beliefs, values, norms, and of signs that include symbols of verbal as well as non-verbal communication (cf., Johnson, 1960).

Anthropologists have sometimes held a broader view of culture and given more attention to the material results of human behavior. Leslie White in a critique of the above-stated concept of culture has called for more attention to "acts, thoughts and things dependent upon symboling." These would include not only the study of the above-mentioned elements, but also those of art, tools, machines, fetishes, etc. (1959). As attractive as White's critique may be, especially for cultural anthropology as an independent science, this approach as related to the cultural study of sport has led more to mere curiosity about things than to theoretical insights. This methodological approach has also dealt more with the cultural diffusion of sport and games than with the social structure of which they are a part. For decades we have learned about all types of games in all types of societies (especially primitive ones), which may well lead to the conclusion that we know more about the games and sports displayed by some Polynesian tribe than those of our own children and ancestors. For an understanding of sport it is less important to find the same games in different cultures as Tylor did (1896). It is more important to analyze, for example, the different meaning of baseball in the United States and Lybia, which in the one culture has at least latent ritualistic functions, while it has also economic functions in the other (Gini, 1939).

Another concept of culture, mainly held in Central Europe, has almost led to the same results for sport. In this concept "higher" culture was separated from civilization and expressed itself significantly in the arts and sciences. On the basis of values attributed to sport *a priori*, it was related either to "Zivilisation" or to Kultur. Physical educationalists through Huizinga's theory on the origin of culture in play saw in the latter approach their main support (1955). Thus defining sport as a special form of play, physical educationalists felt safe in their implicit attempt to justify sport for educational purposes. Yet Huizinga's theory has not only been criticized on the basis of ethnological findings, (c.f., Jensen, 1942), but he himself was very critical about the play element in sport. Those that believed in the role of sport within higher culture were hardly able to prove their hypothesis. So, as recently as Rene Maheu (1962), they often expressed their hope that sport in the future would contribute to "Kultur."

One can hardly deny that sport has indeed some impact on "higher" culture, as may be shown by symbolic elements from sport to be found in script and language. In an analysis of the cultural meaning of the ballgame of the Aztecs and Maya, Krickeberg found that in their script there were elements related to this game. The symbol for movement for example, was identical with the I-shape of the ball court (1948). "To get (take) a rain check" refers to baseball, but has now become in American English symbolic for any situation where you get another chance. "That's not cricket" refers to a dishonest procedure in everyday life. And though German is not as idiomatic as English, it contains elements which originated in sport and games as well. "Katzbalgerei," and the phrase "sich gegenseitig die Bälle zuspielen," refer to a game which today is still known in the Netherlands as "Kaatsen" and perhaps appears in the New York children's game of one-o-cat. As did football in Shakespeare's "King Lear," so appeared this game and its terminolgy in the 16th century poetry of J. G. Fischart.

How weak these relationships of sport indeed are to "higher" culture may be shown by the relatively unsuccessful attempts to establish through special contests in modern Olympics, a relationship between sport and the arts. Sport only rarely expresses itself in the material aspects of culture. It is what I would like to call a momentary activity. Just from a certain level on, an event may have its appearance on such a short range cultural element as the sports page of the next day's newspaper. This appearance of sport in the media of mass communication, in language, poetry, and the arts is significant for the overall meaning of sport within society, but these manifestations tell us little about sport itself and its interdependence with general culture as we define it.

It may also be interesting to discuss cognitive elements such as scientific insight coming out of sport. Also religious beliefs and ritual found in sport would be an interesting point of analysis. Yet after showing how sport is indeed bound to society and structured by general culture, we will mainly discuss our problem on the level of cultural values and their related social structure.

SPORT AS PART OF CULTURE AND SOCIETY

That sport is structurally related to culture and society has sometimes been questioned. Yet it is quite easy to show how strong this relationship is. Sport is indeed an expression of that socio-cultural system in which it occurs. David Riesman and Reuel Denney describe how American football was changed through the American culture from rugby to a completely different game. It is now well integrated and quite obviously shows in its vigor, hard contact and a greater centrality on the individual the basic traits of the culture of American society (1954).

On the level of the so-called primitive societies we see the same dependence of sport and games on culture and its underlying social structure. The Hopi Indians had 16 different terms for foot races which nearly all referred to one aspect of the social organization of that tribe (Culin, 1907). A recent socio-historical study on three Illinois subcultures finds the same close relationship between socio-cultural system and sport (Hill, 1966). And Käte Hye-Kerkdal outlines the tight structural relation between the log-races of the tribe of the Timbira in Brazil and their socio-cultural system. This ritualistic competition between two teams has symbolic meaning for nearly every aspect of the dual organization of this tribe. It refers to all kinds of religious and social polarities and is so strongly imbedded in this religious-dominated system that winning or losing does not have any effect on the status of the team or individual, nor are there any other extrinsic rewards. Yet these races are performed vigorously and with effort (1956).

Now that we have proven that there is a structural relationship between sport and culture, the first question is that of sport's dependency on culture. What factors make for the appearance of sport? Or more specifically, what are the underlying cultural values?

CULTURE VALUES AND SPORT

By values we mean those general orientations in a socio-cultural system that are not always obvious to its members, but are implicit in actual behavior. On the level of the personality system they are expressed partly in attitudes. Values should be separated from norms which are derived from values and are actual rules for behavior. For instance, health is a high value in the American culture, as it seems to be in all young cultures, while death is higher in the hierarchy of values in old cultures like India (Parsons, 1960). On this continuum we may explain why sport as an expression of the evaluation of health is more important in American than in Indian society. The whole emphasis on physical fitness in the United States may well be explained by this background, and the norm "run for your life" is directly related to it.

Sport, Industrialization and Technology

In comparing the uneven distribution and performance level of sport all over the world, one widely accepted hypothesis is that sport is an offspring of technology and industrialization. The strong emphasis on sport in industrialized societies seems to show that industrialization and technology are indeed a basis for sport. This would be a late confirmation of Ogburn's theory of social change, as well as of Marxian theory that society and its structure depend on its economic basis. However, there are quite a number of inconsistencies. Not all sport-oriented societies or societal subsystems show a relation to technology and industrialization, and historically games and sport have been shown to have existence prior to industrialization. Yet it can hardly be denied that certain conditions in the later process of industrialization have promoted sport, and technology has at least its parallels in modern sport. The above-stated hypothesis may, despite its obvious limitations, lead us to the independent variables.

Sport, A Protestant Subculture?

In an investigation that because of its methodological procedure turned out to be a profound critique of Marxian materialism, Max Weber studied the interrelationship of what he called "The Protestant Ethic and the Spirit of Capitalism." (1920). This investigation about the underlying values of capitalism in Western societies quoted data on the over-representation of Protestants in institutions of higher learning, their preference for industrial and commercial occupations and professions and the stronger trend towards capitalism in Protestant-dominated countries (most obvious in the United States). Weber found not the material basis but Protestant culture, with achievement of wordly success and asceticism held as the basic values, caused industrialization and capitalism. In accordance with the Calvinistic belief in predestination, the Protestant felt that he was blessed by God once he had achieved success. Thus, need for achievement became an integrated part of his personality and a basic value in Protestantism. Together with the value of asceticism this led to the accumulation of wealth and to Western capitalism. If we turn to sport, we find the same values of achievement and asceticism. Even the puritans, generally opposed to a leisurely life, could therefore justify sport as physical activity that contributed to health (cf., McIntosh, 1963). Today we find significance for this relationship in the YMCA, in a group like the American Fellowship of Christian Athletes, and also in the Protestant minister who in Helsinki became an Olympic medal winner in the pole vault. He showed the consistency between Protestantism and sport in his prayer right after his Olympic winning vault. Max Weber's findings about the relationship between the Protestant ethic and the spirit of capitalism may thus well be extended to the "spirit" of sport. Not only Weber was aware of this relationship, but also Thorstein Veblen who described the parallels in religion and sport ritual (1899).

The relationship between sport and Protestantism is not only to be observed in the emphasis on sport in the Scandinavian and other Protestant countries. A rough compilation of the probable religious preference of Olympic medal winners on the basis of the percentage of different religious groups in their countries also shows the dominance of Protestanism up to 1960. Protestantism accounted for more than 50 per cent of the medal winners, while its ratio among the world population is less than 8 per cent (Lüschen, 1962). Furthermore, in 1958 a survey of young athletes in West Germany by Lüschen showed the following distribution according to religious preference:

	Whole Population West Germany	Sport Club Members 15-25	Track Swimming	High Achievers Track/ Swimming
Protestants	52%	60%	67%	73%
Catholics	44%	37%	31%	26%
Others	4%	3%	2%	1%
n =	universe	1,880	366	111

These figures indicate the overrepresentation of Protestants in German sport. Moreover, they indicate a higher percentage in individual sports, and an even higher percentage of Protestants among those that have achieved a higher level of performance. Thus it may be concluded that there is a correlation between Protestanism and sport and the culture of both. This was obvious for individual sports, but less for team sports where in the German sample Catholics appeared quite often. Since in Catholicism collectivity is highly regarded, this inconsistency is to be explained by the value of collectivity in team sports. It is consistent with this hypothesis that Catholic Notre Dame University has been one of the innovators of football in America. At present, it is a leading institution in this discipline. And internationally Catholic-dominated South America is overall rather poor in individual sports, but outstanding in team sports like soccer and basketball.

This result on the overall, strong relationship between sport and Protestantism is, despite support by data, theoretically insufficient. As was the case with sport in its relationship to industrialization, there are many exceptions. The high achievement in sport of the Russians, the Poles, the Japanese, the Mandan Indians, the Sikhs in India, or the Watusi in Africa cannot be related to Protestantism though in Japanese Zen-Buddhism there are parallels.

The Centrality of the Achievement-Value

Since again Protestantism cannot be specifically identified as being the independent variable, we may hypothesize that there is a more general system of values as the basis for Protestantism, capitalism and sport. In his critique of Max Weber, McClelland has considered the ethic of Protestantism as a special case of the general achievement orientation of a system, this being the independent variable. Achievement orientation (or, as he puts it on the personality-system-level, need-achievement) precedes all periods of high cultural achievement in ancient Greece, in the Protestant Reformation, in modern industrialism and, as we may conclude, in modern sport. He referred in his analysis also to the related social structure of the achievement value (such as family organization), which should also be studied in relationship to sport.

If we turn again to the cross-cultural comparison of those systems that participate and perform strongly in sport, we find that in all of these societies achievement-orientation is basic. In Russia this value is expressed in the norm that social status should depend only on achievement. The Sikhs and the Watusi are both minority groups in their environment. In order to keep their position, they have to achieve more than the other members of the societies they live in. The Japanese (Bellah, 1957) and the Mandan Indians (McClelland, 1961) also place a heavy emphasis on achievement.

Similar results appear in cross-cultural investigations of different types of games as related to basic orientations in the process of socialization. Roberts and Sutton-Smith find in a secondary analysis of the Human Relation Area Files of G. P. Murdock that games of chance are related to societies that emphasize routine responsibility in the socialization process. Games of strategy are found in societies where obedience, games of physical skill in those where achievement is stressed (1963). Individual sports would mainly qualify as games of physical skill and again show achievement as their basic cultural value. Team sports as well are games of strategy. Their relation to training of obedience would support exactly what we called earlier the value of collectivity.

It remains an open question, for further research into the value structure of sport, as to which other values are related to this system. It is to be expected that the structure of values will be more complex than it appears on the basis of our limited insight now. Roberts and Sutton-Smith briefly remark that games of physical skill are related to occupational groups that exert power over others (1963). Thus, power orientation may be another value supporting sport. This would cross-culturally be consistent with power-oriented political systems that strongly emphasize sport. Here we could refer to countries like Russia or the United States, as well as to a tribe like the Mandan Indians.

The Culture of Societal Subsystems and Its Relation to Sport

Within a society we find subsystems that have their own subculture, which will be another condition for sport. The female role in modern societies still depends on a culture that stresses obedience as the main value-orientation, while the male culture is strongly oriented towards achievement. Thus we find a disproportionately high participation of men in sport which in most of the disciplines is a male culture. One of the most male-oriented sports, however, is pool, a game supported mainly by the subculture of the bachelor. This has, with the general change in the number of people marrying, lost its main supporting culture (Polsky, 1967).

Another subsystem which in its culture shows a strong relationship to sport is that of the adolescent age group (cf. Coleman, 1961). Sport is dependent more on the culture of the adolescent than on that of any other age group. Helanko raises the point, referring to his studies of boys' gangs in Turku, that sport has its origin in the gang-age and in boys' gangs. The fact that there are no rules for early sports to be found is seen as one of the supporting factors (1957). Generally speaking, achievement is again more central as a value in adolescence and early adulthood than later, where the main response to sport goes not so much towards achievement but towards values of health and fitness.

The different social classes have a culture of their own. The greatest emphasis on achievement, and thus the highest sport participation, is to be found in the upper-middle class. It is considerably less important in the lower class where routine responsibility is valued. The notion that there is no way to gain higher status accounts for the high regard for games of chance or those sports where one may just have a lucky punch, as in boxing (Weinberg and Arond, 1952). Loy has related the different types of games and the passive and active participation in sport to different modes of adaptation and to the members of social classes (1966). His theoretical analysis as to "innovation" found in the lower class, ritualism in the lower-middle class and conformity in the upper-middle class is supported by data (cf. Lüschen, 1963; Loy, 1969) that show the same ways of adaptation in sport. However, in responding to the social class system and its culture as related to sport one should have in mind that class determined behavior may not follow the traditional class lines in sport. Sport may indeed show or promote new orientations in the class system (Kunz and Lüschen, 1966).

Finally, sport is organized within, or relates to different associations whose cultures sometimes have a profound influence on sport itself. This is especially true for physical education in schools where, with the same skills and rules, we may find a completely different culture as compared to sport in the military establishment. And while intercollegiate and interscholastic athletics are overall a surprisingly well integrated subculture within American schools and universities, the different values held by an educational (the school or university) and a solely success-oriented unit (the team) may well lead to strong value conflicts. This could result in a complete separation of school and athletics.

FUNCTIONS AND DYSFUNCTIONS

After we have found achievement, asceticism in individual sports, obedience (collectivity) in team sports, and exertion of power, the basic value orientations that give structure to this activity, we may then proceed to the second question: How does sport influence the socio-cultural system at large? Though we have little evidence through research, we may on the basis of structural-functional methodology b eable to outline the basic functions of sport for pattern maintenance, integration, adaptation and goal attainment.

The Functions of Sport Within Culture and Society

As in the case of the Timbria, Hye-Kerkdal states that the basic values of that culture were learned through the log-race. Furthermore, the participants were functionally integrated into the social system (1956). Thus, we may hypothesize that the main functions of sport are pattern maintenance and integration.

Since sport implies (as we saw) basic cultural values, it has the potential to pass these values on to its participants. We know from studies of the process of socialization that the exposure of children to competitive sport will cause these children to become achievement-motivated; the earlier this exposure occurs, the more achievement-motivated they become (Winterbottom, 1953). And the child's moral judgment may, for instance, be influenced through games such as marbles. Again, according to Piaget, the child not only becomes socialized to the rules but at a later age he also get an insight into the underlying structure and function of the rules of a game, and thus into the structure and function of social norms and values as such (1965). Overall, from the level of primitive societies to modern societies, sport not only socializes to the system of values and norms but in primitive societies it socializes towards adult and warfare skills as well.

Since we mentioned that sport is also structured along such societal subsystems as different classes, males, urban areas, schools and communities, we should say it functions for integration of these systems as well as for the society at large. This is most obvious in spectator sports where the whole country or community identifies with its representatives in a contest. Thus, sport functions as means of integration, not only for the actual participants, but also for the represented members of such a system.

Sport in modern societies may function for goal-attainment on the national polity level. In primitive societies, sport functions for adaptation as well as goal-attainment since the sport skills of swimming, hunting and fishing are used to supply food and mere survival.

Possible Dysfunctions of Sport and Social Control

A question should be raised at this point asking whether sport is dysfunctional for culture and society as well. Th. W. Adorno called sport an area of unfreedom ("ein Bereich der Unfreiheit"), (1957) in which he obviously referred to the differentiated code of rules which earlier led Huizinga to his statement that excluded sport from play (1955). Both seem to overlook what Piaget called the reciprocity and mutual agreement on which such rules rest (1965). And they may also be considered as an expression of a highly structured system.

Another dysfunctional element for culture and for the sport system itself could be the centrality of achievement. It has such a high rank in the hierarchy of values of sport that, by definition, the actual objective performance of a member of this system will decide the status he gets. In the core of sport, in the contest on the sports field, there is only achieved status. It seems that there is no other system or any societal subsystem, with the exception of combat, where achievement ranks that high. It may create conflict once this value-orientation is imposed on the whole culture, and it may create conflict within the system of sport itself since its members bring other values into this system as well. M. Mead in an investigation of competition and cooperation (the first concept of which is related to achievement) of primitive peoples, however, finds that there seems to be no society where one of these principles existed alone (1946). And on the micro-sociological level, small groups seem to control this value by discriminating against those that deviate from the group norm of a fair performance (Roethlisberger and Dickson, 1939). Thus, one would notice some kind of a mechanism built into a social system like a group that keeps it in a state of balance. Exactly this seems to happen within sport where the sporting groups themselves and their differentiated organizational and institutional environment exert social control on those participants achieving beyond a certain level.

In a survey of sport club members in Germany, it was found that the norms expressed for an athlete's behavior referred surprisingly less to the achievement value but more often to a value of affiliation, which is to be defined as a positive orientation towards other group members or opponents. Fair play was the one mentioned most frequently. The value of affiliation expressed by the respondents was found more in normative statements the higher their level of performance. On the basis of the hypothesized mechanism of social control, they are under stronger pressure to affiliate with others (Lüschen, 1963). This may explain (on the basis of this structural relationship) why in the culture of sport we find not only the value of achievement but also that of fair play and other affiliative orientations.

However, achievement and affiliation may not necessarily be related. It depends on the amount of social control imposed on sport from the internal as well as external system, whether this relationship will be strong or weak. In professional boxing these controls are very weak; while in golf with the handicap rule, they seem to be comparatively strong (Lüschen, 1970).

How much this pattern would influence the culture as such is an open question. Yet it seems not so mis-oriented as often thought when Oetinger stated that sport would provide a good model for political partnership

(1954). We may on the basis of our findings hypothesize that also on the political level the amount of social control will decide whether two or more systems will coexist or not.

Sport and Socio-Cultural Change

After we have discussed the culture and underlying social structure of sport and its function, we are left with Radcliffe-Brown's third programmatic point—that of social and cultural change. We know little about the role of sport in socio-cultural change, though we hypothesized earlier that it may have a function of innovation, or at least structural relationship to changes in the system of social classes. Sport has also functioned as an initiator for the diffusion of technical inventions, such as the bicycle or the automobile (Kroeber, 1963). The same holds true to a degree for conduct in regard to fashion and a healthy life. Typically, this question of change has been highly neglected so far.

Sport and Cultural Evolution

If we finally try to explain the different cross-cultural appearance of sport on the basis of an evolutionary theory, it is hard to justify on the basis of our present knowledge about the appearance of sport that there are such things as primitive and developed cultures of sport. The Mandan Indians had a highly developed sport culture, the Australian aboriginals, as perhaps the most primitive people know to us today, know quite a variety of recreational activities and physical skills, and the variety of competitive games in Europe and America in the past was perhaps richer than today.

An evolution can only be seen on a vertical level which on the one hand shows in a state of mechanic solidarity rather simple rules in sport and games, while in a state of organic solidarity, as in modern industrialized societies, the code of rules and the structure of games get more differentiated.

What we may furthermore state is that, on the level of primitive cultures, sport's function is universal, often religious, collectively oriented, and in the training of skills, representative and related to adult and warfare skills; while modern sport's function may be called specific for pattern maintenance and integration, is individual oriented and nonrepresentative in the training of skills. The rewards are more intrinsic in primitive cultures, while they are more extrinsic in the sport of modern cultures. Thus, referring to our definition at the beginning, one may well differentiate between physical and recreational activities of primitive cultures and sport in modern cultures (c.f. Damm, 1960).

SUMMARY AND CONCLUSION

The interdependence of sport and culture, up to now mainly outlined on the basis of sport's contribution to higher culture (Kultur), was discussed on sport's relation to culture with the emphasis on values, sport's function for the socio-cultural system and its relation to change and evolution.

The system of sport, an integrated part of the socio-cultural system, seems to depend on the industrialized, technological or Protestant religious system. Yet cross-culturally it appears that these systems as intermediate variables are just special cases of a more general system. This is determined for sport by the achievement-value, a value of collectivity and supposedly power orientation. On the basis of these cultural value orientations one may explain the uneven distribution of sport as such, and of team sports versus individual sports in certain socio-cultural systems.

Sport's function for a socio-cultural system can mainly be seen for pattern maintenance and integration, in modern polity dominated societies as well for goal attainment. In primitive cultures it is universal and thus functions for adaptation as well.

Though a relation of sport to social change is obvious (sport fulfills a certain role for innovation), this neglected question of social change needs more careful investigation. Evolutionary theories applied to sport need more study as well; this might contribute to evolutionary theories as such. It appears that physical activity on the level of "primitive" cultures should be kept apart from sport in modern cultures since meaning and manifest functions are as universal on the one level as they are specific and segmentary on the other.

RELATED LITERATURE

Adorno, T. W. *Prismen.* Frankfurt, 1957.
Bellah, R. N. *Tokugawa Religion: The Values of Pre-Industrial Japan.* Glencoe, Ill., 1957.
Coleman, J. S. *The Adolescent Society.* Glencoe, Ill., 1961.
Culin, S. *Games of the North American Indians.* 24th Report, Bureau of American Ethnology, Washington, D. C., 1907.
Damm, H. "Vom Wesen sogenannter Leibesübungen bei Naturvölkern." *Studium Generale* 13 (1960): 3-10.
Gini, C. "Rural ritual games in Lybia." *Rural Sociology* 4 (1939): 283-299.
Helanko, R. "Sports and socialization." *Acta Sociologica* 2 (1957): 229-240.
Hill, P. J. A cultural history of frontier sport in Illinois 1673-1820. Unpub. Ph.D. Dissertation, University of Illinois, 1966.
Huizinga, J. *Homo Ludens.* Boston, 1955.

Hye-Kerkdal, K. Wettkampfspiel und Dualorganisation bei den Timbira Brasiliens. J. Haegel, ed. *Die Wiener Scule der Volkerkunde*. Wein, 1956: 504-533.

Jensen, A. E. "Spiel und Ergriffenheit." *Paideuma* 2 (1942): 124-139.

Krickeberg, W. "Das mittelamerikanische Ballspiel und seine teligiose Symbolik." *Paideuma* 3 (1948): 118-190.

Kroeber, A. L. *Anthropology*. New York, 1963.

Kunz, G. and Luschen, G. Leisure and social stratification. Paper at *International Congress for Sociology*. Evian, France, 1966.

Loy, J. W. Sport and social structure. Paper at the *AAHPER Convention*. Chicago, 1966.

Luschen, G. "Der Leistungssport in seiner Abhangigkeit vom sozio-kulturellen System." *Zentralblatt für Arbeitswissenschaft* 16 (1962): 186-190.

———. "Soziale Schichtung und soziale Mobilität." *Kölner Zeitschrift fur Soziologie und Sozialpsychologie* 15 (1963): 74-93.

———. Leisungsorientierung und ihr Finfluss auf das soziale und personale System. In Luschen, G. ed., *Kleingruppenforschung und Gruppe im Sport*. Koln, 1966: 209-223.

———. "Cooperation, association and contest." *Journal of Conflict Resolution*, 14, 1970 (forthcoming).

Maheu, R. "Sport and culture." *International Journal of Adult and Youth Education* 14 (1962): 169-178.

McClelland, D. C. *The Achieving Society*. New York, 1961.

McIntosh, P. C. *Sport and Society*. London, 1963.

Mead, M. *Competition and Cooperation Among Primitive Peoples*. Berkeley, 1946.

Oetinger, F. *Partnerschaft*. Stuttgart, 1954.

Parsons, T. *Societies*. Englewood-Cliffs,-N.Y., 1966.

———. "Toward a healthy maturity." *Journal of Health and Human Behavior* 1 (1960): 163-173.

Piaget, J. *The Moral Judgment of the Child*. New York, 1965.

Polsky, N. "Poolrooms and poolplayers." *Trans-action* 4 (1967): 32-40.

Radcliffe-Brown, A. R. *Structure and Function in Primitive Society*. Glencoe, Ill., 1952.

Riesman, D. and Denney, R. Football in America. Riesman, D., ed. *Individualism Reconsidered*. Glencoe, Ill., 1954: 242-251.

Roberts, J. M. and Sutton-Smith, B. "Child training and game involvement." *Ethnology* 1 (1962): 166-185.

Roethlisberger, F. J. and Dickson, W. J. *Management and the Worker*. Cambridge, Mass., 1939.

Stumpf, F. and Cozens, F. W. "Some aspects of the role of games, sports and recreational activities in the culture of primitive peoples." *Research Quarterly* 18 (1947): 198-218, and 20 (1949): 2-30.

Sutton-Smith, B. Roberts, J. M. and Kozelka, R. M. "Game involvement in adults." *Journal of Social Psychology* 60 (1963): 15-30.

Tylor, F. B. "On American lot-games." *Internationales Archiv für Ethnographie* 9 (1896 supplement): 55-67.

Veblen, T. *The Theory of the Leisure Class.* Chicago, 1899.
Weber, M. *Gesammelte Aufsätze zur Religionssoziologie.* Tubingen, 1920, I.
Weinberg, S. K. and Arond, R. "The occupational culture of the boxer." *American Journal of Sociology* 57 (1952): 460-463.
White, L. "The concept of culture." *American Anthropologist* 61 (1959): 227-251.
Winterbottom, M. R. The relation of childhood training in independence to achievement motivation. Unpub. Ph.D. Dissertation, Univ. of Michigan, 1953.

Theses toward a Political Sociology of Sport

Jean-Marie Brohm

1. SPORT AND IMPERIALISM

(a) The Origins of Modern Sport

Modern sport, organised into national and international sports federations, is an *imperialist phenomenon,* in the marxist sense of the term. Sport developed in this form essentially from 1880-1900 onwards, in other words, at the beginning of the age of imperialism, analysed by Lenin.

The first modern Olympic games were held in Athens in 1896 and then in Paris in 1900, while the first major sports competitions such as the Tour de France or the FA Cup were organised at around the same time. Sport was directly linked to the interests of imperialist capital. The early Olympic games, in Paris, Saint Louis and London, were organised in conjunction with Universal Exhibitions or Trade Fairs.

(b) The Organisation of Sport

From the start, the international organisation of sport was tied to imperialist international organisations. Sport served as both a supportive institution and as an ideological cover. Following both the 1914-18 and the 1939-45 World Wars, the organisation of international sport benefited from imperialist attempts to control the world. Since then, international sport has been inextricably linked to super-national organisations, in particular the UN and UNESCO. Today, the Olympic Movement and the IOC (International Olympic Committee) are closely tied to the UN and more specifically to U.S. Imperialism. Brundage, the President, is American [This article was written in 1971—Ed.]. Within the framework of peaceful coexistence, the International Olympic Movement fully reflects the interests of imperialism. The cosmopolitan, 'pacifist' ideology expressed in the Olympic ideal is in reality none other than the hypocritical ideology of imperialism, which 'leads to war, as surely as the storm clouds lead to the storm'.

The set-up of world sport is not just held together by its own ideology of 'peace between peoples' and by its own organisation. For imperialist sport is closely dependent on imperialist institutions and treaties such as NATO, SEATO etc. There are very close links between civilian and military sport. For instance, Western military sport is tied directly to NATO and constitutes a spearhead of North-Atlantic imperialism. The international organisation of sport constitutes a 'World Government of Sport', responsible for:

- organising international competitions,
- dealing with relations between national federations,
- laying down rules for different sports and supervising their application, settling disputes, deciding sanctions, etc.,
- recognising world records,
- developing an ideological Charter for 'universal sport'.

(c) Sport and Peaceful Coexistence

As an international reality, sport is a very *precise reflection of the relation of forces between imperialism and the bureaucratic state-bourgeoisie of the 'socialist' countries* (or to use Trotskyist terminology, the Stalinist bureaucracy).

In 1921, at the Third Congress of the Communist International, a 'Red Sports International' was set up, with the aim of organising working-class sportsmen and women against the bourgeoisie. For a whole period, the USSR refused to establish sporting relations with the imperialist countries. But following the stalinisation of the USSR and the adoption of the counter-revolutionary policy of 'socialism in one country' and 'peaceful coexistence', the USSR established sporting relations with more and more countries, particularly following the end of the Second World War.

In 1952, one year before Stalin's death, the USSR took part in the Helsinki games, thereby coming into the Olympic Movement. Since that time, world sport and the Olympic games have been regarded by both the imperialist states and by the Stalinist, bureaucratic states as an important element of peaceful coexistence. The Olympic sports ideology is a hypocritical ideology which seeks to hide the reality of the class struggle behind so-called 'brotherhood between the peoples'. The reality behind the 'peace' of the sports field or the 'truce' of the Games is that sport is a grim analogue of the permanent state of war under imperialism, as can be seen by looking at the recent Olympics.

Thus the Olympic games in Melbourne in 1956 were unable to conceal the fact that the French and British imperialists were in the course of intervening in favour of the Zionist imperialists of the state of Israel with Suez adventure. At the same time, tanks sent by the Russian Stalinist bureaucracy were bloodily crushing the revolution of the workers' councils in Hungary.

Then in 1968, all the imperialist countries sent their Olympic teams to Mexico, shortly after the Diaz Ordaz government had had student demonstrators shot down. Earlier that year, the Stalinist bureaucracy had betrayed the great general strike of May and June in France, while American imperialism was bombing, burning and killing in Vietnam. Meanwhile, the troops of the Red Army and the Warsaw Pact were invading Czechoslovakia to put down the Czech intellectuals and workers and smash the popular mobilisation of the Prague Spring.

On a world scale, sport has always been linked to the twists and turns of the international class struggle. And sport itself, notably the Olympic Movement, is an important ideological element in this struggle.

2. BOURGEOIS SPORT AND THE CAPITALIST STATE

(a) All the Structures of Present-day Sport Tie it to Bourgeois, Capitalist Society

Sport is dependent on the development of the productive forces of bourgeois society. Technical progress in sport closely follows the technological and scientific development of capitalism. Bourgeois sport is a class institution, totally integrated into the framework of capitalist production relations and class relations. Like other class institutions, such as the University, the Army etc.

And finally, as a phenomenon of the superstructure, sport is linked to all the other superstructural levels of capitalist society. The organisational unity of sport is ensured by the repressive grip of the bourgeois state. Moreover, sport as an ideology, transmitted on a huge scale by the mass media, is part and parcel of ruling bourgeois ideology.

(b) Sport and the State

From the start, the development of sport has been tied to that of the state. Like all other class institutions and structures, sport is mediated through the state which locks in all the structures of society as a whole. When the process of establishing bourgeois nation-states has been set in train by bourgeois revolutions such as the French Revolution of 1789, *sport has tended to participate in the process of development of these states.*

Most major national liberation movements which have fought for the establishment of nation-states have consciously made use of physical activities and mass sport *as a means of creating a national identity*.

First Example: *Jahn*[1] and anti-Napoleonic, German nationalism—the establishment of a German nationalist movement, leading to the national unification of Germany under Prussian rule.

Second Example: Mao Tse-Tung, whose early work, 'A Study of Physical Education', was to help to strengthen Chinese youth physically and mentally in the struggle against Western Imperialism and local, feudal reaction.[2] Physical education was thus a factor in the process of the bourgeois democratic revolution.

Third Example: Today all colonial and semi-colonial countries which achieve independence *structure the population by means of mass, State-run sport,* as an integral part of the establishment of their nation-state.

In situations where the state dominates all political existence, as under fascist or military/police régimes, or under the dictatorship of a Stalinist, bureaucratic state-bourgeoisie, sport is simply a structural part of the state repressive apparatus, particularly the army.

In this type of state, mass sport is merely a para-state institution for regimenting youth, which operates along with other reception organisations such as state-controlled youth movements, Scouts, the army, etc. This was the set-up, for example, in Hitler's Germany, Stalinist Russia or in France under the Vichy régime. In this case the basic political functions of sport are:

- to control youth activities,
- ideological regimentation,
- pre-military training on nationalist lines: preparation for the 'defense of the fatherland'.

In the period of the death-agony of imperialism, bourgeois states tend increasingly to become strong, police-states, like for example the DeGaulle/Pompidou régime. In this case too, sport shares the general aims of the bourgeois state, in the widest sense of the term: sport becomes *State Sport:*

- sports structures, federations, clubs etc., are closely tied into the state apparatus;
- the state itself promotes state sport through a state doctrine: an official approach to sport which is enforced by the creation of a special administrative structure: the Ministry of Youth and Sport;
- top ranking sportsmen and women are state athletes with the job of promoting the state's official propaganda;
- the state imposes competitive sport in schools as the compulsory mode of physical education.

(c) Sport and the Capitalist Organisation of Production

Sport as an activity characteristic of bourgeois industrial society, is an exact reflection of capitalist categories. And as Marx explained:[3] economic categories reflect the structures and principles of organisation of the capitalist mode of production. The vertical, hierarchial structure of sport models the social structure of bureaucratic capitalism with its system of competitive selection, promotion, hierarchy and social advancement. The driving forces in sport—performance, competitiveness, records —are directly carried over from the driving forces of capitalism: productivity, the search for profit, rivalry and competitiveness.

Sport as a technology of the body structurally reproduces capitalist repressive techniques: the division of labour, ultra-specialisation, repetition, training, the abstraction of space and time, stereotyped movements, the parcelling up of the body, measurement, stop-watch timing, Taylorism, Stakhanovism. . . .

Sport treats the human organism as a machine, in the same way as the worker becomes a mere appendage of the machine in the capitalist system.[4] Sport as an ideology reproduces and strengthens the ideology of alienated labour: work, continuous effort, struggle, the cult of transcending one's own limitations, the cult of suffering, the cult of self-denial, self-sacrifice etc. Sport is a morality of effort which conditions people for the oppressive work of the factory.

(d) Sport and State Monopoly Capitalism

(i) Sport as an activity involving the circulation of money and capital is thus totally tied up in the financial and economic network of monopoly capitalism. Professional sport with its show-business, its betting and its financial speculation, is just the most glaring aspect of this process.

(ii) Trusts, banking groups and monopolies use major international competitions to reinforce their domination, as for example, in the skiing events at the Grenoble Winter Olympics. Moreover major national and international competitions require huge mobilisations of capital and economic resources: thus the choice of site for the Olympic Games is the object of fierce competition between multi-national firms.

(iii) Sport also develops its own industries on a broad, capitalist basis, through the manufacture of equipment and the promotion of sporting goods. Financial trusts, such as Rothschild, were quick to develop and profit from the sports and leisure industry, Winter Sports and the 'Club Méditerranée'.

(e) Sport and Capitalist Showbusiness

Spectator sport is a commodity sold along normal capitalist lines. Sportsmen and women themselves are commodities, bought and sold according to the law of supply and demand, viz. the famous 'transfers' of professional footballers.

As soon as spectator sport becomes caught up in the capitalist web, the door is inevitably open to every kind of 'abuse' and 'fiddle': shamateurism, the star-system and the hunt for high fees.

As a form of mass entertainment, sport is a process whereby the population is reduced to an ideological mass. Sport is a means of regimentation and de-humanisation—see, for example, the role of football in Brazil, Britain or Spain, or of cycling in Italy and France, or of baseball in the USA etc. Spectator sports are a mass political safety-valve, a system of social diversion and an element in pre-military conditioning. Moreover, it is worth noting that most major competitions are controlled, if not actually run, by the police and the army, as was the case at the Mexico and Grenoble Games. In other words sport, as one of the factors for maintaining law and order, is usually controlled by the forces of law and order.

The ceremonies at major sports competitions are just like big military parades or pre-fascist rallies, with their 'traditional' or military music, the flag rituals, rhythmic marches, national anthems and medal ceremonies. The best examples of this kind of ceremonial are provided by the Hitlerite Games of 1936 in Berlin and the Mexico Games, controlled by the same *Granaderos* who had taken part in the repression of the student movement.

(f) Sport and the Ruling Ideology

Sport is a concentrated form, an officially promoted microcosm, of all the ideological prejudices of bureaucratic, bourgeois society:
- the cult of the champion and the star-system;
- the cult of promotion, social advancement and the hierarchy;
- the myth of transcending one's own limitations through effort;
- character building;
- sexual repression—the healthy life etc.;
- the brotherhood of man—everyone united on the sports-field;
- nationalism and chauvinism.

3. INSTITUTIONAL REPRESSION

- Sport is a social process for the continuous repression of childhood drives. As a socialising institution, sport channels the sexual drives of the adolescent in a repressive direction, through sublimation, unconscious repression and diversion.
- As Freud showed, sport replaces libidinal pleasure with the masochistic pleasure obtained from movement. As sports trainers are constantly stressing: 'It's when it hurts that it's doing you good!'
- Sport is a process whereby codified, stereotyped 'bodily techniques' are imprinted with the aim of producing automatic, adaptive reflexes.
- Sport is the repressive cultural codification of movements.
- Sport helps to shape the super-ego of the adolescent: external repression is internalised through the mediation of the trainer, the representative of bourgeois values and the bourgeois social order.
- *Sport is alienating. It will disappear in a universal communist society.*

NOTES

1. This is an expanded version of an article which first appeared in *Le Chrono Enraye* No. 8 (May-June 1972).
2. On this question see: J. Ulmann, *De la Gymnastique aux Sports Modernes*, PUF, Paris, 1965, pp. 277 on.
3. One can find some extract and a commentary of this text in S. R. Schram, *The Political Thought of Mao Tse-Tung*, Penguin Books, London, 1969, pp. 152-160.
4. 'Just as in general when examining any historical or social science, so also in the case of the development of economic categories is it always necessary to remember that the subject, in this context contemporary bourgeois society, is presupposed both in reality and in the mind, and that therefore categories express forms of existence—and sometimes merely separate aspects—of this particular society, the subject; (. . .) This has to be remembered because it provides important criteria for the arrangement of the material.' Karl Marx, *Introduction to a Critique of Political Economy*, in *The German Ideology*, part I, Lawrence & Wishart, London, 1970, p. 146.
5. 'Owing to the extensive use of machinery and to division of labour, the work of the proletarians has lost all individual character, and, consequently, all charm for the workman. He becomes an appendage of the machine, and it is only the most simple, most monotonous, and most easily acquired knack, that is required of him.' K. Marx and F. Engels, *Manifesto of the Communist Party*, in K. Mark/F. Engels, *Collected Works*, Vol. 6, Lawrence and Wishart, London, 1975, p. 490-91.

Towards an Anthropology of Play[1]

Brian Sutton-Smith

At the 1973 meeting of the American Anthropological Association, in a symposium on play, Margaret Mead presented the opinion that from any worthwhile scientific point of view, anthropologists had never really studied the subject. There were a few records here and there of high quality, there were the many accounts in the Human Relations Area Files, but in general, these records did not tell you how this play was functioning in the lives of the players. It was too cursory to allow any very clear interpretations in most cases.

Unfortunately, although there has been more activity on this subject, in psychology, the interpretation might well be the same. For both cases, I think there are at least two reasons. First, there has been the general neglect in social science of the expressive and nonserious subject-matters, a neglect there is now some signs will be remedied. Secondly, there is the inherent difficulty in studying these subject matters. They tend to be ephemeral. They tend more easily to freeze under observation. Thirdly, they are related to the rest of life in ways we are not easily able to understand. Because of our work-oriented way of life which makes us see the world in characteristic ways, it seems particularly difficult for us to generate a theoretical framework which is appropriate to play. In the face of play we are like anthropologists in a strange place, with a strange group and in a state of culture shock.

In our book, *The Study of Games*, Eliot Avedon and I reviewed the major work of the early anthropologists (Wiley, 1971), in particular the work of Tylor and Culin who used games largely as a part of their larger arguments over cultural diffusion versus the independent invention of cultural traits. In the same book we demonstrated that early folklorists also used games in a similar tendentious way believing that through games scientists could reconstruct the character of early history. The

From The Association for the Anthropological Study of Play *Newsletter*, 1974, 1:2, pp. 8-15. Reprinted by permission of the author.

names of the American scholar, William Newall, and the British folklorists, Gomme, Betts, and Spence are remembered in this light. Even the more recent British folklorists Peter and Iona Opie give us a version of the same notion, when they say that although games may not be used to reconstruct the past, they can at least be used to show the continuity with the past. They say, "From this point of view the study of games remains important, not for the purpose of reconstructing history, but for the purpose of illustrating the continuity of human nature." (Avedon and Sutton-Smith, 1971, p. 161). Let me say of the Opies that their interest in what they term "Child Life and Literature" to which they devote almost every day of both their lives is a totally admirable preoccupation. Their home in England is a most impressive library of every thing associated with children in the history of recent centuries. More than any one else I know they seem to realize that the changing treatment of children is a focal point for understanding the history of civilization.

But, my point here, is that like Tylor and Gomme, they perpetuate the notion that there is one *language of play and games*, and that we can understand what that language is simply by putting those plays and games on record. If we could actually achieve such a goal, then Margaret Mead's skeptical review of the facts would be out of order. But, of course, she is right. All these esteemed scholars were not really concerned with play and games, they were concerned with other more important and serious subject-matters, such as diffusion. They were neglecting play at the very moment it was being studied. While this is a less fair charge to bring against the Opies, it still holds true. Although their focus is more completely on play and games, their functional assumptions lead to the same result. Because they take their human nature for granted, they in effect always *study text without also studying context*. So we never really do know how or what these plays mean to those that use them. We have the record of play and games they provide, but little insight into what they mean to the players, which is Mead's point about the anthropological literature on the subject.

It is not my business here to deal with the psychology of play, but in the book *Child's Play* (with R. E. Herron, Wiley, 1971), I came to very similar conclusions. The collections of children's play and games in the early part of this century were meant to be illustrations of the necessary stages through which children must go. They were meant to indicate facts about human evolution. In the thirties most of the study of play had to do with the management of the kindergarten. Who plays with blocks; who plays with sand? Do children fight more or less when they have play apparatus? In the psychoanalytic studies of play, which constitute the largest body (if we take doll play therapy and diagnosis into account) of play studies in any subject-matter, play is conceived of as a *projection* of those other more important human subjects: aggression, eroticism, dependency, anality and the like. Here we have *context without text*. The play is studied to tell us once again only about human nature that is not play. This time not about diffusion, evolution, nor management, but about human conflict. Actually there is probably more information about the way play functions in human nature in this body of material than there is any where else. But the problem is one can not always tell with those who write about play diagnosis and therapy which of their intuitions are brilliant insights and which are simply their own projections. When the theory of play as projection is confused with the projections of the theorist as player, the rest of us must necessarily be a little uncertain about the conclusions that are offered. In the more recent studies of play as a cognitive or a voluntary behavior, there continues, I have argued, to be a reduction of play to cognitive structures on the one hand or exploratory behaviors on the other, such as care in *Child's Play*, Wiley, 1971, Section 8. Once again we are not able to focus on play without using it as an illustration of something else that is more important, although I would hasten to point out that I think the increasing intensity of this circumjacent activity is having a cumulative effect on our knowledge. When you look at those who give us only text, like the Opies and the folklorists, and those who give us only context, like most psychologists, some glimmering of the relations between both begins to merge.

In *The Study of Games* Avedon and I suggested that the new studies of Roberts and others, that is the cross cultural studies of games, represented a new start in the anthropology of play. Yet while this was certainly true on an empirical level because much new information was added, one has to question whether any real breakthrough was accomplished on a theoretical level; or whether Roberts, myself and others, did not simply serve once more to reduce games to some other more important functions, and in doing so have the subject-matter elude us once more. Let me briefly review what we did achieve in our studies.

The Roberts-Sutton-Smith Studies. These studies show:

1. That in cross-cultural studies there are hundreds of statistically significant associations between the presence of games and other cultural variables.

2. Different types of games (strategy, chance, physical skill and central person) have different patterns of association. There are also patterns asssociated with the absence of games and with the presence of more types of games.

3. The cultural variables with which associations have been made include child training variables, economic, technological, political and sociological variables.

These are in brief the major cross cultural findings. The *interpretations* from the more simple to the more complex are as follows:

1. That games are in some way functionally related to culture. They are not trivial or unessential or random.

2. That more complex cultures have more complex games and more types of games and that these various associations are merely an index of general complexity (cultures with no competitive games are very simple; cultures with all types are the most complex). This argument has been amplified by Don Ball of the University of British Columbia, Vancouver, Canada.

3. That there are meaningful structural relationships between each type of game and its patterns of association. Thus strategy is linked with obedience, training and social system complexity; chance is linked with responsibility, divination, nomadic habits and economic uncertainty; physical skill is linked with the tropics and hunting; central person games are linked with independence, training and marriage.

4. That the way to explain the linkages both with child training variables and cultural variables is in terms of the *conflict-enculturation hypothesis*, which says that conflict engendered by child training procedures (one is both rewarded and punished for interest in certain behaviors) leads to a readiness to be aroused by symbolic systems (games) which configure the conflict (in their role reversals). Involvement over times in these rewarding game patterns leads to mastery of behaviors which have functional value or transfer to culturally useful behavior.

5. That the way to prove this pattern of hypothesis is to show that the same patterns hold within our own culture as were to be found cross-culturally in the original studies (sub-system replication). Studies of adult preferences for games, of children's preferences, and of children's play appear to provide support for the original patterns of relationships. See, in particular, the studies of Tick Tack Toe in *The Folkgames of Children.* (op cit.)

6. That the way the enculturation aspect of this thesis occurs is through the games acting as models of cultural power relationships, that is those involving strategy, chance, force or arbitrary status. Studies of the character of power in games when compared with the exercise of power in the family suggest that there is no simple parallel between the two spheres, although factor analytic studies of such family power do yield some factors that are interpretable as strategy, force and chance. (These studies are described in Sutton-Smith and Rosenberg, *The Sibling*. Rinehart and Winston, New York, 1971, chapter 4.)

Now let me return to my original point about most of the work in anthropology and psychology—that it is a study of context without much reference to text. These studies of mine with Roberts are susceptible to the same criticism. What is textual here are the determinants of outcome (strategy, chance, etc.). That is all we have to say about games. What is contextual are the asserted relationships about psychogenic and sociogenic correlates. We are saying, like Durkheim or Malinowski, that games do not exist randomly in the structural fabric, they are there for a cultural purpose. As models of power, they replicate the larger systems of power of which they are a part and serve their purpose within these as buffered training systems, to use our phrase. To say this is to subordinate the game to the larger system. Granted we make it more than the sort of ephemera that the word "projection" implies. Our acquaintance with the vigor of play in the cross cultural materials saves us from that. We put more life into play as the notions of miniature power systems and buffered models suggest, and we do imply that they are larger systems for learning. Our games are systems for the socialization of conflict, as I have recently argued, and the socialization of power, as we argued earlier.

What has been occurring recently within sociology and anthropology, and has existed for a long time within literature, is the realization that these minor cultural systems such as games, and more obviously novels, do not exist simply to socialize members into the normative systems of the culture of which they are a part. On the contrary, the very nature of many of these systems is to challenge and even to reverse the systems of which they are a part. This thesis was taken up in a two part seminar of the American Anthropological Association in 1973 entitled "Forms of Symbolic Inversion." Here there was a study of the role of the trickster in folklore, of the fool at court; of the role of festivals such as the Mardi Gras; of inversion within ritual in simple cultures; of reversal in the power terminology of marginal groups; of reversals in the alienated groups of hippies, addicts and communes; of reversals in sex groups in all their current variety; and finally; of reversals in leisure, including a study of my own which I have called games of order and disorder.[3]

Games of Order and Disorder. What all the investigators were concerned with in these papers was to attempt to understand the role of such inversions in culture. By and large, these phenomena were pictured as anti-structure set off in a compensatory or cathartic relationship to the rest of the culture, a point of view originally, but no longer, taken by Victor Turner in his outstanding work on these problems, *Ritual Process* (Aldine Publishers, 1969). I took the view that these phenomena could also be considered as *proto structure*, that is as a source of novelty or as a source of new culture. To quote, "The normative structure represents the working equilibrium, the anti-structure represents the latent system of potential alternatives from which novelty will arise when contingencies in the normative system require it. We might more correctly call this second system the proto cultural system because it is the precursor of innovative-normative forms. It is the source of new culture."[4]

To briefly summarize my argument. It was that the anomalous class of pastimes, if considered in conflict terms, could be viewed as a set of oppositions between order and disorder, between anarchy and chaos. That these pastimes were in effect games in which the players did not compete with each other, but with the forces of chaos. That children between the ages of three and six years are preoccupied with such games. That there are four stages in their development: (1) games in which all act in concert and then collapse (Ring-a-Ring-a-Roses, Hand holding and Winding up and out amongst the Trobrianders);[5] (2) One or more players has a central role in bringing about the collapse (Poor Pussy, Jack-a-Balan) usually by causing them to laugh by absurd mimicry, etc.; (3) There is a coordinated series of actions leading to a climax of chaos (Consequences, My Aunt Went to Paris); (4) Actions are coordinated toward the downfall of a central figure (King of the Golden Sword, Queen of Sheba). This series of one to four covers the age levels in order from about four years to fourteen. There are many examples in the Human Relations Area Files from all culture areas, but insufficient to use in any statistical sense. The games have been, by and large, just too ephemeral for anthropologists and others to note seriously. They are, however, just one part of a more general concern with chaos, tumult, and vertigo in mankind's leisure which was first focussed for us, I believe, by Roger Callois in his book *Man, Play and Games* (Free Press, Glencoe, Illinois, 1961) and are exampled by all the arts of clowning, acrobatics, fun fair vertigo, danger, hazard, and dizziness with which we are familiar in the worlds of play and entertainments.

In my analysis of these and other games I suggested various ways in which role inversions could occur and thus provide the player with a novel experience (rather than simply with a replication of cultural experience). *First*, each player gets a turn at roles he may not get usually. Most cultural relationships are asymmetrical. Most game relationships are symmetrical. They model equality of turn taking, where life does not. There is more reversibility of roles in games than is to be found in the normative structure. Dominant persons tend to hold on to their dominance in every day affairs. What is usually inverted, therefore, is not the cultural dimensions (success or failure) but access to the roles within it. At least that is true for competitive games which both model power relationships as we said, but give leeway of access to these where that does not always exist elsewhere. *Secondly,* games of order and disorder are a special case, because they model the system only to destroy it. Their ambivalence is much more fundamental. They are both the most fundamental form of games (establishing for the young the roots of cooperation) and the most radical (upsetting the orders of motor, conventional impulse and social hierarchical control). *Thirdly,* all games provide a great deal of leeway within any given role for tactical variations and innovation. There are always new ways to be more strategic, to deceive or to cheat. These may be miniscule in the larger scale of the game, but they are indeed often reversals of the usual procedures for life and not unsuggestive of the way things might be done differently.

So in sum, we have in games behavior in which conventional roles are mocked (the games of order and disorder); we have in games an unconventional access to roles; and we have in games access to novelty within role. All of which I would contend could be seeds of potential novelty for the larger society, which is a thesis in the interpretation of play to which I will return shortly.

The Six Cultures Studies. It was always my hope that the extensive work of John and Beatrice Whiting would ultimately provide us with sufficiently convincing evidence on children's play that we might finally begin to get some idea of how we might resolve the various issues of cultural replication and reversal in children's play. It does not look as if it will do this, although there are some important relationships to be found there. The work on the Nyansongo of Kenya, for example, shows that in cultures where the children are an important cog in a fragile economic machine, there is little scope for them to play. The major job for these children is herding the cattle. It is reported that "fantasy play is almost non-existent among these children." (B. B. Whiting, 1963, p. 173) All that was observed was some fairly desultory physical play such as blocking streams and swimming, climbing trees, shooting birds with slings, fighting with each other, tussling, chasing and exchanging blows, watching cars on the roads. This is consistent with the studies of Dina Feitelson who reports that in the carpet weaving cultures of the Middle East where children are an economic asset, they also begin early in direct imitation of adult activity and do not indulge greatly in what you or I might call play.[7] The studies of Sarah Smilansky of hierarchical cultural groups in Israel are of similar importance.[8] This does not mean that all relatively simply cultures do not play, because the records of play amongst Australian aboriginal groups are very extensive. What seems to be critical is whether or not the adults have a direct economic need to train the children in highly normalized means of survival. In such cultures the "work ethic" makes real sense. The adults know what must be done to survive and they cannot afford the wasted time of child play. Children are an important cog in the machine. The same position prevailed in England in the early half of the nineteenth century when pauperism was widespread and young children were exploited in mines and factories as a necessary way of helping each family to survive. The Australian aborigines, as Michael Salter's collection shows so clearly, have an open ended environment for their children. There is much they can teach, but much also the child must learn through self reliance, including the fact that he must deal with novel circumstances. Play seems to be most relevant in such "open" societies and much less relevant in "closed" ones. It has more value for foragers than for tillers.

Even within complex societies when there is more leeway for the children to roam about and choose their own companions, there seems to be more play activity. In the Whiting's study when the Taira of Okinawa are compared with the even more culturally complex Rajputs of India whose children are restricted to sibling play in back yards, the former show much more activity. The Taira have tag, marbles, rope jumping, races, team chasing, houses, robbers and peddlers, kick the can, hopscotch, ball bouncing, tip cat, wrestling and prisoner's base; whereas the Rajputs have much less: the imitation of parent cooking or farming, dolls, small toy models, bows and arrows, hoops, wagon grinders and scales, plus some chasing and seesaw.

Nevertheless, as a society gets to be more complex, there are more problems, more novel contingencies which must be managed; so not surprisingly, the more complex cultural groups in the Whiting study (USA, India, Okinawa) exhibit more types of play than the less complex groups (Mexico, Philippine and African). One can manage this in the simplistic terms of arousal theory and say that novelty prompts exploratory activity; and then add the recent findings that more exploratory activity is usually followed by more play. Or we can break it down as we did in the cross cultural studies, showing what sorts of games go with what sorts of complexity. Or we can suggest, as I have more recently, that there are certain varieties of play which are relevant to certain types of cultural problems. Thus, there is exploratory play, imitative play, testing play and constructive play, and there are the social forms of sociodrama, contesting and make-believe.[9] It is possible to look at, for example, the aborigines and see that most of their play involves exploration and testing; whereas, in a symbolic and achievement oriented culture like ours, most play involves make-believe and contesting. It is my opinion that future research in the anthropology of play will go further along these lines into the careful specification of types of play and the type or subset of the cultural system to which it is related either directly or inversely.

There are some other possible differences between the society with the most observed play in the Whiting study, the Taira of Okinawa, and the society with the least observed play, the Nyansongo of Kenya, and these are worth mentioning as leads to future research. The family unit in Taira is nuclear, there are private courtyards so privacy is possible. Children can wander in an open and friendly society of other children; they meet more children who are not their kin. There is a school and there are competitive games at the school. There is more interaction with the father. There are more outsiders in the playgroups. Children under five are seldom given chores; they do not have to look after younger children to any extent. There are various specialized buildings such as shops. Children are self assertive. In the Nyansongo, by contrast, where subsistence agriculture prevails, the children must help with the work; they must help with the care of the younger children. Under the mother's control they help with many chores, getting fuel, cooking. They are members of an extended family and they are discouraged from leaving their immediate home environment. There is no school and no organized play; however, there is some dirt throwing and rough-housing by boys. There is little interaction with the father. The children are very much under the mother's control and dominance. These are all interesting contrasts. It is simply not possible yet for us to know which of these variables is intrinsic to the difference in play and which merely is an accidental associate. Intuition suggests the complexity, the play groups, the privacy, the father stimulation, and the lack of chores might all be important contributors.

A Theory of Play. As well as a clearer specification of types of play and types of relationship to cultural system, clearly we need a more useful theoretical account of play. We need an account which focuses on all the issue of both text and context. I have elsewhere set out what I think are some of the requirements of an adequately research oriented description of what this play theory should be.[10] It must pay attention to the antecedents of play, the structure of play, the consequents of play, and the relationship of all of these within larger ideological frames of reference. Within this approach it needs to focus separately on cognitive, motivational and affective variables as these have entered into different research programs. The antecedents and consequents and the involvement with ideology have to do with the context of play, the sort of thing that psychologists and anthropologists usually care about. The structure has to do with the text which has traditionally been the concern of folklorists and recreationists.

Let me deal first and most briefly with *text.* Here I have found it useful to think of playing cognitively as a form of *abstraction.* By this I mean a novel formulative process by which the child creates meaning and organization out of his prior experience, following here Vygotsky's interpretation of play rather than Piaget's. Conatively, I believe it is best thought of as a form of *power reversal.* Affectively, as a form of *vivification* of experience.

The *antecedent context* can emphasize the relationship to prior exploratory activity, as does Piaget, to antecedent power relationships or to antecedent signal activity, following Bateson. It can stress the nature of stimulus, motivational and affective quiescence as necessary for play. Or it can emphasize the paradoxical carry over of long-term enduring motives and conflicts into the play itself. My own preference is for finding parallels first between dreams and play, and, secondly, between play, games and sports and other forms of human expressive activity, such as narrative myth. Whether or not and how these systems emerge depends pretty much on the sort of cultural context, work-oriented or open-oriented, that I have been describing above.

The *postcedent context* includes the novelty to which play as abstractions give rise (now confirmed by a developing body of research), the flexibility which is an outcome of the power reversals, and the sense of revival which comes from the special quality of vivifying affective experience in play.

The transfer of these outcomes depends on the prevailing ideology. In a closed work ethic society there is no scope for the novelty and facetiousness to which play gives rise. In an open society this novelty is a source of potential adaptation, albeit an overproductive source being no guarantee of preparation, as Groos thought, but at least of the promise of being ready.

In this interpretation as seen in the analysis of games above, the play, games and sports both mirror and provide potential novelty about the larger society. In this interpretation also, social scientists, including anthropologists, have been mainly concerned with what I would like to consider the *integrative* functions of play in society. They have been concerned, as were Roberts and I, with normative socializing. The more static the society the more relevant that type of play theorizing is. What an increasingly open society like ours needs, however, is to consider the *innovative* functions of playing and try to account for the ways in which novelties introduced into the text ultimately transfer back to the society at large. What are the laws by which text is re-introduced to context? These should be able to be handled in probabilistic terms at least.

Any anthropology of play is in danger of succumbing to integrative theories because anthropology has tended to deal with relatively static societies. Perhaps in a complex culture such as our own we might be in danger of paying too much attention to novelty, although this is hardly to be feared as yet. The normative view of culture is still too strong with us.

In this paper what I hope to have indicated, if not always spelled out, are some of the areas into which research must probe as well as some of the theoretical problems with which play students must cope if we are, indeed, to overcome the relative ineffectiveness to date of research in the anthropology of play.[11]

NOTES

1. Prepared with the support of a grant from the National Institute of Education to study the "Enculturation of the Imagination in Early Childhood," # NE-G-00-3-0133.
2. The single best source for these studies in B. Sutton-Smith, *The Folkgames of Children*. University of Texas Press, Austin, 1973.
3. Gruppe, O. (ed.) *Sport in the Modern World: Chances and Problems.* Springer-Verlag, Berlin, 1974, pp. 70-75.
4. To be published under the editorship of Barbara Babcock Abrahams, University of Texas, Austin. B. Sutton-Smith article "Games of Order and Disorder."
5. Trobriand references from Malinowski, Bronislaw, *Sex Life of Savages*, 1969. Other references in B. Sutton-Smith, *The Games of New Zealand Children*, University of California, Berkeley, 1959. (Republished in *The Folkgames of Children*, op cit.)

6. B. B. Whiting (Ed.), *Six Cultures: Studies of Child Rearing.* Wiley & Sons, N.Y., 1963.
7. These references plus a more extensive discussion are to be found in B. Sutton-Smith, "Play as Adaptive Potentiation," *Sportswissenschaft,* in press.
8. Sutton-Smith, B., "The Games of Two Cultures," *Folkgames of Children,* op. cit.
9. Sutton-Smith, B., "Children at Play," Natural History, 80, 1971, pp. 54-59.
10. Sutton-Smith, B., "Play, Games and Sports in Industrial Society," Paper to International Sociological Association Meeting, Toronto, Canada, August, 1974.
11. A fuller treatment will be provided in the forthcoming *Dialectics of Play* to be published by *Sportswissenschaft,* University of Tubingen, Tubingen, West Germany.

Part II

Sport in Cultural Context

Section A

Socializing Institutions: Sport and Moral Education

Participation in sport requires the outlay of resources, such as time, money and effort, which are in relatively limited supply to each individual. Because sport appears to be a somewhat frivolous activity, the rationalistic nature of our modern society requires some social legitimation for the expenditure of such scarce resources. Probably the most common legitimation of sport is that sport is an agency of socialization and thus serves an important purpose in the social system.

Socialization is a social learning process through which the individual learns system goals, roles, values, attitudes, and comes to share common expectations about them with others in the social system. The process is complete when the values, roles, and the like are internalized by the individual and become unconscious determinants of his or her behavior.

The process of socialization continues throughout the individual's life, but some of the earliest agencies of socialization include the systems often referred to as socializing institutions: the family and the school. Much of the activity which takes place within their jurisdiction has to do with the learning of socially appropriate values, attitudes, and behaviors. Mindful as they must be of this responsibility, these systems could be expected to welcome other systems or activities which aid them in their socializing efforts. One can logically argue that, given the costs of sport, parents and school administrators would not condone, endorse, or encourage sport participation unless they perceived it as an activity consistent with the ends they were seeking. Without parental support, most children could not afford lessons or the access to some necessary facilities, could never obtain equipment, would never be allowed to rearrange the family vacation plans in order to play Little League baseball. Without support from school officials, students might never have the opportunities to learn certain team sports, might never receive the coaching necessary to achieve their athletic potential, might never be part of such adolescent rituals as pep rallies and homecoming parades. The very cooperation of the family and the school in presenting opportunities for sport involvement to children indicates a positive assessment by those groups of the value of sport. Moreover if asked why they endorse or sponsor sport for their children, parents will not reply that they do so because it is fun for their children (although surely that is an important consideration to them): rather they will respond with a vertible catalogue of reasons related to socialization.[1] School officials can also provide a formal rationale for their support of sport which often revolves around the educational value of scholastic sport.[2]

Much evidence can be presented to support the contention that sport is endorsed by some systems because it is perceived as an agency of socialization. Moreover, a common assumption of the family and the school appears to be that sport will teach positive values such as striving toward goals, sportsmanship and teamwork; the possibility that negative or undesirable values, such as winning at any cost, cheating, or the desire for personal glory, might be taught through sport is often overlooked. One way to reconcile both arguments is to acknowledge sport as a system comprised of symbolic messages. Sport may be an activity through which values may be taught, but *which* values are taught is determined by the individuals or systems which have power over the content of the message carried through sport. If one coach encourages and rewards winning regardless of the illegal means required to attain that goal while another encourages and rewards fair play even at the cost of victory, the athletes influenced by these two coaches may learn different lessons from sport. When discussing sport as a socializing agency, then, care must be taken to ensure that the analysis includes a thoughtful assessment of the social context in which sport is being used as an instrument of moral education.

Sherif's article emphasizes that concern, and she urges scholars to pay closer attention to the process through which sport teaches values. Specifically Sherif is concerned with competition. She notes "psychological effects of competition depend on its social context," and she considers sport as an obvious situation in which to explore the dynamics of the competitive process. Although she discusses several field studies in which the competitiveness endorsed in sport appeared to generalize to other situations and manifest itself in less desirable ways, Sherif does not

1. For example, see Geoffrey G. Watson, "Games Socialization and Parental Values," *International Review of Sport Sociology,* 1977, 12:1, pp. 17-48.
2. An excellent example of such a formal rationale is quoted in Walter Schafer, "Some Social Sources and Consequences of Interscholastic Athletics," in G. S. Kenyon, ed., *Aspects of Contemporary Sport Sociology,* Chicago: The Athletic Institute, 1969, p. 31.

condemn the competition in sport, as some commentators have done. Instead she advocates more thoughtful scholarly examinations of the social context of competition.

Jerome and Phillips address a familiar topic related to sport in the educational system: what is the relationship between participation in interscholastic sport and the educational goal of academic achievement? Their review of research on the topic reveals important cross-cultural differences. In the United States, sport involvement and academic achievement are positively related, but in Canada the pattern is reversed and sport involvement is negatively related to academic achievement. Jerome and Phillips discuss the differences in terms of the different cultural climates of the two nations, and their approach once more supports the argument that the lessons taught through sport are dependent upon the system which places those values into the sport system.

Comparing data collected from amateur baseball teams to those from amateur theatre groups, Stebbins demonstrates that socialization is not a problem handled only by children. Stebbins concentrates on one feature of socialization into a role, or stage fright: "the problem of sustaining an identity in the face of apprehensiveness about one's ability to do so." Stebbins isolates six preconditions that result in stage fright and then goes on to generalize this framework to other social situations.

Fine focuses on organized sport for children, in this case Little League Baseball. As an activity endorsed not only by the family, but also the community, Little League Baseball might be expected to represent an opportunity for socialization. Fine concentrates on one aspect of socialization—the moral education of the child—and he explores Little League Baseball as an arena where such values as effort, sportsmanship, teamwork, and coping with victory and defeat are advocated. More significantly, Fine explicitly demonstrates that moral values are controlled by those who are in a position to define the meaning of the social situation to others. From this perspective, Fine illustrates the significant amount of power entrusted to volunteer coaches, for they possess "explicit authority for assigning meaning to game events."

The Social Context of Competition

Carolyn W. Sherif

Confession of ignorance may be a step toward wisdom. Let me confess, then: I am ignorant about the field of sports and recreation. With colleagues in psychology and other social sciences, I share great information gaps about the effects of competition on children, for gaps exist in research into these problems.

It may be, however, that if we start naively, vision unclouded by preconceptions, we can avoid blind alleys that lure the sophisticated—in this case, those knowledgeable of all the pros and cons about various sports and recreation programs, philosophies, or the virtues and hazards of specific sports. Our view is guided, instead, by research on competitive processes among children. Assuredly, the consequences of severely strenuous activity on children should be a major preoccupation for physiologists, to determine whether or not children at any age are engaging in activities so strenuous as to be detrimental to their physical growth and development.

But let us be candid. Most discussions of competition among children do not concern the strenuousness of activity; they concern the social-psychological effects of competition on the developing human personality. Futhermore, such discussions too frequently bog down in irreconcilable controversy after the first few words are spoken. The participants almost always start with preconceived judgments about the effects of competition that no amount of talk can alter. To some, competition is regarded as natural, healthy, and essential for building character. To others competition is regarded as harmful, psychologically injurious, and detrimental to cooperative activity, which is endowed with all manner of beneficial effects and seen as the highest state of human relations.

The person who butts into such controversies with simple-minded observations (such as the terrifying consequences for social life if everyone competed all of the time, or the obvious fact that cooperative activities are integral to anything from a good ball game to a ghastly war) is regarded as a maverick who just does not get the point.

The point of such controversies is, of course, that the proponents have axes to grind. Their arguments are tools to support schemes of social arrangements—political, economic, or even recreational. Serious analysis of competitive processes involving children has no place for such ax-grinding. First, bias inevitably hampers viable research into a sorely neglected problem of major importance in child development. Second, it prevents planning for the most felicitous contexts for the development of human personality. But do-or-die defenders of competition or of cooperation are seldom as interested in such plans as they are in defending their own assumptions.

Try to find an instance of competition that does not involve cooperation with someone. Try to find an instance of cooperation, either within a group or with another group, that involves no competitive activity. According to the dictionary, competition stems from the Latin verb meaning "to seek together." In the most general sense, therefore, competition implies its supposed obverse: cooperation.

Trying as best we can to proceed without prejudgments, our task is to examine and to study the effects of competitive processes by inquiring into the *social context* in which children come together to seek, and then to examine, the effects of such contexts on the psychological outcomes of competition.

An occupational hazard of being a professor is to gain the comfortable feeling that a high-sounding definition of a problem solves the problem. At the risk of being so interpreted, a characterization of competition is here proposed because it seems conducive to our task, and because it will permit us to integrate a variety of research findings related to that task. *Competition consists of activities directed more or less consistently toward meeting a standard or achieving a goal in which performance by a person or by his group is compared and evaluated relative to that of selected other persons or groups.*

A few words of clarification will permit us to proceed to the major points in this discussion. The clarification consists of emphasizing two words in the characterization of competition. *Consistently* emphasizes patterns of activity that, with no more than occasional diversion, weave toward a standard or goal. *Selected other persons or groups* implies that consistent patterns of activity are not compared to or assessed by everybody, or by just anybody. By its very definition, competitive activity implies a social context involving *certain* other people and a selective process determining who they are or shall be.

Research bearing on the social context of competition and its effects will be summarized in the remainder of this paper. In brief, the themes of the successive sections are as follows:

1. Very young children cannot compete; competition develops during socialization in a specific social context.
2. Competitive processes and their outcomes vary according to the structure of standards and goals which, in turn, differs enormously from culture to culture, group to group, sex to sex, and even sport to sport.
3. Aspiration levels, achievement, success or failure and their psychological consequences depend upon the social context of the competitive process, the effective social context consisting both of the structure of standards and goals and of those persons and groups who count for the child.
4. Since they neglect the social context, most research models for studying effects of competition, particularly in sports, are inadequate and probably misleading.
5. Research specifically analyzing the social context of competition over time indicates that the psychological consequences for the child generalize far beyond the specific competitive activities themselves.

By analyzing the effective social context of competitive processes, alternative plans are suggested, conducive to the widest realization of human potentialities.

In discussing each of these themes, I shall be summarzing large bodies of specific research, without embroidering the discussion with copious footnotes and references. The reader with serious research interests may find ample documentation and references in Sherif and Sherif, *Social Psychology* (1969: esp. Chs. 6, 7, 11, 12, 17, 18, 19), and in my *Orientation in Social Psychology* (forthcoming).

CHILDREN LEARN TO COMPETE

Very young children cannot compete in the sense defined here. The capacity to direct behavior consistently toward an abstract standard for performance or a distant goal develops only with age and, as Piaget has suggested, through interaction with peers. Through such interaction, especially with peers who lack the overwhelming power of adults to impose standards for behavior, the child develops the ability and the desire to attain some defined level of performance or to reach a goal that does not automatically follow a short-time sequence of action ("a cookie after you eat the spinach"). Competition involves goals that are remote in time, carry abstract reward value, and are only probably attainable.

This does not mean that little children don't play, run, throw balls, swim, wrestle, hit, kick, suffer disappointments, or bask in the warm glow of approval. Infants treat one another much as objects, but soon learn games such as "I hand the toy to you and you hand it back, and I hand it to you," and so forth. Young children's play is solitary or side by side. Interaction has little to do with improving the actual performance underway. In fact, studies have shown that the presence of another child in an activity intended by adults to be competitive may actually lower performance level. The pleasure of each other's company takes precedence over sticking to the business at hand.

Usually during the preschool years, the child becomes capable and often absorbed in role-playing games—house, cowboys and Indians, war, or (as I overheard in my own neighborhood a few years ago) "let's kill Bobby Kennedy." They have reached a new level of play. They can take the roles of others, switch roles, follow and even change the rules. The play begins to take on the outward appearance of competition as the children bicker over who gets to be mommy, daddy and baby; who gets to be on the side of the good guys and who has to be bad, all the time with each side attempting to escape or bang-bang the other dead. Seldom is such play competitive in the sense defined, or in the sense that an adult intervening to set criteria for winning or losing will have much success.

Of course, the young child will respond to praise and correction in an activity that is enjoyable, such as throwing a ball or running. He responds when that praise or correction comes from an adult, older brother or sister, or playmate whose words, smiles, and frowns count a great deal in his young life. But in these early preschool years, behavior directed consistently toward attaining a standard or reaching a goal to be compared with the performance of others is only an occasional happening. You may have heard, as I did, young children playing a game in which the rules specify winning in terms of speed, time, accuracy, or the like. The winner announced "I won," whereupon another child joyously proclaimed "I won too." Then, with the pronouncement "We all won," the children turned to another concern—in this case, a devout hope that the ice cream man would soon be on their block.

Ordinarily, by about the age of six in our society, a child can and does compete. Still, the consistency of competitive behaviors varies enormously. Research has shown, for example, that middle-class children with schoolteacher and business parents compete consistently at an earlier age than children of working-class families. Perhaps even more important for our theme, the quality and persistence in competition depends upon the nature of the activity and its significance to the child. This point was driven home to me recently by an experienced recreation major at Pennsylvania State University, who expressed regret that she had not fully considered the developmental processes in competition. Working with second graders (seven-year-olds), she organized a relay race. The children were quite mature enough to grasp the rules and to understand the criterion for victory. They had a wonderful time running the relays, followed the rules, but they couldn't have cared less who won. As a result, the relays were a fun game but a shambles from the viewpoint of anything that might be called competition.

Several implications emerge from this brief account of the development of competition among children. First, the capacity to direct behavior consistently toward abstract standards or remote, uncertain goals in which one's behavior is compared and evaluated relative to others develops with age. The crucial evidence supporting this conclusion stems from a body of research showing that not only consistently competitive behavior, but also consistently cooperative behavior, consistent helping behavior, consistent sympathetic actions at the distress of others, and—most unfortunately—consistent prejudicial hostility toward groups traditionally discriminated against in our society all emerge at about the same period in the child's development.

Second, the process of development occurs in a social context in which parents, siblings, and peers are very important in providing the medium for testing one's own performance and for learning the reciprocal nature of rules and standards. Recreation leaders and teachers are important— but all of these significant figures are surrounded, like it or not, by a cultural context that is at least equally significant for the child's development. How else are we to understand the earliest buds of competition in rivalry over who gets to be father or mother, in divisions into good guys and bad guys for bang-bang conflict when the good guys and bad guys are precisely those whom the children meet in storybooks and on television? Evidence indicates that the social context for competition is crucial; if so, it is utter nonsense to speak of "born winners and born losers." There are, and always will be, individual differences. But the winners and the losers are shaped in a variety of ways by their social context, at times obviously and at others more subtly. It is more accurate to state that winners and losers are made by their experiences in a social context of other people who, to a major degree, determine the targets for their efforts and the structure of standards and goals related to those efforts.

Finally, the social context in which competitive behavior develops affects not only its rate of development but also the targets for competition—that is, what is important to the child and what can be left to the birds. In this country, at a very early age boys learn that sports of various kinds are *the* avenue for recognition to a far greater extent than girls. As a result some boys are placed in untenable situations psychologically, and many girls simply fail to persist in sufficient physical activity to develop strong and healthy bodies. We need to inquire into the variations in the social context that may produce strikingly different outcomes in what is regarded as important for competition and the behavioral outcomes of the competitive process.

DIFFERENCES IN THE NATURE AND STRUCTURE OF STANDARDS AND GOALS

Particularly in a society such as ours, it is important to recognize that the nature of activities deemed important enough to warrant competition and the structure of the relevant standards and goals differ from culture to culture, group to group, sex to sex, and even sport to sport. Too frequently we assume that what is worthy of competition (the "good life," in our terms—athletics to build body and character) is and should be a universal norm and ideal. In fact it is not. Consideration of such differences may reveal some failings in our society and suggest guidelines in planning for needed changes.

It is commonplace to point out that societies differ enormously in the prizes they offer for different activities, including sports and recreation. What is not so obvious is that societies that prize physical activity and health need not place enormous value on organized competitive sports. In some societies, physical fitness is prized for everyone and may be encouraged through universal physical activity, including work as well as fun and games. In others, excellence in sports is prized but rewarded indirectly through extra time for practice, opportunity to instruct, while those most outstanding are expected to be self-effacing in directing their efforts to the general improvement of physical well-being rather than personal aggrandizement and public acclaim.

Let us look at our own society. Sports compose a major value complex that the child encounters at an early age, especially if he happens to be male. Furthermore, sport is defined as competition to win. For the individual, the aim is to make the first team and, at all costs, to be on the winning team. If the varsity is winning, there is consolation even in being second or third or fourth string. Barring any of these positions, it is the rare boy who does not become absorbed as spectator of amateur and professional athletics, which may well mean that his own physical activity is limited to walking to the school bus or riding a motorbike. In our own extensive research on informal groups of adolescent boys studied in their natural habitats between 1958 and 1970 in the southwestern and eastern United States, we found only one group of teenage boys with no visible interest in ssports. These were sons of recent Mexican immigrants of peasant origin. Other Chicano youths in the same city were intensely interested in sports: with the hope of making a team, one group even entered a high school reputed for its magnificent athletic teams but located halfway across the city of San Antonio. While their relatively small stature precluded this goal, the youths actually stuck to that school through thick and thin, working to maintain passing grades and walking a couple of miles back and forth each day—all for the pride of identification with those glorious winners.

With girls it is different. After about the age of twelve, they quickly learn that actual participation in sports brings little glory. Their claim to fame comes through feminine attachment to the male team members, the booster clubs, or—thrill of all thrills—being a cheerleader. We will refer to girls again in the next section. Here it is sufficient to note that, in the past, their recognition in sports came chiefly from swimming, diving, ice skating, and other such graceful (hence lady-like) activities.

Among the so-called minority groups, excepting the rare Jim Thorpes, it has been primarily the blacks who have warmed their hearts through embracing the sports complex. How long and difficult has been the struggle of those pioneers who finally made it in the terms dictated by the dominant white sports complex! Black stars and superstars register their resentment at the second-class status that plagues our black citizens, even sports demi-gods. We may well sympathize, protest, and support their efforts to alter what is but one system of a dominant-subordinate relationship that permeates our national life. However, in analyzing competition in the lives of children as the sports complex is presently organized, there are issues of larger import that affect the average boy and girl regardless of race.

These larger issues center around the extreme importance attributed to organized competitive sports in our society, and the structure of goals integral to that organization. Of course, our more intelligent, confident, and successful sports educators realize that there are problems. Joe Paterno, the Penn State football coach, has said, "I don't think society would fold up if football would disappear"; he has even declared that he sees no excuse for extramural competitive sports before the high school level. He can say such things; but, as an outsider, I cannot do likewise without risking all sorts of disapprobation. This in itself is testimony to the power, prestige, and exclusiveness of the sports complex as now organized.

As a social psychologist I can, however, point to the structure of the goals that create problems in personal development for large numbers of young people. At present, the goal structure is a win-lose (or, if you wish, zero-sum) game. The aim is to win, thereby utterly defeating the opponent. This goal structure is clear enough in organized team sports; it is equally clear in the path that the individual child must take to succeed. He (or occasionally she) must gain exclusive hegemony over all competitors for the available slots on the team.

The tragedy for black youth is not that the sport complex encourages physical activity and the improvement of skills: it is that, with a few other exceptions (music, for example), the goal structure of sports provides the major, if not the only, means for him to improve his lot. Those who do not make the first string, and do not get courted for scholarships or pro teams, are assigned to perdition if they retain their devotion to the sports complex. Someone ought to question the long-range human consequences of failing in the sports lottery, both for black and for white children. How many of those hooked on the sports complex, with all their devotion of time and energy as second- and third-string players or water boys or cheerleaders, might be first-rate politicians, writers, scientists, mechanics, artists, musicians, electronic technicians, or piano tuners if the structure of goals and social support even began to approach the compelling structure of organized sports? How many useful citizens with dreams that could become realities have lost those dreams in the hours and hours of trying, hoping, sitting, and waiting to compete in sports with "I win—you lose" goal structure?

To contend that the prevailing structure of goals is necessary, normal, or natural can be countered even within the sphere of sports and recreation activities. The win-lose, beat-everyone-out-for-the-best-slot complex may indeed be characteristic of much of American life. But it is not true in many sports activities—mountain climbing, fishing, jogging, backpacking, nature hiking, many water sports, some snow sports, modern and folk dancing, calisthenics, and a good many others. Enjoyment or even excellence in golf or tennis is not dependent on the win-lose law of the organized sports jungle.

I am concerned that more children become actively involved in sports and recreation activities for both health and pleasure. I resent the undeniable fact that somewhere early in my own development I ended up out of sports activities, feeling inadequate and therefore unworthy of trying. I would like to see sports and recreation activities a part of my life and the lives of our children. Let us learn from social-psychological research just what psychological processes are involved in the effects of competition among children.

PSYCHOLOGICAL EFFECTS OF COMPETITION DEPEND ON ITS SOCIAL CONTEXT

Competitive activities refer to performance that is compared to standards set by certain other persons, and to the assessment of performance by certain other persons. These reference standards and persons, along with the structure of goals awarded to the competitors, are the effective social context of the competitive process.

The psychological effects of the competitive process can readily be inferred from the substantial body of literature on levels of aspiration and the experiences of success and failure. Experiencing success or failure is always relative to standards to which the child aspires. Like it or not, these standards are influenced decisively by significant adults, peers, and the images portrayed through the mass media of communication. Thus the child is seldom entirely free to establish a standard that fits his interests and abilities. He cannot remain immune to the judgments of parents, teachers, and peers in setting the level of his aspiration for performance.

Long ago William James defined the experiences of success or failure in relative terms, as the ratio between one's actual performance and his pretensions or aspirations in that field of activity. Much later Kurt Lewin, F. Hoppe, J. D. Frank, and others initiated research into the relationship between aspiration level and performance. Several findings from this substantial body of research have definite implications for the effects of competition.

First, in a given activity, there is a strong tendency to maintain the same level of aspiration regardless of actual performance. Experiences of failure are in a sense inevitable on those occasions when performance falls below the standard. This failure to adjust one's standards to actual performance (or, if you like, this rigidity of the aspiration level) is typical both of the performer and of others with personal investments in his performance. For example, in a study I conducted some years ago with children and their parents in a dart-throwing task, the parents tended to maintain a rigid aspiration level for their children, as did the children for themselves, regardless of actual performance.

Although this may not be true for the professional athlete, the child's aspiration is typically set at a level that has the peculiar and unfortunate effect of assuring the better performer more frequent experiences of success than the child whose performance is average or below. Typically, the more adequate performer sets his aspiration level slightly below his performance level and keeps it there. The average or less adequate performer, on the other hand, sets a standard considerably above his typical level of performance, thereby practically insuring a continuing sense of failure and frustration. Improvement in performance, therefore, has quite different psychological meaning for the child who is able and the child who has less aptitude.

The level at which standards of performance for an activity are set by adults or older children reflects a social norm that may or may not be realistic for the developmental level and skills of the child. Many years ago Dwight Chapman and John Volkmann, then later Leon Festinger and a number of other researchers, used carefully designed experiments to show what happens when performance is compared to that of a group too advanced or too low for the person's actual potentialities. Quite simply, if the person is told the expected level of performance for a group that he considers inferior in a specific activity, he raises the standard for his own performance. However, if the comparison group is one that he regards as superior to his own, his aspiration level is sharply lowered. An adult who holds up the performance level of the varsity high school team as a standard to sixth graders may inspire the exceptional few to work harder, but the majority will simply lower the level to which they aspire. Similarly, as Joe Paterno remarked in *Football My Way*, the standards of professional sports may instigate great efforts from the ambitious few, but for most players such standards simply remove the fun of sports by producing an aspiration level recognized as inferior, hence offering little joy when it is attained.

Thus far, the summary of research on aspiration levels and performance has been abstracted from recognition of actual attainments. Of course, this is not the case. As N. T. Feather has shown, consistent improvement in skill is tracked by consistent raising of the standard set for one's performance. Conversely, consistent trends toward decreasingly adequate performance are tracked by lowering of one's expectations. This may happen to even the best athlete when he begins to lose his stride. Much more significant for young children, however, is Feather's finding that the aspiration level tends to be maintained rigidly at a high level when the actual level of performance over time is fluctuating and least predictable. This state of affairs is highly probable for the young child, whose performance is likely to vary considerably from day to day or week to week, with the result that the child faces the continuing hazard of experiencing failure for reasons that are seldom clear to him or her.

The effects of continuing experiences of success or failure in young children have been documented, notably beginning with the research of Pauline Sears. The child who experiences success at a level approved and rewarded by significant adults and peers is able to tolerate an occasional failure or an "off day," recognizing it as such. But the child whose persistent experiences are defined as less than successful, or as failures, suffers considerably from a temporary drop and the resulting disapproval from persons significant in his or her eyes. Over time, the level of aspiration set for performance drops lower and lower, and pretensions may even vanish altogether. The child simply stops trying.

The outcomes summarized above certainly have import for the planning of sports and recreation programs. Currently, the great emphasis on interscholastic competition, varsity sports, and professionalism means that the vast majority of children are doomed to be very small frogs in enormous pools. Surely, for the developing human personality, it is important to create pools in which most children can have the experience of growing and gaining because they were not pressured to maintain a constantly rising aspiration level.

The problem suggested is compounded tenfold when we focus specifically on girls' sports and recreation. As girls approach adolescence, the double standard emerges with a vengeance. The little girl who is active and skilled may be called a tomboy, but she need not suffer unduly except from the scorn of boys who don't want a girl tagging around. If her skills are directed toward sports such as water ballet, ice skating, diving, or gymnastics, she can make it through early adolescence and beyond without detracting from what she and many of her peers and adults think of as feminine. But if these graceful and accepted feminine activities are not her forte, she faces a dilemma: be typed by peers as one of those athletic oddballs, or drop out. The vast majority choose the latter course, to the great misfortune of their health, physical development, and future enjoyment. They even develop (in the sense used by

Matina Horner in her doctoral thesis) a *fear* of success. If you play tennis and like it, go ahead and play, but not too well—certainly not so well that you beat male opponents.

The girl who remains devoted and who persists during her adolescent years in improving her skills in "unfeminine" sports faces a situation analogous psychologically to that of the successful black athlete. (I emphasize the psychological effects, because the sociological causes and consequences are quite different.) By striving toward and attaining a high level of performance, she experiences success in one respect but faces failure in others—namely, in those spheres traditionally defined as feminine. For the successful black athlete, of course, this impossible feat of high self-esteem and sense of accomplishment in sports is accompanied by the denial of rights and privileges that should be available to any athlete of attainment. For the female athlete in "unfeminine" spheres, the denial is psychologically painful, but perhaps less important from an educational and sociological point of view than the statistically more frequent fact that girls simply lose interest in sports, drop out, or try hard not to succeed too well. Let me enter a plea to those involved in the improvement of the status and quality of girls' physical activity. Their opportunities should be enhanced. More girls should enter and continue in sports. However, please do not fall into the traps already set by the structure of boys' sports. In achieving greater opportunity for girls, please do not merely imitate the existing male models. The task is not to imitate, but to innovate. Who knows; perhaps the boys' sports programs will be altered to imitate the new female programs.

THE INADEQUACY OF TYPICAL RESEARCH MODELS FOR STUDYING EFFECTS OF COMPETITION

As a researcher, I shall be brief and harsh in commenting on most research available on the effects of competition in sports. Too frequently the social context of competition is ignored in the research design. It is unnecessary to cast blame for this state of affairs on researchers in sports, recreation, or the sociology thereof. My point can be made from an entirely different problem area.

Consider the vast bulk of research on juvenile delinquents. Much of this research studies a sample of youth labeled as delinquents by legal authorities (and hence by their peers, school, families, and communities) and compares certain of their personal characteristics or social relationships with those of a sample labeled nondelinquents (because legal authorities have not so labeled them). In good research procedure, one matches the two samples in certain important respects, such as socio-economic class, sex, family size or status, etc. Almost invariably, some differences are found between the two samples—usually differences that make the nondelinquent sample seem better adjusted, better students, and so forth. I am not saying that such findings are invalid; I am saying that such a research design tells us nothing at all about why the delinquent sample became labeled delinquent, why they differ from the nondelinquents, or, for that matter, why the nondelinquents are nondelinquents.

To make the point clear, let us design studies by this model in which we could show that those who engage in sports to a significant extent do not exhibit superior personal characteristics and social skills. Select a school that, for any reason, deemphasizes competitive sports and strongly emphasizes the arts, scholarship, or scientific investigation. Compare a sample of athletes in that school with non-athletes. Or, in almost any large high school, compare the girl members of the basketball or hockey teams with a sample of nonmembers. It is highly probable that the students who are not athletes would come out looking better adjusted, more sociable, and with certain more desirable personal characteristics.

This small exercise is intended to emphasize that research into competitive sports must consider the social context as a part of the research design and must trace, over time, its role in the competitive process and its effects. For this reason Thomas D. McIntyre's "Field Experimental Study of Cohesiveness, Status, and Attitude Change in Four Biracial Small Sport Groups" (Ph.D. dissertation, Pennsylvania State University, 1970) should be read seriously by researchers. While he did not find (as he had quite frankly hoped) that participation on interracial teams greatly altered the attitudes of blacks and whites toward one another, he did discover a great deal about the effects of the social context in inhibiting and permitting the formation of biracial teams, about the development of group and team organization, about the formation of friendships across racial lines, and about the competitive process. Any researcher interested in the effects of competition, for good or for evil, must undertake investigations that include the social context and study the competitive process over time. There simply are no shortcuts or easy answers to our questions in this regard. Meanwhile, our traditional cross-sectional studies comparing selected samples of athletic participants and nonparticipants will continue to tell us that conformity to and success in a highly valued activity ordinarily brings rewards and felicitous personal experiences.

PROLONGED COMPETITION ON WIN-LOSE BASIS
GENERALIZES BEYOND THE GAME

In his writings on the "split-level American family" and on the goal structures that pit child against child, age group against age group, and social group against social group, Urie Bronfenbrenner of Cornell University has made it poignantly clear that we have neglected to take the broad view of the effects of competition on children. Both he and other social psychologists who have commented on childhood in general (in contrast to simply analyzing the child at home, or the child at school, or the child in sports as though the child's development were split into compartments) have illustrated some of their main points through a series of experiments directed by Muzafer Sherif (see Ch. 11 in *Social Psychology*).

In three separate experiments conducted in natural circumstances in summer camps, Sherif and his associates demonstrated that prolonged competition on a win-lose basis between groups of children had effects that extended far beyond the specific context of the games played. It should be emphasized that these experiments used sports as a medium for prolonged competition, not as the butt of criticism. The participants in each case were American boys about twelve years old to whom sports were already of central interest, along with camping and outdoor recreational activities. To compete in sports was not only a natural but also a highly desirable activity.

The camps were organized by research personnel and arranged over time so that the structure of goals between groups of boys were systematically changed to study, first, the effects of prolonged win-lose competition and, second, the change of those effects in more creative directions. For this reason I believe that they have definite implications for the possibilities of planning and programming in sports and recreational activities.

For reasons of theory and hypothesis testing, which need not be our main concern here, the participants in each of the three experiments were carefully selected to be unacquainted with each other at the outset, well adjusted in school and on the playground, and members of stable middle-class families of similar religious and ethnic backgrounds. The choice of such a homogeneous bunch of typical, normal American boys permitted us to rule out explanations of the results of their interaction on such possible bases as their being already unduly frustrated, insecure, poor losers, or divided by striking differences in background when they came to the camp.

Research personnel all functioned in the roles of regular camp personnel, securing the research data through a variety of unobtrusive research techniques that insured that the boys were not aware that their words and deeds were being studied, and that conclusions were not based selectively on events that supported the research hypotheses. (In brief, the latter was accomplished by using a combination of research methods, the outcome of some being beyond the researchers' control, and then basing conclusions on these converging sources of data.) While the boys did not know that they were being constantly studied, their parents were aware of the study nature of the camps. All possible safeguards, including medical precautions, were taken to insure the boys' safety and welfare.

Since the research concerned group competition, the first stage (about a week in each case) focused on group formation. The selected participants were divided arbitrarily into two bunches, matched as closely as possible in terms of size, skills, and interest. The sole conditions for activities, most of which were actually chosen by the boys themselves, were that they focus on interaction within the developing groups and that they encourage activities requiring that all members participate actively in order to reach their goal, enjoy themselves, or whatever state of affairs described the satisfactory outcome of the activity. For example, to use a canoe left by their cabin, the boys had to figure out a way to transport it through the woods. Or, when very hungry, they were given food in bulk form—ground beef, uncut buns, a watermelon, unmixed powdered drinks—whose transformation into a meal required their division of labor and cooperation.

In each case two groups formed; each group had little contact with the other and, in the last experiment, neither group actually knew of the existence of another group in camp. The groups had distinctive organizations (leader-follower relations) and norms (customs, preferred territory, nicknames for members, and names for themselves). One group developed a complex of norms centering around tough, brave masculinity that flinched at no danger and willingly endured discomfort, while the other (closely matched initially on an individual-by-individual basis) developed its little culture in a fashion that forbade swearing, emphasized moral uplift, and encouraged regular prayer.

The goal structure in which these groups first met was transformed to a win-lose structure very naturally when they discovered each other's presence and asked to compete in organized sports. A tournament of games was organized to accede to this request and "make it more fun"; highly attractive prizes were available for the winning group. The tournament lasted for several days, including a variety of sports events selected by the boys plus a few (tent-pitching, cabin inspection, etc.) that permitted the research personnel to keep the cumulative scores of events close to the very end. This particular structure of highly desirable goals that one group could attain only at the expense of the other's loss had a number of effects that far exceeded the bounds of the sports competition itself.

As good American boys and experienced competitors, the games started in the spirit of good sportsmanship, graceful winning and losing. However, they quickly turned into vicious contests in which the sole aim was to win and in which the competitors became increasingly seen as a bunch of incorrigible cheats, quite outside the pale of that brand of humanity identified within one's group. (In the experiment mentioned, in which the culture of one group was toughness and the other of piety, this outcome applied equally to both groups, regardless of the difference in their norms for internal group behavior.)

The prolonged competition between groups had a decided impact on the leader-follower relations, norms, and focal concerns within each group. The daily concern was developing strategy and tactics to defeat the other group. Leaders or other high-status members who shrank from the intense forms of conflict that developed were replaced; erstwhile bullies who had been "put in their place" within their own groups now became heroes of combat.

Outside the athletic competition, and against adult rulings, raids and acts of aggression were organized by the boys themselves. Such acts included messing up the rival's cabin, painting derogatory slogans on the stolen blue jeans of the opponent's leader—"The Last of the Eagles"— and hoarding small green apples to be used "in case" of attack by the other group.

Upon the victory of one group in the tournament, boys in each group possessed attitudes of extreme prejudice and hostility, universally condemning the individual characters of members of their rival group. In fact, each wanted nothing at all to do with the other group.

Appeals to moral values ("love thy enemy") had no effect at all at this point. In religious services organized separately by each group, the local minister conveyed such messages and appeals in forms which the boys appreciated and understood—but immediately afterward they turned to renewed cursing of their opponents.

Cohesiveness, solidarity, self-initiated responsibility, and democratic procedures greatly increased within each group during the conflict. However, the norms of brotherhood and supporting one's fellows which were so strikingly apparent within each group did not apply to the other group.

Democratic procedure, loyalty, and friendship at home need not be transferred to the treatment of those not within the magic bounds of one's own group or team.

In the experiments, several changes in goal structure were tried in the attempt to change this dismal state of affairs. First, there was a series of events that were highly appealing to each group separately (common goals) and in which they had to participate together as equals. However, these contact situations involved no interdependence between the groups. Each could eat the greatly improved food, shoot July Fourth fireworks, use new sports equipment, see a movie, etc., side by side without so much as speaking to the other group. In fact, they did speak. While they conducted their affairs separately, they used these contact situations as opportunities for recriminations, for accusations of "who's to blame" for the existing state of affairs, for hurling invectives, and when food was present, for "garbage wars" that had to be stopped when the weapons changed from mashed potatoes and paper to forks and knives.

The change that was effective, over time, in altering the generalized state of hostility and aggression created from prolonged win-lose competition was the introduction of a series of goals, each profoundly appealing to each group but whose attainment required the participation and the resources of both groups. To distinguish these from merely "common" goals, they were termed "superordinate goals": goals urgently desired by each group but unattainable without cooperation. In the first study, this condition took the form of a "common enemy." A team from another camp competed with teams selected from both of the rival groups. The short-term effects of this common enemy were to induce cooperation for "our camp" to beat theirs. However, when the common enemy was gone, the two rivals quickly retreated to their own in-groups, still unwilling to cooperate in other activities across group lines. Further, had we continued the "common enemy" approach, we would have ended by merely enlarging the scope of the generalized effects of win-lose competition that had already occurred within our camp. In effect, we would have had a bigger war.

The superordinate goals that were effective were problem situations —an apparent breakdown in the water system at a time when outside help was not immediately available; how to get another movie when the camp was short on funds and neither group had enough canteen funds left to sponsor a movie alone; a stalled Mack truck that was the sole vehicle to go for food when everyone was hungry and which was far too large for one group to push or pull alone; food preparation at a time

when everyone was very hungry, even though "separate but equal" facilities were available but less efficient; tent pitching when all were
tired and when the poles and stakes had somehow gotten all mixed up.

Such superordinate goal structures did not have an immediate effect
on the hostility between the groups. They induced immediate cooperation, which dissipated into separate exclusiveness once the goal had been
achieved. It required a series of such goals over time for a genuine and
lasting change in the relationships between the groups to occur. Such
a series of superordinate goals was effective; the boys not only learned
to cooperate with each other as groups, but also took initiative to do so
on their own. Over time, their views of the other group's immorality and
ruthlessness were altered. They learned to take turns in camp activities
and actually initiated campfire entertainments in which each group alter-
nated presenting the best and funniest of their talent.

Between the alternative structures of win-lose conflict and superordinate goals, there are many other possibilities. I offer the results of
these experiments to stimulate thinking, planning and, I hope, revising
of the programs of the sports and recreational competitions in which
our children participate. The advantage of superordinate goals, when
these are genuine for each group (not imposed by adults), is that other
measures which have been tried, often vainly, to keep competitive outcomes within bounds are transformed. Information is exchanged across
group lines; friendships can form; leaders of groups can initiate new
programs and actions without fear of being called traitors by their own
groups; the creative potentials of the groups are given the broadest possible scope.

Particularly with young children in community and school contexts,
the full understanding of the meaning and the potentialities of superordinate goal structures has the possibility for building competitive sports
programs in which children learn the sorts of responsibility, loyalty, skilled
efforts, practice, and teamwork that we believe build character, while
avoiding some of the generalized consequences that accrue from competition in actual life. If seriously translated into action, these desirable and
potentially fruitful experiences for development toward adulthood could
create situations in which everyone can win—if not a total victory, at
least enough to lift self-esteem, skills, and experiences that may universally benefit the bodies and minds of our youth. I leave the creation of
superordinate goal structures to those who know much more than I about
sports and recreation. I am convinced, however, that their planning requires not sheer individual genius, but cooperation and competition
among those charged with such planning to produce the most effective
and viable programs. I am further convinced that many of those so
charged would find great joy in the experience of trying.

The Relationship between Academic Achievement and Interscholastic Participation: A Comparison of Canadian and American High Schools

Wendy C. Jerome and John C. Phillips

Interscholastic athletics have been considered an anti-intellectual influence by some authors (Henry, 1963; Coleman, 1961, 1965) who argue that school athletic programs encourage a diversion of school resources, parental support, and student energies away from the mission of scholastic excellence. Recent studies of American high school athletic programs, however, provide compelling evidence that participation in athletics is associated with better grades, higher aspiration levels, and a more positive attitude towards school.

A variety of plausible explanations for this phenomenon have been suggested which center around three basic themes: (1) selection—the better, more proschool students try out for, and are selected to membership on school teams; (2) "spill-over"—there is a transfer of positive work habits, attitudes, and values from sports to school work; and (3) differential school experiences—athletes are more visible, acquire increased status, and receive more encouragement from school personnel than do non-athletes.

This paper will review some of the evidence concerning athletic participation and scholastic achievement in American and Canadian high schools and discuss certain cultural differences which may explain the variation noted in the relationships between sports and studies.

Schafer and Armer (1968) found that high school athletes achieved slightly better grades than their non-athlete matches and that this ad-

From *Journal of the Canadian Association for Health, Physical Education and Recreation.* 1971, vol. 37: 18-21. Copyright 1971 Canadian Association of Health, Physical Education and Recreation. Reprinted by permission of the publisher.

vantage increased among boys from blue-collar homes and boys who were not in a college-preparatory program. Bend (1968), in a nationwide study of American high school athletes, found substantially the same pattern. Athletes got slightly better grades and the advantage of the athletes was most pronounced among "low endowment" (low IQ, blue-collar) boys. Buhrmann's (1968) study of junior high school boys in Oregon also found that participation seemed to encourage students from poor and disadvantaged groups to achieve scholastically at a much higher level than their non-participating peers.

There is strong evidence to indicate that athletes aspire to attend college and succeed in attending college more than do non-athletes. Bend (1968) found that 81.8% of his superior athletes aspired to at least some college work compared to 56.1% of his non-athletes. The figures for low-endowment superior athletes were 39.8% and 13.3% respectively. Of the superior athletes, 71.4% actually attended college while 50% of the non-athletes attended. Figures for the low-endowment athletes and non-athletes were 14.8% and 6.9%. Rehberg and Schafer (1968; 1970) found similar patterns in aspirations and expectations for college attendance.

In a recent study of one American high school, Phillips and Schafer (1970) found that athletes, when compared to non-athletes, shared attitudes which were somewhat more favourable toward the school and its traditions. They concluded that the better academic performance by athletes could be explained by the greater pressures toward conformity to school rules and traditions expected of athletes, as well as a more positive attitude toward the school among athletes. Since athletics, to a greater degree than scholarship, also provides entry to elite school status in American schools (Coleman, 1960; Clark, 1957; Horowitz, 1967), we should not be suprised at the athletes' relatively strong support for school rules and traditions.

It should be noted that there is some support for the concept of the "all-round" individual. Both Coleman and Horowitz found that the "athlete-scholar" rated highest on measures of interpersonal popularity. In comparisons between the "pure" athlete and the "pure" scholar, however, both found that the athlete was accorded much higher status. Explaining this phenomenon, Coleman presents the view that because members of the school and community identify strongly with the success and failure of "their" team, the athlete gains status because he is doing something for the community. Success in scholastic matters, on the other hand, is obtained at the expense of classmates and often results ridicule and rejection of the achiever, unless balanced by athletic contributions.

These, and other recent studies, have provided some insight into the relationship of high school athletic participation to scholastic achievement. However, the results of these studies conducted in American high schools are often applied to the Canadian high school, perhaps because of the apparent similarities between the two countries and the fact that little research has been conducted on the Canadian high school athlete.

It would appear from the results of the few studies that have been conducted that a difference does exist. Jerome, in a study currently underway in Sudbury, Ontario finds that while the majority of students would aspire to be "athlete-scholars," in comparisons between the "pure" athlete and the "pure" scholar, the athlete was far down the line. This attitude among Canadian students is further supported by Zentner and Parr (1968) whose study of social status among high school students in Calgary led them to conclude that high academic performance was a positive factor in the student status structure. In that study, students with high academic achievement were overrepresented in the leading crowds.

As for the relationship between academic achievement and athletic participation, Jerome found that when final grade averages obtained by students prior to opportunity for interscholastic competition were compared to those achieved after this opportunity was available, the non-participants' grades changed in an upward direction while those of the athletes became lower. The differences between the two groups were significant at the .05 level. Further, when socio-economic status and academic program were considered, it was found that non-participant's grades improved to a greater degree than did those of athletes of the same social class and academic program. Again the differences were significant.

A further study by King and Angi (1968) of the hockey playing student in Ontario found that in Grade 9 hockey playing students achieved similar marks to non-hockey playing students, were slightly lower on achievement and aptitude tests, and had higher academic and vocational goals. However, by the time these hockey players had reached Grade 12 they had significantly lower school marks than the non-players, significantly lower achievement and aptitude scores,and had lowered their academic and vocational goals. It should be noted that these hockey players were not involved in interscholastic hockey, but in highly organized Junior A, B, C, and D hockey programs in the community which are not conducted to fit around the students' academic responsibilities as are interscholastic sports.

Why these differences between school athletes in the two countries? On the surface it would appear that the interscholastic programs in Canada and the United States are similar. A wide range of activities, competitive leagues, school awards, state and provincial championships are common to both. Certified teachers coach the teams. The local news media cover the competitions and report on the results.

Returning to the three explanations posed earlier, if the better, more motivated students tend to go out for, and be selected to athletic teams, we would expect the positive relationship between athletic participation and academics to hold in both American and Canadian schools. Also, if, as Schafer and Armer (1968) have suggested, good habits and application to sports carry over to academic matters, we would expect athletes from both cultures to do better in school. If we accept this reasoning, we can expect students to do better in studies as a result of participation in athletics regardless of whether they receive special attention form the school. This does not appear to be so in Canadian schools. It would seem, then, that the third explanation offered, differential school experiences, would be the most plausible.

It is clear that in the American secondary school high recognition and accompanying status are achieved directly through athletic activities. Athletes are more likely to be members of the leading crowds than are scholars. Coleman (1960) showed that athletic success was clearly and consistently the most important means .to achievement of status in every school he studied. Schafer and Armer (1968) feel that for the blue-collar boy the most certain means of entry into the "leading crowd" is athletics. This does not appear to be the case in the Canadian school. The athlete is visible, but not to the same degree, and his acceptance into the leading crowd appears to be dependent to a greater degree on his scholastic aptitude.

Downey's (1960) study of cultural differences between various regions of the United States and Canada sheds some light on why this situation may be present. He found that Canadians placed a greater emphasis on the pursuit of knowledge and scholarly attributes as an outcome of schooling than did Americans. The American schools tended to emphasize physical development, citizenship, and social skills. The reward structures of the schools would tend to reflect these emphases. Spady (1970) has suggested that many students may view athletics as an alternative to, rather than complementary to, the academic mission of the school. Canadian schools, by increasing the rewards available to participants in academic areas may encourage the less interested students to use athletics as an alternative.

Schafer and Armer (1968) reason that another positive effect participation in athletics may have upon the grades of American students is the "lure" of a college career in sports provided through athletic scholarships. This financial assistance available in almost every post-high school institution in the United States is not common in Canadian institutions of higher learning. The availability of these scholarships to American students might well encourage them to maintain their grades at a level which would assure them of consideration by college coaches.

In addition, the degree of emphasis and support from the American community for the high school athletic program is much greater than that found in Canada. American communities identify with "their" team. It is not uncommon to see a large number of adults mixed with students at high school athletic contests. In most Canadian schools, it is uncommon to see a large number of students in attendance. Local news media in both countries provide coverage for high school sports; however, in the United States this coverage extends to national sports magazines. These periodicals carry results of high school competitions, they publicize all-stars, and carry articles on high school athletes of national calibre. Rarely does one see a Canadian high school athlete mentioned outside the high school column of the local newspaper.

The findings suggest that the positive relationship between athletic participation and academic achievement in American high schools can probably best be explained by special rewarding experiences in and from the school and community. Athletes, like all other creatures, appear to become positively attached to sources of rewarding experiences, in this case the school. Perhaps, too, as Schafer and Armer (1968) suggest, the high prestige that American students obtain from sports participation gives them a better self-concept resulting in a more positive attitude towards themselves and their abilities—both athletic and scholastic. In the absence of a differential reward structure favouring athletics, one cannot expect athletes, as a group, to excel in their school work to a greater degree than other students.

REFERENCES

Bend, Emil. *The Impact of Athletic Participation on Academic and Career Aspiration and Achievement.* (New Brunswick, New Jersey: The National Football Foundation and Hall of Fame, 1968).

Buhrmann, Hans G. "Longitudinal Study of the Relationship Between Athletic Participation, Various Social-Psychological Variables, and Academic Achievement of Junior High School Boys" (Microcarded Ph.D. dissertation, University of Oregon, 1968).

Clark, B. R. *Educating the Expert Society*. (San Francisco: Chandler, 1962), pp. 244-258.

Coleman, James S. "Adolescent Subculture and Academic Achievement," *American Journal of Sociology*, Vol. LXV (January, 1960), pp. 337-347.

———. *The Adolescent Society*. (New York: The Free Press, 1961).

———. "Peer Cultures and Education in Modern Society." In Theodore M. Newcomb and Everett K. Wilson (eds.), *College Peer Groups: Problems and Prospects for Research*. (Chicago: Aldine, 1966), pp. 244-269.

Downey, L. W. "Regional Variations in Educational Viewpoint," *Alberta Journal of Educational Research*, Vol. VI, No. 4 (December, 1960), pp. 195-199.

Hargreaves, David H. *Social Relation in a Secondary School*. (London: Routledge and Kegan Paul, 1967).

Henry, Jules. *Culture Against Man*. (New York: John Wiley and Sons, 1963).

Horowitz, Herbert. "Prediction of Adolescent Popularity and Rejection from Achievement and Interest Tests," *Journal of Educational Psychology*, Volume 58, No. 3 (1967), pp. 170-174.

Jerome, Wendy C. "A Study to Determine the Relationships Between Participation in Organized Interscholastic and Community Sports and Academic Achievement," (Unfinished Ph.D. dissertation, University of Oregon).

King, A.J.C., and Carol E. Angi. "The Hockey Playing Student," *CAHPER Journal*, Vol. 35, No. 1 (October-November, 1968), pp. 25-28.

Phillips, John C., and Walter E. Schafer. "The Athletic Subculture: A Preliminary Study." Paper presented at the annual meeting of the American Sociological Association, Washington, D. C. 1970.

Rehberg, Richard A., and Walter E. Schafer. "Participation in Interscholastic Athletics and College Expectations," *American Journal of Sociology*, 73 (May, 1968), pp. 732-740.

Schafer, Walter E., and J. Michael Armer. "Athletes are Not Inferior Students," *Trans-action*, (November, 1968), pp. 21-26, 61-62.

——— and Richard A. Rehberg. "Athletic Participation, College Aspirations and College Encouragement," *Pacific Sociological Review*, 13 (Summer, 1970), pp. 182-186.

Spady, William G. "Lament for the Letterman: Effects of Peer Status and Extracurricular Activities on Goals and Achievement," *American Journal of Sociology*, 75 (January, 1970), pp. 680-702.

Zentner, Henry, and Arnold R. Parr. "Social Status in the High School: An Analysis of Some Related Variables," *Alberta Journal of Educational Research*, Vol. XIV, No. 4 (December, 1968).

Toward a Social Psychology of Stage Fright

Robert A. Stebbins

Lyman and Scott's (1970) pioneering essay on stage fright is the first attempt by social psychologists to analyze this emotional state. It refers in general to the problem of sustaining an identity and in particular to the problem of sustaining that identity in the face of apprehensiveness about one's ability to do so. Stage fright is generated in two ways:

> Knowing in advance that a situation will open one to a total inspection of self, or anticipating that a slip or flaw will suddenly thrust one into a position that invites challenges to a claimed identity, or both (Lyman and Scott, 1970: 160).

Their statement, though it contains some awkward inconsistencies and omissions, has nonetheless laid a solid foundation for further theorizing and research on the social psychological antecedents and consequences of stage fright. The aim of the present article is to build on this foundation by identifying the preconditions of stage fright and relating them to certain observations made by Lyman and Scott later in their paper. Participant observation of the activities of two adult amateur baseball teams and an amateur theater company plus interviews with fifty-five players, actors, and actresses provided the empirical source for the ideas presented here.

PRECONDITIONS

Before considering the preconditions it should be pointed out that stage fright appears to develop in another way besides the two mentioned by Lyman and Scott. Research with the baseball players indicated that, beyond pregame jitters, many of them also grow apprehensive over their

This paper was originally presented at the Canadian Sociology and Anthropology Association meetings, Frederickton, N. B., 1977. Reprinted by permission of the author.

potential inability to perform in a way that would bring immediate honor. For instance, a baseball player nervously realizes that he could bungle the opportunity to win the admiration of his teammates and the spectators by failing to get the hit that would drive in the winning run. Or a relief pitcher becomes aware of the prospect that by striking out the next three batters he could be the hero of the game because he has deftly eliminated the possibility that his team will lose the game. Stage fright results here not from an apprehension that the individual might be unable to perform in routine circumstances, but from an apprehension that he might miss the opportunity to show how well he can do under tense conditions where fellow players and spectators expect less from him.

Common sense usage of the term suggests that stage fright emerges prior to the *performance* of a *critical activity*. Further, stage fright develops when the performer knows in advance that the performance of this critical activity could place him in one or more of three threatening situations: where he is open to a total inspection of self by others, where a slip or flaw invites a challenge to a claimed identity, or where he must perform exceptionally well. The observations of and interviews with the baseball and theater amateurs suggest six preconditions that must pertain if these three situations are to be defined as threatening. They are importance, imminence, audience, control, difficulty, and freezing. Lyman and Scott (1970:186) mention only the first of these.

The critical activity must be *important* to the individual. That is, honor and other significant rewards are seen by him to hinge on his conduct of it. Importance comes from taking the activity seriously, from the thought that an inadequate performance is embarrassing and out of step with one's image as a participant in that pursuit. This definition of importance exists even among baseball and theater amateurs, for they take their avocations seriously. One significant value affected by stage fright is the group product or performance. A dropped line onstage or a badly aimed throw to first base, owing to stage fright, blemishes the overall quality of the dramatic production or reduces the chances of winning the ball game.

Secondly, conduct of the critical activity must be close enough at hand to dominate the individual's thoughts. In other words the activity must be seen as *imminent*. Still, he is not actually doing it, since both interviews and observations indicate that stage fright usually disappears at this time. Nor is the threatening situation so distant that other more immediate events occupy the person's mind.

About half the theater sample of twenty-seven respondents said they experience stage fright prior to a performance, especially opening night. Typically, it is most acute between the time of the individual's arrival at the theater and the time of his or her first entry onstage. Some expand this period of tension in one or both directions, by fretting the entire day (and even more) or by growing apprehensive before every performance in the run.

Stage fright among the theater amateurs generally disappears once they have delivered a couple of lines to the house. For most baseball players their butterflies leave once they take their first turn at bat, or field or pitch their first ball. But, as in theater, there are differences in the duration of this state. For a few players one or more innings must pass before they begin to relax. A couple of players said they lose their apprehension once the game commences, even though they have yet to bat or field a ball. Others say they feel little of it beyond the first two or three games of the season. The level of nerves also varies with the level of conditioning and training. Needless to say, a crucial game, particularly if the competition is keen, is apt to intensify the apprehension that players experience and generate it in those who normally escape it.

A third precondition is that the critical activity be conducted before an audience considered by the person as able to evaluate his efforts. The most critical audience for the amateurs of this study are their fellows in the dugout or the wings of the theater. But the spectators for the baseball player and the house for the thespian are also regarded as sophisticated enough about the activities taking place before them to spot at least some flaws in their execution. A middle aged actress commented on the difficulties of acting before a well-informed audience:

> I think probably the worst audience would be one that is completely sophisticated. In other words if you had an audience—if every seat in that house was filled with old pros that really know their business—they would probably be so critical that your performance would have to be so marvelous that you wouldn't have an applaud in the house all night. Whereas, if you get your run-of-the-mill people who come to be entertained—just like most people go to movies or watch TV or go to the ballgame—if you get a good response from that group of people, then you've done a good job.

Yet actors and actresses tend to lament the absence of a minimum degree of sophistication among members of the audience, for those people miss many subtleties in the script and the acting.

Another precondition of stage fright is that the critical activity be seen by the audience as within the individual's *control*. But he must also believe that the audience holds this expectation. One actress, for instance, related how she worried before each performance over the possible behavior of a dog she was required to carry onstage. Objectively, it would have been difficult for her to control every move of the animal. Subjectively, she felt that the audience expected her to do just that. Whatever the perspective, the scene would have been ruined had the dog wriggled free and scampered across the stage contrary to the playwright's intentions.

Fifth, the critical activity must be of sufficient *difficulty* to be potentially unmanageable when under pressure to conduct it well before a knowledgeable audience. If all the baseball player had to do was swing a bat, and hitting a pitched ball was irrelevant, there would be little cause for stage fright. In itself swinging a bat is easy. Getting a hit becomes problematic when it means striking a pitched ball with English on it to a place in the field where his opponents are unlikely to retrieve it before he reaches first base. This is difficult. And players are often apprehensive about the thought of having to perform it as a group of informed and observant spectators look on. A seasoned pitcher discusses the precondition of difficulty in the following passage:

> Once you get that first inning over with—the first inning's my worst. Controlwise or anywise the first inning's always the worst. I seem to pick up steam. I feel like I throw the ball better and harder in the seventh inning than I did in the first. That's the reason I don't like to relieve. You go out and pitch one or two innings; those are my worst innings.

Given the audience's expectation that he be able to control what he knows is a difficult activity to conduct, the individual is apprehensive that he may *freeze* while executing it. That is, he fears he may lose confidence, becoming unable to act, speak, or think at the level necessary to conduct the activity as expected. One baseball player's account of his "nervousness" illustrates the nature of freezing in that sport:

> Pregame nervousness is usually pretty good. You get out there and you start warming up and your legs feel like rubber and your old arms just don't want to throw right, you know. You get ready to go up to the plate and bat and you're swinging the bat and it feels like you've got a hunk of lead in your hands instead of a bat. Yeh, nervousness does play a great part in it. Later on during the season it does seem to go away, I guess because fatigue sets in and the nervousness goes away [laughter]. Later in the game you're not near as nervous either.

In theater actors and actresses say they can tell immediately when one of the cast goes up on his lines by, among other cues, the look in his eyes.

When these six preconditions are met stage fright is the result. What then are the implications of this elaboration of Lyman and Scott's ideas for their remarks on embarrassment and stage fright, audience stage fright, and stage fright in everyday life?

EMBARRASSMENT

Though stage fright and embarrassment produce similar symptoms, they are analytically distinct (Lyman and Scott, 1970:160). Embarrassment, on the one hand, occurs while when one's identity is under attack; the crucial concern being the impression one is making on others in the present (Goffman, 1965). Stage fright, on the other hand, is an anticipatory state; one knows in advance that a major identity will somehow be threatened.

The observations of the baseball and theater amateurs suggest that a sequential relationship exists between stage fright and embarrassment. To the extent that stage fright produces a self-fulfilling prophecy—that is, the individual does freeze as he thought he might—embarrassment is the outcome. The worst has happened; he has lost control and now must suffer abasement before the audience. Thoughts of possible embarrassment in the future undoubtedly help intensify stage fright in the present as well.

AUDIENCE STAGE FRIGHT

Lyman and Scott (1970:174-177) identify three kinds of audience stage fright. One of these is an empathic reaction for the performer that takes place among some members of the audience. Here there is a "fusion of identities," especially among intimates, which encourages an altruistic expression of apprehension over the possibility that the focal person may freeze and spoil his or her performance. Another kind occurs when the audience is apprehensive that it will be unceremoniously converted to performers, as when entertainers roam through the house unexpectedly involving certain of its members in spontaneous public exchanges. Thirdly, audience stage fright is also said to be engendered by watching what is widely defined as "unwatchable." Examples include observing a family quarrel for a domestic outsider or viewing a pornographic film scene for the moviegoer who is unaccustomed to such explicitness.

Do these varieties of audience stage fright meet the six preconditions set out earlier? Are they anticipatory responses to one or more of the three threatening situations? The answer to these questions is no. The first is more accurately called "group sympathy," through which members of the audience understand, emotionally and rationally, the performer's aims and feelings. The former are not performing before an audience a difficult activity whose control is problematic. They are merely observing such a performance.

The second kind of audience stage fright refers to what is, in fact, an unknown activity. The pertinent question is how can one grow apprehensive over a future performance the nature of which one is ignorant? The preconditions of control, difficulty, and freezing are inapplicable here. This kind of audience stage fright is more aptly seen as anticipated embarrassment. The individual is apprehensive alright, and he is apprehensive over the possibility that he will somehow behave in a way that leads the rest of the audience to lower their estimation of him. But the apprehension hinges on a condition missing in genuine stage fright; namely, a fear of the unknown. The stage frightened person knows all too well what is expected of him. The person anticipating possible embarrassment in the circumstances considered in this variety of audience stage fright is better described as "anxious"; the cause of the apprehension is vague, or unknown altogether.

The third kind of audience stage fright—collectively watching the unwatchable—lacks the element of anticipation. It is embarrassment, not stage fright, that follows from beholding an unexpected family quarrel or act of sexual intimacy. These incidents happen on the spur of the moment for the person, giving him or her no time to prepare for them, including the development of apprehension.

Lyman and Scott's idea of audience stage fright also fails to mesh logically with the three threatening situations. The individual either has no advance knowledge of what will be expected of him or has no direct role in the activity. It must be concluded that audience stage fright, at least as conceptualized so far, is an impossibility, given the future reference of pure stage fright and the preconditions for its occurrence.

STAGE FRIGHT IN EVERYDAY LIFE

Lyman and Scott (1970:177-182) go on to identify several situations in daily life that engender stage fright. In one of these the individual's claimed identity is tested in a critical performance or set of performances; for example, as a new employee, as a sexual partner on the first night of marriage, or as an upwardly mobile guest at a high-class party.

Nonetheless there is one situation discussed in this part of their essay that fails to meet the preconditions we have been considering. When a critical performance occurs in the presence of high-status others, the lower-status person, Lyman and Scott hold, tends to experience anxiety over if and how he should acknowledge the real differences that separate him from those others. Labeling as stage fright the emotional state that develops here presupposes that the lower-status person is thinking prior to the critical situation of whether or not to acknowledge these differences and, if so, how best to do this. Such planfulness seems unlikely. It seems more likely that the possibility of an acknowledgement of this kind strikes him while in the critical situation, forcing him to ponder the immediate and long-range consequences of such a move as he struggles to do his best in the present. Lyman and Scott have identified a difficult interactive problem that undoubtedly troubles some people, but it appears not to be a form of stage fright as the latter is defined in their paper and the present one.

CONCLUSIONS

Several of the preconditions suggest certain practical strategies for coping with stage fright, some of which have already been mentioned in the theoretical and applied literature on the subject. For instance, the performer might try, where feasible, to redefine the importance of the critical activity. He might tell himself that this is, after all, only a game or that there will be other opportunities to perform this role in the play or field a ball in this particular situation. One's social image may not rest solely on doing well at this moment.

The individual might also try to ignore the audience, advice better suited to athletics than to the performing arts. The latter's effectiveness is tied in part to their conscious communication with the audience. As an alternative the artistic performer might try to adjust to the audience's presence through a series of dry-run performances.

Difficulty can be minimized, possibly even eliminated in some instances, by preparation, practice, rehearsal, and the like. Confidence is built in this manner (Brantigan, 1975; Eisenson et al., 1963). As diffifulty is reduced control is increased. It follows that the prospect of freezing also declines.

These strategies seldom, if ever, eradicate stage fright. We rarely have so much control over our thoughts as to make this possible. Perhaps this is for the better. The respondents in the present study indicated overwhelmingly that some preliminary apprehension is desirable if they are to do their best publicly. It makes them alert. It is only the debilitating kind of stage fright they wish to avoid.

In the end stage fright, whether in art, sport, or everyday life, is a type of definition of the situation. In Znaniecki's (1952:251) words it is a "prospective definition," a form of mind that sociologists and social psychologists have neglected. As John Dewey and George Herbert Mead pointed out so often, though in terms different from Znaniecki, prospective definitions are uniquely human meanings that help motivate us in the present and help establish personal continuity as we pass through the countless situations of everyday living. This alone is ample reason to give further scientific attention to stage fright wherever it is found.

References

Brantigan, Thomas A.
    1975   "Stage fright; do we teach our students to be nervous?" *The AGO-RCCO Magazine* (November): 34-35.
Eisenson, Jon, J. Jeffery, and John V. Irwin
    1963   *The Psychology of Communication.* New York: Appleton-Century-Crofts.
Goffman, Erving
    1956   "Embarrassment and social organization." *American Journal of Sociology* 62: 264-274.
Lyman, Stanford M. and Marvin B. Scott
    1970   *A Sociology of the Absurd.* New York: Appleton-Century-Crofts.
Znaniecki, Florian
    1952   *Cultural Sciences.* Urbana: University of Illinois Press.

Preadolescent Socialization through Organized Athletics: The Construction of Moral Meanings in Little League Baseball

Gary Alan Fine

Most adult-child interaction is considered by adults to be fundamentally a moral enterprise. Adults, because of their role relationships in regard to children, and because of their own normative beliefs, feel that they have a moral obligation to inculcate a sense of social propriety to those children with whom they regularly come into contact. These moral messages are translations of the world-view of adults, at least the ideal or 'ought' form of that moral order. Traditionally the adult presents moral dicta in the form that they allow for no negotiation and for no situational variability; however, preadolescents by examining these statements in their situational context learn that they are only raised in certain situations, that they are situationally grounded, and that they are rhetorics as much as absolute statements about social truths. By the time that children have passed through preadolescence they have become quite adept at verbally manipulating moral messages to present and describe situations in ways which are favorable to an interpretation supporting the impression which they are hoping to foster.

The adult makes a fundamental assumption that underlies the teachings which they provide children that the world as given must be an ideal world, that this world view must be accepted by the child (even though it is empirically unfounded), and that the actions of the child must be

From *Dimensions of Sport Sociology: Proceedings of the 1978 Big Ten Symposium of Sport Sociology* (March Krotee, ed.), West Point, New York: Leisure Press 1979. By permission of the publisher.

Part of the research dealing with Little League baseball was supported by National Science Foundation Grant No. SOC7-10394. The author would like to thank Sherryl Kleinman for a critique of a draft of this paper.

capable of being interpreted as stemming from this belief. In other words, children are not instructed in the situational contingencies of moral decisions.

The socially accepted assumption is that adults will profess the ideal moral rules of society (for which each adult has his own variant) while in the presence of children, and that these moral rules, even when used in strained situations will be presented as unbreachable by "good people." Children, at least by the time that they have reached preadolescence, are not so naive as would be necessary for this rather transparent staging to be convincing. Thus, children, particularly when they are amongst their peers, often behave more in accord with the world as observed, than with the world as professed by adults, and this leads to disciplinary difficulties with children. As Dreitzel (1973, p. 13) suggests, by preadolescence children will have developed a peer culture which has become resistant to many adult pressures in peer group settings. However, this facet of childhood socialization is generally decided by adults, and attempts at conversion ("socialization") are seen as both desirable and necessary (see Speier, 1973), and most children are willing to be parties to this exercise in power maintenance—at least in part because of the rewards provided to convincing actors. Successful socialization on the part of the children consists of learning in what situations to express the moral verities proclaimed by adults, learning which ones they "really" mean (and are sanctionable in all circumstances—which are few indeed), and what moral rhetoric to use when they are caught. Like all examples of presentation of self, this does not necessarily presume a cynical exploitation on the part of the participants—rather it stems from the coercive power of situations over the absoluteness of moral statements. Thus adults use moral statements situationally, and pretend that they are absolute; preadolescents learn to take and use these rhetorics situationally, but again pretend they are universalistic.

Moral exemplifications (or indoctrination) is particularly prevalent in social institutions which have character-building as an explicit goal (e.g., schools, summer camps, religious groups, families, and in this case, athletic teams). While all of these agencies are worthy of study to determine the interactionist relevance of socialization, we shall focus upon the moral education given by adults as a function of children's participation on Little League baseball teams. With its emphasis on competition and goal orientation, organized sports provide an arena ("a social world") in which the child can learn "character" (or proper behavior) from adults —both localized to the specific sports setting and generalizable to nonathletic settings.

Athletic proponents frequently proclaim that participation in organized sports is an excellent way for children to build character, although some researchers have come to doubt the validity of this untested verity (see Ogilvie and Tutko, 1971), and others (Edwards, 1973, p. 103) complain about the vagueness of the concept of sportsmanship. The character building aspects of sports are heavily emphasized in Little League rhetoric. The Officials Rules of Little League Baseball, Incorporated proclaim that the purpose of the organization is explicitly didactic:

> Little League Baseball is a program of service to you. It is geared to provide an outlet of healthful activity and training under good leadership in the atmosphere of wholesome community participation.
> The movement is dedicated to helping children become good and decent citizens. It strives to inspire them with a goal and to enrich their lives toward the day when they must take their places in the world. It establishes for them rudiments of teamwork and fair play (1977 Official Rules: Little League Baseball Rules and Regulations, p. 2).

Whether Little League baseball does achieve its stated motto of "Character, Courage, Loyalty" has been vigorously debated. Critics claim that participation in the Little League program may be potentially damaging to the child. Devereux has maintained that in Little League "the risks of failure are large and wounding, and in the pyramidal structure of League competition, only a few can be winners: everybody else must be some kind of loser" (Devereux, 1976, p. 50). Further, he suggests that Little League competition kills the spontaniety of children, and that Little Leaguism threatens to destroy the culture of childhood in its most psychologically and educationally beneficial aspects (cf. Knapp and Knapp, 1976). The dispute over the value of the Little League program for its participants is unlikely ever to be resolved—in part because adults disagree on the proper goals of the organization. At present we can state with confidence (Fine and West, 1978) that children enjoy playing Little League baseball, and prefer it to informal baseball games, but its social and psychological effects are less known, and probably undramatic, compared to more intensive forms of moral education, such as the family or the school.

Both defenders and critics of Little League agree, despite a notable paucity of data, that this organization, with some 600,000 preadolescent participants (ages nine to twelve), has a significant effect upon children's behavior and beliefs. While there are four major sources for these effects (the coaches, players, fans and umpires), only the coach shall be examined here. The coach (or manager) has extensive contact with his players and is given particular responsibility for inculcating his charges with the proper techniques for playing baseball and teaching the value of hard work, sportsmanship and good citizenship. This does not deny the potency of the other sources for socialization within the Little League setting—the players particularly play a major shaping role in controlling and altering behaviors and beliefs. However, the presence and role of the adult coach makes Little League baseball and parallel sporting institutions distinct from the informal recreation of children. The coach accepts the responsibility for teaching his players baseball skills and teaching them to be upstanding youngsters who will be a credit to themselves, their parents, their community, and to the coach himself— as references to unruly players may be used to denigrate a man's managerial ability. The boy should learn from his coach "how to handle feelings and situations. The coach is a voice—guiding, teaching, offering opinions on the boy's progress and assessing his value as a person." (Johnson, 1973, p. 1).

Despite general discussions of the socializing effect of sport (viz Kenyon, 1968; Loy and Ingham, 1973), there exist no ethnographic reports on the process of socialization of sport. The learning of "sportsmanship" is treated in general terms with little attention paid to the situational reality of the transmission of values, norms and behaviors. We shall focus on four basic themes which managers frequently employ in the course of Little League to instruct their players in what they perceive as the moral order of sport. These are 1) effort, 2) sportsmanship, 3) teamwork, and 4) coping with victory and defeat. These four are seen as central elements of the ethnography of the moral enterprise called Little League baseball, and also have general implications for the preadolescent's mastering of presentation of self for the adult world. Obviously these four concepts are glosses for complex constellations of attitudes and behaviors; yet the terms serve as markers for goals which managers feel are important to implant in their charges.

METHODOLOGY

The research to be described derives from three years of intensive data collection with five Little League "major leagues" in New England and Minnesota. The primary methodological tool employed was participant observation; the author (and, in one league, a research assistant) interacted with the players and coaches over the course of the Little League season (see Fine and Glassner, 1978). This participant observation data was supplemented by in-depth interviews with players, coaches, and parents, and with questionnaires distributed to players. Within each league two teams were observed in detail; during practices and games the observer stayed with the team in the dugout or on the field. The five leagues chosen for study represent several distinct types of communities: 1) Beanville; an uppermiddle class professional suburb of Boston, Massachusetts, 2) Hopewell, an exurban township outside of the Providence, Rhode Island metropolitan area — consisting of small towns, beach front land, farms, and a campus of the state university, 3)Bolton Park, an upper-middle class professional suburb of St. Paul, Minnesota, similar to Beanville except for geographical location, 4) Sanford Heights, a middle to lower-middle class suburb of Minneapolis, consisting primarily of developers' tract homes, and 5) Maple Bluff, an upper-middle class neighborhood within the city limits of St. Paul, Minnesota, examined by Harold Pontiff. While these five leagues obviously do not represent a random sample of Little League organizations in the United States, they do cover a moderately wide range of environments, and the observations can serve as an indicator of socialization patterns in other leagues. Unlike Watson's research (1973; Watson and Kando, 1976), our data do not reveal distinctive social class divisions; it is not clear whether this is due to data collection procedures, communities that are not truly comparable (none of our leagues can legitimately be called working class, and Watson presents no income data on his committee), or the issues being examined. What is striking in these data are how similar the socialization techniques are across communities and geographical region. For the purpose of this paper all leagues shall be discussed together—working from the assumption that coaches and players generally come from the broad American middle-class. To be sure many personal differences in coaching style exist, yet several basic themes are repeated across teams.

EXEMPLIFYING THE MORAL ORDER

Socialization in sports, like all interaction, is situated in a particular meaning context, and results from the attempted enforcement of a definition of the situation by the coach. Moral statements are the result of attributions that coaches make about their player's motivations. Thus, the coach is not responding to the events occuring in the context of a Little League game, but to the meanings that these events have for him and to the meanings of the events that he ascribes to his players. This attribution provides the cognitive stance from which the coach will derive his moral tone and content. This ascription process by the coach is in theory problematic, although it is conventionalized in practice. Coaches have no mechanisms for achieving certainty about players' motivations or future actions—even though they may feel confident in their beliefs, and treat these beliefs as empirically justified and as a charter for action. The actual beliefs and feelings of the players are inaccessible to the coaches and are only available through behavioral indicators of internal states and conventionalized understanding about what preadolescents "should" be feeling in such situations. Thus, coaches comments are social constructions of the game reality, and are designed to regulate on-going interaction. Their general acceptance by players suggests the existence of common behavioral indicators and social conventions, and indicates the coercive power of the situational definition promoted by the coach.

These moral constructions occur in two classes of settings. Coaches may impart these messages as "set-pieces" in formal talks before and after games, or the messages may be part of the on-going interaction between coach and player during the activity of the game. In general, the comments during the game tend to be less global than the declamations which bracket game events; however, both refer to basic moral verities, and both are generated from adult attributions of preadolescent beliefs.

For purposes of clarity of presentation we shall assume that each of the four themes is analytically separable. This is not wholly accurate, and very nearly wholly false, in that analyzing any statement for its component meanings involves the same interpretive process that the coach is using to understand his players. Our categorization is pragmatically useful, but not totally adequate in that statements frequently have several layers of meanings, and may refer to several themes simultaneously.

THE IMPORTANCE OF EFFORT

A belief common to American culture is that "if something is worth doing, it is worth doing well." In sports, where emphasis is placed on winning and personal success, the proverb is seen as being dramatically appropriate. Yet knowing whether an action is being "done well" is problematic—what criteria can be used to judge the doing? The assumption, embedded in this truism, is that trying is recognizable, and is distinct from success and failure (see Iso-Ahola, 1976, p. 43). Some Little League coaches make this distinction explicit in their remarks, suggesting that they do not really care about winning or losing as long as their players do their "best":

> "There are several ways to play baseball. Some people play to win. But I believe that if a game isn't fun, it isn't worth doing. Other people believe that the only reason to play baseball is to have fun and they often fool around and play baseball only half the time. I believe that baseball is a game to learn, to learn to develop your skill, to get

the most out of yourself, and if you do that, baseball will be more fun than you imagine. Your goal for the year is to be a winner. That doesn't mean winning every game. Sometimes you will be up against teams that are better than you. It does mean to give everything you've got. If you give everything that you've got, you're a winner in my book. The only one who cares is the man who made you, and he made both teams, both winners and losers. Give everything you got." (Field notes, Royals, Bolton Park, 5/9/77, first practice)

"I believe in taking Little League baseball seriously; there is a time to horse around and a time to be serious. I take the Little League pledge of doing your best seriously. If we play good ball and lose, you'll never hear a cross word from me. You will hear from me if you play bad ball and win. That's as bad as losing." (Field notes, Cards, Sanford Heights, 4/20/77, first practice)

The coaches through these statements assume that the player will "fool around" or "horse around" if given the opportunity, and thus there is perceived to be a need to warn players that Little League is an activity on a different order than "play". Also, the adults assume that the determination of "doing one's best" will be simple. Since most coaches emphasize the importance of trying one's hardest, it follows that coaches may perceive a lack of effort when team records are unsatisfactory. Coaches in other words seem to postulate a linear dimension of effort on which teams may differ, and any given team may differ from game to game. Some coaches explicitly note the connection between effort and succession discussing the season:

"Whenever you guys are inside the fence I want to see you hustle. The name of the game is hustle. I promise you that if you hustle, you're going to win this year." (Field notes, Sharpstone, Hopewell, 3/27/76, first practice)

"Only three words—hustle, pride, and class and everything will fall into place." Field notes, Pirates, Maple Bluff, 5/12/77, first practice)

Thus, defeat may be seen as *prima facie* evidence of lack of effort or "hustle." While coaches may praise their team for good effort in a losing cause, this is relatively rare, and often involves a poor team almost vanquishing a team considered far superior.

ASCRIPTION OF EFFORT TO INDIVIDUAL PLAYERS

Efforts by individuals are often interpreted not as physical inadequacies but as a lack of hustle, and therefore, being motivational can be more easily correctable than a lack of physical ability:

Coach to eleven year old utility outfielder after he misses a catch at practice: "David, you got to want to, you know." (Field notes, Transatlantic Industry, Hopewell, 4/29/76)

Assistant coach to ten year old after he misses an outfield catch in practice: "I'm not mad at you that you made an error, but you just stood there; you gotta hustle." (Field notes, Sharpstone, Hopewell, 4/7/76)

Assistant coach to twelve year old after he is called out attempting to stretch a single to a double: "If you hadn't loafed on the way to first, you would have made it." (Field notes, Dodgers, Sanford Heights, 4/23/77)

These comments, and others like them, locate the problem in the player's motivation. To some extent this assumption is legitimate, and occasionally players admit that they should have tried harder. Effort is one component of well-executed baseball; however, it is significant that this can be a legitimate explanation for failure even if it does not apply. On other occasions, hustle is employed as an explanation for success and is a compliment used to reinforce this supposed motivation:

Assistant coach to twelve year old starting pitcher pitching well after losing his previous game: "You're pitching like you mean it." (Field notes, Orioles, Bolton Park, 5/31/77)

Generally, as in this case, the compliment is noted after the boy's motivation has been questioned. To imagine a Little League pitcher not throwing as if he "means it" is difficult, although intensity may vary across games. Attribution of a lack of hustle is a routine criticism, and frequently the comment is spoken without any indication of how the player should strengthen his skills so as to improve—the implication being that the player has the requisite physical skills, but needs to activate them.

These attributions may be exaggerated as when the coach criticizes a boy for being "asleep" while playing—indicating a general dissatisfaction and indicating that the player neglected to perform some action while playing that he should have, or performed it too slowly, rather than performing some action which should have been avoided:

Coach to eleven year old utility outfielder: "Come on, Rich, be a hitter. You're not even awake up there." (Field notes, Giants, Sanford Heights, 4/27/77)

Coach to twelve year old starter batting, "Come on, Al, play ball now. You went to sleep that time." (Field notes, Cards, Sanford Heights, 4/28/77)

Coach to twelve year old catcher in practice game after he delays too
long on a throw to second to throw out an opposing runner: "Todd,
you were sleeping on that pitch. You should have had him dead to
right. (Field notes, Orioles, Bolton Park, 5/12/77)

All of these comments were directed to boys who seemed not to be paying attention, or at least to boys who made decisions not to act (swing
or throw) in situations which their coaches defined as ones in which
swinging or throwing were the only appropriate actions. The lack of
action was directly attributed to the player's lack of attention. From
the assumption of the coach, an attribution to the player is easily drawn,
and the player in turn becomes socialized to the fact that situational definitions are not interdeterminate, but have some absolute normative component. Indeed, a similar process of attribution occurred between two
preadolescents when one boy said to his teammate after a strikeout in
practice: "Hugh, you looked a little dreamy." (Field notes, Padres, Bolton Park, 5/9/77), suggesting that by preadolescence players can assess
each others' internal motivation. Reputational factors impinge on the
coach's attribution of motivation; some boys have biographical backgrounds which include reputations as "hustlers" or "gutsy little ballplayers," while others are suspected of manifesting a lack of interest and
concern ("goof-offs"). Behavior is interpreted through the coach's understanding of the "stable" traits which he feels his players exhibit, and
his desire through his comments is to shape their future behavior to a
standard which he feels is normatively justifiable. Attribution theory suggests that people may be relatively willing to attribute dispositional, rather
than situational, causes to the actions of others (Nisbett et al., 1973);
at least when that public attribution is congruent with their own desired
presentation of self (Friedman, Fine and DiMatteo, 1978).

A criticism of a lack of hustle is a particularly potent weapon on the
part of the coach because it effectively allows for no adequate response
by the player. A denial of a lack of hustle can be taken as symptomatic
of a lack of hustle by many coaches; even when the charges are not appropriate, the truly motivated player would accept them as just and
would attempt to do better. How many people can claim to be doing
their absolute best? Also, the player has no observable evidence to point
to in his own defense, since motivation is an internal state. The cues
that the coach employs as the basis of attribution are not such as to be
the grounds for an adequate defense. The player is not in the position
to judge his own behavior for its motivational components—at least in
this adult-child situation. Players rarely dispute motivational attributions, even though they may privately not accept them, whereas they

will dispute judgments of the coach in regard to external, physically observable events ("that pitch was outside," "you should have backed up further to catch that"). Ironically that which the preadolescent player should know best (his internal state) is that for which he can claim least defense. The player is socialized in this fashion of how to construct criticism and accounts of behavior; one can not adequately defend oneself from an internal accounting but needs to point to some externally verifiable contingency which led to the event; similarly one can sanction the behavior of another by impuning their internal state, and this is how preadolescents defend themselves (by contending that they should not have swung at a particular pitch because of the spatial characteristics of that pitch) and sanction others (by asserting that others are lazy or not trying).

This discussion does not deny that individuals are actually affected by internal contingencies for action (or motivation), and that motivation affects baseball ability. That must be accepted as a given; what is problematic is the interpretation of this motivation by others. Here a set of conventionalized cues, such as not swinging at a ball thrown over the plate or not running sufficiently fast to catch a fly ball, must serve as indicators of motivation, with perceptual variation not conceived of as a significant variable. The interpretive process shapes the behavior of the coach toward his players.

ASCRIPTION OF EFFORT TO THE TEAM

Coaches make attributions not only to individual players, but also to the team as a unit, and preadolescents in turn learn that such ascriptions are normatively acceptable. An additional assumption is necessary here: that there is some concordance among the motivations of the players. In terms of our observations, it appears that the coach relies not so much upon attributing a lack of motivation or desire to all players, but the ascription of lack of motivation to one or two of the players usually considered most motivated, coupled with the lack of disconfirming evidence (notable examples of high motivation) from other players. Thus, the attribution to the team is a generalization, rather than a description, and represents a process parallel to stereotyping. Again there is a linkage of success and desire:

> Assistant coach after several errors during practice: "I'm glad I'm working nights so I won't get to see you fellows play, because I think you guys are going to get racked up. . . . Play the game like it's supposed to be played." (Field notes, Jamesville Lumber, Hopewell, 5/2/76)

> Coach, after team allows four runs to score in the first inning: "Are you sure you guys want to play ball this morning?"

> Assistant coach: "We played that time like we were asleep. Is anyone ready to quit and go home?" (Team in semi-unison responds: "No!") (Field notes, Orioles, Bolton Park, 6/11/77)

> Coach after his team lost what was considered to be an easy game: "You didn't have any pep out there. . . . You guys didn't want it." (Field notes, Cards, Sanford Heights, 6/24/77)

Past events in which no criticism was given or implied can be reinterpreted by the coach as indicating a lack of motivation by the team, and of course players learn to do this as well in summarizing the position of their team. This suggests that the team history is a construction of the interactants, particularly those with the authority to set the definition of the situation:

> Coach after his team (with a 6-3 record) loses 5-1: "You guys are sleeping out there. If you have no pride in yourself, I don't want you. . . . In other games, even in games in which you guys won, there was a lack of hustle. . . . I won't quit on you, don't you quit on me." (Field notes, Dodgers, Sanford Heights, 6/1/77)

Of course, coaches may use this technique of retrospectively rewriting history to denigrate the effort of other teams, although this tends to be somewhat rarer because the actions of other teams generally have less moral relevance:

> Before an important game the coach of the second place team refers to the actions of the first place team which his team had beaten earlier in the week, as a model for his team to avoid. The Astros (the first place team) had scored two runs in the top of the first inning, and the Orioles (the second place team) had come back to score three runs in the bottom of the first inning, eventually winning 5-4. The Orioles coach refers to the Astros behavior in the bottom of the first inning: "There was no chatter. There was no nothing. Their heads were down like lost dogs. . . . To me I think we're a better team than them. . . . If we play the way we played last week, we can win." (The coach's assertions about the Astros behavior in their previous game is contrary to the evidence reported in my earlier field notes—and seems to be a social construction by the coach), (Field notes, Orioles, Bolton Park, 7/14/77)

The supposed behavior of the Astros is being used strategically to contrast to the hustling attitude of the Orioles. Coaches will employ a variety of strategies to cope with their own frustrations at what they judge is a team lacking in motivation to win, and draw from current themes of pop psychology:

Coach to his team before a game, after losing two consecutive games: "I don't know what to tell you. Just go out there and have fun. If you want to swing, go ahead and swing; if you don't want to swing, don't swing. If you want to catch the ball, go ahead; if you don't want to catch the ball, that's OK too. If you want to drop the ball behind your head, that's OK. . . . We've tried everything and nothing seems to work, so go ahead and do what you want. If you want to swing, go ahead; if not, go ahead. . . . (about fifteen minutes later this talk is continued; players had become rowdy again after being silent at first): "I only ask one thing of you tonight; like I said you can go out and do anything you want: drop the ball, swing if you want, I don't care. Just do me one favor: no excuses tonight. None of this he threw it too fast—no excuses. I'll tell you one thing: you're wrong. That's not the problem. It's not the umpire's fault or because it's too low or too high or any of that. It's nobody else's fault. It's your own fault because you're not trying." (Field notes, White Sox, Maple Bluff, 6/30/77)

While the content is variable as befits different contexts and participants, the basic moral themes of the remarks are similar. Success is seen by the coach as being determined by effort—not external factors (the situational self-attributions that Nisbett finds), such as the umpire or the opposition, or by ability deficits. Motivation is the only available variable the coach can manipulate, and thus these comments may give the coach a sense of efficacy. The athletic credo, empirically incorrect, that "you are only limited by your desire" indicates the stress on this aspect of play. Such an emphasis on motivation is highly conducive to blame and scapegoating, and it should not be surprising that players blame others for baseball lapses, since their sports socialization emphasizes the intentionality of victory. Events which in themselves have no moral implications (victory and defeat) are imbued with a moral meaning, and players' actions are given a moral worth which spreads to the evaluation of the player himself. Iso-Ahola's research on players' attributions of success and failure (1976, 1977a, 1977b) reveals that success and failure (winning and losing) did not influence player's judgments of their own effort, but did affect judgments of team effort. The potential danger in competitive sports may lie less in the direct effects of competition on the self-image, than in what the aftermath of competition indicates about the proper evaluation of others. Physically unable athletes or teams are not much criticized; the problem arises in that few boys or teams are defined as physically unable. Rather they are defined as unmotivated and thus are subject to blame.

This scapegoating can be observed in the reactions of players to a marginal eleven year old player who stole second base while his team was behind 4-1 in the fifth inning (of a six inning game). The boy finds himself in a maelstrom of criticism, generated as a result of the coach's questioning of the team's attention to the game.

> After a marginal eleven year old player steals second base (successfully), the coach yells at the team: "Who sent him?! Who sent him?!" The twelve year old catcher yells at his teammate: "Dickie, knock it off!" This is followed by the twelve year old pitcher yelling: "Brickman, there are two outs, get with it!" (It is never determined who, if anyone, sent the boy) (Field notes, Dodgers, Sanford Heights, 6/1/77).

The premise of the team members is that the runner should have understood the situation, but didn't care enough to learn what was going on, and thus was personally blameworthy (thus, success and praise are not always connected. Preadolescents learn methods of understanding social reality and of depicting and manipulating the moral order. The players have the verbal skills to announce their conclusions; it is the interpretive skills for judging athletic performance that are being taught. Note that a questioning of the group's concentration is the stimulus which produces the scapegoating—an attempt to shift the blame.

Team attributions need not always be negative. Teams which triumph under trying circumstances may be praised for their motivation, although more often the praise seems to emphasize skill. Motivation seems of particular relevance when there is a contrast drawn between present effort and past indolence.

> Assistant coach after team wins following several defeats: "See what hustle can do?" Coach: "All you did differently was hustle." (Field notes, White Sox, Maple Bluff, 6/21/77)

> Coach of a last place team after a close defeat: "You played real well. Heads up ball. I think we'll beat the Tigers." (Field notes, Red Sox, Bolton Park 6/4/77)

Once again situations are redefined so that motivation was made the crucial variable producing success. This is despite the competitive nature of the Little League set-up in which it is hard to imagine teams not motivated to win, and in which this motivation is reinforced by parents and peers.

SPORTSMANSHIP

Sportsmanship is easier to operationalize and to observe than is motivation. However, it is emphasized by the coaches less frequently than other themes, and is in fact somewhat tangential to the socialization process of Little League baseball, despite emphasis in the official Little League literature. The reasons for this may not be entirely self-evident: first, Little League is oriented to success, and losing (the only time when sportsmanship is perceived as problematic) is not easily handled by adult supervisors. The second explanation casts a more positive perspective on Little League baseball and its participants. Sportsmanship is rarely mentioned because it is rarely seen as an issue. Coaches begin the season suggesting the importance of a sportsmanlike attitude toward umpires and other teams, and preadolescent participants generally abide by this. Most grumbling and anger is expressed within the context of team interaction, and is not publically displayed (i.e., it occurs within the walls and fences of the dugout). The number of public unsportsmanlike actions in which players engage is relatively small. A third explanation for the lack of general comments about sportsmanship concerns the way that problems which do occur are handled. They are treated as specific cases, rather than as symptomatic of a deeper structural disorder in the game setting, and therefore are generally dealt with individually.

This third explanation suggests that coaches' behaviors in regard to sportsmanship contrast with their behaviors regarding effort. A particular instance of lack of hustle is often treated as a potentially major problem, whereas a specific unmannerly action is treated as a temporary disturbance. Coaches in the two leagues in which interviews were conducted were unanimous in their assessment of their players as being basically well-mannered, whereas several coaches criticized their team for not exerting enough effort. Thus, the coach's picture of the preadolescent is of a boy who is a good sport except under extreme situational contingencies, but as an individual who may not work as hard as is necessary without adult pressure. Thus, the perceived steady-state of the preadolescent is that of a good-natured, playful boy. The image of the players influences the subject matter on which they are to be lectured.

Two major problems develop which may motivate the coach to emphasize sportsmanship in the game setting. First, players as a result of team or personal failure, may become visibly agitated, and may display behaviors which are judged by coaches to be inappropriate for their age and in the context of play. The preadolescent may forget that he is part of a social situation, a situation in which the standards of presentation of self are based upon adult conceptions of the ideal world—a world in which hostility is considered inappropriate and sanctionable. This situation may be difficult for the coach because of his own emotions and attitudes. He may at this time be similarly agitated and upset, and not be thinking about instilling sportsmanship, but about his primary goal of victory. Further, criticizing a boy for a lack of sportsmanship when the player is already upset is by no means a pleasant task, for it requires facing the boy's unpleasant emotions and being the target for part of his anger. Finally, the boys who are most likely to engage in these behaviors tend to be those who are seen as most difficult to "reach", that is who refuse to share the moral order of the adult world, and for whom any criticism may aggravate the situation. Thus, in situations in which such players become visibly agitated, the coaches frequently spend time "talking them down", but in this process feel that even an implied criticism of a lack of sportsmanship might be counter-productive. Thus, coaches regularly overlook a lack of sportsmanship, or treat it as a situation which requires a maximum of personal support for the boy and for his playing ability, and not criticism. Coaches vary in terms of the techniques which they find most efficacious for handling the situations that develop and it is hard to suggest a general picture of adult attitude to sportsmanship as a function of failure:

> Assistant coach to nine year old after striking out: "Don't throw your bat. Even Mickey Mantle strikes out." (Field notes, Sharpstone, Hopewell, 5/5/76)

> Assistant coach to eleven year old after striking out: "Don't throw the bat—if you're going to stand there and not swing, don't throw the bat. It's not the bat's fault." (Field notes, White Sox Maple Bluff, 7/11/77.)

The significant point is that these comments, which occur in the course of Little League play, are generally not directly related to the global concept of sportsmanship. While coaches begin the season with the admonition to be good sports, or gentlemen, this emphasis is rare during the season. By any standards Little League players are "well behaved" in the presence of adults, and attention to sportsmanship" is seen as more necessary to limit the actions of parents and spectators when they fail to maintain appropriate role distance.

The second area in which reference to sportsmanship occurs is in regard to the appropriate public attitude towards the opposing team. Here coaches have a certain ambivalence, and some very marked individual differences are noticeable. A player is expected to cheer for his team, and is subject to being charged with a lack of motivation and team spirit if he (and his fellows) are "dead" or if the dugout is "like a morgue."

Simultaneously some coaches distinguishing between "rattling" the opposing team, which is considered legitimate baseball, and harrassing the other team, which is not. The distinction is based upon the coach's definition of the situation, a definition based in part on the importance of the game, the score, and the attitude toward the other team (even in Little League there are vigorous rivalries):

> In one game the two top teams in the league were playing, and the coaches of these two teams had a fierce rivalry which extended over five years. In this game, which would mean the championship if the team then in first place won the game, and in which the son of the second place team's coach is pitching, the assistant coach of the first place team tells his players: "Get him rattled. Get him rattled." He later tells his players to ask the umpire for the count of balls and strikes: "That rattles him to think about the count." (Field notes, Astros, Bolton Park, 7/14/77)

> In a game which had to be played over because of darkness, and in which the team that was ahead thought the coach of the other team had been stalling, the assistant coach of the team which had been ahead told his players to rattle the opposing pitcher who was having pitching problems: "Can't you see this guy's having problems. Get on him." (Field notes, Sharpstone, Hopewell, 5/15/76)

> Coach to his team in the last game of the season—a game which will make no difference in the standings: "Guys, you got a big lead—I don't want any monkeying around out there, I want no talking to them. I want you to be good sports." (Field notes, White Sox, Maple Bluff, 8/4/77)

It appears that the relevance and depiction of sportsmanship is situationally determined—and not objective as sometimes suggested (Jackson, 1949). Behaviors which are considered legitimate in one circumstance are considered sanctionable in another, and players must come to recognize the cues which indicate the legitimacy of "unsportsmanlike" behavior. Player will learn from this not that sportsmanship is important or unimportant, but that it is a rhetoric which may be raised in certain situations in which it is in one's self-interest to do so. Indeed, preadolescents do become quite adept at sanctioning adults whom they feel are behaving with intents inimical to their own, and frequently the rubric of sportsmanship and similar concepts are employed to demonstrate the moral weakness of the adult's behavior, indicating that sportsmanship has been learned as a tool for managing impressions:

> Twelve year old first baseman says to his teammates in a sarcastic tone of voice about the opposing coach in a closely contested pre-season practice game: "Real sportsmanship. He goes to the catcher: 'If that guy in the batter's box doesn't get out of the way (when the catcher

is throwing to second base, trying to catch a base runner), I want you to take his head off.' " (Field notes, Orioles, Bolton Park, 5/21/77)

After the opposing coach calls the twelve year old player "bush" for stealing home in a runaway game, the player turns to his teammates and says sarcastically: "I know a coach who wears a yellow hat who thinks that Little Leagues is the pros." (Field notes, Sharpstone, Hopewell, 5/15/77)

Coaches' actions are thus subjected to the same sort of evaluation that the players are subject to. Although it happens rarely, the preadolescent's coach may be subject to this moral evaluation, as when one twelve year old claimed this coach "has the worst manners of any coach" after having become involved in a rather unpleasant altercation with a rival coach (Field notes, Orioles, Bolton Park, 7/14/77). Preadolescents are able to grasp that whether the sportsmanship refers to the individual or to the team, the situational constraints determine its evaluative components.

THE VALUE OF TEAMWORK

Preadolescents are often conceived of by adults as being egocentric, or only beginning to develop a sense of others' needs and desires. Adults can explain preadolescent action as being oriented towards the fulfillment of personal goals, rather than group ends. Developmental psychologists see preadolescence as a time of transition in terms of orientation to others. The young child is highly self-centered; however, by late preadolescence this has generally become transformed into an overriding concern with the peer group and with the good opinions of others (Kohen-Raz, 1971, p. 119). This corresponds to a change in orientation to game rules noted by Piaget in his developmental examination of children's marble playing (Piaget, 1962).

However, even older boys do not always display the orientation to teamwork that their coaches feel is appropriate. Twelve year olds, who are very conscious of their self-presentation, may orient themselves to peer groups which are different from the team. Thus, the boy might be able to gain more status by being a "prima donna" (a term generally used by coaches) or a "hot dog" (generally used by players), then by being a "team player." The preadolescent's reference group provides his orientation towards his behavior and he is behaving in accord with the normative perspective on the game situation that this group provides.

Because coaches believe that players may be thinking primarily of personal glory, rather than team success, coaches feel that teamwork is part of the moral order in which his players must be instructed. This belief is stated explicitly, as for example by one Sanford Heights coach when asked about what the goals of Little League baseball are:

> You know, you got the opportunity for cooperation with other people and to try to accomplish something as a team; being part of a team effort is very important whether you're a good player or not. . . . This teamwork is very important. That's one of the things that life's all about, is working as a team. Little League is that opportunity. (Interview, Astros manager, Sanford Heights, 8/10/77)

To be sure there is a pragmatic aspect to this emphasis on teamwork, in that teamwork is believed to correlate with success, but the goal of learning teamwork is a moral goal unto itself. One coach commented that Little League baseball was as important for preadolescents as the army was for the young men in that it taught them to work as a unit (Interview, Giants manager, Sanford Heights, 8/16/77). The Little League team (or a similar sports team) may be the first organization in which a boy is a member, where the organization has an overt collective task, which is enforced, and which can only be achieved with the direct participation of the preadolescent. In this, the Little League team differs from families, church groups, school classrooms, and Boy Scout troops.

The importance of teamwork is stressed at the beginning of the season and at several points during the year whenever the coach attributes a lack of cooperation to his players:

> Coach to players at a preseason practice: "For the past three years we have been the big team, but this year we're the little guys. . . . This year we've got to play together as a team. We've got a good hitting team; we've got a good fielding team." (Field notes, Expos, Sanford Heights, 4/18/77)

> Later the same coach reminds his players during the practice: "Pull for your team. We don't have room for a bunch of individuals. Everyone of us must do our best. Last year we had a lot of prima donnas, and we only came in third." One of his returning twelve year old players deliberately belches, and the team laughs uproariously. (Field notes, Expos, Sanford Heights, 4/18/77)

The reaction of the Expos players to the coach's remarks indicates that the charge made to them is problematic, and is capable of being accepted or rejected. Because of different personnel and situations, teams respond differently to coaches' comments. The symbolic (and actual) belch by the Expo player served as an indication of the lack of teamwork that was evident that year; the raucous laughter was the team's ratification of that orientation of unconcern with competitive Little League baseball. While one must be wary of cause and effect explanations which are based on the experience of a single team, the Expos finished mired in last place, winning only three of eighteen games, well below what was predicted of them at the beginning of the season (their coach predicted they would win ten games).

The Expos were known throughout the season for their lack of team spirit—a factor which their coach commented on in the post-season interview to explain their dismal record, along with the team's negative attitude and discouragement before the season began: "They're weren't really problem kids; it's more with attitude. It's not that they were creating problems, but they really weren't playing the best they could together." (Interview, Expos Manager, Sanford Heights, 8/18/77). Whether their last place finish could be said to be caused by their lack of teamwork, it was attributed to that by other players and coaches.

Other coaches with similar philosophies but different players found that their players would accept teamwork as a desirable goal:

> Coach to team before the first game of the season: "On the Cardinal team everyone plays. We're not the Cardinals. We took the I out. We're the Cards, or you'll have to say Cardinals without the I which sounds funny." Players laugh approvingly. (Field notes, Cards, Sanford Heights, 5/2/77)

The laughter in this conversational slot is a ratification of the manager's moral order of baseball, and not an affront to it, as was the case on the Expos.

As with effort, the determination of the presence or absence of teamwork is believed to be obvious and easily defined. Again, the proof of the pudding is in the eating, as a successful team may be praised for demonstrating admirable teamwork:

> Coach to team after victory: "I was very proud of some of you guys. It was a good team effort." (Field notes, Cubs, Sanford Heights, 6/24/77)
> Coach after a come-from-behind victory: "Isn't that nice to come back and win it. It was a team effort. Everybody played well." (Field notes, Red Sox, Bolton Park, 7/31/77)
> Coach to team after they finished tied for third in the major Minnesota Little League tournament: "I'm proud of you guys. You guys showed more togetherness and guts than any team in the tournament. . . . You got nothing to be ashamed of. . . . You gave it everything you had; I'm proud of every one of you. More proud than I can say." (Field notes, Dodgers, Sanford Heights, 8/5/77)

One can contrast this to statements made by coaches when their team is not judged to be playing well—in this case by the same coach as above:

> Coach to team after a pre-season loss, while the entire team is angry and depressed: "Some of you guys played yourselves out of jobs. No thinking out there. No aggression is being shown on balls. Nobody wants to take charge out there. You're a team; you got to play as a team. You got to start to think. You can't stand there with two outs and let the ball go by." (Field notes, Dodgers, Sanford Heights, 4/29/77)

Examining these quotations, and listening to them in context, convinces the observer that the coach is not responding to a clear indicator of a concrete phenomenon. Rather, it is a situationally constructed criticism, indicating that several players are making mistakes, or that there is a confluence of superior plays, and that these are occurring within an athletic sequence. One boy making an exceptional throw and his teammate making an exceptional catch is defined as an example of teamwork. If the two actions occur in separate play units, the coach might not use the construct of "teamwork" but rather that of "hustle" to describe the behavior, and of course both constructs point to successful outcomes.

The usage of the rhetoric of teamwork and team spirit is connected with that of effort in such activities as cheering for one's teammates and avoiding fights with them. Whereas "effort" is linked to personal responsibility and group actualization, teamwork is considered to be social responsibility, as exemplified in the analogy with a family: "We are a team. We are a family. We got to pull together." (Field notes, quote from Assistant Coach, Orioles, Bolton Park, 5/31/77). This analogy explicitly places the coach in the position of moral exemplar for the players, and defines the sporting enterprise as a moral enterprise. As with effort and sportsmanship, the appropriate mention of teamwork is a part of the adult's interpretative process—an interpretive process that creates morally significant issues from the physical movements of children.

WINNING AND LOSING

The final moral issue that we shall discuss incorporates the other three within its scope. One of the major aspects of Little League baseball that critics and proponents attend to is the circumstance that in Little League children learn how to win and lose. They learn how to behave in situations of victory and defeat, although because of team structure, ability, and coaching, some teams must learn to deal with victory more often than defeat, while others must learn the reverse. In addition, players must cope with this in light of their expectations for their teams and themselves.

Both victory and defeat pose moral issues, although no doubt the former are considerably more pleasant to deal with. Coaches frequently begin the season by officially downplaying the importance of the specific win-loss record of the team as long as the other moral factors, discussed above, are met:

> The coach during the team's second practice gathers his team around: "What would you say if I said you have to win all your games to satisfy me?" (Some of his players say they can do it) "What would you say if I said you would have to win the pennant to satisfy me?" (Some overly agreeable players, not trained in adult rhetoric, say "sure"). "You won't have to do any of those things. There are four things that you have to do to satisfy me. The four things have to do with integrity. Do you know what it has to do with?" (One player says "honesty"). "That's basically right. It means being what you claim to be. You do the same things when we're [the coaches] looking, and when our backs are turned. It also means not cheating. We want you to be an encourager. Mainly to the other guys on the team. Third is sportsmanship. That means not griping when you lose. That means not griping when the umpire makes a call against you. That means not riding the other team. That's the way some teams win, but that's not the way I want you to play. The fourth is dedication. That means playing as hard as you can, and dedication means playing as hard as you can in practice as well as in games. That's what I expect out of you. I'm not dissatisfied with last night's practice, but if you don't improve from last night, I will be dissatisfied. If you lose a game to a better team, I don't care. I don't want us to beat ourselves." (Field notes, Royals, Bolton Park, 5/10/77)

However, the issue of what constitutes a better team becomes problematic, particularly in that most coaches expect to win many more games than they lose, to come in first or second, and many coaches find these expectations frustrated. These global statements may be systematically different from the conduct of the coaches within the game situation—As the overarching concert of integrity takes a backseat to the pragmatic concerns of winning particular baseball games. Players can be expected to learn that the concept of integrity is a rhetoric that one should raise only in particular times and places.

The adults involved with Little League tend to be very oriented towards winning and losing, and the importance of competition, and reveal this in symptomatic behavior:

> The coach of the Astros arrived at the field on opening day at 8:00 a.m. (the opening day ceremony starts at 9:30 a.m.). He tells me that he always drives around all night before opening day. One of the other coaches told me that the year before he drove to Duluth, and another year to Eau Claire, Wisconsin. This other coach claims

that he too gets nervous before opening day, and that last year he stayed up all night and painted his team's helmets. (Field notes, Opening Day, Bolton Park, 5/21/77)

The emotions that the coach is attempting to discuss with his players are the same ones that he faces in himself. Several coaches have indicated privately that they must make a serious and sustained effort to control their personal drive for "victory at all costs," in order to be what they conceive of as a proper role model for their players (thus, adapting to the criticism of Little League).

Different moral factors will affect the interpretation of a victory as opposed to a defeat. In a victory the success of the team is described as symptomatic of some positively evaluated trait that the team revealed that day or in general. The interpretation of a victory will involve reinforcement of team behavior. Something (obviously) has been performed correctly. It is extremely difficult to specify what the team did that provided success, since a large part of victory at this age is inevitably ascribable to luck and idiosyncratic factors such as vacation schedules or pitching rotation. Thus, the coach's comments are often vague and do not reinforce any particular skill—other than teaching the child that he is good when he wins—for whatever reason:

> Coach to poor team after a close victory: "You guys played exactly the way you're capable of playing. . . . You're back in the groove." (Field notes, Red Sox, Bolton Park, 6/27/77)

> Coach to successful team after 1-0 victory over a generally unsuccessful team: "This was one of the best played games I've seen down here." (Field notes, Orioles, Bolton Park, 7/9/77)

> Coach to team after an important victory following several defeats: "Guys, I want to tell you something—I'm proud of you guys for your game tonight. I don't care what happened the rest of the year—you guys were superb . . . and I'm talking about each and everyone of you did something. You guys were superb, and I don't care if we lose another game or what happens the rest of the year; first of all, we deserve this one. You guys were super. That's what you call hustling, and that's what you call going off and getting 'em. Every single one did something; everyone did something. You guys were super . . . You guys were unbelievable. You guys can be proud of yourselves tonight. That made up the whole season right there; one game made up the whole season." (Field notes, White Sox, Maple Bluff, 7/26/77)

These statements suggest the difficulty that individuals have assigning meanings to diffuse causes. While coaches can and do refer to specific aspects of a successful performance, these specific events are taken as symptomatic of the successful playing in general. The cause of these victorious performances are as hard to determine as judging hustle or teamwork.

The coach also must on other occasions explain defeat to his team, and there are as many explanations for defeat as there are ways for pre-adolescents to lose baseball games. Defeat provides a signal that something went wrong, and that an evaluation is necessary. Obviously some defeats are more galling than others. It is possible to some degree to state that the team as individuals played either well or poorly, and if well to compliment them on a game well played but lost (see Iso-Ahola, 1976). Also, the coach may feel that even in defeat the team may need some moral support so as not to take the loss too hard, or on the other hand may feel that they lost because they were over-confident and thus need to be brought "down to earth." Finally, the reactions of the coach may vary according to the team situation—a last place team that loses a close game may be complimented and told that they played a fine game, while a first place team which loses an important game in the same manner may be lashed for a sloppy job. Post-game comments are thus situationally constructed—both from the observable game events and also from the social meanings that those game events have for the coach and his players.

Under favorable situations the coach may actually be quite complimentary to a vanquished team:

> After his last place team loses 10-5, the assistant coach comments: "You guys are right on the edge of hitting well. It's just a matter of reducing errors, and a little luck. We're jelling as a baseball team." (Field notes, Red Sox, Bolton, Park 6/4/77)

> Coach to team after a close, well-played 5-3 loss to their league rivals (who are now in first place while they are in second place): "We played a good game. Everybody makes errors. That's why you play together as a team. The game today was a good played game. . . . If the man upstairs don't want you to win, you don't win. . . . They know we got a good ball team." (Field notes, Orioles, Bolton Park, 6/11/77)

> Coach to average team after losing to one of the best teams in the league by one run: "Boys, you played excellent. Absolutely excellent. Charlie, that was an excellent hit in the end; Roger, you played just super. Great. You all played excellent. That's the kind of baseball I don't mind losing by one run to them, because really if we didn't make that mistake in the first or second inning, we gave them two runs right there. That was a super game, guys. That's the way to play baseball. That's a super game." (Field notes, White Sox, Maple Bluff, 6/30/77)

Thus losing does not necessarily produce attributions of inadequacy by the coach. However, if some element of the players' motivation or behavior is seen as representative of team troubles, negative attributions may occur. Players believe that they can sense an attack coming and may discuss this among themselves:

After a pre-season game loss, players on the Cubs see their coaches meeting on the field obviously discussing the game that has just ended:

> Barry (11): "They're gonna give us a lecture on how to play baseball."
> Bob (12): "I'm not gonna listen."
> Barry: "Me neither . . . They're getting their guns out." (He dives for the floor with Bob laughing)
> The coaches in fact do not berate the team for losing.
> (Field notes, Cubs, Sanford Heights, 4/30/77)

Coaches may employ a number of strategies to criticize a team for losing, and these include citing a lack of hustle or a lack of team spirit—particularly in games which are defined as symptomatic for the rest of the season, or in which inconsistency of team play is evident, such as games in which a team plays particularly poorly ("falls apart") in one inning. Losing is attributed, not to ability deficiencies, but to a perceived deficiency in motivation by the players, and coaches believe that these are "moral" rather than technical problems, and thus subject to conscious control:

> Coach to team after loss because of one poor inning: "We played five good innings of baseball. The first inning we didn't want to play." (Field notes, Giants, Sanford Heights, 5/7/77)

> Coach to team after losing a practice game: "The lack of thinking cost us this game." (Field notes, Dodgers, Sanford Heights, 4/25/77)

> Assistant coach to team after they lose a post-season game by a considerable margin supposedly played in preparation for them to attend a post-season championship tournament: "I told you a while ago we're not fully committed to this tournament. I'll take the time to take you fellows down to that tournament, but only if I see some very significant improvement in attitude, in hustle, and most of all in team spirit. Save your arguments and fights for your bedroom, the wrestling, the boxing, whatever you want to compete in there; that's where that stuff belongs. That's an individual effort and you can do what you want, this isn't. One bad attitude begets another bad attitude, and I don't believe in it." (The assistant coach speaks seriously and deliberately to a sullen, depressed team) (Field notes, Dodgers, Sanford Heights, 7/21/77)

Playing Little League baseball is defined as a moral enterprise by parents, adults, and the organization. Thus, the game outcome can be ascribed to the character of the players. This view is not only common to Little League baseball, but seems relevant to other aspects of life in which the Just World Hypothesis is applicable. That is, the belief that those who have success—for whatever "actual" reason—are virtuous; and those who face defeat are liable to charges that their circumstances are attributable to personal culpability. Since the victims are likely to be unwilling ·to accept this "given" (attributing these events to situational, rather than dispositional causes), they must be instructed in this belief. This is a central reason why Little League coaches (and other athletic leaders) hold post-game meetings to review the game—not only to discuss modes of physical improvement (which is rarely the topic of these meetings), but to establish (and enforce) a moral consensus on the players. While it is unrealistic to determine the "true" cause for success and failure, an important ingredient of sports socialization is for players to believe that there are such definitive causes, and to internalize the belief that they are in control of their own outcomes—a sense of efficiency. Players are willing to accept these interpretations and are praised for their maturity and spirit, while others who refrain from embracing the coach's explanations are branded as arrogant, stubborn, or poor sports. The fact that most coaches consider most of their team to be mature and spirited indicates the power of the coach in enforcing social meanings for game events. However, the player listening to these situationally grounded explanations may find in them a message, generally unexplicated, that the game meaning will not be a function of an objective view of player's own actions as physical movements, but will be an interpretation based on the context of the entire game situation. Thus, the player, as well as being socialized to the moral order of Little League baseball as seen by their adult mentors, is also socialized to the rhetorical devices involved in the construction of moral meanings in social situations.

ADULT SOCIALIZATION OF MORAL ORDER

Little League baseball has been seen as an arena in which the moral basis of social action is brought to bear on individuals' behavior by legitimate arbiters of the social order. While this analysis could be extended to sports participation generally, it seems particularly evident in the case of youth sports, such as Little League baseball, in which one purpose of the league program is explicitly didactic and devoted to "character building". However, as we have indicated above, this process is problematic for it assumes knowledge of emotions and motivations which are partially hidden from those who are doing the instruction. The coaches must interpret the meanings of the behavior of their charges, and then must filter these meanings through a culturally-established moral order.

The approach could cogently be applied to other universes of discourse, as well as sports—areas, such as school or family-life, in which a "moral" education (or normative socialization) is the putative goal. In such situations there are occasions on which sweeping and inclusive moral statements are made, but more often guidance is generated through interaction, and has its meaning interpreted by reference to these specific events. Coaches' comments are understood by the players in the particular context in which they occur, and players may respond to (negotiate) these statements, bringing to bear their own perceptions of ongoing events. Coaches are therefore judged by the similarity between the perceived appropriateness of their moral messages and the player's view of their own abilities and motivations (which in the context of preadolescent discussion is evaluated by reference to the coach's "knowledge of baseball" and "fairness"). Together coaches and players attempt to construct an approved social identity for the preadolescent—often explicitly related to athletic situations, but sometimes more general. This, in effect, means that coaches may have license to criticize players because of the supposed long-range outcomes of such criticism. Thus, one coach explained to his players: "We may yell at you more than you like. It will make you a better lad, and eventually a better man." (Field notes, Cards, Sanford Heights, 4/20/77), and another commented: "We're not hollering at you guys to be hollering at you; the object is to help you boys learn." (Field notes, Phils, Sanford Heights, 4/20/77). Most, though not all, of the players will accept this definition of the coach's behavior, and both of these coaches were generally popular with their teams because of their desire to win, their "strictness," and their coaching ability (again a problematic attribution—this time by the players, which can perhaps in part be confirmed through results: the Phils finished first; the Cards tied for second).

We have underplayed the reciprocal socialization of preadolescents on their coaches, although this rather subtle process does occur. Players make public their attributions of other players and other teams, and these meanings may be accepted by the coach; however, since players don't have the explicit authority for assigning meaning to game events, this process of socialization is difficult to describe, and rarely mentioned explicitly by coaches or players. Interaction, even when structured by a formal status hierarchy inevitably affects all participants—even those with legitimate authority. The moral order of a society or subsociety does not consist of definitive rules, but rather it is a social construction which continually is expanded and specified in order to deal with on-going events. From the particularistic nature of the application of the moral order it is generalized to other social situations, and thus what is learned in Little League has a wider significance for the child's interaction.

We argue for a different conception of socialization than that which characterizes much of the literature on sports sociology. Rather than emphasize the prevalence of general core values discussed in general terms, the emphasis here has been on how these values are communicated in the course of on-going game-based interaction. Rather than assuming that deviation from these core values is obvious, it has been suggested that the attribution of motivations which express these cultural attitudes is problematic, and is in itself a fit object for examination.

Further, we suggest that the preadolescent player can understand the situationally grounded character of these utterances. Not only are preadolescents being socialized to these moral values, but also they learn how to manipulate these values—when to use the rhetoric of the moral order. Preadolescents are learning not only how to do what adults think best, but how to manage impressions by the situated usage of moral concepts, a central feature of preadolescent sports interaction, not sufficiently examined by sociologists.

REFERENCES

Devereux, E. C. Backyard Versus Little League Baseball: The Impoverishment of Children's Games. In D. M. Landers (Ed.), *Social Problems in Athletics*. Urbana: University of Illinois Press, 1976.

Dreitzel, H. P. Introduction: Childhood and Socialization. In H. P. Dreitzel (Ed.), *Childhood and Socialization*. New York: Macmillan, 1973.

Edwards, H. *Sociology of Sport*. Homewood, Il.: Dorsey Press, 1973.

Fine, G. A. & Glassner, B. The Promise and Problems of Participant Observation with Children. *Urban Life*, 1978, in press.

Fine, G. A. & West, C. S. Do Little Leagues Work: Player Satisfaction with Organized Preadolescent Baseball Programs. *Minnesota Journal of Health, Physical Education, and Recreation*. 1978, in press.

Friedman, H. S., Fine, G. A. and DiMatteo, R. Self-presentational Influences on the Actor-observer Difference, unpublished manuscript, 1977.

Iso-Ahola, S. Evaluation of Self and Team Performance and Feelings of Satisfaction After Success and Failure. *International Review of Sport Sociology*, 1976, *11*, 22-44.

Iso-Ahola, S. Effects of Team Outcome on Children's Self-perception: Little League Baseball. *Scandinavian Journal of Psychology*, 1977a, *18*, 38-42.

Iso-Ahola S. Immediate Attributional Effects of Success and Failure in the Field: Testing Some Laboratory Hypotheses. *European Journal of Social Psychology*, 1977b, *7*, 11-32.

Jackson, C. O. What About Sportsmanship? *Physical Educator*, 1949, *6*, 12-15.

Johnson, T. P. *My Coach Says* . . . USA: Little League Baseball, Inc., 1973.

Kenyon, G. C. Sociological Considerations. *Journal of Health, Physical Education, and Recreation*, 1968, *39*, 31-33.

Knapp, M. & Knapp H. *One Potato, Two Potato* . . .: *The Secret Education of Children*. New York: Norton, 1976.

Kohen-Raz, R. *The Child From 9 to 13*. Chicago: Aldine, 1971.

Loy, J. W. and Ingham, A. G. Play, Games, and Sport in the Psychosocial Development of Children and Youth. In G. L. Rarick (Ed.), *Physical Activity: Human Growth and Development.* New York: Academic Press, 1973.

1977 Official Rules: Little League Baseball Rules and Regulations. Williamsport, PA: Little League Baseball Incorporated, 1977.

Nisbett, R. E., Caputo, C. G., Legant, P., and Marecek, J. Behavior as Seen by the Actor and as Seen by the Observer. *Journal of Personality and Social Psychology,* 1973, 27, 154-64.

Ogilvie, B. C. and Tutko, T. A. Sport: If You Want to Build Character, Try Something Else. *Psychology Today,* 1971, 5, 61-3.

Piaget, J. *The Moral Judgment of the Child.* (M. Gabain, trans.) New York: Collier, 1962. (Originally published, 1932).

Speier, M. *How to Observe Face-to-Face Communication.* Pacific Palisades, CA: Goodyear, 1973.

Watson, G. Game Interaction in Little League Baseball and Family Organization. (Doctoral dissertation, University of Illinois, 1973). (University Microfilms, No. 74-12, 235).

Watson, G. G. & Kando, T. M. The Meaning of Rules and Rituals in Little League Baseball. *Pacific Sociological Review,* 1976, 19, 291-316.

NOTE

All proper names of communities and their inhabitants used in this account are pseudonyms.

Section B

Political Institutions and Sport

Events in the near future will reveal whether that ultimate showcase of international sport—the Olympic Games—will ever again exist as a truly international contest and festival. With the boycott by the United States of the 1980 Summer Games in Moscow, perhaps the final political death-blow has been dealt to that sporting festival which Baron de Coubertin optimistically, and innocently, intended as a symbol of peaceful international competition.

But even before the U.S. boycott to protest Soviet aggression in Afghanistan and similar action by some of America's allies, few people would have argued with the statement that sport and politics are often significantly linked. Even the most cursory review of the history of the Olympic Games reveals a virtual compendium of political overtones to sport. Nations look to the "unofficial" medal tallies as a symbolic restatement of the international power structure; countries vie for the opportunity to host the Games in order to demonstrate the resourcefulness of their country, often when they fear their national prestige is low; nations employ exclusionary tactics to deny access to the Games to those nations considered morally or politically offensive, or, as was the case in 1980, dramatize their displeasure with other nations through withdrawal tactics; and splinter groups grasp the opportunity to make the Games a platform for the statement of their own political commitments.

Few would deny that some relationship exists between sport and politics; however, precisely how the two are related, and why, are questions of considerable complexity. Perhaps one should begin with some thoughts on the nature of political systems and ask if there are elements of sport which make it conducive for use by political systems.

Political systems are concerned with jurisdiction or the problems of who shall have the right to make important decisions for the group. Power, or the ability of one individual or group to realize its will over another, even in the face of resistance,[1] is a central element in jurisdictional matters. That group which is empowered, which has jurisdiction over system goals and priorities, acts under the guiding influence of a program of system values referred to as the political ideology. Sport may be likened to politics insofar as power is the central theme of action. In many, though not all sports, this is so. However, it is with reference to ideology that the relationship between sport and politics can best be explored.

Sport itself is devoid of inherent ideology, which is why it has been an equally effective means of demonstrating the values of fascist, socialist, communist, and capitalist governments. But when sport is understood as a symbolic system capable of carrying messages, it can be understood as a system capable of carrying ideological statements as well. Sport can be used to these political ends precisely because of its symbol-carrying nature. Moreover, when teams or individuals are seen as representatives of political systems, as they inevitably are, group identification and the development of group pride, or nationalism, is invited.

The co-option of sport for political purpose can be both positive and negative. At its best, sport can serve as a means for effecting international friendship—an original aim of the Olympic Movement and a process exemplified by the "ping pong diplomacy" which led to renewed diplomatic relations between the United States and Communist China. Achievement in sport can also serve as a rallying point for a community or disadvantaged nation: a symbol of their emerging national identity and pride. But at its worst, sport can be a tool of aggressive nationalism. Success in an athletic contest, particularly when competing against those whose ideologies are diametrically opposed to one's own, is often taken as indicative of more significant political successes. Thus success in sport is often attributed to the superior ability of one group to mobilize its resources to action, and this in turn is often claimed to be the result of a better political and ideological system.

Most of these themes are expanded by McIntosh, Helmes, and Guttmann. McIntosh reminds us that "International sport is like an iceberg; a small part consisting of the Olympic Games and other world championships is seen, but most international contests go on unnoticed by press or people." Nevertheless, even at this unheralded level, McIntosh takes the view that "very seldom has sport been free of politics."

Helmes takes a more specific focus and concentrates his analysis on the ideological implications of sport on one country—Canada. Helmes' analysis proceeds from his observation that "In Canada . . . sport has

---

1. Jonathan H. Turner, *Patterns of Social Organization: A Survey of Social Institutions* (London: McGraw Hill) 1972, p. 262.

always been (and continues to be) a class-based area of human activity that contains significant ideological overtones." Working within a Marxist perspective, Helmes investigates the meaning of ideology and develops the thesis that ideologies reflected by sport serve as a subtle form of social control.

Guttmann's essay deals with his attempts to explain the rise of modern sport. Discussing and rejecting arguments following from Marxist (sport and capitalism) and Weberian (sport and Protestantism) perspectives, Guttmann offers the thesis that the rise of sport is attributable to the acceptance of a scientific *Weltanshauung* which stresses the importance of progress and achievement.

Sport, Politics and Internationalism

Peter C. McIntosh

In 1956 the armed conflicts in Hungary and Suez caused six nations to withdraw from the Olympic Games which were to be held in Melbourne, Australia. Mr. Avery Brundage, President of the International Olympic Committee commented: "By their decisions these countries show that they are unaware of one of our most important principles, namely that sport is completely free of politics." A superficial glance into the past is enough to show that very seldom has sport been free of politics. Certainly Baron de Coubertin did not see sport completely free of politics when he founded the modern Olympic Games. On the contrary, he hoped that sporting activities might improve the political relationships between nations. He addressed a circular to the governing bodies of sport in January, 1894, expressing the hope that every four years the athletic representatives of the world might be brought together and that the spirit of international unity might be advanced by the celebration of their chivalrous and peaceful contests. If sport was to influence politics it was hardly conceivable that the interaction should be in one direction only and that politics should have no bearing at all upon sport. The naiveté of Mr. Brundage's statement, however, must not be allowed to obscure the relationship between sport and politics which is felt to exist by many people besides the members of the I.O.C.

The relationship may turn bad in at least two ways, by too much interaction and by the debasement of either one of the two agents. The injection of too much sport into politics might reduce the most serious of human activities to puerilism, while the seriousness of politics, if carried into sport in too great measure, could destroy its playfulness and so change its very nature. Again, corruption in sport might lead to corrupt pressure being brought to bear upon local or national politicians which could harmfully affect the life of the community. The greater danger, however, is from corruption acting in the opposite direction. If the political life of a community is corrupt or is organized for unworthy or inhumane ends then it will hardly be possible for sport to remain unaffected; it will be harnessed, however loosely, to the same unworthy ends. The ideals of sportsmen may for a while pull the polity back or slow down its regress but observation of Germany in the 1930's and of South Africa in the decades since World War II suggests that sportsmen share the corrupt political and social ideas of their community in about the same measure as other citizens. Even if they do not share those ideals they tolerate them and their application to sport in order to be able to continue to play. There is at least one noble exception to this generalization which ought not to pass unnoticed. When in 1848, the German State of Baden attempted to implement a liberal constitution, Prussia and the other big states at once invaded Baden. The provisional government appealed for help to oppose the aggressors. The *Hanau Turnverein* sent three hundred armed gymnasts, who increased their number to six hundred *en route*. For a time they held out against the best-trained army in Europe. The end was inevitable. Some escaped to Switzerland. The rest were killed in action or shot as rebels after capture. The collapse of the political movement for a united, free and democratic Germany caused many gymnasts to flee across the Atlantic. In America they reestablished their clubs. Their liberal ideals caused them to declare forcefully in favour of the abolition of slavery. They supported Abraham Lincoln politically and then enlisted in the armies of the North in considerable numbers.

Sport has certain characteristics which perhaps impel it more readily than other human activities towards an association with politics. Sport, especially competitive sport, tends to identify the individual with some group and the individual welcomes this identity. Even the lone runner cannot escape his association with club or town, county or country. The member of a team inevitably sinks some of his individuality in the group. In the great age of sports development the extent to which the individual was submerged was an indication of merit in a game or sport. The young master in *Tom Brown's Schooldays* was made to say about cricket: "The discipline and reliance in one another which it teaches is so valuable, I think. It ought to be such an unselfish game. It merges the individual in the eleven; he doesn't play that he may win, but that his side may," to which Tom replies: "That's very true and that's why football and cricket, now one comes to think of it, are such much better games than fives or hare and hounds, or any others where the object is to come in first or to win for oneself and not that one's side may win."

The political significance of discipline, reliance on one another, and merging the individual in the group was not lost upon educators and statesmen in Victorian England. Furthermore, competitive sport fitted in well with the Victorian pattern of industrial and political rivalry. A belief in collisions, collisions of political parties, religious sects, industrial firms and teams of sportsmen was the light to illumine the broad road of social progress.

The merging of the individual in the group was not confined to the players themselves but to some extent was experienced by those who watched and those who shared a common club membership, a geographical location, or a racial affinity with the performers. In the later nineteenth century the growth of urban areas was so rapid and so amorphous as almost to smother the individual's sense of belonging to any group larger than the family, but on Saturday afternoons he could at least identify himself and his interest with those of eleven figures on the football field as he took his place on the terraces with thousands of others. Some transference of identity from local club to local government almost certainly helped the growth of civic sense and pride in cities such as Birmingham and Manchester. Local politicians who advocated measures to encourage or promote sport did so in the realization that they were helping the political development of their great towns.

In the United States the influence of sport on politics has been considerable. The line taken by German-American gymnasts has already been noted. In a broader sphere sport gave cohesion to a great variety of immigrants with different racial, religious and political backgrounds. It developed in America at about the same time as in Britain, in the latter part of the nineteenth century. Success quickly became an important matter of local prestige, and often the local representatives would be the high school or college; it thus united in rivalry different communities and townships. If the immigrants themselves retained some of their cultural isolation their sons found sport an easy avenue to the American way of life.

Success in sport was important to Americans and it is to their credit that in a community with a history of racial discrimination the racial complexion of the performer was not allowed to prevent his rise to the top in sport. He could represent his town, his state, his country if he were good enough. In boxing the Negro Jack Johnson was heavyweight champion of the world from 1908 to 1915 at a time when the heroes of the American Negro were almost all in sport because here could he meet and beat the white man on equal terms. Johnson himself in vaunting his superiority left a legacy of hatred. By 1937 the inarticulate and shy Joe Louis, the next Negro heavyweight champion, was as beloved by white men as by Negroes. In 1962 Floyd Patterson, the third of a great line, could write; "For myself I can truthfully say I feel no differently inside if I am fighting a white man or another Negro." Later in that year he lost the world heavyweight title to the fourth Negro to hold it, Liston.

In the Olympic Games many Negroes have represented the United States with distinction. When in 1936 at the Olympic Games in Berlin Hitler refused to receive Jesse Owens because he was a Negro after his great victories on the track, the action of the Führer was taken by Americans as an insult to them all.

North of the forty-ninth parallel the Canadians, with their federal constitution, provincial autonomy and large self-conscious minority population of French Canadians, have long experienced the lack of a sense of nationhood. In 1962 a government campaign for fitness and sport was launched by the Minister of National Health and Welfare who included this significant remark in his speech to Parliament: "Canadian participation in international competitive events is emerging as an important aspect of a growing spirit of nationhood."

Sport then has been found to be a cohesive agent and in countries where it is the policy of governments to keep a people divided as in South Africa or in Germany the community of interest in sport between different racial or political groups has been an embarrassment to the politicians.

In the planned societies of communist countries the interaction of sport and politics is deliberately carried a long way and the interaction is from politics to sport rather than in the opposite direction. At first, after the October revolution of 1917, the communist government in Russia took no official interest in sport. In 1925, however, sport was officially recognized and encouraged and in 1930-1 a number of tests in games and sports were instituted leading to the award of G.T.O. Badges ("Ready for Labour and Defence"). Sport was organized under an All Union Committee of Sport and Physical Culture, a government organ responsible to the Council of Ministers of the U.S.S.R. From then onwards there was no suggestion in communist countries that sport was or ought to be "free of politics." On the contrary, sport and training for sport were used extensively for political education so that it became impossible to train as a coach without instruction in Marxism-Leninism and it was impossible to compete in a stadium great or small without being bombarded with the political slogans and ideas of the government of the day. Many sports meetings were organized by political organizations for political purposes.

In countries where sport is organized piecemeal by voluntary bodies and is, to all appearances, independent of political organization and indoctrination, it cannot be inferred that interaction between sport and politics does not take place. The difference is rather in the pattern of organization rather than in the presence or absence of interaction. The pattern of sport in Eastern and Western Germany exemplifies extremes of political organization.

All the German sports organizations were dissolved by order of the Control Commission after the war ended in 1945. In East Germany the government party then decreed that anyone who wished to take part in sport must do so as a member either of the new political youth organization (F.J.D.) or of the workers organization (F.D.G.B.). In 1948 the *Deutscher Sportausschuss* was set up with an avowed political aim. This was followed in 1952 by a State Committee for Sport and Physical Culture.

By contrast, in the Western Zone the *Deutscher Sportsbund* was set up in 1950 with the stated object of solving its problems without reference to party political, religious, racial or military considerations. The establishment of the *Sportsbund* was the result of efforts to find an organization which would enable sportsmen to govern themselves and pursue their interests without control or interference from the government.

Whatever may have been the differing patterns of organization of sport the interest of government organs in West Germany has been no less than in the East. In 1960 the German Olympic Association published a *Memorandum on the "Golden Plan" for Health, Sport and Recreation.* The Golden Plan was based on nation-wide surveys of sports facilities and asked for expenditure of £568,900,000 (6,315,000,000 D.M.) over fifteen years. The first four years were to be used in building up a combined federal and provincial government expenditure of £28,000,000 in direct grants to local communities. By 1961 grant aid from government sources already totalled £13,500,000 (150,000,000 D.M.) or forty-eight per cent of the target for 1964.

To a greater or lesser degree the governments of all western European countries and many others besides now finance sport for their people, all but three of the European countries drawing the revenue to do so from football pools. In Great Britain annual direct aid to sport from the government in 1962 still amounted to no more than £670,000 and that sum was reached only after the Chancellor of the Exchequer had announced an increase of £200,000 on the original sum budgeted. The Wolfenden Committee Report, comparable in some ways to the German Golden Plan but much more modest, had asked for £10,000,000.

Undoubtedly the parsimonious treatment of sport by the British Government has been largely the result of firmly held beliefs that financial aid would involve government interference and that interaction between politics and sport must stop well short of this point. The same beliefs caused the Wolfenden Committee to reject vigorously the suggestion that there should be established a new Department of State called the Ministry of Sport. Yet the Ministry of Education is already, within limitation, a Ministry of Sport. It accepts or rejects all plans for new schools and colleges and so determines the facilities which are provided there for sport in school and out. It provides some of the money for their construction; it sets limits on expenditure on sport by local authorities; it makes a small grant, already mentioned, to voluntary organizations. It helps to finance the coaching schemes of governing bodies of sport and it helps to maintain three national recreation centres. Where sport is educational, and, broadly speaking, is being taught or learned rather than played for its own sake the Ministry of Education already exercises the functions of a Ministry of Sport by permitting, assisting, controlling, inspecting and, some would say, by interfering. When sport is educational it is considered worthy of political direction and some measure of control, but when sport becomes an end in itself it has so far ceased, in Britain, to be an activity which is appropriate for political support.

There have been three occasions when the political disinterestedness of the British Government has been breached. In 1927 the Air Ministry entered an official team for the Schneider Trophy Air Race. It did so again in 1929 and 1931. The race was at this time an international sporting contest, nothing more, and the intervention of the British Government in a sporting event preceded similar intervention by any other government of whatever political complexion. In 1954 the British Government once again broke its principle of non-participation in the world of sport. Roger Bannister had just become the first man to run the mile in less than four minutes. The Foreign Office sent him on a "good will" visit to the United States in order to improve Anglo-American relations.

In January, 1963, the British Prime Minister, having rejected the recommendation of the Wolfenden Committee for a Sports Development Council with funds to allocate, assigned to Lord Hailsham the task of co-ordinating the aid given to sport and recreation by different Government departments, such as the Ministries of Education, Health, and Housing and Local Government. It looked as if Lord Hailsham was to be in fact but not in name a Minister of Sport. At almost the same time there appeared on the horizon a cloud no bigger than a man's hand in the form of a small sum in the estimates of the Commonwealth Relations Office, a government Ministry, to meet a deficit which had been incurred by the British Empire and Commonwealth Games organization in participating in the Games in Western Australia in November, 1962. Whether this was a precedent of political significance was not clear at the time.

It is in the international sphere that the modern development of sport has most significant political implications, for it is here that the hazard to the true nature of sport is most acute and it is here that sport may make its most significant contribution to human welfare and sanity. The rise of international sport has been meteoric. The America's Cup race instituted in 1857 for friendly competition by yachts of different countries was probably the first modern international sporting contest of any consequence. Before the end of the century other international events had appeared, but at the first modern Olympic Games in 1896 there were only thirteen competing nations. In 1960 the number was eighty-four and it has been during the first sixty years of the twentieth century that international sport has come into real prominence.

One of the most considerable achievements has been the setting up of International Federations for the organization and control of individual sports. In sports where times and distances can be measured it soon became necessary to have a body to ratify records so that the claimant to a record could enjoy world-wide acceptance and recognition. In all competitive sports, however, as competitors from one country met those from other countries it became necessary to agree upon the rules and the eligibility of competitors to ensure even competition. The desire for this international competition at all levels of ability became so strong and so widespread that differences of language, of local practice, of social and educational background and of political outlook were not allowed to stand in the way of agreement on an essential basis for competition. Federations were set up for athletics, football, swimming, lawn tennis and many other sports. From the start the decisions of these bodies enjoyed a remarkable acceptance and obedience from constituent bodies all over the world. Whatever defects there may be in international sport there have at least been forms of democratic world government which have had tolerable success within their own limited jurisdictions. Since 1960 there has also been an International Council of Sport and Physical Education under the aegis of UNESCO which was already in 1962 beginning to bring together the international federations and organizations of teachers, coaches and leaders in a further limited world organization.

The desire for international competition is not confined to the richer and more highly developed countries but is shared by these countries which might be thought to be preoccupied with the basic needs for survival. A complete analysis of participants in the Olympic Games of 1952 was carried out in Helsinki and showed that one hundred and sixty competitors came from countries so poor that the annual *per capita* income was less than $100. Rich countries with a *per capita* income of more than $750 sent one hundred and ninety-four competitors.

The best performers anywhere want to test their skill against the best from elsewhere, but because at international level the best performer merges some of his identity in the nation itself, whether he wants to do so or not, success in sport has political importance. This is true for the emergent nation as well as for the more highly developed countries. In February, 1959, the Indian Parliament debated a motion expressing concern at the deterioration of Indian sports, especially cricket. The motion was provoked by the previous failures of the Indian cricket team in the West Indies. One Member of Parliament suggested that no Indian team should be sent abroad for five years, to enable them to improve their standards. Canada, at the other end of the national income scale, launched a government campaign for fitness and amateur sport in 1962 in full recognition that "those who compete in the Olympic Games, the British Empire and Commonwealth Games, the Pan American Games and other international championship games are ambassadors of good will for Canada." The Prime Minister expressed the hope that the programme would add not only to the happiness and health of all people of Canada but to the international athletic prestige of Canada.

Direct intervention by a Head of State in sport because of its international and political significance took place in December, 1962. At that time in the United States disagreement between two rival governing bodies of sport, the Amateur Athletic Union and the National Collegiate Athletic Association, reached a climax. The Attorney General failed to reconcile the two bodies. President Kennedy himself warned the American people in a press conference on 12th December that the United States might not be represented at the next Olympic Games if the two factions refused arbitration. He said: "The governing bodies of these groups apparently put their own interests before the interests of our athletes, our traditions of sport and our country. The time has come for these groups to put the national interest first. Their continued bickering is grossly unfair. On behalf of the country and on behalf of sport I call on the organizations to submit their differences to an arbitration panel immediately." These were strong words, but the political importance of the statement lay not so much in the words used as in the fact that directions were given by the President of the United States to voluntary sports organizations which realized less clearly than he did their own inescapable political responsibilities.

Communist countries have long openly regarded their sporting representatives as political emissaries who can do more than diplomats to recommend the communist philosophy and way of life to those who have not adopted it. East and West sportsmen, whether they like it or not, are "ambassadors of good will" and are under pressure to vindicate not merely their own prowess but the ideology of their country. There are few governments in the world which do not now accept the political importance of success in international sport.

The desire to win is sometimes so strong that sport cannot contain it; when this natural human desire is reinforced with political pressures it is small wonder that on occasion the structure of the sporting event bursts assunder. It was argued in an earlier chapter that play is an essential element in all sport if it is to retain its intrinsic value, and that play implies a defined area of unreality in which the rules of ordinary life are superseded for the time being. It is possible for very great tension to be built up in a game or contest without the illusion of unreality being shattered. Often, however, it is shattered in international sports. A game of ice hockey may develop into an unregulated fist fight as it did in the Winter Olympic Games at Squaw Valley in 1960. A game of water polo may turn into a bloodbath as it did in the Olympic Games in Melbourne in 1956. Cricket or football matches may be destroyed as sporting events by bottles thrown by spectators. On these occasions the illusion is shattered and the contest. has all the aggression, humiliation and bitterness of real life.

On the other side of the balance sheet there are many occasions when "strife without anger and art without malice" are maintained in the most intense competition. There have been numerous occasions at the Olympic Games when competitors from different ideologic blocks, even from countries in open hostility with each other have stood on the victor's rostrum to receive their medals. Their nations' flags are flying while the whole crowd stands to do honour to them. These moments and many honourable and friendly contests, unnoticed by the press of the world, nevertheless enhance the dignity of man.

While competitors and spectators sometimes fail to sustain the unreality of sport, there are from time to time political forces which seek to destroy it. There is no reason in any sport why those who know and accept agreed rules and who have the necessary skill should not play together, yet in South Africa black and white races are not permitted to play together for fear of breaching the political doctrine of apartheid. In Europe, too, the political division of Berlin and the tension there in

1962 led to restrictions on movement between communist and non-communist countries which implied that no international sport would be possible between the two blocks.

In both these situations there was interaction from sport to politics as well as from politics to sport. The South African Olympic Committee was warned that it would be suspended by the International Olympic Committee if the South African government persisted with racial discrimination in sport. In the European situation the I.O.C. in March, 1962, stated that the Olympic Games would be held only in cities which would guarantee free access for all recognized teams. As no city in a country of the North Atlantic Treaty Organization would be permitted to admit East Germans, all these countries were debarred from holding the Olympic Games until they agreed to recognize the special and "unreal" nature of sport. The International Council for Sport and Physical Education urged UNESCO to try urgently to secure that the youth of the whole world and its officials might meet freely in sport. The Council cancelled its own general assembly which was to be held in Manila because the Government of the Philippines would not guarantee entry to delegates from communist countries.

The essential nature of sport is in danger internationally not only from restriction but also from domination by the two great power blocks, the U.S.A. and the U.S.S.R. It is inevitable in the present situation that they should be more than anxious for success and that this anxiety should be shared by their citizens and allies. In 1962 both global and local wars are likely to be suicidal ways of influencing people and winning support, and sport as a means of influence has assumed correspondingly greater political importance. The situation was anayzed in essence by Arnold Toynbee in 1948. In *Civilization on Trial* he wrote: "Communism is a competitor [with the West] for the allegiance of that great majority of mankind that is neither communist nor capitalist, neither Russian nor Western but is living at present in an uneasy no man's land between the opposing citadels of two rival ideologies. Both nondescripts and Westerners are in danger of turning communist today, as they were of turning Turk four hundred years ago, and, though communists are in similar danger of turning capitalist—as sensational instances have shown—the fact that one's rival witch doctor is as much afraid of one's own medicine as one is afraid oneself, of his, does not do anything to relieve the tension of the situation.

"Yet the fact that our adversary threatens us by showing up our defects, rather than by forcibly suppressing our virtues, is proof that the challenge he presents to us comes ultimately not from him, but from ourselves."

It may be that sport will provide opportunities for all people to meet this challenge but it may also happen that the Olympic Games and other top-level international competitions will change their character. There are indications that the U.S.S.R. will press for more and more sports to be included in the Olympic programme, for instance, parachuting, aerobatics and motor-racing, so that the Games become too vast for staging by any city other than one supported massively by a wealthy central government. The Russians may also press for the enlargement of the I.O.C. to such dimensions that it will be too unwieldy to exercise effective control and be a happy hunting ground for big powers. What could then happen is that the Olympic Games would be no more than a testing ground for two great political units. There would be no difficulty in training *élite* teams of participants whose efficiency and skill would be superb but who would cease to be sportsmen, just as the professional athletes of the Mediterranean arenas ceased to be sportsmen during the last five hundred years of the ancient Olympic Games. The competitions would be keenly contested but as predominantly political occasions they would cease to share with humbler events that playful unreality which is essential to sport. It remains to be seen whether the international bodies can so frame their regulations that a limit can be set to the political and financial exploitation of the best performers which will preserve their character as sportsmen. Most of these bodies have not so far shown signs of recognizing the problem and the International Olympic Committee, which has begun to see it, has not been markedly successful in finding a solution.

International sport is like an iceberg; a small part consisting of the Olympic Games and other world championships is seen, but most international contests go on unnoticed by press or people. It is at this level that sport may have its greatest impact on world affairs. In his *Reith Lectures* in 1948 Bertrand Russell argued that the savage in each one of us must find some outlet not incompatible with civilized life and with the happiness of his equally savage neighbour. He suggested that sport might provide such outlets and that what was wrong with our civilization was that such forms of competition formed too small a part of the lives of ordinary men and women. Men must compete for superiority and it is best that they do so in contests which yield utterly useless results. This is not to say that the results do not matter. They matter supremely and if they do not they will not satisfy man or nation, but in sport victory is never for all time nor is defeat irreparable. The individual, the team, the nation, even the ideological block lives to fight another day.

The enormous growth of sport as a World-wide phenomenon may herald the birth of a new Olympic ideal and a new asceticism, an asceticism which looks to achievement and prowess in play as an end in itself.

The final conclusion then is a paradox; sport, if it is pursued as an end in itself, may bring benefits to man which will elude his grasp if he treats it as little more than a clinical, a social or a political instrument to fashion those very benefits.

REFERENCES

MOLYNEUX, D. D., *Central Government Aid to Sport and Physical Recreation in Countries of Western Europe* (University of Birmingham, 1962).
JOKL, E. *et al.*, *Sports in the Cultural Pattern of the World* (Helsinki, 1956).
COZENS, F. W. and STUMPF, F., *Sports in American Life* (Chicago, 1953).

SEE ALSO

INTERNATIONAL OLYMPIC COMMITTEE, *Bulletins*.
RUSSELL, BERTRAND, *Authority and the Individual* (London, 1949).
TOYNBEE, A., *Civilization on Trial* (London, 1948).
UNESCO, *The Place of Sport in Education* (Paris, 1956).

Ideology and Social Control in Canadian Sport: A Theoretical Review

Richard C. Helmes

INTRODUCTION

Recently, there has been a resurgence of interest in Marxian political economy in Canada. Marxist scholars, by stressing rather than obscuring the centrality of class conflict as a force in Canadian social development, have challenged liberal conventional wisdoms about the historical evolution of Canadian society.[1] One central concern of these Marxist analyses has been to demonstrate the important role that ideology plays in the legitimation of the capitalist social order. In Canada, particular attention has been focussed on the ideological role of the mass media, the educational system and the state. One "ideological institution" which has received very little attention, however, is sport.

Now Marxists have never accepted the liberal conventional wisdom that sport is an aspect of culture standing outside of and separate from "real life," or that sport is a "functional" milieu for the healthy release of energy and emotion and the learning of "beneficial" values. Marxists have consistently argued that sport, like all other institutions, both creates and is created by the matrix of material and ideational influences specific to any particular period in history. Yet, despite recognition of this point, Marxists do appear to have accepted the liberal notion that sport and other forms of leisure activity are somehow not worthy of serious attention by the academics. Study of activities related to alienation, the state, work, and so forth are regarded as far more essential to the development of an understanding of capitalist hegemony than is the study of sport. This is unfortunate, for while I am in some agreement with the general sentiment of such an argument, I do believe that there are some

This paper is an abridged version of "Ideology and Social Control in Canadian Sport: A Theoretical Review," by Richard C. Helmes, Working Papers in the Sociological Study of Sports and Leisure, Volume 1, No. 4. Reprinted by permission of the author and the Sports Studies Research Group, Queen's University.

issues which should be further considered before casting sport aside and designating it as a comparatively trivial aspect of the social life-worlds of citizens in modern liberal democracies.

Most significant among these issues, perhaps, is the nature of sport's long-standing ties to the class structure and of sport's significance in the maintenance of political order. In Canada, for example, there is now a good deal of literature which demonstrates that sport has always been (and continues to be) a class-based area of human activity that contains significant ideological overtones. Consider the following arguments:

i. There were quantitatively and qualitatively different rates and styles of involvement in the "folk" and "elite" recreational pastimes of frontier Canada—organized sports were almost solely the prerogative of the colonial mercantile elite (Wise, 1974; Metcalfe, 1976; Gruneau, 1976b and 1978).

ii. The majority of urban sporting clubs of the last half of the nineteenth century were upper middle class institutions run by and for members of the urban commercial bourgeoisie (mostly in finance and retail/wholesale trade) (Wise, 1974; Metcalfe, 1976; Gruneau, 1978).

iii. The present-day split between professional and amateur sport originated during the latter half of the nineteenth century and was the result of a class-rooted conflict between members of the commercial community who favoured a Victorian, morally-utilitarian concept of amateur sport and those upward-striving members of the working-class and business community who regarded sport as a more rational utilitarian business enterprise and venue for the dramatization of the principles of free-market competition (Gruneau, 1978).

iv. Contemporary involvement both in high-level amateur sports and organized physical recreation still seems to be strongly influenced by socioeconomic factors (Curtis and Milton, 1976; Gruneau, 1976b; Beamish, 1978).

v. There are structural ties between elite groups in different sectors of the Canadian economy (most notably financial capital) and elite positions in Canadian amateur and professional sport (Clement, 1975; Gruneau, 1978).

vi. The "ideological content" of organized Canadian sport seems to parallel closely the values of meritocratic liberalism, the dominant ideology of capitalist society (Helmes, 1977).

All of these findings point to the class-based character of Canadian sport and, thus, raise the issue of the ideological role sport might play in social control. I shall argue in this paper that highly structured, rationalized sport *does* play an important ideological role in Canadian society by aiding in the legitimation of the status quo. Sports provide an arena of political socialization in which system-stablizing liberal values are reinforced.[2] This strong liberal ideological bias is not simply the product of blind, deterministic, historical forces but is, rather, the result of intervention by dominant classes in Canadian society. I argue that individuals who occupy (and have occupied) positions of power within the formal organizational structure of sport and other related institutions have *used* sport to protect their vested interest in the maintenance of an institutional framework which guarantees their privileges.

It will become obvious in the presentation of this argument that I am making an assumption upon which the validity of all of my conclusions rests. I am assuming that sport *is* sufficiently "meaningful" to a sufficiently large number of individuals that it *does* possess potential to act as a medium of political socialization (Berger, 1962). And, given the complexity of the process of value "transfer" and the dearth of information available on the influence of sport involvement *per se* on political orientation (Zureik, 1976), it is recognized that this assumption may be rather tenuous.[3] The widespread popularity of sport *does not,* as is often assumed, automatically render it significant as a force in the formation of value structures; rather, individuals must strongly *identify with* sport in order that "transfer" occur. However, given that we recognize the subtlety of the processes by which domination and legitimation occur in advanced capitalist society, we must not simply assume by the same token, that sport is of only secondary significance in the maintenance of capitalist hegemony.

The analysis which follows is divided into three sections. Part one of the discussion outlines a number of preliminary considerations on sport and social control in capitalist societies. Part two of the discussion focusses on the nature of ideology and outlines some specific relationships between ideology, sports and social control in Canadian society. The final section of the essay includes a summary statement and some concluding comments on the relationships between sport, social control and the forces of legitimation in the modern capitalist state.

THE PROBLEM OF IDEOLOGY

Social order in Canada is not the result of spontaneous, universal agreement on a set of shared values. Rather, order in Canadian society hinges, to a considerable degree, on the extent to which those in control of the institutional structure (power which emanates from control over the means of production) are able to *justify* existing social and economic conditions and power relationships. This process of "legitimation" is achieved, in part, via the dissemination of liberal ideology through the institutional structure. In most capitalist societies, the process of legitimation appears to have been so successful that capitalist political economy has become widely accepted as a "given"—the "natural" and most "just" type of socio-economic system possible.

For those who do not doubt the viability and morality of modern capitalism and the hierarchical class structure which is so much a part of it, this legitimation of the status quo is not a problematic issue. And, indeed, over time, those being ruled under the guise of "the rule of the majority" come to regard the pattern of *public* legitimation as being in their *private interest*. Accordingly this pattern takes on the characteristics of something which stands both above and outside of human intervention.

> The subordination of the self to the labour process itself takes on the appearance of blind economic law, so that the domination of man by man no longer appears as an injustice but a biological or legal necessity. . . . Moral systems that constitute the rules of ordinary behaviour assume the status of natural law; they become reified as commands for individual conduct (Aronowitz, 1973: 7-8).

The reason that this reification occurs is that, for all intents and purposes, only *dominant* ideological interpretations and explanations of social order are "allowed." All others are "structured out" with the result that the institutional order tends to become characterized by a range of value orientations supportive of the status quo (Miliband, 1969: 220).[4] Marxists contend that the ideological content of these values is far from fortuitous; the institutional order is repressively supportive of such "negative" features of capitalist society as alienated labour, the fetishism of consumption, and highly structured, intergenerational patterns of political and economic inequality *only* as the result of the manipulation of ideological "master symbols" by a dominant class (Mills, 1957:36).[5] Moreover, some Marxist-inspired writers contend that an ideological veneration of the status quo has created a citizenry made up of unthinking, unaware "cheerful robots" (Mills, 1957:171) or "one-dimensional men" (Marcuse, 1964) incapable of applying their critical capacities to an extent sufficient to allow them to challenge the political-economic status quo. A narrowing of the universe of political discourse has occurred and virtually any possibility for the development of a more cooperative, humanely rational form of social organization—and the consequent liberation of man—has been precluded.

While I agree with the general sentiment of this argument, I believe it unwise to overestimate the power of ideology to create "cheerful robots" (i.e., to view man as the creature rather than the creator of society), for doing so underestimates the active role that man plays in the shaping of his own history. Conversely, however, it seems even more unwise to complacently argue (as many liberal theorists do) that individuals freely shape their own destinies. For while the second argument fails to acknowledge the existence of the repressive class constraints to individual and collective freedom characteristic of capitalist society, the first prematurely and incorrectly absolves man of the right—and duty—to shape the future.

Regardless of the degree to which one agrees with the notion that man in capitalist society has been rendered politically impotent, there is some consensus that a dulling and narrowing of political awareness has occurred. How does this process of "dulling" and "narrowing" occur? First, there is an element of overt coercion involved.[6] Also, there is a degree of relatively obvious and overt political socialization and ideological censorship that takes place in the educational system, the mass media, and so on. Far more significant than either of these, though, by virtue of both its "will-o-the-wisp" character and its profound success, is the actual *content* of capitalist ideology—meritocratic liberalism, technological rationality, the rational-legal form of domination and so on. It is these *contents* of ideological systems in capitalist societies that are the foundations of social control.[7]

Canadians, for example, have come to identify with liberal ideological master symbols to the extent that alternative, socialist master symbols are rejected automatically. Without understanding the basic view of the nature of man and society upon which socialist forms of social organization are based, most Canadians have been taught to condemn them blindly. This aversion is certainly not the result of a conscientious, knowledgeable consideration of socialist political theory and philosophy. Rather, it is the result of repeated exposure to a variety of political socialization experiences peculiarly liberal in content and character and generally patterned by institutional elites hostile to socialist thinking.

As noted earlier in this discussion, some neo-Marxists have viewed sport as one of the institutional mechanisms by which citizens in capitalist countries are socialized in this manner. They have viewed sport as a simple reflection of the capitalist infra-structure which is manipulated by media and sport elites as a tool of political socialization. Indeed, many have regarded sports as a new "opiate of the masses" (cf., Hoch, 1972; Laguillaumie, 1972). While such interpretations of sport are of value in

the sense that they have stimulated some re-examination of the contention that sport is an apolitical institution, they do not provide a very systematic or even accurate assessment of sport's role in social control. Richard Gruneau's (1976a:28) assessment of Paul Hoch's "vulgar materialist" analysis of sport in the United States sums up the shortcomings of
much of this literature rather aptly:

> Moral indignation and a commitment to progressive change are hardly
> guarantees of objective reasoning or even of factual accuracy, and
> the victimization of Marxist scholarship by a facile polemic like Paul
> Hoch's *Rip Off the Big Game* (1972) testifies to the dangers of com-
> mitment without content.

This paper attempts to approach the subject matter of sport and social control in Canada from a neo-Marxist perspective, like Hoch and the
others, but with the hope of: (a) providing a corrective to some of the
vulgar materialist work; and (b) dispelling some of the myths perpe-
trated by liberal theorists who see sport as a "beneficial" institution by
which individuals are integrated into a non-problematic social order.[8]

IDEOLOGY AND SOCIAL CONTROL IN CANADIAN SPORT

(i) Basic Principles of Ideology

The sociological literature is dominated by two different views of the
nature of ideology. According to one view, clearly exemplified in the
work of Karl Mannheim, ideology is used in a totally non-evaluative sense
to describe the basic philosophy or *Weltanschauung* of a particular age
or concrete historical group. The alternative interpretation, that is expressed in the work of Karl Marx, employs the word ideology in a highly
negative sense. Marx argues that ideology is clearly partisan. In capitalist
society, it is a tool of class domination that works for the bourgeoisie to
maintain the proletariat in an advanced state of false consciousness and
thus perpetuates an exploitative relationship between classes. Despite this
fundamental difference of opinion regarding the character of ideology,
however, there is considerable agreement among sociologists regarding
the way in which ideology works. That is, ideology is generally regarded
as having a dual character, to be working at two "levels of consciousness."
This distinction is particularly well-outlined in Mannheim's discussion
of "particular" and "total" ideology in *Ideology and Utopia* (1936:49).

According to Mannheim, "particular ideology" is largely superficial
in nature and tends to operate at the most obvious, conscious level of
personal awareness. Attempts to transmit ideology at this level of aware-

ness, he argues, are often recognized as partisan by both the sender and receiver of the message. As such, both perceive the message as a distortion of social reality (1936:49).

> The particular conception of ideology is implied when the term denotes that we are skeptical of the ideas and representations advanced by our opponent. They are regarded as more or less disguises of the real nature of a situation (Mannheim, 1936:49).

"Total ideology," by contrast, does not operate at a personal, conscious level of awareness but is, instead, more pan-societal and all-pervasive. It is, Mannheim states, "the ideological composition of the total substructure . . . of a particular age or concrete historical group" (1936:49). It influences the individual at a subconscious level of awareness.

In the following discussion of the social significance of the character of the ideological content of Canadian sport, Mannheim's conceptual and terminological distinction between these two different kinds of ideology is used as a rough guideline for understanding sport and social control in Canada. However, while this terminological distinction is invoked for ease of presentation and analysis (it provides an excellent sense of the two-fold character of ideology), I must stress that the interpretation of the political nature and role of ideology used throughout the discussion borrows heavily from Marxism.

(ii) Canadian Sport and Particular Ideology

The political use of sport as a mechanism of social control in Canadian society has been recently discussed by Roger Levasseur (1976). In his essay, "Sport: Structure, Représentations idéologiques et symboliques," Levasseur argues that "les promoters et producteurs du sport . . . (ont developee) également un discours idéologique spécifique" (1976:51) in order to shape the "particular" political consciousness of Canadian sports consumers. And, among the most important of the "promoteurs et producteurs du sport" is the federal government, whose *formal* involvement in sport, fitness and recreation in Canada began in 1943 with the National Fitness Act.

Bill C-131, the National Fitness and Amateur Sport Act has formed the basis of *direct* Canadian governmental involvement in sport since 1961.[9] In 1969, the federal government began to regard its involvement as more essential than had historically been the case. So, following strong and explicit references made to the importance of sport at the particular level of ideology by Prime Ministers Lester B. Pearson and Pierre Elliott Trudeau, the Liberal government established the *Task Force on Sports for Canadians*. This task force was commissioned to determine how (Note: not *if* but *how*) the federal government should become more involved in sport in Canada.[10] The decision to become involved was based on the desire to see amateur sport become a more potent vehicle of "social development" (*Sports Policy*, 1970:11) in Canadian society.[11]

Careful reading of the *Task Force* report and the "Proposed Sports Policy for Canadians" which emerged from it, indicates that the Canadian government had two very explicit goals in mind when discussing "social development"—"national unity" and "international prestige." From a content analysis of selected Canadian printed media and sports policy documents conducted in 1977 (see Helmes, 1977), I was able to determine that "nationalism" was a dominant ideological component of the "Sports Policy"—direct references to "unity," "national goals" and "Canadianism" made up a large percentage of the coded entries. This finding would seem to support the contention made above regarding the explicit goals of federal governmental sports policy. Yet, the view that sport in Canada plays a poltical role *only* in relation to nationalism seems rather facile. Levasseur, for example, argues that while sport may play a role in maintaining "an intrinsically Canadian sense of community" (*Task Force*, 1969:13) and that governmental involvement in sport in Canada may be important for the development ot national consciousness and unity, the underlying importance of the promotion of unity through sport is that it tends to assist in the maintenance of system stability.

> Certain États peuvent également utiliser l'élite sportive comme élément d'affirmation d'une conscience nationale . . . Enfin, signalons que les élites sportives sont récupérées implicitment ou explicitement par les gouvernements comme une élément de plus en plus important de stabilité sociopolitique (Levasseur, 1976:55).

In addition to reinterpreting the *Task Force* view of the role of sport in maintaining system stability through the promotion of national unity, Levasseur argues that there is an important role played by sport in contributing to system stability through the development of international prestige.

> (L'État), en tant que principal agent de d'appareil politique utilise à des fins multiples la symbolique sportive. Il se sert en premier lieu de l'élite sportive comme élément d'affirmation du *prestige national* (1976:55 emphasis added).

The accuracy of Levasseur's analysis of the role of the federal government in employing sport at the level of "particular" ideology for purposes of "social development" becomes even more obvious when one examines the nature of government involvement after 1970 and the publication of the recommendations of the *Task Force*.

The most important of the recommendations of the *Task Force* was the establishment of *Sport Canada*, a federally and privately-funded, non-profit organization set up "to provide a focus for the administration, support and growth of sport in Canada" and designed "to lift Canadian sports into a new era of *accomplishment*" (*Task Force*, 1969:75, emphasis added). A brief look at the policy decisions after the establishment of Sport Canada illustrates that the choice of the word "accomplishment" was not a fortuitous one in this instance. For, throughout the *Task Force*, the authors emphasized the importance of the development of "elite" athletes, and did not (despite much of the rhetoric in both the *Task Force* report and the "Proposed Sports Policy for Canadians") promote the development of broad public recreation and sports programs.[12] This emphasis on "elite" sports was especially evident in the content analysis that I conducted of Canadian media and sports policy documents (Helmes, 1977). Over 28 percent of the coded entries in this analysis emphasized the significance of "skill" and "victory" where only 2 percent of the coded entries emphasized recreational "participation."

From Levasseur's arguments, a review of the *Task Force* and the "Sports Policy," and my own research in this area, I would argue that at the specific level of "particular" ideology the Canadian state has attempted to *use* sport for political purposes in its recent programs (e.g., the "Sports Policy," "Game Plan '76," etc.). The patriotic, nationalistic concerns of government sports policy are scarcely disguised by terms like "social development" and this emphasis on politics has far-reaching implications.

For example, Gruneau (1976b) indicates that, following the controversy over the invocation of the War Measures Act in 1970, the theme of the Canada Winter Games became "Unity Through Sport" in order to promote, in particular, "anglophonic and francophonic unity" (1976b:122). Similarly, if one accepts the notion of the expenditure of skilled effort in a competitive hierarchial marketplace as the "ideal typical" pathway to individual salvation in capitalist liberal democracies, then the very fact that *competitive, commercialized, professionalized* sport merits the moral and financial support of the Canadian government legitimates the activities as the "proper" form of leisure-time activity for Canadians.

(iii) Canadian Sport and Total Ideology

On the question of ideological legitimation, the relationship between sport and the mass media goes far beyond the simplistic assertion that sport plays a "gate-keeping" ideological role. Aronowitz (1973:11), for example, points out that the strong relationship which has developed between sport and the mass media has not only increased the mass appeal and popularity of sport, but has also increased both the range and depth of the impact of sport on political consciousness.

> To fully understand the ideological impact and manipulative functions of current media presentations, it is necessary to appreciate the *multi-layered* (emphasis added) character of contemporary mass culture. In addition to the *overt* ideological content of films and television . . . there is also a series of *covert* messages contained within them which appeal to the audiences largely on an unconscious level . . . sexually explicit or violent films . . . advertising . . . (and) sports serve similar functions.

Those who have contended that the logic, structure and ideological content of sport in capitalist society (particularly the United States) is the product of manipulation by a "power elite," "monopoly capitalist elite" or "dominant class" who seek to maintain existing patterns of property and power distribution have not always provided the empirical justification required to make such statements. Providing a number of examples of the "manipulation" of sport at the level of particular ideology and then simply extending this to the covert level of total ideology by inference and assumption is not adequate.

There are several pre-conditions which must be met before it can be argued that the ideology and structure of sport has been framed *for a specific purpose* by a "dominant class" or "power elite" in society. First, the membership of this elite group would have to be explicitly identified.[13] Second, it would be necessary to demonstrate that those individuals filling the elite positions in the bureaucracy of institutionalized sport (for example, the federal and provincial sports-governing bodies and professional leagues) were recruited from, or had strong ties to, the economic elite and the dominant class. If such ties could be found, it would remain necessary to prove that this group had identified and agreed upon an ideological perspective which they felt would be most advantageous to them in terms of its capacity for the maintenance of system stability. In addition, it would be necessary to demonstrate that most members of the "dominant class" understand the nature of ideology and that they understand the learning processes involved in political socialization. Finally, it would be necessary to identify the specific structural mechanisms and procedures by which the manipulation of sport at the level of "total" ideology might be effected. That is, it would be necessary to outline the "chain of command" (the decision-making hierarchy) and the actual institutional structures through which the program of broad ideological manipulation is formulated and carried out.

Is it possible to identify a group in Canadian society with both a vested interest in the maintenance of the status quo and with the power to allow them to achieve their goal? Two arguments have been advanced in answer to this question. The first of these was offered in *The Vertical Mosaic* (1965) by John Porter. In that book, Porter argued that there is a "plural elite" system operating in Canada; that is, there are several groups of institutionally-specific elites each with a functionally and structurally differentiated power base and role. In addition to the structural separation of these elites, there is, according to Porter, a degree of normative differentiation and separation which precludes wholesale mingling and cooperation. In sum, then, Porter's argument is that Canada's power structure follows a classic pluralist model; a set of countervailing powers or checks and balances exists which prevents any one particular group in society from gaining an over-riding influence over any of the others.

In a more recent (1975) examination of this issue, Wallace Clement has disputed Porter's conclusion, arguing that there is a single group in Canadian society, the "corporate elite" (composed of members of the "economic" and "media" elites), which loosely corresponds to the top stratum of a "dominant class" in the Marxian sense.[15] Clement quarrels with the two pluralist interpretations of the roles of the government as either: (a) an arena for the solution of major group conflicts in capitalist society; or (b) as an impartial umpire, arbitrating conflicts and maintaining an effective balance between power blocs and interest groups. He disagrees with this argument on two grounds. First, he disputes the claim that in a pluralist democracy "free willed individuals . . . will come together when they detect injustice and voice their concerns through the many 'access points' in the state." He argues that, contrary to this view, "individuals are not 'free-willed' but subject to dominant ideological systems" and that such a theory "fails to acknowledge . . . the unequal allocations of resources necessary to mobilize and realize concerns" (1975:359). Similarly, he disputes the pluralist contention that "the state will be an unbiased mediator of interests" (1975:359) and approvingly cites Ralph Miliband's argument that it is necessary to understand that "the state might be a rather special institution, whose main interest is to defend the predominance in society of a particular *class* (1969:3, emphasis added. In conclusion, Clement argues that:

> To argue that liberal democracies (like Canada) are characterized by a "mixed economy" of public and private capital is to miss the point of how they are "mixed" and in what proportions. When public capital is used to support private capital, the mixture is not "balanced" but has the effect of reinforcing and maintaining inequalities. The gains

to be made are still private gains and the power is still private power. . . . Top decision making positions in the economy and mass media in Canada are dominated by a small upper *class*. Through dominant corporations they maintain a hierarchically ordered corporate system by which they are able to extract surplus allowing them to continue and expand their control (1974:364, emphasis added).

However, while the information presented by Clement in *The Canadian Corporate Elite* seems to render Porter's "plural elite" model somewhat problematic, it must be stressed that the mere identification of "interlocks" between elites in Canadian society does not constitute "proof" that these groups act in concert to maintain their privileged positions—least of all through control over the "state." For, as Panitch (1976) points out:

> an interpretation of the Marxist theory of the state as claiming that the state merely acts on the direct instructions of the bourgeoisie is a crude caricature of the concept of the modern state as "a committee for managing the common affairs of the bourgeoisie," a caricature which fails to distinguish between the state acting on *behalf* of the bourgeoisie, from its acting on their *behest* (Panitch, 1976:3).

Similarly, the mere provision of the structural potential for similarity of elite value orientations is not sufficient evidence to assume that the members of elite groups in Canadian society possess similar value orientations.

Clement deals with this second criticism by delving into what he refers to as "the private world of powerful people." He examines the socialization experiences common to the elite groups in Canadian society and concludes that their social class, educational, occupational, etc., backgrounds provide them with a relatively uniform world-view and a sense of "collegiality" (Weber, 1947:396). Moreover, this "collegiality," according to Clement, is highly reminiscent of "class consciousness" and is a stronger force of "in-group" solidarity than exists in any of the other classes in Canadian society. That is, while there are other groups in Canadian society whose "objective" position suggests that they belong to the same class, it is only among the corporate elite that this "objective" position ("class in itself," in Marx' terms) is transformed via socialization experiences into a "subjective" recognition of class position and a realization of the necessity for *directed*, communal class action ("class for itself," in Marx' terms).

Is there any information to suggest that such "collegiality" has influenced decision-making processes in Canadian sport and what, if any, are the structural links between elite groups which allow this involvement to occur? According to Gruneau (1978), a considerable number of structural (personal, corporate and political) ties bind those who hold high-ranking positions in Canadian sport to other elite groups in Canadian society. For the most part, these ties are strongest between sport and indigenous Canadian financial capital, but, in the case of professional team sports, many of these ties are to elite groups outside the country. These ties, Gruneau argues (1979:in press), merely re-affirm Canada's traditional role as a dependent state:

> Boards of directors of most Canadian professional sports teams (except for a few teams in the C.F.L. and W.H.A. where control lies in the hands of business and professional interests in the local community) maintain readily identifiable ties with indigenous Canadian capital in the areas of finance, trade, the food and beverage industry, transport and communications, but (again excepting the C.F.L.) the major leagues that these franchises operate within are controlled by American interests. Hockey and baseball, in particular, represent a classic dramatization of the doubly exploitative nature of Canada's association with the American metropole. The accumulative interests of Canadian capital in areas where these interests have always been strong are enhanced by their association with organizations where control lies in American hands. And, whereas Canadian capital is involved in a profitable relationship that maintains patterns of dependency, the interests and forms of cultural expression of most Canadians remain largely underdeveloped. This is not to say that Canadians as a whole have "lost" control of commercial sports to foreign interests, rather . . . it is doubtful if any real collective control by Canadians has ever been present. With few exceptions, modern commercial sports have always been owned and controlled by private individuals (or at best by a representation of individuals from middle or upper class fragments in communities) and have represented the organization of the interests of these individuals in corporate entities that function in an international capitalist system.

Gruneau also refers to data which suggest ties between the dominant class in Canada and strategic amateur organizations like the Canadian Olympic Association. Yet, while these data reveal the existence of structural ties between organized sport and the Canadian elite and class structures, there is little in Gruneau's analysis that deals *specifically* with questions of "class consciousness" or "collegiality." Gruneau simply notes the homogeneous character of the backgrounds of sports leaders of different types, their memberships in Canada's dominant class and suggests how "volunteer" and "state" sports provide excellent "elite forums" where collegiality might possibly be established (see Gruneau, 1978 and 1979). This conclusion is buttressesd by a socio-historical discussion which introduces a framework for understanding sport's changing relationships to "elite" and "class" interests in Canadian society.

In each of five periods of Canadian history, Gruneau argues, Canadian sport has been characterized by an historically-specific structural "form" and ideological orientation. During each of these periods, it has been under the control of particular (dominant) segments of the Canadian class structure. Especially important for our purposes here are the several references he makes, in his broader analysis of class and power in Canadian sport, to sport's historical role in the process of social control. He sees sport's role in this process as a dual one.

First, he argues that sport assumes an historically-specific organizational "form" which, over time, assumes a degree of ontological status. As a structure with ontological status, it then develops a certain degree of resistance to material and ideational influences operant in larger society. Thus, though changes in the mode of production, class structure and ideological orientation of larger Canadian society are reflected by changes in sport, they tend to lag somewhat in their evolution because of the organizational and ideological inertia of the previous form.[16] Second, sport serves a socially-stabilizing role in the process of social control not only in this way, but also as the result of overt attempts by members of the dominant class to maintain social order through the manipulation of sport. In the outline of the historical role played by sport in this capacity, he emphasizes that there has been a strong, continuing and mutually-supportive relationship between the two tendencies throughout Canadian history.

> For each period, I have attempted to suggest how the development of new social and productive forces and relationships have demarcated a progressively dominant "form" or set of conflicting "forms" for sport's organizational character and relationship to the class structure. Since each "form" tends to establish an organizational legacy, I indicate how the conflict and accommodation that has occurred between them has led to an increasingly complex structure of organizational leadership—a structure whose complexity and apparent "pluralism" in the present day belies a continuing association with the dominant classes and status groups in Canadian society (Gruneau, 1978: 210).

The significance of Gruneau's work, in this instance, is two-fold. First, the image of Canadian sport as an apolitical, democratized institution is one which suffers sorely from the influence of myopic historical hindsight and the effects of contemporary ideological blinders. For, as Gruneau stresses throughout his analysis, to accept pluralist theories, or theories of "post-capitalism" and impute to them the ability accurately to describe the reality of Canadian society is to demonstrate methodological and theoretical wishful thinking. Indeed, as he concludes, the evidence suggests that pluralist and post-capitalist theories are "prematurely and falsely disillusioned with the utility of *class* analysis as a viable approach to the study of sport, and the comprehension of general issues and problems of societal development" (1978:237). Second, the examples he provides illustrate that the relationship between the recruitment of elites in Canadian sport and the structural organization and ideological nature of Canadian sport is one which may well allow sport to be examined as an agent of culturally hegemonic domination along the lines of Third World dependency models (1978:237).

For purposes of the presentation at hand, however, the most important issue which arises from a consideration of Gruneau's socio-historical discussion concerns the fit between the ideological orientation which dominates policy in the institutional spheres of Canadian life and its relationships to the value-orientation of those who hold "elite" positions within the Canadian class structure. Earlier in this paper, I argued that in order to accept the notion that sport is consciously used as an "ideological institution" by the dominant class (at the level of total ideology), it is necessary to: (a) ascertain the personal ideological orientations of members of the elite and from this try to determine if some type of "elite" or "class" consciousness exists; and (b) provide evidence that "liberal ideology" (which may differ from the "corporatist" ideology which may be found among the elite) was being promoted in the institutional structure as a conscious means of maintaining social order (and, therefore, vested interests). While there can be little denying sport's relationships to manipulative policies that work at the level of "particular" ideology, and while sport's organizational leadership seems to have been almost exclusively recruited from the dominant class, we may still only make inferences about the degree of "conscious manipulation" in sport's relationships to "total ideology." Some additional considerations on this question are raised in the concluding statement which follows.

SPORT AND SOCIAL CONTROL: SUMMARY AND CONCLUSIONS

In this working paper, I have attempted to examine the argument that contemporary sport performs a social control function in capitalist society by acting as a vehicle of political socialization employed by elites within the dominant class. It can be concluded, I would argue, that *at the level of "particular" ideology*, the role of such elite groups in Canada (in particular, political and media elites) is essentially one of "gatekeeping"; sport *is used* as a means of social control but only in that those who control the staging of athletic events limit the exposition of ideological perspectives to those supportive of the prevailing political economic order. Sport tends to be regarded as a "beneficial" institution through which essentially integrative, valuable learning experiences occur. Thus, insofar as elite groups "control" sport via their positions at the top of sports organizations, their decisions tend to *maintain* a logic in sport and a structure which has resulted from material and ideological changes in political economy that have occurred during the last two hundred years. That is, in the same way that other institutional structures grew out of the interplay between a changing material base (growth in urbanization, technology, transportation) and evolving ideational influences (ascriptive conservatism, meritocratic liberalism), sport developed characteristics reflective of and supportive of a capitalist liberal democracy. The extent of sport involvement on the part of media and government elites does not go beyond attempts to maintain system stability through the promotion of Canadian national unity and international prestige.

Yet, there is very little evidence to suggest that *conscious* manipulation of sport occurs at the level of "total" ideology. In addition to the fact that arguments in favour of this contention tend to ignore or play down the effects of historically significant material and social influences at the level of political economy, there is only scattered information to suggest that the elite groups in Canadian society possess sufficient structural control to develop a coherent program of planned political socialization through sport. Thus, the actions of the individuals who man the command posts of Canadian sport appear to be better explained by a multiplicity of factors not considered by those who espouse a "conspiratorial" theory of the political manipulation of sport. As Hargreaves points out, such a position is a rather simplistic one.

> It is not that Machiavellian capitalists deliberately get together to compensate workers for the deprivations of work by expanding the leisure industries so that the work force will be better motivated to produce, having been compensated by a more satisfying leisure. It is that the alienating nature of work in a capitalist society itself produces in the worker a reaction to it, which takes the form of a demand for compensation in leisure. *This demand is formulated within the terms of a pre-existing autonomous cultural tradition, of which sporting pastimes are an important part.* (Hargreaves, 1975:56, emphasis added).

How, then, may we explain the persistent "recruitment" of sports leaders from the dominant class. One answer might proceed as follows. Members, of the various elite groups in Canadian society may well have developed, through childhood and adolescent socialization experiences, an affective attachment to sport. They regard it as an essentially benign social institution, other than at the level of "particular" ideology (to use Mannheim's term), and strive to maintain its "neutrality" by preventing the intrusion of "radical politics" into sport. Any affective attachment to sport that they might have is rooted in their involvement in sport as *individuals*—not as a *class*. For example, sport offers to them as individuals the opportunity for enjoyment through physical activity and for some, it provides for a display of status through the "conspicuous consumption" of sports-related clothing and equipment and through attendance at important sporting contests. Sports also provide the opportunity to mingle on a personal level with media "celebrities" and they provide investment opportunities in the form of team ownership, facility development and ownership, and concession management.

On a more personal, subjective and "meaningful" level, sport is exciting and may well have been a significant feature of these individuals' early lives, for example, via participation in "character-building" athletics at the schools (many of them "private") they attended. Similarly, these individuals may believe that sport reinforces "desirable" character traits and this may stimulate their promotion of sport as a "worthy," personally meaningful endeavour (using, obviously, a decidedly ideological interpretation of the term "worthy"). These "explanations" of elite involvement are more palatable than any conspiratorial theory which would explain involvement on the basis of an identified need to control the logic, structure and ideological content of sport and "use" it as a means of social control at the level of total ideology.

Indeed, it seems more likely that sport could be termed one form of "complementary" behaviour in the sense that Baldus (1977) uses the term. Baldus argues that in modern capitalist society there are two strategies which have developed that allow the dominant class to secure "periphery" behaviour in a fashion compatible with system-stability.[17] The first is "interventive control" which "comprises all efforts by the dominant class (or by institutions acting on its behalf) to create needed periphery behaviour through the use of persuasion or coercion" (Baldus, 1977:250). With regard to this strategy, Baldus notes that it is necessary to demonstrate "an empirical connection between a dominant class intervention and resulting change in periphery behaviour" (1977:250) in order to prove that interventive control has been employed. This is the form of social control discussed above vis-à-vis "total" and "particular" ideology.

There is, though, a second strategy which involves "the use of already existing conditions in the periphery which are *not* the intended result of a prior control initiative by the dominant class, but are complementary to its interest" (1977:250); that is, the use of *complementary* periphery behaviour.[18] According to Baldus, complementary behaviour "represents an unsolicited contribution by the periphery to dominant class objectives . . . (and) require(s) only minimal efforts of guidance or exposure to have (its) desired effects" (1977:250-1). Further, it may be extremely diverse, both in form and in the subjective meanings and personal goals attached to it" (1977:251), because it is judged by the dominant class purely in terms of its *instrumental* utility.

> The personal intent which made the periphery unit engage in the behaviour, therefore, can be disregarded. In fact, the use of complementarity usually involved a situation where behaviour directed toward a particular goal of the periphery is used by the dominant class as a means for reaching an entirely different goal. Consequently, periphery units are not aware of the complementarity of their own behaviour. Moreover, the use of complementary periphery behaviour does not require an interaction between dominant class and periphery. It is often the very absence of actions in the periphery, for instance as a result of ignorance because internal strife preoccupies or weakens the periphery, which facilitates the realization of dominant class interests. The use of complementary behaviour therefore allows the dominant class to obtain needed means from a periphery which appears to pursue goals of its own choice, and free of outside interference (Baldus, 1977:251).

Sport's status as a freely chosen leisure time activity, *supposedly* existing separate from political influences, would seem to make it an ideal form of complimentary behaviour. Also, its direct role in the process of capital accumulation, its uncritical promotion of consumption, its tendency to legitimate patterns of competition, power, authority and hierarchy, and its tendency to stifle political involvement on the part of the periphery (with only a minimal "gate-keeping" involvement by the dominant class) would seem to support the "complementarity" thesis.

Leo Panitch's examination of the Canadian state reveals a point that can be related to the discussion of this issue. As noted earlier, Panitch argues that the relationship between the *ideology* and *actuality* of corporate capitalism in Canada reveals that the state plays a very important role on the *behalf* (not on the *behest*) of the bourgeoisie. The state's main role in Canada has been, according to Panitch, to provide an environment suitable for *capital accumulation,* to perform a *coercion* function, and to perform a *legitimation* function. With regard to ideology, liberalism dominates the institutional structure and, therefore, state involvement in the aid of the private sector (contravening liberal "laissez-faire" doctrine) must be justified in terms of its contribution to the "public interest."

Similarly, corporate capitalists only tend to object to governmental interference and invoke liberal "laissez-faire" ideology when it is to their advantage. As Nelles (cited in Panitch, 1975:15) points out:

> The positive state survived the nineteenth century primarily because businessmen found it useful. The province . . . enjoyed the appearance of control over it, while industrialists used the government . . . to provide key services at public expense, promote and protect vested interests, and confer the status of law upon private decisions. . . . The structures established to regulate business in the public interest . . . contributed to a reduction of the state—despite an extension of its activities to a client of the business community.

Panitch stresses throughout his discussion that the Canadian state has been particularly involved in the accumulation function with the result that each of the other two functions—coercion and legitimation—have been left somewhat unattended. If Panitch's argument regarding the neglect of the legitimation function in favour of capital accumulation by the Canadian state is accurate, increasing present-day Canadian government involvement in sport and other forms of cultural policy may be evidence of the beginnings of a more concerted move in the direction of legitimation. I refer here not only to the involvement of the Canadian bourgeoisie as businessmen in the highly lucrative leisure-industrial complex so well described by Hargreaves (1975), but also to recent attempts to promote mass "democratized" sport in Canada as an aspect of the "good life." Indeed, the increasing involvement of the federal government (as part of the state system) in such areas as sport, broadcasting, cultural policy, etc., may well be indicative of a growing necessity for some form of legitimation to be undertaken in order that more overt forms of interventive social control (including physical coercion) do not have to be used to maintain an order which, given contemporary economic difficulties and social upheavals with relation to language rights, regional disputes and so on, is undergoing some considerable stress and criticism.

NOTES

1. See, for example, the Marxist-inspired (but not Marxist) essay by R. T. Naylor, "The Rise and Fall of the Third Commercial Empire of the St. Lawrence" in Gary Teeple's book *Capitalism and the National Question in Canada*. Work on national and continental corporate elite structures has been completed by Wallace Clement, *The Canadian Corporate Elite* (Toronto: McLelland and Stewart, 1975) and *Continental Corporate Power* (Toronto: McLelland and Stewart, 1977). One specific institution which has recently received a considerable amount of attention is the Candian state. Examples of such work include Leo Panitch, "The Role and Nature of the Canadian State" in *The Canadian State: Political*

Economy and Political Power, Leo Panitch (ed.), (Toronto: University of Toronto Press, 1977, pp. 3-27) and Dennis Olsen, *The State Elite in Canadian Society,* Ph.D. dissertation, Carleton University, Ottawa, Ontario, 1978. Much of the work dealing with the analysis of particular historical events relates to the history of Canadian labour; for a good example see David Frank, "Class Conflict in the Coal Industry: Cape Breton 1922," in *Essays in Canadian Working Class History,* G. S. Kealey and P. Warrian (eds.), (Toronto: McLelland and Stewart, 1976, pp. 161-184).

2. In doing so, however, no attempt will be made to evaluate sport's *relative* significance or success in this capacity in comparison with other institutions. Such an evaluation, even if considered plausible at some future date, would be very premature at present given the paucity of theoretical and empirical sociological and social psychological research which has been done on sport and political socialization.

3. The only study I know of dealing with the political attitudes of athletes in Canada is one done by Brian Petrie and Elizabeth Reid, "The Political Attitudes of Canadian Athletes" (1972). It is of questionable value however because of sampling and other methodological difficulties, most notably the use of an *American* political attitude scale (McClosky) to measure the attitudes of *Canadian* athletes.

4. Frank Parkin (1971), Michael Mann (1970, 1973) and Richard Sennett and Jonathan Cobb (1973), among others, while basically in agreement with the argument that there is a "mainstream" ideology characteristic of the institutional structure, caution that it is somewhat of an over-simplification to talk in terms of a coherent, inter-institutional ideology. Parkin (1971) argues that there is a "set" of ideological orientations which generally "accommodate" capitalist political economic organization. More specifically:

> the various agencies of political persuasion . . . do not operate in concert. Many of them are not even 'political' and resolutely shun 'politics'. And none of them, whether 'political' or not, propagates a closely-defined and tightly-woven conservative ideology, let alone an officially-sanctioned one (1971:195).

Similarly, Mann (1970) has provided a degree of empirical support for the argument that at any one point in time there may be a range of value orientations in existence in a capitalist democracy which do not markedly impair general accommodation to the dominant ideology. Indeed, he contends that the working class recognizes the inapplicability of the liberal ideology to their own situation and tends to adopt a purely "pragmatic" acceptance of dominant value structures. Aspects of the argument of Sennett and Cobb echo these sentiments as well.

5. These ideological master symbols or symbolic legitimations of authority vary with historical context. The "divine right of kings" and the "will of the majority," for example, have carried equal ideological clout but have legitimated different, historically-specific forms of political-economic organization.

6. Two observations should be made in this regard. First, it is important to remember that the state is the only institution which has both a legal right and the concrete capacity (via the use of the army, police, etc.) to uses physical coercion to maintain social order. Secondly, though, as T. B. Bottomore has pointed out there have been many instances in which the state has found it necessary to employ physical coercion in order to maintain social order.

> . . . (T)here has grown up an idea that a sympathy with movements of rebellion is somehow more ideological, and a greater threat to sociological objectivity, than is attachment to the status quo. This is obviously not the

case. Nor is it evidently true that violence and the use of force are more prevalent in revolutionary movements than in counter-revolutions or in the defense of an established order. It would be difficult, no doubt, to draw up a balance sheet of violence, but there are numerous historical examples of the savage repression of radical, or even reforming groups in modern societies, . . . and it appears quite probable that the *status quo* is generally defended much more violently than it is attacked (1972:223).

7. "Structural legitimations" of the social order may also exist. In his book, *The Fiscal Crisis of the State* (New York: St. Martin's Press, 1973), James O'Connor argues that the state is playing an increasingly direct and important role in the maintenance of social order and in the creation of conditions amenable to profit-making in the monopoly sector of the capitalist (specifically, American) economy. The crisis of "underconsumption" has resulted, for example, in increased state spending on defence and bureaucracy. Similarly, the growth of unemployment has resulted in an increase in the range and predominance of various kinds of social security. The outcome of the growth of monopoly capitalism in the U.S.A., then, is the growth of what he referred to as the "warfare-welfare state" (1973:99). This would seem to be a variety of structural legitimation.

8. Hargreaves (1975:58) points out that the traditional "liberal" view that sport is apolitical until "tampered with" by the state is a rather naive idea. Thus he argues that:

> "(the) kind of invidious comparison between those societies in which government unambiguously uses sport as a political tool by organizing sport directly on a massive scale, and societies like our own (e.g., Britain, Canada and the United States) where government plays an increasing, but still marginal role in the organization of sport for the masses, is misleading in two ways. First, it directs attention away from the political importance of sport not organized by the state . . . (and) secondly, it considerably underestimates the political significance of the role already played by the state in sport in these societies. There is no good reason for the belief that sport is of less political significance in the west than it is in totalitarian regimes.

9. For specific discussions of early federal government involvement in sport, physical education, recreation and fitness, see Semotiuk (1970), Gear (1973), Sawula 1973), West (1973), and Bedecki (1971).

10. Both the "terms of reference" and the individuals chosen to do the study clearly indicated that the government was not interested in determining if government should become involved in sport, they were interested in determining how government should become more involved in sport. The terms of reference, for example, stated (in part) that the Task Force was directed to ". . . explore ways in which the government could improve further, the extent and quality of Canadian participation in both sport at home and abroad" (1969:ii). Similarly, the individuals chosen to direct the Task Force were Dr. W. Harold Rea, Dr. P. W. des Ruisseaux, and Nancy Greene, each of whom had been very intimately connected with Canadian amateur sport for many years. The following passage from the introduction to the Task Force Report illustrates their collective orientation toward sport.

> Each of us began the task with a conviction that sport is important—important to individuals, communities, and the nation. Thus the expectation would be that we should favour policies which sustain, extend and aggrandize sport. Indeed, persons cool or hostile of sport could accuse us of a lack of objectivity (1969:1).

11. The character of such "social development" is clearly outlined not only in the *Task Force* and the *Sports Policy* but also in the C.O.A. *Record*. There is a tendency in all of these sources to describe the positive contribution of sport vis-a-vis its role in the growth of nationalistic chauvinism and competitiveness.

12. An interesting study would be to determine the amount that has been spent by all levels of government on the provision of programs and facilities for mass involvement as opposed to the recruitment and training of elite athletes. Gruneau makes an interesting observation in this regard.

> . . . Such programs as *Participaction* notwithstanding, funding seems overwhelmingly directed to sporting associations, the majority of which are especially concerned with the production of quality athletes. For example, in 1972-73 according to a pamphlet detailing the membership and functions of the "Canadian Sports Federation" *Sport Canada* was to receive 6.5 million in grants and *Recreation Canada* 2.3 million. Most of Sport Canada's money was earmarked for (elite-oriented) sporting associations. . . . Moreover, given that the period from 1970 to the present has involved a major push for Olympic success—*production* has clearly superceded *participation* as *the* major goal for sports policy (1976b:135).

13. Note that this and other of the preconditions mentioned in this "model" are discussed by Panitch (1977) in his outline of a preliminary theory of the Canadian state (1977).

14. In Chapter Nine of *The Canadian Corporate Elite,* Clement poses the rhetorical question, "Can it, in fact, be said that the economic and media elite are actually one: the corporate elite?". His answer?

> . . . the overlap (of the media elite) with the economic elite is extensive, almost one half the members are the same people. Moreover, those not overlapped resemble very closely the economic elite. The conclusion must be that together *the economic and media elite are simply two sides to the same upper class* (Clement, 1975:325).

It is necessary to point out that Elizabeth Baldwin (1977a, 1977b) has disagreed with Clement's figures. Via a more consistent and stringent set of decision rules and by including the C.B.C. in the analysis of the media elite, she was able to reduce the overlap from 49% to 26.2%.

15. Interestingly, it appears that material conditions are such that this liberal ideological perspective, so evident in the institutional structure, does not correspond at all to the corporate collegial value orientation espoused by many of the elite. That is, entrepreneurial capitalism has given way, in Canada, to corporate capitalism. This appears to have resulted in a situation where the structural characteristics of corporate capitalism are being justified by a flourishing but somewhat anachronistic free-market liberal ideology. The Canadian economic elite, it might be argued, has reaped the benefits of a situation where ideology "lags behind" structural and material conditions in Canadian society. They espouse a competitive, liberal, free-market ideology and a "laissez-faire" government policy toward business while at the same time they have continued to expand and centralize their operations to such a degree that they have developed almost monopolistic control over many of the different sectors of the Canadian economy. They are thus placed in the ironic position of having obtained a position of power through the progressive exploitation of the system of "free enterprise" (and can publicly invoke liberal "laissez-faire" ideology) despite the fact that they have guaranteed themselves a position of considerable economic, political and social influence by having limited the economic growth of competitors through the use of monopoly capitalist practices.

16. Baldus defines the "periphery" as all those who do not own productive capital—that is, the means of production. Those who do have access to private ownership of productive capital are the "dominant class."

17. Baldus describes his framework for analysis as follows:

   If the dominant class in capitalist societies has as its major objective the maximization of surplus profit and the accumulation of capital, three specific means requirements have to be met. They represent the main areas of contact between dominant class and periphery, because in all three the cooperation of the periphery has to be secured. The first is the protection of the institution of private property, of the means of production, and of the rights connected with it. The second requirement is the delivery of a sufficient flow of work inputs and members of the periphery. These two means requirements existed of course in feudal societies as well. The third—peculiar only to capitalism—is the need to assure the consumption of the surplus product created in the capitalist mode of production (Baldus, 1977: 249).

18. It is not my intention here to claim that many of the features of sport in capitalist society are not also characteristic of sport in communist countries—nations where sport is an excessively competitive, *hierarchical* institution *should not* be found. It is clear, however, that sport in the Soviet Union and in other communist countries throughout the world is as intensely competitive and as much a vehicle for the development of nationalism and international prestige as it is in capitalist society. To develop an explanation and analysis of this state of affairs is not within the scope of this paper. However, so as not to completely avoid the issue, I offer the following observations for your consideratioin. The process of revolution, as Marx stated, is a continuous one. The simple establishment of the dictatorship of the proletariat and the abolishment of private property is a necessary but insufficient condition for the "positive transcendance" of capitalist society. By placing all property and power in the hands of a centralized state, the capitalist order has been only quantitatively and not qualitatively transcended. Such is the situation, for example, in the Soviet Union. Until the revolutionary process removes the State from its position as (effective) capitalist and until more of the nations of the world experience similar proletarian revolutions, competition and hierarchy will continue to be the hallmark of all areas of social endeavour, including sport, both nationally and internationally. The sport of the Soviet Union reflects many characteristics of bourgeois sport simply because the process of revolution has not gone far enough to create the conditions necessary to allow for the growth of a more informal, participation-oriented form of involvement in recreative physical activity. Indeed, given that "sport" as we know it seems by nature, if not by definition, to be hierarchical (that is, always involving a winner and a loser) it might be argued that in a truly communist society, sport as we know it would not exist.

REFERENCES

Aronowitz, Stanley. *False Promises: The Shaping of American Working Class Consciousness.* New York: McGraw-Hill, 1973.

Axthelm, Peter. *The City Game.* New York: Harper's, 1970.

Baldwin, Elizabeth. "The Mass Media and the Corporate Elite: A Re-analysis of the Overlap Between the Media and Economic Elites." *Canadian Journal of Sociology,* 2(1), 1977 (a).

————. "On Methodological and Theoretical Muddles in Clement's Media Study." *Canadian Journal of Sociology*, 2(2), 1977 (b).

Boileau, Roger, Y. Trempe and F. Landry. "Les Canadiens francais et les grands jeux internationaux." In Richard S. Gruneau and John G. Albinson (eds.) *Canadian Sport: Sociological Perspectives*. Toronto: Addison-Wesley, 1976.

Bottomore, T. B. *Classes in Modern Society*. New York: Vintage Books, 1966.

Brohm, J. "Sociologie politique du sport." In G. Berthaud et al (eds.), *Sport, Culture et Repression*. Paris: Petite Maspero, 1972.

Clement, W. *The Canadian Corporate Elite: An Analysis of Economic Power*. Toronto: McClelland and Stewart, 1975.

Curtis, J. and B. Milton. "Social Status and the 'Active Society': National Data on Correlates of Leisure-Time Physical and Sport Activities." In Richard S. Gruneau and John G. Albinson (eds.), *Canadian Sport: Sociological Perspectives*. Toronto: Addison-Wesley, 1976.

Frank, David. "Class Conflict in the Coal Industry in Cape Breton, 1922." In G. S. Kealey and P. Warrian (eds.), *Essays in Canadian Working Class History*. Toronto: McClelland and Stewart, 1976.

Gardner, Howard. *The Quest for Mind*. London: Quartet, 1976.

Geertz, Clifford. "Deep Play: Notes on the Balinese Cockfight." *Daedalus*, Winter, 1972.

Gruneau, Richard S. "Sport, Social Differentiation and Social Inequality." In D. Ball and J. W. Loy (eds.), *Sport and Social Order*. Reading: Addison-Wesley, 1975.

————. "Sport as an Area of Sociological Study." In Richard S. Gruneau and John G. Albinson (eds.), *Canadian Sport: Sociological Perspectives*. Toronto: Addison-Wesley, 1976 (a).

————. "Class or Mass: Notes on the Democratization of Canadian Amateur Sport." In Richard S. Gruneau and John G. Albinson (eds.), *Canadian Sport: Sociological Perspectives*. Toronto: Addison-Wesley, 1976b.

————. "Elites, Class and Corporate Power in Canadian Sport: Some Preliminary Findings." In W. Orban and F. Landry (eds.), *Sociology of Sports*. Miami: Symposia Specialists, 1978.

————. "Power and Play in Canadian Social Development." *Working Papers in the Sociological Study of Sports and Leisure*. Kingston: Sports Studies Research Group, Queen's University, Vol. 2, No. 1, 1979 (in press).

Hall, M. Ann. "Sport and Physical Activity in the Lives of Canadian Women." In Richard S. Gruneau and John G. Albinson (eds.), *Candian Sport: Sociological Perspectives*. Toronto: Addison-Wesley, 1976.

Hare, Nathan. "The Occupational Culture of the Black Fighter." In J. Talamini and Charles Page (eds.), *Sport and Society*. Boston: Little Brown, 1973.

Hargreaves, John. "The Political Economy of Mass Sport." In Stanley Parker et al (eds.), *Sport and Leisure in Contemporary Society*. School of the Environment, Polytechnic of London, 1976.

Heller, C. S. *Structural Social Inequality*. Toronto: Collier-Macmillan, 1969.

Hellison, Donald R. *Humanistic Physical Education*. Englewood Cliffs, New Jersey: Prentice-Hall, 1973.

Helmes, Richard C. "Canadian Sport as an Ideological Institution." Unpublished M.A. thesis, Queen's University at Kingston, 1977.

Henricks, Thomas. "Professional Wrestling as Moral Order." *Sociological Inquiry*, Vol. 44, No. 3, 1974.

Hoch, Paul. *Rip Off the Big Game: The Exploitation of Sports by the Power Elite*. New York: Anchor Books, 1972.

Howell, Max and F. Cosentino. *A History of Physical Education in Canada*. Don Mills: General Publishing, 1971.

Huizinga, Johan. *Homo Ludens: A Study of the Play Element in Culture*. Boston: Beacon Press, 1955.

Ingham, Alan G. "Occupational Subcultures in the Work World of Sport." In D. Ball and J. W. Loy (eds.), *Sport and Social Order*. Reading: Addison-Wesley, 1975.

Jay, Martin. *The Dialectical Imagination*. Boston: Little Brown, 1973.

Jobling, Ian. "Urbanization and Sport in Canada, 1867-1900." In Richard S. Gruneau and John G. Albinson (eds.), *Canadian Sport: Sociological Perspectives*. Toronto: Addison-Wesley, 1976.

Johnson, Leo. "The Development of Class in Canada in the Twentieth Century." In G. Teeple (ed.), *Capitalism and the National Question in Canada*. Toronto: University of Toronto Press, 1972.

Kealey, G. S. and P. Warrian. *Essays in Canadian Working Class History*. Toronto: McClelland and Stewart, 1976.

Laguillaumie, Pierre. "Pour une critique fondamentale du sport." In G. Berthaud (ed.), *Sport, Culture et Repression*. Paris: Petite Maspero, 1972.

Lenin, V. I. *Imperialism, the Highest Stage of Capitalism: A Popular Outline*. Peking: Foreign Languages Press, 1973.

Levasseur, Roger. "Sport: structures, representations ideologiques et symboliques." In Richard S. Gruneau and John G. Albinson (eds.), *Canadian Sport: Sociological Perspectives*. Toronto: Addison-Wesley, 1976.

Listiak, Alan. "Legitimate Deviance and Social Class: Bar Behaviour During Grey Cup Week." In Richard S. Gruneau and John G. Albinson (eds.), *Canadian Sports Sociological Perspectives*. Toronto: Addison-Wesley, 1976.

Lucas, Rex. "Sport and Recreation in Communities of Single Industry." In Richard S. Gruneau and John G. Albinson (eds.), *Canadian Sport: Sociological Perspectives*. Toronto: Addison-Wesley, 1976.

Mallea, John. "The Victorian Sporting Legacy." *McGill Journal of Education*, 10 (2), 1975.

Mann, Michael. "The Social Cohesion of Liberal Democracy." *American Sociological Review* (XXXV), 1970.

———. *Consciousness and Action Among the Western Working Class*. London: The Macmillan Press, 1973.

Mannheim, Karl. *Ideology and Utopia: An Introduction to the Sociology of Knowledge*. London: Routledge and Kegan Paul, 1936.

Marchak, Patricia. *Ideological Perspectives on Canada*. Toronto: McGraw-Hill Ryerson, 1975.

Marcuse, Herbert. *One-Dimensional Man: Studies in the Ideology of Advanced Industrial Society*. Boston: Beacon Press, 1968.

Marx, Karl and F. Engels. "The German Ideology." In R. Tucker (ed.), *The Marx-Engels Reader*. New York: W. W. Norton, 1972.

Metcalfe, Alan. "Organized Sport and Social Stratification in Montreal." In Richard S. Gruneau and John G. Albinson (eds.), *Canadian Sport: Sociological Perspectives*. Toronto: Addison-Wesley, 1976.

Miliband, Ralph. *The State in Capitalist Society*. London: Quartet Books, 1969.

Miller, D. M. and K. Russell. *Sport: A Contemporary View*. Philadelphia: Lea and Febiger, 1971.

Naylor, R. T. "The Rise and Fall of the Third Commercial Empire of the St. Lawrence." In G. Teeple (ed.), *Capitalism and the National Question in Canada*. Toronto: University of Toronto Press, 1972.

———. *The History of Canadian Business*. Toronto: James Lorimer, 1975.

O'Connor, James. *The Fiscal Crisis of the State*. New York: St. Martin's Press, 1973.

Orlick, Terry and C. Botterill. *Every Kid Can Win*. Chicago: Nelson-Hall, 1975.

Page, Charles. "The World of Sport and its Study." In J. Talamini and C. Page (eds.), *Sport and Society: An Anthology*. Boston: Little, Brown and Co., 1973.

Panitch, Leo. "The Role and Nature of the Canadian State." In L. Panitch (ed.), *The Canadia State: Political Economy and Political Power*. Toronto: University of Toronto Press, 1977.

Parkin, Frank. *Class Inequality and Political Order*. London: Paladin Books, 1971.

Petrie, Brian. "Sport and Politics." In D. Ball and J. Loy (eds.), *Sport and Social Order*. Reading: Addison-Wesley, 1975.

Petrie, Brian and Elizabeth Reid. "The Political Attitudes of Canadian Athletes." Paper presented at the Fourth Canadian Psycho-Motor Learning and Sport Psychology Symposium, Waterloo, October 22-25, 1972.

Porter, John. *The Vertical Mosaic*. Toronto: University of Toronto Press, 1965.

Real, Michael R. "Super Bowl: Mythic Spectacle." *Journal of Communications*, (Winter), 1975.

Rigauer, Bero. *Sport und Arbeit*. Frankfurt: Suhrkamp, 1969.

Sahlins, Marshall. *Stone Age Economics*. Chicago: Aldine, 1972.

———. *Culture and Practical Reason*. Chicago: Aldine, 1976.

Scott, Jack. *The Athletic Revolution*. New York: The Free Press, 1971.

Seeley, J. R., R. A. Sim and E. W. Loosely. *Crestwood Heights: A Study of the Culture of Suburban Life*. Toronto: University of Toronto Press, 1956.

Sennett, R. and J. Cobb. *The Hidden Injuries of Class*. New York: Vintage Books, 1973.

Teeple, Gary. "Land, Labour and Capital in Pre-Confederation Canada." In G. Teeple (ed.), *Capitalism and the National Question in Canada*. Toronto: University of Toronto Press, 1972.

Veblen, Thorstein. *The Theory of the Leisure Class*. New York: Macmillan, 1953.

Webb, Harry. "Professionalization of Attitudes Toward Play in Adolescents." In G. S. Kenyon (ed.), *Aspects of Contemporary Sport Sociology*. Chicago: The Athletic Institute, 1969.

Weber, Max. *The Protestant Ethic and the Spirit of Capitalism*. New York: Scribners, 1958.

Wise, S. F. "Sport and Class Values in Late Nineteenth-Century Canada." Paper presented at the Annual Meetings of the North American Society for Sport History, Windsor, 1974.

Zureik, Elia and R. M. Pike. *Socialization and Values in Canadian Society* (Vol. I). Toronto: McClelland and Stewart, 1975.

Zureik, Elia and A. Frizzell. "Values in Canadian Magazine Fiction: A Test of the Social Control Thesis." *Journal of Popular Culture*, Vol. 10, No. 2, 1976.

Capitalism, Protestantism, and Modern Sport

Allen Guttmann

Modern sport, a ubiquitous and unique form of nonutilitarian physical contests, took shape over a period of approximately 150 years, from
the early eighteenth to the late nineteenth centuries. Speaking historically,
we can be reasonably precise about place as well as time. Modern sports
were born in England and spread from their birthplace to the United
States, to Western Europe, and to the world beyond. The origins of modern sports have been chronicled in hundreds of books and articles and
particular sports have had their industrious historians, but only a handful
of scholars, mostly Europeans, have attempted to *explain* the rise of modern sports. The most persuasive explanations have been stimulated by the
insights of Karl Marx and Max Weber, neither of whom wrote very much
about sports.

1. A MARXIST INTERPRETATION

Marxist interpretations of the rise of modern sports begin with the
materialist conception of history. In the Marxist view, sports are invariably related to the organization of the modes of production. Even in
the Stone Age, "Physical exercises . . . were originally one with the means
of production (*Arbeitsprozeß*)."[1] Men ran, heaved rocks, and cast spears
in order to improve their skills as hunters. Survival depended on physical
prowess. What was true of the "sports" of the Stone Age remains true, in
different circumstances, today. Marxist historians have consistently analyzed the rise of modern sports from this materialist perspective. Medieval sports mirrored feudal society and modern sports are the product
of Liberal capitalism, that is, of bourgeois society. There is enough truth
in this interpretation to reward an investigation of it. I shall, for the rest

of this section, write from their point of view, without constant qualifications such as "from a Marxist perspective." My criticisms appear in section 3.

Medieval sports served the interest of the feudal nobility which was the effective ruling class of the Middle Ages.[2] Sports were of many kinds; even the peasants had their rude games, their running, wrestling, fighting with staves, their rough-and-tumble version of what eventually became modern soccer. The sports of the peasantry tended to be those which kept them physically fit for the strenuous tasks of agricultural labor. Sports were one means to maintain their labor power (*Arbeitskraft*) at a suitably exploitable level.

The sports of the nobility also bore the marks of their origins in the world of work. On the one hand, there were hunting, fishing, and hawking—all of which were pastimes open to ladies as well as to lords, all of which were injurious to the lower orders of society who were often dependent on hunting or fishing to supplement their diets or who suffered economically when their rulers pursued game through cultivated areas. Frequently, the right to hunt or hawk was restricted to the nobility. Poachers were cruelly punished. In addition to the "field sports" which evolved directly from the world of productive work, there were sports immediately related to the realities of political power. There were tournaments and jousts, the first a miniature battle between a large number of armored horsemen, the second a combat between two mounted knights. In a world based on rule by physical force, play itself symbolized the relationship between classes. The tournament was mock warfare, sport, a demonstration of martial ability, and a subtle warning to those who might dream of a more egalitarian social order.

The class relationships of capitalist society are governed by different modes of production from those of the Middle Ages. Different social imperatives led to different kinds of sports and, more importantly, to different conceptions of the nature of sports.

The gross disparities in the distribution of wealth obtained from industrial and financial capitalism led to increased differentiation in the kinds of sports enjoyed by the rich and the poor. The lords of the land became landlords, and they laid aside the weapons of a feudal age. Sports lost their directly political function—it is impossible to crush a rebellion with a golf club—and certain sports became the expression of a leisured class.[3] Golf and tennis continued to be the prerogative of the ruling class, but there was no longer any need to confine them to the wealthy by royal edict or by threats of dire punishment. Economic cost sufficed. Tennis, for instance, requires an expensive court and must be learned slowly,

which often implies professional lessons and always means the investment of considerable time. The traditional clothing of tennis, immaculate
"whites," was a subtle reminder to upstarts that proper dress was in itself
beyond the means of most people. For the very rich, for whom even golf
and tennis had become too popular, there was always polo or yachting.
Consider, for example, *The Book of Sport,* published in New York in
1901. This sumptuous, lavishly illustrated tome contains essays on golf,
court-tennis, racquets, hand-fives, squash, lawn-tennis, polo, fox-hunting,
yatching, and coaching. Of the last, driving about in horsedrawn car-
riages, Oliver H. P. Belmond opined, "No sport which requires the perfection of skill and dash and the exercise of nerve will ever be abandoned
by Americans."[4] Absent from *The Book of Sport* was any mention of the
sports that most Americans played.

In capitalist society, sports like soccer and baseball are reserved for
the laboring classes. These sports have as their major goal the maintenance of a maximally productive work-force. "What happens or is allowed
to happen in the worker's leisure time is determined by the necessity,
in a capitalist society, for labor power (*Arbeitskraft*) to be reproduced."[5]
It is also necessary to provide some kind of compensation for the cramped
physical conditions of assembly-line production, lest illness reduce the
worker's labor power to zero.

The sports of the elite are means of socialization by which the rulers
can develop those traits of character and leadership necessary for dominion at home and abroad. The sports of the proletariat, on the other
hand, are vehicles for a different sort of socialization. They tend to be
team sports which inculcate subordination and acceptance of authority,
authority symbolized most immediately in the person of the coach. They
initiate youth into the routines of the industrial system and they act to
divert potentially revolutionary energies from politics.

It was inevitable, therefore, that England, the homeland of industrial capitalism, was also the birthplace of modern sports. The aston-
ishing readiness of the English to wager money on horse races, foot races,
and boxing was commented upon by many observers. In the words of
an eighteenth-century French commentator on English customs, "The
probability of life, and the return of ships, are the objects of their arith-
metic. The same habit of calculating they extend to games, wagers, and
everything in which there is any hazard."[6]

This readiness to wager on horses, cocks, bears, ships, and pugilistic
butchers paralleled the increased willingness to risk venture capital in
the development of England's expanding industry. From the eagerness

to risk and wager came the need to measure time and space. The capitalist's ledgers are close kin to the scorecard. We suddenly enter the world of the bookkeeper and the bookie.

In the nineteenth century, public schools like Rugby, Eton, Harrow, and Winchester joined with Oxford and Cambridge to create an ethos of fair play, good sportsmanship, and business acumen. Thomas Hughes' famous novel, *Tom Brown's Schooldays* (1857), is the dramatic embodiment of the regnant values of Thomas Arnold's Ruby School, where the sons of the middle class learned the lessons of bourgeois Liberalism. To Oxford and Cambridge went the graduates of the public schools. From Oxford and Cambridge the energetic British soldier, civil servant, or businessman went forth to Vancouver, Madras, Cape Town, or Melbourne. And brought with him the marvels of modern sports.

As early as 1830, Englishmen resident in Germany founded the Hamburg Rowing Club. Within five years after Major (Ret.) Walter Wingate invented lawn tennis in 1873, the exciting new game had spread to Germany, the United States, Brazil, India, and Australia. The British founded the Dresden Football Club in 1890 and the following year they founded the White Rovers at Paris. Three years later, the son of an English family living in Brazil brought soccer to Sao Paulo. In 1896, the son of Hungarian immigrants to England visited his relatives and introduced soccer to Hungary. A similar story can be told about a dozen other sports, from rugby to badminton. We can sense the force of the British model when we note that the Hamburg Sport Club of 1880 held its races in English distances, and when we see that the most famous athletic clubs of France tended to have English names, like le Racing-Club de France (1882).

TABLE 1

The Diffusion of Modern Sports

(By year of organization)

	English	U.S.	French	German	Swedish
Football Assoc.	1863	1913	1919	1900	1904
Amateur Swimming Assoc.	1869	1878	1889	1886	1904
Bicyclists Union	1878	1881	1881	1884	1900
Metropolitan Rowing Assoc.	1879	1872	1890	1883	1904
Amateur Athletic Union	1880	1888	1887	1891	1895
Lawn Tennis Assoc.	1888	1881	1889	1902	1906

The receptivity of a nation to the ecological invasion of modern sport is in itself an index of that nation's industrial development. Despite the accidents of historical transmission and all the other uncertainties of such an investigation, it is nonetheless remarkable how the spread of modern sports organizations correlates with the rise of industrialism. According to W. W. Rostow's study *The Stages of Economic Growth* (1960), the first five nations to "take off" into the stage of sustained economic growth were Great Britain, France, the United States, Germany, and Sweden. Table 1 clearly demonstrates that the first nations to industrialize were also the first to establish national organizations for modern sports, in almost the same order.[7] By concentrating on *national* organizations, I have sought to minimize the distortions caused by such factors as a group of British businessmen setting up a single soccer club totally out of character with the indigenous sports of the host country. If we calculate Kendall's coefficient of concordance, which will be 1.0 if the sequence is always England-America-France-Germany-Sweden and 0 if the sequence is always reversed, the coefficient of concordance is quite high, .637, which strongly suggests *some* relationship between the pace of industrialism and the spread of modern sports.[8]

In the early nineteenth century, modern sports were—like capitalism itself—a progressive force, more democratic than the medieval sports they superseded, but the development of industrial capitalism led to forms of exploitation which were even grimmer than those of feudalism. Sports began to play an increasingly conservative and reactionary role. One sign of this has been the intense commercialization of sports everywhere outside the orbits of the Soviet Union and the People's Republic of China. The tendency to transform human behavior into transactions of the marketplace has made sports into a matter of profit and loss. The structure of amateur sports demands on ticket sales to college games and to meets sponsored by sports organizations like the AAU. The sporting goods and recreation industries are large and complex. The structure of professional sports is openly rather than covertly commercial. Corporations and wheeler-dealer millionaires own teams and take advantage of the tax laws to profit economically while complaining all the while of the unprofitability of their franchises. Major-league baseball depends on the Supreme Court's special exemption from antitrust legislation while other professional team sports must limp along with depreciation allowances on their players, with enormous revenues from commercial television, with stadiums donated by gratefully bilked municipalities, and with the leverage of extralegal rather than wholly legal monopolies. The result? Teenagers sell themselves into semibondage for millions of dollars, "amateur" athletes earn enough *sub rosa* to grumble about their losses when they become professionals, drug-abuse accompanies the desperate desire to share in the winner's bonus. All in all, an unattractive picture.[9]

In addition to commercialism, Western sports have increasingly been vehicles for the inculcation of militarism, nationalism, and imperialism. In the 1920s and 1930s, the leaders of sports were ready to welcome Fascism. The French novelist Henry de Montherlant wrote *Les Olympiques* (1920, 1938) and *Le Songe* (1922) in which athleticism was a metaphor for a Fascist view of the world. Edmund Neuendorff, leader of the *Deutsche Turnerschaft*, congratulated Hitler on becoming chancellor and affirmed that the German gymnastics movement marched side by side with Hitler's Storm Troops.[10] The 1936 Olympics, staged in Berlin under Hitler's aegis, symbolize the marriage of Nazism and modern sports. Since World War II, the United States and the nations of Western Europe have continued to use sports as a means to indoctrinate the masses with the virus of militarism, nationalism, and imperialism. On the occasion of the founding of East Germany's national sports organization, the *Deutscher Turn- und Sportbund* (1957), its president announced, "The DTSB incorporates social democracy in sports and finds its firm basis in the principle of democratic centralism. In West Germany, on the contrary, democracy is ground under foot. A small group of imperialists and militarists rules over the majority of the people. These conditions are mirrored in sport."[11] Nearly twenty years later, in the new era of détente, East Germany's chief theoretical journal for sports studies, *Theorie und Praxis der Körperkultur*, continued to denounce the militarism and imperialism of bourgeois sports.[12]

The final stage of historical development comes with the emergence of socialism, which eliminates the exploitative relationship between the capitalist and the worker. Since the mode of production is transformed, it is inevitable that sports too are transformed. In the Soviet Union and in the nations of Eastern Europe, sports continue to be a means of socialization (in the psychological sense), but the lessons learned are utterly unlike those of the past. In addition to their recreational function, sports are elements in national security and economic productivity. In the Soviet Union there is an entire system of physical culture, beginning with compulsory exercises for preschool children and including organized sports within the schools and universities as well as in factories and offices, regular "Spartakiades" which involve tens of millions of contestants throughout the entire area of the USSR, seven levels of athletic achievement ranging from "Youthful Achievement Second Class" to Honored Master of Sport," advanced research at dozens of university-centers, and constant supervision by governmental and party authorities. Ideologically, the system can be traced back to the Third Congress of Komsomol (Young Communist League) in October 1920, when, in Lenin's presence, the delegates resolved that[13]

> the physical education of the younger generation is an essential element in the overall system of the Communist upbringing of young people, aimed at creating harmoniously developed people, creative citizens of Communist society. Today, physical education also has direct practical aims: (1) preparing young people for work; and (2) preparing them for military defense of Soviet power.

In line with this policy, Ministers of Sport and Tourism urge the people of every Communist country to maintain their physical fitness through calisthenics and sports in order to raise the level of industrial output and to contribute to the defense of socialist society. The importance of this theme is reflected in constitutional provisions. Article 18 of the Constitution of the German Democratic Republic affirms, for example, that "Physical education (*Körperkultur*), Sports, and Tourism are elements of socialist culture and further the citizen's all-around physical and spiritual development."[14] A less official but scarcely less prominent goal is competition with athletes from capitalist nations in order to demonstrate the superiority of the socialist way of life.

Under socialism, sports are available as never before to both sexes, to all races, and to all classes. "Universal sport," comments a leading Polish sociologist, "requires the removal of all kinds of social divisions. . . . Sport for all assumes the abolition of every social, national, class-linked, sexual, and racial discrimination."[15] Sports cease to be associated with nationalism and imperialism. They contribute to the creation of what Marxists refer to as "New Socialist Man." "As is generally known, the Soviet Union is successfully resolving the task of an all-round development of man."[16] Sports are an integral part of that success.

This, briefly, is the historical development of modern sports as interpreted by Marxist scholars. Before evaluating this interpretation, it will be helpful to examine the work of the Neo-Marxists.

2. THE NEO-MARXIST CRITIQUE

The Marxist interpretation of the rise of modern sports begins in more or less objective analysis and ends in polemics. The closer the discussion comes to the present, the less disinterested, the more passionate. The Neo-Marxist critique commences with the fundamental criticism of Western sports made by Marxist scholars and extends the criticism into a wholesale indictment not simply of the alleged perversions of sport under contemporary capitalism but of the very idea of sports. While Marxist theorists condemn the alleged militarism and imperialism of West-German sports, while American radicals such as Jack Scott and Harry Edwards expose the authoritarianism and racism of the "sports estab-lishment" of the United States, the Neo-Marxists are still more radical. They reject not merely the abuses of the institution but the institution it-self. They hold that sports in their *ideal* form—sports as described by coaches, physical educators, and administrators—are a perversion of the human spirit.

The theoretical sources of Neo-Marxism lie partly in Marx, especially in the early, more philosophical writings, and partly in Freud, whose the-ory of the unconscious is a necessary element in the argument that workers (or athletes) who seem satisfied with the status quo are victims of "false consciousness," i.e., they do not really understand their own interests. In-stitutionally, Neo-Marxism flourished in the 1920s at Frankfurt's *Institut für Sozialforschung,* where Theodor Adorno, Max Horkheimer, and Her-bert Marcuse labored in fruitful collaboration. Although none of the great figures of prewar Neo-Marxism has devoted an entire book to the phe-nomenon of sports, passages in Adorno's *Prismen* (1955) and *Erziehung zur Mündigkeit* (1970) have been an important stimulus for Bero Ri-gauer, Gerhard Vinnai, Jean-Marie Brohm, and other spokesman for the Neo-Marxist critique of sports which sprang up in Germany and France in the 1960s.

As in the previous section, it is important to understand the Neo-Marxist position before we attempt an evaluation of it. Once again, I shall synthesize from their point of view and hold my own criticisms in abeyance.

Of the seven characteristics of modern sports, the Neo-Marxists are quite ready to accept the first two—secularism and equality—but spe-cialization represents the beginnings of evil. Consider, for instance, the field-goal kicker of an American football team. Is there a more absurd symbol of specialization in modern sports? Is he an athlete or a figure from a film by Charlie Chaplin? Can he be held up as an example of *mens sana in corpore sano?* Does he feel a surge of animal pleasure as his foot meets the ball and his five seconds of "play" come to an end? Consider, similarly, the single-minded dedication necessary to become the world's best highjumper or hammer-thrower. Consider the months and the years of rigorous training, the abnegations, the self-discipline, the asceticism, the cultivated onesidedness. How different is the high-jumper or the hammer-thrower from the exploited bolt-tightener on the assembly line? Marx wrote in *Die Deutsche Ideologie* (1845-1846) of the whole man, of the fully developed human capable of an infinite variety of activities:[17]

> As soon as the division of labor sets in, each man develops a certain exclusive range of activity, which is imposed on him, which he cannot avoid or escape. He is a hunter, a fisherman, or a herder, or a critic, and he must remain what he is, if he doesn't want to risk his livelihood, but in the communist society of the future, where no one is restricted to a limited range of activity, it will be possible to do one thing today, another tomorrow, to hunt in the morning, to fish in the afternoon, to be a herdsman in the evening, to criticize one's meal—without becoming a hunter, a fisherman, a herder, or a critic.

The Neo-Marxist extends the list of limited identities—hunter, fisherman, herder, critic, sprinter, left tackle, relief pitcher, goalie.

Simultaneously with the advent of specialization, man becomes mechanical, the athlete is metamorphosed into a cog in the machinery of sports. "The champion," writes a French critic, "is fabricated in the image of the worker and the track in the image of the factory. Athletic activity has become a form of production and takes on all characteristics of industrial production."[18] A German scholar makes a similar point: "Man becomes an interchangeable part on the playing field as in the office and the factory. . . . Man becomes a kind of machine and his movements, controlled by apparatus, become mechanical."[19] The final result of specialization is, paradoxically, a mechanical perfection with no human quirks to hinder replacement or substitution.

Rationalization in sports is equally incompatible with spontaneity and inventiveness. There is no modern sport which does not have codified rules and regulations, but why shouldn't we play whatever game we want to play, in whatever manner and spirit we choose? The rule-boundedness of modern sports is thus the athletic equivalent of a paint-by-the-numbers kit.

There is more to rationalization than the coercion of the spontaneous impulses of *Homo ludens*. Bourgeois theorists boast that sports offer a model of fair play through adherence to the rules of the game. The Neo-Marxists maintain that society's rules are exploitative, grossly unfair, and immoral. Sport helps to socialize us into accepting rules which are inherently unjust and unfair and into assuming falsely that justice can be subsumed under fair play. "The individual is compelled to follow 'the rules of the game' upon which he has had no influence and through which the privileges of the ruling class are preserved."[20] The real task is to realize the class nature of society's rules and regulations. They are rational means to an irrational end, namely, the maintenance of the repressive power of the capitalist class.

Bureaucratic organization? The phrase itself reeks of inhumanity. Individual athletes become helpless pawns in the hands of a power structure composed of retired athletes, government functionaries, or wealthy businessmen with an interest in (and frequently a profit from) sports. Decisions are made in an authoritarian way by officials accountable to no one, certainly not to the athletes whose lives they callously manipulate. Edicts are handed down and there is neither discussion nor appeal. "The individual athlete shrinks into the object of alienated centralized administration."[21] The AAU and the NCAA struggle for power and the helpless athlete finds himself barred from contests, suspended, thwarted, humiliated.

Quantification? The living, breathing person, the simple, separate person praised by Whitman and evoked by Wordsworth and the German Romantic poets disappears into the abstraction of numbers. "Into all human relationships, into all sectors of social life, capitalism begets quantification."[22] In a capitalist society, the human personality becomes a salary, a serial number, a batting average. Despite the elegant rhetoric about playing the game rather than thinking about the numbers, the spectator's attention becomes fixed in a relentless search for quantification. There is no time left for considerations of grace, no room for fair play, no chance to respond to the kinesthetic sense of physical exuberance. The phenomenon of alienation, by which the worker disappears into the fetish of the commodities he produces, can be seen most clearly when the individual athlete vanishes into the abstraction and becomes the ten-second man or the .300 hitter. Jimmy Brown, surely one of football's greatest running backs, reveals as much when he admits, "I hold more than a dozen records and as a result have been turned into a statistic."[23]

The extreme form of this tendency is, as we have seen, the emphasis on records, on the most repressive form of quantification. The fetish of achievement is no longer satisfied by victory in the contest itself. In capitalist society, even the winner of the race becomes a loser when his time disappoints the crowd's expectations. What are the Olympic games or the Super Bowl without a harvest of records? The quest for records fuels the drive for more intense specialization, for longer, harder, more physically punishing training. The result is that almost everyone, except the handful of athletes who set the (always temporary) records, is left with a sense of frustration and failure.

To the Marxist critique of sports under capitalism and to the rejection of the distinguishing characteristics of modern sport, the followers of Adorno and Marcuse add specific charges about the insidious function of sports. The most important charge is that sports are designed as sexual sublimation. Sports release sexual impulses in the form of aggression. If these impulses had been left repressed, they might have exploded in the form of political revolution, which is, of course, the outcome to be avoided if capitalism is to survive. Sexual repression is, according to Marcuse, a necessary part of capitalism, but sports provide a safety valve when the repression becomes excessive. Sports drain off repressed sexual energy which cannot, for whatever reason, be profitably utilized by the economic system. Through the psychological mechanism of identification, the spectators join vicariously in the sublimation achieved by the players on the field.

The precise form of this sublimation is important. Sexual repression produces aggression and it is aggression that is directly released through sports, aggression which might otherwise destabilize the entire system of political control. "The aggression derived from sexual repression can thus be released (*kompensiert*) through the athletic achievements and competitions."[24] Unfortunately, the transformation of sexual energies into physical aggression is imperfect. Sexuality appears in sports as sexuality—but only in the forms of perversion, as sadism, masochism, narcissism, and homosexuality. "The erotic life of the athlete demonstrates a strange schizophrenia; in its physiological aspects, it is heterosexual, but in its psychic aspects it corresponds to the erotic dispositions of early childhood, and it is accordingly homosexual."[25] The athlete's wife may satisfy his lust, but his teammates are the objects of his love. Football, argues Paul Hoch, is "America's Number One fake-masculinity ritual," an ironic, unconscious display of the very perversions that athletes and spectators most despise.[26]

In short, sport is "the capitalistically distorted form of play."[27] Sport is not an escape from the world of work but rather an exact structural and functional parallel to the world of work. Sport does not offer compensation for the frustrations of alienated labor in capitalist society; it seduces the luckless athlete and spectator into a second world of work more authoritarian and repressive and less meaningful than the economic sphere itself. Capitalist society is essentially achievement-oriented and competitive and sports present to us the purest model of that society—and that is just what is wrong with sports. What society needs is not greater pressure for more achievement, but freedom from the incessant demands for achievement, from the "inhumane absurdity . . . of the will to win."[28] What society needs is not sports but play, not the *Realitätsprinzip* but the *Lustprinzip*. Sport represses, play emancipates. Under Communism, sport will disappear and play will resume its rightful place.

3. A CRITIQUE OF CRITIQUES

I should never have begun this book if I were not convinced of the proposition that there is a relationship between sports and society. The question is, what kind of relationship? One way to answer the question is to examine the characteristics of modern sport and to demonstrate that they are to a remarkable degree the characteristics of modern society as described by Max Weber and Talcott Parsons. This we have attempted in chapter 2. Another way to answer the question is to examine the historical process by which modern sports evolved out of the folk-games and aristocratic sports of the Middle Ages. The Marxists and the Neo-Marxists agree that the evolution of modern sports can be explained by the development of industrial capitalism. Supported by the undeniable fact that England was the birthplace of both modern sports and the industrial revolution, the theory has a great deal to recommend it, but I am prepared to advocate an alternative explanation. It is important, however, that we know exactly why we cannot accept the Marxist and the Neo-Marxist interpretations *in toto.*

The Marxist claim that the nature of sport is determined by the means of production is not persuasive. Despite its wealth of detailed information, this analysis remains vague about the exact relationship between a given sport and a given economic system. The joust between the armored knights on horseback was undeniably an aspect of the feudal order, but the mode of production was essentially agricultural, as it had been for centuries and as it would for centuries remain. Since an agrarian economy preceded and followed the sport, the connection between the joust and agricultural labor is by no means clear. If it is argued that jousts and tournaments are martial exercises which relate directly to the status of the ruling class which ruled by direct physical force, then the argument has shifted from economic to political-military determinants. This turn in the argument leads to other problems. If the political purposes of the ruling class are the clue to the kinds of sports in medieval society, then we must ask why the English ruling class persistently emphasized *archery* as the preferred sport for the yeomanry. Was it sensible to encourage the disadvantaged to practice the very weapon which was to end the supremacy of the mounted knight?

More vague and less persuasive still are the arguments made about the specific kinds of sports practiced in the modern world. Generalizations must be challenged by specific questions. What is the exact relationship between industrial capitalism and the game of soccer? The game itself can be traced back to medieval times. It is popular today in countries which remain almost entirely agricultural as well as in the most industrial cities of Europe. It is popular in Poland, Czechoslovakia, and other Communist nations which are, indeed, highly industrialized but which can scarcely be called capitalist. If the game of soccer by its internal structure contributes to the exploitation of the working class, then it is difficult to see that the enthusiastic players of the Soviet Union are exempt from the same exploitation as those of Sao Paulo and Liverpool. If it is argued that the social context makes the difference, then it is the social context that matters and not the kind of sport. The humane society makes all sports humane. But to admit this is to abandon the thesis that different kinds of sports reflect different modes of production.

Similarly, it is true that empirical studies of rates of participation give statistical support to the common-sense observation that kinds of sport vary with social class.[29] We can go further and establish the fact that English soccer is, indeed, more popular among factory workers than among professionals while the contrary is certainly true for cricket, but it remains difficult to perceive the necessary connection between these correlations and the socialization of the players to rule or be ruled. If there were something about American football which encouraged the players to accept their inferior lot in life, why was the game popular at Harvard, Yale, and Princeton at a time when it was scarcely known among the working class? Long after the establishment of the National Football League in 1920, American football continued to be regarded as typically collegiate, and today the sport continues to be considerably more popular among managers and executives than among factory workers.[30] If the game inculcates subservience and docility, the ruling class, led by none other than Richard M. Nixon, has victimized itself. Marxist and Neo-Marxist interpretations of the values transmitted through particular kinds of sports are the product of ideology rather than the result of careful empirical analysis.

Equally unpersuasive is the allegation that Western sports have been schools of nationalism and imperialism. If it is true that American or Italian athletes and sports administrators are more militaristic and nationalistic than their counterparts in Cuba or Yugoslavia, then the explanation must lie elsewhere than in the kinds of sports because, once again, the kinds are essentially the same. It is, of course, theoretically possible that athletes in the West are manipulated into the adoption of undemocratic values while those of the East are encouraged in the opposite direction, but considerable empirical evidence points to the conclusion that militarism and nationalism are more strongly associated with the sports of Communist than with those of non-Communist countries.

While the United States Army and the armies of Western Europe commonly introduce sports into their leisure-time programs, the organization of sports in the Soviet Union and its allies has frequently taken a directly military turn. The twelve "friendly armies" of the Warsaw Pact nations compete in sports, just as the soldiers of NATO do.[31] Civilians learn military along with athletic skills. Motocyclists in the sports clubs of the Soviet Union learn to drive quickly and well; they also learn to drive with "gas masks, throwing grenades, and shooting, all from the motorcycle."[32] The Russians award the GTO badge for men ("Ready for Work and Defense") for physical fitness in eight categories. Six of the categories are pacific enough, but the seventh calls for profiency in shooting and the eighth offers a choice: one can throw a discus, a javelin, a shot, or a hand grenade.[33] While critics of American sports point to military metaphors like the "long bomb" in football, Chinese sports include marksmanship, running the obstacle course, bayonet charges, grenade throwing, parachuting, and anti-aircraft defense—all for civilians.[34] In 1960, the East Germans awarded the "touristic" pentathlon badge for children from twelve to fourteen years of age. The five sports of the pentathlon were the eight-kilometer orientation run, the obstacle course, throwing clubs at a target, long-distance swimming, and shooting with air guns.[35] In a speech, the East-German Minister of Education reminded his audience:[36]

> It is no accident that Friedrich Engels placed great weight on the premilitary education of youth through gymnastic exercises. We have up to now underestimated the importance of premilitary education. . . . We must overcome the pedagogic pacifism in physical-education classes. These classes must become a part of the premilitary education of our youth.

Finally, athletes from Communist countries are far more likely than their Western counterparts to say that they compete for their homelands. The Chinese credit their achievements to the inspiration of Chairman Mao, the East-Germans to the model of Walter Ulbricht, and the Cubans to the exemplary leadership of Fidel Castro. In the words of an East-German "Master of Sport," "The finest and most beautiful aspect of achievement-sport (*Leistungssport*) is the possibility of representing one's country in a national or international competition."[37] Quite naturally, much is made in Communist publications and broadcasts of their athletes' success in international competition.[38] Given the Communists' emphasis on the symbolic social significance of athletic superiority over capitalist nations, this attitude should surprise no one.

The claim that Western nations have organized their sports in a militaristic and nationalistic manner must be taken *cum grano salis,* but there is another accusation whose truth we must acknowledge. Western sports, especially American sports, are commercialized to an extent unknown elsewhere. What the state does in the Soviet Union or Bulgaria, what the private club does in West Germany or France, a combination of schools and private enterprise does in the United States. And the line between "big-time" college sports and the openly professional sports leagues is often a faint one, difficult for foreigners to trace and impossible for the NCAA to enforce. Nonetheless, we must not mistakenly assume that commercialization is solely responsible for all the ills of modern sports. There are many evils specific to commercialism: the neglect of sports that do not prove profitable, excessive costs which limit access to facilities that should be available to all, the mutilation of televised games and meets by advertisements, and the manipulation of scheduling in order to cash in on "prime-time" television audiences. Most of the diseases of modern sports, however, have infected all modern societies and cannot be associated simply with commercialization: an overemphasis on winning, cheating, the use of drugs, the training of small children for highly competitive sports, and the tendency to turn every form of play into some kind of contest.

This brings us back to the fundamental postulate of chapter 2. The characteristics of modern sports are essentially invariant in every modern society, whether that society is Liberal, socialist, or Communist. Differences do exist, and they will occupy us in chapters 4–6, but these differences are minor in comparison with those distinguishing modern from primitive, ancient, and medieval sports. This fact seriously undercuts the Neo-Marxist critique. It is true that American and French sports are characterized by a high level of quantification, but this social fact cannot be explained simply by capitalism when an equally high if not higher level of quantification exists in Poland and the Soviet Union. It is true that bureaucratic organization governs the competitive sports of West Germany, but we must be permitted considerable skepticism when a leading East-German sociologist asserts, "It is a fundamental principle of socialist democracy that the athletes themselves should work out, discuss, agree upon and finally realize their plans and intentions for the further development of sporting activities."[39] Fundamental principle it may be, but the principle of "democratic centralism" has made present practice in Eastern Europe even more bureaucratic than that of Western Europe—and capitalism cannot be the reason. It is true that Western sports institutionalize the achievement principle and frequently carry it to extremes, but achievement is also the proud slogan of Communist nations: "Everywhere in our social life the achievement principle increases in strength. . . . Achievement-sport mirrors the humanistic character of our socialist physical culture."[40] If capitalism accounted for the stress on achievement rather than on ascription, then Marxism must have found a more than adequate substitute. To a degree unknown in the West, the sport psychology of Eastern Europe is devoted to the scientific study of motivation, a study itself motivated by the intense desire to raise levels of athletic achievement.[41]

No wonder, then, that the West-German Neo-Marxists have concentrated their critical fire on the West rather than on the specialization, rationalization, bureaucratic organization, quantification, and quest for records in the Communist world. Their theoretical model simply cannot cope with the institutional reality of Communism. Final proof of this can be observed in the *Marxist* response to Neo-Marxism. Communist scholars have repudiated the entire Neo-Marxist critique of sports with much the same impatience that Lenin showed for "infantile Left-Wing deviationism." They have denounced the Neo-Marxists as "left-radical Trotskyites" whose work contains "political weaknesses and errors deriving from the anti-Marxism and anti-Leninism of their basic assumptions."[42] Meanwhile, French Neo-Marxists have not hesitated to carry the logic of their argument to the ineluctable conclusion that Communist sport is as bad (almost) as capitalist sport. The French have excoriated the Parti Communiste Français for its worship of the heresy of modern sports. The PCF has found words with which to defend itself. The ideological pot boils.[43]

That the Soviet Union cannot be excluded from any rational criticism of modern sports, however, does not imply that modern sports cannot be rationally criticized. It is one thing to say that the Neo-Marxists are wrong to explain every abuse in terms of capitalism and another to say that there are no abuses. The crux of the matter for us is whether the abuses represent the distortion of modern sports or the very essence of the phenomenon. *Are* sports a modern curse? Do they alienate the athlete from the product of his labor? Are they a form of sexual sublimation?

When we move from the world of play and noncompetitive games to the world of contests, we have made an important transition, have crossed a kind of ludic Rubicon. The cooperative Japanese ball game *kemari* has neither winners nor losers, but modern sports are by definition structured to produce a won-lost outcome. Ties are possible, but the entire tendency of modern sports is to eliminate them by extra innings in baseball, by "sudden-death" overtimes, by rematches, by *some* device that will end the ambiguity. From the psychological need to win, a thousand distempers grow. Here are the roots of what psychiatrist Arnold Beisser calls "the madness in sports."[44] It is the desire to win at all costs which eats away at the simple pleasures of play, which leads ultimately to illicit violence and use of drugs. When eight-year-old hockey players skate out on the ice and begin by prearranged plan to "take out" the star of the opposing team by breaking his ankle with their hockey sticks, the "achievement principle" has clearly gone too far.

Let us grant this. Let us also note that the structure of modern sports makes it all but inevitable that half the participants in any contest will lose. In leagues and in championship meets, the proportion of losers necessarily rises. When the Olympic race has been won, the victor receives the gold medal and all the others have lost, but the losers live with their disappointment. They quote Pierre de Coubertin on the rewards of participation. Unless we take the sportsmanlike quotation to be utter hypocrisy, we must conclude that winning isn't always everything. There must, in other words, be some psychological mechanism which enables all of us to endure defeat and to live with the fact that not everyone can be the best. While the stress on athletic victory is often destructive, especially when children are the actors involved, it may be that sports are a valuable means to socialize us into a world where disappointment and frustration are inevitable. I am not anxious to overpraise the "good loser" of Victorian homily, but I insist that the winner cannot be the only one who profits from the contest. Defeat is simply too common for it to be as destructive to the psyche as some have claimed.

Similarly, the allegations of alienation in sports have been hyperbolic. To the thesis that modern sports alienates the athlete from himself, Hans Lenk has countered that there is less alienation in sport than elsewhere in the modern world. Sports remain a subdivision of the realm of freedom in that the athlete chooses whether or not to participate. It is precisely in this freely chosen world of sports that one *can* identify with "the product of one's work," i.e., with one's performance as an athlete. In the achievements of sports one can experience a sense of wholeness denied elsewhere. Here, as in the arts, one submits to a discipline which liberates. "Athletic achievement is . . . unambiguously one's *own*, contrary to the achievements of assemblyline production."[45] On the field of sports, one's achievements are intelligible to everyone, as those of the physicist are not, and one can win recognition beyond the circle of specialists. It is the athlete who is able, in Erving Goffman's sense of the term, to "present himself" to others.[46]

The alleged extinction of personality within the abstraction of the record is also an overstatement. If the athlete is a colorless person, it is probably true that his moment of glory will last only as long as his record, but it is also true that the recognition received by such a colorless person would have been unattainable elsewhere. Better fleeting glory than none at all. It is, moreover, undeniably the case that the fame of many athletes has survived despite the fact that their achievements have been surpassed. Hans Lenk asks the right question: "The records of Nurmi or Zatopek or Wilma Rudolph have been surpassed and forgotten, but have the names and the image of personality disappeared along with the records?"[47] Quite obviously not. The names of Jim Thorpe and Babe Ruth and Big Bill Tilden may not last so long as those of Milo of Croton and Theagenes of Thasos, but the relationship between records and personality is clearly a complicated one.

Unless we are to assume that men and women are so victimized by "false consciousness" that they have lost all awareness of their own emotions, we must pay attention to what people say about their athletic experiences. Let us be distrustful of the published biographies and autobiographies of famous athletes, most of which exude enthusiasm for the world of sports. Let us look at the carefully assembled evidence in Michel Bouet's phenomenological study, *Les Motivations des sportifs* (1969) and at the painstaking empirical investigations of Hartmut Gabler, whose quantitative studies of swimmers must be among the most thorough ever conducted.[48] The results are clear. From Bouet's protocols, gathered from 1,634 sportsmen and sportswomen, sports appear to be means of "feeling that one exists," "discovering oneself," "realizing oneself," "finding an expression of the self," "knowing oneself," "communicating nonlinguistically," "obtaining recognition from others," and "dominating others." (Bouet is too honest to censor out the unpleasant motivations.) Sports "offer to man a chance to prove his existence to others in an authentic manner."[49] Gabler's psychological tests are less dramatic, but they ought to suffice against the popular notion that athletic achievement is correlated with neurotic personality.[50] Since we began our inquiry into the nature of modern sports by quoting Roger Bannister's description of a magical moment of spontaneous play, it is perhaps appropriate to single him out from among the thousands of athletes who have tried to communicate what they felt about sports. Bannister tried to portray his emotional state as he neared the end of the first four-minute mile:[51]

> I had a moment of mixed joy and anguish, when my mind took over. It raced well ahead of my body and drew my body compellingly forward. I felt that the moment of a lifetime had come. There was no

pain, only a great unity of movement and aim. The world seemed to stand still, or did not exist. . . . I felt at that moment that it was my chance to do one thing supremely well. I drove on, impelled by a combination of fear and pride.

And when it was over, when the time was announced, Bannister grabbed his friends Brasher and Chataway "and together we scampered round the track in a burst of spontaneous joy."[52]

Although athletes are sometimes thought to be rather inarticulate, it is truly remarkable how many of them have attempted to express themselves in poetic form, especially in the pages of professional physical education journals like *Quest*. The poems are almost invariably attempts to communicate what is, of course, essentially incommunicable—the joy of physical action. In her book of poems, *My Skin Barely Covers Me* (1975), ex-swimmer Barbara Lamblin dramatizes both the joy of sports and the destruction of that joy by an excessive stress on winning.

Barbara Lamblin is not alone. Many athletes have become disillusioned with the practice and even with the ideals of modern sports. Some have testified to a sense of victimization and alienation.[53] The Neo-Marxist insists that athletes avowing a sense of alienation experience reality while the voices of affirmation speak from "false consciousness." There is, ultimately, no way to resolve a disagreement of this sort. A similar impasse awaits us in the rocky terrain of psychoanalysis. What can we reply to the charge that repressed heterosexual energy is sublimated into homosexual athletic aggression? Like much psychoanalytic theory, the Neo-Marxist interpretation of sexuality and sports is impossible to invalidate. The best response seems to be that Victorian sexual morality did look to sports as a substitute for sexual activity. Strenuous play and a cold shower tamed the savage adolescent. But modern sports have long since freed themselves from Victorian views of sexuality. Whatever coaches and physical educators may now say in their public statements, athletes have made it abundantly clear that heterosexual activity is a prerequisite of the sporting life. What Babe Ruth did on the sly, screened by the cooperation of moralistic journalists, Wilt Chamberlain and "Broadway Joe" Namath now do openly, even boastfully. Let a runner give what seems to be the almost universal opinion: "Athletes love physical expression, and sex is one of the best forms of it."[54] To the evidence of predominantly heterosexual behavior, the Neo-Marxist countercharges that the heterosexuality of the athlete is inauthentic, a "repressive cosmetics-and-commodity sexual pseudo fulfillment."[55] The argument has become positively ptolemaic. Such indictments cannot be answered.

Ironically, the Neo-Marxist radicals have not ventured to defend the rights of homosexuals in sports. For that, we can turn to a remarkable American novel by Patricia Nell Warren, *The Front Runner* (1975), but the Neo-Marxist will find cold comfort in a book which celebrates both the joy of sports and the homosexual love of an Olympic champion and his coach.

At least one aspect of the Neo-Marxist critique is susceptible to an empirical test. The argument that sports function to render apathetic and to divert from political activity can be invalidated by the evidence. Numerous studies have demonstrated a strong correlation between active and passive sports participation. Those who participate directly in sports are more likely than nonparticipants to be spectators, both in person and through the electronic media.[56] Since active participants are invariably a minority of the total population of a society, this does *not* mean that most spectators are also active participants. They *are,* however, more likely to be participants than their fellow citizens who avoid the spectator's role. Even in soccer, where the ratio of active to passive participation is much lower than in most other sports, studies have shown that as many as two-thirds of the spectators in the stadium are themselves active players.[57] An even larger number of empirical studies have indicated that active participation in sports is positively correlated with various other cultural activities, including involvement in politics.[58] This last point is especially important. The best data now available tend strongly to disprove the charge that an interest in sports "infantalizes" or "cretinizes" the athlete or the spectator.

We can carry the discussion further. If sport *in general* is repressive, alienating, and apathy-inducive, which is the Neo-Marxist thesis, then we must conclude that the ruling class of modern society has decided to alienate itself rather than those whom they most oppress. There is overwhelming evidence to demonstrate conclusively that managers and professionals participate in sport at higher rates than members of the working class; the educated participate at a higher rate than the uneducated; men participate more than women.[59] These relationships hold for Communist as well as non-Communist countries and they hold more strongly for highly competitive than for more recreational sport. If sport is an engine of alienation, we can only conclude that the advantaged have turned it upon themselves rather than upon the disadvantaged.

A final comment on the Neo-Marxist critique. The preference for play rather than for modern sports is one which the "New Left" shares with Johan Huizinga, who more than a generation ago lamented that the instinct for play had atrophied "with the increasing systematization

and regimentation of sport."[60] The preference for play is part and parcel
of a Romantic rejection of the basic characteristics of modern society.
On this issue, the Neo-Marxist position is much closer to the conservatism of *Homo Ludens* than to the radicalism of *Das Kapital*.

4. A WEBERIAN INTERPRETATION

The critique of the Marxist and Neo-Marxist critiques brings us once
again to the fact that there is undoubtedly some relationship between
the rise of modern sports and the development of modern society. What
relationship? The answer must, inevitably, be a generalization of a rather
large order. Such generalizations are certainly subject to close scrutiny
and hard questions about detailed interactions, but there is at least one
interpretation which does not founder upon the shoals of blatant contradiction of theory by fact.

The entire discussion of the difference between primitive and modern sports (chapter 2) was informed by what I refer to in shorthand as
a Weberian view of social organization. Max Weber's analysis of the transition from traditional to modern society has its analogues in Ferdinand
Tönnies' classical formulations of *Gemeinschaft* and *Gesellschaft* ("community" and "society"), in Sir Henry Maine's theory of the movement from
status to contract, and in Talcott Parsons' distinction between particularistic and universalistic modes. My choice of the term "Weberian" is motivated partly by convenience.

One great advantage of the Weberian model is that it enables one
to see in the microcosm (modern sports) the characteristics of the ma-
crocosm (modern society)—secularism, equality, specialization, rationalism, bureaucratic organization, and quantification. These six characteristics, plus the quest for records which appears even more strikingly in
sports than in the rest of the social order, are interdependent, systematically related elements of the ideal type of a modern society. They derive
from the fundamental Weberian notion of the difference between the
ascribed status of traditional society and the achieved status of a modern
one.

Another advantage of the Weberian interpretation is that it does not
reduce explanation to the economic determinism which is Marxism's ever-
present beast in the jungle. The trouble with economic determinism in
this particular case is that the explanatory factor, industrialization, does
not explain enough. Although the first nations to industrialize were, indeed, the first to develop national organizations for modern sports, other
countries, like Bulgaria and Cuba, have reached impressive levels of ath-

letic achievement without extensive industrialization (not to speak of industrial *capitalism*). Industrialism no longer seems to be the key, if it ever was.

A recent statistical study by Hilmi Ibrahim attempts to correlate national success in Olympic competition, on a points-per-capita basis, with industrialization as measured by Robert Marsh's Index of Societal Differentiation, which ranks nations by the percentage of their nonagricultural labor and the level of their energy consumption. With these admittedly imperfect variables, Ibrahim found that nations high on Marsh's scale have done well at the Olympics, but less industrialized nations have often done better, especially in recent years.[61] Using Ibrahim's data, we can calculate the Spearman rank-order correlation for Olympic success and industrialization. If the rank order in the first category is the same as in the second, the correlation is 1.0. If the order is reversed, the correlation is − 1.0. For the top five medal-winners in 1968, the correlation of athletic success to level of industrialism was actually − .8.

Economic factors remain, however, absolutely essential to any satisfactory interpretation of the nature of modern sport. In every modern society, for instance, the middle class is overrepresented in its active and passive participation in sports. This overrepresentation cannot be unrelated to economic factors like wealth and income and occupational category. Marxist scholarship has alerted us to this relationship. But it is also true of modern sports that the young are more intensely involved than the old, men more than women, the educated more than the uneducated, Protestants more than Catholics, and the upwardly mobile more than the downwardly mobile. Class is important, but age, sex, education, religion, and mobility are also important factors which cannot be neglected if we seek to comprehend the nature of modern sports. Once again, the common thread that ties these factors together is the emphasis on achievement. If status is awarded on the basis of age or sex or religious affiliation, then social mobility—if there is any—will hardly be a function of achievement and the educational process will not stress individual effort as the route to success. Obviously, we do *not* now and never will live entirely in what the psychologist David McClelland calls "the achievement society." Not even in the achievement-oriented world of sports are the influences of ascribed status completely absent. Coaches will always play favorites and officials will never be completely unbiased. But the Weberian model is more congruent with social reality than is any other model. The congruence is especially close in modern sports.

For a Weberian interpretation, however, the relation of sports to religion is a particularly sticky wicket, just as the relationship between economics and religion proved to be a classical problem in Weber's own sociological work. We know that modern sports spread from Protestant England and that they spread more quickly to Protestant than to Catholic countries (although France is an important exception here). We also know that Protestants are more likely than Catholics to be involved in sports and also more likely to be athletes of international calibre (which is not to deny that Catholics are overrepresented in some sports, like American professional football). Tables 2 and 3, taken from studies by Günther Lüschen and Hans Lenk, demonstrate the overrepresentation of Protestants in German sport and in Olympic competition.[62] Given such data, we are tempted to seize upon Weber's own concept of "secular asceticism" and to explain disparities in the rate of participation and achievement by the self-discipline of physical training, which is therefore the equivalent of the deferred gratification necessary for the accumulation of capital and the reinvestment of profits.[63]

TABLE 2
Sport and Religion in West Germany

	General Population (%)	Members of Sports Clubs (%)	Members Involved in Track & Swimming (%)	Members in High-Level Track & Swimming (%)
Protestants	52	60	67	73
Catholics	44	37	31	26
Others	4	3	2	1
Number		1,880	366	111

TABLE 3
Sport and Religion at the Olympic Games

	Share of Olympic Gold Medals (%)	Share of World's Religious Population (%)
Protestants	54.5	7.6
Catholics	40	23.6
Mohammedans	1.6	15.5
Buddhists, Shintoists	1.2	7.3
Jews	1	.4
Others	1.6	45.4

Unfortunately for this line of reasoning, we quite properly think of the English and American Puritans as among the most Protestant of Protestants and we know that the Puritans were bitterly hostile to sports. John Bunyan's autobiography dramatizes his conversion to righteousness at the very moment when he wickedly indulged in a "game of cat" (an ancestor of baseball). The Puritans of Massachusetts and Connecticut "banned dice, cards, quoits, bowls, ninepins, 'or any other unlawful game in house, yard, garden, or backside, singling out for special attention 'the Game called Shuffle Board, in howses of Common Interteinment, whereby much precious time is spent unfruitfully."[64] The interdiction of shuffle board does not suggest a string disposition toward sports.

James I of England urged in his *Book of Sports* (1618) that the people of his realm should not be disturbed "from any lawfull Recreation; Such as dauncing, either men or women, Archeries for men, leaping, vaulting or other harmless Recreation . . . ," but the Puritans of the Commonwealth had the hangman burn the king's book.[65] Dennis Brailsford, in a history of sport and society from Queen Elizabeth to Queen Anne, sums up the Puritan view: "The Puritans saw their mission to erase all sport and play from men's lives."[66] This may sound like Macaulay's quip that the Puritans banned bear-baiting not because of the pain suffered by the animals but because of the pleasure experienced by the spectators, but Brailsford's study is a meticulously researched piece of scholarship. Other historians have commented on the sudden revival of English sports in 1660 when Charles II, "the Merry Monarch," returned to restore the banished pleasures of the stage and the turf.[67] There is ample evidence of Protestantism's reluctance, before the twentieth century, to look favorably upon modern sports.[68]

This hostility poses one problem. Another arises when we ponder the enthusiasm for modern sports in the Soviet Union and in Japan, two nations quite definitely out of the orbit of Protestantism, nor can we explain the achievements of Polish, Cuban, Bulgarian, and Hungarian athletes by references to Protestantism any better than by assertions about the imperatives of capitalist development. The clue of this explanatory labyrinth may well be found in Robert Merton's famous essay, "Puritanism, Pietism, and Science" (1936). In this essay, Merton demonstrated that Protestants were much more likely than Roman Catholics to have been partisans of the "new science" of the seventeenth century:[69]

> Empiricism and rationalism were canonized, beatified, so to speak.
> It may very well be that the Puritan ethos did not directly influence
> the method of science and that this was simply a parallel development
> in the internal history of science, but it is evident that through
> the psychological compulsion toward certain modes of thought and

conduct this value-complex made an empirically-founded science commendable rather than, as in the medieval period, reprehensible, or at best acceptable on sufference.

The implication for our present purpose is that the correlation between Protestantism and participation in sports disguises the fundamental causal relationship between these two dependent variables and the independent variable which acts upon them. The basic explanatory factor is the scientific world-view, a world-view which has since been espoused by the Japanese and by every Marxist society. Indeed, Marxists like to think of themselves as the only scientific philosophers.

In other words, the mathematical discoveries of the seventeenth century were popularized in the eighteenth century, at which time we can observe the beginnings of our modern obsession with quantification in sport. During the Age of the Enlightenment, we can see the transition from the Renaissance concept of "measure," in the sense of moderation and balance, to the modern concept of measurement. The movement is philologically visible in German as well, i.e., from *Maß* to *Messen*.[70] The emergence of modern sports represents neither the triumph of capitalism nor the rise of Protestantism but rather the slow development of an empirical, experimental, mathematical *Weltanschauung*. England's early leadership has less to do with the Protestant ethic and the spirit of capitalism than with the intellectual revolution symbolized by the names of Isaac Newton and John Locke and institutionalized in the Royal Society, founded during the Restoration, in 1662, for the advancement of science.

This interpretation was suggested by Hans Lenk: "Achievement sport, i.e., sport whose achievements are extended beyond the here and now through measured comparisons, is closely connected to the scientific-experimental attitudes of the modern West."[71] The suggestion was further developed by Henning Eichberg in *Der Weg des Sports in die industrielle Zivilisation*.[72] Equipped with this insight into the role of the scientific *Weltanschauung* in the rise of modern sports, we can satisfactorily account for the post-World-War-II surge of athletic achievement in the nations of Eastern Europe, where the vestiges of premodern social organization and ideology were suddenly, even ruthlessly, challenged by a relentlessly modern attitude.

To the degree that religious tradition induces a nonscientific or even an antiscientific orientation, the transition from folk-games to modern sports will be inhibited and retarded, but the reason for this inhibition and retardation has less to do with the positive in religious faith than with the negative assessment of modern science. This can be seen in the case of Canadian sport, where the French population has been drastically underrepresented. In France itself, Roman Catholicism interacted with the rise of mathematical science in such a manner that the French, from the time of Descartes and Pascal to that of Poincaré and de Broglie, have made great contributions to the natural sciences. In France itself, modern sports appeared early and developed fairly quickly (despite the opinion of some that sport "has made no real impression on the soul of the French nation").[73] In Canada, however, Catholicism seems to have encouraged a kind of parochial antagonism to the modern world, a negativism which appears in the statistics on sports participation. Although roughly 30 percent of Canada is ethnically French, this group has provided only 8.1 percent of the 4,297 athletes representing Canada at the Commonwealth, Pan-American, and Olympic games. Since we know that economic factors play an important role in rates of participation in modern sports, we cannot simply say that religion alone is responsible for this striking disparity, but it would be a mistake to discount the powerful influence of the Catholic Church in Quebec and the Maritime Provinces. The sociologists whose empirical study I have just cited offer the following explanation for Quebec's athletic backwardness: "Among French Canadians, the traditional mentality has long rested on an agricultural ideology and on a vision of the world which is essentially religious, which venerates the past."[74]

The persuasiveness of this explanation is increased by the few studies to analyze the rates of sports participation of a student population in relation to the field of academic study. Looking at 387 students at two Swiss universities, authors of one survey found that theology majors were, by a wide margin, the least involved in sports, while students of the natural and social sciences were among the most active.[75] A study of 345 students at Amherst College looked specifically at the relationship between academic major and rate of participation in sports. It was found that social-science majors participate most frequently, followed by natural-science majors. Students of the humanities were significantly less active ($t = 2.366$, $p < .01$; $t = 2.087$, $p < .025$).[76] If these findings are typical, which only empirical research can establish, the correctness of my argument about sports and a scientific *Weltanschauung* will be supported.

Henning Eichberg has pointed to the importance of a mathematical-empirical world-view, but he has also, less persuasively, attempted to find a correlation between the rise of modern sports and the Romantic Revolution which swept over much of Europe and America at the end of the eighteenth and the beginning of the nineteenth centuries. It is, in my view, more probable that Romanticism, with its pervasive antiscientific bias, encouraged the survival of premodern sports like hunting and fishing and hindered the emergence of modern sports. We can see this clearly in a movement strongest in Germany, where the Romantic Revolution was also quite intense. I have in mind the German variety of gymnastics known as *Turnen*.

The origins of *Turnen* are conventionally traced to the innovative educational work of Johann Christian Friedrich GutsMuths and Friedrich Ludwig Jahn. Both men believed in the importance of physical education. Both set up systems which included a wide range of gymnastics and what we know as track and field sports. Both were ardently nationalistic. When GutsMuths republished his *Gymnastik für die Jugend* (1793) in 1817, he dropped the Greek word from the title and replaced it with a German word, he substituted a nationalistic for a universal reference, and the book became *Turnbuch für die Söhnes des Vaterlandes*. In it, he wrote, "We must give our youth a patriotic education for the spirit and a truly paramilitary education for the body."[77] In the foreword to his *Deutsches Volkstum* (1810), Jahn proclaimed, "A state without a people is nothing, a soul-less artificiality; a people without a state is nothing, an airy, disembodied abstraction."[78] Jahn himself was committed enough to become an active participant in Germany's national revolution against the Napoleonic occupation of the fatherland.

From Jahn's *Turnplatz* in the fields near Berlin, established in 1811, the movement spread quickly throughout Germany and from Germany to the rest of Europe and even to the United States. The movement was always political as well as athletic. Although the early *Turner* were often Liberal nationalists, which brought them into a protracted conflict with the Prussian authorities, the political orientation of the movement gradually shifted to the right, especially after the failure of the Liberal revolution of 1848 and the fight of the more radical *Turner* to America.[79] The *Turner* became increasingly committed to Romantic nationalism, to the celebration of the mysterious German spirit, which is born of the mystic unity of *Volk* and *Vaterland*. The mysticism reaches a kind of crescendo in Hermann Burte's novelistic evocation of the ideal *Turner* in *Wiltfeber: Der ewige Deutsche* (1912), surely one of the most Romantic novels ever written.

Although GutsMuths and Jahn had not been immune from the tendency to quantify, to seek records, or to encourage competition, the *Turner* became increasingly hostile to what their most famous twentieth-century leader called "the anti-spirit of noisy championships."[80] The *Turner*, as defenders of Romantic nationalism, became the enemies of modern sport, which they perceived as Liberal, rational, international, and un-German. "*Der Sport ist undeutsch.*"[81] This rejection of modern sports by the *Turner*

is of crucial importance. Their journal, *Die Deutsche Turnzeitung*, condemned boxing and running and they denounced modern sports as se-
mitic.[82] When word of the revived Olympic games reached Germany,
the *Rheinische-Westfälische Zeitung* voiced opposition: "A sports club or
any individual German who embarrasses his country by furthering or
even visiting these games deserves to be cast out by his morally indig-
nant people."[83] When the invitation to Athens arrived, the *Deutsche
Turnerschaft* rejected it.[84] When a group of gymnasts went anyway, they
were subsequently expelled from membership.[85] Four years after the
first modern Olympics, the *Deutsche Turnerschaft's* chairman announced
that sport was "a passionately pursued form of physical exercise as alien
to German behavior as its name, for which there is no German word."[86]
As late as 1933, a writer in *Die Schar* called for the renunciation of "concrete stadium, cinder track, tape-measure, stopwatch, manicured lawn,
and track shoes. . . . In their place comes the simple meadow, free nature."[87]
Even the *Turner* of the working class, despite their Marxist vision of a
modern, social-democratic Germany, declared their reluctance to endorse
competitive gymnastics, especially high-level competition.[88] Competition,
both team and individual, did eventually become a part of German gymnastics, but modern sport remained suspect. From the late nineteenth
century until the dissolution of the *Deutsche Turnerschaft* under Hitler,
there was the repeated accusation that sport was English, not German,
a symbol of Liberal internationalism, a threat to the Romantic unity of
the German *Volk* upon the native soil of the *Vaterland*. And England,
birthplace of modern sports, returned the "compliment" by an almost
complete neglect of *Turnen*.[89] It was, therefore, a perverse historical irony
that Adolf Hitler, the personification of Romantic nationalism in its most
irrational and destructive form, was persuaded to set aside his initial reluctance to sponsor the Olympic games of 1936. In order to allow *der
Führer* a propaganda coup, sport finally received its German apotheosis.[90]

In Romantic nationalism's opposition to modern sport, we have seen
the other side of the coin, the obverse of the scientific world-view. In
our search for the roots of modern sport, we have moved in an explanatory regression from abstractions like the Industrial Revolution and the
Reformation to a still more abstract formulation—the scientific world-view.
And now we confront a paradox. The quest for records is in itself one
of the most remarkable forms of the Faustian drive, one of the most extraordinary manifestations of the Romantic pursuit of the unattainable.
Sports themselves, originating in the spontaneous expression of physical
energy, have their source in the irrational. We are all familiar with the
frenzy of an athletic encounter, with the atavistic enthusiasm of football

fans, with the naked aggression of the boxer's punch, with the inexplicable determination of the entranced runner who staggers on despite the spasms of his tortured body. Paradox, yes. Contradiction, no. Sports are an alternative to and, simultaneously, a reflection of the modern age. They have their roots in the dark soil of our instinctive lives, but the form they take is that dictated by modern society. Like the technological miracle of Apollo XI's voyage to the moon, they are the rationalization of the Romantic.

NOTES

1. Wolfgang Eichel, quoted in Horst Überhorst, "Ursprungtheorien," *Geschichte der Leibesübungen*, ed. Horst Überhorst, 6 vols. (Berlin: Verlag Bartels und Wernitz, 1972-   ), 1, 17; see also Dieter Voigt, *Soziologie in der DDR* (Cologne: Verlag Wissenschaft und Politik, 1975), pp. 29-31.
2. The best account is by Andrzej Wohl, *Die gesellschaftlich-historischen Grundlagen des bürgerlichen Sports* (Köln: Pahl-Rugenstein Verlag, 1973), pp. 9-30.
3. *Ibid.*, pp. 30-57.
4. "Coaching," *The Book of Sport*, ed. William Patten (New York: J. F. Taylor Co., 1901), p. 219.
5. Gerhard Vinnai, *Fußballsport als Ideologie* (Frankfurt: Europäische Verlagsanstalt, 1970), p. 13. Vinnai is a Neo-Marxist, but this remark is Marxist.
6. J. B. LeBlanc, quoted in Marie Kloeren, *Sport und Rekord* (Leipzig: Verlag von Bernhard Tauchnitz, 1935), p. 272.
7. The idea for such a table came from Peter C. McIntosh, *Sport in Society* (London: C. A. Watts, 1963), pp. 63, 85; the use of Rostow was suggested by Hilmi Ibrahim, *Sport and Society* (Long Beach, Ca.: Hwong Publishing Co., 1975), p. 117.
8. For the coefficient of concordance, see George A. Fergusosn, *Statistical Analysis in Psychology and Education*, 3rd ed. (New York: McGraw-Hill, 1971), pp. 312-14.
9. The fullest documentation of commercialism comes from non-Marxist sources, especially from Joseph Durso, *The All-American Dollar* (Boston: Houghton Mifflin, 1971); Bernie Parrish, *They Call It a Game* (New York: Dial Press, 1971); Peter Douglas, *The Football Industry* (London: George Allen & Unwin, 1973); Roger G. Noll, ed., *Government and the Sports Business* (Washington: Brookings Institute, 1974); Gary Davidson and Bill Libby, *Breaking the Game Wide Open* (New York: Atheneum, 1974); and Sheldon M. Gallner, *Pro Sports: The Contract Game* (New York: Scribner's, 1974).
10. Jürgen Dieckert, *Die Turnerjugendbewegung* (Schorndorf: Karl Hofmann, 1968), pp. 111-16; Horst Überhorst, *Edmund Neuendorff* (Berlin: Bartels und Wernitz, 1970), pp. 69-72.
11. Rudi Reichart, "Zur Gründung des 'Deutschen Turn- und Sportbundes,'" *TPK*, 6 (1957), 481-88.
12. See Rudolf Volkert, "Zur burgerlichen Theorie der 'Leistungsgesellschaft' und zu dem dieser Gesellschaftstheorie unterstellten Modellcharakter des Sports," *TPK*, 24 (1975), 1082-95.
13. Quoted from James Riordan, "Marx, Lenin, and Physical Culture," *JSH*, 3 (1976), 159.

14. Cited from Hermann Josef Kramer, *Körpereziehung und Sportunterricht in der DDR* (Schorndorf: Karl Hofmann, 1969), p. 29.
15. Andrzej Wohl, "Prognostic Models of Sport in Socialist Countries," *IRSS*, 6 1971), 26; Wohl, *Die gesellschaftlich-historischen Grundlagen des bürgerlichen Sports*, p. 181.
16. N. I. Ponomarev, "Free Time and Physical Education," *IRSS*, 1 (1966), 167.
17. *Die Frühschriften*, ed. Siegfried Landshut (Stuttgart: Alfred Kröner, 1971), p. 361.
18. Pierre Laguillaumie, "Pour une Critique fondamentale du Sport," *Sport, culture, et répression*, ed. Ginette Berthaud et al. (Paris: Francois Maspero, 1972), p. 41.
19. Vinnai, *Fußballsport als Ideologie*, pp. 17-18.
20. Jac-Olaf Böhme, Jürgen Gadow, Sven Güldenpfennig, Jörn Jensen, and Renate Pfister, *Sport im Spätkapitalismus*, 2nd ed. (Frankfurt: Limpert, 1974), p. 47.
21. Vinnai, *Fußballsport als Ideologie*, p. 39.
22. Jean-Marie Bröhm, "Sociologie politique du sport," *Sport, culture, et repression*, p. 23.
23. Jimmy Brown and Myron Cope, *Off My Chest* (Garden City: Doubleday, 1964), p. 63.
24. Böhme, Gadow, Guldenpfennig, Jensen, and Pfister, *Sport im Spätkapitalismus*, p. 37.
25. Vinnai, *Fußballsport als Ideologie*, p. 65.
26. Paul Hoch, *Rip Off the Big Game* (New York: Doubleday-Anchor Books, 1972), p. 154.
27. Ulrike Prokop, *Soziologie der Olympischen Spiele* (Munich: Hanser Verlag, p. 21.
28. Jean-Marie Brohm, *Critiques du sport* (Paris: Christian Bourgeois, 1976), p. 23.
29. Among the best studies are John W. Loy, "Social Origins and Occupational Mobility Patterns of a Selected Sample of American Athletes," *IRSS*, 7 (1972), 5-23; Günther Lüschen, "Social Stratification and Social Mobility among Young Sportsmen," *Sport, Culture, and Society*, ed. John W. Loy and Gerald S. Kenyon (New York: Macmillan, 1969), pp. 258-76; John Eggleston, "Secondary Schools and Oxbridge Blues," *British Journal of Sociology*, 16 (1965), 232-42.
30. See George H. Gallup, *The Gallup Poll*, 3 vols. (New York: Random House, 1972), 3, 1699-1700.
31. Heinz Keßler, "Die I. Sommerspartakiade der befreundeten Armeen . . . ," *TPK*, 7 (1958), 758-63.
32. Henry Morton, "Soviet Sport: School for Communism," Ph.D. dissertation (Columbia University, 1959), p. 273.
33. Peter Sendlak, "Leibesübungen und Sport in der Soviet Union," *Geschichte der Leibesubungen*, ed. Überhorst, 4, 114-15.
34. See Jonathan Kolatch, *Sports, Politics, and Ideology in China* (Middle Village, New York: Jonathan David, 1972), pp. 148-64.
35. Krämer, *Körpererziehung und Sportunterricht in der DDR*, p. 55.
36. Dietrich Martin, *Schulsport in Deutschland* (Schomdorf: Karl Hofmann, 1972), p. 88.
37. Siegfriede Weber-Dempe, "Die Frau als Leistungssportlerin," *TPK*, 4 (1955), 820.
38. See, for example, Dietrich Denz et al., "Zur Entwicklung von Körperkultur und Sport in der DDR," *TPK*, 13 (1974), 589-601.
39. Günther Erbach, "Physical Culture and Sport in the Social Planning Process," *Sport in the Modern World*, ed. Ommo Grupe (Berlin: Springer Verlag, 1973), p. 415.

40. Paul Kunath, "Persönlichkeitsentwicklung und Sport," *TPK*, 17 (1968), 596; Fred Gras, "About the Way of Life and Development of Personality of Competitive Sportsmen," *IRSS*, 11, no. 1 (1976), 77-81.

41. See Horst Smieskol, "Sportpsychologie in den sozialistiscen Ländern Europas," *Sport im Blickpunkt der Wissenschaften*, ed. Helmut Baitsch (Berlin: Springer Verlag, 1972), pp. 160-72.

42. Quoted in Josef N. Schmitz, *Sport und Leibeserziehung zwischen Spätkapitalismus und Frühsozialismus* (Schomdorf: Karl Hofmann, 1974), pp. 21-23.

43. See Jean-Marie Brohm, "Une Politique ouvrière: le PCF et la collaboration de classe," *Sport, culture et répression*, pp. 141-69; Guy Hermier, Roland Passevant, Michel Zilbermann, *Le Sport en questions* (Paris: Editions sociales, 1976).

44. Arnold Beisser, *The Madness in Sports* (New York: Appleton-Century-Crofts, 1967).

45. Hans Lenk, "Leistungssport in der Erfolgsgesellschaft," *Leistungssport in der Erfolgsgesellschaft*, ed. Frank Grube and Gerhard Richter (Hamburg: Hoffmann & Campe, 1973), p. 21. See also Hans Lenk, "Sport, Arbeit, Leistungszwang," *Leistungssport*, 1 (1971), 63-70; Lenk, "Notizen zur Rolle des Sports und der Leistungsmotivation in einer künftigen Gesellschaft," *Die Leibeserziehung*, 20 (1971), 82-87; Lenk, *Leistungssport: Ideologie oder Mythos?* (Stuttgart: Kohlhammer, (1972); Lenk, " 'Manipulation' oder 'Emanzipation' im Leistungssport," *SW*, (1973), 9-40; Lenk, *Sozialphilosophie des Leistungshandelns* (Stuttgart: Kohlhammer, 1976); Howard S. Slusher, *Man, Sport and Existence* (Philadelphia: Lea & Febiger, 1967); Michel Boutron, *La grande Fête du sport* (Paris: Andre Bonne, 1970); Harold J. VanderZwaag, *Toward a Philosophy of Sport* (Reading: Addison-Wesley, 1972); Karl Adam, *Leistungssport: Sinn und Unsinn* (Munich: Nymphenburger Verlagshandlung), 1975.

46. See Helmuth Plessner, "Die Funktion des Sports in der industriellen Gesellschaft," *Leibeserziehund und Sport in der Modernen Gesellschaft*, ed. Gottfried Klöhn (Weinheim: Julius Beltz, 1961), pp. 18-32; Gunter Gebauer, " 'Leistung' als Aktion und Prasentation," *Philosophie des Sports*, ed. Hans Lenk, Simon Moser, and Erich Beyer (Schorndorf: Karl Hofmann, 1973), pp. 42-66; Christian Graf von Krockow, "Selbst-Bewußtsein, Entfremdung, Leistungssport," *SW*, 4 (1974), 9-20.

47. "Zu Coubertins Olympischen Elitismus," *SW*, 6 (1976), 410.

48. *Les Motivations des sportifs* (Paris: Editions universitaires, 1969); Gabler, *Leistungsmotivation im Hochleistungssport* (Schorndorf: Karl Hofmann, 1972); Gabler, "Zur Entwicklung von Persönlichkeitmerkmalen bei Hochleistungssportlern," *SW*, 6 (1976), 247-76.

49. *Les Motivations des sportifs*, pp. 45-55.

50. There is, of course, the other popular notion that athletes are psychologically healthier and "better adjusted" than nonathletes. Gabler concludes in the above-noted works that athletes are simply like nonathletes.

51. *The Four Minute Mile* (New York: Dodd, Mead, 1957), pp. 213-14.

52. *Ibid.*, p. 215.

53. See especially David Meggysey, *Out of Their League* (Berkeley: Ramparts Press, 1970); Ralph "Chip" Oliver, *High for the Game* (New York: William Morrow, 1971); Gary Shaw, *Meat on the Hoof* (New York: St. Martin's Press, 1972); Franz Dwertmann, "Sporthilfe: eine gemeinnützige Einrichtung," *Sport in der Klassengesellschaft*, ed. Gerhard Vinnai (Munich: Fischer Taschenbuch Verlag, 1972), pp. 56-81.

54. Lynda Huey, *A Running Start: An Athlete, A Woman* (New York: Quadrangle, 1976), p. 209.

55. Hoch, *Rip Off the Big Game*, p. 199.

56. See Hans Bloss, "Sport and Vocational School Pupils," *IRSS*, 5 (1970), 25-56; Dieter Hanhart, "Freizeit und Sport in der industriellen Gesellschaft," *Arbeit, Freizeit, und Sport* (Bern: Paul Haupt, 1963), pp. 13-68.

57. See Helge Anderson, Aage Bo-Jensen, N. Elkaer-Hansen, and A. Sonne, "Sports and Games in Denmark in the Light of Sociology," *Acta Sociologica*, 2 (1956), 1-28; Leopold Rosenmayr, "Sport as Leisure Activity of Young People," *IRSS*, 2 (1967), 19-32.

58. See Hanhart, "Freizeit und Sport in der industriellen Gesellschaft," pp. 13-68; Urs Jaeggi, Robert Bosshard, and Jürg Siegenthaler, *Sport und Student* (Bern: Paul Haupt, 1963), pp. 119-22; Anderson et al., "Sport and Games in Denmark," 1-28; Stefan Grössing, *Sport der Jugend* (Vienna: Verlag für Jugend und Volk, 1970), p. 26; James E. Curtis and Brian G. Milton, "Social Status and the 'Active Society,'" *Canadian Sport*, ed. Richard S. Gruneau and John G. Albinson (Don Mills, Ontario: Addison-Wesley, 1976), pp. 302-29; Voigt, *Soziologie in der DDR*, p. 55.

59. See Marek Zürn, "Tourism and Motor Activity of Cracow Inhabitants," *IRSS*, 8, no. 1 (1973), 79-92; N. I. Ponomarev, "Free Time and Physical Education," *IRSS*, 1 (1966), 167-73; John P. Robinson, "Time Expenditure on Sports across Ten Countries," *IRSS*, 2 (1967), 67-87; Andrzej Wohl, "Engagement in Sports Activity on the Part of Workers," *IRSS*, 4 (1969), 83-121; Joffre Dumazedier, "Sport and Sports Activities," *IRSS*, 8, no. 2 (1973), 7-34; Ladislav Lopata, "The Structure of Time and the Share of Physical Education," *IRSS*, 3 (1968), 17-35; Kyuzo Takenoshita, "The Social Structure of the Sport Population in Japan," *IRSS*, 2 (1967), 5-18; Klaus Prenner, "Leistungsmotivation im Spitzensport," *Leibeserziehung*, 20 (1971), 370-75; Richard S. Gruneau, "Sport, Social Differentiation and Social Inequality," *Sport and Social Order*, ed. John W. Loy and Donald W. Ball (Reading: Addison-Wesley, 1975), pp. 121-84; Gruneau, "Class or Mass," *Canadian Sport*, ed. Gruneau and Albinson, pp. 108-41; Barbara Krawczyk, "The Social Role and Participation in Sport," *IRSS*, 8, nos. 3-4 (1973), 47-59; Inge Bausenwein and Auguste Hoffmann, *Frau und Leibesübungen* (Mühlheim: Gehörlosen Druckerei und Verlag, 1967); Günther Lüschen, "Social Stratification and Social Mobility among Young Sportsmen," pp. 258-76; Lüschen, "Soziologische Grundlagen von Leibeserziehung und Sport," *Einführung in die Theorie der Leibeserziehung*, ed. Ommo Grupe et al. (Schorndorf: Karl Hofmann, 1968), pp. 93-111; John W. Loy, "The North American Syndrome," *Sports or Athletics?*, ed. J. Alex Murray (Windsor, Ontario: University of Windsor Press, 1974), pp. 76-96; Raymond Thomas, *La Réussite sportive* (Paris: Presses universitaires, 1975), pp. 17-25; Hans Linde and Klaus Heinemann, *Leistungsengagement und Sportinteresse* (Schorndorf: Karl Hofmann, 1968).

60. *Homo Ludens* (London: Temple Smith, 1970), p. 223. John M. Hoberman has suggested that the rejection of records may also be typical of Fascism; see "Political Ideology and the Record Performance," *Arena Newsletter*, 1 (February 1977), 7-11.

61. *Sport and Society*, pp. 108-13.

62. Günther Lüschen, "The Interdependence of Sport and Culture," *IRSS*, 2 (1967), 132; Hans Lenk, *Werte, Ziele, Wirklichkeit der modernen Olympischen Spiele*, rev. ed. (Schorndorf: Karl Hofmann, 1972), p. 77. Both tables reproduced by permission of the publisher. See also Paavo Seppänen, "Die Rolle des Leistungssports in den Gesellschaften der Welt," *SW*, 2 (1972), 133-55.

63. See Christian Graf von Krockow, *Sport und Industriegesellschaft* (Munich: Piper, 1972), pp. 28-32.

64. Foster Rhea Dulles, *America Learns to Play* (New York: Appleton-Century-Crofts, 1940), p. 6.
65. *Ibid.*, pp. 10, 12. See also Robert W. Malcolmson, *Popular Recreations in English Society, 1700-1850* (Cambridge: Cambridge University Press, 1973).
66. *Sport and Society* (Toronto: University of Toronto Press, 1969), p. 141. See also H. Mayer, "Puritanism and Physical Training," *IRSS*, 8, no. 1 (1973), 37-51.
67. Kloeren, *Sport und Rekord*, pp. 19-37, 205-65.
68. For example, William R. Hogan, "Sin and Sports," *Motivations in Play, Games and Sports*, ed. Ralph Slovenko and James A. Knight (Springfield, Illinois: Charles C. Thomas, 1967), pp. 121-47.
69. *Social Theory and Social Structure* (Glencoe: Free Press, 1957), p. 579.
70. Henning Eichberg, "Der Beginn des modernen Leistens," *SW*, 4 (1974), 21-48.
71. *Leistungssport: Ideologie oder Mythos?*, p. 144.
72. *Der Weg des Sports in die industrielle Zivilisation* (Baden-Baden: Nomos Verlag, 1973), pp. 135-37.
73. Edgar Joubert, "Sport in France," *Sport and Society*, ed. Alex Natan (London: Bowes & Bowes, 1958), p. 29.
74. Roger Boileau, Fernard Landry, and Yves Trempe, "Les Canadiens Français et les Grands Jeux Internationaux," *Canadian Sport*, ed. Gruneau and Albinson, pp. 158, 163.
75. Jaeggi, Bosshard, and Siegenthaler, *Sport und Student*, p. 27.
76. Computed by me from data gathered by Daniel Lundquist, Fall 1976.
77. *Turnbuch für die Söhne des Vaterlandes* (Frankfurt: Wilmans, 1817), p. xvii.
78. *Werke*, ed. Carl Euler, 2 vols. (Hof: Verlag von G. A. Grau, 1884-1885), 1, 160.
79. Hannes Neumann, *Die Deutsche Turnbewegung in der Revolution 1848/49 und in der amerikanischen Emigration* (Schorndorf: Karl Hofmann, 1968).
80. Edmund Neuendorff, quoted in Jürgen Dieckert, *Die Turnerjugendbewegung*, p. 20.
81. Quoted in Gerd Kramer, *Wie Fern Ist Uns Olympia?* (Osnabrück: A. Fromm, 1971), p. 17.
82. Carl Diem, *Weltgeschichte des Sports*, 3rd ed., 2 vols. (Frankfurt: Cotta, 1971), 2, 945.
83. Krämer, *Wie Fern Ist Uns Olympia?* p. 28.
84. Arnd Krüger, *Sport und Politik* (Hannover: Fackel-Träger Verlag, 1975), pp. 30-31.
85. Horst Überhorst, "Return to Olympia and the Rebirth of the Games," *The Modern Olympics*, ed. Peter J. Graham and Horst Überhorst (Cornwall, New York: Leisure Press, 1976), p. 14.
86. Quoted by Horst Geyer, "Stellvertreter der Nation," *Die Vertrimmte Nation*, ed. Jörg Richter (Reinbek bei Hamburg: Rowohlt Verlag, 1972), pp. 80-81.
87. Quoted in Eichberg, *Der Weg des Sports in die industrielle Zivilisation*, p. 120; see also Überhorst, *Edmund Neuendorff*, p. 19.
88. Horst Überhorst, *Frisch, Frei, Stark und Treu* (Düsseldorf: Droste Verlag, 1973), pp. 50, 136.
89. McIntosh, *Sport in Society*, p. 58.
90. Mandell, *The Nazi Olympics;* Hajo Bernett, *Sportpolitik im Dritten Reich* (Schorndorf: Karl Hofmann, 1971); Arnd Krüger, *Theodor Lewald* (Berlin: Bartels & Wernitz, 1975); Krüger, *Die Olympischen Spiele 1936 und die Weltmeinung* (Berlin: Bartels & Wernitz, 1972).

Section C

Economic Institutions and the Work Order of Sport

A nation's economic system is the system responsible for the production and distribution of important resources, beginning with the necessities of life—food and shelter—and eventually including the niceties and luxuries of life—goods designed for our comfort and leisure items designed for our pleasure. Like the political system, which also distributes a commodity, i.e., power, the economic system can operate under a number of ideologies, in one extreme stressing the equality of distribution and at the other extreme allotting resources on some other basis, such as merit, ascribed status or whim.

The economic overtones of sport involvement can be viewed from many directions. One could focus upon recreational sport and discuss the boom and bust cycle of the equipment and facilities markets, highlighting such trends as the miniature golf boom during the Depression, the skateboard fad of the 60's and boom of the late 70's, and the tennis boom and mild bust of the 70's. It is fascinating to observe, for example, how marketing techniques attempt to convince a person who has been running for 15 years that the old gym shoes and sweatshirt will no longer do: one simply must have five-star running shoes and $200 Gore-Tex running suits.

Or one could focus upon amateur sport, examining the economic aspects of pursuing a successful, high level amateur sport career. The heavy influence of social class membership would require serious attention in such an approach[1] as well as the ethical implications of the dilemma between governmental support of amateur sport, professionalized training at the university level, or under the table payments to amateur athletes.

1. See Richard Gruneau, "Class or Mass" in Part III, Section C, for a full discussion of this topic.

Or one could focus upon the economic elements in the professional sports scene, conceiving of sport as a business and moving on to discuss the repercussions of that fact upon the individuals for whom financial success in sport is a matter of vital concern: the owners and the athletes.

In this section, emphasis is placed mainly, though not exclusively, upon the realm of professional sport. The selections are organized into two sections. Both emphasize the notion that sport is a business, but the first section concentrates upon the institutional implications of that fact, while the second section deals with more personal elements of sport as work.

Staudohar introduces the first focus by furnishing a good overview of the issues important to an understanding of the relationship between management (the owners) and workers (the players). Staudohar bases his analysis on the sport of baseball, but similar principles apply to other league-format team sports such as football, basketball, and hockey.

Holahan also deals specifically with baseball. He focuses upon one particular issue which has long been the cause of heated debate between management and players. The players argue that the reserve system, which binds them to a baseball club, restrains their economic freedom; they argue that they should have the right to bargain with any club interested in them. Management holds that if such a system were implemented only the rich teams could afford to bid for good players in what would become a highly competitive market; moreover, they argue that sport is a special kind of business which requires some degree of performance equality between teams in order to keep the outcome uncertain, and the reserve system is necessary to insure this situation. In a more restrained analysis, Holahan presents an economist's view of the debate.

The final two readings concentrate on some personal aspects of sport which are often overlooked. For many athletes, sport is a career and as such it presents to those involved certain work-related problems which must be solved. In general, this requires continual demonstration that the athlete is equal to the challenge and to the unique demands placed upon him or her by the sport world.

Theberge isolates one of the major problems with which athletes must come to terms if they are to be successful: structured uncertainty. Focussing upon women in professional golf, Theberge observes that the golfer's career is remarkable for the "extreme variability and indeterminacy" of the setting: each week the golfer must contend with a new course, distinguished by differences in length, layout and terrain. Theberge notes that because of their need for continual adjustment to novel work settings, the golfer's career is dominated by her need "to reduce this uncertainty and standardize (her) work situation." That observation provides the key to understanding the meaning of many of the actions and interactions of professional athletes.

Ludtke explores the fascinating interaction that occurs between the catcher and the plate umpire during the course of a baseball game. Using real-life examples of catcher-umpire repartee, Ludtke demonstrates that these exchanges are more than emotional flare-ups, angrily blurted and then forgotten: in effect, the catcher and umpire are negotiating important matters, such as the dimensions of the strike zone, which may ultimately influence the outcome of the game.

Player Salary Issues
in Major League Baseball

Paul D. Staudohar

COLLECTIVE BARGAINING

The Major League Baseball Players Association (MLBPA) was formed in 1952. Like its predecessor, the American Baseball Guild, the association was initially dominated by the team owners. Negotiated agreements were reached on a limited number of issues, such as pensions and insurance. But in 1966, Marvin Miller, a former steelworkers' union official, was hired as the MLBPA director. Miller took a more traditional trade union stance with the club owners, and in 1968 negotiated an agreement on a broad range of issues.

Then, in the 1970 agreement, a significant breakthrough occurred when the MLBPA negotiated a provision for a tripartite grievance arbitration panel with a permanent impartial chairman. This replaced the old system under which disputes over the interpretation of the collective bargaining agreement were finally ruled on by the commissioner of baseball.

The more forceful posture of the players' union became apparent to the public in 1972 when the season was delayed ten days as a result of the first players' strike in baseball history. In the ensuing 1973 agreement, another key change was negotiated by the union. This was a clause providing for determination of individual players' salaries by neutral arbitrators, if the player and club were unable to come to terms.

When the 1973 collective bargaining agreement expired on December 31, 1975, the parties were unable to come to terms on a replacement until July 1976.[1] This new contract, in effect through the end of 1979, continues grievance and salary arbitration. An important new provision revises the reserve clause, which previously tied a player to a particular team. Players are now permitted, under certain conditions, to become free agents, selling their services to the highest bidder.

From *Arbitration Journal* 33, 1978, pp. 17-21. Copyright 1978. American Arbitration Association. Reprinted by permission.

FREEDOM ISSUES

Professional baseball is covered by the National Labor Relations Act. While the National Labor Relations Board has the statutory power to decline jurisdiction if the impact of an industry on commerce does not warrant it, it has ruled that baseball is subject to its jurisdiction.[2] Coverage of the antitrust laws, on the other hand, has not been extended to baseball because of a 1922 U.S. Supreme Court decision.[3] The court ruled that playing exhibition games was not within interstate commerce. Exemption from the antitrust laws is unique to baseball. It does not apply to football, basketball, or hockey.

Thus, for a long time, the owners were able to maintain full control over the market through their exclusive rights to bargain with players allocated to them. If a player sought to challenge the reserve clause, the courts, citing the 1922 decision, would find for the club.[4] This had the effect of partially negating the power of players achieved through the collective bargaining process.

The antitrust exemption continues to apply formally to baseball, but it is coming under close scrutiny. In January 1977, the joint Senate-House Committee on Professional Sports stated that there is no justification for baseball's immunity from the antitrust laws, and recommended that Congress remove the exemption.[5] Meanwhile, other changes have taken place that have reduced the effect of the antitrust exemption, and given more market freedom to the players. Under the reserve clause, when a player signs a contract, he becomes the property of the club. If traded or put on waivers, the acquiring club obtains exclusive rights to the player. Even if a player retires and later decides to return to the game, he is bound to the last club with which he had a contract.

A weakness in the enforcement of a contract was exploited by Jim Hunter of the Oakland A's. Hunter had agreed with club owner Charles Finley that half of his salary would be set aside in 1974 in an insurance trust. When a dispute arose and the matter was brought to arbitration, the chairman of the arbitration panel, Peter Seitz, ruled that Finley had not met the conditions of the agreement, and declared Hunter a free agent. Although this decision did not deal directly with the reserve clause, it showed that arbitration gave players whose contracts were not properly followed added protection. Hunter subsequently signed a contract (estimated at $3.75 million) with the New York Yankees, and the Seitz decision was upheld in court.

In 1975, another ruling by Arbitrator Seitz made a direct assault on the reserve clause. The case involved Andy Messersmith and Dave McNally, who contended that since they had played for one year with their clubs without a contract, their employment-status could not be further extended unilaterally by the club. Seitz agreed, declaring the players free agents; the owners' appeal to the courts was again unsuccessful.

With the reserve clause thus negated, the settlement was reached in the 1976 collective bargaining agreement for a modified system that ties the player to the club for a limited period. For contracts executed before August 9, 1976, the club is allowed to renew for one additional year after the expiration date of the contract. Then, if the player remains unsigned, he becomes a free agent. For contracts executed on or after August 9, 1976, any player with six or more years of major league service at the end of the contract date may become a free agent by giving notice.

The clubs meet between November 1 and 15 to select the rights to negotiate with free agents. Selection is made in inverse order of team standings in the previous year. Each of the 26 teams makes one selection in each round of drafting, with individual players to be chosen by a maximum of 12 clubs. The clubs are limited in the number of players they may sign from the draft.[6]

Approximately 150 players were unsigned at the start of the 1976 season. Many were seeking to become free agents at the end of the season, so that they could sign a contract with the highest bidder. Contrary to predictions, however, most of these players signed contracts during the season. By the end of the 1976 season, 24 out of the 600 players in the major leagues had become free agents. This led to a much-publicized financial bonanza for some players who profited from a bidding war among clubs competing for their services. In 1977, three players received contracts of more than $2 million each.[7] Most observers thought that the salaries in the second reentry draft would be moderated. Several free agents in the 1978 season, however, were able to get contracts that far exceeded the previous levels. There were 35 major league players in this reentry draft. Some of the top salaries received are summarized in Table 1.

In the first and second reentry drafts, the two teams spending the most money for free agent players were the New York Yankees and the California Angels. In a recent 15-month period, the Yankees spent an estimated $9 million for four free agents.[8] The Yankees were the major league champions in 1977, but the Angels had a mediocre year, largely due to injuries sustained by key free agent draftees.

It is too early to determine whether free agents with seven-figure contracts will perform well enough to give the club owners a return on their investments, since many free agent contracts have several years to run. Although most of the free agents have played well, a majority of them have not provided the box-office rewards that the owners expected.

TABLE 1

Salaries in Baseball's Second Reentry Draft

Player	Team	Salary ($ million)	Term (years)
Lyman Bostock	California Angels	$2.2	5
Oscar Gamble	San Diego Padres	2.8	6
Rich Gossage	New York Yankees	2.75	6
Larry Hisle	Milwaukee Brewers	3	6
Doc Medich	Texas Rangers	1	4
Mike Torrez	Boston Red Sox	2.5	7
Richie Zisk	Texas Rangers	3	10

Source: Data compiled from Sports Illustrated, Vol. 47, No. 23 (December 5, 1977), p. 15.

AVERAGE SALARIES

The MLBPA negotiates minimum salaries ($21,000 in 1978 and 1979), and the maximum amount that salaries can be reduced from one year to the next. Otherwise, salaries are negotiated by the individual players. The player seeks a salary increase that is at least adequate to provide sufficient income in his productive years in the game. To most players and their agents, this means the maximum amount obtainable. Although many former players get high-paying jobs in a second career because of their sports status, they try to offset the future negative effects on income caused by loss of experience in the nonsport job market.

Average major league salaries tripled between 1969 and 1977. During this time, the Consumer Price Index increased by about two-thirds. The gain in salaries thus considerably exceeds over-all price rises (see Table 2).

As shown in Table 2, the average major league baseball player's salary in 1977 was $76,349, an increase of $24,848 over 1976. In 1977, there were nine teams that had a salary average that exceeded the overall average (see Table 3).

The escalating salaries in baseball do not appear to reflect qualitative differences in the players. Rapid expansion of the major leagues has brought in many players who would not have qualified a decade ago. Apart from economic consideration, such as lucrative television contracts for the clubs, tax advantages to owners, and improved stadium facilities,

TABLE 2
Major League Baseball Salaries, 1969-1977

Year	Average Salary
1969	$24,909
1970	29,303
1971	31,543
1972	34,892
1973	37,606
1974	40,956
1975	44,676
1976	51,501
1977	76,349

Source: Data provided to the author by the Major League Baseball Players Association.

TABLE 3
The Ten Highest Salaried Teams in Baseball, 1977

Team	Payroll	Average
1. Philadelphia	$3,497,900	$139,916
2. N.Y. Yankees	3,474,325	138,973
3. Cincinnati	2,759,800	110,392
4. Pittsburgh	2,485,475	99,419
5. Los Angeles	2,444,700	97,788
6. California	2,415,050	96,602
7. Kansas City	2,399,050	95,962
8. San Francisco	2,204,500	88,180
9. Texas	2,099,825	83,993
10. Boston	1,907,350	76,294

Source: Los Angeles Times, January 10, 1978, Part III, p. 1. Incentives, signing bonuses, and deferred payments were prorated over the terms of the players' contracts in arriving at the data.

labor relations has been a key factor in the salary increases. Especially important has been the opportunity to achieve free agency status, negotiated by the union. Also contributing to salary increases in baseball is the availability of arbitration of individual player salaries.

SALARY ARBITRATION

Use of the salary arbitration feature negotiated by the MLBPA began with the 1974 season. Under this arrangement, if an agreement is not reached between the club and player, the dispute may be submitted to an impartial arbitrator for final decision. Each side makes a final offer and the arbitrator then chooses one offer or the other. Arbitrators cannot compromise, selecting another position in the middle. In theory, this procedure would seem to stimulate bargaining. Under traditional forms of arbitration, the decision may fall somewhere between that of the two parties. This can have a chilling effect on negotiations, since the parties adopt extreme positions in anticipation of arbitration. Under the final-offer procedure, however, taking an extreme position is likely to result in the other side's offer being selected.

To be eligible for salary arbitration, the player must have a total of two years of major league service in at least three different seasons. Submission to arbitration is made between February 1 and 10. Hearings are held before February 20. Criteria for decision are (1) the player's contribution during the past season, including overall performance, leadership qualities, and public appeal; (2) length and consistency of career contribution; (3) past compensation; (4) comparative baseball salaries; (5) existence of any physical or mental defects; and (6) recent performance of the club.

The agreement provides that the arbitrator shall *not* consider the financial position of the player or club, press comments or testimonials, offers made before arbitration, costs of representation, and salaries in other sports. The player and club divide equally the cost of the arbitration hearing.

Results of the use of baseball arbitration are summarized in Table 4. Because salary arbitration was not available for use in 1976 and 1977, there are no cases reported in Table 4 for those years.

The effect of salary arbitration has been to increase the players' bargaining power. Although decisions have favored the owners on the whole, the players have prevailed in several cases where large salaries were involved and where there was a wide spread between the two final offers. Also, it is likely that the existence of the salary arbitration process contributed to higher salaries for the players who did not go to arbitration.

TABLE 4
Arbitration in Major League Baseball, 1974-1978

Year	Arbitration Awards	For the Player	For the Club
1974	29	13	16
1975	14	5	9
1978	9	2	7
Total	52	20	32

Sources: *The New York Times,* March 3, 1974, sec. 5, p. 1; James B. Dworkin, "The Impact of Final-Offer Interest Arbitration on Bargaining: The Case of Major League Baseball." In James L. Stern and Barbara D. Dennis, eds., *Proceedings of the Twenty-Ninth Annual Winter Meeting* (Madison: Wisc.: Industrial Relations Research Association, 1977), p. 167; and data provided to the author by the Major League Baseball Players Association.

In the three years this procedure has been used, the number of players involved has declined each year, from 29 in 1974, to 14 in 1975, to nine in 1978. This indicates that the final-offer procedure is stimulating negotiations, and that the chilling effect associated with conventional arbitration has not been a problem.

CONCLUDING REMARKS

The inflating salaries of players have forced higher ticket prices in many cases. For the 1978 season, 16 of the 26 clubs in the major leagues raised ticket prices.[9] Thus far, there has not been a reduction in attendance, which set a new high in 1977. Yet, when players seek to renegotiate contracts or play out their options, obtaining salaries that are nearly incomprehensible to the average worker, feelings of envy and contempt are bound to occur. There is a sense of disenchantment with the player as an American folk hero.

If the bidding war for players that occurred prior to the 1977 and 1978 seasons continues, as it almost certainly will, salaries will escalate further. Already some clubs are showing signs of weakening financially. The Houston Astros were taken over by creditors, and other franchises may go under in the next three or four years. Whether disgruntled fans will continue to support baseball if prices go sharply higher is uncertain. If support dwindles, the salary pendulum may swing back as market forces necessitate an adjustment. There is little, if any, evidence that the restrictions on the player market, which have now been modified, did much to promote competitive balance between clubs. There is also reason for optimism in that the compromise reached between the clubs and union provides some protection to the fan by limiting the extent to which players can become free agents. After the dust settles, this may well represent a reasonable and tenable middleground between the extremes of monopoly control of players and complete free agency status.

NOTES

1. The contract was made retroactive to January 1, 1976.
2. American League of Professional Baseball Clubs, 180 N.L.R.B. 189 (1969).
3. Federal Baseball Club v. National League, 259 U.S. 200 (1922).
4. Flood v. Kuhn, 407 U.S. 258 (1972).
5. *Los Angeles Times,* January 4, 1977, Part III, p. 1.
6. Basic Agreement between The American League of Professional Baseball Clubs and The National League of Professional Baseball Clubs and Major League Baseball Players Association, effective January 1, 1976, pp. 34-39.
7. *Sports Illustrated,* December 5, 1977, p. 15.
8. *The New York Times,* March 6, 1978, p. C-1.
9. *The Sporting News,* March 11, 1978, p. 55.

The Long-Run Effects of Abolishing the Baseball Player Reserve System

William L. Holahan

Professional sports have been exempt from United States antitrust laws governing restraint of trade because of an important industry characteristic: a good season results only if teams are fairly well matched and play exciting games with uncertain outcomes. The antitrust exemption has allowed owners to develop the reserve system for the ostensible purpose of attaining and maintaining league balance. The reserve system consists of two components:

(a) noncompetitive amateur draft selection by professional teams, the teams with the poorest records selecting first;

(b) the signing of a professional player contract which gives the team owner the right to retain or sell the skills of the player.[1]

The question of interest in this paper is what effect the abolition of the reserve clause will have on league balance and the existence of teams which are marginal when the system is in operation. Rottenberg[2] and Demsetz[3] argue that the reserve clause does not affect player trades or team balance because the same allocation of players will result regardless of who owns the players' skills. Rottenberg further argues that the player draft in which the worst teams select first is equivalent to income redistribution among clubs and that a system of money transfer can be substituted. But industry spokesmen argue that due to high competitive salaries, which would be paid if the reserve clause were abolished, the wealthiest team would sign up all the best players and the marginal teams would go out of business. Obviously the allocation of players *will* be affected if some cities lose their teams! In their powerful articles, Rottenberg and Demsetz do not give a complete analysis of the baseball market—they do not address the long-run problem of possible team dissolution should the reserve system be abolished. This paper briefly re-states the Rottenberg-Demsetz analysis in Part I and then, in Part II, builds upon their analyses to defend a stronger, more complete statement of the impact of the abolition of the reserve system on the ability of teams to survive financially. Since the net effect of the reserve system is to provide monetary transfers among teams, if equivalent monetary trans-fers among teams are retained after abolition of the reserve system, the abolition will cause a one-time devaluation of the club but will not affect team existence or location. Part III refines the analysis to consider the impact of abolition on the functioning of the minor leagues. It is argued that abolition of the reserve clause will not affect the minor leagues but will alter the identity of the investor. Since the player can market his skills when the reserve clause is abolished, he will pay to play for a minor league team and bear the risk of failure. Alternatively, he could contract with a sponsor in return for deferred payment if he is a success. The same incentive to invest will exist as with the reserve system in effect.

I. TRADES AND LEAGUE BALANCE

Rottenberg and Demsetz argue that trades will be unaffected by the ownership of players' skills—if a player is worth more to team A than team B he will be traded to A if not already there. To see this, assume that a player is worth $500,000 a year to Milwaukee and $400,000 a year to Los Angeles (and even less to all other teams) but due to the reserve clause is paid a wage of $100,000 a year to play for Milwaukee. With the reserve system in effect Los Angeles will be unwilling to offer enough to induce Milwaukee to trade the player's contract. Without the reserve clause, Los Angeles will bid the player's salary up to $400,000 but no higher. Milwaukee will match these offers because the player is still worth a net $100,000. Similarly, had the player started out playing for Los Angeles, he would have been traded to Milwaukee with or without the reserve clause.[4]

The argument that the wealthiest team will buy all the superstars if the reserve system is abolished can be shown to be false in a similar way. If team A's second superstar is worth more to team A than he would be worth to team B if he were team B's first superstar, he will not be traded to team B with or without the reserve clause. Otherwise, he will be traded to team B regardless of the reserve system. There is no reason to expect the reserve clause to affect the ability or willingness of the wealthiest team to assemble superstars.

Furthermore, as Rottenberg points out,[5] the effect of letting drafting teams select in reverse order of the preceding year's performance is to redistribute income among clubs, and this can be done through transfers from good clubs to bad in the form of money instead of the equivalent monopsony rents. Suppose team A, the worst team in the league, drafts a player who is worth an estimated $500,000 to team A, $400,000 to team B and less to all other teams, and team A signs him for $100,000. The reserve system has resulted in a net gain of $400,000 for the owner of team A and the player will play for team A. If instead the owner of team B decides that the player is worth $600,000 to him, he will pay team A at least $400,000 for the player's contract, which team A will accept. Thus, the player will play for team B, and team A will enjoy a net gain of at least $400,000 due to the reserve system. The net effect of the reserve system is to bring money to team A, not to individual players. A player selected in the draft will play for the team which values his services the highest, not necessarily the team which drafts him. Team balance can be maintained by organized money transfers among clubs for the development of exciting competitive games. In fact, as we will see below, monetary transfers are essential if the league size is to be unaffected by the abolition of the reserve clause. The team balance argument is not sufficient to justify monopsony rents in the form of subcompetitive wages for players because the reserve system can be replaced without affecting team balance.

II. TEAM SURVIVAL

The Rottenberg-Demsetz argument presented in Part I has been based on the analysis of a short-run phenomenon—the trading of players. It is widely agreed upon by economists. But industry spokesmen often argue that without the reserve clause some teams will go out of business or change their location (*i.e.*, the reserve rent is required for some teams to survive). If so, the Rottenberg-Demsetz argument that trades are unaffected by the reserve system is wrong since the list of trading partners will be changed. This part of my paper shows instead that if the monetary transfers inherent in the reserve system are retained, the abolition of the system merely results in a one-time decapitalization of each franchise equal to the owner's rent bestowed by the reserve system—the present value of the difference between the wages paid under the reserve clause and the highest alternative bid for the players. Players' wages rise

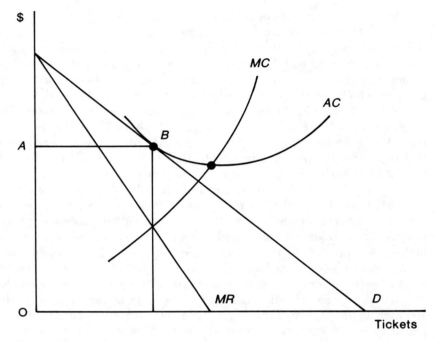

Figure 1

when the system is abolished and the owner absorbs the loss, whether by selling the club at a lower price than he would obtain under the reserve system or by retaining the devalued club. In neither case will the team be dissolved.

Consider Figure 1 where the demand and marginal revenue curves for tickets are drawn with the cost curves of the baseball team. Assume that the reserve clause is in effect and that the price of tickets is OA which clears the market when $MC = MR$. The proof of this assertion is achieved by demonstrating that the properly constructed marginal and average cost curves of the club owner are unaffected by the abolition of the reserve system.

The first step is to show that the equilibrium price and quantity of tickets will not change when the reserve clause is abolished and wages rise. This is surprising since the marginal cost of output is equal to the wage rate divided by the marginal product of labor. Using this formula, one would expect marginal cost to rise when wages rise due to the abolition of the draft-reserve system. This expectation is in the spirit, if not the articulation, of the industry's defense of the reserve system. The argument is incorrect because the owner will evaluate a player at the highest alternative evaluation by other teams. This is true whether or not the reserve system is in effect. Recall the Milwaukee player considered in Part I. If the reserve clause were abolished, the player's wages would be bid up to $400,000. But even with the reserve system, which allows the owner to pay only $100,000 for the player's talents, the club owner will evaluate the player at $400,000 because the owner forgoes the opportunity to sell the contract for $300,000 and to escape $100,000 salary payments by not trading. The owner will always impute the marginal opportunity cost of labor whether it be greater than or equal to the actual wage. For this reason the marginal cost curve in Figure 1 will be unaffected by the abolition of the reserve system and hence the equilibrium price and quantity of tickets will be unaffected.[6] This figure is the graphical equivalent of Part I.

Baseball industry spokesmen argue, however, that due to the high competitive wage levels which would result from the abolition of the reserve system, some teams that are now only marginally profitable will be forced to change their location or go out of business. In effect, the reserve rent is required to enable some teams to break even. In graphical terms, this means that the average cost curve in Figure 1 rises, requiring a long-run adjustment. If this were true, then certainly the price and quantity of tickets would change—both would be zero because the team would be gone! Instead, as shown below, the abolition of the reserve clause results only in a one-time decrease in the value of the club equal to the present value of the stream of reverse rents. The value of the club (purchase price) with the reserve system in effect will always be at least as great as the reserve rents for any team which exists with the system in effect. Hence, the owner can absorb a loss of that size without dissolving the club. The decision to dissolve the club or move it to another city is unaffected by the loss of reserve rents. The average cost curve does not shift.

To see this, assume that the reserve system is operating. Equation (1) expresses the purchase price of a club as a fraction α of the rent V bestowed on owners by the reserve system.

$$P = R - W^a - E = \alpha V, \tag{1}$$

where

R = revenue,
W^a = actual wages of players when the reserve system is in effect,
E = accounting profits which the entrepreneur forgoes in order to own the club,
V = rent bestowed on owners by the reserve system.

But if W^o is the competitive wage level,

$$V = W^o - W^a, \tag{2}$$

rent equals the difference between competitive wages and actual wages. Using (2) in (1) to eliminate W^a and rearranging yields:

$$P - V = R - W^o - E = (\alpha - 1)V. \tag{3}$$

If $\alpha < 1$ with the reserve system operating, then $R < W^o + E$; revenues do not cover the owner's accounting profits in his next best alternative plus the opportunity value of the ballplayers' contracts. In this case, the owner would dissolve the club. He will not sell the club intact because the highest bidder will only pay P, which is smaller than the gain from selling the player contracts individually, i.e., if $\alpha < 1$ then $P < W^o - W^a < W^o$. Hence, it must be true that $\alpha \geqq 1$ for all clubs which exist when the reserve system is in effect; economic profits must be at least as great as the rent component derived from the reserve system or else the team will be dissolved by the selling of players' contracts to other owners. The economic effect of the abolition of the reserve system is a one-time loss of rent V. Since $\alpha \geqq 1$, we see in (3) that $P \geqq V$; there is sufficient surplus for the owner to absorb the loss of V, whether he sells at the lower price or retains ownership of the devalued club.[7] The abolition of the reserve system does not cause teams to dissolve if they were not going to do so with the reserve system.

To see this graphically in Figure 1, let the cost function of the club owner be written:

$$Full\ Cost = W^o + E - V + P, \tag{4}$$

where E, V, and P enter as fixed opportunity costs. To constitute an accurate model of the entrepreneur's decision to enter or exit an industry, the properly constructed cost curves must be based on opportunity costs rather than out-of-pocket expenditures. Since purchase price P is equal to profits, we can write $R - W^o - E + V - P = 0$. Therefore, the average cost curve which includes E, V, and P must be constructed tangent to the demand curve at point B in order to depict a zero-profit equilibrium. When the reserve clause is abolished, this average cost curve does not shift since P is merely lowered by the amount V; the devaluation of the club is equal to the loss of rent. Since $P \geqq V$ under the reserve system, the abolition of the reserve clause and devaluation by amount V will not result in $P < 0$ and force the dissolution of the club. Team net revenues are still at least as great as the entrepreneur opportunity cost, $E + W^o$, and the owner will absorb the loss but the club will remain in business in what is still its profit-maximizing location.

III. TRAINING OF NEW PLAYERS

The industry claims that the reserve clause is necessary for the compensation of clubs for new talent development. A simple application of Becker's theory of human capital[8] points out that this is the correct answer to the wrong question. What is of interest is whether new talent will be developed as it would be under the reserve system, not whether the club makes the investment. Economic theory predicts no change in the amount or type of investment, but it does predict that the players will invest instead of the clubs.

When the reserve system is in effect, the return on the development of the player's talent is specific to the club that invests in his talent. The clubs invest in players by recruiting them to play for minor league teams. Part of the difference between competitive players' salaries and the lower wages paid under the reserve clause is the competitive return to this risky investment. The rest is monopsony rent. Abolition of the reserve clause wipes out the full difference. Without the reserve system, the training is general training—the player can market his own skills and gain the return on his skill development. With a perfect capital market, he has the same incentive to invest in his skill development after the abolition of the reserve clause as the club does with the clause in effect. Capital market imperfections can be corrected by a system of competitive talent agencies with large portfolios of ballplayers, which would spread the risk investment over successful and unsuccessful players. The talent agency's function would be to identify talent and apply to minor leagues to accept the player and let him develop his talent by playing. This is analogous to applying to college. Upon acceptance of the player by a team, the talent agency will pay his tuition. The minor league teams will accept a mix of players that will maximize the expected return to entrepreneurship of the major league team net of the payment of competitive wages. Following the argument of Part I, this mix will be the same as it now is under the reserve clause since the teams place the same marginal value on the player with or without the reserve clause.

The return to the talent agency would be payments from the successful ballplayers—those who make it to the major leagues. The payment would be a simple fraction of the players' salaries for a specified number of years, or a simple fixed amount, or some complicated combination of payments. Competition among agencies would bring the return to the agency down to competitive rates of return equal to the training costs plus the talent agency's entrepreneurial opportunity cost, including a risk premium. Such agencies exist in most forms of entertainment.

We need not think of the talent agency as necessarily distinct from the baseball club. It may be that using capital markets to facilitate the investment in training by ballplayers may be more costly than investment by ball clubs and that many young players would opt for arrangements directly with ball clubs. The club could offer tuition scholarships to a portfolio of promising ballplayers in return for future payments from the players who succeed. The clubs would compete with outside talent agencies and among themselves for such contracts. To sign with a club instead of an outside sponsor would not be equivalent to the current reserve clause. The club's expected return to sponsorship would be competitive. The player could market his skills to the highest bidding team within the bounds of contracts that he selects.

The algebraic argument of Part II becomes only slightly more complicated when the development of young talent is included in the analysis. Let the training costs required to produce a team be C. Then using the notation of Part II, the purchase price of a club as a fraction α of the reserve rent V is:

$$P = R - W^a - C - E = \alpha V. \tag{5}$$

The rent V is now:

$$V = W^o - W^a - C. \tag{6}$$

The investment C must be made by the club since the player cannot gain return to training which is specific to the club under the reserve system. Therefore rent (6) is the wage differential minus the investment required to produce the differential. Using (6) in (5) to eliminate W^a and rearranging yields:

$$P - V = R - W^o - E = (\alpha - 1)V. \tag{7}$$

Since (7) is identical to (3), the argument following (3) still holds: the abolition of the reserve system does not cause teams to dissolve if they were not already going to do so under the reserve system. The rearrangement of investment incentives does not change this result.

IV. POLICY STATEMENT

The baseball player reserve system is a reassignment of the ownership of players' skills to club owners, allowing them to pay subcompetitive wages for players' services. The draft, which permits the teams to choose in inverse order of their performance, amounts to a redistribution of money, not players, and can be replaced by equivalent money transfers. Quirk and El-Hodiri estimate that in the period from 1920 to 1950, four of the sixteen baseball teams had net sales of players which exceeded their net profits.[9] These teams would have folded without either the reserve system or a system of equivalent monetary transfers. The analysis of this paper demonstrates that operations under the reserve system are sufficiently profitable that the loss of monopsony rent generated by the system would not force any club out of business or alter the investment in new talent provided that the monetary transfers equivalent to the draft of the reserve system are put in its place. If these interteam monetary transfers are instituted, the abolition of the reserve system will not affect trades, league balance, the existence of teams, or team location. Hunt and Lewis have shown that industry behavior is consistent with the hypothesis of profit maximization by owners in maintaining league balance, even in the case of those who are in a position to dominate leagues by sacrificing profits and buying a team that is too good.[10] This evidence indicates that the required monetary transfers would be instituted in the interests of baseball and profits. The reserve system can be replaced by systems which allow both good baseball games and player salaries that are equal to marginal product.

NOTES

1. Recent labor-management disputes and court decisions have centered on the years of active service in the sport which must be served before the player can be a free agent and negotiate his own contract. In fact, in 1977 the owners granted that present players can become free agents after only one year, but they did not grant this concession to future players.
2. Simon Rottenberg, The Baseball Players' Labor Market, 64 J. Pol. Econ. 242 (1956).
3. Harold Demsetz, When Does the Rule of Liability Matter?, 1 J. Leg. Studies 13 (1972).
4. Baseball teams are permitted by the Internal Revenue Service to depreciate the skills of the players over the expected length of active service. The loss of the contract-depreciation right due to the abolition of the reserve clause is merely another component of the devaluation of the purchase price of the club. If all teams must use the same formulae for such depreciation, a player's value ranking among different teams will not change when the reserve system is abolished, and hence the above result still holds.
5. Simon Rottenberg, supra note 2, et. 248-49.
6. An equivalent argument can be made for a modification of the reserve system, such as an upper bound on the number of years which a player must serve before he may market his own skills. Each such modification will result in a devaluation of the ball club but will not affect marginal decisions.

7. A related problem is that by depressing wages the reserve system is a barrier to worker ownership. The higher competitive wages which would result from abolishing the reserve system would increase the likelihood of player ownership of some or all teams due to the increased availability of investment capital owned by players, as well as increased access to the large amounts of loanable funds required for takeover. The probability of player ownership would also be increased by the lower purchase price of the ball clubs brought about by the abolition of the resesrve system. A possible conflict of interest exists if a player transfers from Team A to B but retains part ownership in Team A—he may "throw" a game to enhance the value of his Team A shares. A blind trust or a rule requiring divestiture of shares in other teams would eliminate this problem.

8. Gary S. Becker, Investment in Human Capital: A Theoretical Analysis, 70 J. Pol. Econ. pt. 2, Supp. at 9 (Oct. 1962).

9. James Quirk & Mohamed El Hodiri. The Economic Theory of a Professional Sports League, in Government and the Sports Business 33, 53 (Roger G. Noll ed. 1974).

10. Joseph W. Hunt, Jr. & Kenneth A. Lewis, Dominance, Recontracting, and the Reserve Clause: Major League Baseball, 66 Am. Econ. Rev. 936 (1976).

The World of Women's Professional Golf: Responses to Structured Uncertainty

Nancy Theberge

All occupational groups are faced with a set of work related contingencies: demands, requirements and responsibilities that members must meet in order to be successful. The specific forms that these contingencies take, vary among occupations, depending upon the work that is performed and the technological, organizational and cultural setting in which it is performed. Regardless of their forms, however, adaptations and responses to contingencies, structure and condition members' work roles and ultimately, career success.

This paper describes and analyzes the contingencies that shape occupational roles in women's professional golf. For professional golfers, as for all professional athletes, sport participation is not play, but work. That is, it is serious and consequential. Thus, the contingencies of golfers' (and other professional athletes') work are also consequential. In the following discussion, some of the contingencies of this occupational world and the ways in which members adapt to these demands are outlined. The purpose of the analysis is to show how social roles are created and defined in a setting that is marked by extreme variability and indeterminacy; that is, in a situation of *structured uncertainty*.[1]

SETTING AND METHODS

The women's professional golf tour is organized and administered by the Ladies Professional Golf Association (LPGA). Approximately 125 women compete on the tour, which is actually a series of three or four day golf tournaments conducted at different locations. In 1976, between February and November, the women on the tour played 31 tournaments, 27 in the United States and one each in Canada, England, the Philippines

Reprinted from *Play: Anthropological Perspectives;* (Michael Salter, editor), West Point, N.Y.: Leisure Press; 1978. By permission of the publisher.

and Hong Kong. The total amount of prize money awarded was $2,524,000, while individual players' earnings ranged from $25 to $150,734.

The data reported here are taken from field observations and interviews conducted at LPGA tournaments in the summer of 1975 and the spring of 1976, a survey of LPGA members conducted in the spring of 1976, and a secondary analysis of related literature. The number of players who were interviewed is 19, while 82 golfers (66 percent of the players on tour) responded to the survey. The secondary analysis of literature is taken from documents supplied by the LPGA and golfing publications.

THE PROFESSIONAL GOLFER'S WORK WORLD

Simply stated, the work of the professional golfer is to complete a number of rounds of play in a tournament. In the majority of LPGA tournaments the number of rounds played is three (54 holes), while in a few "major" events (and in most men's tournaments) four rounds (72 holes) are played. The tournaments are contested at stroke (also called medal) play, which means that scores are calculated on the basis of the total number of strokes taken over the three or four rounds played.[2] The object of the competition then, is to complete a tournament by taking the fewest number of shots, and final placement is determined by the inverse ordering of scores.

While the object of the sport may be simply stated, its accomplishment, of course, is not so simple. The occupational setting in women's professional golf is best described as one of structured uncertainty. In many and often disparate ways, the golfer's work world is conditioned by variability and continual adjustment to a set of unknowns. For this reason, many of the important contingencies of the occupation are grounded in members' attempts to reduce this uncertainty and standardize their work situation. The types of uncertainty that players face, and the means by which they attempt to reduce it, are discussed below with respect to four different features of the work world: the support structure, the task structure, work roles and relationships, and life style.[3]

THE SUPPORT STRUCTURE

Competing on the professional golf tour requires a considerable financial investment. At the same time, monetary returns from this investment—winnings—are marked by uncertainty and fluctuation. The result of these two conditions is that the golfer's financial situation is precarious.

The expenses involved in playing the LPGA tour (including the costs of travel and lodging, tournament entry fees and caddy fees) average approximately $15,000 a year.[4] While this sum varies among individual players, the costs of playing the tour are relatively inelastic. In contrast, the rewards from tournament play vary greatly. As noted above, in 1976, players' winnings ranged from $25 to more than $150,000. Only 42 players, however, won $15,000 or more. Thus, the first condition of the support structure is that income from winnings is limited and in a given year many players will not win enough to cover the costs of competing on tour.

Financial support is also conditioned by the instability of the golfers' earning power. This is a product of many factors: the threat posed by injury and illness, the unpredictable playing slump, the inevitable decline of skills with age, and the rigidly objective system of rewards from tournament play.

The insecurity associated with the rewards from tournament play warrants special explanation. Each week golfers enter a different tournament where they are tested anew and rewarded only for their play in that event. With some few exceptions, there is no carryover in reward from one tournament to the next and a player may win one week and finish out of the money the following week.[5] Few occupations do not guarantee their members some amount of financial stability, either in the form of job security, a minimum wage or an annual salary. None of these features is present to diminish the insecurity of tournament winnings.

This feature of the tournament reward structure is not accidental. Historically, the reward systems in professional golf and other individual (non-team) sports have been grounded in the belief that athletes should be rewarded solely on the basis of their actual (as opposed to expected) performance. Accordingly, the golfer's winnings are based upon one simple measure—final placement in a tournament.

This type of reward system is different from that present in team sports, where athletes sign contracts for one or more years. Moreover, the measurement of a player's performance in team sports is not always totally objective. While precise measures of performance are available in the form of playing statistics, team-sport athletes are also evaluated on more subjective qualities, such as, leadership and aggressiveness or "hustle". No amount of effort, or any other admired trait, will yield winnings for the golfer, except insofar as these are reflected in her score at the end of a tournament.

In response to the limitations and instability of tournament winnings, there has arisen on the golf tour a secondary or auxiliary set of income sources. These income sources include sponsorship, fees for endorsing commercial products and representing golf and country clubs, and income from giving golf lessons and clinics.

Data from the survey of golfers indicate the importance of these secondary income sources. Sixty-one percent of the players have been sponsored at some point in their careers. Typically, sponsorship arrangements involve an agreement whereby an individual or group guarantees to support a player for a specified sum, in return for which the sponsor(s) is repaid according to the player's winnings. In general, players accept sponsorship when they first come on tour and until they can support themselves with winnings or other sources of income.

These other sources of income are more prevalent. Eighty-four percent of the players earned part of their 1975 income from at least one of these sources and forty-four percent benefited from both. Usually, the amount earned was moderate. Only six percent of players earned more than half their total income from endorsements and eleven percent earned more than half from other golf-related work.[6]

TASK STRUCTURE

The task structure in professional golf is the work done on the golf course. The uncertainty of this feature is due to the variability in the courses played and the conditions under which they are played, and the fluctuations which mark an individual golfer's performance over time.

Each week, as golfers move to a new course, they face a different set of work conditions. Some of the features that distinguish golf courses are length, layout (e.g., Is the course "tight," with narrow fairways requiring extreme accuracy in shot making? Where are "trouble areas" like water hazards and sand traps?), and terrain (e.g., Are the putting surfaces or greens "slick," so the ball "runs"? How high is the rough?). Each course the women play on tour presents a unique combination of these and numerous other factors. Thus, every week players must contend with a new work setting.

Still other factors change during a tournament. For example, pin placements (the locations of the 18 holes) are relocated for each day's play, necessitating daily re-analysis of the putting surfaces. The weather also changes, not daily, but continually. Wind and rain can affect playing conditions considerably and players must learn techniques for working under variant weather patterns. Even the time of day that a player begins her round or "tees off" can be important. A golfer with a late starting time plays a course already heavily traversed by other players and caddies. This will affect the playing conditions on the course and especially, the putting surfaces. After several hours of play, the greens are likely to be matted down or "slick." This causes the ball to "run" and makes the shot more difficult to control and hence, more difficult to execute.

In addition to contending with variability in the courses and the conditions, the golfer must also deal with personal fluctuations in performance. In completing a round, a player brings to bear a variety of skills, involving the execution of several types of shots using fourteen different clubs. Most players' "games" include strengths and weaknesses, shots and clubs that they are more proficient with than others. Even this is marked by change, however, as a player may periodically "lose" a stroke, for example, her putting stroke (in the same way that a tennis player temporarily loses his or her serve). One of the best players on tour explained the difficulties of "putting it all together."

> In order to put it all together, everything has to be working. Now, the problem I have is that when my long game is working, my putting is not working, or when my putting's working, I'm having trouble with some other shot, or getting out of some other problem. But someday, this year I think, I'm going to put it all together and I'll break [i.e., score below] 65 (Personal interview).

In the face of the uncertainty arising from these features of their occupation's task structure, golfers work at standardizing their performance—being consistent. Golf courses cannot be standardized; they can, however, be "managed." Course management is the term players use to denote the tactical and strategical aspects of the sport. It involves club and shot selection and the ability to "read" or analyze the course being played, so the golfer may employ her skills most effectively.

Players develop proficiency in course management as they gain experience, or "seasoning." One player described her development in this respect during her first two years on tour. She prefaced the explanation by indicating that her most extensive day of preparation for a tournament is Tuesday. This is the day she obtains the information she will need for course management:

> Tuesday I go out with my caddy, and we get yardages, check the holes for trouble, where we should be in different positions, we check the green, we check the traps, we hit practise shots out of traps.
> Q.: Do you work differently on Tuesdays now than when you first came on tour?

I think . . . I've used Tuesdays more than my first year. I've used Tuesdays more in making myself aware of course management. Like I say, knowing where to be and where not to be. And if I'm not to be in that spot, well for crying out loud, don't put myself there. Whereas, before, I would just eye the whole hole, instead of picking a spot where I want to be in and blocking out a spot where I don't want to be. And I think I've used my course management a lot better in my play this year than I did my first year.

Q.: So it's a matter of becoming more aware of the kinds of things you have to be conscious of and using this knowledge?

Right, like in Ft. Myers there's a par 5 hole and I hit a great drive and the pin [hole] was tucked on the right hand side by a bunker. So I said to myself, "You do not want to be on the right hand side, because you'll have to hit over that bunker and you don't have much room to work with, to stop the ball close to the pin." So I said "Just hit the ball dead left and open that whole green up, instead of putting your ball here and having to go over, put your ball here and you'll have all this area, and you don't have the trap to worry about at all. And you can run it up and maybe run it up close and make par" (Personal interview).

In short, the golfer's work involves continual adjustment to a new work setting and to fluctuations in her own performance. In working to manage a course and their games, players seek to control the uncertainty of their task structure. This occurs as players become proficient in course management and develop the knowledge that allows them to employ their skills most effectively.

PROFESSIONAL ROLES AND RELATIONSHIPS

The content of the golfer's relationships with persons who fill other roles in the occupational setting is open-ended. In order to stabilize their working conditions, players attempt to standardize their relationships with, respectively, caddies, colleagues, coaches and tournament audiences.

Caddies. The working relationships between golfers and their caddies vary greatly. At one extreme, some players rely extensively upon their caddies for information and consultation throughout their preparation and play in a tournament. An example is this player's caddy:

[He] gets to the course early and looks after everything. He measures [course yardage], he knows where all the trouble is and if I can't get to a tournament early enough he'll plot a meaningful practice round (With the Tourists 1977:6).

At the other extreme, some players want their caddies simply to carry and hand them their golf clubs. Rather than asking their caddies to assume an active and contributing role in their games (as described above), these players define the caddy's role negatively — his job is not to do anything that would disrupt his player's concentration and performance.

To this range of work relationships caddies bring different amounts of skill and knowledge of the sport. Some of the men who caddy regularly on the tour have played or caddied on the men's professional circuit, while others have never played golf and profess to know very little about the sport, beyond identification of the clubs. Because of the variability in caddies' responsibilities and skills and the range in players' temperaments and abilities, each player and her caddy must negotiate a common definition of their working relationship. Most importantly, they must agree upon how much the caddy can and should contribute to the work effort.

One way that players stabilize their relationships with caddies is by working with the same person week after week. The caddies who work at LPGA tournaments are of two types: club caddies, who are recruited locally at each tournament, and tour caddies, who travel regularly with the LPGA. In general, the more successful players employ tour caddies, a practice usually explained in two ways. First, tour caddies are paid more[7] and successful players can afford this expense. Secondly, some players believe that working with the same person regularly can help their game. One player described the comparative advantage of hiring a "professional" tour caddy, as opposed to a club caddy:

> Q.: Do caddies make a difference in your play?
> Oh yeah, yeah. If you have a local boy, a lot of times you're worrying about where he puts the golf bag, or if he's stepping on people's lines on the green. I had one boy in Portland, I hit my ball in the trap and he stands my bag by the trap and leaves it. If that bag had ever tipped and fell into the trap, I don't think I would have been penalized but it would have just annoyed me. And then caddies that start walking your line on the green, it just can be annoying. It can just be an added hindrance.
> Q.: Is it a help to work with the same person week after week?
> It is a help in that if you have a fellow, week in and week out, he knows how you think. He knows how you play. He knows what you're like in different situations. He knows, . . . how far you hit the ball and things like that. And that's a help, there's no doubt about it, because then he knows how to react when the situation comes up. . . . So, a tour caddy, if you can get along well, is very good. . . . It's just easier, a lot easier (Personal interview).

As this player indicates, by hiring a person who caddies regularly and "knows her game," golfers reduce the possibility of "annoyance" or distractions. In turn this counteracts one form of the structured uncertainty of the work world.

Coaches. The coaching role is usually filled by the teaching professional.[8] The "pro's" contributions to a player's game are both technical and mental. Technically, the pro works with the player on her swing and shot making. The more proficient a golfer is in these areas, of course, the more consistent her game will be.

Coaches also help players with their "mental" game and one way they do this is by developing the confidence of players. Athletes in all sports cite confidence as a prerequisite to success. Confidence arises from many factors, one of which is success itself. And yet in order to break into the cycle of "confidence arising from success, and success breeding confidence," players seek assistance from other sources. One of these sources is the teaching professional. A player described how her pro helps her confidence and why this is important. Speaking of their meetings when she takes a break from the tour, she said:

> John always wonders "Well, what kind of mood is she [the player] coming home in this week?" 'Cause usually when I come home, I make a mountain out of a mole-hill. I might feel like I'm not hitting the ball well, but I'll get to John and he'll say, "You are hitting the ball so strong and so good." And, you know, I just need a little added confidence. I just need somebody to tell me. Because I don't think of my swing out there. I just do it. And John helps me mentally. He helps build me in saying "You're swinging so strong, it looks great. You're not doing anything wrong. You've got a great leg movement. Your hands are strong. The plane of the club is strong." Now see I don't think of those things when I am out there (Personal interview).

She went on to explain further why confidence in the coach is so important. During a period when she was playing poorly, she met with her pro:

> I had a week off. And I was able to talk to my pro, collect my thoughts and work on some things. . . . I have so much confidence in my teacher and that's what you need; you need total confidence in your teacher.
> Q.: Why is that important?
> Well, because he's telling you how to improve, he's telling you what the right way to swing and hit the ball is. And if you don't have confidence in him, then you won't play well, you won't even hit it well.
> Q.: So confidence is important because without believing he knows what's best for you, you won't follow through and do it?
> Right, right, exactly (Personal interview).

This player is fortunate because her teaching pro is the person who has coached her since childhood and she has continued to profit from their association. Other players work successfully with different pros over a period of time. Not all players are so fortunate, however, and a common observation among slumping players is that they would like to find someone who "knows their swing" to observe and analyze it. As this suggests, all golfers experience slumps, but their responses to these problems differ. Players who have developed a trusted and working relationship with a coach often are more readily able to get their games back in order. Thus, the coach is an important aid in the reduction of the variability in the golfer's work.

Colleagues. The weekly travel required of golfers reduces their interaction with non-golfing friends. In addition, this itinerancy dictates that players spend much of their off-course lives with other members of the tour, in traveling, lodging and leisure activities. At the same time that players provide friendship and companionship for one another, however, they also face each other in competition each week. The occupation thus presents an extreme form of colleague-competitor relationship, with a potential for dissonance between these two relationships.

Golfers reduce the dissonance that may arise from competing against their friends by rigidly separating the roles of colleague and competitor. That is, while competing they attempt to concentrate on "playing the course" and to disregard their opponents. One player observed that "you can be friendly before and after playing. But when you're playing, you have to forget everyone else" (Personal interview). In short, the possible dissonance from the juxtaposition of the friend and competitor roles is reduced by leaving friendship off the golf course.

The Audience. Attracting an audience is central to the financial success of a tournament, thus, player relationships with the gallery at LPGA tournaments are somewhat paradoxical. On the one hand, golf is considered to be a sport requiring intense concentration, justifying players' inattentiveness to their surroundings, including the gallery. On the other hand, women's golf is also actively seeking public support and interest and it is argued that this effort would be aided by the appearance of "personalities" on tour comparable to Arnold Palmer and Lee Trevino in men's golf and Billie Jean King in women's tennis.

This issue speaks to two facets of the woman golfer's work life — the competitive element requiring concentration upon the game, and the entertainment factor requiring attention to a public image and public relations. A young player described how she was trying to deal with both these features:

> There's one thing that kind of bothers me when I'm playing. Now there are people like Lee Trevino who can joke with the crowd and play well as he jokes. OK? Well, for me, I'm trying to find what's good

for me. And I don't joke with the crowd, but I do try to acknowledge them when they appreciate something that I do. But to go up to the crowd and start talking to them, start a conversation, I don't do that. And I always wonder if, you know . . . I never want to get stonefaced out there. I'm trying to find that happy medium where I can let loose a little bit but yet still stay in the frame of mind where I can keep my concentration.

I remember there was one time where I played a tournament and I did joke with the crowd, and . . . not fooled around, but, you know . . . and then I lost all my concentration from that. Then there was a time when I just went on with my business and never looked out at the crowd at all and I didn't like that. So, I'm trying to find my happy medium, where I can acknowledge the crowd, but yet also keep my concentration at the same time. I'll never be a Lee Trevino, happy-go-lucky, talking-all-the time type person. But I don't want to be a stoneface out there either (Personal interview).

As this player indicates, golfers develop different patterns of interaction with tournament audiences. Each player, however, works to routinize her own mode of interaction, to develop a pattern that is consistent and effective for her and that allows her to concentrate fully on her round of play.

LIFE STYLE

Because the women on the tour move to a different tournament location each week, their life style is marked by constant dislocation and disruption. Insofar as they can, players also try to stabilize and routinize this. An experienced player recently wrote about the advice she offered to a friend who had just joined the tour:

I offered what I thought would be her major adjustments. . . . She would have to develop a routine: her own. Would she prefer private housing or motels? Rent a car or bring her own? She would have to learn which places to stay in which cities, determine her own practice routine, and so on. Tour life is not as glamorous as TV and many stories would make it. It cannot be. A player has to establish a routine and stay with it. Depart from it and you chance breaking your game plan as well (Alcott 1977:6).

As this suggests, the importance of routinizing daily life is to minimize the distractions which might interfere with performance.

Although the constant travel required in professional golf complicates efforts to routinize activities, there are ways in which schedules can be regularized. During each tournament-week players follow much the same playing and practicing schedules. A typical work week includes: travel on Monday, practice on Tuesday, participation in an exhibition Professional-Amateur (Pro-Am) tournament on Wednesday, practice on

Thursday, and tournament play on Friday through Sunday. There will of course be exceptions to this. For example, some players do not qualify for play on Sunday and not all players compete in the Pro-Am event. Nevertheless, this general pattern provides a measure of weekly regularity to players' work lives. Each Monday the pattern starts again. The challenge posed by the travel and disruptions, then, is to minimize the variability within each week as much as possible.

SUMMARY AND DISCUSSION

Several features of the world of women's professional golf are marked by uncertainty: the reward structure, the task structure, work roles and relationships, and life style. The content of the golfer's role takes shape as she attempts to deal with these uncertainties and specifically as she works to control the variability. In order to manage variability, players utilize several organizational and cultural resources. These include sources of income in addition to winnings, the development of course management, standardization of relationships with those who fill other work-related roles, and routinization of the life style. In sum, the structured uncertainty of the occupation and the resources available to deal with this uncertainty, provide the occupational features that players respond to in defining and filling their roles.

In general, players learn to manage the indeterminacy of their work world as they gain experience and are socialized into the culture of the golf tour. Through trial and error and interaction with veteran players, novices or "rookies" learn to adjust. One player has described some aspects of this socialization process:

> In professional golf, you work to stay on top every week, adjust to travel, to practice schedules; you learn to deal with people, with weather. It's all a big mystery at first, but if you want to remain on tour, you learn to cope (Alcott 1977:6).

Learning to "cope" with the demands of the tour is of no small import. A primary function of standardizing and routinizing the various features of this work world is to allow golfers to "play the course." As indicated earlier, the golfer's job consists basically of completing a number of rounds of tournament play by taking a minimum number of shots. In order to do this players develop technical skills but they also strive to reduce the variability of their occupational world. This in turn maximizes their capacity to perform the task at hand. In short, the ability to manage the uncertainty of their work is directly related to career success.

The analytic import of the management of uncertainty extends beyond its relationship to career mobility. More broadly, the above account of responses to indeterminacy provides an illustration of the process of role definition and creation. All social behavior requires actors to interpret their roles. In settings which are marked by indeterminacy, the latitude allowed the individual in this process is considerable. Women's golf provides this type of social setting, for latitude in the construction of her role is not simply allowed the golfer but is forced upon her. Here social roles are defined and created as they are enacted. To be sure, throughout this process these women utilize the various resources which are available to them to deal with this indeterminacy. But these resources, by themselves, are inadequate for describing how people deal with uncertainty. Rather, it is the golfer's interpretation and utilization of these resources which results in the creation of their social roles.

This view of the process of role fulfillment is consistent with Turner's emphasis upon role-making as the creative aspect of role-taking. "In attempting from time to time to make aspects of . . . roles explicit, [the individual] is creating and modifying roles as well as bringing them to light; the process is not only role-taking but **role-making**" (1962:22). As Turner indicates, the freedom allowed the individual in determining the content of his or her role, varies depending upon the organizational setting where interaction occurs. In formally organized settings, where behavior is subject to the constraints of organizational prescriptions, the "tentative character of interaction" (Turner 1962:27) is lessened. No social situation, including what Goffman (1961) has described as total institutions, is completely determined. There are, however, degrees of indeterminacy. Where uncertainty is a dominant feature, that is, in situations of **structured uncertainty,** the clearest insights into the creative aspects of role-making can be gained.

Professional sports, especially individual sports such as golf, provide such a setting. As Page has noted, one of the significant features of organized sport is the combination of "disciplined skill and personal creativity" (1973:34) that is brought to bear. This is true within the confines of the athletic contest — the match, the game or the tournament — but also often within the broader organizational and cultural setting. This combination of discipline and individuality makes sport subcultures a useful setting in which to examine some basic features of social life.[9]

NOTES

1. It should be noted that the analysis provided here is taken from research on the *women's* golf tour only. While there are clear similarities between the culture and social organization of men's and women's golf (and probably many more similarities than differences), these are not discussed here. It is likely, however, that much of the analysis probably applies to men's golf, although research to show this has not been conducted.

2. The other major form of competition is match play, more often found in amateur golf. Match play is hole by hole competition between two persons or two teams.

3. Charles Perrow (1967) has suggested that all work organizations seek to standardize the materials they work with; in Perrow's terms, the "raw materials" of their work. The analysis provided here is consistent with Perrow's observation, although by examining the structured uncertainty of several features of this occupation, this analysis extends the framework provided by Perrow.

4. This figure is reported in Lassila (1976:1-B); *Sports Illustrated,* (1976:12); and Stockbridge (1976:3-D).

5. The few exceptions where there is a carryover in reward from one tournament to the next involve the recent introduction of selected tournaments where entry is restricted to players who have performed well in previous competitions. For example, participation in the Colgate-Dinah Shore Tournament is limited to players who have finished among the top three in an LPGA event during the preceding three years. Tournaments which impose a qualifying standard are the exception to the women's tour, however. (This is in contrast to the men's tour where weekly qualifying rounds are held for nonexempt players, that is, those who have not met any one of several standards which provide exemption from the Monday qualifying round.) In 1976 only five LPGA tournaments imposed qualifying standards and four of these were sponsored by the Colgate Company.

6. A more detailed account of sources of financial support in women's golf is contained in Theberge (1977).

7. On the average, tour caddies are paid about $10,000 a year, plus five percent of players' winnings (With the Tourists 1977:6). Club caddies are paid a daily fee of $15 or $20 and at the player's discretion, a bonus based on her winnings.

8. Exceptions to this are players who coaches are friends or relatives and who are not paid, hence, technically, they are not professionals.

9. I would like to thank Susan Birrell, Robert Faulkner, John Loy and Richard Martin for their comments on an earlier draft of this paper.

REFERENCES

Alcott, Amy, 1977. The Alcott Report. Golf World 18:6.
Goffman, Erving, 1961. Asylums. Garden City: Doubleday Anchor.
Lassila, Alan, 1976. Pro Golf Tour is no Joy Ride. Sarasota Journal 17:1-B.
Page, Charles, 1973. The World of Sport and its Study. *In* Sport and Society.
     J. T. Talamini and C. H. Page, eds. Boston: Little Brown. Pp. 1-40.
Perrow, Charles, 1967. A Framework for the Comparative Analysis of Organizations. American Sociological Review 32(2):194-208.
Sports Illustrated, 1976. Sports Illustrated 26:12.

Stockbridge, Dorothy, 1976. Thriftiness Important Virtue for LPGA Rookie
    Pros. Sarasota Journal 20:3-D.
Theberge, Nancy. 1977. The System of Rewards in Women's Professional Golf.
    Paper presented at the meeting of the American Sociological Association,
    Chicago.
Turner, Ralph, 1962. Role-Taking: Process Versus Conformity. *In* Human Be-
    havior and Social Processes. A. M. Rose, ed. Boston: Houghton Mifflin.
    Pp. 20-40.
With the Tourists, 1977. With the Tourists. Golf World. 4:6,7.

The Despot and the Diplomat

Melissa Ludtke

Catchers and home-plate umpires are almost certainly the oddest of all sport's odd couples. Crouching and sweating together beneath layers of padding and suffering like bruises from foul tips and curves in the dirt, they play a game within a game, one in which other players are seldom involved. The catcher acts as his team's diplomat, his words usually as guarded and as subtly delivered as his signs to the pitcher. The umpire is an autocrat, often congenial, sometimes unyielding. However, the peace between the diplomat and the benevolent despot is tenuous and often destroyed. When this happens, their masks fly, and what began as a discussion inaudible to virtually everyone else in the park becomes as much of a show as an Ali weigh-in. That's exactly what happened one day late last season when Umpire Don Denkinger miscalled the first pitch of a game.

Red Sox Catcher Carlton Fisk caught that pitch, a fastball, after it crossed the middle of the plate.

"Ball one," said Denkinger.

Fisk, outraged and astounded, leaped straight up, hitting Denkinger under the chin with his catcher's helmet. "How in hell can you call that a ball?" he screamed.

"Take it easy! Take it easy!" Denkinger said.

"You're in for a bleep day if you keep calling pitches like that," said Fisk.

"It's the first pitch. What do you want to do? Hang me?"

"The first pitch. If I let you get away with that, the entire afternoon will be awful."

"So I blew it," said Denkinger. "Relax. I know I missed it."

"You sure as hell did miss it. And I'm jumping on you simply to wake you up."

Rarely does a catcher greet the umpire with such an outburst. The early innings are a period when players become acquainted with the umpire's strike zone and the tempo of his calls. Denkinger was flabbergasted by Fisk's eruption, and that was precisely what Fisk intended. He wanted to startle Denkinger and he did it by abrogating the unspoken rules of home-plate conduct. By quickly throwing the ball back to the pitcher, by not turning around, by not jumping up, the catcher obeys these rules. For his part, an umpire will have an easier time of it if he answers a catcher's questions, which is child's play compared to the alternative—jawing with a discontented pitcher 50 or 60 feet away.

"The umpire is not a machine. He is not a computer and he is not a robot," says Dodger Catcher Steve Yeager, whose six seasons have taught him the value of a gentle approach. "The umpire is human and entitled to a few mistakes." No matter how firmly he believes that, Yeager, like other catchers, cannot let umps' mistakes go entirely unchallenged, because he is literally caught in the middle, his face toward the pitcher, his back brushing against the umpire. It is his deftness at public relations—his ability to satisfy his pitcher's need for an advocate while not enraging the ump—that maintains harmonious working conditions for all. The tactics and tone he employs can be as violent as Fisk's outburst, which was tantamount to rebellion, or as subdued and inventive as those used by former Dodger Tommy Haller in 1971.

Umpire Bruce Froemming was a rookie then. Haller had spent 11 seasons behind the plate, and he had an umpire in the family—brother Bill in the American League. For five innings Haller asked Froemming about every close pitch, not showing him up but testing his judgment. Finally he popped the question.

"Bruce, what's your last name?"

"Froemming."

"Spell it," demanded Haller.

"F-r-o-e-m-m-i-n-g."

"That's with one 'I'?"

"Yep," replied the unsuspecting ump.

"That's exactly how you've called the game all night."

Froemming still chuckles about the incident, and aficionados of umpire-catcher repartee consider it a classic. It was a perfect tension breaker during a game in which Haller had been doing what umpires like least—carping about ball and strike calls.

"We are paid to call the close ones," says American Leaguer Marty Springstead, "not the ones a guy can see from the third deck." And it is those decisions that rile a pitcher, whose motion has left him off balance and without a good view of the pitch. If he needs the strike and the call is a ball, nothing will persuade him that the umpire was right. A few catchers, Yeager among them, help out the ump by signaling to their pitchers, telling him where the pitch was. "That saves the umpire wear and tear," says Yeager. "If I sit there doing nothing while my pitcher yells and screams, all that does is rile the dugouts and the fans and get them on the umpire's back." For similar reasons, Thurman Munson of the Yankees spends a lot of time gesturing to his manager, Billy Martin, whom he describes as "having umpires down his throat."

In some circumstances catchers will even side with the umpire to keep the peace. San Francisco Catcher Marc Hill does that when he is catching for John Montefusco, who, Umpire Billy Williams says, "wants everything to be a strike." As the Count stares at the umpire, Hill either hollers, "Hey, it was inside," or tells the ump, "Don't pay attention to him, he's crazy anyway."

All pitchers, flaky or otherwise, feel persecuted by umpires. The successful umpire—the one nobody notices—is supposed to handle gripes while still controlling the game. "For me to be able to run a game smoothly, the catcher must throw the ball back before he asks me anything," says American Leaguer Steve Palermo. "Naturally, he will say something on close pitches, because he is looking through tinted glasses. As someone once said, 'It ain't necessarily so, but he wants it to be.'"

Palermo's crew chief, Nestor Chylak, a 24-year veteran, says, "A catcher has the right to ask me on any call, but I get upset when I know he is 100% wrong. Then he is putting the monkey on my back. I don't mind a challenge. If he questions it nice, he'll get an honest answer."

Umpires and catchers both demand honesty. However, each has an additional request. Catchers ask for consistency from umpires—"Call the pitch the same in the ninth as in the first." Umpires demand fairness— "Don't wait for a tense moment in the game to challenge me on a pitch." An umpire prefers a catcher who quizzes him early and tosses around harmless phrases like "Stay with that pitch" and "Don't give up on it." The catcher who complains only when he desperately needs a favorable call is disdainfully referred to by umpires as a "situation catcher."

"He is the one who puts the hangman's noose around our necks," says Springstead. "He is the one we dislike tremendously, and the one we don't forget." The situation catcher, according to umps, is the one who quarrels even though the umpire's strike zone is the same as it was earlier in the game when the catcher made no comment. "Often you'd think the whole game is played in the ninth inning," says Chylak. "I call a consistent game for eight innings, and then all of a sudden a catcher needs the pitch and he starts climbing all over me."

Equally unpopular is a catcher who holds the baseball while jawing with the umpire. "If he gets rid of it, that's fine," says Palermo. "All the attention reverts to the pitcher. What goes on between me and the catcher is not even noticed." By holding the ball a catcher invites a hasty end to peaceful negotiations. "If he holds it, he gets the dugout riled," says Froemming. "Instead of throwing it back and then saying, 'Bruce, I think the ball caught the corner,' he has now told everybody that he thinks I missed the pitch."

Such incidents occur in almost every game. Chalk it up to the human element, to the fact that an umpire cannot be infallible or even completely consistent. And a catcher, though he may try, can never be totally objective. Keeping their relationship cool is further complicated by the fact that, from the moment the umpires step on the field, the animosity of the fans is apparent from the boos that are heard from the stands. It is difficult for a catcher, particularly the one for the home team, to resist the temptation of bringing his allies in the stands into play in his relationship with the ump.

Although the fans' taunts are often irritating, umpires are much more concerned about the players' reactions. "I want the players to say, 'Here they come,' instead of 'Holy Toledo, it's not them again,'" says Chylak.

No matter what the greeting, the home-plate umpire—an assignment an ump draws every fourth game—must familiarize himself during the warmups with the starting pitchers' tempos and repertoires. "Chylak is particularly loose for those eight pitches," says Boston Catcher Fred Kendall. "Instead of standing away from the plate or behind me, as the others do, he stands at the plate like a hitter."

Regardless of his viewpoint, each home-plate umpire searches for clues. If a highballer is working on a sinker or breaking ball, the ump wants to know. The umpires swap information in their locker room before the game, but the best source is the catcher. It often helps both sides if the receiver shares what he knows with the umpire.

"At San Diego I caught Randy Jones," says Kendall. "The first thing I told the umpires was that Randy keeps the ball low. He throws that way all game, so the ump might as well get used to calling it. They like me telling them, because it helps them stay with the pitch."

But there are times when clues are better left undiscovered. Palermo found that out one day in Boston when he listened to Fisk ramble on about "a real good sinkerball." They were watching Bob Stanley warm up.

"It was early in the season and I figured that Fisk had caught him in spring training," says Palermo, who had never seen Stanley pitch. "His pitches did more tricks than a spinning top, but Stanley *never* threw a sinker."

Idle chatter between umpire and catcher consumes the rest of the time before the game begins. It is the kind of talk overheard in hotel elevators and lobbies, but it is crucial to a good working relationship because it is the start of a dialogue that should last the whole game. As Yeager says, "Once we lose our track of communication, we've lost a major battle."

If a battle does ensue, it is likely to be triggered by an argument about the strike zone. "There are games when my strike zone may seem a bit different from the last time these teams saw me," says Springstead. "If a catcher asks me early if I'm planning to stay with a particular pitch, I tell him, 'Well, I have so far.' Usually that's good enough for him."

If the umpire's definition of the strike zone does not cause a catcher and his pitcher to complain, the tempo of the umpire's calls often will. Every umpire develops a rhythm. It is like a metronome activated on the first pitch. The pitch smacks the mitt—boom!—and the call is made. This is not as easy as it sounds. When Nolan Ryan and his fastball are matched against Wilbur Wood and his knuckler, the adjustment an umpire must make every half inning is like the one a dancer makes in switching from the Charleston to a waltz.

"In the first half of an inning the ball is on top of me in a flash," says Springstead of Ryan's pitching. "After three outs I'm thinking bing, bing, bing. Along comes Wood, his knuckler taking its sweet time drifting up there. I get anxious and I tend to lean into the plate, which is bad because it means my head is moving and I'm not keeping a firm vision of the strike zone. I can't allow that to happen. It's a tremendous adjustment, but I must make it."

And when a reliever comes in, the umpire suddenly finds himself dancing to still another tune. During a game at Minnesota, Jim Shellenback came out of the bullpen while Rich Garcia was working the plate. Garcia had no idea what to expect because it was Shellenback's first appearance of the season. "His catcher, Butch Wynegar, told me nothing," says Garcia. "Roy White of the Yankees came to bat, and all of a sudden along comes a palmball. It was high, then—boom!—it dropped, causing me to delay my call for a fraction of a second. Because I did something different, it threw White off. He turned to me with a suspicious look, like he was asking whether I really knew where the strike zone was.

"Geez, I didn't know he threw a palmball," Garcia said to Wynegar.

"I guess I should have told you," Wynegar said.

No one has to tell an umpire when he misses a call, he knows he has erred just as surely as a player knows when he has mishandled a grounder. It is just that the ump has many more chances to blow one. As the Specialized Umpire Training Center handbook says, "An infielder must play

32 games of errorless fielding to have as many opportunities as an umpire has in one game of calling balls and strikes." And it is not as easy for an umpire to redeem himself, because a player can make up for a mistake either at the plate or in the field. If an umpire attempts to balance out a bad decision by altering his calls on future pitches, he sacrifices his objectivity—and, inevitably, his control of the game. The ump is far better off when he forgets about the miscall.

Johnny Bench says, "It's rare that an umpire says, 'I missed that one,' but when he does I don't say another word. What else can a man admit? It's when an umpire doesn't acknowledge the error that I feel like I'm butting my head against a wall."

Not all catchers agree with Bench, but, then again, no two catchers respond to a blown call in the same manner. Some acknowledge an umpire's mistake with a quick "ooooh" or "aaaah." Yeager usually lets out a sharp grunt, which veteran umpires know is his most derisive expression. However, in last season's third playoff game between the Dodgers and Phillies, Umpire Harry Wendelstedt "missed a call" that Philadelphia parlayed into three runs when Los Angeles Pitcher Burt Hooton, rattled by Wendelstedt's call, walked four batters in a row. In that case Yeager replaced his grunt with, "Harry, it was a good pitch." In light of the importance of the game, that was a mild remark. "There was no need to make a big commotion about it," says Yeager. "It was just one pitch, and it was the third inning. If it had been the ninth, I might have screamed. Even that probably wouldn't have done any good, because the umpires know my personality and know what I do."

A catcher may also gauge his response by who is standing behind him. Munson offers a gruff "No it wasn't" when Ron Luciano, whom he doesn't get along with, calls a close pitch a ball. But when Chylak makes a similar call, Munson tones down his tactics. "If I say to Nestor, 'Damn it, you blew it,' I am likely to rub him the wrong way," says Munson. "I simply tell him, 'You missed it,' and Nestor, who has a lot of confidence in himself, says, 'I didn't.' If I think he blew it very badly, I'll say, 'Nestor, I'm telling you the truth.'"

As Garcia found out, debates at home plate can sometimes involve both catchers. Just such a round-table discussion occurred last September during the opener of a three-game series at Yankee Stadium, with the second-place Red Sox trailing the Yankees by three games. Garcia had the plate assignment. Munson and Fisk, arch rivals, were catching. The Sox were behind 4-2 in the seventh inning when Rick Burleson, representing the tying run, came to the plate. Garcia's strike-three call ended the threat, and Burleson argued with him.

When Fisk came out to warm up his pitcher for the bottom half of the inning, he interrogated Garcia, who in turn asked Fisk if he thought the ball had dipped.

"Yeah, I thought it was low," said Fisk. "It looked like a slider."

"Yeah, it was."

"It looked like it broke out of the strike zone," said Fisk.

"It might have."

"Perhaps you called it before it broke."

In the top of the eighth it was Munson's turn to get into the discussion.

Said Garcia, "That strike I called on Burleson. It might have been low. It was a slider and it sunk."

"That pitch didn't sink. Guidry doesn't even have a slider," Munson said.

Truth is, New York Pitcher Ron Guidry has a pretty good slider, but Garcia did not expect Munson to agree. All he wanted the Yankee catcher to know was that the pitch was a ball, and it would remain one for the rest of the game. Yes, he had called it a strike. No, he would not do so again.

When diplomacy fails, an umpire has another tactic he can use to try to cool off a seething catcher—brushing off the plate whether it needs it or not. This puts the antagonists face to face, instead of back to front and it lets them do some heavy jawing without making their disagreement all that apparent to everyone in the park. Vic Voltaggio, an American League rookie umpire last season, once used the maneuver in the first inning when the plate did not need a brushing off as badly as Oakland Catcher Jeff Newman needed a talking to. A's Pitcher Rick Langford was already in trouble, and, in trying to calm down Langford, Newman had put the blame for the pitcher's inability to throw strikes on Voltaggio.

"We're not going to battle for nine innings," Voltaggio told Newman as he bent down to sweep the plate. "You might as well curse me out now, and I'll unload you. Otherwise, we're going to play this game."

The tactic worked, preventing a first-inning rhubarb without embarrassing either party. Newman lasted the game, and Langford found his stride and went on to win in extra innings.

The fact that Voltaggio did not unload Newman is hardly surprising. Very few catchers are ejected. In 1977 only five American Leaguers (Ray Fosse of Cleveland, Darrell Porter of Kansas City, Charlie Moore of Milwaukee, Manny Sanguillen of Oakland and Munson) were thrown out for offenses ranging from loudmouthing to fighting. The National League had nine ejections—Houston's Joe Ferguson, Cincinnati's Bill Plummer and Philadelphia's Tim McCarver leading the league with two apiece. The previous season only one major league catcher, Fosse, was ejected, for the unpardonable offense of angrily bumping an ump.

Normally there is very little physical contact, even by accident, between catchers and umpires. The Crawford family—father Shag, who retired in 1975, and son Jerry, who now works in the National League—is an exception. In the Crawford style, the umpire rests a hand between a catcher's hip and rib cage. "It keeps him under control," says the younger Crawford, "and it lets me know where he is going. I ask the catcher if it bothers him, and only Jerry Grote has complained." But as all National League umpires attest, grousing is part of Grote's game.

Where and how an umpire positions himself depends on what type of protector he wears. All National Leaguers must use one that is worn inside the uniform shirt, while American Leaguers can choose between the inside pad and the balloon protector, which is worn outside the uniform. (Those who favor the pad say it is less cumbersome than the balloon, which the umpire must prop up with his hands before each pitch. Those who use the balloon feel it gives better protection.) An insider positions his head in what is called the slot, the gap on the inside corner of the plate between the catcher's head and the batter's shoulder.

"If my slot isn't there, I adjust," says American Leaguer Jim Evans. "All the catchers are right-handed, so when a lefty is at bat and the sign is given for an inside pitch, the catcher wants to avoid moving his glove across his body and catching the ball backhanded. Instead, he slides his body over to block the ball and field it squarely. By doing this he also narrows my slot, which forces me to move with him to get a full view of the pitch."

Outsiders call balls and strikes by looking straight over the catcher's head—if the receiver is squatting directly behind the plate. The catcher may move to set an outside or inside target or to field a pitch, but a balloon ump should never budge from his original position.

"When a catcher slides over I have to look over his ear or shoulder even though I'm accustomed to working over his head," says Springstead. "It throws me off, but it doesn't happen a lot."

It is important to umpires that the catcher stay low. If he obscures any portion of the plate from the ump's view he risks having the strike zone shrink, because there is an umpire's axiom that says, "If I can't see it, I'm not going to call it a strike."

Oriole Catcher Elrod Hendricks is 6′ 1″ and long-legged. "I can steal pitches by getting down real low," he says. "By steal, I mean I get strikes called on pitches that other catchers my height may not get even though the pitches really were strikes. That's because a lot of tall catchers block the umpire's vision."

Stealing pitches is as integral a part of Hendricks'—or any other catcher's—game as stealing second base is of Lou Brock's. By positioning himself on the outside corner, for example, the home-team catcher sets up a situation in which the umpires' judgment—and courage—are pitted against the crowd's reaction.

If the pitch is outside, if the umpire sees it miss, if the hitter doesn't swing, but if the catcher doesn't budge, fans assume it was a strike. And if the catcher wants to "get cute" he can hold the ball there for the entire ball park to judge.

"I can't cheat and give him a strike," says Springstead. "The pitch is out of the strike zone, exactly where the catcher wanted it, in hopes that the batter would swing. But the batter didn't swing, and I'm not going to call a strike. I can't let the catcher use the 30,000 people in the stands to intimidate me."

The setup to steal outside pitches falls apart when the pitcher unintentionally throws a strike on the inside. "Then the catcher reaches across the plate, and there isn't anyone in the park who thinks it was a strike, when it was," says National Leaguer Paul Runge. "Sure, catchers try to cheat, but it's nothing personal against umpires."

To prevent being misled, an umpire must keep a level head. "Once I start moving my head I lose perspective," says Springstead. "The toughest one to call is the one right at my eyes. My tendency is to flinch. If I do, there is no way I can call the pitch correctly."

"Umpires don't have lights that blink on to give them an automatic strike zone," says Yeager. So on every pitch the umpire must mentally redefine the zone and defend it against attacks from the catcher. For the system to work the catcher must also remain as still as a rock. "If I constantly jump up and down or move from side to side, I'm not giving the umpire his best look," says Yeager. "So I have no right to disagree with his call."

For the most part, in recent seasons conciliation has replaced confrontation behind the plate. "I don't want to get into arguments with umpires," says Munson. "I need them when I'm hitting. I need them when I'm catching. But I can't let my pitcher and manager down by letting a bad call go by and not saying anything. I don't bitch just to bitch."

In the days when there were Boston Braves and Brooklyn Dodgers, tradition has it that umpires would cut off a catcher by saying, "You think that was bad. Wait until you see this one." When the next pitch flew across the plate, the umpire would get his revenge: "Ball two!"

Says Garcia, "They got away with it simply because there was no television, no cameras and no instant replay. I can't imagine that happening today."

Electronic surveillance may curtail heavy-handed behavior by umps but it cannot prevent grudges from arising. Take the case of Larry Barnett and Fisk. Since the third game of the 1975 World Series, the two have been about as friendly as John Dean and Richard Nixon. That night 40 million TV viewers watched as Barnett didn't call interference on Reds pinch hitter Ed Armbrister after Armbrister had collided with Fisk on a bunt play. Fisk's subsequent overthrow of second base allowed the eventual winning run to move into scoring position.

"Ever since that game our relationship has been strained," says Barnett. "If I didn't say that, I'd be lying. Fisk says hello, I say hello, and we limit it to that."

Keeping the conversation to greetings is not always that simple. Last September, Fisk and Barnett were together again. First Barnett called Fisk out on a 2-2 pitch that Fisk thought was inside. Then, when Boston was in the field, Barnett made another call that Fisk felt was incorrect. An argument ensued.

"I'll tell you one thing," Barnett said to Fisk. "You open your mouth once more and I'll run you."

"That's the way you are," Fisk said. "Just because you wear a blue uniform you think you have the right to command the game whether you're right or wrong. You can't think you are calling the game right. You just can't."

"I'll give you one more chance. Either get back in the game or you're gone."

At that moment Red Sox Manager Don Zimmer arrived on the scene.

"I don't want you getting tossed," he told Fisk.

"Zimmy, I'm keeping him," said Barnett.

"That's real nice, Larry," said Fisk. "You're really doing me a great big favor. But why don't you try calling the pitches correctly."

Fisk survived the nine innings. So did the Red Sox, beating Detroit 6-2.

Barnett and Fisk are not alone in their mutual animosity. Froemming cannot forget a game in 1973 when the irascible Grote, then catching for the Mets, let a fastball get by him that almost hit the hot-tempered Froemming in the throat. Because they had spent the three previous innings in a non-stop argument, Froemming accused Grote of intentionally moving aside in hope that the pitch would hit the umpire.

"Are you going to throw me out?" snapped Grote.

Mets Manager Yogi Berra charged from the dugout.

"He made no attempt to stop that pitch," Froemming told Berra. The umpire's accusation was tough to prove and he knew it. Grote remained in the game.

Aside from catchers who gripe, steal pitches and sometimes miss them, an umpire must contend with bellyaching batters. Catchers can be the worst of the lot, because they are more attuned to an umpire's strike zone and his frame of mind than other hitters. One umpire, Jim Evans, classifies hitters as follows:

"There's the alibier, the guy who tries to put the monkey on my back. Then there is the phony beefer, the guy with the superstar complex who thinks if he doesn't swing, it can't be a strike. And there's the legitimate beefer. He sincerely believes he is right. I never mind an argument from him."

According to umpires, worst of all is the two-strike-zone catcher, who sees one strike zone while working behind the plate and another, smaller version while standing alongside it.

"Joe Ferguson hardly ever questions me when he's catching," says Dick Stello. "But when he's a hitter, he has a wholly different strike zone, one that's so small I can't call a strike on him."

Once when Umpire Paul Runge called Bench out on strikes he heard about it for the rest of the game. Seems that Bench was going for his 1,000th RBI. When the third strike was called, with a man in scoring position, Bench disagreed. Walking back to the dugout, he complained.

"I came out to catch, and we talked some more," says Bench. "Runge was ready to throw me out. I caught a pitch he called a ball. I held it there to show him that it was the same as the pitch he struck me out on."

"Don't show me up," the umpire said.

"If I were trying to show you up, I sure would've said more when I walked away."

It was the sixth inning.

In the ninth Bench was still around. Runge leaned over as the game neared its end and left Bench with these parting words: "Before you go, good luck in the All-Star Game."

Section D

Media, Messages and Sport

A medium is a channel of communication that is usually analyzed in terms of its two primary components: the form it takes and the content, or message, it carries. In North America, the media forms with which we are most familiar include print media such as books, newspapers and magazines; electronic media such as television and radio; and other artistic media such as films and graphic art. Because it acts as a message-carrying system, sport also can be considered a medium and investigated sociologically as other media are.

Sociologists study media in terms of the personal fulfillment they provide to individuals (the "uses and gratifications" theories referred to in many journals) and the value they serve within the social system. In that context, media are generally acknowledged to provide opportunities for socialization and for community solidarity through the transmission of uniform images.

The selections included in this section analyze sport as a medium as well as content matter for other media. As a specific media form, sport might profitably be analyzed with reference to the research concerning the social uses of media. Once again, the theme of sport as a symbolic system (i.e., a medium) emerges. But sport also serves as content for other media; the sports sections of our daily newspapers, the hours of television programming devoted to sport, the thousands of sport stories and novels such as the Chip Hilton series, the plethora of sport films which have followed closely on the heels of the financial success of *Rocky*, all attest to the fact that sport is considered "good copy" by the other media. As both medium and message, then, sport deserves scholarly attention.

Birrell and Loy examine the theories of one of the most fascinating scholars writing about media, Marshall McLuhan. McLuhan contends that societies can be characterized by the media forms prevalent within them, and Birrell and Loy begin by investigating sport from that perspective. Then they offer ideas about sport as content matter of other media, specifically television, and make predictions about the future of media sport.

Palmer elaborates on the theme of sport as content of other media by focusing upon sport in the novel. By analyzing the way sport is depicted in fictional accounts, the social analyst can learn much about the way sport is perceived by the artistic interpreter of society. Palmer provides an overview of the themes most significant in sport novels and throws light on the image of the athlete and the image of sport in society.

Comisky, Bryant and Zillmann investigate the increasingly prominent role of the sportscaster and discover disconcerting evidence that for many in the sport audience, hearing is believing. As they conclude, "viewers' perception of the hockey play was greatly influenced by the nature of the accompanying commentary."

Media Sport: Hot and Cool[1]

Susan Birrell and John W. Loy, Jr.

MCLUHAN'S VIEW OF MEDIA IN SOCIETY

McLuhan's celebrated statement, "the medium is the message," represents the essence of his thinking. McLuhan's basic thesis is that the real message of any medium is not the content but what the form of the medium itself reveals about the society. McLuhan discerns fundamental relationships between the historical development of a society and its media forms, and he divides human history into three eras: pre-literate, literate and post-literate. Each era is typified by the media found within it.

Pre-literate society is primarily on oral tradition society, rich in folklore and intimate communication forms. The invention of the printing press ushered in the literate era with its emphasis upon linear styles of communication. In recent years the invention of television, computers, and other electronic devices marked the beginning of the post-literate period and the development of the "global village."

Pre- and post-literate societies have much in common, particularly the sensory experience associated with their respective media. Both feature a diffused pattern of sensory stimulation, while the print-oriented experience of the literate phase of society features a linear, step-by-step progression.

McLuhan's term for media suited to literate societies is "hot" media, while post-literate media are classified as "cool." The basic criterion for McLuhan is the sensory participation demanded from the audience. Hot media—such as books, newspapers, and films—are media of "high definition," requiring low participation from the audience. The "low definition" of cool media such as television, theatre, and cartoons calls for higher sensory participation. As McLuhan states:

> A hot medium is one that extends one single sense in "high definition."
> High definition is the state of being well filled with data . . . hot

From *International Review of Sport Sociology* 14, 1979, pp. 5-19. Ars Polona, Krakowskie Przedmiescie 7, Warsaw, Poland.

media do not leave so much to be filled in or completed by the audience. Hot media are, therefore, low in participation, and cool media are high in participation or completion by the audience. Naturally, therefore, a hot medium like radio has very different effects on the user from a cool medium like the telephone.[2]

For McLuhan, a medium is broadly conceived as any sensory extension of man. Among his interesting list of media (in addition to the expected examples—television, radio, movies, photographs, the printed word —he includes clothing, money, clocks, and the electric light bulb), McLuhan cites games, including sports, as "media of interpersonal communication."

McLuhan's conjectures about sport as medium and sport as content matter of other media are interesting and highly original. In general they can be dealt with as two separate issues and the implicit hypotheses made explicit for a more serious evaluation of the validity of McLuhan's ideas.

SPORT AS MEDIUM

Like many others, McLuhan contends that sport reflects the culture in which it is found: specifically, he argues that certain sports are "hotter" than others and thus best suited to the literate stage of societal growth. According to McLuhan, football has predictably overtaken baseball in popular appeal in America because baseball is a hot sport, developed in the literate society, while football is a cool sport, well-suited to the post-literate era. He observes:

> It is the inclusive mesh of the TV image, in particular, that spells for a while, at least, the doom of baseball. For baseball is a game of one-thing-at-time, fixed positions and visibly delegated specialist jobs such as belonged to the now passing mechanical age. . . . When cultures change, so do games. Baseball, that had become the elegant abstract image of an industrial society living by split-second timing, has in the new TV decade lost its psychic and social relevance for our new way of life. The ball game has been dislodged from the social center and been conveyed to the periphery of American life.
> In contrast, American football is nonpositional, and any or all of the players can switch to any role during play. . . . It agrees very well with the new needs of decentralized team play in the electric age.[3]

Thus, one hypothesis about the relationship of sport and the media which McLuhan offers is that certain sport forms suit certain societal forms: cool sports are more popular than hot sports in post-literate society. That hypothesis might be testable if one could indeed classify sports according to "heat." McLuhan does not offer such a taxonomy but perhaps it is possible to refine his concept of "definition" to the point where it can be applied to sport.

McLuhan distinguishes media of high definition from media of low definition in terms of the participatory demands made on the consumer. Sports make the same demands upon spectators and audiences: the sport experience can be conceptualized as relatively more diffuse or more focused—diffusion being defined as a function of the demands put on the secondary participant in terms of sensory acuteness and sensory involvement. Thus diffusion can be understood as a sensory variety show: the spectator is bombarded by many aspects which demand his attention, but he must limit himself to only one. The more diffuse the choices, the more demanding is the involvement experience for the spectator.

The basic concept can be further clarifed along two dimensions: locational diffusion and action diffusion. Locational diffusion is simply the amount of space required by the sport. Diving and boxing are low on this dimension; golf and football are high. Action diffusion is inversely related to the degree of linear progression of the game. Sport in which the ball moves freely between two teams, as in soccer and hockey, are the best examples of high action diffusion. Baseball, on the other hand, features a distinctively linear type action sequence.

To a degree, action diffusion is a function of the pace of the game action and the proportion of unexpected or unpredictable action. Generally, races are linear by nature and thus low in action diffusion. But auto racing is an exception because of the potential for action and accidents to occur anywhere on the track. For the fan intent on experiencing the sport event most fully, highly diffused action demands a great deal of attention and acuteness. A football fan, for instance, is called on to make some important decisions at each play in order to enjoy the game experience to its fullest.

Table 1 illustrates the diffusion dimensions of selected sports. Those high in diffusion across both dimensions, like hockey and soccer, are most diffuse overall, while sports such as wrestling, diving and bowling are the most focused or linear.

According to the hypothesis inherent in McLuhan's statements on sport, the popularity of different sport forms should vary according to historical and cultural factors. There is only mild support for the historical thesis. For example, the late nineteenth century, the literate era for most of Western society, was a period of codification of sport. Specific rules were spelled out, and the approach to sport during this era was overshadowed by this very linear interpretation of sport. However, that thesis is less salient when applied to a more modern period.

The thesis would predict that Class III sports ought to have died out in American society or at least be suffering a severe loss of popularity because their forms are antithetical to the tenor of the times. However,

TABLE 1

Diffusion Ratings of Selected Sports

Sports	Diffusion Dimensions	
	Locational diffusion	Action diffusion
CLASS I		
auto-racing, basketball, football, hockey, lacrosse, roller derby, rugby, soccer	high	high
CLASS II		
baseball, golf, most races, tennis	high	low
CLASS III		
bowling, boxing, diving, fencing, field events, gymnastics, pool, wrestling	low	low

this is decidedly not the case: witness the recent surge in popularity of tennis (Class II) and gymnastics (Class III), and the resurgence of baseball (Class II).[4]

Furthermore, if McLuhan hopes to convince his readers that the thesis has some validity from a cross-cultural perspective, he will have to furnish a more precise argument than this:

> Offhand, it might be supposed that the tight tribal unity of football would make it a game that the Russians would cultivate. Their devotion to ice hockey and soccer, two very individualist forms of game, would seem little suited to the psychic needs of a collectivist society. But Russia is still in the main an oral, tribal world that is undergoing detribalization and just now discovering individualism as a novelty. Soccer and ice hockey have for them, therefore, an exotic and Utopian quality of promise that they do not convey to the West. This is the quality that we tend to call "snob value," and we might derive some similar "value" from owning race horses, polo ponies, or twelve-meter yachts.[5]

Actually, McLuhan's thesis might provide an interesting basis for a study of sport forms as they reflect the developmental stage of a society. Unfortunately, he has failed to provide a reasonable interpretation of football as opposed to hockey and soccer (are the latter really "very individualist forms of game"?), and falls back on a rather dogmatic explanation to justify his conclusions. A similar fault is evident in McLuhan's analysis of football as "nonpositional" and as a game in which "any and all players can switch to any role during play."[6] In fact, football has become even more structured and position oriented in the dozen years since McLuhan made his comments, a trend exactly opposite to what he would predict.

SPORT AS MEDIA CONTENT

McLuhan claims that "the content of any medium is always another medium"[7] so it is not surprising to find sport as content matter for other forms of media, most notably television. By its very nature, sport should be successful as television content. McLuhan states, for example, that

> . . . because the low definition of TV insures a high degree of audience involvement, the most effective programs are those that present situations which consist of some process to be completed.[6]

Indeed, the steady increases in the amount of sport on television in the past ten years, increasing network budgets for sport, and the success of such TV sport creations as Monday Night Football and Wide World of Sports attest to the general validity of McLuhan's argument.[9] Yet some sports are more popular television sports than others (see Table 2) and their popularity does not reflect their diffusion classification as might be expected. Indeed no discernible pattern emerges. Hypotheses derived from McLuhan have little power in explaining the data.

Another aspect of the problem is the notion of the translation of one medium into another. McLuhan is quite explicit in his belief that the translational powers of media can change the course of history. He states that certain politicians translate better into different media than do others. Compared to the cool Kennedy, he argues, Nixon was too hot for the television cameras, thus his poor showing in the Presidential debates of 1960.[10] Even more dramatically, McLuhan contends that Hitler's hot personality was perfectly suited to the hot medium of radio. McLuhan declares:

> Had TV occurred on a large scale during Hitler's reign he would have vanished quickly. Had TV come first there would have been no Hitler at all.[11]

What are the effects, then, of translating the live sport event, generally a very cool medium into another, hotter medium? Specifically, what changes in the sport experience arise when the spectator follows sport through television rather than live attendance? In short, what does television do to the sport experience of the fan in terms of McLuhan's ideas?

TABLE 2

Average U.S. Audience Per Cent by Sport Type for Three Years[a]

Year Diffusion Ratings	1970		1973		1975	
	%	N	%	N	%	N
CLASS I						
football[b]	13.9	101	15.2	110	15.5	116
basketball[b]	8.0	47	7.4	72	8.0	71
auto racing	4.7	2	11.1	3	10.0	6
ice hockey	4.2	16	5.0	24	3.9	21
soccer					4.6	2
class average	11.2	166	11.3	209	11.7	216
CLASS II						
horse racing	13.7	3	9.3	9	10.8	6
baseball	11.4	36	13.4	53	12.0	52
golf	5.6	69	5.5	81	6.8	58
tennis	4.2	5	5.1	321	4.1	64
skiing	5.8	16	5.2	1		
class average	7.4	129	8.0	176	7.5	180
CLASS III						
bowling	7.2	13	8.9	14	8.6	18
boxing			5.2	6	5.3	8
fishing	8.1	1				
class average	7.3	14	7.8	20	7.6	26
HYBRID TELECASTS						
multi sport	9.2	54	8.9	84	9.2	113
track and field	5.6	15			6.0	1
Pan Am Games					5.8	1
World Games			5.4	8		
class average	8.4	69	8.6	92	9.1	115

Figures compiled from "Let's Look at Sports, 1975;" "Let's Look at Sports: The 1973 Season," and "A Look of Sport: The 1969-1970 Season," Nielsen Television Index, Media Research Division, A. C. Nielsen Company.

[a]These figures include both regular season games and special events such as the Super Bowl, the World Series, and the Stanley Cup. The Riggs-King tennis match is included in the 1974 figures and the Ali-Lyle heavyweight boxing championship is included in 1975.

[b]These figures include both professional and college games.

The coolness or diffusion of television as a medium, relative to the medium of the event itself, must therefore, be examined. The model in Figure 1 suggests that movement from the sport event as medium to television as medium should change the nature of the sport experience somewhat, through a focusing of diffuse action which is unavoidable due to limitations of broadcasting translation.

Time Dimension	Immediate	Simultaneous		Delayed
Form of Sport Media	Event	TV	Radio	Newspaper
Degree of Coolness	Cool ⟶			Hot
Degree of Diffusion	Diffuse ⟶			Focused

Figure 1. Relative "coolness" and diffusion of sport media

In the earlier days of television, effectiveness of sport coverage with only one camera varied from sport to sport. The singular focus was disastrous for sports such as baseball but had an almost negligible effect on a relatively more focused event such as boxing.[12] Increasing the number of cameras used to cover an event might appear to foster greater diffusion. But the action is still previewed by the producer who selects exactly which part of the total picture will be broadcast.

Other complex advances in technology have continued to limit the diffusion effect of television. Instant replay, isolated camera, stop action, slow motion, wide-angle lens, and split screen have all transformed the sport spectacle, disrupting the natural rhythm of the game and synthesizing the action through highlighting to enhance the excitement value.[13]

In general, television produces the following effects which are unavailable to the line event audience:

1. Changing the size of the image and permitting a greater range of vision (wide-angle lens, split screen).
2. Concentrating time diffuse events into a more manageable time span (highlights).
3. Manipulating time to dramatize action (instant replay, slow motion, stop action, highlights).
4. Focusing on one isolated action (isolated camera, instant replay).
5. Providing more statistical information.

What television can not do is allow the spectator the freedom to choose the segment of action he wishes to follow. In addition, television does not provide the fan with the high degree of social integration with other fans and, more important, integration with the nature of the game experience itself.[14] As Orrin E. Dunlop, Jr., a writer for the New York Times, lamented in the early days of televised sport:

(The fan) does not see the half of what is going on to make baseball the pleasure it has become in 100 years. The televiewer lacks freedom; seeing baseball by television is too confining, for the novelty would not hold up for more than an hour, if it were not for the commentator. . . . What would old-timers think of such a turn of affairs—baseball from a sofa! Television is too safe. There is no ducking the foul ball.[15]

A more recent interpretation continues in the same vein:

The networks with their zeppelins and zoom lenses, their dreamlike instant replays of color and violence have changed football watching from a remote college pastime to something very much like voyeurism.
. . . No matter how fine his TV reception, no beer and arm chair quarterback can hope to see the true game. For all the paraphernalia, the tube rarely shows an overview; pass patterns and geometric variations are lost in a kaleidoscope of close-ups and crunches.[16]

Live sport spectation is a diffuse experience; media sport are focused events. How the spectator has resisted or adjusted to such shifts serves as a basis for speculation as to the future of media, sport, and the sport experience of the fan.

THE FUTURE OF MEDIA SPORT

With McLuhan as prophet, one might assume that the new electronic age with its diffuse and demanding nature drives people further and further from a linear interpretation of the world. Surely the media of the future will offer increasingly diffuse media experiences to the media sport consumer. But will super spectator ever abandon his television set? Will the media sport experience of the future be hot or cool? Speculative models for both positions exist; surprisingly some are beginning to creep into reality as well.

Through its technological breakthroughs, television is bringing a higher and higher degree of focus to a diffused sport world. In effect, television is providing the fan with a greater amount of information, both visually and through statistical recitations, and depriving him of the integrative aspects of the sport experience. Thus the close link with the game in its natural spectatorial form is broken in order to provide a higher informational picture of the game. Taken to an extreme, this will eventually lead to a homogenization effect on the media.

But contrary to McLuhan's theory, the new techniques of sport broadcasting seem to enhance the sport experience for the fan rather than diminish it. Although it removes him from the true context of the sport situation, the American spectator seems more than happy to accept the television sport experience.

If McLuhan's literate/post-literate society theory is correct, this first generation of television children to come of age—those in their early thirties, the first wave of the post-literates—should be expected to shun a hotter media experience for a cooler one. This does not seem to be the case. Instead, it is more likely the case that the first television generation has been brought upon the television sport experience, and that this has fostered a linear orientation to sport. Television has trained America to focus on particular bits of action and ignore, or perhaps never come into meaningful contact with, a live event experience. Perhaps this explains why many disgruntled fans leave a live game complaining that they could have seen it better on television.

Techniques such as isolated camera, instant replay, stop action, and split screen are designed to provide the spectator with knowledge, not an integrative sensory experience. Perhaps the American fan with his increasing mania for statistical information is being fed the diet of data he requests. Other revolutionary techniques or practices may go even further to satisfy him.

One innovation which has yet to make its actual debut is a method of telecasting sport events called "retarded live action television."[17] According to the news report of the invention, "at regular intervals, a frame of perhaps one second duration is discarded, and the blank space is filled by stretching out the others. The action can be slowed by 15 or 20 per cent without the viewer being conscious of any delay."[18]

Another potential change in sport due to television lies in the area of officiating. It has become obvious to the fan as well as the coaches that instant replay can not only recapture isolated action but rule violations as well. A replay can either confirm or contradict the judgement of the referee, and nowadays a referee is often more relentlessly monitored than the players. The camera can be used not only to confirm a ruled decision but to make one. During the 1974 NFL play-offs, the most memorable and spectacular play was the controversial last minute catch of a deflected pass by Pittsburgh Steeler Franco Harris. To be legal, the ball had to touch an opposing player between the initial contact with the intended Steeler receiver and Harris. The referee was not quite sure; he ran to the sidelines to confer with relay men in contact with the television production box. For the first time in media sport history, instant replay and slow motion techniques were used to confirm the officials' decision.

Despite agitation from many coaches, including Woody Hayes, to make regular use of instant replays for officiating purposes, the issue has not yet been seriously discussed.[19] In fact, arenas such as Capital Center in the Washington, D. C. area which are equipped with telescreens for instant replay purposes generally refrain from replaying controversial calls by the referees.[20]

On the other hand, in 1973 the American Horse Shows Association introduced an experimental system for judging dressage championships. The system involved the video-taping of events at locations around the country and submitting them for review to a panel of judges. The measure is intended to allow riders to compete without the inconvenience and expense of transporting horses across country.[21]

Weibe[22] has attributed America's appetite for the media to the difficulty individuals have in trying to divest themselves of their fundamental egocentrism and acquire the concept of the "other." Their reluctance to deal with others is manifested in their susceptibility to the media. The media provides the illusion of interaction while actually removing the other and replacing it with "printed symbols of sounds or images, but never persons."[23] Perhaps this theory is personified by super spectator.

Followed to an extreme, this high information/low interaction orientation results in studio sport. Studio sport or scripted sport would eliminate all chance elements and all integrative aspects of sport contests. All that would remain would be the distillation of the contest, the results and that data. Sport, like the entertainment product it is, would become an athletic "Playhouse 90," with the Super Bowl featured as "Masterpiece Theatre." Plays would be repeated until the perfect take had been satisfactorily accomplished. Several examples can be cited which indicate that this orientation to sport is not as unrealistic as one might suppose.

To some extent, television already controls important game elements such as time outs. One special individual is designated to walk along the sidelines and signal the referee when the station needs time for a commercial.[24] Often these arbitrary interruptions can work to the detriment of a team. When Bill Russell was player-coach of the Celtics, he was once fined for refusing to call time out for the broadcasters because his team was enjoying the momentum of a catch-up victory and he realized that an interruption at that point could cost him the game.[25] The extreme of this sort of manipulation occurred during the 1967 Super Bowl when the half time kick and return were replayed because the audience had been detained by a commercial message.[26] Who knows how the live audience dealt with their bewilderment at the repetition.

Evidence to support a trend toward "process theatre" is exemplified in the coverage of the USC-UCLA football game in 1974. During one running play, one instant replay camera followed USC back Anthony

Davis to the line where the second camera smoothly picked up the coverage. The resulting spliced tape was highly effective and similar to techniques presently being used by sport film producers.

In another instance, television producers restaged the start of a 500 meter swimming event they were taping because the cameras had missed the real thing. The staged start was then spliced in with the footage of the actual race.[27]

Another piece of evidence supporting a belief in the increasing focus of media sport is the increasing use made by fans of hotter media to supplement or replace their media sport experiences. The increased portability of electric media makes this more commonplace every day. Thus those in the stands often bring along a portable television so they can "see the game better," while those who watch the game on television at home are apt to turn down the television audio and listen to the broadcast on the radio.

Clearly the fan who uses supplemental media is demanding more input. This could lead to a more diffused experience (in fact, that argument is propounded below). But in most cases, the fan uses a hotter, more focused medium to provide the information lacking in the cooler experience. Thus even in a situation in which the potential for diffusion is high, the media fan relies increasingly on hot, focused media.

In some situations, the fan's options are limited for him. An example can be drawn from the sky boxes in the Astrodome in Houston. Because the ridiculous distance from the live action all but prohibits the box owner from viewing the sporting event, box owners are virtually forced to watch the closed circuit broadcast of the live event in order to follow the game. Those who purchase skybox tickets are thus virtually forced to trade the cool media experience of watching the game itself for the hotter experience of television.

Moreover, a startling finding by Comisky et al.[28] reveals that sport spectators are more attuned to the commentary of the announcers than to the visual portion of the game. In fact, in actual segments of a hockey broadcast devoid of exciting play, viewers were easily convinced by the announcer that they were watching a fiercely competitive game. In contrast, a more action-filled segment of the game was judged less exciting by the viewers because the announcers let the action speak for itself and offered little dramatic commentary. It would seem that when the information gained from one medium conflicts with that offered by another, the spectator relies more heavily upon the sense most attuned to hotter messages—the ear.

On the other hand, perhaps Americans are still captivated by sport on television only because a cooler medium has not yet presented itself. Future developments in television or in other media used to cover sport events might provide a more diffuse and demanding experience for the spectator.

Forty years ago, essayist E.B. White speculated about the sport experience of the future. His concept of sport in the future was a totally diffuse one: "Not only did sport proliferate but the demands it made on the spectator became greater. Nobody was content to take in one event at a time, and thanks to the magic of radio and television nobody had to."[29] White illustrates the development of media sport through a super spectator who sits in the stands viewing the Yale-Cornell football game while simultaneously listening to the radio broadcast of the World Series from New York, monitoring the horse race presented on video sets located at either goal line, and glancing occasionally at the scores of other major or minor sporting contests being constantly revised by skywriters. "The effect of this vast cyclorama of sport was to divide the spectator's attention, over-subtilize his appreciation, and deaden his passion."[30]

Aldous Huxley's conception of the "feelies," his medium of the future, is in many ways similar. Apparently no senses are left unstimulated by the future total-experience medium. Society has progressed through an oral and a visual stage. Soon taste, feel and smell will also be incorporated, or as Huxley advertises: "Three Weeks in a Helicopter, an All-Super Singing, Synthetic-Talking, Coloured, Stereoscopic Feely. With Synchronized Scent-Organ Accompaniment."[31]

Amusing as their ideas must have seemed years ago. White and Huxley have proved to be accurate prophets. "Sensurround," the cinema technique used to enhance the viewers's experience of Earthquake and Midway, is the first step in the direction of Huxley's "feelies," and some practices and innovations can be cited as evidence of White's perceptiveness, e.g., the fan who buys two televisions so he can watch two sport programs at once. Charles Sopkin[32] experienced the ultimate in this regard. He closeted himself in a room with seven televisions, each tuned to a different network, and monitored all for "seven glorious days, seven fun-filled nights."

Wherever possible, the media keeps pace with demands for media variety. Telescreen, the huge replay screen in the Capital Center, makes it possible to fulfill White's predictions, for it is not limited to replaying action occurring on the floor below but might be used to broadcast another altogether.

Similarly, because of a contract conflict during the 1973 season, CBS found itself in the unwitting position of presenting to its viewers their most diffuse sport experience to date. The lifting of the blackout required CBS to broadcast into the Oakland area both the Detroit-SanFrancisco and the Giants-Raiders games in the same time slot.

> The network does not plan to let momentum govern its coverage staying with long drives and periodic swingbacks. Instead it plans constant changing to show as much action as possible just as dial switchers of the past did before affluences led to two television set families and the piggyback concept.[33]

The best model of the super spectator of the future is the sport show producer. Anyone who has seen Two Minute Warning would have to be impressed by the cacophony and confusion of the sport producer's world. Seated in a control booth, he continually monitors the image from each camera being used while receiving a constant relay of information through an earphone. His function is to predigest sport for the viewer. He determines when to insert instant replay and which camera's image gives the most effective picture. It is he who sees the diffusion and makes the focus decision. He is perhaps the only person for whom the media sport experience matches the live event in terms of diffusion. Roone Arledge is the archtype of the media man of the future.

SUMMARY

Why the individual feels less removed from the sport event beamed into his living room than the experiences of being physically present at the event is a function of the way in which he defines the sport experience. Several possible factors such as information, integration, arousal, and escape have been considered above. A model based on McLuhan's theory of media has been presented suggesting that an informational predisposition fosters an affinity toward linearity, focus and hot media sport experiences, whereas integrative and arousal predispositions incline the individual toward a more diffuse or cool experience. With that dichotomy in mind, speculation about the media sport experience of the future was presented. If, as McLuhan claims, this is truly a post-literate society, with all that implies in terms of focus and diffusion, innovations aimed at an increasingly diffuse media experience will appear and take their place in the consciousness of the sports fan. Some such innovations have already made their entry. In general, however, American sport fans are fed a greater and greater diet of predigested, focused sport events. And so far, none of the post-literates is complaining.

NOTES

1. A portion of this paper is adopted from a presentation given at the Popular Culture Association Meetings in 1974.
2. Marshall McLuhan, Understanding Media (New York: New American Library, 1964), p. 36.
3. Ibid., pp. 211-212.
4. See Ron Fimrite, "Grand New Game," Sports Illustrated, August 11, 1975, pp. 10-13.
5. McLuhan, p. 212.
6. Ibid.
7. Ibid., p. 23.
8. Ibid., p. 278.
9. The prominence of sport on television probably requires little documentation. However, it might be noted that well over 1000 television broadcast hours per week are devoted to sport (Advertising Age, October 22, 1973); that a record 76 million Americans tuned in the last game of the 1976 World Series (James P. Forkan, "Nets, Sponsors Ready to Play Ball," Advertising Age, March 15, 1976, p. 84); that the rights to broadcast the Olympic Games rose over 300 per cent, from $25 million in 1976 to $85 million in 1980 (William Leggett, "Commercializing the Games," Sports Illustrated, August 9, 1976, p. 47; William Oscar Johnson, "A Contract with the Kremlin," Sports Illustrated, February 21, 1977, pp. 14-19); that television revenues for major team sports have risen 1000 per cent in the past twenty years (Ira Horowitz, "Sports Telecasts," Journal of Communication, Vol. 27, 1977, p. 160); that cost per minute for advertising during the Super Bowl in 1979 will be $350,000 (James P. Forkan, "Football Ad Prices Way Up," Advertising Age, January 16, 1978, p. 2); and that reliable sources estimate that the rights to telecast NFL contests during 1978-1981 will cost about $640 million (Forkan, 1978, p. 2).
10. McLuhan, p. 288.
11. Ibid., p. 261.
12. See William O. Johnson, Super Spectator and the Electric Lilliputans, (Boston: Little, Brown and Company, 1971).
13. See Brien R. Williams, "The Structure of Televised Football, Journal of Communication, Vol. 27, 1977, pp. 136-137, for a similar view.
14. Again Williams (Ibid.) reflects the same idea when he contrasts "stadium event" to the "medium event".
15. Orrin E. Dunlop, Jr., New York Times, May 21, 1939 as quoted in Johnson, Super Spectator, p. 39.
16. Stephen Kanfer, "Football: Show Business with a Kick," Time, October 8, 1973, pp. 54-55.
17. "Retarded Live Television, New York Times, April 14, 1973, p. 43.
18. Ibid.
19. Sports Illustrated has argued for the use of TV cameras to make officiating decisions. See "Scorecard: Eye in the Storm," November 18, 1974, p. 26; "Scorecard: Delayed Relay," January 12, 1976, p. 6; and "Scorecard: Seeing is Believing," January 2, 1978, p. 7.
20. Peter Carry, "Big New E for Big New Eye," Sports Illustrated, March 11, 1974, p. 16.
21. "Video-Tape Helps Judges Pick Dressage Champion," New York Times, December 16, 1974, p. 73.
22. Gerhart D. Weibe, "Two Psychological Factors in Media Audience Behavior," in Alan Wells, Mass Media and Society (Palo Alto: National Press Book, 1972), pp. 208-217.

23. Ibid., p. 210.
24. William Leggett, "Stop the Game, I Want to Go On," Sports Illustrated, October 21, 1974, p. 73.
25. "TV Influences Sport," Newsweek, June 5, 1967, p. 66.
26. Johnson, Super Spectator, p. 59.
27. Leonard Shecter, The Jocks (New York: Paperback Library, 1969), p. 86.
28. Paul Comisky, Jennings Bryant, and Dolf Zillmann, "Commentary as a Substitute for Action," Journal of Communication, Vol. 27, 1977, pp. 150-153.
29. E. B. White, "The Decline of Sport," Second Tree from the Corner (New York: Harper and Row, 1954), p. 41.
30. Ibid., p. 42.
31. Aldous Huxley, Brave New World (New York: Bantam, 1932), p. 113.
32. Charles Sopkin, Seven Glorious Days, Seven Fun-Filled Nights (New York: Ace Publishing, 1968).
33. Jack Craig, "CBS Juggling Act," Boston Sunday Globe, November 4, 1973, p. 88.

The Sports Novel:
Mythic Heroes and Natural Men

Melvin D. Palmer

Sports have occupied a place in long narrative fiction since Drona of the *Mahabharata* taught the royal sons of Bharata to play games, since Achilles called the epic games to honor the memory of Patroklos, and since Nausicäa played ball with her hand-maidens in the *Odyssey*. But such episodes are not fundamental to the epics. Similarly, one finds sports referred to in secondary ways in the medieval romance and early novel, as in the stone-throwing contest in *Havelok the Dane* and the physical education of Gargantua in Rabelais' masterpiece. From the fox hunt of *Tom Jones* to the cricket field of *A Portrait of the Artist as a Young Man*, sports can hardly be said to constitute the focal metaphor of a single adult novel, nor does a single adult novel focus on an athlete hero.

But with the rise of mass spectator sports, it is not surprising that writers of serious intent are now coming to sports to see what they can find. The sports novel intended for adult audiences is a phenomenon of our time; and even though this sub-genre of modern fiction was slow getting off the ground, it has been rising rapidly over the last thirty years, attracting writers of more than common merit. The earliest sports novels— not surprisingly about the most mythic of American sports, baseball—are Ring Lardner's *You Know Me, Al* (1916) and Heywood Broun's *The Sun Field* (1923).[1] Both authors employ a measure of stylistic sophistication to bring sports fiction out of the world of adolescent wishful-thinking; but neither can be regarded as writers of really first-rank distinction and they did not seem to encourage an immediate following. In fact, years of literate opinion seems to have been summed up in the words of a *New York Times* Review (1923) of Broun's novel: "Somehow, one does not asso-

This is a revised version of "The Sports Novel: Mythic Heroes and Natural Men" by Melvin D. Palmer. Copyright 1973 by QUEST board (The National Association for Physical Education of College Women and the National College Physical Education for Men). Reprinted by permission of the author and publisher.

ciate baseball players [or any athlete, he would add] with the graver problems of life [p. 8]."

But writers of the forties, fifties, and sixties have proved this posture wrong. In these decades, among American and British writers—I can find no continental sports novels—the sports novel has come into existence and is probably here to stay. The genre has been dominated by American novelists: Nelson Algren, Bernard Malamud, John Updike, Budd Schulberg, and Irwin Shaw, supported by lesser figures and by such British writers as David Storey and Brian Glanville. Further, the first Delta Prize Novel Contest was won by a sports novel, Jeremy Larner's *Drive, He Said* (1964). Such activity is enough to demand our reckoning seriously with the sports novel. What are these novels like? Why do these writers turn to sports for central metaphors and to athlete-heroes for central figures? Let us take the first question first by surveying the works individually.

We need to make an initial distinction between sports novels about athletes and novels dealing with sportsmen or athletic people. For example, Ernest Hemingway would seem to merit scrutiny in such a study as this—and he does to a degree—but Hemingway did not write a sports novel *per se*, and he is primarily concerned with sportsmen who are fishermen, game hunters, or the like. We are concerned in this analysis primarily with organized, spectator sports. Hemingway does deal with athletes at times, however. For example, in the short story *The Killers*, the ambiguous "natural" fighter hunted by the corrupting hangers-on of the sports world does give us a theme we shall see often. And in the egotistical Cohn, the boxer of *The Sun Also Rises*, we find a picture of the man who plays the game badly, for bad reasons—another though less prominent theme of the sports novel. Perhaps the most important contribution of Hemingway to the sports novel, though, is his general emphasis on the sports arena as a place of initiation, a place where man is existentially forced for good or bad to confront himself alone.

Before Hemingway, the novels of Lardner and Broun introduced some of these same themes and a variety of minor themes that were to be treated by other writers later. Lardner clearly pushes the sports novel out of the realm of juvenile fiction through the creation of an unglamorous but very human hero who does not come out on top of the heap. Further, the human quality of the "hero" is narrated and dramatized in the very form of the novel, a series of entertaining, naive, very colloquial letters from major league pitcher Jack Keefe to his friend Al. In a sense, though, the novel is a typically American success story of the young man from the country who comes to the city and makes his mark. This concept of the natural man versus the machinations of civilized society and organized sports will reappear as the main theme of the sports novel. Lardner also strikes a new note by depicting his hero in domestic situations, as he goes through two girlfriends before marrying and having a child. The basic sports metaphor therefore expands beyond the arena to become an analogue for the game of life, which is another idea attractive to sports novelists. Another realistic theme that Lardner introduces is that of the fickle crowd which seems both to desire heroes and to desire their toppling down. All in all, however, the free-swinging naive humor of the tale is in the tradition of Mark Twain and looks forward to the three baseball novels of Mark Harris. Lardner sees the farcical aspects of the sport as well as its seriousness.

Heywood Broun's *Sun Field* (1923) consolidated the gain made by Lardner in a more serious context. In Broun's Tiny Tyler we see the other half of the ideal baseball star, the homerun slugger (as distinct from the shutout picture). It is a traditionally-written third-person novel, but the style is all that is traditional, for Broun complicates sports fiction by introducing, in the person of Judith Winthrope, an intellectual and a writer. The resultant clash between the intellectual and the sports world created yet another theme of sports fiction, one to which we shall return. In fact, Broun seems as much intent on tracing Tiny's and Judith's marital difficulties as with writing about baseball. Lardner and Broun touch a nerve that goes far beyond the mere telling of a good action-packed story and thus send sports fiction off in new and more realistic directions.

Chronologically, the first two sports novels of the past thirty years are about boxing: Nelson Algren's *Never Come Morning* (1942) and Budd Schulberg's *The Harder They Fall* (1947). Not as popular as these authors' *Man With the Golden Arm* and *What Makes Sammy Run*, respectively, these stories nevertheless picked up after a hiatus of about twenty years and got the rise of the sports novel well underway. Neither author treats sports as a dream realized. Algren's story is the naturalistic account of a prizefighter, also a baseball player, "Lefty" Bicek of Chicago's Polish ghetto. Bicek emerges as a sympathetic but lower than average specimen of humanity attracted by the great dream of the New World to find quick fame, success, money, and girls; but he finds instead that Sports, the only area where he has much competence, cannot fulfill this dream except in dreams, as he remains trapped in his environment.

Similarly a story of protest is Schulberg's prize-fighting novel, which is actually an exposé of the fighting racket. Schulberg focuses on three characters. First there is the boxer himself, Toro Molina, another natural man from the provinces (here, Argentina), who is duped into thinking he is actually winning a series of set-up matches. The second is Nick Latka, the mobster who has outlined an amazingly thorough publicity stunt to get Toro to a championship fight, knowing Toro will lose, so that he can clean up on the bets. The third is the intellectual, the writer Ed Lewis, who handles the publicity for Nick and is torn by his sensitivity to Toro but rationalizes all by thinking himself superior. It is from his point of view that the story unfolds, and he comes to realize at the end that he too is a mere pawn of the mobsters and is too weak to do anything about the evils he sees. The novel depicts the utter degeneration of the American Dream. The corrupt elements emerge victorious; the natural man loses; and the crowd's cries for blood are satisfied.

From this brutally realistic situation seen in Algren and Schulberg, a later writer about boxing tried to snatch a measure of saving grace: William Heinz, whose *The Professional* (1958) both borrows from and goes beyond the earlier boxing novels. Heinz's point of view is also realistic—he tries to depict boxing as it is—but he salvages a measure of dignity for his protagonists. The main characters are again three: Eddie Brown, a clean-cut, polite fighter; Doc Carroll, the aging manager who sees in Eddie his last chance to cop a championship; and Frank Hughes, the writer-intellectual assigned to cover Eddie and do a story on him. Like Schulberg, Heinz takes a writer to narrate the story; but unlike Schulberg's Lewis, the writer here seems to represent the author's point of view. The novel traces the preparation for the big fight and the fight itself, which ends in failure for Eddie and Doc. But both emerge as sympathetic characters, not defeated by the mob as in Schulberg, but by chance. Incidental to the novel is a topic sports novelists sometimes deal with. There is some social protest in Heinz's seeing has-beens as ignored and Blacks as discriminated against in the sports world. But the main theme enters as the narrator-author says that boxing is "the basic law of man. The truth of life. It's a fight, man against man and if you're going to defeat another man defeat him completely. Don't starve him to death like they do in the fine clean competitive world of commerce [p. 126]." It is well to believe in reason and prospects for the future, but for the present, the law is the law of the jungle, "and as long as that's true, I find man revealing himself more completely in fighting than in any form of expressive endeavor [p. 126]." This sounds almost like Hemingway at times. Here the athlete and the arena are superior to life outside, life being what it is. The logic here may border on the cynical, but the novel is nevertheless an attempt to go beyond Algren and Schulberg to find value in the endeavor of sports. These are our three boxing novels.

As might be expected, baseball dominates sports novels, just as American writers dominate the writing of them. In fact, of the eighteen sports novels of the forties, fifties, and sixties, eight are about baseball and fourteen are by American novelists. It is not hard to see why baseball would dominate the sports novel, what with the mythic proportions and early origins of the sport in America. And as for American dominance of the sports novel, perhaps one finds a reason in the very fact that massive interest in modern spectator sports and the leisure to pursue such an interest simply came to America first, for good or bad, as a result of technological progress and democratic attitudes. It is interesting to note that only one novel deals with football, and not in a professional setting. Only two deal with basketball, and one of those only loosely. Of the four British novels in this survey, one takes rugby as its metaphor, another takes soccer, and two focus on long-distance running.

Like the three boxing novels, the baseball stories are realistic, some rather heavily so and others, like Harris's three novels, realistic in the sense of Lardner's, that is, with a strong admixture of humor. The first of these, Malamud's *The Natural* (1952), has not been surpassed as a sports novel and may be best seen after we look at the other baseball novels. Without Harris and Malamud, then, we have four: Eliot Asinof's *Man on Spikes* (1955), Charles Einstein's *The Only Game in Town* (1955), Martin Quigley's *Today's Game* (1965), and Irwin Shaw's *Voices of a Summer Day* (1965). The first three deal with the actual sport in professional leagues; the last is the recollections of a middle-aged father as he watches a little league game involving his son.

The novels of Asinof, Einstein, and Quigley—writers of generally lesser stature than Harris, Malamud, and Shaw—are pretty much of a piece. All tell action-packed stories with little attempt to delve into social commentary or psychological analysis. They are what we call pot-boilers, though intended for adult consumption. Of the three, however, Quigley's novel does seem superior, partly because he captures the drama of a single game, but mainly because the author attempts to explore something of the mythic quality of the sport. At one point, the central figure of the story, the manager of the team, demands of a sports writer: "Why do you and all the millions of people in America . . . care so much about something that is just a game played for your amusement [p. 23]?" The answer is:

> It's because we know what the game is and who you are. We sit in the stands and look down and watch you struggle, man against man, and man against the fates. Perhaps you are to us what the demi-gods and heroes were to the ancient Greeks, and perhaps baseball is to us what the theater was to them—a drama with familiar heroes in familiar situations [p. 24].

But the reference to Greek theater is later deflated when the manager tells visiting foreign professors that the Greeks "played with heroes, and we play with people [p. 70]." These three novels deal with players as people rather than as heroes.

Irwin Shaw's *Voices of a Summer Day* occupies the time of about four hours while the main character watches his son play a ballgame and through the sounds of the game recalls forty years of his life. On the surface, sports is simply a framework for the recollections and not the focal metaphor. Symbolically, however, the central figure watches a ballgame in the sense of watching the game of his life. There are parallels between the wanderings of the mind and the rambling of the game. For example, in the section of the novel called *1964*, the author narrates the happenings of the game and then juxtaposes them with a section called *1926*. This type of division suggests the inning-by-inning analysis of a ballgame. The novel moves in sporadic bursts of action instead of following a normal story line. There is no regular plot, no climax, just specific occurences covering specific periods of time, much like innings in a ballgame. All in all, the protagonist comes off as a man who, in spite of errors, has managed to hold his own in the game of life.

Mark Harris picks up where Ring Lardner left off and brings a large degree of native American, Twainian, humor to the baseball diamond. His novels are *The Southpaw* (1953), *Bang the Drum Slowly* (1956), and *A Ticket for Seamstitch* (1957). All three are the fictional, autobiographical accounts of Henry Wiggin, a major league pitcher turned to writing. Further, we are told in a headnote that "punctuation [was] freely inserted and spelling greatly improved" by Mark Harris. Much like Lardner's Jack Keefe, then, Henry Wiggin reveals himself in his own way and with a good degree of simplicity, or naiveté. Another young man from humble parents and the provinces, Henry makes it big in the big leagues. And in his initiation to city ways and the unsavory aspects of organized sport, he becomes disillusioned with the game but matures without losing his natural sensitivity. Henry comes off at first as the All-American boy (He was born on the 4th of July!) with an enormous appetite. His appetite is also symbolic in that it is really an appetite for the great American dream of success. He finds the dream hollow and drops it, but the experience does not crush him. A major influence on him is his childhood sweetheart, Holly, whom he later marries. Holly is constantly telling Henry that the best man is a "soft" man. Here, indeed, we have a softening of the harsher, more masculine emphasis that one finds, for example in Heinz's *Professional* or, even given Hemingway's own brand of sensitivity, in Hemingway himself.

The Southpaw traces Henry's youth, his rise to the majors, and the ultimate capturing of the pennant, which, because Henry has changed, does not seem worth the hardships that purchased it. The novel touches on social and political problems of the time when we see Henry made fun of by the other players for taking a Black roommate and when Henry rejects an offer to play post-season ball in Korea. The latter decision was made in disgust at the sport but was interpreted as an attack on U.S. involvement in the Korean war. In this novel, the sports world often is cut down, but Henry finds something more valuable: himself. The other two Henry Wiggin novels do not seem to live up to the first one, but they are nevertheless among the best available novels to deal with sport.

Bang the Drum Slowly is the touching tale of the lingering illness and death of a minor member of Henry's team, Bruce Pearson. The team's indifference to Bruce (Henry is the only one to attend the funeral) serves to undercut the traditional attitudes toward sports heroes. In fact, by bringing illness and death into the playworld of sports, Harris may very well be suggesting that organized, spectator sports and the American dream they promise are disease-ridden, if not moribund. Interesting is the novel's comment that "baseball is . . . a game rigged by rich idiots to keep poor idiots from wising up to how poor they are [p. 207]." It is a dream, a mere illusion. In fact, Harris goes so far as to suggest that people do not want heroes at all. The crowd boos and jeers, without knowing why. The crowd is a herd that would rather see its heroes fall than rise to distinction.

In *A Ticket to Seamstitch,* Henry Wiggin focuses on the career of a young rookie who glamorizes the game. In fact, he's a young Henry Wiggin. Seamstitch is the name of a fan whose one desire is to make the long trip to see a major league game. Henry turns the arrangements over to the rookie, Piney; and the whole sequence ends in disillusionment for all three characters as Piney and Seamstitch come to see the unglamorous features of sports. In these three novels, Harris gives a realistic picture of professional baseball, but he goes beyond this picture by analyzing basic problems of the human condition. And he does it all with a happy blend of humor and sensitivity.

Even so, the Harris novels do not analyze sport as profoundly as does Malamud's *The Natural* (1952). In the story of Roy Hobbs, Malamud combines the folklore of baseball with the mythos of epic and romance. He explores the archetypal layers of "hero." One finds in the novel hints of Babe Ruth, Lou Gehrig, and the infamous "Shoeless" Joe Jackson; but one also finds a team called the Knights, a manager called, mythically,

Pop Fisher, and Roy Hobbs himself, whom Podhoretz (1953) called "Achilles in left field [p. 321]." Roy's bat even takes on mythic proportions: given a name, "Wonderboy," in the manner of the ancient hero's lance or sword, the bat is the product of a lightning-struck tree, almost a gift from the gods. Roy, like Henry Wiggin, has an enormous appetite; but his is a bigger, more epic appetite, and it extends to women as well as food. Further, it is this appetite (for food and women) that causes him to take a bribe, break training, lose everything, and end up in tears. In the context of folklore and myth, Roy Hobbs comes through as indeed the natural, a natural man from the provinces, with an epic appetite for a dream; but he ends up crushed by his own weakness as it flashes head-on with the mutable and corrupt elements of the sport and the city.

When we turn to football and basketball novels, we turn away from the world of professional sports but not away from an analysis of some of the same problems encountered there. *The Hero* (1949) was a first novel in which the author, Millard Lampell, traced ground that has by now become familiar: the situation of the talented young athlete from a modest background (here, he is Steve Novak, son of a humble immigrant) who expects to find in sports a golden key but instead finds disenchantment. The author places his hero in the context of a southern school where he is not accepted fully by the aristocratic children of Old America. After some initial difficulty, however, he is accepted by his English professor (the intellectual of the tale, who is immediately cynical about athletes) and by the daughter of one of the school's wealthiest, most influential, and most sports-minded alumni. After realizing that he is simply a paid performer and after suffering the pain of having to play a tough game with a bad shoulder, he pulls out with the alumnus's daughter and his new wisdom, buttressed by the influence of his English professor.

John Updike's *Rabbit, Run* (1960) is not a sports novel in the same sense that these other novels are. Except for the opening sequence, where Rabbit interrupts his trip home to play basketball with some young kids, and except for the episodes on the fairway, the novel treats the domestic and existential problems of this ex-basketball star, a has-been as a young man. The basketball metaphor, however, runs, feints, changes direction, backs up, runs again, seeking the basket to recapture the feel of the clean swish. He does not find it. Instead of the freedom and joy he felt in his hero-days in high school, he found himself in an impossible zone-defense, with no way out.

Like *The Hero*, Jeremy Larner's *Drive, He Said* (1964) has a college setting, but it gets into more topical problems than the earlier college novel. In the context of free-wheeling campus sex, the New York liberal establishment, drugs, and practically everything else from the current campus scene, Larner traces in a semisurreal style the experiences of two different but complementary heroes. Hector Bloom is an All-American basketball player; and his roommate, Gabriel Reuben, is a young student transformed by modern tensions into an unstable rebel. Hector is another natural man, and Gabriel is the overly sophisticated intellectual. As we shall see, however, Hector moves into the mean between these extremes to emerge as the novel's main hope for the future. Hector becomes disillusioned with the mechanical, impersonal style of basketball he has been taught. He calls it "White-boss" ball; it lacks the freer, more natural, more enjoyable qualities of "Black-boss," the Black athlete's style of playing. In fact, under Larner's hand, the game itself becomes a microcosm of a rules-imposed superstructure that is modern society in general and the Cold War in particular. Hector makes this transition from game to life, and at the end of the novel he seems ready to take over the causes that Gabriel leaves behind. Gabriel, who becomes a sort of angel/martyr, dies in a fire while posed on top of a float celebrating a sports event. His treasured ticket to the Land of Revolution, created as a kind of cynical joke, floats from his hands down to the hands of the now mature hero Hector.

The four British novels in this survey were all written in the sixties and all are realistic. The most realistic is the angry statement of David Storey (who is, in fact, one of Britain's generation of "Angry Young Men"). *This Sporting Life* (1960)—like *The Hero,* an ironic title—begins with an injury and ends as the aging hero contemplates his aching feet. By the end of the story, practically nothing of importance has happened to Arthur Machin, professional rugby player. Between the opening injury and the concluding focus on aching feet, the story traces one long metaphor of boredom and pain, including the suffering and death of the only person to whom Machin showed any human feeling, his landlady turned misterss. The words human feeling are perhaps ill-chosen, however, for Machin is like a machine, as his name suggests. And this is nowhere more apparent than at the end where he stands robot-like on a field of other human-automata. But he is not completely a machine. In the naturalistic tradition of the novel, he is also an animal, acting instinctively (much like Rabbit, another animal) when his territory is threatened and sensing not much more than appetite and pain. The sports arena of this novel is the setting for a calloused ego trip and its frustration. Storey's Machin is Updike's Rabbit stripped of any redeeming features that Rabbit might have.

Brian Glanville's *Rise of Gerry Logan* (1965) is also the tale of an ego trip, but one in which the egoist ends up on top, looking to climb even higher and without compunction about stepping on others to get there. Through professional soccer, Gerry Logan becomes a celebrity in Great Britain and on the continent. He is thereby duly lionized by press and public. At the novel's conclusion, he has ahead of him a successful career in television. Glanville places himself into the novel as a sports-writer and states the novel's theme after Gerry was outclassed on a tele-vision show. Glanville is amazed, however, that neither Gerry nor the mass television audience was aware of Gerry's poor performance:

> It was the night he appeared on the Brain Trust that his progress seemed finally out of control. . . . Could one really be right while everyone else was wrong? And if one *was* right, was this any conso-lation? For it meant that one was living in a . . . world so bored with itself, so void of standards, that it rejoiced in its own deception [p. 206].

Gerry is more of a heel than Storey's Machin or Updike's Rabbit (if Rab-bit is in fact a heel). How can one blame an animal or a machine? But Storey's novel is blacker, for it does not even have the ray of awareness that Glanville injects through himself into his novel.

British writers seem to be particularly drawn to long-distance run-ning. The metaphor has excellent potential, for here the author can con-centrate on his hero in a truly existential situation as he runs, quite alone, far away from the crowd, the arena, and even teammates and foes. But only one writer has explored in depth the existential possibilities of the metaphor, and that is in a short story rather than a novel: Alan Sillitoe's *Loneliness of the Long-Distance Runner* (1960). Here, Smith (the only name he has) is a "bad" reformatory school boy who participates in long-distance running at the behest of the school's governor. Ostensibly a kind of rehabilitation privilege, the running is actually intended to gain glory for the school. This dishonesty symbolizes to the sensitive but un-educated Smith what is wrong with society in general, why he is in re-form school, and why his family has had such a hard time. Sillitoe and his runner vent their mutual rebellion at what they see as a phony society. On the very brink of victory, in view of the small but cheering finish-line crowd, Smith suddenly stops and heroically throws the race. Smith comes off as the human product of an inhuman society.

In *The Games* (1967), Hugh Atkinson picks up this motif, but he does other things too. He has three runners, all of whom meet a different fate. There are four story lines, one each for the three runners and one for the international intrigue over preparations for the Olympic Games at which the three runners ultimately converge. One runner, the egoist of the group, finds poetic justice by getting too wound up in his over-confidence and crashing to his death into a concrete wall. Another comes to realize through the loneliness and difficulty of the race that his life had been one of taking rather than giving. He rights matters by turning down an alley and refusing to win. The third is the natural man, an Australian Aborigine, who had become interested in third-world discrimination and student rights. He gracefully wins the race.

In *The Olympian* (1969), Brian Glanville returns to the sports novel and chooses long-distance running this time. It is another story of the rise and fall of a great athlete. Ike Low is another natural man who wins as long as he remains uncorrupted; but when he loses his spontaneous simplicity through the worlds that sports opens to him, he loses the big race to another natural, a primitive African.

Such is the sports novel to date and the main themes running throughout it. The dominant theme seems to be that of the natural man in pursuit of a dream. But he does not remain a natural, nor does he usually achieve the dream. These writers could have made the same point on the failure of dreams by writing about the business world, the world of music, or practically any other world. But in the sports world, one finds better examples of the natural man working with more elemental qualities than are found in most other situations. That seems to be what has attracted writers to the athlete hero. Further, perhaps it is the age-old attraction that the body has for the mind, the physical and natural for the intellectual. It is a romance of opposites, an attempt to resolve some of life's polarities.

Why, then, is the writer so often critical of the sports world? He does not like everything that he finds there. He finds tenderness and brutality, humor and sadness, but most often brutality and sadness. He finds a microcosm where man, through native strength and skill, tries to come to terms with things on a rather elemental level. But he finds this quest often frustrated by other things. Most often, he seems to find documentation for some of the ideas advanced by Johan Huizinga (1938), one of this century's foremost analysts of play: "Ever since the last quarter of the nineteenth century, games in the guise of sport have become increasingly strict and elaborate [p. 197]." And Huizinga sees this as a "fatal shift toward over-seriousness [p. 198]." He goes on to conclude: "More and more the sad conclusion forces itself upon us that the play-element [is] on the wane [p. 206]."

In short, most often, the sports novelist finds that sports have squeezed out play, just as civilization has squeezed out the natural man. Again, a comment of Huizinga's is to the point: "In the sphere of . . . play, the child . . . [is] at home with the savage [p. 188]." It is worth stressing, however, that the writer does not blame the game itself; he likes both the game and the natural. Rather, it is the extremely organizational context of the game that all too often takes the natural player and changes, corrupts, or destroys him by killing the child-like and primitive spontaneity and joy that should characterize games.

A NOTE ON "THE SPORTS NOVEL: MYTHIC HEROES AND NATURAL MEN"

Since publishing this article in 1973, I have felt the need to add comments on several other American novels—some printed before my 1970 cut-off date and some printed afterwards.

The minor vogue for basketball fiction initiated by John Updike in 1960 and contributed to by Jeremy Larner should include mention of Jay Neugeboren's *Big Man* (Boston: Houghton Mifflin, 1966). In this, the first sports novel with a black hero, we enter the world of the point-shaving scandals as Mack Davis tells the story of his dreams and frustrations. Similarly, boxing continued to be a metaphor for sports fiction in the sixties with Leonard Gardner's *Fat City* (New York: Dell, 1969), a popular novel about boxers who do not approach championship status.

The year 1968 witnessed three major publishing events in the history of sports fiction. Frederick Exley's *Fan's Notes* (New York: Harper and Rowe)—indirectly a sports novel—deals with a hero whose father had been a star athlete but who himself is doomed to the life of a fan. He illustrates some of the frustrations of the 1960's as he sits in bars, watches the New York Giants on television, and picks fights. Also in 1968—and for the first time in over a decade—baseball came back into the mainstream with Robert Coover's *The Universal Baseball Association* (New York: Random House). Like Exley's hero, the protagonist of this story, Henry Waugh, was not an athlete; unlike Exley, however, he was not even a fan. His baseball is limited to a highly complicated game he had invented. His preoccupation with this game causes him to lose his few friends and his job. Here, significantly amid the hottest year of the turbulent 60's, the great American dream, as symbolized by baseball, had become only a remote item of the past. The third sports novel of this crucial year, Gary Cartwright's *Hundred Yard War* (New York: Doubleday), strikes a new note. It is the first sports novel I can find about professional football, and it depicts a world of hard knocks, big money, and abundant sex. This new hedonism contrasts sharply with the innocence of the old-fashioned baseball hero; and it heralded the ascendancy of football over baseball in fiction (just as football had outpaced baseball in gate receipts and other indexes of popularity). With Coover, the year 1968 seemed to signal the end of the old baseball world; with Cartwright, the year seemed to anticipate an entirely new ethos.

Football reigned supreme in sports fiction for a few years. Excluding Coover's unusual story, from 1956 until 1973 there was not a single novel whose central metaphor was baseball. On the other hand, the early 70's saw a succession of six football stories: Joseph Pillitteri's *Two Hours on Sunday* (New York: Dial Press, 1971); James Whitehead's *Joiner* (New York: Knopf, 1971); Don Delillo's *End Zone* (Boston: Houghton Mifflin, 1972); Dan Jenkins' *Semi-Tough* (New York: Athenaeum, 1972); Frank Deford's *Cut 'n Run* (New York: Ballentine Books, 1973); and Peter Gent's *North Dallas Forty* (New York: Morrow, 1973).

A couple of these are little more than pot-boilers; others made important contributions to sports fiction. *Joiner* stands out as an attempt to "join" the body and the mind in an effort to update the Greek ideal of a sound mind in a sound body. The hero, Sonny Joiner, is a star student, an avid reader, and an outsanding athlete. *End Zone* uses football as a basic metaphor in relation to the campus unrest of the time, as the author seems to find America hovering in the end zone of its greatness. The novels by Jenkins and Gent, of course, had a large following—the former apparently for its hedonistic kicks and the latter as a fictional exposé. Both have recently been made into first-run movies.

It should not be surprising that the nostalgia craze of the early 70's would bring baseball back into American fiction. This, the most mythically American of all sports, came into prominence again along with nostalgic movies like *The Summer of Forty-two,* television series like *Happy Days* and *The Waltons,* and non-fictional treatments of baseball like *The Boys of Summer.* This brand new vogue for baseball made itself felt in the novel in John Graham's *Babe Ruth Caught in a Snowstorm* (Boston: Houghton Mifflin, 1973) and in Phillip Roth's *Great American Novel* (New York: Holt, Rinehart, Winston, 1973), an appropriately titled story for the great American sport.

All in all, the early 70's saw the continued flowering of the sports novel as an important sub-genre of modern American fiction. Not only did authors continue to take sports and athletes as relevant metaphors for and reflections of modern society, but they seemed to do so more prolifically than ever before.

NOTE

1. Here I exclude the numerous dime-novels and juvenile novels from the late 19th century on. These, as might be expected, are full of adolescent fantasy and stock characters, actions, and themes. I also exclude, from this study of the novel, the numerous short stories dealing with sports. For further commentary on these areas of sports fiction—in the context of baseball—see Graber (1967) and Coffin (1970). There is practically no secondary material on the sports novel in general.

REFERENCES

Algren, N. *Never come morning.* New York: Harper, 1942.
Asinof, E. *Man on spikes.* Hightstown, N. J.: McGraw-Hill, 1955.
Atkinson, H. *The games.* New York: Simon and Schuster, 1968. Orig. 1967.
Broun, H. *The sun field.* New York: Putnam, 1923.
Coffin, T. P. *The old ball game: baseball in folklore and fiction.* New York: Herder and Herder, 1970.
Einstein, C. *The only game in town.* New York: Dell, 1955.
Glanville, B. *The Rise of Gerry Logan.* New York: Delacorte Press, 1965.
Glanville, B. This sporting life. *New York times book review,* July 18, 1965, 2.
Glanville, B. *The olympian.* New York: Dell, 1969.
Graber, R. S. Baseball in American fiction. *English Journal,* 1967, *56,* 1107-1110.
Harris, M. *The southpaw.* Indianapolis, Ind.: Bobbs-Merril, 1953.
Harris, M. *Bang the drum slowly.* New York: Knopf, 1956.
Harris, M. *A ticket for Seamstitch.* New York: Knopf, 1957.
Heinz, W. C. *The professional.* New York: Harper, 1958.
Huizinga, J. *Homo ludens.* Boston: Beacon Press, 1950. Orig. 1938.
Lampell, M. *The hero.* New York: Messner, 1949.
Lardner, R. *You Know me, Al.* New York: Scribner's, 1916.
Larner, J. *Drive, he said.* New York: Delta, 1964.
Malamud, B. *The natural.* New York: Harcourt, Brace, 1952.
New York times book review, Oct. 21, 1923, 8.
Podhoretz, N. Achilles in left field. *Commentary,* 1953, *15,* 321-326.
Quigley, M. *Today's game.* New York: Viking, 1965.
Schulberg, B. *The harder they fall.* New York: Signet, 1947.
Shaw, I. *Voices of a summer day.* New York: Delacorte Press, 1965.
Sillitoe, A. *The loneliness of the long-distance runner.* New York: Knopf, 1960.
Storey, D. *This sporting life.* London: Longmans, 1960.
Updike, J. *Rabbit, run.* Greenwich, Conn.: Fawcett, 1960.

Commentary as a Substitute for Action

Paul Comisky, Jennings Bryant, and Dolf Zillmann

> *On the strength of the sportscasters'*
> *play-by-play account, the viewers may "see"*
> *fierce competition where it really does not exist.*

It is generally assumed that the sports spectators in front of the television set are seeing *the game,* that is, an unbiased and reliable, "true" representation of the game that the fans in the stadium or arena see. But are they? It can be argued that they are not. Whereas the viewers in the stadium perceive the event as is, the home viewers are exposed to a "media event" that is the product of a team of professional gatekeepers and embellishers. In choosing from among the several close-ups, long shots, replays, cutaways and various segments of action at his disposal, the director is certainly an editor of the game. Moreover, yet another crew, the sportscasters, is in charge of embellishing the drama of the affair, thereby making it more palatable to the action-hungry audience.

The sportscasters help create the media event by embellishing the actual happening with play-by-play, color commentary, and what have you. It is commonly assumed that sports commentary serves to compensate for imperfections of the visual modality of the medium in creating the live game: much sports commentary indeed serves this function. In fact, the announcer's description and analysis are often so useful that there are numerous accounts of fans in the stadium monitoring broadcast transmissions to verify that what they had just seen was really what they thought they saw (cf. 1, pp. 310-312). However, the audio portion of the sports telecast tends to provide the spectators with much more than restatement of what they just saw (or would have seen had they been at the game). The role of the contemporary sports commentator has expanded to include the responsibility of dramatizing the event, of creating suspense, sustaining tension, and enabling the viewers to feel that

From *The Journal of Communication,* Summer 1977, copyright Annenburg School of Communications, 1977. Reprinted by permission of the author and publisher.

they have participated in an important and fiercely contested event the fate of which was determined only in the climactic closing seconds of play (cf. 1, p. 309). It would appear that these dramatic embellishments might provide the spectators at home with a very different impression of the game than that received by the viewers in the stadium or arena, yet, in spite of this possibility, there apparently has been no research on how television commentary contributes to the spectators' perception of the game or how it affects their appreciation of the play.

Our own research into the impact of commentary on the perception and appreciation of sports events came about somewhat by accident.

After examining videotapes of several ice hockey games for various types of violent interactions (cf. 2), we selected two segments that we had tentatively identified as containing different degrees of aggressiveness: one with normal play and the other with aggressive exchanges. We had selected these segments while watching the monitor in much the same manner that the typical sports fan observes televised sports, with at least a moderate amount of attention given to both the audio and visual portions of the presentation. Upon more systematic examination of the audio and video tracks of our segments, however, we discovered that the segment that we had initially identified as showing aggressive action contained only a little explicitly violent behavior. The announcers, however, had managed to convince us that we were witnessing rough and tough ice hockey at its best, with the action threatening to turn into fisticuffs at any minute, when in fact there was little action. The segment that we had identified as showing normal action, on the other hand, actually presented several very rough incidents (hard checks, etc.). The announcers, however, when play was intense, had let the action carry the game with little commentary of a dramatic sort. It appeared that we had bought into the commentary of the game more than the visually present action.

In order to more systematically examine the effects of commentary on perception, and specifically, in order to determine what effect the viewer's perception of roughness of play has on overall appreciation of the ice hockey, we subjected the two twelve-minute segments to a laboratory test. To be more certain about the magnitude of the differentiations in perceived roughness in the audio and video portions of the two segments, two pretests were performed. In the first pretest, 1 female and

2 male undergraduates recorded the frequency of rough incidents while watching only the video portion of the segment. With perfect agreement, they identified 11 rough incidents in the rough-action segment and 3 in the normal-action segment ($\chi^2(1)=4.56$, p<.05). They then listened to the audio portion of the segments for the frequency of references to roughness (e.g., "hard hitting"). They recorded *no* reference to roughness for the rough-action segment and 6 references to roughness for the normal-action segment (χ^2 with Yates Correction $(1)=4.17$, p<.05). In the second pretest, a panel of 5 male and 5 female judges rated the audio and then the video portion of each of the two segments on a scale ranging from 0 ("not at all rough") to 100 ("extremely rough"). Results were as follows. For video only, $\bar{x}=64.5$ in the rough-action condition, and $\bar{x}=26.5$ in the normal-action condition ($t(18)=6.25$, p<.001). For audio only $\bar{x}=16$ in the rough-action condition, and $\bar{x}=63$ in the normal-action condition ($t(18)=6.64$, p<.001). Roughness in action and in commentary were then indeed negatively related.

In the main experiment, participants were exposed to one of the two segments in one of two presentation modes: with or without commentary. In all, 139 undergraduates in Communications at the University of Massachusetts participated in the study. They were randomly assigned to one of the four treatment conditions, with males and females at an approximately constant ratio. Upon entering the laboratory, the participants were asked to be seated and .not to interact with one another in any way. They then viewed a television segment in one of the four treatment conditions. After viewing, they rated the segment on a series of scales presented on a questionnaire. Four of the questionaire items were designed to measure alterations of perception and two were included to assess appreciation of the sports events shown. All scales ranged from 0 (labeled "not at all _____") to 100 (labeled "extremely _____") and were marked and numbered at intervals of ten. The participants could make their rating at any point on the scale. The four scales relating to perception were: (1) How much *action* did the segment contain? (2) How *enthusiastic* were the participants shown in the segment? (3) How *rough* was the action in the segment? (4) How *violent* was the action in the segment? The two scales relating to appreciation were: (5) How *entertaining* did you find the segment? (6) How *enjoyable* was the segment?

The results showed that viewers' perception of the hockey play was greatly influenced by the nature of the accompanying commentary.

The data were analyzed by the analysis of variance method of unweighted means as shown in Table 1. The F ratios (all associated with 3 and 135 degrees of freedom) for the six measures specified above were: (1) 3.56, p<.05; (2) 3.73, p<.05; (3) 11.94, p<.001; (4) 18.5, p<.001; (5) 3.33, p<.05; (6) 2.31, p<.10.

The strength of the effect of the dramatic commentary on the viewer's perception can be seen from an examination of the mean scores of perceived roughness of play. In the normal-action condition, the commentary stressing the roughness of play made the normal play appear rough; actually it made it appear rougher than the rough play. In the rough-action condition, on the other hand, the commentary that did not emphasize roughness made rugged play appear less rugged. The other measures of perception of play show very similar effects. There can be no doubt, then, that commentary can substantially alter perception of play.

The mean values on the measures of appreciation show substantial effect as well. The condition perceived to be most entertaining was that featuring normal play which the commentary presented as rough. It is

TABLE 1
Perception of Roughness and Appreciation of Play in Professional Ice Hockey as a Function of Broadcast Commentary

Dependent Measure	Normal play		Rough play	
	Commentary stressing roughness	No commentary	Commentary ignoring roughness	No commentary
Perception of play:				
Action-packed	70[b]	66[b]	54[a]	69[b]
Enthusiastic	76[b]	60[a]	74[b]	75[b]
Rough	67[d]	39[a]	47[b]	61[c]
Violent	62[c]	28[a]	41[b]	58[c]
Appreciation of play:				
Entertaining	54[c]	35[a]	38[a]	44[b]
Enjoyable	54[a]	39[a]	40[a]	43[a]

Note. Means having different superscripts differ at p <.05 by Neuman-Keuls' test. The game was the Boston Bruins vs. Detroit Redwings at Detroit, a regular game of the 1976-1977 season as broadcast by the Boston Bruins' Network. The commentary was that of the original broadcast.

interesting to note that the differences in the ratings of entertainment value follow the degree to which play was *perceived to be* rough. Since this perception was largely a function of commentary, the commentary stressing roughness of play proved to increase the entertainment value of the sport event in question more than the variation in actual roughness.

These findings are suggestive of the great potential of sports commentary to alter the viewers' perception of the sport event. The viewers seem to get "caught up" in the way the sportscaster interprets the game, and they allow themselves to be greatly influenced by the commentator's suggestion of "drama" in the event. The viewers, in the end, may "see" fierce competition where it really does not exist.

Not only does dramatic commentary affect perception of play, but it is apparently a factor in the enjoyment of televised sports as well. Our findings suggest that the enjoyment of televised sports events closely corresponds with perceptions of roughness, enthusiasm, and even violence in play. With the perception of all these aspects of play being strongly influenced by broadcast commentary, it appears that, to a high degree, the sportscaster is a critical contributor to the spectator's appreciation of televised sports.

REFERENCES

Michener, J. A. *Sports in America*. New York: Random House, 1976.
Zillmann, D., J. Bryant, and B. S. Sapolsky. "The Enjoyment of Watching Sport Contests." In J. H. Goldstein (Ed.) *Sports, Games and Play*. Hillsdale, N.J.: Lawrence Erlbaum, in press.

Section E

Religion, Ritual and Sport

The relationship between sport and religion has intrigued many people, so that it is not uncommon to hear the assertion that sport is a modern day religion. Indeed, many personal accounts exist which stress the asceticism of training and the feeling of transcendence which occurs when one has reached his or her total capabilities. Moreover, in a more social frame of reference, one could point to the institutionalization of sport as a significant element in social life by noting the enshrinement of our sport heroes in awe inspiring halls of fame replete with stained glass windows. But if one is to investigate in a more systematic matter the statement that sport is a modern day religion, it seems appropriate first to come to terms with the meaning of religion in society.

Religion is an institution which revolves around a network of beliefs and rituals pertaining to the sacred. Durkheim, who was the first to explore religion as a social rather than personal experience,[1] conceived of religion as a system which bound the individual to the community by means of ritual behavior towards symbols which represented the values of the community. Thus religion was conceived by Durkheim as a symbolic system. In this case, the content or messages carried by the system pertain to the beliefs or values of the community. To Durkheim, the ritual or special treatment of symbols of the community was the core of religion. However, Durkheim was quite open-minded about what comprised religion, and his work can be readily extended to apply to secular rituals as well. If sport serves the same purpose, i.e., if it serves as a bridge between the individual and the value system of the community, it can be interpreted as a significant secular ritual and perhaps can be conceived of as a modern day religion.

1. Emile Durkheim, *The Elementary Forms of the Religious Life* (New York: The Free Press) 1915.

Both Fiske and Cheska discuss football as a "ritually elaborate" activity. Using a framework from the renowned anthropologist Van Gennep, Fiske analyses American football as a masculine rite of passage, noting the presence and significance of the full ceremonial cycle from separation, to transition, to incorporation.

Cheska also focuses upon American football as a significant ritual. Cheska concentrates her analysis on the concept of power, which she finds celebrated in the spectacle of college football.

Pigskin Review: An American Institution

Shirley Fiske

INTRODUCTION

> We anthropologists treat a familiar culture as though it were a strange one . . . we consciously choose this approach so that we may view the culture from a new angle and throw into relief features obscured by other forms of study. (Nadel 1951:7)

This statement succinctly sums the prime impetus for writing this paper: it is imperative to adopt the analytic framework of anthropology in order to explain in proper perspective events which occur in our own culture. Let us consider what we Americans think to be a harmless athletic contest: when closely inspected through the Truth-Lens of anthropology, it is actually a stealthy type of ritual behavior escaped from "primitive" camps. American traditions are ethnologically cubby-holed curiosities paralleling those found in pre-literate cultures throughout the world. Basic cultural processes which produce behavioral similarities across technological gulfs may manifest themselves in forms somewhat sheltered from the awareness of the natives, but they do not cease to operate.

Having direct contact with several football players and the coaches of a well-known university, I observed many of their quaint customs and beliefs; as the season progressed, my Anthopology-Eyes brightened, for the various ritual behaviors closely resembled that which in other cultures is labeled "puberty rites," or "initiation ceremonies." Further investigation along these lines has supported my hypothesis—this study is an effort to demonstrate that the actual nature of a football season is an initiation into adulthood. The format for the body of this paper is first, a brief review of the theoretical background of initiation ceremonies, the presentation of the data gathered, and the analysis and interpretation of it. Finally, perhaps some alteration may be made in the models as a result of studying the rite in our own culture.

Reprinted with permission of the author.

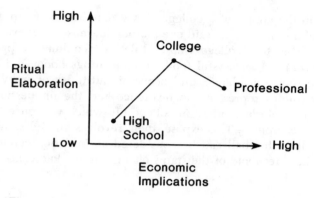

Figure 1

Before embarking on the major discussion of this paper, it might be well to justify the relevance of *collegiate* football to initiation ceremonies, and also the choice of the University of Southern California as the subject of analysis. Football events range in ritual content on a continuum from the football of high school to that of college and then professional ball. A cross-cutting dimension is that of athletic entertainment, an economic criterion relating to the outside society. High school football and professional football are at the extremes of these axes: high school football does not have the elaborate ritual of collegiate football, and furthermore it is primarily an athletic contest, without important economic ramifications. Professional football is on the other end of the economic extreme —its very existence is determined by the economic conditions it creates. It rates lower on ritual concomitants than college, but higher than high school; it is not a temporary status during one's lifetime, but is a mode of living for the players, so it has not the symbolic content of initiation ceremonies. Professional football is a specialized type of entertainment of a very different nature than collegiate football, where team members are competing among themselves for a livelihood.

The justification for the choice of schools from among many colleges is twofold: first, the proximity of location, and the accessibility of data; secondly, and more importantly, the University of Southern California is the epitome of a college enmeshed in football tradition. The fervor and pride generated by the football team are evident to an extreme degree. USC represents college life and the football centrifuge at its peak development, approximately as it was across the nation previous to the current trend to de-emphasize athletics in favor of intellectualism. *Middletown*, although published in 1929, illustrates the strength of the American pride even in the choice of a college: " 'My daughter plans to go to the University of ....,' said one mother, 'because, she says, 'Mother, I just *couldn't* go to a college whose athletics I couldn't be proud of' " (Lynd 1929:214). A successful football team brings honor and develops pride in the social, academic, and economic attitudes of individuals at SC; these attitudes represent the reverence and the unquestioning importance of the role of football in college life which was once the norm on all college campuses. This exposé, then, revolves around showing that American college football can be considered an initiation ceremony, occurring on the threshhold of the status change from adolescence to adulthood.

THEORETICAL BACKGROUND

The occurrence of ritual at puberty has posed a rather complex problem for anthropologists. It reflects both the physical aspect of reproductive maturity; as well, it is at this point that the individual has attained the socio-emotional responsibility of adulthood. In most societies, there is some association in peoples' minds between the notion of sexual maturity and that of social maturity: for this reason, the puberty ritual is described by anthropologists as an "initiation ceremony," or "rite of passage" from one role to another. Puberty is a sign of the final and completed difference between the man's body and the woman's—a time when both sexes must assume their respective masculine and feminine roles.

The flexibility of these rites in marking both a cultural and physical change in the individual has shown amazing variability in the types of ritual of the event. The adaptability of the initiation ritual is one of its foremost features, for it is found in some form, however, sublimated, in all societies. One group may stress the aspects of proper training for parenthood and emphasize appropriate role assumption. All primitive societies have some method of marking this dual change; the same process is at work in familiar institutions within our own society.

A consideration of initiation rites reveals many types, for each society marks the initiations of the individual throughout his life cycle without recognition of the modes of transition—e.g., baptism, confirmation, graduation, puberty, marriage. Most of these examples indicate a transition from one social role to another to be adopted. In our American society, a frequent, and one of the most obvious, types of initiation, is that into a closed group, club, or fraternity—often, interestingly, with a sex-linked membership requirement[1]—where there is some form of testing or hazing connected with entering the group. Naturally, sororities and fraternities stand as good examples of this type of initiation, as well as Shriners, Elks, and secret societies. These initiation ceremonies share much in common with the transition into adulthood, *viz.*, the individual is given new duties, rights, and responsibilities, and a new set of people with which to interact in a new role; nonetheless, they differ fundamentally from puberty rites, with which we are concerned, for they do not apply equally over the vast majority of men or women in that particular age-grade. The ceremony and the adoption of the new role has no wider significance than the small sub-group of the society to which it pertains, and would not be understood by the wider audience.

Hence the passage from one social situation to another is often accompanied by some form of *rite de passage*. However, the most important transition for any society is the transition from adolescence to adulthood, because it is here that the cognitive-emotional training for adult roles is condensed, and this is the most crucial period for transmission. The childhood bonds, especially with parents, are broken and adult values are instilled in both young men and young women. Each society must have a way of dramatizing the importance of adopting these values which will perpetuate the society; for if there were no importance attached to the way to become a proper adult person—if there were no values inculcated in growing citizens—then that society would function less than economically.[2]

Due to a desire for brevity, I will summarize only three of the authors who have written definitively on the anthropology of initiation into adulthood; Van Gennep (1909), Whiting (1958, 1960, 1964), and Young (1962, 1965).

Since the first major treatise elucidating the subject in 1909, Van Gennep's comprehensive *Les Rites de Passage*, no one has seriously shaken his basic postulates concerning the generic category of rites of passage. Throughout an initiation ceremony, Van Gennep emphasized the importance of the transition from the profane world to that of the sacred. The person who enters a new status at variance with one formerly held becomes "sacred" to the others who remain in the "profane" world.

The rites have a common function, in easing the individual in transition from one social role to another, and they also have common stages. There is a separation or death from the old state of being, a transition between the two states, and an incorporation or rebirth into the new one. An important feature is often that of symbolic dramatization of the stages: separation or death is often symbolized in physical seclusion (a bush camp, or a separate building or corporal punishment (whipping, beating, etc.) of the initiates; "the purpose is to make the novice 'die,' to make him forget his former personality and his former world" (Van Gennep 1909:81, n. 2). The transition period allows the initiates to interact with the other members of the society, but often on a markedly different level—i.e., with special favors, compensations, etc., from others, for the novices are still in the "sacred" sphere relative to the rest of the society. Rebirth or incorporation is a phase which occurs variably in different societies. During this period, initiates may act as though they are newly born, and must relearn all the gestures of ordinary life. The individual is symbolically reintegrated into the ways of the society, only this time with a new social role—adulthood.[3]

While Van Gennep considers initiation to be a dramatization of role change through the opposition of profane and sacred worlds, the two authors who we will consider next felt that initiation emphasizes *sex* role adoption in adulthood. In three consecutive articles (Whiting, Kluckholn, and Anthony 1958, Burton and Whiting 1960, and Whiting 1964), Whiting, through cross-cultural research, upheld what has become known as his "cross sex identity" hypothesis. This hypothesis maintains that in those societies where it is necessary to switch the child or adolescent abruptly from an identification with his mother to that of the father, then this will be marked by a severe initiation ritual. That is, where children grow up emotionally very close to their mothers, then, if they are male, in order to insure proper adult behavior, the former bonds must be broken in favor of male role assumption.[4] The dimensions of a ceremony necessary to call that event an adolescent initiation are the presence of one of the following: (1) painful hazing by adult males; (2) genital operations; (3) seclusion from women; (4) tests of manliness (Whiting, Kluckholn, and Anthony 1958:360).

Frank Young also looks at initiation ceremonies via cross-cultural methodology, and concludes somewhat similarly that initiation ceremonies serve to dramatize sex role recognition and reinforce social solidarity of adult males. Young removes the causation from the realm of infantile fixations and places it on a societal level.

Sex role dramatization is necessary where there is a high degree of male solidarity, defined as the consensus among the men regarding the purpose and activities of males (Young 1962:387).[5] Young notes that this situation usually occurs in soceties where resources are exploited by cooperation, and where intergroup hostilities are conducive to male solidarity.

The social meaning of male solidarity must be dramatized in a memorable way; the candidate must participate intensely. Young offers a scale of degrees of dramatization of initiation rites, from the lowest step of customary minimal social recognition (gifts, party, change of names), to the next step, social seclusion (physical or social separation), then personal dramatization (initiate is ceremoniously dressed and/or gives a public performance), organized social response (group dresses ceremonially and/or performs), and finally the most dramatic step—emotionalized social response (beating or hazing) (Young 1962:385).

Whiting and Young led a spirited controversy over their respective interpretations of initiation ceremonies. Using the techniques available through their methodology, they come to a close agreement on the ultimate value of initiation as a technique of male sex identification: their main disagreement resides in the interpretation of systems of causation—Whiting emphasizes childhood patterns of behavior and motions and the necessity of breaking them, and Young chooses to place causation on the societal level in the form of male solidarity.

CEREMONIAL DATA

I would like to demonstrate that the "athletic" phenomenon of American collegiate football may be considered an initiation ceremony celebrating the status change from adolescence to adulthood.

The data is of two kinds: first, the actual descriptions of the formal content of the ceremony itself. This data is derived from interviews with the players and coaches, and from my own observation. To clarify, the actual strategy employed in the defensive-offensive maneuvers on field during a game does not concern us except symbolically; the many plays and formations are relatively unimportant except inasfar as they demonstrate the elaborate and highly ritualized nature of the ceremony. I have interviewed four players, consulted manuals, and observed behavior. There is little or no disagreement among the sources about the formal characteristics of the program—these are explicit, clear-cut events.

The second type of data is what is generally referred to as the "native's viewpoint" of the reasons for and the effects of the ceremony. This aspect necessarily involves interpretation on the part of both informant and the anthropologist, so I spoke to many more individuals to get a representative view. As well as the four initiates, I spoke to three of their coaches, the head yell leader, and engaged innumerable individuals in informal discussion about the importance of the football festivals.

The duration of the ceremony is eight months, each year, with the activity concentrated in the first four months. During the four weeks of intense ritual activity, there are discrete weekly festivals. Membership in the novice group is a desirable goal for all young males, although only the most fit are allowed to participate. A boy may enter the activities

356   Sport in Cultural Context

for one year or up to four years, but not more; and once he has begun the yearly cycle, quitting it is accompanied by a heavy stigma both among the initiates and in the society at large.

The Setting: The sacred ground upon which the public part of the ceremony occurs (weekly for eleven weeks) is a rectangular field, 100 yards long. The spectators gather on all sides to watch the ceremony. Public rites occur in this setting.

The Personnel: These people of the ceremony can be classified into the actual participant, the affiliates, and the spectators; each of these is removed one degree further from emotional identification with the novice group, respectively. The first group is the most important, obviously. It is composed of a set of seven directors (elders), one of which is the head co-ordinator who is oldest and who has accumulated vast wisdom. He is revered and respected. The other participants are the initiates themselves—usually about seventy—who are ranked internally according to ability to perform properly and according to seniority. The hierarchy, from the top down, is composed of groups referred to as the "varsity," the "red shirts," and the "j.v's."

The affiliated personnel travel with the novices when ceremonies occur at fields other than their own. They do not participate in the ceremony directly, nor are they admitted to the secret meetings or secluded areas. The affiliated personnel are of two kinds: there are specialized individuals hired to care for certain needs of the novices (team "trainers" and "managers"), and there are individuals whose goal is the interpretation of the novices' actions to the audience during public performances. These virginous dancers and their male counterparts ("yell leaders," and "song girls") lead organized chants and incite emotionalized responses from the crowd during the performance.

The last group is the audience, which is composed of multitudes of people, both kin and non-kin. They must remain off the sacred ground whenever the novices occupy it, but are encouraged to react vocally and with gestures to the movements of the novices on the field.

Various phases of the ceremony emerge from the data, and are given below along with a brief synopsis of their import.

Yearly Ceremonial Cycle

Phase I: "Double Days"

The official schedule starts in early September, for a period of two weeks before the first public ceremony. This period is termed "Double Days" (because the novices practice two times a day) and is designed to promote unity among the group through hard work, fatigue, and practice. There is a set number of gatherings which can occur, ruled by higher authorities in the nation. The novices are confined to a strict daily schedule. They are secluded from women, and their diet is controlled—the initiated eat all meals together in an institution known as "Training Table"—and certain foods with a high concentration of starch and carbohydrates are taboo. This period is characterized by the initiates as a very trying, tiring time, and very tense because all the novices are living in such close quarters. The daily schedule is reproduced below. There is a four-day break before the first public ceremony.

7:00 A.M.	Awakened
7:30	Eat first meal of the day together
9:00	On a secret field, dressed in costumes, participate in rigorous physical activity for two hours
11:00	Off field
12:00 P.M.	Eat second meal together
2:00	On field again, repeat same physical punishment as earlier
4:00	End punishment
5:30	Eat third meal together; the meals have been planned by the elders according to specific regulations
6:00	Meeting of all novices, presided over by elders, to discuss the inadequacies of the novices; psychologically harassed.
8:00	End of gathering; the novices are now free to mingle with each other, but they cannot leave the building.
10:30	Bed check by the elders to see if all novices are in bed.

Phase II: "The Season"

The cycle now enters a period lasting through December 7, characterized by weekly confrontations between the initiates of this group and those of the same age-group, but of a different locality. Traditionally, these are considered hostile encounters, varying in degree of hostility between the groups. Open hostility is precluded by the set ritual of the game in which the groups engage.

This period, where the initiates are once again interacting with society, is still characterized by numerous taboos, such as sex on the nights preceding the contest, and on diet, and even implicitly on their personal appearance. There are secret meetings daily for two hours, during which time there is continued physical punishment. On the evenings and mornings before each public ceremony, the novices are secluded. In addition, they are also exempt from many of the requirements of their peers. Within their living groups (most noticeably, frats) they are excused from duties, both physical and mental. In interaction with their peers, they are given great deference and respect. Even in interaction with their superiors such as administrators of the educational institution and their instructors of formal education, they are excused from duties which others must execute, such as tests, papers, etc. On an even higher plane, the novices are exempt from induction (armed service) while they maintain their ability to participate (through mediation of the elders).

There are two variants of the weekly schedule; one is adapted for ceremonies which will occur on the sacred field of another institution, and the other is adapted for events which will occur on the home field. The major difference in the schedules is that the rally is usually moved up to Thursday, and the novices fly to the other field and back again. The generalized schedule is reproduced here:

Mon: 3:00 Meeting of all novices
          3:30 On field in secret session; wear "sweats"
          5:30 Off field
          6:00 Eat dinner together
Tues: 3:00   Meeting
          3:30 On field, with more elaborate dress than Mon., called "full dress"
          5:30 Watch films
Wed: Same as Tues.
Thurs: 3:00 Meeting
          3:30 On field, work on entire ceremony together
          5:30 Off field
          6:00 Eat together
Fri: 3:00 Meeting
          3:30 Brief practice
          4:00 Off field—Nearing the culmination of the weekly routine, the peers of the initiates express their appreciation and devotion, loyalty and admiration, to the novices. The affiliates organize a crowd around the players as they exit from the secret practice and pass through their admirers, always showing extreme modesty, into another sacrosanct area called the "Locker Room." At this time, the elders take little part in the ceremony; they call upon the weekly leader ("team captain") of the novices, who speaks to the crowd. The crowd responds with traditional chants of encouragement to the novices, urging them to honorable victory in the forthcoming contest.

6:00   Eat dinner together

7:00   Seclusion (in the "Sheraton Wilshire Hotel")

7:30   Entertainment (motion picture) viewed by the novices as a group, and apart from the rest of society. The lodging and entertainment are of the finest quality available.

10:30   Elders "bed check" to make sure the novices are in bed

Sat: 8:00   Orange juice served in bed

9:00   Last meal served before the contest: steak and eggs

11:00   Meeting of the entire group; the *chief elder* (in a rare appearance) talks to the team

12:00   Novices go to the sacred field, where they are dressed in colorful costumes and protective padding of debatable protectiveness. At this time the "trainer" lovingly massages, tapes, and wraps the bodies of the participants. The costumes are symbolic in that the whole team is identified by a particular color of the costumes, but each individual is given specific recognition by his identifying number.

1:00   The novices warm up, doing various gymnastics

1:30   The novices emerge as if by magic from the bowels of the stadium, and are greeted by the cheers of the crowd; there is much that is symbolic in the actual maneuvers, the setup of the players on the bench, the hierarchy of coaches, the acceptance of authority. by the novices, the actions of the affiliates (especially the virgins and their male counterparts), and the reaction of the crowd, but space does not permit its analysis here.

4:00   End of contest—the novices are free.

Sun: 6:00   Novices assemble to watch "films," a magical method which can recreate the events of the last contest, and put the individuals' actions up for scrutiny and ridicule by the elders.

Ritual Elaboration: The novice group being victorious in all its confrontations, (USC was National Collegiate Champions in this year of 1967) was invited to perform publicly in opposition to another champion group. Since this is a *very* desirable goal (i.e., to play in a "Bowl" game), the novices were further honored and lauded, and there was further ritual elaboration of their initiation.

The daily schedule is the same as the one during "Double Days," and it continues for two weeks previous to the celebrate game. The novices are again secluded in an all-male residence, they eat their meals together, and are subjected to two brutal practices daily. During the first week, they are free to leave the buildings in the evenings (until 10:00 P.M.); during the second week, they must remain with the elders at all times.

The second week marks the highest degree of seclusion in the entire ceremonial cycle: the novices change their residence from the first week (dorms) and are secluded in the luxury accommodations formerly reserved for the night before the event. They are to speak only to their elders or another novice, they may not receive messages, or send them, or speak to anyone in the outside society.

The entertainment which is provided the novices is symbolically important. Two events are of special interest, although others occurred; there is no attempt to analyze them here. On the first Tuesday there is held a gigantic feast, specifically for the novices, and hosted free by a local merchant (Lawry's Prime Rib). The object of the feast is to consume as much beef as possible; for there is a myth accompanying the feast which states the prophecy that the group of novices which consumes the greatest quantity of beef will triumph in the contest. The feast is termed the "Beef Bowl," and the two groups of novices compete on different nights. (USC consumed 349 lbs.: Indiana consumed 280 lbs.)

An evening festival (closed party) was hosted for the novices, with various performers entertaining them. The highlight of the evening was the presentation of gifts to the novices, from representative groups in the outside society. Each novice received a silver platter (Chrysler Corp.), a transistor radio (RCA), a watch (Jurgenson), a pair of binoculars.

Phase III: Latency

After the final public ceremony, the novices are released from their authoritarian submission, and re-enter the social network, ostensibly free from the restrictions once imposed. However, they are in effective communication with the elders at all times, and constantly under their surveillance. The coaches are omniscient: they know the families, the girls the players date, the brawls, and the problems of all the players.

The novices now enter a latency period, with no formal structure intervening between the novices and their directors; the taboos, though implicit, are no longer agents of direct punishment. There is still much contact between the novices and directors, but its nature has changed—the novices are now entrusted to help with jobs which the coaches would ordinarily do themselves (recruiting); and there are scheduled conferences between the novice and his coach every two weeks.

Phase IV: "Spring Ball"

This is the final phase of the yearly cycle, and involves an emphasis on the role played by the *individual* novice and his skills, in contrast to the unity emphasis during Double Days. There are few restrictions placed on him in the form of seclusion or taboos. The main object is the competition between individuals, to beat out the other person who is competing for the same position.

The two-week phase is culminated on May 5 by a public ceremony, which is intra-novice; the top-ranked novices are pitted against the second-ranked. There is little ritual elaboration associated with this ceremony. After this event the novices are freed of all formal restrictions, taboos, etc.; they are on their own to use their best judgment in all situations. The summer may be a period of trial of the effectiveness of the indoctrination and internalization of the precepts passed on by the elders.

INTERPRETATION AND CONCLUSIONS

Having presented the data on the formal mechanics of the ceremony, I would like to show that football, as expressed by USC, may be considered an initiation ceremony, according to the criteria of Van Gennep, Whiting et al., and Young. Ultimately, all these analyses involve a re-identification with the adult role, so it is necessary first to show this transition.

The period of adolescence in the U.S. has long been known as a turbulent transition period. The teen-age period reaches a culmination toward the end, from ages seventeen to twenty, and a symbolic rite is necessary to focus attention of the adult dogma to be assimilated . . . this is the role of football.

Ralph Linton makes an important observation when he states that the puberty ceremony in the U.S. depends to a great extent on the social class of the individual. For the lower levels, the parents ask children to extend down the bottom level of adulthood and become wage-earners early. Conversely, professional groups and people who send their children to college treat adolescence as a continuum of childhood, with economic dependence on parents perpetuating the submissive role of childhood. "For males in the higher social levels, a similar transition comes when the individual leaves the sheltered environment of college and embarks in the cut-throat competition of modern business" Linton (1942:602).

Or, as Talcott Parsons notes, values of the young male must change rather abruptly from the youth culture with its emphasis on fun to a "prosaic business executive or lawyer" (Parsons 1942:8). The young man is expected to assume the mundane responsibilities of adult status, and football prepares him for this.

In terms of Van Gennep's scheme, the three phases which occur in rites of passage are evident. During Double Days the novice is separated from his previous environment, in relation to which he is "lost from the world," according to Coach Marv Goux. The comments of the novices also emphasize the death state: "It kills you," "You have to eat, sleep, think football," i.e., the novice is dead to the rest of society (Oliver, Mc-Connell). There is grueling physical and mental punishment. The object of this period is the separation (mentally and physically) of the initiates from society, and to create among the novices a sense of working as a *unit* for a desired goal. The behavior stressed during Double Days is opposed to the normal individually-oriented goal behavior, and hence symbolizes the death of the novice as an isolated individual, and entrance into a cooperative unit (*viz.* society).

The rites of transition are saliently marked by the increased interaction of the novice in the society. No longer is he secluded, except for about three hours daily, and for the night before the public ceremony. The novices still eat together one meal daily, and the restrictions are more implicit than forced on them; the elders determine the right to dismiss any boy who by their judgment has not adhered to the taboos and whose behavior shows it. The transition period, then, swings from short periods of seclusion and ceremonial action to semi-normal interaction within the society.

Rites of reintegration are accomplished during the third phase of the yearly cycle—Spring Ball. The reintegration does not utilize such drastic behavior as the novices pretending not to know how to walk, eat, etc. The rites are composed of the same elements of which the other phases are composed, but the emphasis is on the *individual,* and lends a contrasting atmosphere to that of Double Days of The Season. Spring Ball prepares the novice for action once again in the society, by concentrating on the skills and performance of the individual player; competition within the group is high—this is a relearning process to prepare for reintegration within a competitive society.

Now let us turn to the dimensions of initiation as outlined by Whiting. Initiation is characterized by *one* or more of the following features according to Whiting's 1958 article: (1) painful hazing by adult males; (2) genital operations; (3) seclusion from women; (4) tests of endurance and manliness (Whiting, Kluckhohn, and Anthony 1958:360). Football has all but the second element, and thus qualifies as an initiation ceremony.

Turning to Young's discussion of initiation ceremonies, we find that his solidarity hypothesis defines initiation ceremonies as dramatic forms of sex role recognition. On his scale of degree of dramatization of male initiation, football rates as one of the most dramatic of all possible rites. In addition, there are three criteria of the ceremonies: (1) it must be periodic in the same general form and supervised by adults. (2) it must apply to all adolescents of one sex only, and (3) of a series of initiation events only the most elaborate are to be considered. Football meets the demands of all three criteria, although the second deserves justification: the performance of football is a symbolic act of initiation for the entire male adolescent group. The college residence of each particular novice is conceived as his local tribal affiliation, although a pan-tribal identity with the age-grades of all adolescents exists above the provincial loyalty. The participation in the actual ceremony where the initiatory principles are displayed publically is limited to the few who are most capable and who represent most obviously the specifications of adult status. Although precipitation is limited to the fittest, the *principles* which are taught the novices apply to *all* adolescents of the tribe. And since the novices are objects of admiration and respect, the values which they represent are emulated by their male peers. The general precepts apply to all males; football is a symbolic rite of transformation for the total adolescent group.

The previous analyses by Whiting, Van Gennep, and Young of the initiation event by a unidimensional model, i.e., in terms of the import on one conceptual level, bypasses much of the important ramifications of the ceremony. To understand the ceremony adequately it is necessary to view it through the cross-cutting levels of the individual, the peer age-grade, and the society. There is a different significance in the ritual for each subgroup of society, and it is inaccurate to interpret initiation as having an immutable or constant meaning for all members of the society. This tripartite view is more profitable to elucidate initiation, for it allows for the interplay of more variables in the explanation of it. The relation of the *individual* to the ceremony: The elders were much more adept and explicit in their answers to this question, having formulated the aims and hopes previously; the novices were more unsure about what it meant to participate in the event, and one novice refused to tell me, saying, "Do you think I'd tell *you*?" (McConnell). It emerged later that this was not a sexual taboo against telling me, but that the novice felt extremely moved by the ceremony and did not feel at ease in expressing his feelings.

There is, obviously, a physical aspect to the ceremony, and bodily fitness must be relevant to the novices. However, this element was rarely stressed when asked to relate their conceptions of the importance of football to their own lives. Instead, the importance of the ceremony to the novice is due to the development of personal qualities, all of which are deemed virtuous in adult society. The compiled list herein covers the most salient reasons why it is felt that the initiation cycle is significant in the lives of the novices.

1. Merlin Olsen, a celebrated post-novice, feels football allows men to concentrate on *work*, and develops a dedication which is carried on through one's life; he stresses that work is the greatest aid to creating *men*.

2. Closely related to this is the view that football forces an individual to become somewhat self-sacrificing for the good of a cooperative effort; it shows how to "sacrifice for the good of the whole organization and not just play for your own sake," as Coach Fertig puts it.

3. Within the general pattern of conformity, football teaches individuality (Kreuger). A player must conform to the training rules, and behavioral standards, but he is encouraged to express himself in his playing formation. The second and third points together constitute a unitary quality: there is a contribution to the group effort wholeheartedly, and yet allowance for the development of individuality *within the norms*.

4. The football ceremonies develop the ability to think quickly and clearly under pressure; the novice must mobilize all his knowledge and physical resources in split-second decisions (Fertig).

5. Leadership is developed, e.g., each weekly team captain represents the group in all public appearances.

6. The equality of individuals is taught, for the novices are judged on ability and performance.[6]

7. Football allows individuals to focus their socially unacceptable drives into something worthwhile (Krueger).

8. The experience of traveling with the group, exposure to public performance, being on display, develops in the novices a sense of social competence. "They are able to meet people in any circle and can handle themselves socially" (Fertig).

9. Football heightens the competitive desire "to win."

10. Of course there are the obvious attributes which are implicitly inculcated and so explicitly demonstrated every Saturday afternoon: the sexual identification provided through the demonstration of manliness, aggressiveness, and prowess on the field. The traditional image of the "All-American male," and the "clean-cut football hero," is emphasized and re-emphasized as a model.

Ideally, then, fotball has the facility to turn out perfect ideal-types, according to the specifications of the older generation. The elders feel that an individual will become a different person through playing the game; the transformation will create adult members of a social organization. Phil Krueger cites the great number of football players who have achieved successful transformation and become leading businessmen. He emphasizes the point that football as a means to an end is all right; but if it represents the high point in a player's life, then he's in trouble. In effect, football should represent a transition phase through which one develops the qualities necessary for successful adult orientation. "You put yourself in a dangerous, yet controlled situation; and you become a better man for having faced the danger" (Krueger).

Relation of the *peer age-group* to the ceremony: Being a symbolic ceremony, the relationships between the novices and their peers is a unique one, a dimension not yet explored in initiation ceremonies. Yet the relation is obvious, and is consonant with the expectations: the behavior and values of the novices serve as a model for males to emulate; they are desirable sexual objects for females, and this fact reinforces the behavior of the age-group in adopting the values.

Interestingly, part of the male image (which the peers also identify with) is the cultivating of the ability "to get away with" as much as possible without being caught. It is considered manly to flaunt authority, but only *up to a point;* and the novices know exactly where that threshold is which will invoke supernatural punishment—expulsion from ceremonial participation.

The relation of the society to the ceremony: One aspect is particularly outstanding when the ceremony is analyzed on this plane—the economic benefits circulated by the occurrence of the event. The ceremonies act as an attraction for financial backing of the university, as well as supporting activities from the profits gained from admission, concessions, etc. The money made in net profit alone from the football season at USC supports all the other athletic programs in the university (Krueger). The economic ramifications of the football season is amazingly intricate, affecting the welfare of the players (through the sale of their tickets), producers of sports equipment, contractors, and even the city council of Pasadena.

People like to identify with a group which shows successful application of the discipline and qualities admired by them; the alumni will support the institution if it can be proud of its accomplishments, and they judge the quality of its accomplishments through the performance of its football team. The primary importance of the ceremony differs for each group—for the individual, it is foremost a program of personal development; for the peer age-grade, it is a model to emulate; for the society, the economic factor looms most important.

The foremost task faced by each society is to perpetuate its ethnocentricity—its values and traditions. It must fashion a sense of *identity* for each adult which will incorporate those elements that must be passed to future generations.

In a culture as heterogeneous as America, this task is not easily accomplished. The diversity of role choice open to the adolescent necessitates a centripetal force, to focus on a coherent and perceivable bundle of adult values with which to identify. Initiation, in the football ceremony, is a symbolic process whereby a confluence of the desired roles of adult life is achieved; and it is expedient to unify the diverse models of identification in order that transformation occur *effectively*.

NOTES

1. The sexes are also segregated in most preliterate societies' initiation ceremonies into adulthood.
2. Since values are usually (historically and in some contemporary societies) passed on from elders to younger generations with little or no questioning allowed, it will be interesting to see what comes out of the current situation where we are questioning the very validity of accepting without questioning the basic assumptions of our social systems that our elders hand down to us.
3. Although the influence of Durkheim's previous work is evident in Van Gennep's theory (in the primacy of the social nature of phenomena, and the division of the world into sacred and profane spheres), Durkheim in his works subsequent to Van Gennep's perceived initiation ceremonies as essentially religious events. In his *Elementary Forms of Religious Life* he states that initiation ceremonies are, foremost, instruments which emphasize the "essential duality of the two kingdoms sacred and profane" (Durkheim 1913:39). It implies a "veritable metamorphosis" for Durkheim, who sees the ceremony as indicative of a transformation of the whole being. The individual leaves the purely profane world and enters the sacred world.
   See also James Bossard and Eleanor Boll (1948), who analyzed the debutantes' presentation to society as a contemporary rite of passage using Van Gennep's criteria.
4. Two conditions which might lead to this situation where there is maximum conflict in sexual identity—where a boy has initial exclusive sleeping arrangements with his mother, but where the domestic unit is patrilocal and controlled by men.
5. The degrees of male solidarity are indicated on the following scale from low to high: (1) informal solidarity that does not attain the behavioral expression; (2) exclusive male activity for adult males, protected by physical or normative perception barriers; (3) ritualization of male activity, at least in part; (4) definite ranking of men within the activity; (5) training for war a part of the activity (Young 1965:67).

6. Perhaps football teaches as well the racial hypocrisy which often permeates the white world—although the black players are treated with all the respect due a white player, and are accepted as equals among the white players, the elders segregate along racial lines during the periods of seclusion: rarely does a white player room with a black player.

References

Bossard, James H. S. and Eleanor D. Boll. 1948. Rite of passage—a contemporary study. *Social Forces* 26:247-255.

Burton, Roger V. and John M. Whiting. 1960. The absent father and cross-sex identity. *Merrill-Palmer Quarterly* 7:85-95.

Durkheim, Emile. 1913. *Les formes elementaires de le vie religieuse.* Paris, Alcan. Trans. by Joseph Swain. *Elementary forms of religious life.* Glencoe, Ill.: The Free Press, 1947.

Fertig, Craig. 1968. Interview February 9, at USC; quarterback coach.

Goux, Marv. 1968. Interview Feb. 23, at USC; defensive linemen coach.

Krueger, Phil. 1968. Interview Feb. 9, at USC; coach of defensive ends and linebackers.

Linton, Ralph. 1942. Age and sex categories. *American Sociological Review* 7:589-603.

Lynd, Robert S. and Helen Merrell Lynd. 1929. *Middletown.* New York: Harcourt, Brace, and Co.

McConnell, Steve. 1968. Interview February 10, at USC; middle guard.

Nadel, S. F. 1951. Foundations of social anthropology. Quoted from Honigmann, John J., *Theory of Ritual*, Chapel Hill, U. of N. Carolina.

Oliver, Ralph. 1968. Interview Feb. 10, at USC; middle guard.

Olsen, Merlin. 1968. Speech delivered to Sigma Chi fraternity at USC, Feb. 7.

Van Gennep, Arnold. 1909. *Rites de passage.* Paris. Emile Nourry. Trans. by Monika B. Vizedom and Gabrielle L. Chaffee. *The Rites of Passage.* Routledge & Kegan Paul, 1960.

Whiting, John M. and Richard Kluckhohn and Albert Anthony. 1958. "The function of male initiation ceremonies at puberty," In *Readings in social psychology.* Eleanor E. Maccoby, Theodore M. Newcomb, and Eugene Hartley, eds. New York: Holt, Rinehart and Winston.

Whiting, John M. 1964. "Effects of climate on certain cultural practices," *In Explorations in cultural anthropology.* Ward H. Goodnough, ed. New York: McGraw-Hill.

Young, Frank W. 1962. "The function of male initiation ceremonies: a cross-cultural test of an alternative hypothesis." *The American Journal of Sociology* 67:379-91.

————. 1965. *Initiation ceremonies.* New York: Bobbs-Merrill Co., Inc.

Sports Spectacular:
The Social Ritual of Power

Alyce Taylor Cheska

> Many Americans worship at the church of sports. Services are held
> for each personal belief, whether it be football, racing, goft, or diving.
> One is thrilled by the splendor of the occasion and the beauty of the
> surroundings. On the walls hang the trappings and accounts praising
> past heroes. The offering freely asked is cheerfully given. The rendi-
> tions of the colorfully clothed musicians stir one to action. Dramatic-
> ally delivered is the powerful message of overcoming the adversary.
> Here each is brought to his own style of fulfillment. As one turns to
> leave, one muses, "It is good to have been here, for I have felt the
> power." (Cheska, 1972)

Socialized man has long used the collective gathering to express and
preserve sociocultural concepts. One such concept is *power* which encompasses one's capacity to accomplish something and thereby obtain
control. As individuals and groups, people have struggled for control and
their success is measured in status, goods, services, resources, and value.
This cultural code of power is expressed and communicated through
ritual action (Munn, 1973, p. 581). The ritual provides through iconic
symbols (acts, words, or things) models of the power process in life situations. The ritual message condenses the various power experiences and
their meanings within a particular society into an objective vehicle which
is understood and shared by individuals on a personal, subjective, valuable level.

Any form of secular activity, whether practical or recreational, can
be stylized into dramatic performance and made the focus of a ritual sequence (Leach, 1961). The concept of power is often objectified in the
sports spectacular, an elaborately colorful ritual ceremony which is found
throughout the modern world. A few examples of such events are the

New Year's Day football Rose Bowl and the Basketball tournament "March Madness" in the United States; the South American national soccer matches; the southeastern Asian colorful sepak takraw[1] contests; the eastern European elaborate sports Spartakiads;[2] and the crowing international grandeur of the modern Olympics.

In the north central region of the United States there are ten large universities which compete against each other in athletic contests. Several years ago this author attended a homecoming football game between two of these schools. On that Saturday afternoon, the stadium was packed with 66,000 brightly bedecked fans. They eagerly watched and cheered 22 player "priests" alternately carry, kick, and pass an eliptical leather ball toward opposing end lines of the oblong playing field. Each eleven-man team attempted to control the ball, advance it the length of the field, and score more goals than its opponents within a prescribed time limit. The crowds in the bleachers shouted and sang encouragement to their respective teams. The 600-member card section flashed in succession a multi-colored design of an Indian chief, its school's name, and words "Go get 'em," "Win." During time-outs acrobatic cheerleaders led the rooters in praiseful chants of the young football players. The combined power of 66,000 shouting voices clapped like thunder. At half-time, the mid-point of the contest, the players left the arena, but quickly the 300-foot long field was blanketed with a smartly uniformed bank of 150 expert muscians who, while harmoniously playing a rousing march, stepped rapidly into a large alphabetic pictogram "I." The music stopped. From the far end of the stadium crept the leathered form of a Plains Indian who bent and swayed to the now muted tones of the band. As the dancer increased the tempo of his high rhythmic stomp, the music built to a mightly crescendo. At this moment the Indian leapt high into the air, landing abruptly in a wide, strong stance with arms crossed, holding his feather head-dressed head proudly. Chief Illiniwek, symbol of great aboriginal strength, received the explosive applause of the fans. He slowly raised his arms high, entreating the Great Spirit's blessing, while the stadium rang with the strains of Alma Mater. In my mind's eye, the impact of that afternoon's sports spectacular still remains today.

Contemplation of the phenomenon of the modern sports spectacular leads to many questions. Why are these events found throughout the world? Can the sports spectacular be regarded as ritual? What underlying message is the symbolism of the event carrying? Has the play form of sports spectacular become for modern man a communitas substitute for sacred ritual?

SPORTS SPECTACULAR AS MESSAGE OF POWER

Geertz (1969) has wisely observed, "definitions establish nothing, [but] they do provide a useful orientation, or reorientation, of thought, . . . such can be an affective way of developing and controlling a novel line of inquiry" (p. 4). In this paper operational definitions of certain key words can increase understanding.

One pivotal word is *sport,* and in this context sport is defined as an institutionalized game (Loy, 1969, p. 56). Basic elements of a game as suggested by Sutton-Smith (1973, p. 5) are rules, opposition of forces and uncertain outcomes. A game can be considered a competitive activity involving skill, chance or endurance on the part of two or more persons who play according to a set of rules, usually for their own amusement or for that of spectators.[3] Synonyms for game include contest, competition, sport. Persons who actively engage in sports are often called athletes. The Greek origin of the word athlete indicates a person who contends for a prize in the public games; hence, this meaning has been ununderstood since then.

The Greeks used the word "agon" to denote a struggle or contest in which prizes were awarded in a number of events (i.e., athletics, dramatics, music, and poetry). Current words of protagonist and antagonist, derivatives of agon, identify the contenders, a classification to which athletes belong. Rooted in ritual, agonistic activities or contests of every description played a dominant part in the culture and daily life of every Greek; Huizinga (1955, p. 30) contends that the competitive impulse pervaded the whole Greek life.

The athletes, contending in a competitive act, endeavor to gain that for which another is also striving. The very structure of sport is a frame or vehicle for modeling the striving for power or control in its broad sense, for the outcome of a contest, as often in life, assures an uneven distribution of power. Basically because one party loses and another gains such prizes as status, goods, resources, or value, this type of contest sometimes referred to as a zero-sum game (Von Neumann & Morgenstern, 1944, p. 641).

Within the context of this discussion, *power* is interpreted to mean control of self and situation.[4] The situation encompasses that which surrounds the individual, as nature and/or other people. The quest for control as an operational habit lends a chronic character to the flow of a person's activity and the quality of one's experience (Geertz, 1966, p. 9). The social code of power as variably and individually expressed in many lives is condensed with symbolic vehicle forms, thus focusing subjective meanings into more objective, simpler communicative messages. One of these vehicle forms, the sports event, enacts the concept of power as maximization, achievement, control. Various degrees of control are expressed. The control may be *direct* as dominance by physical qualities, manipulation, or confinement of others by players in the athletic arena. The modern Olympics motto, "swifter, higher, stronger" (Citius, Altius, Fortius) conceived by Father Didon in 1895, glorifies this kind of control. Control may be *indirect* as making a goal, winning a contest, or showing improvement over past individual or group accomplishments. Each of these intermediate outcomes or steps as part of the sequence of power may serve as separate or integrating symbols. Control may be *associated* as identification and involvement of spectators with participating athletes in the enactment of the power process directly or indirectly. Within the sports event as a cultural vehicle, the associative and accumulative interaction and integration of symbols, whether person, process, act, or thing carry the message of ritualized power. It is to be noted that the sports spectacular can exist as a cultural entity; however, when the elements of ritual are fulfilled a meta-social or projective message system is brought into circulation.

Another aspect of power is observed in the concept of opposition with its dichotomous conflict of forces. This opposition is associated with primordial universal dualism: good/evil; order/chaos; man/woman; have/have not. This distinct separation of these categories is accentuated in the sports enactment. The moral interpretation of good/evil is played out in the ritual of "my" team as representing good and the opposing or "other" team as bad or evil. The concept of order/chaos is exemplified in verbal as well as non-discoursive actions of spectators of a contest. Cheerleaders and rooters alike in the United States shout "stomp 'em," "knock 'em cold," "kill 'em." The assumption is that "my" team will be able, through organized action, to disperse, rout, destroy the "other" team. The man/woman dualism is implied in the man's appropriate realm (Schafer, 1975) of contact sports as football, soccer, wrestling, while the women's realm consists of the "pretty" non-contact sports, as gymnastics, skiing, swimming, ice skating (Metheny, 1972, pp. 277-290). The female role is frequently exemplified in cheerleader (Herkimer, 1967). The have/have not dichotomy is seen in the reward system of sports with material (extrinsic) and non-material (intrinsic) pay-offs for the winners, while the losers must be satisfied with "de-feat" which literally means "away from achievement."

The word *"spectacular"* or "spectacle" is defined as anything presented to the sight or view, especially something of a large-scale, impressive kind, as a public show or display.[5] Spectacular adds the dimension of being dramatically daring or thrilling. Seemingly the emotional conductibility of the mass may be intensified by the bodily contagion in the spectator crowd. Symbols of almost every conflict can be presented to consciousness, accompanied by all the allurements of light, color, rhythm, or sound (Howard, 1912). The sports spectacle has historically carried the stain of vainglory display concept. Athletes as performers or entertainers exemplify the debasing, predetermined, immoral, brutalizing spectacle rather than the unpredictable, dignified, moral contest (Stone, 1958). This author disagrees with Stone's generalization. His examples of the ancient Roman gladiatorial bouts and the modern professional wrestling matches are extreme examples of exploitation for individual profit. The sports spectacular to which this paper refers is an elaborate recurrent community event in which human and material resources are directed in a celebration of art, song, drama, music, and movement. The festive atmosphere is shared by observers in attendance or by mass media. Aspects of communitas are much more apparent in this concept of sports spectacular than are aspects of alienation as claimed by Stone. In considering the derivatives of spectacle, the word spectator identifies a person who is present at and views a spectacle, display, exhibition, or the like. When a spectator is observing a sports event, the term often used is "fan" (an enthusiastic devotee or follower). A fan is described as one who goes into a frenzy about a particular sport or interest. During the Roman times priests sometimes became so inspired because of the goddess who worshipped in the fane or temple, that they tore their robes and slashed their bodies in frenzied zeal. This was referred to as "fanaticus." The literal meaning is "inspired by the fane" or "fanatic"; the shortening of the term resulted in "fan" (Bucher, 1972, p. 293). This author argues that the cyclical sport event conducted as a large scale impressive public show or display can be called a *sport spectacular* and a *social ritual of power.*

A *ritual* is defined as an established or prescribed procedure for a religious or other rite (Winick, 1966). Ritual is considered the observance of set forms in public worship or a code of ceremonies in general. A rite encompasses a prescribed formal or customary ceremonial act, while a *ceremony* applies to more or less dignified acts on religious or public occasions.[6] Rite is synonymous with ceremony; ritual is the form or procedure of that rite, and the sports spectacular is considered the event or context in which the act and procedure take place.

ELEMENTS OF RITUAL IN THE SPORTS SPECTACULAR

The actual ritual or form of a rite serves as an important factor in preserving and transmitting the emotional experience of non-verbal social values (Klapp, 1956, p. v.) that we call expressive or non-rational. The use of actions rather than logic as methods of persuasion may be described as expressive behavior. In other words, ritual carries a symbolic message which communicates a commonly interpretive meaning to those involved. Through the utilization of symbols of unification of response is possible, but only if these symbols are perceived similarly as important and elicit common mental images and, in turn, corresponding overt actions. To "set the stage" for common response and subsequent action of persons involved, there are certain conditions necessary.

The sports spectacular as a vehicle of symbol contains the basic elements of ritual. According to Klapp (1956, p. 13) the elements of ritual are: 1) repetition, 2) regularity, 3) emotionality, 4) drama, 5) symbolism.

Repetition: A ritual is appropriate at specified times and is repeated then, and only then. Ritual can give a pattern to time, dividing it into recurring cycles, and hence providing a calendrical framework for society. The period of ritual is determined partly by memory, because a thing must be repeated before it is forgotten. Ritual functions as an agency of society's sentimental memory (Klapp, 1956, p. 11). In primitive agricultural peoples the planting and harvesting ceremonies mark important economic pursuits and provide community gathering points. Because of technological cultures' acute consciousness of the passage of time, a decrease in the need for time-marking celebrations has been claimed. This may be exactly why ritual events are desirable; for the monotonous minutia of time-awareness actually blurs its passing and fails to provide societal punctuation marks.

Repeated rituals in our society include national celebrations as New Year's, Independence Day, Thanksgiving (Spicer, 1969); personal rites of passage (Van Gennep, 1960; Turner, 1969) as birth, marriage, death; and holy days as Christmas, Easter, Sunday (Lee, 1964).

Sports spectaculars often mark calendrical division of the year. In the United States, football bowls come during the latter part of December and first part of January (near the winter solstice); basketball championship tournaments take place in March (near the spring equinox); the baseball World Series is held in early October (near the fall equinox). Two and four year cycles are found in the biennial World University Games and the quadrennial ancient and modern Olympics.

Regularity: One procedure in ritual is usually considered the correct, acceptable or best. Culturally this consensual standardization insures that group norms and sanctions are accepted as inherent in the ritual pattern. Frequently a particular ritual's authenticity and potency are judged on exact replication of past rituals. One needs only to examine the duplication of the modern Olympic rites with the ancient Greek Olympics to recognize this belief. Pierre de Coubertin, founder of the modern Olympics, fashioned its ceremony after the Greek festival. It appears that ritual itself begets its own authenticity.

In various sports spectaculars a specific format or order that has been established previously persists over time and changes are "unthinkable." Within the contest, for example, the procedure is set; the actual regulations or rules of play, once stylized, are repetitive and adhered to steadfastly. The sports rule book, with official "ritual" for handling any contingencies which might occur, is considered the "bible." Interpretation is prescribed, not left to whim. If the "ritual" is violated, the offender loses advantage or power by enforcement of penalties; therefore, compliance is essential. The act of cheating is the breaking of the rules or format by not following the ritual, and, therefore, not tolerated. The organized rules help determine who is the legitimate winner of the contest; winning by any other method is not acceptable to participants or spectators of the event. A sport event probably represents the most remarkable display of fair play known today. The reason for this insistence on morality may be that sports are idealized make-believe versions of the real world. This is overwhelmingly true, even though the strategy of contestants includes pushing against the "legal" edge of regulation.

Within the rite or ceremony, ritual or rules persist over time; when change seems necessary, it is approached with resistance. In the United States the changing of a women's basketball rule from the limited dribble to the continuous dribble was met with major opposition for several years. The rule was finally changed only when the continuous dribble was proven physiologically harmless to the female. Rule modification of football and basketball to better accommodate television time modules may in part exemplify an even more prescribed regularity.

The chronological patterning of a sports spectacular shows a set form. Generally the audience or spectators fill the arena before the appearance of the opposing participants; the warm-up of both the participants and spectators follows. Participants warm-up physically by repeating anticipated actions of the event while the spectators eat, drink, chat, cheer, sing, and chant. The sport arena's seating arrangement often divides the opposing spectator groups so they face each other. Each group sits in bleachers behind its team. Persons who mix with opposing fans, and make this fact known, are often jeered and sneered, or even bodily ejected. The concept of stranger in the group is worth further investigation, but space prohibits. The flag salute and singing of the Star-Spangled Banner has become part of the pre-contest ritual in the United States. This, followed by the officials—the regulators of the event—moving to a prominent place in the arena, signifies commencement of the contest. The game is succinctly divided into equal time parts during which the participants contend for the prize. This author views the drama as a symbolic message of power.

Emotionality: In ritual is the involvement of emotions or feelings regarding a situation, thing, idea or person. Emotionality is not used as a substitute for practical or rational control, but as another level of behavior in which personalized feeling is elicited by involvement. Large scale sporting events create a dramatic atmosphere where conflicting powers meet head-on in a very emotional setting (Kilmer, 1976, pp. 34-35). In sports spectaculars feelings run "high"; anticipation and immediate involvement represent a commitment to the striving toward control or the symbolization of power. Huizinga (1955) describes the element of tension as meaning "uncertainty, chanciness, a striving to decide the issue and so end it. The player wants something to 'go', to 'come off'; he wants to 'succeed' by his own exertions" (pp. 10-11). Uncertainty needs to be resolved. A resolution—who is in power or control—is acted out in the game situation.

Another aspect of emotionality, the expression of individual energy, unites with others toward a common focus. The ritual response of energy arousal and canalizing toward power is part and parcel of the emotional excitement of the event; this can be termed communal participation or group unity transcending individual existence. Contributing to this communal effect are the symbolic cues found throughout the arena. During the game at prescribed moments of non-play, forms of entertainment are provided, i.e., music, marching, acrobatics. The presence of pom pom girls and cheerleaders is unique in United States' football and basketball sport competition. In performing their role they direct the audience's aggregate emotional power. The transfer of this collective explosion of energy from spectators to participants is an unfathomed phenomenon. Individuals and groups report that such transfer seems to take place either physically or psychically, but logical explanations are lacking. To date scientists do not know if the nebulous concept of fan power might have a physiological or chemical base. Could the emission of separate physiological or chemical force fields of each fan cumulatively result in transmission of collective energies? A starting point might be the determination of the cohesive qualities in differing group types. Mu-kerjee (1959, pp. 9-10) classifies groups as: crowd, interest-group, community, and commonality.

The dualistic contention for the prize is the paramount symbol of the sports event. The fundamental social phenomenon, binary opposition, as symbolized in the context of the sports contest, can be understood as a cultural code with condensed meaning in particular societies. The ritual game exemplifies clearly the state of opposition and the process of striving between groups (Munn, 1973, p. 581). Contributing symbols include the spatial organization of the arena into opposing areas, interstices, boundaries and barriers; the temporal sequence of playing time, time-out, and intermission; visual and auditory cues of color, shape, direction, focus, sound, sequence, and climax. Visual perception is heightened by the display of opposing teams' color schemes throughout the arena, i.e, contestants' uniforms, cheerleaders, and band costumes, banners. The officials' uniforms set them aside as special from all others. The auditory display is conducted by the bank, singers, cheerleaders, and the fans.

The excessive consumption of food and alcohol by spectators at sporting events (and other festival celebrations) can be construed as showing consummation power. The dress and gyrations of pom pom girls and cheerleaders at football games suggest sexual symbolism (Ferril, 1974, p. 71), as do the actions of the players (Arens, 1975). The close relationship of fertility and power in the sports event needs further investigation. Caillois' theory of festival (1959, pp. 97-127) which proposes that fertility is born of excess may provide a reference point for further study.

Drama: Ritual is dramatic because it is performed for an audience. The elements of drama—participants, ritual, plot, production, symbolism, social message—are all brilliantly choreographed in the sports spectacular. A more detailed analysis can be found in the work of Toohey (1974).

The primary actors involved in the sports spectacular are the players and the spectators. Each realizes that role-taking in ritual performance is not reality; a quality of pretense, mimicry, identification with other than self pervades. This is especially true of sports spectators who vicariously become absorbed with the athletes as performers of feats beyond ordinary man. When these "super-men" through role errors show mundane or real human qualities, make mistakes, or give mediocre performances, the dramatic aura is shattered. The observers are jerked back to reality and the imperfection is felt sharply. The play is marred. The spectator may utilize the sports spectacular to act out the concept of control, mentally fleshing out dreams of achievement as exemplifed in the sports arena. However, the significance of this role-playing is much wider; it is the actual trying on of success—or failure—in relation to power as a base of an individual's interpersonal operation methodology. This is an example of behavior also found in other roles the individual assumes in life. The drama of power or control between two opposing forces played out in the magic circle of the stadium, arena, field or court carries with it the personally significant symbolic message.

Symbolism: A social idea which can be shared by people can be communicated by ritual. The ritual is symbolic and mnemonic. In the sports spectacular the meaning or symbol is the message of power, a cultural code in many cultures of the world. It is here where the myriad of unique personal experiences of power become reorganized, simplified, condensed, and narrowed into creative images shared by many. The meanings of power or control are iconically symbolized, and in turn communicated through these vehicles. The nodes of meaning are compressed into a particular image and then transferred back to the individual as conscious, objective meanings. The message or cultural code is communicated through ritual and iconic metaphor; in this instance the carrying vehicle is the sports spectacular.

The sports event is a simulated striving for power. The message of the sport event is that the conflict is like the real world, but the actual game is not the real world (Bateson, 1972, p. 183; 1977, p. 3); therefore, the consequences, success or failure, are not as serious as in real life situations. Involvement in the sports spectacular, with its encompassing emotional expression, is appealing to the individual because of the low cost or investment for practice of handling control or power. The sports spectacular is a superb "playground" for use and display of power. This time of participation in simulation is very appealing to a great majority of people. In the United States the annual attendance at sports spectaculars, including attendance made possible via the mass-media, exceeds that of any other public event. Recently an estimated 76% of the total population of the United States observed the first professional football superbowl. In 1976 a total of 314 million spectators attended sporting events in the United States ("The boom in leisure," 1977). In 1976, the World Cup soccer match was observed by approximately 400 million people. Why do these events attract so much attention?

FUNCTIONS OF RITUAL IN SPORTS SPECTACULAR

The apparent fulfillment of ritual functions in the sports spectacular may help show why there appears to be such great interest in this seemingly insignificant entertainment ceremony. What a ritual symbol means can be discovered by observing the diverse uses of that symbol in both sacred and profane contexts. Benedict (1937) proposed that in most civ-lizations certain dominant and intensively developed themes are repeti-tiously elaborated in ritual after ritual. Radcliffe-Brown (1948) postu-lated that human beings always manipulate their thought categories consistently. Leach (1968, pp. 523-526) lists functions of ritual as com-munication, power and belief. *Communication* and *power* will be used to develop the proposition that the functions of ritual are elaborated in the sports spectacular. *Belief* as a function of sport ritual is treated elsewhere (Cheska, in preparation).

Ritual as Communications: Actions that occur within the magic circle of sporting events are full of symbolic meaning. The whole event is de-signed to distinguish social relationships between people attending and within the process. How ritual messages are actually communicated is not well understood. Why do the colors blue and orange bring to mind for many individuals a similar concept—the image of a specific university? It is known that each person's perception and subsequent interpretation of an event is unique, yet to share meaning there must be an integrative image that carries enough similarity in all involved individuals to be commonly identified.

The illusive product of this process is akin to communitas (Turner, 1974, p. 89) or flow quality whose features Csikszentmihalyi (1975) has identified as an experience of: merging action and awareness; the cen-tering of attention on a limited stimulus field; the loss of ego as in re-ligious ritual, artistic performances, and games; the control of personal actions and of the environment; the non-contradictory demands for ac-tion and clear, unambiguous feedback; the need for no goals or rewards outside itself. Turner (1974) points out that in pre-Industrial Revolution societies, ritual could always have a flow quality for communities (tribes, moieties, clans, lineages, families, etc.); but in post-Industrial societies, when ritual gave way to individualism and rationalism, the flow experi-ence was pushed mainly into the leisure genres of art, sport, games, pas-times (p. 90). The apparent shift of ritualistic flow (feeling of integra-tion) from the total community to leisure situations may indirectly point out a methodological survival process or a paradigmatic shift.

The ritualized message of hierarchial social relationships can be read-ily shown. For example, at a basketball event teams are distinguished from each other and from officials by position, color, costume, actions. Oppos-ing sides are identified by such things as selective seating and color com-binations. The auditory collectivity of band, cheerleaders, and spectators in tribute to their team is a very powerful communicative ritual. They communicate the "belongingness" of each distinctive group and "sepa-rateness" between groups, and serve as boundary markers.

The thematic social message of conflicting forces is dramatically ritualized, for in the game there is a tenseness of victory and defeat communicated within the compressed arena of time and space (Kilmer, 1976, p. 37). In the contest, the relative hierarchical power relationship is played out, showing who wins and who loses. The behavior of individuals at the conclusion of a sporting conflict conveys the message of which group is in ascendency. Jubilative, effervescent, expansive behavior easily marks the winners; a dejected, subdued, withdrawn attitude readily identifies the losers. These kinds of behavior have become ritualized in American sports scenes. The emotion of pleasure is a feeling of power; that of displeasure is a feeling of impotence (Howard, 1912, p. 42). The sport spectacular, with its symbolic pageantry, conveys dramatically the social theme of power and its converse, impotency. The distinct message of hierarchy—the winner/loser paradigm—differs from life where lines are not as discrete. The game is a simpler, more distinct model of control. The steps toward and the gaining of the prize in a game are stated in non-compromising terms (i.e., inches, yards, seconds, points). In life one is not always sure who has won, what has been won, or how this was accomplished. In this light, the sports event is more "real" than reality.

Ritual as Power: In this paper the dilemma of sacred vs. profane ritual has not yet been addressed. Ritual as power can be considered not only as a statement of interpersonal relations, but as relations ranging from a superb human that is able to perform feats beyond those of an ordinary human to a super-human or super-natural agency which can perform feats not attainable by humans. The extraordinary human is considered a hero/heroine, while the super-human or super-natural agency is considered a god/goddess, spirit or force. The distinction is one of sacred vs. profane. The sacred ritual involves entreaty and/or demand by humans to supernatural or superhuman powers for help in accomplishing some significant act (Ember & Ember, 1973, pp. 270-273). The profane ritual involves entreaty and/or demand by humans to extraordinary humans for help in accomplishing some significant act. In this author's mind the distinction is erroneous, for the relationship between sacred and profane is rather one of continuity than category. This point is confirmed by Leach (1968), who feels that ideas about the relations between supernatural agencies and human beings or about the potency of particular ritual behaviors are modeled on first-hand experience of real-life relationships between real human beings. Conversely, Leach suggests that every act by which one individual asserts his authority to curb or alter the behavior of another individual is an invocation of metaphysical force. The submissive response is an ideological reaction. The power of ritual is just as actual as the power of command (p. 525).

When this is acted out in sacred ritual, it may be seen in the efficacious power of the cross in the Christian religion or of the mana in objects in the Malayan Polynesian tribes. Each symbol carries the power of the original in its perception by the believers. In Western countries the erosion of church ritual has taken place in recent centuries; ritual symbols of supernatural power have diminished. (This does not imply that belief in them has necessarily diminished, but their ritualistic representation has decreased.) However, because humans need significant symbolic ritual to synthesize social themes, and specifically ritual of power, profane examples of this have increased. A shift from the sacred to the profane ritual can be seen in the ritual trappings of power developed by the nations of the world. The increase of the pageantry of nationalism can be seen in the modern Olympics, as the raising of the flag and playing of the national anthem of the winning athlete's nation. The attempts to set up distinct international athletic games by the U.S.S.R. in creating the Spartakiad and China's promulgation of the Asian Games have intensifed the model of power in athletics.

The use of profane ritual for personal profit has led to a general distrust of ritual. The specific benefit of the "ritual makers" is in violation of the common benefit of ritual performance. Examples of the profit motive can be seen in many ways (i.e., the scapegoating ritual of secret societies as the Ku Klux Klan; the false sense of success promised during ritualistic shenanigans of politicians, palm readers, faith healers; the ritualized cults of strange prophets; and similar events). It is interesting to note the efforts of the Soviet Union to create secular ritual, such as hero awards and civil palaces of marriage. In spite of mistrust of certain practices, ritual's ability to re-create conditions of powerful emotional experience, to dramatize or personify certain vital ideas on which society is based, makes ritual essential to people (Klapp, 1956, pp. 12-13).

The fundamental hierarchy of power as a pan-human theme seems to be played out increasingly in profane rituals. Among these is the sports spectacular. As a celebrative ritual enactment of power, the sports spectacular has become for common man a substitute for sacred ritual enactment of power. The use of sports spectaculars in the transfer of ritualization of power from the sacred to the profane is historically consistent. In the past the playing of ritual games was used to influence the supernatural agencies. For example, Homer recorded that the early Greek funeral games in honor of Patroclus were competitive events related to death (Gardiner, 1910, p. 14); the eastern North American woodland Indian tribes played lacrosse to gain the Spirit's help in curing the sick (de Brébeuf, 1897); the captain of the losing team in the pre-Columbian

Aztec rubber ball court game (*tlachtli*) was sacrificed to the gods (Kemrer, 1968). Power—either entreaty for or transfer of it—has been the theme in these and similar game rituals. The sports spectacular is a logical medium or vehicle in which to carry the symbolism of power.

Sacred and profane ritual enactments are both symbolic messages of power, the sacred representing the super-human and the profane representing the superb human. This ritual re-enforcement of the cultural code of power is needed by humans; therefore, when one method of symbolization is diminished, another will increase. Sharing of the cultural code of power as a viable human interactive concept is continually imperative. Currently the profane ceremony of the sports spectacular has become one acceptable method. The above discussion suggests that the basic essentials of ritual are indeed contained in the sports spectacular. The modern sports spectacular, by means of symbolic ritual, dramatically conveys the social message of power.

NOTES

1. Sepak Takraw (sepak means kick; takraw means ball in Thai) is a variation of an ancient circle ball game in which a 4-6″ diameter light open woven bamboo ball was kicked by the inside foot area sequentially between players. The object was to keep the ball airborne. The modern game, reflecting five centuries of competition, is similar to foot volleyball. National and international sepak takraw (sometimes called sepak raga) is held in Southeast Asia, and is one of the popular sports competitions in the Asian Games.
2. Spartakiads, competitive sports festivals, have been held in Russia since early 1900s. They were held in various republics, colleges, trade unions, and among school children; accompanying the sports competitions were gymnastics, calisthenics, dance, and mass formation displays. In 1956 the U.S.S.R. national Spartakiad, modeled after the Olympiads, was initiated, and competition was held in the year preceding each quadrennial Olympics. In the 1970-1971 national Spartakiad, there were approximately 18 million competitors.
3, 4, 5, 6 After reviewing numerous writings, encyclopedias, and dictionaries to gain the essences of the words game, power, spectacle (spectacular, spectator), and ceremony, the *Random House Dictionary of the English Language College Edition,* 1968, was used because of its precise terminology.

REFERENCES

Arens, W. The great American football ritual. *Natural History,* 1975, *84,* 72-80.
Bateson, G. A theory of play and fantasy. In G. Bateson (ed.), *Steps to an ecology of mind.* New York: Ballantine Books, 1972.
Bateson, G. Play and paradigm. *The Association for the Anthropological Study of Play Newsletter,* 1977, *4*(1), 2-8.

Benedict, R. Ritual. In E. R. A. Seligman (ed.), *Encyclopaedia of the Social Sciences* (Vol. 13). New York: Macmillan, 1931.

The boom in leisure. *U.S. News and World Report*, May 23, 1977, pp. 62-76.

Bucher, C. A. *Foundations of physical education* (6th ed.). St. Louis: C. V. Mosby, 1972.

Caillois, R. *Man and the sacred.* Glencoe, Ill.: The Free Press, 1959.

Cheska, A. *In the service of sport.* Unpublished free verse, 1972.

————. *People at play—An anthropological viewpoint.* In preparation.

Csikszentmihalyi, M. Play and intrinsic rewards. *Journal of Humanistsic Psychology*, 1975, *15*, 41-63.

de Brébeuf, J. Huron relations of 1636. In R. G. Thwaites (ed.), *The Jesuit relations and allied documents* (Vol. 10). Cleveland: The Burrows Brothers, 1897.

Ember, C. & Ember, M. *Cultural anthopology.* Englewood Cliffs, N.P.: Prentice Hall, 1973.

Ferril, T. H. Freud, football and the marching virgins. *Readers Digest*, September 1974, pp. 71-73.

Gardiner, E. N. *Greek athletic sports and festivals.* London: Macmillan, 1910.

Geertz, C. Religion as a cultural system. In M. Banton, *Anthropological approachs to the study of religion.* London: Tavistock, 1966. (A.S.A. Monographs, 3)

Herkimer, L. R. Cheerleading. In R. Slovenko and J. A. Knight (eds.). *Motivations in play, games and sports.* Springfield, Ill.: C. C. Thomas, 1967.

Howard, G. E. Social psychology of the spectator. *American Journal of Sociology*, 1912, *18*, 23-50.

Huizinga, J. *Homo ludens, a study of the play element in culture.* Boston: Beacon Press, 1955.

Kemrer, M. J., Jr. A re-examination of the ball game in pre-Columbian mesoamerica. *Ceramica de Cultura Maya et al.,* 1968, *5*, 1-25.

Kilmer, S. Sport as ritual: A theoretical approach. In D. F. Lancy and B. A. Tindall (eds.), *The anthropological study of play: Problems and prospects; proceedings of the First Annual Meeting of the Association for the Anthropological Study of Play.* Cornwall, N.Y.: Leisure Press, 1976.

Klapp, O. E. *Ritual and cult.* Washington, D. C.: Public Affairs Press, 1956. (Annals of American Sociology)

Leach, E. *Rethinking anthropology.* London: Athlone Press, 1961. (London School of Economics. Monographs on social anthropology, no. 22)

————. Ritual. In D. L. Sills (ed.), *International Encyclopedia of the Social Sciences* (Vol. 13). New York: Macmillan and Free Press, 1968.

Lee, R. *Religion and leisure in America.* New York: Abingdon Press, 1964.

Loy, J. W. The nature of sport: A definitional effort. *Quest, 10*, May 1968, pp. 56-71.

Metheny, E. Symbolic forms of movement: The feminine image in sports. In M. M. Hart (ed.), *Sport in the socio-cultural process.* Dubuque, Iowa: Wm. C. Brown, 1972.

Mukerjee, R. *The symbolic life of man.* Bombay: Hind Kitabs, 1959.

Munn, N. D. Symbolism in a ritual context: Aspects of symbolic action. In J. J. Honigmann (ed.), *Handbook of social and cultural anthropology.* Chicago: Rand McNally, 1973.

Radcliffe-Brown, A. R. *The Andaman Islanders.* Glencoe, Ill.: The Free Press, 1948. (first published in 1922)

Random House dictionary of the English language college edition. New York: Random House, 1968.

Schafer, W. E. Sport and male sex-role socialization. *Sport Sociology Bulletin,* 4, 1975, 47-54.

Spicer, D. G. *The book of festivals.* Detroit: Gale Research Co., 1969. (reprint of 1937 ed.)

Stone, G. American sports: Play and display. In E. Larrabee and R. Meyersohn (eds.), *Mass leisure.* Glencoe, Ill.: The Free Press, 1958.

Sutton-Smith, B. and Avedon, E. M. The function of games. In B. Sutton-Smith and E. M. Avedon (eds.), *The study of games.* New York: John Wiley, 1971.

Sutton-Smith, B. Games, the socialization of conflict. *Canadian Journal of Sport and Physical Education,* 1973, 4(1), 1-7.

Toohey, D. M. *Basketball, its dramatic ritual, ceremonies and social function.* Paper presented at The Association for the Anthropological Study of Play conference, Detroit, 1974.

Turner, V. W. *The ritual process.* Chicago: Aldine Press, 1969.

———. Liminality, play, flow, and ritual: An essay in comparative symbology. In E. Norbeck (ed.), *The anthropological study of human play.* Houston: Rice University, 1974. (Rice University Studies, *60*(3), 53-90)

Van Gennep, A. *The rites of passage.* Chicago: University of Chicago Press, 1960. (first printed in English in 1909)

Von Neuman, J. and Morgenstern, O. *Theory of games and economic behavior.* New York: Wiley & Sons, 1944.

Winick, C. *Dictionary of anthropology.* Totowa, N.J.: Littlefield, Adams, 1966.

Part III

Subgroups, Subcultures and Sport

Section A

Ethnic Groups and Sport

Not all groups and individuals in a society participate in sport to the same extent or with the same style. Sometimes these variations in involvement can be attributed to individual differences, i.e., for reasons of personality or motivational differences, some individuals enjoy particular sports and certain styles of competition while others express contrasting preferences or prefer not to be involved in sport at all. But sometimes the key to understanding differential rates of participation is to be found in social category membership. This section and the two following it are concerned with the effect membership in certain social categories has on sport involvement and the manner in which the sport experience of individuals is shaped by their awareness of social category membership.

Social categories are based on the fact that individuals can be identified and differentiated on the basis of biological or ascribed social characteristics and that their identification as members of such groups has effects upon many aspects of social life.[1] Social category membership is usually related to social characteristics which are assigned an individual at birth and which constrain his or her opportunities, aspirations and world view. Among those categories most often discussed are age, ethnic origin, racial background, socio-economic status, and sex.

Social characteristics are often related to discrimination, or unfavorable treatment on arbitrary grounds according to a group or individual. Discrimination can take many forms, but two general types of discrimination are based upon legal and conventional constraints. Legal discrimination is formal discrimination and refers to such written or institutionalized practices as private clubs, quota systems, and financial barriers. Because it is formal, legal discrimination can be challenged in courts as

1. For a full discussion see John W. Loy, Jr., Barry D. McPherson, and Gerald Kenyon, *Sport and Social Systems*, Chapter 9, (Reading, Mass.: Addison-Wesley Publishing Company) 1978.

has been demonstrated by recent cases seeking legal decisions concerning whether girls should be allowed to play on previously all-male Little League teams or whether it is possible for a Canadian quarterback such as Jamie Bone, to get a fair try-out in the Canadian Football League. However, conventional restrictions are more subtle and harder to combat, for they consist of normative statements or beliefs about how things should be. Conventional arguments often reduce to the attitude that certain things—a *girl* playing Little League baseball? a *Canadian* quarterback good enough to play in the CFL?—just aren't done.

Examples of discrimination based upon social category membership remind us that discrimination occurs when one group feels that it is superior in some way and thus deserves jurisdiction over important aspects of social life. This includes control over the distribution of opportunities, such as who shall have access to sporting facilities. Thus the exclusion of certain social categories from access to opportunities and facilities can be understood, though somewhat simplistically, as a function of the "dominant" group who control sport: in North America, for example, this is the young, white Anglo-Saxon Protestant male. Moreover, not only are these subgroups in danger of losing full access to sport, they are in danger of losing control of the symbolic message system that sport is, for the group which encodes sport with its social meaning commands great, though subtle power. Subgroups must choose a strategy for handling such exclusion. There are several choices.

First, the group can drop out of sport (or the particular sport, positions or style of involvement at issue). In many cases, this has been the historical response: we find few laborers playing polo, few Blacks playing ice hockey, and few women pole vaulting.

A second response is to fight to overcome the arbitrary inequities. The woman's movement in sport is an obvious example of an increasingly successful attempt to respond in this manner.

A third response is to promote alternative opportunities based upon social category membership. In this manner, the group can take pride in its separate status and use sport as a symbol of group unity and identity. The Black power salute of the 1968 Olympic Games is one example of sport being used by a minority group to state its own divergent message; the retention of the games of their old country by immigrants, particularly in the face of pressure to assimilate to the new culture, is another.

The readings in this section focus upon many of these issues as they relate specifically to ethnic and racial groups. In the first two selections, the topic is discrimination. In a classic study which has often been replicated Loy and McElvogue discuss a significant aspect of racial discrimination in American baseball and football: the exclusion of Blacks from positions of centrality and power.

Ball uses the Loy and McElvogue model of centrality to explore the discrimination of Canadians in Canadian football. However, Ball finds the model less satisfactory in explaining patterns of discrimination in Canada and proposes an alternative model: the primary-supporting model.

Pooley focuses on the role sport takes in the assimilation of immigrant ethnic groups. Studying soccer teams in Milwaukee, Pooley found evidence that sport does not necessarily aid in the cultural assimilation of ethnic groups; rather it can also serve as a symbol of identification with the ethnic heritage of the group, thus preserving the boundaries of the group.

Racial Segregation in American Sport

John W. Loy, Jr. and Joseph F. McElvogue

INTRODUCTION

Numerous journalists have commented on the social functions which sport fulfills for minority groups in American society. Boyle, for example, forcefully writes:

> Sport has often served minority groups as the first rung on the social ladder. As such, it has helped further their assimilation into American life. It would not be too far-fetched to say that it has done more in this regard than any other agency, including church and school (1963, p. 100).

Recently, journalists have placed special emphasis on the many contributions sport has made for the Negro. As Olsen observes:

> Every morning the world of sport wakes up and congratulates itself on its contributions to race relations. The litany has been so often repeated that it is believed almost universally. It goes: "Look what sports has done for the Negro" (1968, p. 7).

In view of the many journalistic accounts of the contributions of sport to the social success of minority groups, it is somewhat surprising that sociologists and physical educators have largely ignored the issue of minority group integration in American sport. The purpose of this paper is to direct the attention of sport sociologists to the issue by presenting a theoretical and empirical examination of racial segregation in America's major professional baseball and football teams.

From *The International Review of Sport Sociology* 5, 1970, pp. 5-23. Copyright 1970 Ars Polona, Krakowskie Przedmiescie 7, Warsaw, Poland.

THEORETICAL OVERVIEW

Theoretically considered, our examination largely draws upon Grusky's (1963) theory of formal structure of organizations and Blalock's (1962) set of theoretical propositions regarding occupational discrimination.

Grusky's Theory of Formal Structure

According to Grusky, "the formal structure of an organization consists of a set of norms which define the system's official objectives, its major offices or positions, and the primary responsibilities of the position occupants" (p. 345). The formal structure ". . . patterns the behavior of its constituent positions along three interdependent dimensions: (1) spatial location, (2) nature of task, and (3) frequency of interaction" (p. 345). The theoretical import of Grusky's model is contained in his statement that:

> All else being equal, the more central one's spatial location: (1) the greater likelihood dependent or coordinative tasks will be performed and (2) the greater the rate of interaction with the occupants of other positions. Also, the performance of dependent tasks is positively related to frequency of interaction (p. 346).

Combining these three criteria, Grusky distinguishes positions of high interaction potential and position of low interaction potential within the social structure of organizations. He defines the occupants of these two types of positions as high and low interactors, respectively.

For our purposes, we prefer to use the concept of "centrality" in dealing with Grusky's three interdependent dimensions of organizational positions. With an extension to permit us to embrace all three of Grusky's criteria, we accepted Hopkins' (1964) definition of this concept:

> Centrality designates how close a member is to the "center" of the group's interaction network and thus refers simultaneously to the frequency with which a member participates in interaction with other members and the number or range of other members with whom he interacts (p. 28) [and the degree to which he must coordinate his tasks and activities with other members].

Blalock's Theoretical Propositions

Several years ago, Blalock (1962) made a very astute analysis of why "professional baseball has provided Negroes with one of the relatively few avenues for escape from blue-collar occupations." From his analysis, Blalock developed thirteen theoretical propositions concerning occupational discrimination which can be empirically tested in other occupational settings. His analysis is an excellent example of how the critical examination of a sport situation can enhance the development of sociological theory in an area of central concern. Blalock was, however, perhaps naive in assuming that professional baseball is ". . . an occupation which is remarkably free of racial discrimination" (p. 242).

We sought to test Blalock's assumption that professional baseball is relatively free of racial discrimination by drawing upon three of his propositions to predict where racial segregation is most likely to occur on the baseball diamond. The three particular propositions which we considered were:

1. The lower the degree of purely social interaction on the job . . ., the lower the degree of discrimination" (p. 246).
2. "To the extent that performance level is relatively independent of skill in interpersonal relations, the lower the degree of discrimination" (p. 246).
3. "To the extent that an individual's success depends primarily on his own performance, rather than on limiting or restricting the performance of specific other individuals, the lower the degree of discrimination by group members" (p. 245).

On the one hand, the consideration of proposition 1 in conjunction with proposition 2 suggested that discrimination is directly related to level and type of interaction. On the other hand, the combined consideration of propositions 2 and 3 suggested that there will be less discrimination where performance of independent tasks are largely involved; because such tasks do not have to be coordinated with the activities of other persons, and therefore do not hinder the performance of others, nor require a great deal of skill in interpersonal relations.

Since the dimensions of interaction and task dependency treated by Blalock are included in our concept of centrality, we subsumed his three propositions under a more general one, stating that: "discrimination is positively related to centrality."

STATEMENT OF THEORETICAL HYPOTHESIS

Broadly conceived, discrimination ". . . denotes the unfavourable treatment of categories of persons on arbitrary grounds" (Moore, 1964, p. 203). Discrimination takes many forms, but a major mode is that of segregation. Segregation denotes the exclusion of certain categories of persons from specific social organizations or particular positions within organizations on arbitrary grounds, i.e., grounds which have no objective relation to individual skill and talent.

Since we were chiefly concerned with the matter of racial segregation in professional sports, we took as our specific theoretical hypothesis the proposition that: *racial segregation in professional team sports is posi-*

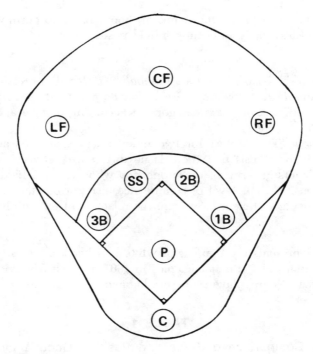

Figure 1

tively related to centrality. In order to test this hypothesis, we empirically examined the extent of racial segregation within major league baseball and major league football.

THE CASE OF PROFESSIONAL BASEBALL

Baseball teams have a well defined social structure consisting of the repetitive and regulated interaction among a set of nine positions combined into three major substructures or interaction units: (1) the battery, consisting of pitcher and catcher; (2) the infield, consisting of first base, second base, shortstop and third base; and (3) the outfield, consisting of leftfield, centerfield and rightfield positions.

Empirical Hypothesis

As is evident from Figure 1, one can readily see that the outfield contains the most peripheral and socially isolated positions in the organizational structure of a baseball team. Therefore, on the basis of our theoretical hypothesis, we predicted that Negro players in comparison to white players on major league teams are more likely to occupy outfield positions and less likely to occupy infield positions.

Methods

Data. On the basis of the *1968 Baseball Register* all professional players in the American and National Leagues who played at least fifty games during the 1967 season were categorized according to race and playing position.[2]

Treatment. The X^2 test for two independent samples was used to test the null hypothesis that there is no difference between white and black ballplayers in terms of the proportion who occupy infield and outfield positions. The .01 level of significance, using a one-tailed test, was selected as being sufficient to warrant the rejection of the null hypothesis.

Findings

Table 1 presents the number of white and black athletes occupying specific positions in the major leagues in 1967. It is clearly evident from the table that Negro players are predominantly found in the outfield.

TABLE 1

A Comparison of Race and Position Occupancy in Major League Baseball in 1967

Playing Position	American League		National League		Both Leagues	
	White	Black	White	Black	White	Black
Catcher	13	0	14	1	27	1
Shortstop	7	0	10	1	17	1
1st Base	11	2	7	5	18	7
2nd Base	10	3	6	1	16	4
3rd Base	9	2	7	4	16	6
Outfield	26	14	12	22	38	36
N =	76	21	56	34	132	55

Race

Position	White	Black	Total
Infield	94	19	113
Outfield	38	36	74
	132	55	187

$$X^2 = 20.32; \ p < .0005 \ (df = 1)$$

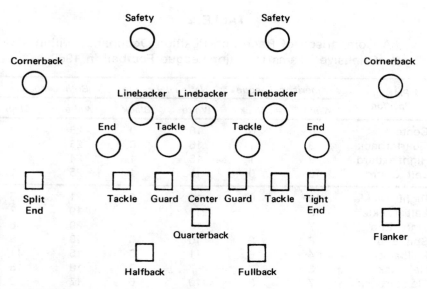

Figure 2

The highly significant X^2, resulting from the test of our null hypothesis, gives strong support to our empirical hypothesis and provides some confirmation of our theoretical hypothesis that racial segregation in professional sports is related to centrality. As a further test of our hypothesis we examined the extent of racial segregation in professional football.

THE CASE OF PROFESSIONAL FOOTBALL

Like baseball teams, football teams have well defined organizational structures. However, whereas the positions in baseball organization are determined by defensive alignment, there exists both a distinctive offensive and a distinctive defensive team within modern professional football organization. Figure 2 shows the constituent positions of the offensive and defensive teams of any given professional organization.

Empirical Hypothesis

It is clear from Figure 2 that the most central positions on the offensive team consist of center, right guard, left guard and quarterback; while the most central positions on the defensive team are the three linebacker positions. Therefore, on the basis of our theoretical hypothesis, we pre-

TABLE 2

A Comparison of Race and Position Occupancy within Offensive Teams in Major League Football in 1968

Playing Position	American League		National League		Both Leagues	
	White	Black	White	Black	White	Black
Center	10	0	16	0	26	0
Quarterback	9	1	16	0	25	1
Right Guard	9	1	15	1	24	2
Left Guard	10	0	15	1	25	1
Right Tackle	10	0	11	5	21	5
Left Tackle	8	2	11	5	19	7
Tight End	7	3	13	3	20	6
Spit End	8	2	10	6	18	8
Fullback	4	6	11	5	15	11
Halfback	3	7	7	9	10	16
Flankerback	7	3	10	6	17	9
N =	85	25	135	41	220	66

Race

Position	White	Black	Total
Central	100	4	104
Noncentral	120	62	182
	220	66	286

$$X^2 = 32.37; p < .0005 \text{ (df} = 1)$$

dicted that Negro football players in comparison to white players are more likely to occupy non-central positions than central positions on both offensive and defensive teams.

Methods

Data. Using the *Official 1968 Autographed Yearbooks* of the American and National Football Leagues in conjunction with Zanger's *Pro Football 1968* we classified all starting offensive and defensive players according to race (black or white) and playing position (central or non-central).[3]

Treatment. The X^2 test for two independent samples was used to test the null hypothesis that there is no difference between white and black occupancy of centrally located positions on either offensive or

TABLE 3

A Comparison of Race and Position Occupancy within Defensive Teams in Major League Football in 1968

Playing Position	American League		National League		Both Leagues	
	White	Black	White	Black	White	Black
Middle Linebacker	8	2	16	0	24	2
Right Linebacker	10	0	15	1	25	1
Left Linebacker	8	2	15	1	23	3
Right End	6	4	12	4	18	8
Right Tackle	7	3	13	3	20	6
Left Tackle	7	3	10	6	17	9
Left End	8	2	11	5	19	7
Right Safety	7	3	10	6	17	9
Left Safety	7	3	10	6	17	9
Right Cornerback	2	8	6	10	8	18
Left Cornerback	1	9	3	13	4	22
N =	71	39	121	55	192	94

Race

Position	White	Black	Total
Central	72	6	78
Noncentral	120	88	208
	192	94	286

$$X^2 = 29.26; \quad p < .0005 \quad (df = 1)$$

defensive teams. The .01 level of significance, using a one-tailed test, was selected as being sufficient to warrent the rejection of the null hypothesis.

Findings

Tables 2 and 3 presesnt the number of white and black athletes occupying central and non-central offensive and defensive positions, respectively, in the major professional football leagues in 1968. It is evident from the tables that very few Negro players occupy central positions, either defensively or offensively. The significant X^2 tests of our null hypothesis give strong support to our empirical hypothesis and provide further confirmation of our theoretical hypothesis.

DISCUSSION

The preceding findings leave little doubt that only a very small proportion of black athletes occupy central positions in America's professional baseball and football organizations. However, notwithstanding our theoretical buttress, a number of telling questions can be raised regarding the revealed relationships between race and position occupancy. Three such questions are: (1) Does the discovered relationship between race and position occupancy indicate the actual presence of racial segregation? (2) If racial segregation is actually present, what are the "social mechanisms" linking it to centrality? (3) If racial segregation does exist in professional sports, what are its social consequences? Let us briefly consider each of these questions in turn.

DOES RACIAL SEGREGATION ACTUALLY EXIST IN SPORT?

One can argue that showing that Negro athletes infrequently occupy central positions does not confirm that they are racially segregated. They may be excluded from central positions for objective rather than arbitrary reasons. On the one hand, Negroes may not have as great a talent or skill for certain tasks as white players, and are thus excluded from selected positions for that reason. On the other hand, Negroes may possess greater athletic ability than whites for certain activities, and are accordingly found proportionately more often in some positions than others. A third alternative, of course, is that Negro athletes exclude themselves from selected positions by personal preference.

Although we are not presently prepared to fully assess the validity of each of these three perspectives, we must frankly state we find them tenuous. For example, we have found no evidence which would lead us to believe that Negro athletes have inferior ability in comparison to white athletes for any role assignment in professional baseball or football. We observe that time and again in the world of sport athletic stereotypes of Negroes have been refuted. It will be recalled that, not too long ago, there existed the myth among track authorities that Negroes were racially suited for the sprints and perhaps the shorter distance races, but did not possess the capabilities for the endurance events. The success of black athletes in long distance running events, including the Olympic marathon, in recent years has dispelled the notion that Negro trackmen are speed merchants without stamina.

Similarly, we have discovered little support for the view that Negro athletes possess certain abilities in greater abundance than white athletes. We have, however, encountered some findings which indicate that a black athlete must be superior to his white counterpart before he is permitted to occupy a given position. For example, a recent study shows that the cumulative major league batting averages in 1968 were higher for Negroes at every position as follows: catcher-whites .238, blacks .279; first and third bases-whites .265, blacks .277; second and shortstop-whites .246, blacks .258; outfield-whites .253, blacks .266 (Los Angeles Times, May 15, 1969, part 3, p. 3).[4]

Finally, we find it difficult to believe that Negro athletes are largely selecting the positions which they occupy in baseball and football on the basis of personal preference. What seems to be operating is a self-fulfilling belief. A black athlete assumes that he doesn't have much chance at being accepted at certain positions and thus tries out for other positions where his estimates of success is much higher. As Olsen succinctly states: "He *anticipates* the white man's categorization of him, and acts accordingly" (1968, p. 170). An interesting study, we suggest, would be to compare the playing positions of white and black athletes in professional football with those they filled in college football. Our prediction is that a greater proportion of black than white athletes will be discovered to have acquired new role assignments.

Some would perhaps contend that we are overstating our case regarding racial segregation in professional sports; because:

> The degree to which Negroes have moved into pro sports is astonishing. More than half the players in the National Basketball Association are Negroes — as were eight of the ten starters in the last NBA All-Star Game. A quarter of the players in the National Football League are Negroes, and the 1967 NFL team was 40 per cent black. Nearly 25 per cent of all players in major league baseball are American Negroes, and here too a disproportionate number of the stars are not white. For example, of the top ten hitters in the National League for the 1967 season, only one was a Caucasian (Olsen, 1968, p. 170).

Nevertheless, we point out that sport seems to mirror American life at large, in that, integration has been very slow, and where it has been rather fully achieved there remain many forms of discrimination other than that of segregation.

Professional baseball is a good example of how slowly the process of integration takes place. Many herald 1947 as the year "the color line was broken" with the entrance of Jackie Robinson into major league baseball. But, as illustrated in Table 4, ten years later there were only a dozen Negro players in the National League and as late as 1960 there were only a half dozen black athletes in the American League. Table 4 does reveal, however, that there has been a substantial increase in the number of Latin American players in recent years and indicates that there exists an intermediate "brown zone" between the "white and black belts" of major league baseball.[5]

WHAT ARE THE SOCIAL MECHANISMS OF SEGREGATION?

Assuming that there is racial segregation in professional baseball and football, one is led to inquire as to what are the underlying causes of this form of discrimination. We have argued that segregation is a function of centrality and its associated interdependent dimenssions of spatial location, rate of interaction and task dependency. Sociologically viewed, our theoretical rationale is probably a fairly satisfactory one; but those of a more social psychological orientation would likely want to know what sort of personal qualities and behavioral dispositions are associated with centrality which influence segregation.

There are no doubt many kinds of normative beliefs and attitudes which act as antecedent and/or intervening variables in the relationship between segregation and centrality. We specifically speculate that there is a relationship between interaction and attitudes regarding personal intimacy; and a relationship between tasks dependency and beliefs concerning the qualities of judgment and decision-making ability.

A major generalization of discrimination research states that: "there is a range within discriminatory practice such that there is most discrimination and most prejudice as the practice comes closer to intimate personal contact" (Berelson and Steiner, 1964, p. 511). Thus, we reason that Negroes may be excluded from central positions because these positions involve high rates of interaction which lead to greater personal contact among players than do peripheral positions in an organization.

We conject, in passing, that there may even be normative beliefs regarding the interaction of Negro athletes among themselves. In the case of professional football, for instance, black athletes are most often found at the two cornerback positions. Similarly, in the case of professional baseball, we point out that in the infield Negroes are most often found at first and third bases. While the relationship may be a spurious one, it is interesting that Negroes are placed in the extreme corners of the field in both baseball and football. A related observation is that seldom does one find two Negroes playing side-by-side in either major league baseball or football.

In treating interaction, one should, of course, distinguish between task interaction and social interaction since there is probably only a moderate correlation between the two. Although we expect that there may be a substantial degree of prejudice regarding the intermixing of white

and black players off the field, we are not sure that there is marked prejudice among players concerning racial interpersonal contact on the field.[6]

We speculate that segregation in professional sports is more a function of management than playing personnel. For example, there appears
to be a myth among coaches that Negro players lack judgment and decision-making ability. This myth results in black athletes being excluded
from positions requiring dependent or coordinative tasks as such activities generally require greater judgment than independent tasks. In short,
the central positions in major league baseball and football are typically
the most responsible or so-called "brains positions." The following quotations from Olsen with respect to central and peripheral defensive positions within football organization well illustrate the matter:

> "Most defensive football players have a single job to do, with little
> variation, but the linebacker has to exercise judgment" says a thought-
> ful NFL player. "He may wind up tackling the quarterback fifteen
> yards behind the line of scrimmage, and he may wind up knocking
> down a pass twenty-yards up the field. He has to be able to read
> plays well, everybody knows all the things the linebacker has to do.
> It's one of the most responsible defensive positions. Therefore, he
> can't be a Negro" (p. 172).

> "Cornerback is not a brains position" says Bill Koman, retired St. Louis
> Cardinal linebacker. "You pick up the split end or the flanker and
> you stay with him all the way. That's it" (p. 173).

> "Yassuh, white man, boss," says one NFL cornerback derisively when
> asked about the situation, "We ain't got the brains to play center,
> 'cause we can't count, but we can follow that flanker's ass all the way
> down the field, *yuck, yuck*" (p. 173).

In our discussion herein we have emphasized the interaction and task
dependency dimensions of centrality; whereas in our empirical examination of racial segregation we stressed the dimension of spatial location.
Additional limitations of our empirical analysis include the fact that our
measure of spatial location was dichotomous rather than continuous in
nature; and the fact that we only looked at major league baseball and
football for specific one-year periods. In an effort to overcome these limitations, we extend our analysis of the racial composition of professional
baseball to cover a twelve year period; and we developed an operational
index of centrality which is continuous in nature and which reflects the
interaction and task dependency dimensions of centrality.

Table 5 shows the approximate number of individual white and
black athletes at each field position in the major leagues over a twelve
year period.[7] The table also shows the rank order of playing positions
in terms of the proportion of Negro players at each position. This rank
order is nearly identical to that given in Table 1.

TABLE 4

Distribution of White, Black and Latin American Players
by Position in Major League Baseball 1956-1967
National League

Year	Catcher	Short-stop	2nd Base	3rd Base	1st Base	Outfield	No. Total
1967	14	10	6	7	7	12	56
	1	1	1	4	5	22	34
	0	1	4	1	3	7	16
1966	13	9	8	8	5	15	58
	2	2	2	3	4	21	34
	0	2	4	2	3	8	19
1965	15	10	10	8	7	13	63
	1	1	1	3	5	19	30
	1	3	3	0	5	8	19
1964	13	8	11	8	8	18	66
	2	2	1	3	5	20	33
	0	3	2	2	2	8	16
1963	14	8	8	14	10	22	76
	1	2	2	2	4	18	29
	0	3	2	0	1	3	9
1962	Date not available						
1961	11	5	8	8	6	18	56
	1	2	2	2	2	11	20
	0	3	2	0	2	5	12
1960	12	6	7	9	9	21	64
	1	2	2	1	2	11	19
	0	1	2	0	2	4	9
1959	Data not available						
1958	12	7	8	9	10	18	64
	2	1	1	0	2	8	14
	2	1	1	0	1	2	5
1957	11	6	8	8	11	25	69
	1	2	1	2	1	5	12
	1	1	0	1	0	2	5
1966	11	9	8	9	9	20	66
	1	1	3	1	1	5	12
	0	0	2	0	0	2	2

TABLE 4 (continued)

Distribution of White, Black and Latin American Players by Position in Major League Baseball 1956-1967
American League

Ethnic Group	Catcher	Short-stop	2nd Base	3rd Base	1st Base	Outfield	Total No.
White	13	7	10	9	11	26	76
Black	0	0	3	2	2	14	21
Latin	2	4	1	1	1	6	15
White Black Latin			Data not available				
White	12	12	10	10	14	29	87
Black	2	0	1	1	1	12	17
Latin	1	3	2	2	1	6	13
White	12	9	13	10	12	29	85
Black	2	0	1	1	2	10	16
Latin	1	2	0	1	1	7	12
White	14	10	11	6	13	31	87
Black	2	0	2	1	1	7	13
Latin	2	2	0	1	1	5	1
Whit	13	11	11	9	11	34	85
Black	2	0	1	2	0	3	8
Latin	2	3	0	1	1	2	9
White	13	9	13	12	12	29	89
Black	2	1	1	1	0	9	14
Latin	1	3	0	0	1	3	8
White	10	6	9	11	11	27	74
Black	2	0	1	0	0	3	6
Latin	0	3	0	0	2	2	7
White	13	12	12	9	10	28	84
Black	0	0	0	0	2	3	5
Latin	0	2	0	1	2	2	7
White Black Latin			Data not available				
White Black Latin			Data not available				
White Black Latin			Data not available				

TABLE 5

Distribution of Individual White and Black Players by Position in Major League Baseball 1956-1967

Playing Position	White Players	Black Players	Total No. of Players	% of Black Players	Rank Order % White Players
Catcher	85	5	90	.0555	1
Shortstop	39	4	43	.0930	2
2nd Base	61	7	68	.1029	3
3rd Base	41	9	50	.1800	4
1st Base	54	13	67	.1940	5
Outfield	129	61	190	.3210	6
$N =$	409	99	508	.1948	

TABLE 6

Ranks for Position Occupancy and Annual Assists in Professional Baseball

Field Position	Rank Order		d_i	d^2_i
	% of Whites*	Annual Assists**		
Catcher	1	1	0	0
Shortstop	2	2	0	0
2nd Base	3	3	0	0
3rd Base	4	4	0	0
1st Base	5	5	0	0
Outfield	6	6	0	0

$$r_s = 1 - \frac{6 \sum_{i=1}^{n} d^2_i}{N^3 - N} = 1 - \frac{6(0)}{6(3)-6}; \text{rho} = 1.00$$

*See Table 5.   **See Footnote 8.   (Siegel, 1956, pp. 202-213)

Having reaffirmed the relationship between segregation and spatial location, we turned our attention to the interaction and task dependency dimensions of centrality. We decided that the total number of "assists" made by occupants of given field positions during a season would serve as an adequate operational indicator of centrality.[8] On the one hand, assists are an indicator of the rate of interaction and the number and range of other group members with whom a position occupant interacts. On the other hand, assists are an index of the degree to which dependent tasks are associated with given positions.

We discovered that the rank order of field positions with respect to number of annual assists remained the same for both leagues for every year covered.[9] More strikingly, however, we found a perfect rank order correlation between our measures of segregation and centrality (see Table 6). Thus, we concluded that we had obtained substantial support for our theoretical hypothesis that racial segregation in professional team sports is positively related to centrality.

WHAT ARE THE SOCIAL CONSEQUENCES OF SEGREGATION?

It is exceedingly difficult to assess the social consequences of racial segregation in professional baseball and football because data is limited; and because the consequences are both manifest and latent, acute and chronic. It would appear, however, that one of the major disadvantageous consequences of segregation is the retardation of upward career mobility in professional sports. Grusky (1963) has shown that approximately three-fourths of all major league baseball managers are recruited from infield positions.[10] Therefore, to the degree that Negro athletes are denied access to central positions, they are also limited in obtaining positions of leadership in professional baseball.[11]

Grusky assumes that the position which an individual occupies influences his development of varying kinds of role skills; and further assumes that the occupancy of central positions enhances the obtainment of key role skills related to Hopkins' (1964) set of fifteen theoretical propositions regarding small groups. For example, Hopkins states that: "For any member of a small group, the greater his centrality:

1. the greater his observability;
2. the greater his conformity;
3. the greater his influence; and,
4. the higher his rank" (1964, p. 51).

Another related proposition is that centrality is positively related to liking (Grusky, 1963, p. 347; Homans, 1950, p. 133).[12]

This latter proposition suggests that there may be a "vicious cycle" operating in professional sports. Negroes, because they are not liked by the white establishment, are placed in peripheral positions; and, as a result of this placement, do not have the opportunity of high rates of interaction with teammates, and do not receive the potential positive sentiment which might accrue from such interaction. In view of the nature of our problem, our discussion is likely too brief and superficial. However, we hope that we have been successful in directing the attention of sport sociologists to the matter of integration in American sport, and in providing stimulation for further theoretical and empirical analyses of the subject.[13]

NOTES

1. Appreciation is accorded to Mr. Schroder, director, and Mr. Dyer, assistant director of Helms Hall for assistance in the collection of data for this paper.
2. The criterion of fifty games was established in order to eliminate the partial participant, such as the pinch hitter or runner, the player brought up from the minor leagues on a part-time basis, the occasional utility man, and the unestablished rookie trying to make the team at any position.

   Players were ethnically classified as Caucasians, Negroes or Latin Americans. The latter group was excluded from most analyses, however, as it was impossible in terms of the sources available to determine which Latin American athletes were Negroes.

   Players at all positions were considered except for pitchers. They were excluded for purposes of analysis because: (1) data comparable to that collected for other players was not available, (2) the high rate of interchangeability among pitchers precluded accurate recording of data, and (3) pitchers are in a sense only part-time players, in that they typically play in only one game out of four, or if relief pitchers, play only a few innings in any given game. In order that the reader may make certain comparisons later in the paper, we note at this point that "only 13 of 207 pitchers in 1968 major league rosters were Negroes" (Olsen, 1968, p. 170).
3. The major difficulties we experienced in data collection were associated with the problems of determining the race of the players and in determining who were the first string or starting players. In the case of major league football, we used the "official yearbooks" to ascertain the race of given players as these sources contained photographs of the members of every team in a given league. Zanger's text was used as a means of determining the first string or starting lineup for each team. However, Zanger's lineups were preseason forecasts based upon the player's performance the previous seasson. A more accurate means of recording would have been to determine the players having the most playing time at each position for every team during the 1968 season.

An indication, however, that the data which we present in Tables 2 and 3 is reasonably accurate are the following facts cited from a study made independently of our own:

"On a typical weekend in the 1967 NFL season, no Negro center started a game. Of the 32 offensive guards in the starting lineups of NFL teams, 29 were white" (Olsen, 1963, p. 171).

". . . (on that same typical weekend in the 1967 season, 48 linebackers lumbered out on the field to start NFL games, and 45 of them, or 94 per cent, were white)" (Olsen, 1968, p. 172).

4. For a more complete account of how Negro athletes must be superior to white athletes in professional baseball in order to maintain their positions, see Rosenblatt, 1967. Finally, we note that the three outfield positions were considered as a single category since data were not available for each of the three outfield positions taken separately.

5. It would be interesting to find out whether or not "darker" Latin American athletes are more often found in the outfield than the "lighter" Latin players. There are some small indications that "quota systems" are operating for American Negro players and Latin American players, in that, if members of one group are prominent occupants of a given field posittion within a league, then the members of the other group tend to be predominant at another playing position. For a discussion of the social relations between American Negro and Latin American players, see Boyle, 1963, pp. 108-113.

6. Charnofsky (1967), for example, presents evidence which suggests that while there exists a degree of racial prejudice among a number of players, the majority of athletes in professional baseball hold favorable attitudes toward minority group members on their teams. We note, however, that off the field the problem of discrimination may be a horse of a different color. For example, the 1969 season is the first where several teams have set forth explicit policies assuring the racial integration of teammates on the road via mixed room assignments.

7. As is evident from Table 4, we were unable to obtain relevant data for a number of seasons for the two major leagues between 1956 and 1967. However, there does not appear to be much change in playing personnel from one year to the next. Moreover, our figures provide a conservative estimate of the racial composition of professional baseball, in that the missing data includes more white players.

It was not difficult to keep track of a small number of players switching leagues over the period sampled, but a small number of players switching playing positions over the period covered did pose a bit of a problem. We arbitrarily assigned them the position where they had played the most games in their major league career.

8. An assist is the official credit awarded in the scoring of a game to a player who throws a ball in such a way that it results in a putout. Data regarding assists were obtained from the *American League Red Book* and the *National League Green Books*. These are annual publications of the two major leagues which report vital statistics about all players, teams and games each season.

9. In the scoring of a game, the strikeouts made by the pitcher which are caught by the catcher are recorded as putouts for the catcher. For purposes of analysis we considered such putouts as assists. We reasoned that the catcher calls the pitch and assists in making the strikeouts by receiving the thrown ball from the

pitcher. We note that a strikeout is recorded regardless of whether the ball is caught or not. An example of the consistency of the number of annual assists by position for both leagues is the following data for the 1963, 1964 and 1965 seasons:

Year	American League	Position	National League
1963	10,508	C	9,946
	4,724	SS	4,749
	4,427	2nd	4,253
	3,176	3rd	3,029
	1,119	1st	1,002
	325	Out	323
1964	10,713	C	10,112
	4,775	SS	4,939
	4,425	2nd	4,404
	3,225	3rd	3,096
	1,059	1st	1,018
	308	Out	322
1965	10,461	C	10,454
	4,696	SS	4,886
	4,274	2nd	4,831
	3,341	3rd	3,093
	1,050	1st	1,045
	274	Out	292

10. In Grusky's study about twenty-five per cent of the managers were found to be ex-catchers. Recent investigations by Loy and Sage concerning collegiate baseball show that college coaches and college team captains are most often recruited from infield positions; especially that of catcher. Moreover, their findings indicate that, although there are relatively few Negroes playing college baseball, there are proportionately more Negroes in outfield than infield positions.

11. It is only recently that a token number of former Negro athletes have been hired as coaches in professional sports; and to date there are no Negro head coaches in major league football or Negro managers in major league baseball.

12. See Hopkins, 1964, pp. 112-117 for a critique of this proposition.

13. This article is based solely on an unrevised paper presented at the International Seminar on the Sociology of Sport, organized by the Research Institute of the Swiss Federal School of Gymnastics and Sports and the University of Bern on behalf of the International Committee for the Sociology of Sport, September 7-13, 1969 at Macolin, Switzerland. Since the presentation of this paper there has appeared two reports which treat the topic in much greater depth and which offer selected findings somewhat different from those given above; see: Anthony H. Pascal and Leonard A. Rapping, "Racial Discrimination in Organized Baseball," (Report for the RAND Corporation, Santa Monica, California, May 1969); and, Garry Smith and Carl F. Grindstaff, "Race and Sport in Canada," (University of Western Ontario, October 1970).

REFERENCES

American Football League Official Autographed Yearbook 1968. Dallas: Sports Underwriters, Inc., 1968.

American League Red Book. Boston: American League Publicity Department.

Baseball Register. St. Louis: Sporting News.

Berelson, B. and Steiner G. A., *Human Behavior—an Inventory of Scientific Findings.* New York: Harcourt, Brace World, Inc., 1964.

Blalock H. M. Jr., "Occupational Discrimination: Some Theoretical Propositions," *Social Problems* 9 (1962): 240-247.

Boyle H. H., *Sport—Mirror of American Life.* Boston: Little, Brown Co., 1963.

Charnofsky, H., "The Major League Professional Baseball Player: Self-Conception Versus The Popular Image," *International Review of Sport Sociology* 3 (1968): 39-55. Polish Scientific Publishers, Warsaw.

Grusky, O., "The Effects of Formal Structure on Managerial Recruitment: A Study of Baseball Organization," *Sociometry* 26 (1963): 345-353.

Homans, G. C., *The Human Group.* New York: Harcourt, Brace World, Inc., 1950.

Hopkins, T. K., *The Exercise of Influence in Small Groups.* Totowa, N. J.: Bedminster Press, 1964.

Loy, J. W. and Sage, J. N., "The Effects of Formal Structure on Organizational Leadership: An Investigation of Interscholastic Baseball Teams." Paper presented at the second International Congress of Sport Psychology, November 1, 1968 in Washington, D. C.

Moore, H. E., "Discrimination," pp. 203-204 in Julius Gould and William L. Kolb (eds.), *A Dictionary of the Social Sciences.* New York: The Free Press of Glencoe, 1964.

Olsen, J., *The Black Athlete—a shameful story.* New York: Time, Inc., 1968.

National Football League Official Autographed Yearbook 1968. Dallas: Sports Underwriters, Inc., 1968.

National League Green Book. Cincinnati: National League Public Relations Department.

Rosenblatt, A., "Negroes in Baseball: The Failure of Success," *Trans-Action* 4 (September, 1967): 51-53, with a reply by Whitehead 4 (October, 1967): 63-64.

Siegel, S., *Nonparametrics Statistics.* New York: McGraw-Hill Book Co., Inc., 1956.

"Study Indicates Cracking Majors Harder for Blacks." Los Angeles: Times, May 15, 1969, Part III, p. 3.

Zanger, J., *Pro Football 1968.* New York: Pocket Books, 1968.

Ascription and Position:
A Comparative Analysis of "Stacking"
in Professional Football

Donald W. Ball

One of the emergent characteristics of the sociology of the sixties was the development of a substantive focus on sport. Among the major reasons for this development were the increasingly large number of persons and volume of resources involved in sport and the recognition of the preeminently social nature of sport as a form of conduct.

Sport as a social activity is particularly amenable to general sociological scrutiny because sports *qua* games may be heuristically treated as closed systems, with explicit and codified normative regulations, for example, rulebooks, and precise and public measures of outcomes, performances, efficiency, and the like. Such an approach is basically one of a "sociology *through* sport," using sport data to address more general sociological questions.

Although sport may be treated "as if" it is a bounded system, empirically it is embedded in the larger society—acting and reacting and mirroring that broader societal context. Sport is neither trivial nor merely a laboratory for the sociologist, but an important dimension of human experience and concern. This perspective is one that focuses on "sport and society" or the "sociology *of* sport," viewing sport as a social reality *sui generis*.

The following discussion will be concerned with patterns of differential treatment of professional football players in Canada and the United States. Such differences will be considered both with regard to (i) the variables of race and national origins, that is, a sociology of sport; and (ii) in terms of which of two thereoretical models can best account for any differences found; that is, a sociology through sport.

Reprinted from *The Canadian Review of Sociology and Anthropology*, 10:2, (1973) by permission of the publisher.

APPROACHING THE PROBLEM

In considering the differential treatment of professional athletes on the basis of race, there are two broad approaches. One, "the Jackie Robinson story" basically says (regarding blacks), "you never had it so good" (Boyle, 1963; Olsen, 1968). This view emphasizes the opportunities for mobility made available to minority group members by professional sport. Thus, professional sport is seen as an accessible "legitimate opportunity structure" (Cloward and Ohlin, 1960).

The other view might be called "the Harry Edwards corrective" (Edwards, 1969). This perspective acknowledges the availability of entrance into sport for minority members, but points to continued discriminatory practices within the context of the structure of sport. Of special attention by this school have been their allegations of "stacking."

Stacking, the practice of positioning athletes in team sports on the basis of particularistic rather than universalistic characteristics has been alleged and described by Edwards (1969), Meggysey (1970), and Olsen (1968); and empirically demonstrated by Loy and McElvogue (1970), along with confirmatory research by Brower (1972). Essentially, *stacking in sports involves assignment to a playing position, an achieved status, on the basis of an ascribed status* (Davis, 1949:96—117). A focal concern by sociologists of sport has been the stacking of team members on the ascriptive basis of race, (for example, Loy and McElvogue, 1970; Brower, 1972; and Edwards, 1969). As is the case with much material of a sociological perspective, the works cited above are primarily or exclusively referring to situations in the United States.

In the following discussion, the theoretical formulation and empirical investigation begun on U.S. professional football by Loy and McElvogue (1970) will be applied to Canadian sport, replicated on race (also see Smith and Grindstaff, 1970; Barnes, 1971), and *extended to national origins* with comparative data drawn from the Canadian Football League (CFL). Additionally, an alternative theory will be proposed as of equal or greater power in explaining Canadian patterns.

THE CENTRALITY THEORY

Drawing upon Grusky's theory of organization structure (1963) and Blalock's propositions regarding occupational discrimination (1962), Loy and McElvogue (1970:5—7) have formulated a theory to explain the disproportionate presence—stacking—of blacks in some positions, and their practical absence from others in professional football and baseball. In doing so, they conceive of teams as work organizations, and the positions within them as analogous to occupations.

Employing baseball teams *qua* formal organizations for his empirical examples, Grusky has asserted that the formal structure of an organization systematically patterns the behaviours associated with its constituent positions along three interdependent dimensions: spatial location, nature of organizational tasks, and frequency of interaction. The major theoretical thrust of Grusky's organizational model is contained in the statement that "all else being equal, the more central one's spatial location: (1) the greater the likelihood dependent or coordinative tasks will be performed and (2) the greater the rate of interaction with occupants of other positions. Also, the performance of dependent tasks is positively related to frequency of interaction" (1963:346).

Centrality, then refers to (i) spatial location and (ii) the attendant kinds of tasks and interaction rates. From a structural standpoint it is best operationalized, at least in the case of fixed-position team sports taken-as-formal-organizations (for example, football, or baseball), by spatial location.

Like Grusky, Blalock's consideration of interaction, task dependency, and occupational discrimination turned to baseball for empirical examples to bolster the theoretical propositions. Blalock's propositions can be readily synthesized with Grusky's model. As Loy and McElvogue put it, "since the dimensions of interaction and task dependency treated by Blalock are included in the concept of centrality, we integrated his propositions under a more general one, stating that *discrimination is positively related to centrality*" (1970:7; emphasis added).

CENTRALITY AND PROFESSIONAL TEAM SPORTS

In professional team sports a specific variant of occupational discrimination is *stacking*: the arbitrary inclusion or exclusion of persons vis-à-vis a playing position on the basis of ascriptive status, for example, race. Thus, Loy and McElvogue predicted as their specific theoretical proposition that stacking, a form of "racial segregation in professional team sports is positively related to centrality" (1970:7).

THE ORIGINAL TEST OF THE PROPOSITION

For their first test of the prediction, Loy and McElvogue turned to major league baseball in the United States. Using 1967 data and treating catchers and infield positions as central, the outfield as non-central (and excluding pitchers as unique and neither), they found that 7 out of 10 white players ($N = 132$) occupied central positions, while only 1 out of

TABLE 1

Central and Non-Central Position on Offence and Defence[a]

	Offence	Defence
Central:	center	linebackers
	quarterback	
	guards	
Non-central	tackles	tackles
	ends	ends
	flankers, wide receivers	backs, safeties
	running backs	

[a]Adapted from Loy and McElvogue (1970:10-12).

3 blacks ($N = 55$) were so located (1970:8—10; also see 15—24). Statistically significant beyond the .0005 level, the baseball data were strongly supportive of their model and the stacking prediction it generated. They next turned their attention to U.S. professional football.

THE CASE OF PROFESSIONAL FOOTBALL

Although there are differences between the rules and positions regarding professional football in Canada and the United States, these are increasingly more historical than actually differentiating (on the convergence between the two games, see Cosentino, 1969). Table 1 indicates the central and non-central positions which characterize both offensive defensive formations, and subsumes the minor differences between the two sets of procedures in force on each side of the border.

DATA

Loy and McElvogue's American football data (1970:11-13) were drawn from yearbooks for the 1968 seasons of the American Football League and the National Football League and classified all starting players (except specialty teams) by offensive or defensive position, along with race, black or white. All data on American professional football employed in the following is taken from their study.

The data on the Canadian Football League personnel presented here is for the 1971 season. It is drawn from the *Canadian Football League Player Photos, Official 1971 Collection*, a widely distributed promotional device, and checked where possible against other and similar sources (on the rationale for using such mass-circulation-based data see Ball, 1967: 452-453). These materials provide a 75 per cent sample of the 32-man roster allowed each of the nine teams in the league, and like the Loy and McElvogue data, are based upon pre-season, but accurate, forecasts. For each player information is available on position, on race (from a photograph), and usually on national origin and on prior education and playing experience. Although a 75 per cent sample should yield an $N = 216$, due to missing information it is reduced slightly here to $N = 209$. On the whole, visual inspection suggests the sample is representative. However, it is slightly biased toward imports in terms of national origins.

Although this attribute, national origin, is an important independent variable, its bias is neutralized by percentaging against the unbalanced marginal totals. However, because of the limitations of the sample, the following is claimed to be no more than a "demonstration" (Garfinkel, 1964), rather than a more rigorous "investigation." (On the methodological problems of using rosters, for example the lack of stability within seasons, see Smith and Grindstaff, 1970:60-62). Finally, though the data cover only one season in each case, other research has shown aggregate sport data to be quite stable over time (on international figure skating, see Ball, 1971; on baseball, see Loy and McElvogue, 1970:15-22).

CENTRALITY, STACKING, AND RACE: A COMPARISON

According to the Loy-McElvogue hypothesis, blacks in professional football will be stacked at non-central positions and excluded from central ones. Comparing their data on the American NFL (columns B and D of Table 2) with data on the CFL (columns A and C) indicates a similar pattern in each case: blacks are virtually excluded from central positions in professional football on either side of the border. The similarity of the patterns is as striking as the moral implications are obvious; neither virtues nor vices are respecters of national borders (also see Smith and Grindstaff, 1970:47-66; and more generally, Cosentino, 1969, on the "Americanization" of Canadian football).

CENTRALITY, NATIONAL ORIGINS, AND STACKING

Unlike professional football in the United States, Canadian football has been historically cross-cut by another ascriptive status of its players; national origin, Canadians and imports (for the latter, read Americans). Americans have been playing football in Canada at least since 1912 in the forerunners of the CFL and the rugby unions (Cosentino, 1969:48-49).

TABLE 2

Race of Players By Centrality of Position for Canadian
and U.S. Professional League (adjusted percentages)[a]

Position	Percentage of whites		Percentage of blacks	
	(A) Cdn.	(B) US[b]	(C) Cdn.	(D) US[b]
Offence				
Central	47	45	06	02
Non-Central	53	55	94	98
Total percentage	100	100	100	100
N	97[a]	220	19[a]	66
Defence				
Central	28	37	—	06
Non-Central	72	63	100	94
Total percentage	100	100	100	100
N	83[a]	192	12	94

[a]Percentage adjusted to compensate for the additional position in Canadian football. This position is non-central; thus the non-central raw number is multiplied by
.875 (7/8) to equalize with US formations. Adjusted base numbers, upon which percentages are calculated are: 97 = 90; 83 = 75; and 19 = 17. This procedure is not
necessary in subsequent tables where comparisons are limited to CFL players only.
[b]US data for 1968 from Loy and McElvogue (1970:10-12).

It should be understood that the categorization of national origins to
be used here, Canadians and imports, is not the same as that used by the
CFL itself. The League's definition emphasizes prior experience as well
as citizenship and nativity, the criterion herein employed. Thus, an American player without US high school or college experience becomes a non-
import under League definitions. Put another way, national origins are
ascriptive, while League definitions may be achieved. Consistency suggests the utility of opting for the former as an analytical variable.

CANADIANS AND IMPORTS: THE DATA

When nativity is considered, the null form of the stacking hypothesis
predicts no differences between the proportion of centrality located Canadians and imports. In other words, the relationship should be one of
parity.

TABLE 3

National Origins of CFL Players and Centrality of Position

Position	Percentage of Canadians	Percentage of Imports
Central, all	27	35
Non-Central, all	73	65
Total	100	100
N	94	110
Offence		
Central	34	41
Non-central	66	59
Total	100	100
N	50	64
Defence		
Central	18	26
Non-Central	82	74
Total	100	100
N	44	46

Following Loy and McElvogue (1970), Table 3 presents the distribution of imports (Americans) and Canadians in the CFL in terms of the centrality model. It is clear that whether one looks at over-all patterns, or at offensive or defensive alignments separately, imports predominate over Canadian players in terms of the proportion of central positions they occupy. The difference on offence is particularly interesting, since almost half of the central Canadians are at one position only ($N = 8$), that of centre. Smith and Grindstaff (1970:36) have described the centre as a position usually manned by Canadians and "generally acknowledged to require less skill." Thus, if central positions are assumed to be in some ways more "difficult" as well as more "desirable," Canadians predominate at only the least of these. Additionally, because of the restictive quota on imports (maximum of 14 out of 32 players *per* team in 1971), quantitative differences are actually more extreme than their apparent magnitude.[2]

To demonstrate that Canadians and imports are differentially distributed is not to demonstrate "stacking" *per se,* however. It is frequently alleged that imports are the more skilled players by virtue of their superior training rather than their ability; especially in terms of their college and university football experience (see former import Hardimon

TABLE 4

Prior Background Experience of CFL Players and Centrality of Position

Position	Percentage US College	Percentage Other
Central, all	31	20
Non-Central, all	69	80
Total	100	100
N	45	44
Offence		
Central	37	21
Non-Central	62	79
Total	100	100
N	32	14
Defence		
Central	15	20
Non-Central	85	80
Total	100	100
N	13	30
Central Positions		
Offence	86	33
Defence	14	67
Total	100	100
N	14	9

Curetan, quoted in Barnes, 1971:43-54). At the same time, although perhaps not widely recognized, the fact is that approximately half of the Canadians in the Canadian Football League played football while attending college or university in the United States. Such "crash courses" have often been the instigation of CFL teams themselves (Barnes, 1971).

Thus, examining Canadian players in terms of prior playing experience would allow for an assessment of a *training* versus *stacking* hypothesis. Table 4 presents data on Canadian players in terms of centrality and whether or not they played collegiate football in the United States or had some other form of prior experience, for example, Canadian university, junior football, or high school participation.

If training accounts for the differential positioning of imports and Canadians, it should virtually disappear in the cases of Canadians with US collegiate experience. From these data can be seen: (i) over-all, American collegiate experience is associated with centrality; (ii) that this association is especially marked on offence; but (iii) slightly reversed for the defensive unit. However, recalling Table 3, neither the over-all nor the offensive proportions of US trained Canadians at central positions reaches the percentage of such positions occupied by imports. Although these data do not compel the acceptance of a stacking hypothesis, they do argue the rejection of one based upon training alone.

The reversal of the association between US training and centrality when the defence is considered is somewhat anomalous. However, upon closer examination it appears to be at least partly artificial. Few US-trained Canadians play defence: less than half as many as the "others" without such experience (13 to 20). Further, most Canadians *cum* American collegians in central positions are on offensive units, while the reverse is true for those without such experience.

This last is part of a more general pattern. "Most teams play more of their imports on offense rather than defense because coaches feel that normally it takes more talent and experience to play offense, and that it is possible to train Canadian players with less experience to do an adequate job of defense" (Smith and Grindstaff, 1970:60). The data in Table 5 substantiate this statement. Imports predominate over Canadians on offence, but US-trained Canadians do so especially compared to those without such experience.

CENTRALITY: AN OVERVIEW

In general, the ascriptive statuses of Canadians and imports do appear to be differentially positioned in terms of the centrality model. Assuming, for whatever reasons, that central positions are more desirable or more rewarding, the ascribed status of imports is associated with such location, and that of Canadian with the alternative of non-centrality. When Canadians are categorized as those with US collegiate football experience, or those without it, the deficit position is explained and reduced, but not removed.

Still, the differences are not of sufficient magnitude to warrant an exclusive employment of the centrality model as an explanatory tool in the case of differential positioning by national origins in the CFL. In sum, centrality shows more power as regards stacking and the ascriptive criterion of race than it does regarding nativity.

TABLE 5

Offensive and Defensive Players in the CFL
By National Origin and Prior Background Experience

Position	Percentage by national origin		Percentage by background, Canadians only	
	Imports	Canadians	US College	Others
Offence	58	53	71	26
Defence	42	47	29	74
Total	100	100	100	100
N	110	94	45	44

PRIMARY AND SUPPORTING PLAYERS:
AN ALTERNATIVE MODEL

As does the Loy and McElvogue model, this model looks at football teams as a set of positions constituting a formal work organization. However, where the centrality model looks to spatial location, the primary-supporting model looks to organizational goals and the nature of organizationally defined tasks.

The overreaching goal of a football team is to win games. To accomplish this, teams are divided into subunits or separate organizations within organizations: the offensive and defensive units.

Within each of these organizations, offence and defence, positions can be differentiated on the basis of task-orientation into primary and supporting positions. The former, the *primary positions* are those within the organization charged with the basic achievement and realization of the organization's goals. *Supporting positions,* on the other hand, are defined as those responsible for assisting the primary positions in their efforts toward goal-achievement, but not ordinarily directly involved in such accomplishment. Put grossly, primary positions (and thus their occupants, the players) are doers: supporting positions are helpers (for a more generalized and abstract, but similar approach, see Etziono, 1961; 93-96).

When the offensive unit of a football team is considered in terms of the primary-supporting model, with its goal of moving the ball and scoring points, the primary positions are the quarterback, the running backs, and the pass catchers, that is, the ends, flankers, and wide receivers. These are the positions sometimes called by the coaches the "skill positions" (see,

TABLE 6

Primary and Supporting Positions on Offence and Defence

	Offence	Defence
Primary	quarterback[a]	tackles
	running backs[a]	ends
	flankers, wide receivers[b]	linebackers
	ends[b]	
Supporting	centre	backs
	guards	safeties
	tackles	

[a]Proactive
[b]Reactive

for instance, Oates, 1972). The supporting positions, whose task is to assist the goal-directed activities of the primary positions, are the offensive guards, the offensive tackles, and the centre. These are the basic positions charged with blocking so that others may advance the ball. Although the centre handles the ball on every play, it is only to deliver it to the quarterback (except in kicking situations), at the quarterback's initiative, and from a symbolically subordinate posture. It may be noted that although the offensive guards and centre are central in terms of spatial location their tasks are supporting rather than primary.

A further refinement within the primary offensive positions is the distinction between those that are *proactive* and initiate goal-directed activity and/or carry it out independently, and those that are *reactive* or dependent upon the activities of other primary positions for participation. Quarterbacks initiate activity and act independently, and running backs act independently once in posession of the ball: these positions are proactive. Ends, flankers, and wide receivers must wait for a pass to realize their primary, goal-related tasks: they are reactive.

The language of football points to the primary-supporting distinction within the defensive alignment. The common collective term for the defensive backs and safeties is the "secondary." By implication other defensive positions are primary—and so they are. In combination or alone it is the task of the defensive tackles and ends, the "front four," along with the linebackers, to stop running plays before the ball carrier can get past them, and/or get to the quarterback before he can throw a pass. Only if these positions fail to do so does the secondary formally come into play to stop a runner who has progressed downfield or to break up or intercept a pass or to stop a successful receiver from making further

TABLE 7

Primary and Supporting Players in the CFL
By National Origin and Prior Background Experience

Position	Percentage by national origin		Percentage by background, Canadians only	
	Imports	Canadians	US College	Others
Primary, all	68	49	47	50
Supporting, all	32	51	53	50
Total	100	100	100	100
N	110	94	45	44
Offence:				
Primary	73	50	47	57
Supporting	27	50	53	43
Total	100	100	100	100
N	64	50	32	14
Defence:				
Primary	61	48	46	47
Supporting	39	52	54	53
Total	100	100	100	100
N	46	44	13	30
Offence, Primary Only:				
Proactive	72	36	47	25
Reactive	28	64	53	75
Total	100	100	100	100
N	47	25	15	8

progress. Thus, on defence the primary positions are the defensive tackles and ends and the linebackers. The supporting positions are the defensive backs and safeties of the secondary. (Table 6 summarizes the above six paragraphs.)

NATIONALITY AND EXPERIENCE: THE DATA

The data in Table 7 array the same information in terms of the primary-supporting model which were shown in Tables 3 and 4 with the centrality model.

As the data show, in all cases imports are more likely to occupy primary rather than supporting positions, while in only one case, offence, do Canadians reach the parity of a 50-50 split. This despite the fact that over half (56 per cent in 1971) of each roster must be Canadian. The difference between imports and Canadians is most dramatic in the case of the initiating, independent proactive offence positions and the dependent reactors: where imports are proactors in almost three out of every four cases, Canadians are reactors two out of three times. The effect of US collegiate experience is mixed and relatively slight except in the case of the proactive-reactive distinction, where US collegiate experience is almost twice as likely to be associated with the occupancy of proactive positions compared to a lack of such experience. But never does this former group equal the proportion of imports at primary positions in general.

Comparison with the Loy-McElvogue centrality model (Tables 3 and 4) indicates that the primary-supporting model shows much greater differentiation with regard to national origins of CFL players. However, the centrality scheme was originally developed to explain racial differentiation in professional team sports. Thus, Table 8 compares Canadians and imports while controlling for race.

As Table 8 shows, we might speak, none too figuratively it seems, about the "white niggers of the CFL" (after Vallières, 1971). If the assumption is again made that, like central positions, primary positions are the more desirable and rewarding—then only in the case of defence where Canadians are stacked (see Table 5 and accompanying discussion) does the proportion of Canadians exceed that of blacks in primary positions. Further, blacks themselves are traditionally stacked in the supporting defensive secondary (Loy and McElvogue, 1970:13).

SALARY

The assumption that central and/or primary positions are somehow more rewarding and more desirable has been invoked several times in the preceding pages (also see Homans, 1950:140-144). If the assumption is valid, the question becomes one of measurement: what data might be brought to bear to compare (i) the differential rewards of central and non-central along with primary and secondary positions in terms of national origins of the players; and (ii) the magnitude of these differences when it is the two models that are compared.

TABLE 8

Primary and Supporting Players in the CFL
By National Origin and Race of Imports

Position	Percentage of imports		Percentage of Canadians
	Whites	Blacks	
Primary, all	71	60	49
Supporting, all	29	40	51
Total	100	100	100
N	80	30	94
Offence			
Primary	71	79	50
Supporting	29	21	50
Total	100	100	100
N	45	19	50
Defence			
Primary	71	27	48[a]
Supporting	29	73	52
Total	100	100	100
N	35	11	44
Offence, primary only			
Proactive	75	67	36
Reactive	25	33	64
Total	100	100	100
N	32	15	25

[a]Includes one black

Salary provides just such a measure. Barnes (1971:144-145) lists average salaries by position for each team and for the CFL as a whole for the 1967 season. Table 9 presents this salary information. In interpreting these figures, a *caveat* should be kept in mind. Barnes's definitions of Canadians and imports are those of the League, not the criterion of national origin used here. Thus, some Canadians as *per* League classification may be imports or Americans in terms of actual nativity. Therefore, salary differentials are, if anything, conservative, since some high-salaried Americans could be classified as Canadians by the League's standards.

TABLE 9

Differences in Average Salaries: Centrality and Primary-Supporting Models by National Origins[a]

	Centrality Model			Primary-Supporting Model		
	Imports	Canadians	Difference		Imports	Canadians	Difference
Offence				*Offence*			
Central	$13,300	$13,200	$ 100	Primary	$13,612	$12,295	$1,317
Non-Central	13,087	8,958	4,129	Supporting	12,783	8,516	5,267
			X=2,114				X=3,483
Defence				*Defence*			
Central	11,375	8,625	2,750	Primary	12,191	8,708	3,483
Non-Central	12,783	8,516	4,267	Supporting	13,750	8,050	5,700
			X=3,508				X=4,591
Combined average			2,811				3,941

[a]Calculated from Barnes, 1971:144-145

424

The findings emerging from Table 9 are of several kinds. First, in all comparisons imports are rewarded more highly than Canadians. Vallières has described "white niggers" as "the cheap labor that the predators of industry, commerce, and high finance are so fond of" (1971:19). Originally applied to Francophones vis-à-vis Anglophones, "white nigger" also fits the salary situation of Canadians in the Canadian Football League.

Secondly, in the case of imports on defence, the expected salary differential is reversed for both models. Since blacks are traditionally stacked here the finding is all the more surprising. In all other cases (six out of eight), however, differences are as expected, with central and primary players, whether Canadians or imports, reported as more highly rewarded.

Thirdly, when the two models are compared, the magnitude of differential rewards is greater for the primary-supporting model compared to that based upon centrality—in effect, validating the greater utility of the former over the latter, at least in the case of Canadian football.

DISCUSSION

The purpose of this paper has been twofold: (i) from the standpoint of the sociology *of* sport, to investigate patterns of stacking of imports and Canadians in the Canadian Football League, using the basic ascriptive difference of nativity rather than race; and (ii) from the perspective of sociology through sport to compare two models of ascription-based organizational-occupational differentiation.

Are Canadians discriminated against in the CFL? The data are relatively clear-cut. They are less likely to occupy central positions than imports, and still less likely to perform at primary positions compared to secondary ones. Further, their average salaries are lower than those of imports, especially within the context of the primary-supporting model. At the same time, Canadian players with US collegiate football experience are more likely than other Canadians to be located at central or primary positions, though never to the same extent as imports. Thus, while US collegiate experience reduces the differences between imports and Canadians, these differences do not disappear. Is this discrimination? Unless discrimination is operationally defined it remains a moral meaning, subject to the relativization of all such terms. However, a majority of roster positions coupled with a minority of primary or central positions does demonstrate a *prima facie* case worthy of further consideration.

Both Loy and McElvogue (1970:18) and Smith and Grindstaff (1970), although referring to race, argue that stacking is a function of team management rather than of the players themselves. In 1969 in the CFL all 9 head coaches were Americans, as were 31 of the 32 assistant coaches, and 6 of the 9 general managers (the most recent year for which data were readily available (Smith and Grindstaff, 1970:4).

In effect what seems to happen is this: when Americans coaching in the CFL have a first-year prospect from the United States, they also have a set of expectations about his abilities based upon their knowledge of the calibre of football characteristics of the rookie's school, the level of competition, the coaching he likely received, etc. Alternatively, a new American prospect may have had professional experience in the States to generate such expectations among the coaches. For the Canadian collegiate football player (or one up from junior football) no such expectations exist. In a word, the American coaches know a lot about American football. They know little about football in Canada outside of the CFL. Thus, they are more likely to (i) go with the American import, who if not a proven quantity is likely to generate great expectations; and (ii) assume that Canadians, especially those without US collegiate experience, are simply less skilled or talented since they haven't been measured on the recognized testing grounds of the US playing fields.

If discrimination is too strong a word, *benign neglect* is not. These same coaches are, after all, responsible for the similar distribution of blacks at central and non-central positions in both American and Canadian professional football.

The question can also be raised as to why the centrality model is most powerful with regard to stacking and race and works best in the United States, and the primary-supporting model is more useful in accounting for stacking by national origin in the CFL.

First of all, though both models are concerned with ascription, there is a vast difference between race and nativity. And although there are many stereotypical assumptions about black athletes, especially in the US (see for instance, Edwards and Russell, 1971; Brower, 1972), it is not clear that there are similarly extensive attributions about Canadians, and by Americans concerning the former's athletic ability (however, see Barnes, 1971).

Secondly, the centrality model was first (and most thoroughly) tested with regard to baseball, while the primary-supporting model was formulated specifically with regard to Canadian football, thus helping to account for its greater power regarding the CFL.

Thirdly, the centrality scheme emphasizes ascriptive differentiation on the basis of extra-organizational social characteristics, for example, race and interaction patterns. The primary-supporting model starts with organizational characteristics and then looks for ascriptive differentiation among members—and in the case of American-controlled but quota-bound Canadian football it finds them.

In the US situation there are no formal rules which require blacks to be on team rosters. In Canada, a fixed proportion of each roster must be Canadian. The primary-supporting model points to where those least talented or skilled will, in effect, be likely to do the least damage. Thus, blacks in the US (and US imports in Canada) play strictly on the basis of ability—in fact they may have to be better than their white counterparts (Rosenblatt, 1967)—but Canadians in the CFL are guaranteed their quota. Therefore, a task-based model should be more useful in predicting where they may be stacked, as the primary-supporting scheme in fact is.

In sum, Canadians in the CFL are stacked: on defence, in supporting and reactive positions; and even with US collegiate experience they are excluded from the more rewarding and desirable positions: This differential treatment is also reflected in the lower salaries they receive compared to those of imports. Whether caused by discrimination or benign neglect is a matter of definition—even if functionally equivalent in terms of consequences.

Needless to say, the usual *caveats* concerning further research apply here. The explanation of stacking which postulates a lack of expectations about Canadian players is speculative, but worthy of further interest. If valid, it is just one more tile in the mosaic of the branch plant economy. Finally, as will be obvious to many, this is not a "fan's-eye" view, but a sociological one. The fan may look for, and to, exceptions such as high-salaried, Canadian-trained quarterback Russ Jackson; the sociologist points instead to patterns. And, as has often been the case, the exposition of deviant-case analysis by laymen often functions to bolster the state of things as they are.

NOTES

1. I am indebted to Cameron Ball, Neil Ball, and Philip Pollard for their help in procuring some of the data on players in the Canadian Football League used in this article. This project was partially supported by a University of Victoria Faculty Research Grant (08518). Helpful comments were received from colleagues when earlier versions of this material were presented in seminars at the University of Alberta and the University of Calgary; from Brian Currie of the University of Victoria, and John Loy of the University of Massachusetts. A more extensive formulation was presented to the symposium on Man; Sport, and Contemporary Society, Queens College of the City University of New York, March 1972.
2. Unfortunately, sample data do not allow for this factor to be weighed or otherwise controlled. Its effect is to minimize actual differences, and to make apparent differences more conservative.

REFERENCES

Ball, Donald W.
  1967   "Toward a sociology of toys: inanimate objects, socialization and the demography of the doll world." *Sociological Quarterly,* 8:447-458.
  1971   "The cold war on ice: the politics of international figure skating." Paper presented to the third Canadian Symposium on Sport Psychology, Vancouver.

Barnes, LaVerne
  1971   *The Plastic Orgasm.* Toronto: McClelland and Stewart.

Blalock, Hubert M., Jr.
  1962   "Occupational discrimination: Some theoretical propositions." *Social Problems,* 9:240-247.

Boyle, Robert H.
  1963   *Sport—Mirror of American Life.* Boston: Little, Brown.

Brower, Jonathon J.
  1972   "The racial basis of the division of labor among players in the National Football League as a function of racial stereotypes." Presented to the Pacific Sociological Association, Portland, April 13-15.

Cloward, Richard A., and Lloyd E. Ohlin
  1960   *Delinquency and Opportunity.* Glencoe: The Free Press.

Cosentino, Frank
  1969   *Canadian Football: The Grey Cup Years.* Toronto: Musson.

Davis, Kingsley
  1949   *Human Society.* New York: Macmillan.

Edwards, Harry
  1969   *The Revolt of the Black Athlete.* New York: The Free Press.

Edwards, Harry, and Bill Russell
  1971   "Racism: a prime factor in the determination of black athletic superiority." Presented to the American Sociological Association, Denver, September.

Etzioni, Amitai
  1961   *A Comparative Analysis of Complex Organizations.* Glencoe: The Free Press.

Garfinkel, Harold
  1964   "Studies of the routine grounds of everyday activities." *Social Problems,* 11:255-250.

Grusky, Oscar
  1963   "The effects of formal structure on managerial recruitment: a study of baseball organization." *Sociometry,* 26:345-353.

Homans, George C.
  1950   *The Human Group.* New York: Harcourt, Brace and World.

Loy, John W., and Joseph F. McElvogue
  1970   "Racial segregation in American sport." *International Review of Sport Sociology,* 5:5-24.

Meggysey, Dave
  1970   *Out of Their League.* Berkeley: Ramparts Press.

Oates, Bob
    1972   Column on the 1971 National Football League all-star team. *The Sporting News*, 173 (January 15):17.
Olsen, Jack
    1968   *The Black Athlete—A Shameful Story*. New York, Time.
Rosenblatt, Aaron
    1967   "The failure of success." *Trans-action*, 4:51-53.
Smith, Gary, and Carl F. Grindstaff
    1970   "Race and sport in Canada." London: University of Western Ontario (mimeo).
Vallieres, Pierre
    1971   *White Niggers of America*. (Trans. by Joan Pinkham). New York and London: Monthly Review Press.

Ethnic Soccer Clubs in Milwaukee:
A Study in Assimilation

John C. Pooley

INTRODUCTION

Sport has shown itself to be a factor in forming a point of contact between ethnic groups who find themselves living in close proximity. Expatriate groups in African countries, missionaries and traders in isolated communities and military forces representing different nations[2] are good examples of this. Immigrants who become lodged in already established "advanced" societies are equally affected. For example, West Indians who emigrate to Britain, Southern Europeans who emigrate to Australia and diverse ethnic groups immigrating to the United States would fall into this category. Whenever members of an ethnic group move to another society, some degree of assimilation occurs and their survival depends upon it.

The primary purpose of this study was to determine the role of sport in assimilation. More specifically, the study endeavored to determine the significance of the structure and function of ethnic soccer clubs in the assimilation of their members.

The terms used in this study are defined below:

Assimilation
Assimilation is a process of interpenetration and fusion in which persons and groups acquire the memories, sentiments, and attitudes of other persons or groups, and, by sharing their experiences and history, are incorporated with them in a common cultural life.[3]

From the definition, it is clear that "acculturation" is included. As Gordon[4] has commented, the phrases "sharing their experiences" and "incorporating with them in a common cultural life" suggest the added criterion of social structure relationships.

430

Ethnic group. An ethnic group[5] is a group with a shared feeling of peoplehood.[6] According to Tumin,

> The term is most frequently applied to any group which differs in one or several aspects of its patterned, socially-transmitted way of life from other groups, or in the totality of that way of life or culture. Frequently, the group in question formerly enjoyed or still enjoys a separate political-national identity as well. Thus, various national-ethnic stocks in the United States would be considered as ethnic groups, e.g., Greeks, Poles, Hatians, Swedes, etc.[7]

Core Society. This term refers to "the dominant subsociety which provides the standard to which other groups adjust or measure their relative degree of adjustment."[8] According to Fishman,[9] the culture of this society is that "into which immigrants are assimilated, and it forms the one accepted set of standards, expectations, and aspirations, whether they pertain to clothing, household furnishings, personal beauty, entertainment or child rearing."

SCOPE AND SIGNIFICANCE

In this study an attempt was made to assess the factors which accelerate or retard the rate of assimilation. Saxon[10] and Warner Srole[11] have recognized that the recreational habits of a group have considerable import in the degree to which such a group may identify themselves with, or be isolated from, the core society. This point has greater relevance in an age when increased leisure time is available to the majority of the population.[12]

The existence of a sport club provides varying degrees of social intercourse between active and non-active members of the same club and between different clubs. The amount and type of social interaction practiced depends upon the size of the club, makeup of its members, arrangement of social events, and type of club accommodation.

More specifically, this study was concerned with determining the factors which influence assimilation. Questions asked were as follows:

1. To what degree does participation in ethnic soccer influence assimilation?
   a. Positively
   b. Negatively
2. What forces within ethnic soccer explain this influence?
   a. Structural factors
   b. Functional factors

While other studies have focused attention on the significance of religion,[13] color,[14] occupation,[15] and concentration,[16] on the acculturation or assimilation of ethnic groups, little has been written on the use of sport as a vehicle in this process. Participation in a single sport, albeit from a professional standpoint, as a means to assimilate, has been discussed by Andreano,[17] Handlin,[18] Saxon,[19] Boyle,[20] Shibutani,[21] and Weinberg.[22] These studies have been directed toward the individual's motives and attitude, whereas the present study was a departure from this approach in that it examined the role of the sport club as exemplified by the constitution of the club through the voice of the committee. Also, researchers have invariably confined themselves to a single ethnic group[23] or they have analyzed the many factors which have contributed to the acculturation or assimilation process of an ethnic group or groups in a city or rural community.[24]

This study was concerned with the role of the sport club (soccer), in a culturally heterogeneous setting; it sought to uncover club policy rather than individual attitude; it incorporated six ethnic groups in a confined area.

Milwaukee was chosen as the location for the study. Soccer was introduced in the city in 1913; the Wisconsin State Football Association was organized in 1914, and the Wisconsin State Soccer Football League was initiated in 1924.[25] With a population of 1,149,977 in Milwaukee, 326,666, or 28.4 percent comprised the element of foreign stock.[26] It was they who originally were responsible for the introduction of soccer into the area.

The choice of soccer allowed the study to pay some attention to the "foreign game" element. Soccer is a world game, being played on all five continents.[27] Of the larger countries, it is probably played least in America. By contrast, the countries of origin of the ethnic groups, represented by the sport clubs in Milwaukee, all have soccer as their major national outdoor game.

Since the sport of soccer is alien to the core society; and since soccer is the major national game of the countries of origin of the ethnic groups; and since members of the ethnic groups in question were involved in the activities of soccer clubs, either in the role of player, club official, manager, coach, spectator or social member; it is, therefore, hypothesized that ethnic soccer clubs in Milwaukee inhibit structural assimilation.

TABLE 1

Dates of Foundation and Ethnic Orientation[a] of
the Soccer Clubs in Milwaukee

Club	Date When Founded	Ethnic Orientation
A	1922	Croatian
B	1926	Hungarian
C	1929	German
D	1947	German
E	1950	Polish
F	1950	Serbian
G	1952	Italian
H	1953	German
I	1961	German
J	1964	Serbian

[a]Demonstrated by ethnicity of committee members, players, ordinary members, original members, or a combination of these.

POPULATION

The population used for this investigation was the ten soccer clubs located within the City of Milwaukee. Some statistical information relating to the ten clubs is included in Tables 1, 2, and 3. It will be seen from Table 1 that only three clubs were founded in the 1920's. Five clubs came into being within a span of seven years from 1947 to 1953 inclusive. The remaining two clubs, founded in 1961 and 1964, respectively, were formed from members of two existing clubs. Club 1 was originally the second team Club C. When friction developed between the first and the second teams, three men contacted members of the second team and invited them to form a new club.[28]

Club J was founded as the result of a split in the Eastern Orthodox Church which served the Serbian community. Club F represented the original community; the splinter group formed Club J because a sufficient number of players wished to play soccer.[29] Therefore, the last occasion when an entirely new club was formed was in 1953.

The ethnic orientation of the soccer clubs is seen in Table 1. Four ethnic groups are represented by one club as follows: Croatian, Hungarian, Polish and Italian. One ethnic group is represented by two clubs: Serbian. Another ethnic group is represented by four clubs: German.

TABLE 2

Details of Club Membership[a]

Club	Total Membership	Membership According to Age				
		Under 18	18-25 Years	25-35 Years	35-45 Years	Over 45
A	84	14	10	10	10	40
B	71	16	0	40	15	0
C	540	150	100	100	100	90
D	300	50	60	50	40	100
E	160	50	20	45	35	10
F	410	100	30	120	60	100
G	135	25	30	35	30	15
H	240	40	45	75	60	20
I	25	0	12	12	1	0
J	200	20	50	50	40	40

[a]Membership figures are an approximation. Several clubs did not have membership lists.

This does not mean that a club represented exclusively a single ethnic group. It does mean that each club in question was predominately represented by a single ethnic group, according to the criteria indicated in Table 1.

Details of club membership are indicated in Table 2. These figures are approximate only because it was difficult to obtain precise figures. Normally the payment of dues provides an exact indication of membership. However, in the case of some of the clubs, committee members indicated that dues were not demanded because clubs did not wish to restrict the use of the term "member" to those who had become paid members. In most instances, therefore, the figures were agreed upon following a consultation between the clubs' committee members. To be classed as a member, a person was required to demonstrate continuous interest in the club through support of club games or social functions, or through payment of dues.

A total of thirty-five teams were sponsored by the ten soccer clubs in 1967. These included eighteen adult teams and seventeen boys' teams. Details are indicated in Table 3.

TABLE 3

Details of the Number of Teams Sponsored by Each Club
and the Leagues[a] in Which They Play

Club	Number of Teams Sponsored	Major Division	Major Reserve	First Division	Junior	Inter- mediate	Midget
A	3	1	1				1
B	3	1	1				1
C	5	1	1		1	1	1
D	5	1	1		1	1	1
E	4	1	1			1	1
F	4			1	1		2
G	3	1	1				1
H	5	1	1		1	1	1
I	1			1			
J	2			2			

[a]The most senior division is the Major Division. At the end of each season, the last placed club is relegated to the First Division. The team which wins the First Division is promoted to the Major Division. Each Major Division team is required to sponsor a reserve team.

NATURE OF THE BASIC VARIABLES

The nature of the dependent variable and the independent variable, and the procedures used for operationalizing them, are given below.

Dependent Variable: Structural Assimilation

The concept of "structural assimilation" was defined for this study as follows: entrance of an ethnic group into primary group relations with the core society.

In his model of the seven assimilation variables, Gordon demonstrates the key role of structural assimilation in the total process of assimilation.[30] He reiterates: "Once structural assimilation has occurred, . . . all of the other types of assimilation will follow."[31] The implication of this is that the price of such assimilation is the disappearance of the ethnic group as a separate entity and evaporation of its distinctive values.[32]

TABLE 4

The Assimilation Variables

Subprocess or Condition	Type or Stage of Assimilation	Special Term
Change of cultural patterns to those of host society	Cultural or behavioral	Acculturation
Large scale entrance into cliques, clubs, and institutions of host society, on primary group level.	Structural assimilation	None
Large scale intermarriage	Marital assimilation	Amalgamation
Development of sense of peoplehood based exclusively on host society	Identificational assimilation	None
Absence of prejudice	Attitude receptional assimilation	None
Absence of discrimination	Behavioral receptional assimilation	None
Absence of value and power conflict	Civic assimilation	None

The level of assimilation of club members was sought by directly questioning the club committees. The committees were asked to state whether the other six stages of assimilation has occurred. These variables, together with a brief definition of each, are listed below. They are taken from Gordon's model.[33]

Cultural assimilation (acculturation): Change of cultural pattern to those of the core society.

Marital assimilation (amalgamation): Large scale intermarriage between club members and members of the core society.

Identificational assimilation: Development of a sense of peoplehood based exclusively on the core society.

Attitude receptional assimilation: An absence of prejudice by the core society.

Behavior receptional assimilation: An absence of discrimination by the core society.

Civic assimilation: An absence of value and power conflict between club members and the core society.

Independent Variable: Club Policy

The concept of "club policy" was defined for this study as follows: Courses or actions of a club, either explicit or implicit, in matters pertaining to its organization and activities, demonstrated by the actions it has taken in the past and the opinions held by its present committee.

It was found desirable to divide the concept into two aspects. These were operationalized by utilizing a number of elements in each case, as follows:

A. Characteristics of and Policies Concerning Membership
   1. Membership characteristics
     a. Naturalization and generation
     b. Occupation
     c. Ability to speak English
   2. Choice of language, either English or ethnic, demonstrated on the following occasions:
     a. At club meetings
     b. When playing soccer
     c. On social occasions
   3. Policy when accepting new members
   4. Policies for the actions taken to attract new members from:
     a. Other ethnic groups
     b. Core society
B. Policies Pertaining to Structure and Maintenance of Club
   1. Need for existence
   2. Election of officers
   3. Changes in organization
   4. Degree to which club perceives itself either as:
     a. Soccer club
     b. Social club
   5. Degree of organized social contact between the club and:
     a. Other clubs
     b. Core society

THE INSTRUMENT

Data collected in this investigation consisted of responses to a structured interview which was employed between April 7-23, 1967. The structured interview schedule consisted of two parts. The question for Part One were sent to the President of each club at last seven days before the date of the interview. These questions related to the club's history, the number of teams being sponsored, the size of the club, the age, and other details concerning members.

The questions for Part Two were answered spontaneously because it was considered that prior knowledge of them might have adversely affected the answers. The questions were related to club policy concerning membership: questions directed toward the assimilation of members; constitutional procedures; and the language used at club meetings, on social occasions and in the dressing room before a game.

The questions used in both parts of the interview were designed by the investigator. The assimilation variables in Part Two were culled from Gordon's paradigm.[34] An average of four committee members were interviewed from each club.

TREATMENT AND ANALYSIS OF DATA

This study utilized the responses of the club committees to the structured interview. Primarily, questions devoted to club policy formed the basis of the analysis. The study examined the relationship between the dependent and the independent variables and a logical analysis of that relationship.

The information accrued was analyzed in two stages: first, a measure of the level of assimilation already achieved by club members was determined by utilizing questions directly related to the six assimilation variables (excluding structural assimilation). Second, the effect of the policies of the clubs on structural assimilation was determined by utilizing the elements defined under the sub-heading "Independent Variable."

The hypothesis stated earlier, namely that ethnic soccer clubs in Milwaukee inhibit structural assimilation, was more specifically defined for this study as: club policy inhibits the structural assimilation of members.

The information was treated descriptively. In the first stage, the level of assimilation which had already occurred was analyzed deductively. In the second stage, each question was analyzed in terms of the independent variable. In conclusion, the relationship between certain elements of the independent variable and the dependent variable were deduced, and the hypothesis tested.

TABLE 5

Degree of Assimilation of Ethnic Soccer Clubs in Milwaukee Based upon the Model by Gordon

Club and Main Ethnic Group Represented[a]	Type of Assimilation[b]						
	Cultural		Marital	Identifi-cational	Attitude Receptional	Behavior Receptional	Civic
	Intrinsic	Extrinsic					
"A"—Croatian	No	Partly	No	Partly	Yes	Mostly	Yes
"B"—Hungarian	No	Partly	No	No	Yes	Yes	Yes
"C"—German	No	Partly	Partly	Yes	Yes	Yes	Yes
"D"—German	Partly	Partly	No	No	Yes	Yes	Yes
"E"—Polish	Partly	Mostly	No	No	Yes	Yes	Yes
"F"—Serbian	No	Partly	No	No	Mostly	Yes	Mostly
"G"—Italian	No	Partly	Partly	No	Yes	Yes	Yes
"H"—German	Partly	Yes	Partly	Partly	Yes	Yes	Yes
"I"—German	Yes	Yes	Partly	Yes	Yes	Yes	Yes
"J"—Serbian	No	Partly	No	No	Mostly	Yes	Yes

[a]Clubs H and I were least representative of a single ethnic group. Club I was the smallest of the ten clubs by a substantial margin.

[b]Although Gordon identified seven types of assimilation, "structural assimilation" was omitted because it will be examined in the role of dependent variable.

TABLE 6

Characteristics of Club Members:
Percentage Naturalized and by Generation

Club	Percent Naturalized	Percent by Generation[a]		
		First	Second	Third
A	90	50	15	5
B	75	90	10	0
C	90	60	20	20
D	75	80	19	1
E	75	75	20	5
F	50	80	15	5
G	70	65	25	10
H	75	90	7	3
I	98	99	1	0
J	65	90	10	0

[a]First generation, i.e., original adult immigrant.
Second generation, i.e., children of the original adult immigrant.
Third generation, i.e., children of the second generation.

RESULTS

The hypothesis was tested by determining the degree of relationship between the dependent variable and the independent variable.

The results of this investigation showed that:

1. The perceived level of assimilation of soccer club members varied among clubs. (See Table 5.) The two clubs whose members had assimilated most represented the German ethnic group, although they were less ethnic oriented than any of the clubs. The two clubs whose members had assimilated least represented the Serbian ethnic group.
2. In terms of three assimilation variables, namely civic, behavioral receptional and attitude receptional, the majority of club members were alleged to have assimilated in large measure. (See Table 5.) In terms of three other assimilation variables, namely cultural, marital and identificational, the record of assimilation was poor. Of these, marital assimilation (amalgamation) had occurred least of all.
3. A review of the characteristics of soccer club members indicated that: (a) a large percentage were naturalized and first generation immigrants (See Table 6); (b) their most frequent occupations was in the

TABLE 7

Characteristics of Club Members:
Most Frequent Occupations[a]

Club	Most 1	2	3	Least 4
A	Unskilled Labor	Skilled Labor	Private Business	Professional
B	Skilled Labor	Unskilled Labor		
C	Skilled Labor	Private Business	Unskilled Labor	Professional
D	Skilled Labor	Private Business	Professional	Unskilled Labor
E	Skilled Labor	Unskilled Labor	Private Business	
F	Skilled Labor	Private Business	Unskilled Labor	Professional
G	Skilled Labor	Private Business	Unskilled Labor	Professional
H	Skilled Labor	Unskilled Labor	Private Business	Professional
I	Skilled Labor	Professional	Unskilled Labor	
J	Skilled Labor	Unskilled Labor	Private Business	Professional

[a]Homemakers and (high school) students not included.

area of "skilled labor" (see Table 7); (c) they spoke English only moderately well (see Table 8); and (d) approximately one-third were playing members and two-thirds were social members (see Table 9).

4. When accepting new members, approximately half of the clubs had developed a clear-cut, if not rigid, policy, whereas the other clubs had a very open policy.

5. Half of the clubs took no action to attract new members, either from other nationality groups, or the core society (see Table 10). Three

TABLE 8

Characteristics of Club Members:
Ability to Speak English

Club	Very Good	Good	Fair	Poor	Very Poor
A	20%	20%	40%	10%	10%
B	10	60	20	10	——
C	40	50	10	——	——
D	15	40	40	5	——
E	50	10	35	4	1
F	25	25	25	20	5
G	30	30	20	10	10
H	30	40	20	10	——
I	100	——	——	——	——
J	15	40	30	10	5

Mean Percentage:

| | 33.5 | 31.5 | 24.0 | 7.9 | 3.1 |

Mean Percentage without Club I:

| | 26.1 | 35.0 | 26.6 | 8.8 | 3.5 |

TABLE 9

Characteristics of Club Members:
Percentage of Playing Members and Social Members

Club	Percentage Playing	Percentage Social
A	45	55
B	65	35
C	12	88
D	25	75
E	45	55
F	25	75
G	40	60
H	35	65
I	65	35
J	20	80
TOTALS	37.7	62.3

TABLE 10

Action Taken to Attract New Members to the Clubs from Other Ethnic Groups and the Core Society

Club	Other Ethnic Groups	Core Society
A	None	None
B	None	None
C	None (unless player)	None (unless player)
D	None	None
E	None (unless player)	None (unless player)
F	Players encouraged Non-players discouraged	Players encouraged Non-players discouraged[a]
G	None (unless player)	None (unless player)
H	None	None
I	Action taken to attract players and non-players, young and old.	Action taken to attract players and non-players, young and old.
J	None	None

[a]Unless parents of players.

clubs took action to attract players to their clubs, but otherwise ignored other potential members. One club encouraged players but discouraged non-players. One club took positive action to attract new members, whether players or non-players.

6. Seven clubs were identified with a specific ethnic group by their choice of name. Three had neutral names.
7. The language used at club meetings, when playing soccer, and on social occasions varied according to the club (see Table XI). Only two clubs spoke English exclusively. Four clubs spoke their own ethnic language for the most part. The remaining four clubs spoke their own ethnic language and English.
8. There was little social contact between the clubs; with one exception, there was no contact between the clubs and the core society.

CONCLUSIONS

Within the limitations of this study, the following conclusions seem warranted:

With some exceptions, involvement in ethnic soccer is not conducive of furthering assimilation, and that more specifically, club policies of ethnic soccer clubs inhibit the structural assimilation of members.

TABLE 11

Language Used at Club Meetings, When Playing
Soccer and on Social Occasions

Club	Club Meetings	Playing Soccer	Social Occasions
A	Croatian	Croatian and Others[a]	Croation and Others
B	English and Hungarian	Hungarian	Hungarian
C	English	English	English
D	English	German and English	German and English
E	Polish	Polish	Polish
F	English and Serbian	English and Serbian	English and Serbian
G	English and Italian	English	English
H	English	English	English and German
I	English	English	English
J	Serbian	Serbian	Serbian and English

[a]This expression was used by the committee of Club A, presumably because English and other languages were spoken according to the ethnicity of those present.

Notes

1. Part of this paper was read at the AAHPER Annual Convention, Boston, April 11, 1969. The author wishes to acknowledge the valuable assistance of Gerald S. Kenyon, University of Waterloo, who acted as advisor for the study which formed part of a Masters Degree at the University of Wisconsin, Madison, completed in 1968. Printed with permission of the author.
2. The point of contact made possible through sport, can lead to discord as Reid found. In his book which tells the story of an Allied prisoner of war camp in Germany, he relates how arguments developed as a result of a "wall game" competition *between* different nationalities, where as in games played by prisoners from within a single group (in this case Britain), arguments never occurred. P. R. Reid, *Escape from Colditz* (New York: Berkeley Publishing Corporation, 1952), p. 64.

3. Robert E. Park and Ernest W. Burgess, *Introduction to the Science of Sociology* (Chicago: University of Chicago Press, 1921), p. 735.

4. Milton M. Gordon, *Assimilation in American Life* (New York: Oxford University Press, 1964), p. 62.

5. From the Greek word "ethnos" meaning "people" or "nation."

6. Gordon, *op. cit.*, p. 24.

7. Melvin M. Tumin, "Ethnic Group" in Julius Gould and William L. Kolb, *A Dictionary of the Social Sciences* (Free Press of Glencoe, 1965), p. 243.

8. Gordon, *op. cit.*, p. 72. Gordon prefers the term "core group," which used by A. B. Hollingshead to describe the old Yankee families of colonial, largely Anglo-Saxon ancestry who have traditionally dominated the power and status system of the community. See August B. Hollingshead, "Trends in Social Stratification: A Case Study," *American Sociological Review* 17 (December, 1952): p. 686.

9. Joshua A. Fishman, "Childhood Indoctrination for Minority-Group Membership," in "Ethnic Groups in American Life," *Daedalus: The Journal of the American Academy of Arts and Sciences* (Spring, 1961): 329.

10. George Saxon, "Immigrant Culture in a Stratified Society," *Modern Review* 11 (February, 1948): 122.

11. W. Lloyd Warner and Leo Srole, *The Social Systems of American Ethnic Groups* (New Haven: Yale University Press, 1945), pp. 254-282.

12. This point is taken up by Martin when he says, "At present, we are participating in an extremely drastic and rapid cultural change, affecting our entire Western society. The rapid advance of technological science, spear-headed by automation, is causing a steady shrinkage of the workaday world. Plans now underfoot for a six-week vacation and a three-day weekend indicate that before long our work force will have 200 free days in the year." He goes on to qualify this as follows: "These changes do not apply, to the same extent, to professional executive and management groups. However, the fact remains that, coincidental with a rising standard of living, higher employment, and a steadily increasing national product, the American people are finding themselves with more and more time off the job. In other words, we have already acquired, in large measure, the latest and the greatest freedom of all—free time, unstructured time, discretionary time, time for leisure." (Alexander Reid Martin, "Man's Leisure and His Health," *Quest* 5 (December, 1965): 26.)
Three publications by Brightbill, Miller and Robinson, and Dumazedier, which discuss societal problems and current theories related to leisure, either directly or indirectly, point to the increase in leisure time during the current era. "It seems curious that at a time when many people have more leisure than ever before . . ." (Charles K. Brightbill, *Man and Leisure* (Englewood Cliffs, N. J.: Prentice-Hall, 1961), p. v. "The twentieth century finds man turning more and more to his increasing free time, to fulfill himself." (Norman P. Miller and Duane M. Robinson, *The Leisure Age* (Belmont, Calif.: Wadsworth Publishing Co., 1963), p. v. "Leisure today is a familiar reality in our advanced societies." (Joffre Dumazedier, *Toward a Society of Leisure* (New York: The Free Press, 1967), p. 1.)

13. For example, Erich Rosenthal, "Acculturation without Assimilation: The Jewish Community of Chicago, Illinois," *American Journal of Sociology* 66 (1960): 275-288. Yaroslav Chyz and Read Lewis, "Agencies Organized by Nationality Groups in the United States," *The Annals of the American Academy of Political and Social Science* 262 (March, 1949). Harold L. Wilensky and Jack Ladinsky, "From Religious Community to Occupational Group: Structural Assimilation Among Professors, Lawyers and Engineers," *American Sociological Review* 32 (August, 1967): 541-542.

14. For example, Harry J. Walker, "Changes in the Structure of Race Relations in the South," *American Sociological Review* 14 (1949): 377-383. Clarence Senior, "Race Relations and Labor Supply in Great Britain," *Social Problems* 4 (1957): 302-312. Michael P. Banton, *White and Colored* (New Brunswick, N. J.: Rutgers University Press, 1960). J. A. Neprash, "Minority Group Contacts and Social Distance," *Phylon* 14, 19 (June, 1953), pp. 207-212. R. B. Davison, *Black British: Immigrants in Britain* (London: Oxford University Press, 1969), p. 170. Martin Luther King, Jr., *Where Do We Go From Here: Chaos or Community?* (New York: Harper and Row), p. 269.

15. For example, Raymond Breton and Maurice Pinard, "Group Formation among Immigrants: Criteria and Process," *Canadian Journal of Economics and Political Science* 26 (August, 1960): 465-477. Alexander S. Weinstock, "Role Elements: A Link Between Acculturation and Occupational Status," *British Journal of Sociology* 14 (1963): 144-149. Wilensky, *loc. cit.*

16. For example, Otis Dudley Duncan and Stanley Lieberson, "Ethnic Segregation and Assimilation," *American Journal of Sociology* 64 (January, 1959): 364-374. Stanley Lieberson, *Ethnic Patterns in American Cities* (New York: Free Press of Glencoe, 1963).

17. Ralph Andreano, *No Joy in Mudville* (Cambridge, Massachusetts: Schenkman Publishing Co., 1965), p. 133.

18. Oscar Handlin, "The Family in Old World and New," in *Social Perspectives on Behavior,* Herman D. Stein and Richard A. Cloward, p. 103. (New York: The Free Press, 1958).

19. Saxon, *loc. cit.*

20. Robert H. Boyle, *Sport-Mirror of American Life* (Boston: Little, Brown and Company, 1963), p. 97.

21. Tamotsu Shibutani and Kian M. Kwan, *Ethnic Stratification* (New York: The MacMillan Company, 1965), pp. 543-544.

22. S. Kirson Weinberg and Henry Arond, "The Occupational Culture of the Boxer," *American Journal of Sociology* 57 (1951): 462.

23. For example, Pauline V. Young, *The Pilgrims of Russian Town* (Chicago: University of Chicago Press, 1932); Joseph S. Roucek, "The Yugoslav Immigrants in America," *American Journal of Sociology* 40 (March, 1935): 602-11; John S. Hawgood, *The Tragedy of German-America* (New York: G. P. Putnam's Sons, 1940); S. N. Eisenstadt, "The Place of Elites and Primary Groups in the Absorption of New Immigrants in Israel," *American Journal of Sociology* 57 (1951): 222-231; Alan Richardson, "The Assimilation of British Immigrants in Australia," *Human Relations* 10 (1957): 157-165; S. Alexander Weinstock, *The Acculturation of Hungarian Immigrants: A Social-Psychological Analysis.* Columbia University, Ph.D. (1962), *University of Microfilms, Inc.,* Ann Arbor, Michigan; R. Talf, "The Assimilation of Dutch Male Immigrants in a Western Australian Community," *Human Relations* 14 (1961): 265-281; Leonard Broom and E. Shevky, "Mexicans in the United States: A Problem in Social Differentiation," *Sociology and Social Research* 36 (1952): 150-158. In some instances, two ethnic groups have been studied allowing some comparative analysis. For example, Wilfred D. Borrie, *Italians and Germans in Australia: A Study of Assimilation* (Melbourns: Published for the Australian National University by F. W. Cheshire, 1954), pp. 217-231.

24. For example, Stanley Lieberson, *loc. cit.*

25. Wisconsin State Football Association, *Soccer Souvenir Book,* issued on the occasion of the United States Football Association Convention, June 30-July 1 (Milwaukee: Wisconsin State Football Association, 1928). Pages not numbered.

26. U.S. Bureau of the Census, *U.S. Census of Population: 1960.* Vol. 1. Characteristics of the Population, Part 51: Wisconsin. (Washington, D. C.: U.S. Government Printing Office, 1963), p. 309.

27. "In May 1904 in Paris, five nations got together to found the F.I.F.A. (Federation Internationale de Football Association) . . . . Those five nations—France, Holland, Belgium, Switzerland, and Denmark . . . have increased and multiplied." There were eighty-one countries controlled by F.I.F.A. in 1954. Dengil Batchelor, *Soccer—A History of Association Football* (London: Batsford Ltd., 1954), p. 139. In 1963, there were ". . . 119 National Associations affiliated to it (F.I.F.A.) . . . ." A. G. Doggart (Chairman of the English Football Association), in *Fiftieth Anniversary Golden Jubilee Journal* (New York: 1963 U.S. S.F.A. Convention Committee, July, 1963). Hackensmith makes explicit reference to soccer on the five continents, C. W. Hackensmith, *History of Physical Education* (New York: Harper and Row, 1966), pp. 59, 89, 159, 233, 235, 258, 266, 280, 292, 303, 368.

28. Personal interview with the committee of Club I, April 11, 1967.

29. Personal interview with the committee of Club J. April 20, 1967.

30. Milton M. Gordon, *Assimilation in American Life* (New York: Oxford University Press, 1964), p. 81.

31. *Ibid.*

32. *Ibid.*

33. See Table IV.

34. *Ibid.*

Section B

Sex-Based Groups and Sport

In sport, as in many other walks of life, girls and women have often had to face the frustrating attitude that "biology is destiny." Because she is embodied female, the girl interested in sport finds many doors to sport participation closed to her. Only recently has research begun to put into proper perspective many of the myths about physiological restrictions on women's potential for sport achievement. Ironically, now that women have been liberated by the news that biological differences are far less overwhelming than was previously thought, the gap in sport performance for males and females has been narrowing dramatically. This pattern indicates some support for the salience of self fulfilling prophecy: we are only as good as we believe we can be.

The most limiting factor in the realization of female sporting potential is not the exaggerated importance given to physiological differences, but conventional beliefs about the psychological differences between men and women. These outdated views about psychological femininity and masculinity result from conceptualizing males and females as separate social categories and applying a rhetoric of belief about the differential abilities, ambitions, and attitudes located in the two groups. Such categorization leads to differential treatment, expectations, and opportunities, and is the major reason that the potential sporting achievements of North American females have been retarded for so many years.

Like the minority groups with whom they have so much in common, women have traditionally been excluded from full participation in sport in North America because of their social category membership. Recent legislation has aided women's fight to combat discrimination from a legal standpoint, but conventional beliefs have been harder to dispel. Specifically, females have had a difficult time justifying their participation in sport because it is an activity over which males have had the power of definition, i.e., males have managed to control sport by defining it in masculine terms. Women have had difficulty identifying and combatting this problem.

Hart begins this section with a personal statement of what it means to be a female in American sport. She confronts the situations, experiences and conflicts which accompany sport involvement for many girls and women. By exposing such practices, Hart hopes that positive change will be facilitated and negative experiences diminished.

Sherif reviews many pertinent research traditions in her attempt to explore the competitive process as it is learned and experienced by females. Sherif deals with certain Freudian myths she sees at the root of the misunderstanding, as well as inaccurate or incomplete research traditions that have prevented social scientists from clearly understanding the achievement and competitive behaviors of women.

Felshin examines what she sees as three options open to women in sport: the apologetic, the forensic, and the dialectic. She clearly advocates freedom from the imprisoning notions of sport as a male domain and the liberation of sport from its restrictive contemporary models.

On Being Female in Sport

M. Marie Hart

The topic of social and sexual roles in sport is a complicated one about which Americans seem particularly sensitive. The sexuality separated facilities and organizations that often accompany sport and physical education activities may be an extension of certain problems in this area. There is an urgent need to consider these problems if we are concerned about the quality of the experience for all those who engage in sport. Many times it seems that people find it difficult to consider such problems with any degree of objectivity. To remove the personal self from the social process being examined requires a thorough grounding in knowledge of self and a deep understanding of one's own personal sport involvement.

This article is particularly concerned with being a woman and being in sport. Although we have isolated and studied "Women in Sport," we have not so separated "Men in Sport" as a special topic. This is because the latter is the accepted, rather than the exception, in sport discussions. It seems well established that much of sport is male territory; therefore participation of female newcomers is studied as a peripheral, non-central aspect of sport. If one aspect of sport is social experience, it seems appropriate to study it in total context and to note the differences of role and reaction in the variety of people taking part. The separation and alienation of women in sport is not the healthiest of situations. It is only through interaction that we can gain awareness and acceptance of differences. Why is it that in most of the rest of the Western world women co-exist with men in sport with less stigma and with more acceptance as respected partners?

Being female in this culture does not necessarily mean that one is perceived or accepted as "feminine." Each culture has its social norms and sex roles which one can recognize, but in the United States this defi-

An earlier version of this material appeared in *Psychology Today* Magazine, October, 1971. Copyright © Communication/Research/Machines, Inc.

nition seems especially rigid and narrow. For longer than one can remember, women in sport have known and experienced rejection due to their failure to live up to a particular concept of "feminine." It has been an unpleasant and painful memory for many.

Why has it been difficult for women to stay "woman" and be an athlete, especially in games emphasizing physical skill? Games of physical skill are associated with achievement and aggressiveness which seem to make them an expressive model for males rather than females. Women are more traditionally associated with high obedience training and routine responsibility training, and with games of strategy and games of chance which emphasize those qualities supposedly desirable in women (9) (11) (12). This all begins so early that the young girl in elementary school already begins feeling the pressure to select some games and avoid others if she is to be a "real" girl. If she is told often enough at eleven or twelve that sports are not ladylike, she may at that point make a choice between being a lady and being an athlete. Having to make this choice has potential for setting up deep conflict in female children, which continues later into adulthood.

The concept of conflict-enculturation theory of games is developed in an essay by Sutton-Smith, Roberts and Kozelka. They maintain that "conflicts induced by social learning in childhood and later (such as those related to obedience, achievement, and responsibility) lead to involvement in expressive models, such as games . . ." (12:15). This process can be applied also to the game involvement of adults. Cultural values and competencies are acquired in games. It would appear that games operate on various levels as expressive models to ease conflict, with the exception of the case of the woman athlete. As girls become more and more proficient in sport, the level of personal investment increases which may, due to the long hours of practice and limited associations, isolate her socially. Personal conflict and stress increase as it becomes necessary for her to assure others of her sexual identity, sometimes requiring evidence. This level of tension and conflict may increase dramatically if a girl makes the choice to be intensely involved in a sport which is thought of as male territory.

In an interview Chi Cheng, who holds several world track records, was quoted as saying, "The public sees women competing and immediately thinks that they must be manly—but at night, we're just like other women" (14:15). Why does a woman (whether American or otherwise) often need to comment about herself in this way and how does this awareness of stigma affect her daily life? Chi goes on to say: "I'm gone so much of the day and on weekends. I give a lot of public appearances—where I can show off my femininity" (14:16).

Numerous occasions have occurred in college discussion groups over the past few years that convince one that we have imposed a great burden on women who are committed to performing or teaching sport. As an example, several married women students majoring in physical education confided to a discussion group that they had wanted to cut their hair but felt they couldn't. Members of the group asked why this was so, if their husbands objected, if they would feel less feminine, if they were in doubt about their own femaleness. In every case they responded that they simply didn't want the usual stereotype image and comments from friends and family in their social lives. Even when hairstyles are short women in sport are judged by a standard other than fashion. If the married sportswoman experiences anxiety over such things, one can imagine the struggle of the single woman. Unfortunately, this often results in a defensive attitude developed as a shield against those who poke and probe.

When young women do enjoy sport, what activities are really open to them? A study done in 1963 (4) shows recommendations made about sports participation by 200 freshman and sophomore college women from four Southern California schools. Although their own background had been strong in the team sports of basketball, softball and volleyball they did not recommend that a girl, even thought highly skilled, pursue these activities at a professional level. They strongly discouraged participation in track and field activities. The sports they did recommend for a talented young woman were those that they had not necessarily experienced personally. They were ranked as follows: tennis, swimming, ice skating, diving, bowling, skiing and golf. All of these recommended sports are identified with aesthetic considerations, social implications, and fashions for women. Physical strength and skill may be important components of these activities but are not their primary identifications.

Some may argue that the past decade has seen great change in the acceptance of women in a larger variety of sports. That is no doubt true, at least to a degree, but some limited observation would indicate that there has been no radical change. In fact, the wave of enthusiasm for women in gymnastics only reinforces the traditional ideal of the striving for aesthetic form as "appropriate" for women in sport—an aesthetic that emphasizes poise, smooth and rhythmic movement. Form is the ultimate criteria, not strength and speed. Could this be indicative of the status quo?

In contrast to the findings of the 1963 (4) study is the situation of the black woman athlete. In the black community, the woman can be strong and achieving in sport and still not deny her womanness. She may

actually gain respect and status as evidenced by the reception of women like Wilma Rudolph, Wyomia Tyus Simburg, and other great performers. The black woman seems also to have more freedom to mix her involvement in sport and dance without the conflict expressed by many white women athletes. This in itself would be a rich subject for research.

The limitations on sport choices for women have been instituted largely by social attitudes about women in sport as previously discussed. These attitudes have a long history which is revealed in the sport literature. Early sport magazines reinforced the idea of women being physically inferior to men in sport and furthermore inferred that their female emotionality rendered them incompetent. As an example, in response to a strong desire of women to be involved in the new and exciting sport of flying in 1912, the editor of *Outing Magazine* was outspoken in his bias:

> Other things being equal, the man who has had the most experience in outdoor sports should be the best aviator. By the same token, women should be barred. . . . Women have not the background of games of strength and skill that most men have. Their powers of correlation are correspondingly limited and their ability to cope with sudden emergencies inadequate. (10:253)

The social process by which women had arrived at this mythic helpless state of being was never mentioned or discussed.

In 1936 the editor of *Sportsman,* a magazine for the wealthy, commented about the Olympic Games that he was ". . . fed up to the ears with women as track and field competitors." He continued, "her charms shrink to something less than zero" and urged the organizers to "keep them where they are competent. As swimmers and divers girls are beautiful and adroit as they are ineffective and unpleasing on the track" (13: 18).

More recent publications such as *Sports Illustrated* have not been openly negative, but the implication is sustained by the limitation in their coverage of women in sport. Content is small and consists mostly of a discussion of fashions and of women in traditionally approved activities such as swimming, diving, ice skating, tennis and golf. The emphasis in periodicals is still largely on women as attractive objects rather than as skilled and effective athletes.

The magazines *Sportswoman* and *womenSports* have been dedicated to presenting a full and fair coverage of women in sport. The efforts of the editors and writers are excellent even though one occasionally gets the impression that the message is "see we're just as good, skilled and tough as the men but still attractive."

Granted the image is somewhat exaggerated but again care must be taken not just to accept and act out the traditional model of sport developed by and for men. There may be more alternatives and dimensions to be explored which would benefit a greater variety of personalities and social groups.

Attitudes toward women in sport have been slow to change because of misunderstandings like the muscle myth. It has been difficult to allay the fear that sport activity will produce bulging muscles which imply masculinity. Young girls are frightened away from sport by "caring" adults who perpetuate this false idea. The fact, well documented by exercise physiologists, is that "excessive development (muscles) is not a concomitant of athletic competition" (6:130). Klafs and Arnheim further affirm this situation, reporting: "Contrary to lay opinion, participation in sports does not masculinize[1] women. Within a sex, the secretion of testosterone, androgen, and estrogen varies considerably, accounting for marked variation in terms of muscularity and general morphology among males and females" (6:128). Participation in sport cannot make changes in the potential of hereditary and structural factors of any individual.

Perhaps what occasionally gives observers the impression that the muscle myth is true is the reality that some girl athletes are indeed muscular. However, it may be due to their muscularity that they enter sport, rather than it being a result of their participation. This is further explained by Klafs and Arnheim:

> Girls whose physiques reflect considerable masculinity are stronger per unit of weight than girls who are low in masculinity and boys who display considerable femininity of build. Those who are of masculine type often do enter sports and are usually quite successful because of the mechanical advantages possessed by the masculine structure. However, such types are the exception, and by far the greater majority of participants possess a[2] feminine body build. (6:128)

It would seem more accurate and scientifically sound to describe this difference in terms of hormone level and individual potential. (RIGHT ON!)[3] This kind of value laden language is used repeatedly by researchers in the fields of sport and physical education.

Some of the most important considerations about women in Western culture have been written by Simone de Beauvoir. In her book, *The Second Sex*, she also discusses sport as a way of experiencing oneself in the world and of asserting one's sovereignty. She says that outside of participation in sport, a girl must experience most of her physical self in a passive manner (2). De Beauvoir makes one point that is worth the serious consideration of all who are concerned about the dilemma of the woman athlete. She states:

> And in sports the end in view is not success independent of physical equipment; it is rather the attainment of perfection within the limitations of each physical type; the featherweight boxing champion is not the inferior of the faster male champion; they belong to two different classes: It is precisely the female athletes who, being positively interested in their own game, feel themselves least handicapped in comparison with the male. (2:311)

Americans seem not to be able to apply this view of "attainment of perfection with the limitations of each" to the woman in sport. Women have been continually compared to males and have had male performance and style set as model and goal for them. Repeatedly young girls and women athletes listen to, "Wow, what a beautiful throw. You've got an arm like a guy." "Look at that girl run, she could beat lots of boys." Father comments, "Yes, she loves sports. She's our little tomboy." It would seem strange to say of a young boy, "Oh, yes, he is our little marygirl." We have ways of getting messages to boys who don't fit the role, but we haven't integrated it into our language terminology so securely.

These kinds of comments carry with them the message of expected cultural behavior. When well learned it results in girls losing games to boys purposely, avoiding dates which show her sports talent or risking never dating the boy again if she performs better than he does.

The male performance standards and the attending social behavior have extended into even more serious problems. In the early international competitions of the 1920's, women were not subjected to medical examinations. After doubt arose over one or two competitors, each country was asked to conduct medical examinations to determine if indeed the performer was female. Countries did not trust the honesty of nonsupervised tests so additional tests began to be employed. In recent international events women have had to pass the "Barr Sex Test" perfected by a Canadian doctor. The test consists of scraping cells from the inside of the cheek and then analyzing them for "Barr bodies." The number fluctuates normally during a month but all women have a minimum percentage of Barr bodies all the time. In the test, if the percentage drops below the minimum for females then the femaleness of the performer is suspect and she is dropped from the competition.

In 1968, the "Barr Sex Test" was administered for the first time at an Olympic Game, causing quite a stir. The scene was described by Marion

Lay, a Canadian swimmer performing in both the 1964 and 1968 Olympics. The line-up awaiting the test in Mexico erupted in reactions ranging from tension-releasing jokes to severe stress and upset. Some performers suggested that if the doctor were good looking enough, one might skip the test and prove their femaleness by seducing him. At the end of the test the women received a certificate verifying their femaleness and approving their participation in the Games. Many were quite baffled by the necessity of the test, feeling that their honesty as much as their sexual identity was in question. Most could not imagine anyone wanting to win so badly that they would create a disguise or knowingly take drugs that might jeopardize their health.

In addition to the concern over proof of sexual identity, there has been much discussion about the use of "steroid" drugs by some women performers, particularly those from Russia and Eastern bloc nations. These drugs are derived from male sex hormones and tend to increase muscle size. The subject of the use of these drugs by women has been somewhat muted with the result that there is not much literature describing the effects of this drug on women performers. There have been continued warnings against its use by men because of its unknown or dangerous side effects but there is still somewhat limited information published about the effects of the steroid drug. It is known to increase body size and also to produce secondary male characteristics in women such as increasing of facial hair and lowering of the voice (1:135).

Why would a women take such a drug? Is it because the values are on male records and performance, and the national pressure to win may cause her to attempt to come as close to this kind of goal as possible? This kind of expectation in regards to performance and the attending social behavior have caused serious problems for women athletes. If the performance of women could be recognized on its own merit without comparison to male records and scores, many painful social and medical experiences for women would be avoided.

If women in sport feel outside of the mainstream of social life in this country, perhaps another question could be posed to representatives of the new movements. Where has the feminist platform been in relation to women athletes? When the role of women is no longer limited to mother, secretary, or Miss America, isn't it about time that women were given not only freedom to be but respect for being successful in sport? Granted the early 1970's has been a time of increased interest and recognition from women's organizations but more support, understanding and coverage is still needed.

It seems apparent that the female athlete in general has much, if not more, to contend with than any other women in the American way of life as to sex role taboos. To entertain doubts about one's sexual identity and role results in more than a little stress. An editorial in *Women: A Journal of Liberation* states: "In America, dance is a field for women and male homosexuals. There is the dancer's cult of starving and punishing one's body (15:65)." In contrast, one might think of sport as a field for men and female homosexuals, or so the social role of the female athlete seems often to be interpreted. The need to change the environment of sport and dance from symbolic cultural territory for the establishing of sexual identity and acceptance to an environment of valued personal experience and fulfillment is long past due.

The aforementioned editorial goes on to say: "My dream is that dance will not have to be an escape from America's sick sexuality but a celebration of all our bodies, dancing" (15:65). What else could one wish for both men and women in sport? Why could not sport be a celebration, both personal and mutual, of the body-self? A celebration—rather than a conflict over best scores and most points, over who is most male and who is least female—a celebration of one's body-self whoever she or he is. The jokes, stories and oppression are old and far too heavy to be carried along further. The present-day woman athlete may soon demand her female space and identity in sport.

Today women *have* begun to enter sport with more social acceptance and individual pride. After World War II the increase in the number of women athletes and their success became more apparent and better received. In 1952 researchers from the Finnish Institute of Occupational Health conducted an intensive study of the athletes participating in the Olympics in Helsinki. Their findings were of major importance in the study of women athletes. After studying their athletic achievements, physiological and clinical data, age, fitness and social status, the researchers stated that "women are about to shake off civic disabilities which millennia of prejudice and ignorance have imposed upon them" (5:84). The researchers concluded that the participation of women was a significant indication of positive health and living standards of a country.

In addition to the physiological and clinical data, the researchers observed other factors apparent in the performance of women athletes. Criteria for describing the performances expanded to include aesthetic considerations because it "added itself" to the researchers data. They stated:

> A third criterion for the evaluation of women's athletics is an aesthetic one. Parallel with the growth of athletic performance standards there has taken place during the past fifty years or so a display of new dynamic patterns of motion and form which contains elements of artistic value and of creative beauty. The great women hurdlers and

discus throwers, fencers, and divers, gymnasts and canoeists have introduced, unwittingly, of course, features of elegance and of power, of force and of competence such as had previously not been known. That sports and athletics should be able to elicit in women categorical values of this kind and that performance and beauty should thus be correlated is a surprising and highly relevant experience. (5:84-85)

In the same vein, Ogilvie, a professor of psychology, stated:

The review of that data upon San Jose State College women swimmers presents evidence that there has been no loss of the feminine traits most valued within our culture. There was strong evidence that at least this small sample of women had outstanding traits of personality in the presence of outstanding success as competitors. I must reject the prejudiced view that would deny women the joys and rewards of high level athletic competition. It appears to this investigator that you would have to search the whole world over before you could find twenty women who measure up to these in both personality and natural[4] physical beauty. (8:7)

Personal fulfillment as expressed by woman in sports and dance experiences must not be manipulated or denied to anyone in the name of archaic cultural roles. They have been binding, limiting and belittling. This is the age of woman in command of her own space and movement. Men will also gain freedom from their role restriction as the process of social change continues.

The argument that "a person is a person is a person" is one to be heeded—and one wishes practiced. However, it seems necessary in this transitional time to name, discuss and research what is practiced so that social roles and systems can be fully understood and exposed. Only when individuals and more generally the society, becomes conscious of behavior can that behavior be changed. Until then it's all just so much talk.

NOTES

1. Even in their effort to dismiss the myth, Klafs and Arnheim seem to buy the cultural myth implying that muscles are masculine. The literature on this topic is loaded with such cultural slips.
2. The cultural norm hits again.
3. Just couldn't edit out this comment by the manuscript typist—a former career woman turned housewife.
4. Again there is the cultural concern and bias toward "feminine" traits and beauty. Conversely, there is full cultural appreciation of excellent male athletes, be they handsome or ugly.

REFERENCES

1. Blythe, Myrna. "Girl Athletes: What Makes Them Skate, Fence, Swim, Jump, Run?" *Cosmopolitan,* (October, 1969), pp. 110-114.
2. de Beauvoir, Simone. *The Second Sex.* New York: Bantam Books, 1952.
3. Hambric, Lois. "To Ski." Unpublished paper. California State College at Hayward, June, 1971.
4. Hart, M. Marie. "Factors Influencing College Women's Attitudes Toward Sport and Dance," Master's Thesis, University of Southern California, 1963.
5. Jokl, Ernst. *Medical Sociology and Cultural Anthropology of Sport and Physical Education.* Springfield, Ill.: Charles C Thomas, Publishers, 1964, pp. 73-85.
6. Klafs, Carl E. and Arnheim, Daniel D. *Modern Principles of Athletic Training.* St. Louis, Mo.: C. V. Mosby Company, 1969, pp. 127-134.
7. Novich, Max M. and Taylor, Buddy. *Training and Conditioning of Athletes.* Philadelphia, Pa.: Lea and Febiger, 1970.
8. Ogilvie, Bruce. "The Unanswered Question: Competition, Its Effect Upon Feminity." Address given to the Olympic Development Committee, Santa Barbara, California, June 30, 1967.
9. Roberts, J. M. and Sutton-Smith, B. "Child-Training and Game Involvement," *Ethnology* 1 (1962): 66-185.
10. "Still They Fall," *Outing* 67 (November, 1912): 253.
11. Sutton-Smith, B., Rosenberg, B. G. and Morgan, E. F., Jr. "Development of Sex Differences in Play Choices During Preadolescence," *Child Development* 34 (1963):119-126.
12. Sutton-Smith, B., Roberts, J. M. and Kozelka, R. M. "Game Involvement in Adults," *The Journal of Social Psychology* 60 (1963):15-30.
13. "Things Seen and Heard." *Sportsman* 20 (October, 1936):17-20.
14. Winner, Karin. "At Night We're Just Like Other Women," *Amateur Athlete.* (April, 1971), pp. 15-17.
15. *Women: A Journal of Liberation* 2 (Fall, 1970):1+.

RELATED LITERATURE

Harres, Bea. "Attitudes of Students Toward Women's Athletic Competition," *Research Quarterly* 39 (May, 1968):278-284.
Higdon, Rose and Higdon, Hal. "What Sports for Girls?" *Today's Health* 45 (October, 1967):21-23, 74.
Krotz, L. E. "A Study of Sports and Implications for Women's Participation in Them in Modern Society," Ph.D. Dissertation, Ohio State University, 1958.
McGree, Rosemary. "Comparisons of Attitudes Toward Intensive Competition for High School Girls," *Research Quarterly* 27 (1956):60-73.
Metheny, Eleanor. "Symbolic Forms of Movement: The Feminine Image in Sport," *Connotations of Movement in Sport and Dance.* Dubuque, Iowa: Wm. C. Brown Company Publishers, 1965, pp. 43-56.

Trekell, M. "The Effect of Some Cultural Changes Upon the Sports and Physical Education Activities of American Women—1860-1960," Paper presented at the History and Philosophy Section of the National Convention of the American Association of Health, Physical Education and Recreation, Dallas, Texas, March 18, 1965.

Watts, D. P. "Changing Conceptions of Competitive Sports for Girls and Women in the United States from 1880 to 1960," Ed.D. Dissertation, University of California, Los Angeles, 1960.

Females in the Competitive Process

Carolyn Wood Sherif

I am a female; one of the some nine percent of all full professors who are female; one of the five percent females among those in this country who earn $10,000 or more a year (which includes all those rich widows) (Bird, 1971); one of about 42 percent of women Ph.D.'s who is married and has children; and I learned recently in an official publication of the American Psychological Association that I am among some 130 or so women in the country who call themselves social psychologists. I guess that I must be a competitive woman, and that is a "bad" thing to admit.

If you are feeling magnanimous, you can ease my confession by pointing out that I am an exception. Factually, you are quite correct. I raise the issue because each of us, by admitting an exception, is referring to more than statistical fact. Our feelings of discomfiture reflect the widespread conviction that females in our highly competitive and individualistic culture do not compete, that it is unfeminine to compete, and therefore probably either unattractive or abnormal. An exception merely confirms this stereotyped view or, if we happen to like or admire the exception, suggests that the woman in question has some unique ability that other mortals do not possess.

The logic in how we deal with exceptions reminds me of a story told at another research conference by Professor Otto Klineberg. It seems that a man was convinced that he was dead. His family offered all possible evidence to the contrary and finally took him to a psychiatrist. The psychiatrist also tested the belief, to no avail. Almost despairing, the psychiatrist suddenly thought of an ultimate test. "Listen," he said, "do dead men bleed?" "No, of course not," replied the man. The psychiatrist seized his hand and pierced it with a letter opener, saying, "You see, you bleed,

"Females in the Competitive Process" by Carolyn Wood Sherif, from Dorothy V. Harris, Ed. Women in Sport: A National Research Conference. Copyright 1972 by The Pennsylvania State University. Reprinted by permission of the author and publisher.

so you can't be dead." The man looked at the blood as if he could not believe his eyes. "What do you know," he muttered. "Dead men *do* bleed!"

Contrary to the stereotyped notion, I am convinced that females do compete. The conditions of our culture are such that many compete in different ways, for different ends and with different standards than males, particularly after childhood. My reading of the research literature has strongly convinced me that, by and large, we have conceptualized the problem in ways such that our research methods tell us very little about what we want to know and what we need to know, if our intention is practical methods for developing human potentiality through sports, or anything else for that matter. My remark applies to competitive processes involving males as well, some of who are telling us today, I think, that prevalent methods are not contributing much to their well-being either.

Lest you think my stance too extreme, let us note that I am not alone. In her book on *Psychology of Women*, Bardwick (1971) inserted a footnote relating the reaction of her colleagues to seminars on that topic. "There is no psychology of women," they exclaimed, to which she replied, "There will be." Or, consider the jolt I received when reading an article by a young Harvard Ph.D., Naomi Weisstein (1971), with the title "Psychology constructs the female, or the fantasy life of the male psychologist." Its central thesis was as follows: "Psychology has nothing to say about what women are really like, what they need and what they want, essentially because psychology does not know" (p. 70). I have to admit that Dr. Weisstein is correct, but add that in the scattered literature on sex differences, social development and social processes, we can glean and assemble material to answer certain more specific questions.

My thesis and the directions it will take us can be summed up briefly: In one sense all normal human beings compete after early childhood, even in societies where individualistic competition for recognition is not prized as it is in our society. Research on competition often misleads us by identifying the directions, the standards, the goals, and the realistic circumstances that limit goal achievement with competition itself. Competition is not a specific kind of behavior; it is not a unitary motive aimed unerringly at certain specific goals; it is not a specific standard or level of performance.

Competition is a *social process* that occurs when the person's activities are directed more or less consistently toward meeting a standard or achieving a goal in which performance, either by the individual or by the group, is compared and evaluated relative to that of selected other persons or groups. Females are part of such processes every day—whether their activities are toward serving better food than other members of their club; enhancing their appearance; getting the most desirable husband;

having a cleaner house; doing a better job in office or factory; improving their ability to get along with other people; contributing to the progress of their club, bowling team, political party; sewing a fine seam; or accommodating themselves with the greatest submission to the plans and desires of husbands, hence being an "ideal wife." If these kinds of competition have not been studied much, the fact certainly tells something about the social sciences, namely that they are not interested in studying such activities. It does not tell us that women are noncompetitive.

Perhaps I can clarify what I mean by saying competition is social process by referring to cooperation, which is often taken as the polar opposite of competition. In fact, cooperation refers to the structure of *activity*, not to specific behaviors at all. Cooperation can occur whenever there is division of tasks or labor in an activity to which individuals contribute differently for a common end. The fact that this is so is readily seen when we consider that no one can cooperate alone. Sport teams, for example, have to cooperate in order to play the game, and they have to cooperate in some degree with another team in order to compete (Lüschen, 1970).

Competition, as I have defined it, does not require the presence of others, as a person can direct activities toward meeting a standard or achieving a goal that she sets herself, as in practicing a skill; but it is still a social process. Such rehearsal implies the evaluation of behavior by other persons or groups, and the standards tend to reflect those set by important reference persons or groups. Cheating at solitaire is cheating because it violates the rules by which others evaluate performance in the game. To the extent that such evaluations are totally lacking, the process ceases to be competitive. However, the evaluation or comparison of performance in competition is not made by just *any* other person, but by *selected* persons, who may be official judges or referees, members of a peer group, or power figures who are capable of handing out the goodies for meeting or exceeding the standard.

If competition is, as I have stated, a social process rather than specific forms of behavior, it follows that to study females competing, we have to study female behavior in the context of other persons who are competitors, standard-setters, judges or evaluators, and even determiners of what activities are valuable enough to the person that she does compete. Very little research of this kind has done so, particularly where females are concerned.

Thanks to Dr. Smith's paper on females and aggression, I do not cover the research in that area, which in any case is appropriately related to competition only under certain circumstances and in certain kinds of activities. All competition is not exemplified by the movie clips now on television showing the gorgeous body of Raquel Welch roller skating in a race with another gorgeous body, while simultaneously in the process of committing mayhem.

EARLY CHILDHOOD WITHOUT COMPETITION

As consistent patterns of activity directed toward competitive performance, competition is simply nonexistent in infancy and early childhood. The genetic code predetermines differences between the sexes before birth, and these include structural and biochemical differences that could affect competition in specific kinds of activities or at different developmental periods. However, girl and boy babies are altogether equal in one respect: both are incapable of competition.

I may add that, at present, there are not sufficient data available to connect genetic differences with very much of the behavioral variation in infancy, according to Maccoby, who has surveyed studies of infants comparing the sexes (1966; revision in progress). Even more seriously, as she points out (1972), the few differences suggested by available data are linked to social behavior in later childhood only by the most tenuous theoretical leaps, and with great difficulties owing to differences in measures and research methods used at different ages. For example, Maccoby has spelled out the tenuous evidence, in some cases lack of support, for data summaries presented by Bardwick (1971) in tabular form as support for the supposedly greater sensitivity of six-month girls to stimulation. Bardwick attributes the supposed greater sensitivity of older girls to social stimuli to this shaky evidence, and finally the supposedly superior empathy, imaginativeness and fantasy life of women. Unfortunately, the infant data do not even support clear sex differences at six months. For such reasons, I believe that at present we are on very shaky grounds when assigning genetic determination to the few fairly well documented sex differences in social behavior of infants, namely the trend toward more aggressive activities by boys and greater dependence of girls (Maccoby, 1966). Data on parental treatment clearly indicate that differential learning experiences are also involved, a fact which in itself does not vitiate genetic accounts. However, the linkage between the sorts of childhood behaviors assigned these labels and important kinds of adult aggression or dependency relationships is so weak as to cast doubt on the usefulness of the knowledge beyond childhood anyway.

The best longitudinal comparisons of the same individuals from birth through adulthood that bear on competitive behavior come from the Fels Research Institute's study from 1929 to 1959 comparing various measures of achievement and of recognition (Moss and Kagan, 1961). Significant though not impressively large correlations with adolescent or adult ratings appear with measures taken in the age ranges we would expect on the basis of other evidence, namely 6-10 years for boys and somewhat earlier for girls. As the measures were heavily weighted for intellectual activities, the somewhat earlier ages for girls are in line with the early sex differences in cognitive development favoring girls. Perhaps I should add that the well-known Terman study of genius also studied boys and girls through adulthood, reporting a relationship for men between IQ and adult achievement occupationally and professionally, but not for women, for reasons that should be too obvious to belabor.

Observations of children's play reveal at first a predominance of side-by-side activity (once the baby gets over the discovery that other children have eyes and mouths) then parallel play before simple role playing and rule following occur (Parten, 1932-33; Salusky, 1930). Competition, however, involves the child's experience of her own performance, the performance of others, and their relationship in a single pattern. This complex attainment requires, as Piaget (1932) pointed out, the ability to compare oneself to others, as well as to appreciate rules of conduct that govern winning or losing, success in some degree, or failure.

According to several studies in different countries, children do not exhibit consistent patterns of competitiveness until around age four, with middle-class American children competing somewhat earlier than workingclass children (e.g., Greenberg, 1932; Leuba, 1933; Hirota, 1953). As concrete evidence that competitiveness is not the bipolar opposite of cooperativeness, note in addition that just at this time (around 3-5 years) cooperative play becomes a predominant form (Parten, 1933; Salusky, 1930), consistent patterns of cooperativeness are reported (Berne, 1930), consistent patterns of cooperativeness are reported (Berne, 1930), and children begin to respond consistently and appropriately with sympathy to others in distress (Murphy, 1937). Somewhat later, children begin to be consistently responsible for their own behavior and, by five or six, to set fairly consistent standards for their own performance (Gesell and Ilg, 1943; Goodenough, 1952).

To add to the apparent mystery, it is around 4-5 years of age that children in settings that discriminate by skin color also start to make invidious comparisons according to skin color (Clark and Clark, 1947; Goodman, 1952). Their gender identity, which Money (1970) believes is established in rudimentary form well before three years, is also becoming elaborated into rather consistently feminine and masculine patterns of behavior (Murphy, 1947), including preference in toys and games (e.g., Sutton-Smith *et al.*, 1963) in which boys tend to be more masculine than girls are feminine.

What does all of this mean? It means that competition, like a host of other social-psychological processes, develops only with age, in which the child's conceptual development as well as his experience are basic (Piaget, 1952). Such consistencies are signs of the developing self system—a system of interrelated attitudes linking the person conceptually and emotionally to others, to activities, objectives and concepts in the social world (Sherif and Cantril, 1947).

CONSISTENCIES AND DISCONTINUITIES FROM CHILDHOOD THROUGH ADOLESCENCE

The search for *patterns* in behavior consistencies in a variety of respects is, I believe, the only hope for making sense out of research data focused on behavior in more specific respects, such as competitive activities. Such conjunction of evidence on consistent patterns of behavior constitutes the basis for the concept of a self system, which is aroused situationally and regulates activities through selective perception and attention, giving the directionality, heightened intensity and focus that are typical of any motivated behavior (*cf.* Sherif and Sherif, 1969, Chapter 19).

The formation of the self system in early childhood is enormously accelerated and forever afterward transformed by the acquisition of language. As a system of rules and categories for differentiating among stimulus events and contrasting their differences, on one hand, and for defining similarities through assimilating slight differences, on the other, language also bears heavy loads of cultural value defining what is self and not self, what one should and should not be, what activities and objects are more and less desirable for one's self and what are definitely to be avoided. With language acquisition, the self system is transformed into a categorical system for relating self and social world, the categories both defining self-other relationships and becoming ranked or structured in terms of their priority or importance.

It is precisely these features—*viz.* the interrelationships among different aspects of the self system and their priorities within the system—that make the problem of social motivation so extraordinarily difficult and complex. For one thing, these features change over time, so that the physical maturation and social transitions of adolescence or aging alter both the relationships and the priorities of various aspects of the self system. In addition, at different ages and times, society itself presents different opportunities and demands upon the person.

Unless we tackle these problems, I believe that theory and research on the development of motives related to competition, achievement, recognition, and the like are bound to remain a hopeless muddle. In the process, we have to recognize the extent to which sex comparisons are simply flooded by mythology.

Two such myths can be typified with reference to Sigmund Freud, who by no means originated them, but who is identified with them owing in part to his capacity for synthesizing and the extraordinary clarity of his writing. The first myth that has permeated many quarters of society through Freudian influences revolves around presumed pathology in female development. Such attribution is only a bit more sophisticated than simple declaration that women are inferior. Freud himself was very frank in such attribution, which he blamed on biology, even though he still confessed that women remained a mystery to him.

Recently, research on personal traits rated by both college students (Rosencrantz *et al.*, 1968) and by clinicians with degrees in psychiatry or psychology (Broverman *et al.*, 1970) as typical of males and females yielded convincing evidence of the prevalence of the myth of pathology. Males were accorded the most favorable traits by both students and clinicians who, incidentally, did not disagree seriously. Females were pictured by a cluster of traits which, while containing a few redeeming positive traits of the kind we assign even to our worst enemies, can only be characterized as pathological. Both men and women characterized women as tending to be *not at all* resourceful, intellectual, competent, or realistic and being immature, subjective, submissive, easily influenced and wracked with inferiority feelings.

It is disturbing that the myth is so readily accepted by women; however, that merely shows how readily females learn the prevalent cultural myths. Apparently, the readiness with which the myth is accepted has very little to do with actual events in early childhood that are supposed to lead to pathology. It is very much related to social role learning by female children through observation and value dictums. Hartly (1970) reports that both boys and girls, ages 8-11, painted a very conservative picture of what women do and are supposed to do, even when their own mothers were working. Similarly, American men agree that marriage and children are the most important aspects of a woman's life, although they are considerably more generous in assessing their ideal woman than American women anticipate they will be. For example, men rejected a subservient woman and accepted activity, creativity, and equality of female opinions (Steinman and Fox, 1966).

Couple the pathological image with the fact that many instruments, particularly the so-called projective tests, are highly susceptible to biased interpretation. Without labels on the cases, qualified clinical judges cannot differentiate accurately test results produced by psychotics or neurotics from normals (Little and Schneidman, 1959) or homosexuals as compared to heterosexuals (Hooker, 1957). We have a situation in which a great deal of sand can be thrown in a great many eyes. This pathological and negative view of women continues even though by almost all social indicators of disturbance (including suicide, alcoholism, drug addiction, and crimes of violence), males lead the parade. Of course, the male statistics call forth floods of explanation in terms of specific pathologies in male development, but without affecting the basic splendor of the male image. Such speculative explanations do violence to males as well, since the probability of their being wrong is exceedingly high.

The second myth permeates social life far beyond psychology and psychiatry, for it insists that human personality is formed basically and irrevocably in very early childhood. Echoing Freud in assigning supreme importance to parental treatment during the very early years, this myth has produced a research literature focused on parent-child relationships to the exclusion of the rest of the social world that the child discovers very early.

I can illustrate the focus through the writing of a non-Freudian who is keenly sensitive to effects of social learning but, as noted earlier, committed to the basic premise of genetic and developmental continuity in personality development. In *The Psychology of Women*, Bardwick wrote: "Perceived in the most general way, the broad reactive tendencies of children, their original response proclivities to the world, seem to form a consistent life style, although specific behaviors will clearly reflect the sophistication and abilities of a particular stage of development. The extraverted, impulsive, motoric child will tend to continue to respond to the world that way—and such a child is not likely to engage in intellectual pursuits when he or she is older" (1971, p. 103) and so forth. Of course, in one sense, this statement tells us nothing specific, as it is framed "in the most general way" about "general reactive tendencies." In another sense, it tells us precisely where to look for solution to the puzzle of human personality, namely in infancy. Therefore, it effectively perpetuates the second myth without generally acceptable scientific evidence.

Such exclusive focus on early childhood ignores another whole body of data having to do with changes in physiological functioning and social roles during adolescence. Without embracing *other* myths about that period, for example, that it is always or necessarily a stormy crisis or rebellion against adults, we must recognize that adolescence involves body changes signaling the arrival of sexual maturity and in modern societies a prolonged transition from childhood to adult status as a full-fledged male or female. These changes require changes in the self system and confront the person with problems that can affect personality enormously. Furthermore, the adolescent period faces the girl or boy with some striking cultural discontinuities, in the sense that the relative importance of various activities for achievement, sexual behavior and conceptions of self as male or female are markedly different from those of childhood.

I know of no evidence that boys and girls differ in competitiveness during the period of so-called middle childhood (roughly the grade school years) except in what they readily compete *for*. Overall, in our culture, girls exceed boys in competing scholastically, while boys at this period compete more readily in active sport and games (Maccoby, 1966). However, despite these average trends, the great majority of boys are competing successfully in school (otherwise I suspect schools would be closed) and girls are by and large active physically, with their games including both male and female typed activities.

Sutton-Smith and Roberts (1970), reporting that games of skill tend to reflect the power structures and struggles of a culture, have ventured to predict that for this reason boys will be more likely to be involved in games of skill than girls, who they suggest are therefore more prone to games of chance. (Are there more female than male gamblers?) I believe that this extrapolation from cultural analysis to the social-psychological level of choice is apt to be an oversimplification. After all, tradition is a very strong force toward choice of male or female activities, and opportunity is another. I am reminded of a summer camp for boys in western Massachusetts where we conducted research a few summers ago. Even for 8-10 year olds and prominently for older boys, the favored sports were tennis and sailing. One simply has to appreciate the affluent upper-middle-class background of these boys to understand these choices. Similarly, in individual sports, opportunity for females is paramount within the bounds traditionally defined as feminine, which now include swimming and diving, figure skating, tennis and gymnastics.

No matter how smooth the middle childhood years may be, the bodily changes and increased growth rate before and after pubescence are, in themselves, powerful impetus for changing the self system. Such changes do not occur in isolation, for the young person is confronted on all sides from mass media, schools and example with images of the changes required in conception of self, increasingly toward adult maleness or femaleness.

It is very easy in describing the adolescent predicament of girls to exaggerate, and to fail to recognize the increasingly flexible, alternative patterns that may be available to individual girls. On the other hand, it is easy to emphasize the flexible alternatives to the point of neglecting the overriding fact that the image of the female and the future that are offered her are sexual and sexually linked, to the point that in the myth a future without marriage and children is a special hell reserved for the unattractive, non-competitive, unachieving, miserable exceptions. As symbolic of what happens, we find in the research literature that the girl who was once active becomes absorbed in nonathletic contexts, her physical performance in running, jumping, and throwing levels off or drops from ages 12-16 (Horrocks, 1969, p. 445); both IQ and academic performance level off or decline during the same years that boys' levels are increasing, on the average (Horrocks, 1969; Kagan and Moss, 1960; Moss and Kagan, 1961); and she discards most of the unusual and/or "masculine" choices of occupations from her earlier childhood to focus on preparation for catching a mate (a competitive activity) and marriage, or preparing for those occupations defined as feminine or at least offering opportunities for female employment (Seward, 1946; Bird, 1968).

This is not a very attractive picture and, without the age specified, might sound like a decline due to aging. Of course, the girls are attractive as they bloom into sexual maturity, taking care of their appearance at least superficially and throwing themselves wholeheartedly into the activities of their peer world. They compete in matters that touch the heart of the psychological pocketbook. Like boys of their age or a little older, they are finding the people who are in the same boat as they and hence can really understand them—those in their own age range.

The exclusive focus on parents or nuclear family as a source of social learning and motivations is nowhere more absurd than during the adolescent period. Conversely, I believe that the genuine importance of the family constellation during adolescence can be understood better if viewed within the context of the adolescent's relationships with peer groups and related institutions. That is why, I believe, so much research investigating quite reasonable hypotheses about family relationships and adolescent behavior produces so few findings of interest. For example, it was quite reasonable to suppose that girls with older brothers might be more likely than girls only with older sisters to be committed to sport participation. Surely, interests expressed in the family are important in channeling adolescent interests. Yet Landers (1970) tested the sibling hypothesis and found it unsupported. He found that girls with *younger* sisters were underrepresented among college girls committed to sports but that older sisters or brothers or birth order had no important effect.

Some of our own research on adolescent girls with Kelly suggests that the best way to predict sports involvement is to observe who the girl regularly associates with in and out of school. In fact, this is also a pretty surefire way to predict many other behaviors at this time, such as participation in athletic booster clubs, school leadership activities and somewhat illegal participations with older boys after school hours (Sherif et al., in press).

Research on peer culture indicates pretty clearly that for girls, joining the active sport enthusiasts is not exactly the best way to achieve recognition from other girls and especially boys. Such recognition goes to girls who are popular and are school leaders (e.g., Coleman, 1961). There are two strikes against every teacher or coach of sport activities insofar as they desire to involve adolescent girls in their programs. Research on adolescence with regard to aspirations for education and occupation also shows that the student composition of particular schools, the school programs and extra-curricular activities form a powerful pattern whose characteristics can together override the effects of parental direction, training and preference (Sherif and Sherif, 1964).

The importance of the peer associations is further shown in research on the various sources adolescents rely upon for advice and decisions. Of course, parents do have influence, particularly in those matters where their authority, financial resources or expertise as adults is of great importance (cf. Brittain, 1963; Gecas, 1972). However, where parental authority cannot intervene, or in matters where peer and parental standards differ but closely concern peer life, reference groups of peers come to be the most potent source of influence on adolescents' decisions (Kardel and Lesser, 1969; Thomas and Weigert, 1970; Emmerich et al., 1971). Here, as in the entire area of adolescent behavior, the value of the activity in the self system is a crucial determinant of whose word will count. For this reason, the call of some researchers on achievement motivation (e.g., Moss and Kagan, 1961) for differentiation in terms of achievement for what is certainly appropriate.

It follows from this discussion that it is terribly important for an analysis of adolescent competition to know something about the specific brands of peer culture in which the male or female is immersed, for these do differ (e.g., Sherif and Sherif, 1964; Gottlieb, 1964; Coleman, 1961). It is equally important to know the specific reference groups of peers whose standards become so important in defining success or failure. Perhaps it is not really surprising that we know much more about reference groups of adolescent boys than we do girls (Sherif and Sherif, 1964, 1967), for boys' groups are sometimes associated with pressing social problems such as delinquency. What is surprising are the genuine contradictions reported in the literature about girls' groups.

For example, the California Growth Study (reported in Sherif and Cantril, 1947) presented sociometric data indicating that at the junior high school level, girls' informal groups of friends were more tightly knit and closed than those of boys of the same age. Yet Horrocks (1969) has reported that girls' associations were smaller and more transient, a conclusion that Bardwick echoes in her book (1971). On the other hand, contrary to the California study, there is considerable evidence that boys' groups from about 13-14 years of age are very closely knit and relatively stable through the high school years (cf. Sherif and Sherif, 1964).

In plain truth, we simply do not know enough about girls' friendships and groups to draw firm conclusions. Furthermore, the obvious fact that boys and girls form, at times, cross-sex groups of great importance to members has been virtually neglected. We do know that when adolescent girls have had very poor relationships with their families, their peer groups of other adolescents and young adults become utterly pivotal in maintaining their psychological identity as a person, as Konopka (1965) has related so compellingly in studies of unwed mothers and delinquent girls. The absence of such ties with a reference group, Konopka found, amounts to a spiral into pathology and even suicide.

Because female groupings are so important in affecting standards of activity and the relative importance of various activities to participants, I believe that the lack of research on female groups is the most serious gap in the literature. Their importance is attested by our own research (Sherif et al., in press) in which we found that by observing girls' behavior and activities as they associated with each other, we could make quite accurate predictions about judgments made individually by group members outside of their groups and in situations where group membership was not mentioned at all. It is such impact of the person's group on individual behavior, even apart from the group's immediate influence, that makes the study of groups so significant psychologically.

Thus, I believe that research on sport offers a very important opportunity to study the structure and dynamics of female groups, including their relationship to competitive behavior. Such research would contribute signally to knowledge about females and sports and would help to fill a near void in the social-psychological research literature.

DYNAMICS OF COMPETITIVENESS AND
ACHIEVEMENT MOTIVATION

My reading of the literature on achievement motivation in females convinces me that we can understand the competitive process only if we determine the priority of the activity in the self system, find *whose* standards count for the person in assessing performance and the level of that standard relative to what the person can accomplish. William James wrote years ago that success or failure was experienced in relative terms that could be expressed as a ratio between the person's actual performance and his pretensions or aspirations in the field of activity. Furthermore, observing that aspirations vary with the importance of the activity for the person, he noted that he cared a great deal what other psychologists thought of him as a psychologist but not a whit what Greek scholars thought about his proficiency in Greek.

Following James' insights, Kurt Lewin and others pursued research into conditions governing the setting of levels of aspiration and the experiences of success and failure (Lewin *et al.*, 1944). I will summarize some of the main findings with relevance for competition of females.

1. The level at which standards of performance are set is governed by standards prevailing in one's reference groups and relative to other groups with whom the reference group compares itself. For example, when female college students were told that their reference groups (in this case Christian or Jewish) tolerated less pain than a comparison group (Jews for the Chrisians, Christians for the Jews), the women responded by tolerating more pain than their counterparts who had not received such instructions, as though they must prove the sturdiness of their reference group (Lambert, Libman and Poser, 1960). Instructions that their reference group could tolerate more pain also increased pain tolerance for Jewish women and had a phenomenal effect on the Christian women, as though they had been told "Go ahead, you're a winner!" If, on the other hand, the comparison offered is one of a group clearly above one's own, through expertise or skill in the task at hand, knowledge of performance by that comparison group leads to lowering one's own level of aspiration (Chapman and Volkmann, 1939; Hansche and Gilchrist, 1956). There is little doubt that in many activities the stereotyped notions of male vs. female abilities coupled with exclusively male examples of success produce a lowered level of aspiration for females, whether the activity be intellectual, mechanical, political, or athletic.

2. When an activity is very important to the person, there is a tendency to maintain a fairly high and inflexible level of aspiration, even though actual performance fluctuates. Two possible consequences come to mind: First, this relative rigidity of aspiration level means that the person has to learn to tolerate the experience of failure as she competes and to persist in the activity despite it. Although speculative, my belief is that our training of females demands considerably less of them in this respect than the training of boys, who are expected to persist and try again in the face of temporary setbacks. Second, this rigidity of aspiration also occurs when one is personally involved with the performance of others, as witness the tears of female cheering sections when their team is losing. In a study I conducted several years ago, I found that mothers were particularly likely to invest themselves in high and rigid aspiration levels for their children's performance (reported in Sherif, 1948). Since females are in fact barred from achievement in a good variety of activities, I would expect them to be particularly prone to such vicarious competition and experiences of success or failure. The schoolteacher in *The Corn is Green* who was determined to get her young Welsh miner into the university is a good example.

3. The effects of continuing experiences of success or failure have been documented, beginning with the research of Pauline Sears. When accustomed to success, a child is able to tolerate occasional failure without breaking up over it. But persistent experiences of failure to meet the expected standards means that almost every drop in performance is soul shattering. Over time, the aspiration level for performance is set lower and lower until pretensions may vanish altogether. This finding would seem to be particularly relevant for female competition in sports, especially if the female follows the trend from late childhood of stabilized or decreased performance levels while standards get higher because she is older. Of course, there is no irrevocable physical reason why these decreases should have occurred, but if they have, the encouragement of sports competition has to take the ensuing experiences of failure into account. The same caution is urged in encouraging reentry of older women into activity programs.

The key concept in understanding level of aspiration and performance findings is the degree of personal involvement in the activity. Neglect of this concept has, I believe, produced one of the so-called puzzles in research findings on the achievement motive inspired by the conceptions of McLelland *et al.* (1953) and Atkinson (1958). The puzzle arose because the great bulk of research was conducted with men, which is not at all atypical when the world is viewed as a man's world and which it certainly is from the viewpoint of power, authority and the great social probelms of our day. In brief, the puzzle arose when female subjects did not behave in the ways predicted by the theory and supported by research on males.

The achievement motive is postulated as a "stable, enduring personality characteristic" formed through experiences in early life that set the basic level of the motive. However, says the theory, in specific situations the effort that will be expended in an activity and the aspiration level set depends upon the motive being aroused, the probability that the person foresees of success, and how important the activity is to the person. Neglect of the last variable has been crucial to the so-called puzzle.

The puzzle was not that females revealed a lack in the achievement motive, for their responses in college samples were typically as high or higher than males. It was that these responses had very little to do with females' actual behavior or competitiveness in concrete situations. Much of the puzzle has turned out to hinge on the failure to specify the importance of the activity to the female. For example, educated Brazilian (Horner, 1970) and Filipino females (Licuanan, 1972) do compete when placed in achievement situations that arouse male competition, as do high-achieving American females when competition involves only other females (Lesser, Krawitz and Packard, 1963). Thus, individual differences in proneness to compete have to be studied relative to the degree of the individual's involvement in the activity at hand (*cf.* Stein *et al.,* 1971).

Working within the McClelland-Atkinson formulations, Matina Horner (1970) developed a new motive largely for females which presumably is also a "stable, enduring personality characteristic." The female's achievement motive, she said, is stifled by "fear of success." She presented brief story lines to college women, typified by the following: "After first-term finals, Anne finds herself at the top of her medical school class." Males received the same verbal lead, except that John was substituted for Anne. Then she assessed the achievement motive through the Thematic Apperception Test (TAT), which involves telling a story about pictures presented to the subject. The assumption is that their fantasy in the story is a projection of their motives, in this case the achievement motive. She found, however, that about 65 percent of the females, as compared with less than 10 percent of the males, told stories that simply could not be scored as achievement motivation. One group of such stories included social rejection and unhappiness for Anne; another group dubbed Anne abnormal, neurotic or physically unattractive; a third group denied that the story line was true, by absolving Anne of responsibility ("it was luck"), inventing a male who got higher grades, or regarding Anne as a hoax created by medical students to fool their instructor. Horner further studied the reactions of students whose fear of success scores put them in the upper or lower fourth of the distribution by assessing their performance in noncompetitive situations and in situations involving competition with males. Those who scored higher in fear of success performed better in a noncompetitive situation (13 out of 17 women), while those who scored low performed better in the competitive situation (12 out of 13). In addition, however, those who scored high in fear of success imagery also rated the importance of doing well on the tasks as less than those who scored low in fear of success.

Horner's findings are both important and provocative; however, I must confess doubts about the usefulness of positioning another motive such as fear of success. Horner says females learn that competition in traditionally male activities is widely believed to require sacrifice of feminine attractiveness and sex appeal that attracts males. Add to that the documented fact that success in medical school is sufficiently demanding to require sacrifice of many other activities and is unlikely for females in the United States owing to barriers placed on entrance (Rossi, 1965). You have, I think, stories about Anne that merely reflect acceptance of prevailing stereotypes about women who succeed in the medical field and recognition of the improbability of the story. The females who responded may not have feared success, but have accepted the cultural truism that you can't have your cake and eat it too.

Related evidence suggests that the female responses interpreted as fear of success may be reflections of such stereotyped views of female achievement. Studies show that identical written passages or abstract paintings are rated higher when attributed to a male (John) than to a female (Joan) (Goldberg, 1968; Peterson et al., 1971). Horner's findings might, therefore, be explained most parsimoniously by the statement that females who accept stereotyped conceptions of male superiority reveal those conceptions in stories by attributing other kinds of failure to successful females or denying the success as an improbable event. Owing to their stereotype, they neither regard activities involving competition with males as so important nor do they try to perform well in competition with males.

A CRITICAL VIEW OF RESEARCH METHODS

Despite disclaimers to the contrary, the entire line of research that relies upon the TAT or similar projective tests for measurement of competitiveness or achievement motives is open to criticism based on the fact that reliability of the measures is distressingly low (Entwisle, 1972). What this means is that measures obtained at different times or based on different pictures are not highly correlated, suggesting that persons are responding to specific features in the different research situations rather than revealing their motives.

Now I should not like to suggest that the more or less enduring attitudes and motives of the person are not important. Nevertheless, the highly individual-centered ideology of our culture contains a pitfall, *viz.* our tendency to rectify the importance of personality measures when, in fact, all they can do is indicate some consistencies in response in given situations. The remedy is not to throw out personality variables, but to assess them over time in a variety of situations and to look for cross-situation and cross-time consistencies.

It is likely that the folklore of our culture attaches too much weight to the determination of behavior by personality and sex role variables, particularly in situations that are highly compelling and well structured. Milgram's research on obedience to authoritative commands to administer increasingly strong electric shocks to another person in a learning experiment (1965) illustrates the point quite well. One would think that mature males would be somewhat reluctant to administer electric shock to a fellow male even when ordered to by a scientific researcher. A sample of psychiatrists in fact predicted that less than one-tenth of one percent would deliver the maximum shock. In fact about 65 percent of the males did deliver what they thought was the maximum shock on the experimenter's orders, although changes in the situation—such as putting the shocker and the victim very close together—reduced that percentage considerably. Although everything that we read in the literature about females might suggest that they would be less likely to deliver such shocks, Milgram (personal communication) found that they were not, as did Larsen *et al.* (1972) more recently. Larsen *et al.* also reported a great under-estimation of the shock that would be delivered by college students to whom the procedures were described. The only significant sex differences were that females administered shock over 60 trials for a total time about 10 seconds less than the males and the maximum shock they administered was about 30 volts less on the average. It is noteworthy, however, that none of five personality tests given to these subjects correlated significantly with behavior in the shock situation. (It should be added that no one in this experimental set-up actually receives shock. The victim behaves as though he had been shocked.)

Another fiction about female personality that has been perpetuated by too little attention to the impact of the situation is that females are, by virtue of their cultural role training, more compliant or conformist than males. This fiction is stated by Gergen and Marlowe (1972) as follows: "Social-psychological folklore has it that women should be used as subjects when one wants easily persuaded or conforming subjects." After discussing the research literature, they concluded: "Perhaps we simply know less about women and why they behave as they do because in psychology, as in most professions, it's a 'man's world'" (p. 32).

In fact, a reading of research on compliance to social influence or persuasion reveals very clearly that sex differences appear when the situation is not well-structured but ambiguous and without clear guides for behavior. Then the attempt to influence behavior is apt to be more effective for both males and females. Typically the matter at hand is not very important or personally relevant in such studies (Sherif and Sherif, 1969). In addition, there is no battery of tests or performances that can predict female or male compliance generally in a variety of specific situations (Allen and Newston, 1972; Beloff, 1958; Hollander, 1960; Miller et al., 1965). For example, Tittler (in Sherif et al., in press) repeated an earlier study on persuasion from which it had been concluded that females could be persuaded more easily and consistently than males, a difference attributed to social role training. In addition to the topics used earlier, which had included such topics as General von Hindenburg's place in history and the probable success of a fictitious TV comic, Tittler included topics related to male and female sex roles. All subjects were persuaded easily to change their opinions about von Hindenburg and the comic, and females and males were equally resistant to persuasion on the sex role issues.

The structure of the situation itself and its personal meaning are thus so significant that a great many blanket generalizations have to be reconsidered. For example, quite contrary to theory on the achievement motive, male students who were high achievers on both college aptitude test scores and academic grades were not significantly less influenced by fictitious group performance standards than high-achieving females when the instructions were designed to arouse the achievement motive. They were more influenced than females when told that the group had been chosen so that the values of individuals were very similar, even though it was stressed that performance was not very important in the task at hand (Wyer, 1967).

A body of literature that bears directly on our topic, namely the choice of competition vs. cooperation in games of strategy, seems to indicate that the structure of the game itself is overwhelmingly important in affecting competitive behavior. The rules of the game, the number of players, the way rewards are or can be distributed and (although this may sound silly when compared to real life) whether or not the players can communicate with each other are examples of such structural properties. For example, in the prisoner's dilemma game the strategy choices are to take a long chance on winning individually, cooperating and losing, or following the surefire cooperative strategy which does not penalize either player. Rappaport and Chammah (1965) reported that in over 300 trials female pairs adopted the surefire cooperative strategy less frequently than males. This finding has been interpreted (Bardwick, 1971, p. 132) as indicating that when faces are hidden, females are really more competitive and aggressive than males, although why they should feel aggressive toward unknown females is not altogether clear. Other research (e.g., Swingle and Santi, 1972) indicates that the crucial fact here is not that faces are hidden but that no communication is permitted. When communication is either permitted or required, female pairs predominantly choose the cooperative strategy.

While the female tendency to cooperate in such games of strategy does vary markedly according to the structure of the game and the situation, the research literature does suggest that males are more likely than females to interpret such game situations as tests of themselves as individuals, and to follow individually competitive strategies more frequently than females (Wrightsman et al., 1972; Grant and Sermat, 1969). This tendency is particularly pronounced when the game includes the opportunity to decide how rewards (usually small sums of money) are to be divided (Vinacke, 1959). While males are more likely to attempt a winner-take-all approach or to form an alliance with another player against a third, females playing together, more often than males, adopt strategies and divisions of reward that divide the rewards equally among the three players. Since I know of no evidence that money is less highly regarded by females than males, the explanation seems to lie in the greater challenge in the activity itself to males than females, as a means of proving himself. I would not expect males to compete so individualistically if the activity was, let us say, baking a cherry pie, nor would I expect females to be so cooperative if the stakes were really high in her eyes.

The importance of such findings is two-fold. First, they suggest that in activity structured so that cooperation is a feasible strategy to win and share rewards, females are if anything more prone than men to cooperate. If such cooperation is aimed at competition with another team, it is, of course, a much better situation than one in which individuals on teams seek stardom at the expense of team cooperation, a tendency reinforced for males by the reward systems prevailing in sports. Second, such research findings suggest feasible approaches to research and planning on female competitive sports, namely systematic consideration of structures of different games and team competitiveness. To this I should add that we should include properties sorely neglected in research on strategy games, such as the group properties (leader-follower relations, norms, solidarity and goals that develop over time). Such systematic examination would greatly expand our knowledge of effective team functioning and may suggest feasible alternatives in building new sport programs.

CLOSING REMARKS

The most honest way to sum up this paper is to say that we have very few firm conclusions to suggest that females are less competitive than males, but that we have a great deal of evidence that competition depends upon the importance of the activities in question to the person, upon whose words and standards count to the person in assessment of performance, and upon the level of the standards as these relate to actual performance capability or potential. We know that in some societies women compete to be submissive and in others they compete to be dominant, as Margaret Mead's anthropological research has shown (1949). We suspect that in a country like the Soviet Union, where 75 percent of the doctors are women, females would compete to be successful and respected doctors. We have every reason to suspect that the same conditions govern competition in sports.

In the United States, something has gone awry in the relationships between sports for females and the reference groups of adolescents and many adult females. Even though there is nothing incongruous at all in sports participation and being physically attractive (in fact, quite the opposite is more likely), the prevailing sentiment among the female adolescents who are likely to be most prestigious is that females who indulge regularly in sports programs are oddballs. In the case of the most popular and feminine sports, outstanding performers are viewed as exceptions whose devotion and performance is to be admired but not emulated. There are many signs that such sentiments are changing, as indicated for example by a revived and widespread interest among adolescent and college-age females in being outdoors, in hiking and camping. It is also perfectly respectable and desirable to be able to hold one's own at tennis, swimming, and in other sports as well.

What I am saying seems more applicable to team play in the more active games. I suspect that one reason females shrink from competitive team play against females may be that it strikes them as a caricature of male team play. Yet, so far as any evidence available, there is no reason to believe that the motivating effects of female groups are any less than those of males. For example, like young males, females in research compete so intensely that blockage of their group goals brings exactly the same sort of hostility that is aroused among boys' groups (Avigdor, 1952; Sherif and Sherif, 1969, Chapter 11). However, the competition in that research involved putting on a play, not sports.

The preferable time to do something about this state of affairs is not adolescence, for pre-pubescent and pubescent girls are among the most conventionally feminine in our population (cf. Seward, 1946; Hartley, 1970). In fact, although the female sex role is more flexible among high school students than it once was, only a couple of years ago the high school was a hotbed of reaction against an attempt to change the role (Farley, 1971). Nevertheless, while I believe that the age to start changing the state of affairs for girls and sports is in grade school and before, the transition to high school must still be made and this transition is likely for a long time to be marked by considerable discontinuity from the role image prevailing for the earlier period. Therefore, I will make some comments that seem to be warranted by the evidence.

First, the alternatives considered by high school and young adult females are likely to continue in the direction of greater flexibility of the female role concept and in the perception of more alternative styles for being female. This projection is based on the probable increased effects of the revived woman's movement as they filter down through colleges to high schools and the larger changes in outlook about identity and worthwhile goals that have already affected many youth and are likely to affect more. The implication is that the current period is probably the most fertile for innovation in female sports programs of any since it was deemed desirable that they exist at all.

Second, particularly since the dominant mythology of female success will continue to be centered on sexual attractiveness and femininity both in securing a mate and in employment, attempts to increase interest in sports competition individually or in teams that place any but the most outstanding female participant in direct competition with males or that produce weak carbon copies of male programs are not likely to make any more headway than they ever have. Here, the catchwords might well be not to imitate, but to innovate. By expanding the concepts of sports competition to include enjoyment in building and strengthening the body with companionship while doing so, I believe that many females could be involved in sports not traditionally included in atheltic programs.

The competitive process, which is really essential for maintaining *élan* and improving performance, does not have to be modeled on either the individualistically oriented winner-take-all model or the varsity-team-is-our-hero model. Competition can occur in activity structures where rewards intrinsic to the activity and rewards for team effort do not hinge on aggressive destruction of the opponents. If there is reluctance for competition with males but a reasonable desire for integrated sports, why not introduce activities in which males and females compete together against others? I am not proposing a female tackle on every football team, but instead the addition of activities in which males and females can appropriately cooperate in competing with others. Research-oriented programs of this kind would be extremely valuable.

Finally, the most fruitful soil for developing and innovating new sport structures and heightening the value of sports is females' reference groups —those whose standards do count and whose encouragement or discouragement is personally important. Here sports programs share with all other adult sponsored or controlled activities the urgent problem of involving youth and being involved *with* youth in the problems that actually move them. The increasingly bureaucratic and compartmentalized structures of large public schools and universities, their increasing divorce from the real problems of youth, and youthful reactions in the form of both protest and mechanical apathy in doing what is required of them, all militant against such involvements. However, if there are determined efforts to give youth, including females, genuinely cooperative roles in planning and execution, I believe that we shall find females and males actively competing to participate in setting new standards for performance that both can genuinely respect because they are their own.

REFERENCES

Allen, V. L., and Newston, D., "Development of conformity and independence," *Journal of Personality and Social Psychology*, 1972, 22, 18-30.

Atkinson, J. W. (ed.), *Motives in Fantasy, Action, and Society*, Princeton, N.J.: Van Nostrand, 1958.

Avigdor, R., "The development of stereotypes as a result of group interaction," Doctoral dissertation, New York University, 1952.

Bardwick, J. M., *Psychology of Women. A Study of Bio-Cultural Conflicts*, New York: Harper and Row, 1971.

Beloff, H., "Two forms of social conformity: Acquiescence and conventionality," *Journal of Abnormal and Social Psychology*, 1958, 56, 99-104.

Bem, S. L., and Bem, D. J., "Training the woman to know her place: The power of a nonconscious ideology," in M. H. Garskof (ed.), *Roles Women Play: Readings Toward Women's Liberation*, Belmont, Calif.: Brooks Cole Publishing Co., 1971, 84-96.

Berne, E. V. C., "An experimental investigation of social behavior patterns in young children," *University of Iowa Studies in Child Welfare*, 1930, 4, No. 3.

Bird, C., *The High Cost of Keeping Women Down*, New York: David McKay, 1968.

Bond, J. R. and Vinacke, W. E., "Coalitions in mixed-sex triads," *Sociometry*, 1961, 24, 61-75.

Brittain, C. V., "Adolescent choices and parent-peer cross-pressures," *American Sociological Review*, 1963, 28, 385-391.

Broverman, I. K., Broverman, D. M., Carlson, F. E., Rosencrantz, P. S., and Vogel, S. R., "Sex-role stereotypes and clinical judgments of mental health," *Journal of Consulting and Clinical Psychology*, 1970, 34, 1-7.

Chapman, D. W. and Volkman, J., "A social determinant of the level of aspiration," *Journal of Abnormal and Social Psychology*, 1939, 34, 225-238.

Clark, K. B. and Clark, M. K., "Racial identification and preference of Negro pre-school children," in T. M. Newcomb and E. L. Hartley (eds.), *Readings in Social Psychology*, New York: Holt, 1947.

Coleman, J. S., *The Adolescent Society*, Glencoe, Ill.: Free Press, 1961.

Emmerich, W., Goldman, K. S., and Shore, R. E., "Differentiation and development of social norms," *Journal of Personality and Social Psychology*, 1971, 18, 323-353.

Entwisle, D. R., "To dispel fantasies about fantasy-based measures of achievement motivation," *Psychological Bulletin*, 1972, 77, No. 6, 377-391.

Farley, J. T. T., "Women on the march against the rebirth of feminism in an academic community," Doctoral dissertation, Cornell University, 1970.

Gecas, V., "Parental behavior and contextual variations in adolescent self esteem," *Sociometry*, 1972, 35, No. 2, 332-345.

Gergen, K. J. and Marlowe, D., (eds.), *Personality and Social Behavior*, Reading, Mass.: Addison-Wesley, 1970.

Gesell, A. and Ilg, F. L., *Infant and Child in the Culture of Today*, New York: Harper, 1943.

Goldberg, P. A., "Are women prejudiced against women?," *Trans-Action*, 1968, April, 28-30.

Goodenough, F. L., *Developmental Psychology*, New York: Appleton Century, second edition, 1945.

Goodman, M. E., *Race Awareness in Young Children*, Reading, Mass.: Addison-Wesley, 1952.

Gottlieb, D., and Ramsey, C., *The American Adolescent*, Homewood, Ill.: Dorsey, 1964.

Grant, M. J., and Sermat, V., "Status and sex of others as determinants of behavior in a mixed-motive game," *Journal of Personality and Social Psychology*, 1969, 12, 151-158.

Greenberg, P. J., "Competition in children: An experimental study," *American Journal of Psychology*, 1932, 44, 221-248.

Hansche, J., and Gilchrist, J. C., "Three determinants of the level of aspiration," *Journal of Abnormal and Social Psychology*, 1956, 53, 136-137.

Hartley, R. E., "American core culture: Changes and continuities," Chapter 6 in G. Seward and R. Williamson (eds.), *Sex Roles in Changing Society*, New York: Random House, 1970, 126-149.

Hirota, K., "Experimental studies in competition," *Japanese Journal of Psychology*, 1951, 21, 70-81, abstracted in *Psychological Abstracts*, 1953, 27, 351.

Hollander, E. P., "Competence and conformity in the acceptance of influence," *Journal of Abnormal and Social Psychology*, 1960, 61, 365-369.

Hooker, E., "Male homosexuality and the Rorschach," *Journal of Projective Techniques*, 1957, 21, 18-31.

Horner, M. S., "Femininity and successful achievement: A basic inconsistency," Chapter 3 in J. M. Bardwick, *et al.*, *Feminine Personality and Conflict*, Belmont, Calif.: Brooks Cole Publishing Co., 1970, 45-74.

Horrocks, J. E., *The Psychology of Adolescence Behavior and Development*, Boston: Houghton Mifflin, third edition, 1969, Chapter 14, Adolescent groups and group membership; Chapter 15, Friendship and interpersonal adequacy; Chapter 20, Physical functioning and efficiency.

Kagan, J., and Moss, H. L., "The stability of passive and dependent behavior from childhood through adulthood," *Child Development*, 1960, 31, 577-591.

Kandel, D. B., and Lesser, G. S., "Parental and peer influences on educational plans of adolescents," *American Sociological Review*, 1969, 34, No. 2, 213-223.

Konopka, G., *The Adolescent Girl in Conflict*, Englewood Cliffs, N.J.: Prentice Hall, 1965.

Lambert, W. E.; Libman, E.; and Poser, E. G., "The effect of increased salience of a membership group on pain tolerance," *Journal of Personality*, 1960, 28, 350-357.

Landers, D. M., "Siblings, sex, status and ordinal position effects on female's sport participation and interests," *Journal of Social Psychology*, 1970, 80, 247-248.

Larsen, K. S., Coleman, D., Forbes, J., and Johnson, R., "Is the subject's personality or the experimental situation a better predictor of a subject's willingness to administer shock to a victim?," *Journal of Personality and Social Psychology*, 1972, 22, 287-295.

Lesser, G. S., Krawitz, R., and Packard, R., "Experimental arousal of achievement motivation in adolescent girls," *Journal of Abnormal and Social Psychology*, 1963, 66, 59-66.

Leuba, C. J., "An experimental study of rivalry in young children," *Journal of Comparative Psychology*, 1933, 16, 367-378.

Lewin, K., Dembo, T., Festinger, L., and Sears, P. S., "Level of aspiration," in J. McV. Hunt (ed.), *Personality and the Behavior Disorders*, New York: Ronald, 1944.

Licuanan, P. B., "The impact of modernization of Filipino adolescents," Manila: Ateneo de Manila University, *IPC Papers No. 10*, 1972, 1-28.

Little, K. B., and Schneidman, E. S., "Congruences among interpretations of psychological and anamestic data," *Psychological Monographs*, 1959, 73, 1-42.

Luschen, G., "Cooperation, association, and contest," *Journal of Conflict Resolution*, 1970, 14, 21-34.

McClelland, D. C., Atkinson, J. W., Clark, R. A., and Lowell, E. L., *The Achievement Motive*, New York: Appleton-Century-Crofts, 1953.

Maccoby, E. E. (ed.), *The Development of Sex Differences*, Stanford: Stanford University Press, 1966.

Mead, M., *Male and Female*, New York: Morrow, 1949.

Milgram, S., "Some conditions of obedience and disobedience to authority," in I. D. Steiner, and M. Fishbein, (eds.), *Current Studies in Social Psychology*, New York: Holt, Rinehart and Winston, 1965, 243-262.

Miller, N., Doob, A. N., Butler, D. C., and Marlowe, D., "The tendency to agree: Situational determinants and social desirability," *Journal of Experimental Research in Personality*, 1965, 2, 78-83.

Milton, G. A., "Sex differences in problem solving as a function of role appropriateness of the problem context," *Psychological Reports*, 1959, 5, 705-708.

Money, J., "Sexual dimorphism and homosexual gender identity," *Psychological Bulletin*, 1970, 77, 6, 425-440.

Moss, H. A., and Kagan, J., "Stability of achievement and recognition-seeking behaviors from early childhood through adulthood," *Journal of Abnormal and Social Psychology*, 1961, 62, 504-513.

Murphy, G., *Personality*, New York: Harper and Row, 1957.

Murphy, L. B., *Social Behavior and Child Personality*, New York: Columbia University Press, 1937.

Parten, M. B., "Social participation among pre-school children," *Journal of Abnormal and Social Psychology*, 1932, 27, 243-269; Social play among pre-school children," *ibid.*, 1933, 28, 136-147.

Peterson, G. I., Kiesler, S. B., and Goldberg, P. A., "Evaluation of the performance of women as a function of their sex, achievement and personal history," *Journal of Personality and Social Psychology*, 1971, 19, 114-118.

Piaget, J., *The Moral Judgment of the Child*, London: Kegan Paul, 1932.

————., *The Origins of Intelligence in Children*, New York: International Universities Press, 1952.

Rosenkrantz, P., Vogel, S., Bee, H., Broverman, I., and Broverman, D., "Sex-role stereotypes and self concepts in college students," *Journal of Consulting and Clinical Psychology*, 1968, 32, 287-295.

Rappaport, A., and Chammah, A. M., "Sex differences in factors contributing to the level of cooperation in the prisoner's dilemma game," *Journal of Personality and Social Psychology*, 1965, 2, 831-838.

Rossi, A. S., "Barriers to the career choice of engineering, medicine or science among American women," in J. A. Mattfeld, and C. G. Van Aken, (eds.), *Women and the Scientific Professions*, Cambridge: MIT Press, 1965, 51-127.

Salusky, A. S., "Collective behavior of children at a preschool age," *Journal of Social Psychology*, 1930, 1, 367-378.

Seward, G. H., *Sex and the Social Order*, New York: McGraw-Hill, 1946.

Sherif, C. W., with Kelly, M., Rodgers, L., Sarup, G., and Tittler, B., "Personal involvement, social judgment and action," *Journal of Personality and Social Psychology*, 1973, 27, 311-328.

Sherif, M., *An Outline of Social Psychology*, New York: Harper, 1948.

Sherif, M., and Cantril, H., *The Psychology of Ego Involvement*, New York: Wiley, 1947.

Sherif, M., and Sherif, C. W., *Reference Groups: Conformity and Deviation of Adolescents,* New York: Harper and Row, 1964.

————., *Social Psychology,* New York: Harper and Row, 1969.

Stein, A. H., Pohly, S., and Mueller, E., "The influence of masculine, feminine and neutral tasks on children's behavior, expectancies of success and attainment values," *Child Development,* 1971, 42, 195-208.

Steinman, A., and Fox, D. J., "Male-female perceptions of the female role in the United States," *Journal of Psychology,* 1966, 64, 265-276.

Sutton-Smith, B., and Roberts, J. M., "The cross-cultural and psychological study of games," in G. Luschen (ed.), *The Cross-Cultural Analysis of Sport and Games,* Champaign, Ill.: Stipes Publishing Co., 1970, 101-108.

Sutton-Smith, B., Rosenberg, P. G., and Morgan, E. F., "Development of sex differences in play choices during pre-adolescence," *Child Development,* 1963, 34, 119-126.

Swingle, P. G., and Santi, A., "Communication in non-zero sum games," *Journal of Personality and Social Psychology,* 1972, 23, 54-63.

Thomas, D. L., and Weigert, A. J., "Socialization and adolescent conformity to significant others: A cross national analysis," *American Sociological Review,* 1972, 33, 305-326.

Vinacke, W. E., "Sex roles in a three-person game," *Sociometry,* 1959, 22, 343-360.

Watson, G., and Johnson, D., *Social Psychology. Issues and Insights,* New York: Lippincott, 1972, Chapter 11.

Weisstein, N., "Psychology constructs the female, or the fantasy life of the male psychologist," in M. H. Garskof (ed.), *Roles Women Play: Readings Toward Women's Liberation,* Belmont, Calif.: Brooks Cole Publishing Co., 1971, 68-83.

Wrightsman, L. S., O'Connor, J., Baker, N. J. (eds.), *Cooperation and Competition: Readings on Mixed Motive Games,* Belmont, Calif.: Brooks/Cole, 1972.

Wyer, R. S., "Behavioral correlates of academic achievement: Conformity under achievement and affiliation-incentive conditions," *Journal of Personality and Social Psychology,* 1967, 6, 255-263.

The Triple Option . . . For Women in Sport

Jan Felshin

Our visions and images of women in sport are circumscribed by existing societal values and sanctions. The dimensions of the possible for the future depend upon contemporary social emphasis. At any particular time, a host of variables of belief, attitude, and action characterize social phenomena. The concept of "women in sport" represents a syndrome of theoretical stances toward both women and sport as well as their interactive relationship.

Beyond analyzing the contemporary status of the concept, the problem of predicting the route of "women in sport" depends upon the ways in which the present and the future are understood to relate. Dichotomous perspectives exist for the prediction of social change and each has differing inferences for the future of women in sport. For instance, if it is assumed that social data are linear and continuous, then the future is predicted to be the present followed to its logical conclusion. In this view, social resolutions and change occur within the framework of existing values and visions and in accord with the flexibility of the prevailing social frame. According to this perspective, social reality of "women in sport" may well change; however, operant notions of both "women" and "sport" will be accommodated. An alternative view suggests that social trends may be discontinuous from the past. Revolutionary modes assume organic social power and imply that newly discovered attitudes may serve as catalysts of sufficient cruciality to negate and/or replace strictures of the past.

The social hypotheses of the present and the possible relationships to change seem to provide a triple option for the future of women in sport. Because these positions contain the potential for ideological compulsion, it is important to clarify them.

From *Quest,* Monograph XXI (January, 1974): 36-40.

THE APOLOGETIC

Although women participate in sport, the conventional wisdom surrounding their athletic efforts and achievements is an apologetic for reality. To the extent that masculinity represents a mode of assertion and aggression, and femininity, passivity and social desirability, women and sport can exist only in uneasy conceptual juxtaposition. Each woman in sport is a social anomaly when sport is seen as the idealized socialization of masculine traits and the ideals of femininity preclude these qualities. Because women cannot be excluded from sport and have chosen not to reject sport, apologetics develop to account for their sport involvement in the face of its social unacceptability.

Women Athletes are Feminine

The cognitive dissonance inherent in traditional conceptions of femininity and athleticism can be dissipated by denial. The women athlete must document the validity of her womanhood within the cultural connotations of femininity. To do this, she frequently denies the importance of her athletic endeavors and avows the importance of her appearance and the desire to be attractive and to marry and raise a family as the overriding motivations of her life.

Women in sport, both the athletes themselves and their sponsors, especially those responsible for school and collegiate programs, have devoted themselves tirelessly to demonstrating that female athletes are real women. The apologetic has been served in countless ways from an insistence on "heels and hose" as an appropriate off-the-court costume to the sacrifice and exile of some women athletes whose non-conforming attitudes or appearance threatened the desired image of femininity. At the least, this point of view accounts for the inordinate attention to how female athletes look and the illogical commentaries on their social and sexual lifestyles.

Women's Sport is Feminine

Personal apologetics are less necessary as social views accomodate a wider range of appropriate role behaviors for women. Insofar as the assumptions that define femininity also imply male superiority, however, this apologetic for women in sport provides a rationale for limited patterns of participation by women. It presumes that women will stay in "their place" in sport; for to be "feminine" means to be less serious and less important, and to recognize men's activities as the consequential ones. Women's sport, then, develops forms unlike the male versions, and emphasizes the so-called "feminine" sport patterns.

Many women have avoided confrontations with their male counterparts in sport by developing programs that emphasize divergent rationales and administrative arrangements that deny any aspirations toward serious athletic endeavor. It is no accident that much of the women's "philosophy" of sport participation implies restriction and control.

THE FORENSIC

It is, of course, the changing sociolegal structures that suggest the possibility of discontinuity in the future roles of women in sport. The contemporary equality revolutions clarify the inequitable and illegal dimensions inherent in many social practices. The framework for change fostered by feminist ideology imply certain logical imperatives for sport.

Women are Equal to Men

The demands for equality for women in sport are predicated upon the inequities of the conventional social wisdom. Sex stereotyping is clearly responsible for differences in self-perception, aspiration, and ability between boys and girls, men and women. Logic demands that once the pernicious effects of stereotypic standards on women are recognized, there must be aggressive efforts to overcome them. The corollary assumption is that in a sexist society, all action is necessarily political.

The feminist point of view emphasizes the assertion of women's rights, and sport is an important focal point because of its significance in society and the fact that the premise of the separation of the sexes in sport is the lesser ability of women. Sport in both school and society is eloquent testimony to the importance of boys and men and the neglect of girls and women. The forensic position demands women's rights to equal protection under the law; to be treated as individuals, not as a group according to commonly held stereotypes. This legal principle is manifest in the diverse challenges that include the right of girls to play on boys' teams in both contact and non-contact sports; the right of women to the enabling licenses to be jockeys, motorcycle racers, wrestlers, boxers, and anything else they wish; the right to equal pay and equal prize monies, to equitable funding and use of public facilities, and to positions, whether as umpires, coaches, sports information directors, or whatever within the sports context.

There is no "Women's" Sport

Generally, feminist ideology has documented the fact that many of the alleged differences between men and women result from social bias. Even experimental findings in psychology and physiology have been demonstrated to reflect male assumptions of women's lesser abilities. It seems logical within this position, therefore, to conclude that the potential of women is unknown and untapped, and that sport particularly should provide opportunities for unhampered aspirations to be manifest.

Equity for women is translated into demands for the privilege and practices attendant to the male competitive model. Once the principle of discrimination as difference was established, women were able to petition successfully for equal treatment in terms of scholarships, budgets, coaching, facilities, and other aspects of athletic opportunity. In some contemporary programs, it is apparent that women's sport is developing in a fashion parallel to men's sport. In addition, the range of sports available to women is increasing, and football, soccer, and ice hockey teams and leagues have expanded.

THE DIALECTIC

The dialectic of women and sport suggests that the concepts themselves and their interactive mutuality may yield unique configurations of social attitudes and sport forms. The position depends on a feminist-humanist assumption, and rejects the model of sport that depends upon a harsh competitive ethic.

Women can be Athletes

Because sport is an enduring human phenomenon, a symbolic domain wherein the interactions of striving, contesting, and excellence are affirmed, it is rooted in human sources. This position suggests that women, no less than men, refresh and refine abilities and sensibilities within sport and that gender is irrelevant to the realm of sport as experience.

The dialectic of women and sport assumes that sexism, like racism, is social and that the disease should not contaminate the relationship between ethical and actual structures of sport as these depend crucially upon commitment and performance. Women, therefore, must be protected from the slander and limitations that arise from sexual stereotyping; they should share equally in athletic opportunities and fully in the testing and stretching of their abilities.

Women can Define Sport

The forensic position does not distinguish between women's rights and goals in the sense that it petitions entry to existing structures, and liberates institutional contexts for women. The androgynous point of view denies any validity for differences between men and women, and its organizing principle is one of access. Carried to its logical conclusion, this view supports the *status quo* of sport except that is includes women.

The dialectic position hypothesizes alternative social definitions for sport. It affirms differences between men and women without assuming genetic cause, and seeks changed visions for both sexes. The dialogue within the dialectic revolves around finding means to preserve the valuable qualities associated with women and actualizing these in human institutions. As the model of sport developed by men is found objectionable for all human persons, the possibilities for new conceptions of sport emerge as alternative options.

THE FUTURISTIC

Although the delineation of these perspectives implies a triple option, there is little doubt that the changing views and roles of women provide a significant element of social discontinuity that must affect sport. The last vestiges of the apologetic effects are presently apparent in the backlash efforts of some organizations to continue to restrict athletic opportunities for women in the face of sociolegal reality. The apologetic is manifest in such stances as the absolute opposition to girls playing on boys' teams, or to scholarships for women, or to women seeking roles as full-time coaches. It is obvious too in the failure of women leaders in sport to pursue the legal sanction for expanded opportunities for the girls and women in their charge, and their continued attitudes of "making do" with limited resources and facilities while their players clamor for expansion and their male counterparts enjoy every financial and actual privilege.

The liberation of women begins with a forensic view of human rights and affirmative action on behalf of self-worth. Only the powerless fear the repercussions of their demands for power, and the young women of the future will not be frightened by the logical conclusions of the apologetic to the effect that if women play on men's teams, there will be no teams for women, and if women insist on their rights, their few freedoms will be lost. It is beginning to be clear that the inflated price paid for sugar and spice is a function of a manipulated market of male superiority.

The immediate future for women's sport derives from the forensic position. Sport will be symbolic of women's rights and gains, and it will develop according to the principle that separate can never mean equal for the second class citizen. For a time, therefore, girls and women will seek access to existing teams in light of their established legal rights to do so. At the same time, the political view supports the idea that women deserve reparations for past inequities and affirmative action principles will be upheld as an antidote to a sexist society and the sport establishment it has created. Both women in sport and women's sport are entering an exciting era characterized by a heady sense of freedom to try anything. As women in sport test their own potential, their freedom to dare will free all sportspersons from the restrictive visions of the technological, predictable, exclusive character of the competitive establishment.

As the "men only" nature of sport is challenged successfully, and as budgets and facilities are shared by legal sanction, men and women will have to learn to co-exist in sport. The entry of women by itself will simply modify men's assumptions and programs. Budget will dictate more shared contests, greater flexibility of scheduling, co-sexual participation and consideration, and, at the same time, will provide a rationale for men to escape the treadmill of the demands for success that have transmuted dreams of glory into nightmares of failure. As women reject their "sex object" image, men may find that they don't have to be "success objects" either.

By the twenty-first century women will have liberated sport both as a male domain and from its contemporary models. Without the assumption of sport as a singular male preserve and the corollary of male superiority, new perspectives must emerge. In a sense, these will diminish the importance of particular contests and contexts, but in doing so they will suggest the attractiveness of the wonderful world of sport for more people in more varied patterns of participation. Because excellence and ability are essential components of the structure of sport, they will never be denied, but both men and women as high level performers will cease to serve as the viable model for all sport. Stadiums, like concert stages, contribute to our cultural life as the arenas for the few.

The shape of sport in the future is not easy to predict. Faith in the dialectic of women and sport implies the development of new and more humanistic modes for social interaction, behavior, and motivation. It also means that women must explore their options; they must be encouraged to try and to be whatever they are impelled to seek; for it is self that is sought, and no apology is required.

Section C

Social Class and Sport

Social class, or socio-economic status, is one of the most obvious forms of social differentiation in North America. The acknowledgement that differentiation into social classes exists often leads to the assumption that one category or class is superior to another. This is reflected in the labels most often applied to designate class: upper class, middle class, lower class.

Although the term, social class, refers generally to the financial resources available to different groups of individuals, class membership is also defined by such salient factors as occupation, education, and place of residence. Moreover, an individual's location within a particular social class has implications for such intangible items as lifestyle, value systems, life chances, and access to power.

As a social category, social class can be related to sport in terms of the access to resources and opportunities differentially available to individuals on the basis of their social background. Before we can learn to sail or to play tennis, someone has to pay for the lessons and the equipment, and we have to move in a social mileau that considers such activities meaningful. The ideas that sport involvement is limited by our financial resources and constrained by the value systems which surround us as social class members are the themes of the readings in this section.

Gruneau discusses the concept of democratization with reference to modern sport in Canada. Gruneau dispels the myth that sport is a meritocracy where only ability counts. Instead, Gruneau argues, a bias toward upper-middle and middle class background exists among elite amateur athletes, indicating that sport is not a true democracy but another area in which access to resources is a significant determinent of opportunity.

Listiak uses participant observation to study Grey Cup Week in Canada as a festival during which normal restraints on behavior are relaxed. Listiak explores the thesis that such secular rituals as Grey Cup Week serve an integrative function in society by providing an opportunity for members of all classes to mix together in a common experience. Contrary to this hypothesis, however, Listiak finds definite class differences in bar behavior during Grey Cup Week, leading him to conclude that the festivities serve as a middle-class binge and thus reinforce social barriers rather than transcend them.

Class or Mass: Notes on the Democratization of Canadian Amateur Sport

Richard S. Gruneau

INTRODUCTION[1]

Sport has long been regarded as a graphic symbol of meritocracy[2] in western industrial societies. On the playing field it has been frequently taken-for-granted that all compete equally under conditions whereby available rewards accrue to the most highly skilled. There is, however, a good deal of historical evidence to suggest that this view of sport as a true "democracy of ability" (to use Baron de Coubertin's famous phrase) has often been a greatly exaggerated interpretation. Research has shown that socioeconomic biases in nineteeth and early-twentieth century sport were commonplace and greatly limited opportunities for participation and performance by underprivileged groups in social life.[3]

Yet, it has become fashionable in recent years to argue that most of the socioeconomic barriers that limited sports participation and performance in the past have now largely eroded. By this reasoning, the major characteristic of sport's general transition from traditional, class-based elite and folk recreational activities[4] to modern "mass sport" has been a widespread process of democratization (cf., Page, 1973). In this paper I examine two contrasting perspectives on this democratization and data which may be of some use in evaluating which of the perspectives has the greatest relevance for explaining the current socioeconomic dimensions of Canadian amateur sport.

PERSPECTIVES AND DEMOCRATIZATION

Generally considered, the term democratization implies the widening availability of, and diminishing separatism in, varying forms of sport involvement. However, this definition, like many in sociology, is analytically imprecise. It resonates better as a shorthand expression of social changes than as a sociological understanding of these changes and therefore allows considerable disagreement over its contours and limitations. Yet, for most sociologists and popular writers the democratization of sport has been narrowly understood. Its primary focus has concerned the declining relevance of social class and status barriers as factors which affect both the differential accessibility of various aspects of sport involvement and the stimulation of mass athletic participation.

What has occurred, the argument runs, is an overall expansion of opportunities in sport which correlates with a broader erosion of aristocratic and bourgeois class inequality in western societies. The class inequalities of the nineteenth and early twentieth centuries have supposedly been vitiated through broad patterns of social mobility and through widespread changes in social conditions[5] brought on by the growth of mass leisure, mass consumption and mass entertainment (cf. Barber, 1957; Kaplan, 1960; Betts, 1974).[6] Of course, not all sociologists have viewed the consequences of such changes in a completely positive manner (see Stone, 1973; Kando, 1975),[7] but for the majority, the growth of a generally democratized "mass sport" has been heralded as a testament to the inherently classless and nondiscriminatory character of modern life. The image of the affluent democracies, where class and other barriers have decomposed, stands as one of the most powerful and persistent themes in the writings of modern sociologists, and sport has recurrently been suggested as both a graphic reflection and symbolic initiator of these changes.

Unfortunately the popularity of such a perspective does not necessarily make it correct. For example, much of the recent sociological literature on social class and other aspects of structured inequality in western industrial societies emphasizes that the decomposition of particularistic barriers in social institutions has not been achieved to the degree that is popularly believed (see Bottomore, 1966; Parker, 1972; Giddens, 1973; Johnson, 1972; 1974; and Clement, 1975).[8] Moreover, recent empirical studies of active sports participation in the United States and Europe have generally indicated that, as an institution, sport appears to have offered little exception to this pattern. Although it is somewhat of an oversimplification the findings here can be classified under two broad headings: (a) those studies dealing with leisure-sport involvement and (b) those studies dealing with more organized competitive sports. Most of the former have indicated considerable differences in the significance of selected correlates of active participation[9] but as a general pattern it appears that the lower fifths of the income and occupational ranges tend to be substantially under-represented in the majority of activities (cf., Clarke, 1956; Stone, 1957; Boston, 1968; Emmett, 1971; Kraus, 1971; Burdge, 1974). This relationship is emphasized even more clearly by data on participation in competitive amateur sports. Despite some recruitment differences among sports, nearly all studies have indicated that active involvement is positively related to middle and upper-middle class income levels[10] (see Loy, 1969: Lüschen, 1969; Webb, 1969; Collins, 1972).[11] Furthermore, a somewhat enduring consistency between the rank ordering of certain competitive sports and the classes and status groups from which they draw their membership seems to hold in a variety of different countries and across a range of different sample groups.

While such findings may allow for the assertion that the "leisure class" (see Veblen, 1953) of the past has been somewhat transformed by the changing social conditions of modern life, it seems premature to assert, as Gregory Stone (1973) does, that the "leisure class" has become a "leisure mass." Such an assertion greatly underplays the consistency of results which suggest how sports participation continues to remain less universalistic than particularistic. In fact, given the consistency of particularistic findings on a range of types of active sport involvement, it may make some sense to develop and argue a contrary perspective on sport's democratization; one that depicts the reduction of barriers to athletic recruitment less as the harbinger of an open and classless society than the result of the appropriation of folk and elite traditions in sport by the ascendant middle classes of the last century. The implication here is not that the broad-scale erosion of social inequalities in sport testifies to the success of contemporary liberal democracy as a levelling form of political economic organization;[12] rather, the implication is that where traditional inequalities actually have eroded they have often been replaced by new forms of social distinction. For example, over the last century market position and increasing tendencies to assess personal worth in terms of exchange value[13] appear to have increasingly made inroads into the legacies of property, lineage, or racial and ethnic status as the dominant conditions for involvement and the allocation of subsequent rewards. These changes, in the context of their association with the rationalistic[14] forces of the contemporary productive process, may well reflect a "bourgeoisification" of sport far more than they demonstrate an association with the widespread class decomposition that is supposedly characteristic of modern "mass society."[15] Such a view does not imply that socioeconomic changes in sport have *totally* excluded the opportunities for the disadvantaged to develop their physical activities, for it is clear that a good deal of democratization has occurred. The argument is simply that the locus of this democratization can be found within the bourgeoisie[16] and that the forces of change have not necessarily been a linear progression toward equality so much as a basic extension and consolidation of middle class privilege in and through the sporting world.

THE CANADIAN CASE

Which of these perspectives on democratization offers a more accurate interpretation of the development of sport in Canada? It must be conceded that there have been great changes in the degree of exclusivity of various sport forms over the last two centuries. As Metcalfe (1976) and others (Wise and Fisher, 1974) have argued, sport in early nineteenth century Canada was greatly affected by class divisions. That is, despite the existence of comparatively egalitarian recreational activities among frontier Canadians or the urban working classes the roots of organized sports participation can be traced to the leisure pastimes of the "soldier-gentlemen" of the early British military garrisons (Lindsay, 1969), the sporting clubs of the urban elites and developing entrepreneurial classes of the nineteenth century (Metcalfe, 1972; Wise and Fisher, 1974), and the private school and university backgrounds of Canada's anglophone charter group. Such circles of influence reflected British gentry-class traditions in a "Victorian Legacy" (see Mallea, 1975) that ingrained a distinctive ascriptive bias to the earliest organization and administration of Canadian sport. This bias manifested itself in the rather clearly defined (and often legally sanctioned) rules of class, racial and ethnic exclusion that guided the organized activities of the period[17] but the bias was given its general expression in simple conditions of scarcity. Most people had neither the time, money, nor opportunity to participate in an organized fashion and when they were involved it was often only through the then "vulgar" alternative of professionalism.

The contemporary scene, of course, appears vastly different. Extreme class and status-linked barriers to sports participation appear to have been greatly challenged by the changing social conditions of Canadian society. At one level, such factors as technological changes in industry and communications, the expansion of economic surplus, shifts in religious values, the historical concern of the military over fitness, the expansion of the educational system, and the rise of industrial and community-based sports programs, have all been important in broadening the exposure of sport to diverse groups in the population.[18] At another level, given the quantitative growth of the Canadian bourgeoisie and the gradual institutionalization of the rational meritocratic values of liberal democracy, achievement, success, and a concern over the *outcome* of sporting events have all been instrumental in re-assessing both the *utility* and the *desirability* of ascriptive barriers to participation[19] and achievement. Finally, in the shape of state intervention in sport, universal access and the equal opportunity for achievement have come to be increasingly defined as social rights of citizenship rather than privileges of class or status. As T. H. Marshall (1950) has argued, governments in most of the modern liberal democracies have developed commitments to move in the direction of the equality of citizen rights, not just in a civil and political sense, but also in the guarantee of comparable degrees of health and welfare for their citizens. Since the early 1960's Canada's expanding federally and provincially supported sports and recreational programs have been designed (in theory) to broaden at least partially the base of athletic participation in Canadian society.[20] In the face of all of these indices of democratization and increased opportunity it appears difficult to argue with the assertion made in the Canadian government's 1969 *Report of the Task Force on Sport for Canadians* that: "The aristocratic conception of sport has democratized; a whole new world of human activity has been born in which millions take part. . . ."

But it is important to reaffirm here that the decline of the "aristocratic" conception of sport does not necessarily mean that *all* "class" standards for participation have entirely eroded or that new standards have failed to develop. A concentration on the social structural and cultural changes in Canadian society which appear to have been so instrumental in democratizing sport virtually predisposes one to underplay the persistence and possible emergence of factors which continue to guarantee some measure of continuity in the advantaged positions of certain groups. Especially problematic in this regard is the fact that most Canadians *want* to believe not only that their sports are freely meritocratic but that they mirror a democratic and classless society. As Marchak (1975:15) aptly puts it:

> Canadians may not quite believe that all people have equality of opportunity, that birth has no effect on rank, or that anyone may rise to the top. But they see these as defects or imperfections in a classless and mobile society to be reformed or acknowledged perhaps, but not to be interpreted as evidence of a class structure. Golf, appliances, deodorants and Beethoven are equally available to all, and the lack of class distinctions is nowhere more apparent than in the market place.

The prevalence of such beliefs, frequently buttressed by the importation of American stereotypes, reinforces the image of Canada as an affluent leisure society where the problems of inequality are best thought of as "personal troubles of milieu" rather than "issues" of social structure.[21] For, the argument runs, if there is still some measure of inequality today, the existence of an expanded opportunity structure implies that differences between individuals and groups can be explained on the basis of individual achievement rather than on the basis of commonly shared social characteristics.

As attempts to speculate on the legitimacy of such beliefs in the context of sport involvement, empirical studies of the current socioeconomic dimensions of sports participation in Canada have been only of limited value. The few studies of sporting pastimes in this country have tended to concentrate on "leisure-sport" involvement, and have generally emphasized a range of background factors like age, sex, and socialization influences, without attempting to integrate these variables into general statements on the relationship of sport to the class structure (see Kenyon and McPherson, 1973; Hobart, 1974; White, 1975). Moreover, because these studies have differentially defined independent and dependent variables and have utilized divergent research strategies and sample populations, it is difficult to summarize coherently their findings for an understanding of the complex relationship between sport and structured social inequality in Canada. Despite these limitations most of the studies are unanimous in their suggestion that specific forms of active sports participation in Canada remain conditioned by socioeconomic factors that seem generally linked to class position. Typical of such findings are those documented in Curtis and Milton's (1976) ambitious secondary analysis of Canadian "leisure-sports" participation. Their findings revealed socioeconomic differences in both active and passive participation and showed that sports tended to *recruit from high social participators in general*. Although the authors advise "caution" in generalizing about differences or lack of differences and about the strength of socioeconomic correlates across different types and dimensions of sporting activity, their data, in common with those of other studies, go some way toward suggesting that the open "leisure society" has yet to materialize in Canada.

But sociologists' concern with dimensions of "leisure-sports" participation in Canada has not been matched by a parallel concern for the dimensions of more organized competitive forms. This inattention is striking because it is frequently the competitive forms of sport which are invoked as having especially revealed the changes in condition and opportunity that have characterized the recent development of the modern liberal democracies. For instance, at one point in his analysis of the club of

"Philadelphia Gentlemen" American sociologist E. Digby Baltzell (1958: 360) notes how "Changing sporting mores and the changing social origins of sportsmen are often sensitive seismographs of social upheavel." Thus, they can be particularly relevant as foundations on which to make general inferences about the equality of life chances in societies where sporting activities appear important. Even more significant, however, is that the socioeconomic contours of competitive sport can be (and frequently are) interpreted as a *symbolic* statement of the effectiveness and meritocratic character of the distribution of rewards in a market society. As such, competitive sport should receive special attention in any analysis of the comparative explanatory power of divergent perspectives on the democratization of sport in Canadian Society. In the passages which follow, data on the social origins of competitors at the 1971 Canada Winter Games are viewed with these issues in mind. Given that the information presented is "cross-sectional" rather than "longitudinal" it would be hazardous to speak directly to the actual question of trends as *specific properties of the data,* but a snapshot of patterns at a fixed point in time does suggest *current* degrees of "class" or "mass" participation.

SOME METHODOLOGICAL CONSIDERATIONS

The Canada Winter and Summer Games are alternating national events which provide inter-provincial competition for junior (and some senior) provincial champions in selected sports. The information presented here is taken from a stratified sample survey (n=877) of the competitors at the 1971 Winter Games in Saskatoon that was administered by DuWors and Gruneau (1972).[22] For the presentation at hand the focus is on possible correlates of social inequality as reflected through occupation of athletes' fathers, parents' educations, reported family income, ethnicity and religion. All of these correlates have frequently been referred to as empirically relevant dimensions of social inequality in Canada (see for example, Porter, 1966) but they are organized here into two conceptually distinct categories: (a) class backgrounds and (b) status-group association. Class backgrounds are indicated by income and education correlates and *especially* father's occupation. As Frank Parkin (1972) points out, the occupational order in all of the capitalist industrial societies is generally the "backbone" of the reward structure and, as such, it must be seen as the foundation of modern class inequality.[23] "Other sources of economic and symbolic advantage do exist alongside the occupational order" but these generally seem to be secondary to those deriving from position in the marketplace (Parkin, 1972:18).[24] Occupational data for this study were coded on a six category occupational ranking index which combines prestige rankings with the comparative weight of education and income for occupational incumbents (Blishen, 1958:1971).[25]

Status-group association includes such factors as ethnicity and religion. Literature on social stratification and inequality in Canadian society affirms that these factors nearly always intrude on the issue of class position (see Porter, 1966; Dofny and Rioux, 1964; Kelner, 1973; Cuneo and Curtis, 1975; Forcese, 1975; Vallee, 1975, and Clement, 1975) but, as Weber (1958) once remarked about status-groups generally, sometimes the loyalties and emotional identifications involved in them rival and surpass those of class, and sometimes they cut across class lines. The ethnicity of Canada Games athletes was determined by their parents' places of birth and the reported national origin of their family name (self-designated ethnicity).

BACKGROUNDS OF CANADA GAMES ATHLETES

(a) Social Class Correlates

Occupational data presented in Table 1 reveal that the fathers of competitors at the 1971 Canada Games came from a wide range of occupational backgrounds. However, when compared to national male labour force percentages athletes' fathers were over-represented in the professional and white collar occupational categories (especially Blishen categories 1, 2 and 3) and under-represented in those categories primarily reflecting blue collar and primary industry occupations.

Establishing the degree of over- or under-representation from Table 1 is complicated by the fact that the only complete classification of the Canadian male labour force by Blishen's categories is based on 1961 figures. Blishen's top three categories roughly include professional, managerial, technical and finance occupations, which in 1961 made up 17% of the male labour force. White collar sales, clerical and service occupations (category 4 approximately) made up 20% of the 1961 male labour force. The remaining 63% included a range of production occupations, primary industries and skilled, semi or unskilled labour (categories 5 and 6). Using Blishen's figures as a reference, the 37% of athletes' fathers who were classified in the upper three Blishen categories contrasts starkly with the 17% of the male labour force who ostensibly engaged in such activities. Similarly the 29% of athletes' fathers coming from the lower two Blishen categories contrasts even more glaringly with the 63% of the labour force which Blishen suggested could be classified at this level.

TABLE 1

Occupation of Athletes' Fathers Compared to
Canadian Male Labour Force (CMLF) Percentages

Fathers Occupation by Blishen Category	CMLF as Calculated by Blishen (1961 figures)[d]	CMLF using 1971 Figures[e] (approximate)	Male Athletes' Fathers	Female Athletes' Fathers	Total (all Athletes)
			(N = 509)	(N = 368)	(N = 877)
1 (70.00+)	4		12	19	15
2 (60.00-69.99) a	4 }	25	{ 9	11	10
3 (50.00-59.99)	9		10	14	12
4 (40.00-49.99)[b]	20	20	23	21	22
5 (30.00-39.99)	32 ⎫		16	16	16
		55	{		
6 (below 30.00) c	31 ⎭		16	9	13
Other			6	6	6
Did not Answer			7	4	6

[a]includes professional, managerial, financial and technical occupations;
[b]includes clerical, sales, white collar and service occupations;
[c]includes production and primary industry, crafts, transport skilled and unskilled labour;
[d]Bernard Blishen, "A Socioeconomic Index for Occupations in Canada" in *Canadian Society: Sociological Perspectives,* Toronto: Macmillan, 1971.
[e]Ministry of Industry, Trade and Commerce, *Perspective Canada* (1974:123)

It would be a study in itself to up-date Blishen's index, thus the comparisons presented above are somewhat tied to 1961 male labour force averages. Yet, (taking a certain degree of methodological license) it is possible to make approximate estimates of how occupational data from the latest Canada census (1971) align with the general occupational groups subsumed under Blishen's categories. Canadian census figures on the 1971 *male* labour force indicate that professional managerial and technical occupations now include 25% of the male labour force. Clerical, sales and service occupations include 20% and production and primary indus-

tries, skilled and unskilled labour 55%.[26] Comparing athletes' fathers occupations to these data makes the pattern of over- and under-representation less striking perhaps but still reveals a distinct association with professional and commercial activities.

One additional feature of Table 1 that seems worth noting is the difference in occupational percentages between the fathers of male and female athletes. Whereas 31% of the fathers of male athletes had upper-
middle and middle class category 1, 2 or 3 occupations, 44% of the fathers
of the female athletes were ranked at this level. At the same time, fewer
of the fathers of female athletes appeared to be working at occupations
that could be classified as lower class. These findings are somewhat compatible with those of Lüschen's (1969) study of athletes in German sports
clubs. Commenting on marked class differences between male and female competitors, Lüschen suggested that there are strong social barriers
for lower class women who are interested in participating and achieving
rewards in competitive sport.

The information detailed in Table 1 is aggregate data containing the
occupations of all athletes' fathers. Since economic disparities between
Canada's provinces tend to be significant, provincial variations in the
occupational characteristics of athletes' fathers are detailed in Table 2.

In the face of disparities in wealth and employment opportunities and
the different market characteristics of regional labour forces, provincial
differences in athletes' fathers' occupations were to be expected. However, in *all* provinces (even the generally disadvantaged Maritimes)
athletes' fathers were substantially over-represented in middle class occupations and substantially under-represented in lower-ranking ones. Particularly noticeable is Alberta where athletes' fathers on over *half* the
provincial team sample were employed in high-ranking professional and
white collar occupations. By contrast, athletes' fathers from British Columbia appear to approximate more closely general male labour force
percentages. The near proportional pattern of the occupations of athletes' fathers from the British Columbia team also contrasts with the middle class over-representation of athletes' fathers from the Maritime teams.
It may be that in those provinces where class and status-group inequalities are most graphic, competitive sport tends to over-recruit from the
highest strata in the middle class. This hypothesis receives some support
in Table 3, which compares Blishen's ranking of provincial male labour
forces (1971:507) on the basis of their average index scores, with the
mean occupational index scores of athletes' fathers. Table 3 indicates that
athletes' fathers from the "poorest" provinces did not necessarily have
the lowest mean occupational index scores.

TABLE 2

Provincial Rankings on Basis of Mean Occupational Index Scores (Blishen) for Athletes' Fathers (Provincial Male Labour Force Averages, as Calculated by Blishen, Included in Brackets)[d]

Rank on Mean Blishen Score for Athletes' Fathers	Subsample sizes (N)	Percentage of Athletes' Fathers in top 3 Blishen categories[a]	Percentage of Athletes' Fathers in Blishen Category 4[b]	Percentage of Athletes' Fathers in Blishen Categories 5 and 6[c]	Other and Did not Answer
1) Alberta	(85)	52(19)	19(20)	24(62)	5
2) Manitoba	(88)	43(17)	17(22)	28(62)	12
3) Ontario	(84)	38(19)	29(20)	21(61)	12
4) Saskatchewan	(91)	44(17)	20(19)	31(64)	5
5) Nova Scotia	(71)	37(12)	16(25)	35(63)	12
6) Newfoundland	(81)	33(11)	21(16)	30(73)	16
7) New Brunswick	(75)	30(13)	21(20)	25(68)	24
8) P.E.I.	(50)	30(10)	44(18)	18(72)	8
9) Quebec	(98)	31(17)	27(19)	37(65)	5
10) Yukon	(43)	25	19	40	16
11) British Columbia	(74)	28(17)	22(19)	43(64)	7
12) North West Territories	(37)	25	14	41	20

[a]Includes professional, managerial and finance occupations;
[b]Includes clerical, sales and service occupations;
[c]Includes production and primary industry, skilled and unskilled labour occupations.
[d]See Blishen, (1971).

TABLE 3

Comparison of Ranks Based on Mean Blishen Socioeconomic
Index Scores for Provincial Labour Forces (Male)
and Athletes' Fathers in Provincial Team Samples

Rank on Mean Socioeconomic Index Scores for Provincial Labour Force (male) (Blishen, 1971:507)	Rank on Mean Socioeconomic Index Scores for Athletes' Fathers in Provincial Team Samples
1 Ontario	1 Alberta
2 Alberta	2 Manitoba
3 Manitoba	3 Ontario
4 British Columbia	4 Saskatchewan
5 Quebec	5 Nova Scotia
6 Saskatchewan	6 Newfoundland
7 Nova Scotia	7 New Brunswick
8 New Brunswick	8 Prince Edward Island
9 Prince Edward Island	9 Quebec
10 Newfoundland	10 British Columbia
Data for Yukon	11 Yukon
and North West Territories	12 North West Territories
not presented by Blishen	

Aggregate data on athletes' parents' educations are presented in Table 4. The data pattern generally supports the upper middle and middle class bias displayed in the distribution of athletes' fathers' occupations. Twenty-nine percent of athletes' fathers and 20% of athletes' mothers, had some university experience whereas the national (1971) percentage for the Canadian population over the age of 35 is approximately 16%. The pattern of over-representation also occurs at the level of high-school graduates. Table 4 also reveals that 40% of middle-aged Canadians had elementary school or less in 1971 but only 17% of the athletes' fathers and 16% of the athletes' mothers were classified on this basis.

The reported incomes of athletes' families are generally consistent with the findings on athletes' fathers' occupations and parents' educations.[27] In Table 5 the 1970 Canadian family income range is divided into quartiles (each contains one quarter of all family income recipients) and then compared to the distribution for athletes' families. Most noticeable is that only 9% of athletes' reported family incomes fall in the bottom quartile of Canadian family income earners. But, the income data

TABLE 4

Highest Level of School Attended by Athletes' Parents
Compared to National Averages for Canadian Adults (in Percent)[a]
(N = 877)

Educational Level	Athletes' Father	Athletes' Mother	Approximate National Averages (1972) (Men and Women 35 and over)
Elementary School or Less	17	16	40
Completed Some High School	23	28	27
Finished High School	23	28	17
Completed Some University	10	9	5
Finished University	19	11	11
Other (i.e., vocational training)	6	7	—
Did Not Answer	2	1	—

[a]Percentages for civilian non-institutional population 35 and over .calculated from data presented in Statistics Canada, *The Labour Force* Feb. 1973, Vol. 29 #2.

are undoubtedly skewed somewhat by the large non-response (23%). However, an examination of the occupations of the fathers of those who failed to respond to the income probe suggests that the majority of non-responses would generally tend to fall in the top half of the range. For example, only about 25% of the 201 athletes who failed to report a family income had fathers whose occupations were classified in the bottom two Blishen categories; 21% of them had fathers whose occupations fell in Blishen category 4; and 33% had fathers whose occupations fell into the top three Blishen categories.

One problem with viewing general social class correlates of any group of athletes has to do with the fact that critical subsample variations become submerged in the aggregate. *Sport* is so wide a category that to assess its relationship to class inequality without examining specific sport differences can be misleading and tends to neglect the "folk" and "elite" traditions of specific activities. Thus, in Table 6 it is relevant to observe that those sports like boxing, weightlifting and wrestling which demand a less expensive venue, or tend to be stereotypically linked up with "folk" and underclass traditions and lifestyles, appear to recruit their participants from families where the fathers' occupation actually does have a lower

TABLE 5

Percentage of Canada Games Athletes' Parents Located by
Quartiles[a] of the 1970 Canadian Family Income Range[b]

Lowest Quartile	Second Quartile	Third Quartile	Highest Quartile	No Answer[c]
9	19	23	26	23

[a]Each quartile contains one quarter of all family income recipients; for example, the lowest quartile contains the quarter of Canadian families with the lowest incomes.
[b]Data calculated from *Statistics Canada Daily*, Wednesday, June 23, 1974.
[c]23% non-response consisted of 201 respondents. Of this group 33% had fathers whose occupations were classified in the top three Blishen categories whereas only 20% of the group had fathers in the bottom two Blishen categories.

ranking than sports like synchronized swimming, badminton, gymnastics or skiing.[28] Such findings are not surprising and they are somewhat consistent with the kinds of rankings detailed in studies of amateur and school sport in other societies (Loy, 1969; Webb, 1960; Lüschen, 1969).

But, it would be misleading to suggest that sports like boxing are necessarily underclass sports simply because they rank *lower* than upper-middle class on the basis of the occupations of the athletes' fathers. Samples of sports participants must be compared to national or regional labour force percentages. When this is done for the sample at hand it becomes apparent that the percentages of athletes' fathers in blue collar, production and primary industry occupations is barely equal to, or does not exceed, the proportion of the Canadian male labour force involved in these activities. Thus, even though fathers from the highest ranking occupations are under-represented in these activities, the pattern of representation tends more to lower-middle class and upper status blue collar recruitment[29] than a clear reflection of underclass dominance. Other sports, however, tend to be much more dominated by the middle and upper-middle class. The mean occupational score for athletes' fathers in all but five sports falls consistently within the range of the top three Blishen categories. Synchronized swimming and badminton are rather startling in this regard, but in at least six activities the percentage of athletes' fathers whose occupations fall in the top three Blishen categories exceeds 40%.

TABLE 6

Type of Sport Ranked by Mean Occupational Index Scores for Athletes' Fathers

Blishen Category into Which Mean Score Falls	Rank on Mean Occupational Index Scores for Athletes' Fathers	Subsample Sizes (N)	Percentage of Athletes' Fathers in Top 3 Blishen Categories	Percentage of Athletes' Fathers in Blishen Category 4	Percentage of Athletes' Fathers in Blishen Categories 5 and 6	Other	Did Not Answer
(60.00-69.99)	Synchronized Swimming	(42)	72	12	12	2	2
	Badminton	(44)	54	16	9	16	4
(50.00-59.99)	Gymnastics	(46)	48	28	15	2	6
	Alpine Skiing	(62)	48	31	16	2	3
	Speed Skating	(52)	43	31	20	2	6
	Figure Skating	(46)	41	33	22	4	—
	Nordic Skiing	(41)	37	12	27	13	12
	Table Tennis	(38)	35	21	34	2	8
	Basketball	(96)	39	19	29	10	3
	Volleyball	(109)	39	21	32	5	4
	Curling	(64)	30	28	37	—	5
	Fencing	(21)	29	10	29	19	14
(40.00-49.99)	Hockey	(84)	22	29	39	4	7
	Wrestling	(43)	21	12	45	12	10
	Judo	(25)	16	12	48	20	4
	Weightlifting	(36)	9	19	59	11	3
	Boxing	(28)	4	21	50	4	22
1961 CMLF Averages (Blishen)			17	20	63	—	—
1971 CMLF Averages (Approximate)			25	20	55	—	—

509

(b) Status Group Correlates

In conjunction with the view that sport has been a significant aspect of class decomposition in Canadian society is the idea that sport simultaneously reduces the social distance between ethnic and religious groups by promoting harmony and friendship between them. Along these lines, I should mention that the particular theme of the 1971 Canada Winter Games was "Unity Through Sport."[30] While this theme distinctly referred to anglophonic and francophonic "unity" it presumably was meant to encompass the range of groups making up the Canadian mosaic. Used in the above sense, the term "mosaic" has gained popularity among Canadians partly as a result of a generalized tendency to view Canada in a socially pluralist fashion. The current "official" version[31] of Canadian society suggests that Canada is a federated mosaic of distinct but equal cultural groupings each sharing in the rewards that their union brings. Under this arrangement differences are bound to arise but, given the equal involvement of all in national events, it is argued that the difficulties can be assuaged in the pursuit of collective goals. Unfortunately, the comparative equality of groups in the mosaic seems to have remained convoluted by the invidious ranking of these groups in the current system of structured inequality. As John Porter (1966) described so clearly in *The Vertical Mosaic*, Canada's cultural groupings—its status groups— are arranged hierarchically such that some groups are far more equal than others. To what degree are any of these cleavages revealed among Canada Games athletes?

Table 7 presents data on the country of origin of athletes' parents. What is immediately obvious is that the overwhelming majority of the athletes who competed at the Games were at least second generation Canadians. Over 80% of the parents of the athletes were born in Canada and when parents born in the British Isles are included, the percentage climbs to over 85%. In other words, perhaps we might question the degree to which high level amateur sport in Canada appears to be heavily recruiting from the Canadian immigrant populations of the last thirty years.

In the sense that country of origin of parents does not really index all possible ethnic or religious differences, athletes were asked to designate their own ethnicity to the best of their ability. This is a particularly crude index of active cultural differences in lifestyle or viewpoint between athletes but it does appear to have some value in providing an overview of general patterns of status group association. These data are outlined in Table 8, although their presentation must be guided by a further caveat. Simply, many athletes either refused to answer or felt that they could not accurately designate their ethnicity. Thus, the "unknown" category in some of the provincial subsamples is substantial

TABLE 7

Birthplace of Athletes' Parents[a]

Place of Birth	Fathers		Mothers	
	(N)	(%)	(N)	(%)
Canada	691	78.8	714	81.4
British Isles	59	6.8	54	6.1
German and Scandinavian	38	4.3	46	5.1
Other	72	9.3	58	6.8
No Answer	7	0.8	5	0.6

[a]Percentages of Countries counting at least 1% of the total.
Note: Required citizenship is not a contaminating variable here since any landed immigrant who had been a resident for two years or more was eligible.

enough to make the patterns displayed of dubious reliability. Yet, in spite of the problems of making overly specific conclusions here the data patterns described in Table 8 are highly compatible with other studies of status group involvement in Canadian life (cf., Vallee, 1975). For example, the under-representation of athletes from French backgrounds even on the provincial teams of Quebec and New Brunswick is striking. This finding corroborates those of Boileau et al. (1976) who have documented the under-representation of francophones on Canadian international sports teams. Moreover, given that studies have suggested that francophones tend to have underclass status more than anglophones, their comparatively small percentages in this sample seem compatible with the data presented on class correlates of involvement. A final observation from Table 8, is that athletes from German and Scandinavian backgrounds are represented in greater proportion than either the French or "other European" categories.

Because ethnicity and religion are relatively consistent dimensions of status group association it is not surprising to find that the underrepresentation of predominantly Catholic groups like francophones or Italians is partially reflected in the religious affiliations of athletes and their parents.[32] Table 9 shows that athletes and athletes' parents were over-represented in the Protestant denominations and under-represented in the Catholic ones. Again, this finding is somewhat compatible with those of other studies. Lüschen (1972:27) has noted that: "Max Weber's findings about the relationship between the Protestant ethic and the spirit of capitalism may thus well be extended to the spirit of sport." Lüschen sampled over 1800 members of German sports clubs and found that just

TABLE 8

Ethnic Composition of Provincial Teams (Percent Reported Affiliation) Compared to Provincial and National Averages (1971) (Provincial Averages Displayed in Brackets)[a]

Provincial Team	Subsample Size (N)	British Isles	French	German and Scandinavian	Other European	All Others	Unknown
Newfoundland	(81)	54(94)	6(3)	3(1)	6(.5)	5(.5)	26(1)
P.E.I.	(50)	48(83)	12(14)	8(2)	6(.5)	6(.5)	20(-)
Nova Scotia	(71)	56(78)	10(1)	10(7)	3(2)	1(2)	20(1)
New Brunswick	(75)	39(58)	20(37)	9(2)	1(1)	6(1)	25(1)
Quebec	(98)	16(11)	40(79)	6(1)	6(7)	20(2)[b]	12(-)
Ontario	(84)	41(59)	4(10)	8(10)	19(16)	7(4)	21(1)
Manitoba	(88)	47(42)	10(9)	15(20)	12(21)	6(7)	10(1)
Saskatchewan	(91)	46(42)	2(6)	24(28)	9(17)	6(6)	13(1)
Alberta	(85)	41(47)	1(6)	23(25)	10(17)	6(3)	19(2)
British Columbia	(74)	45(58)	4(4)	8(18)	17(12)	4(6)	22(2)
Yukon	(43)	42(49)	2(7)	11(17)	5(10)	5(15)	35(2)
North West Territories	(37)	27(25)	5(7)	22(7)	(5)	11(54)[c]	35(2)
Total All Athletes	(877)[d]	41(45)	10(29)	13(10)	9(12)	7(3)	20(1)

[a]Data compiled from Ministry of Industry, Trade and Commerce; Perspective Canada, (1974:264-265).
[b]17% of Quebec team listed ethnicity as "Canadian."
[c]Large percentage for "all others" here due to substantial Indian and Inuit population.
[d]Averages may not work out exactly due to rounding.

512

TABLE 9

Religious Affiliations of Athletes and Athletes' Parents
Compared to National Averages (in Percent)

Religious Affiliation	Athletes' Father	Athletes' Mother	Athlete	Canadian Population (1971)[a]
Catholic	33	34	31	46
Protestant	32	32	26	18
Anglican	12	14	12	12
Reformed Bodies[c]	5	5	5	7
Lutheran	4	4	3	3
Other	4	4	4	10
No Religion	2	2	9	4
No Answer	7[b]	6	11	—

[a]Data compiled from Ministry of Industry, Trade and Commerce; *Perspective Canada* (1974:281).
[b]Numbers do not add up to 100% because of rounding.
[c]Includes Presbyterians and Baptists.

under two-thirds of the total sample and three-quarters of the *high achievers* were Protestant. By contrast, the religious data were less striking in the Canada Games sample. While Protestant religions were over-represented when compared to national percentages, they comprised less than half of all athletes. Moreover, the class correlates of involvement detailed earlier appear to suggest that socioeconomic level might well be a far better predictor of high level competitive involvement than religious affiliation.

Finally, given the myriad of cultural stereotypes about sports participation (ranging from skiers named Hans or Stein to francophone weightlifters) possible relationships that might exist between ethnicity and type of sport participated in are examined in Table 10. Again, the previously suggested caveats apply especially in the case of those sports where the percentage of unknown responses is excessive. Within these limitations, however, some interesting data patterns are displayed in Table 10. Somewhat striking, for instance, is that synchronized swimming and badminton, the two highest ranking sports on the basis of fathers' occupation, are greatly over-represented in the British Isles category.[33] Among athletes from French backgrounds the only sports that appear to be represented in or near proportion are weightlifting and boxing. Interestingly Boileau et al. (1976) have reported a higher than usual percentage of

TABLE 10

Type of Sport Participated in by Ethnic Groups (Percent Reported Affiliation)

Sport	Subsample Sizes (N)	British Isles	French	Highest Percentage in Addition to British Isles or French		All Others	Unknown
Badminton	(44)	64	2	7	(Canadian)[a]	11	16
Basketball	(96)	46	12	12	(Germanic)	18	12
Boxing	(28)	32	21	7	(Germanic)	4	36
Curling	(64)	53	3	14	(Germanic)	18	12
Fencing	(21)	56	14	20	(Germanic)	6	4
Figure Skating	(46)	35	17	13	(Other European)	13	22
Gymnastics	(46)	35	9	11	(Canadian)	15	30
Hockey	(84)	32	16	12	(Germanic)	9	31
Judo	(25)	44	8	16	(Germanic)	8	24
Alpine Skiing	(62)	37	14	14	(Germanic)	14	21
Nordic Skiing	(41)	44	5	27	(Germanic)	4	20
Speed Skating	(52)	33	6	13	(Germanic)	19	29
Synchronized Swimming	(42)	71	2	10	(Germanic)	12	5
Table Tennis	(38)	37	5	24	(Asian and Other European)	8	26
Volleyball	(109)	38	11	19	(Germanic)	21[b]	11
Weight Lifting	(36)	28	31	8	(Germanic)	5	28
Wrestling	(45)	42	5	16	(Other European)	18	19
National Averages		45	29	10	(Germanic)	15	1

[a]Athletes listed ethnicity as "Canadian."
[b]High percentages in "Others" column refer primarily to "Other European."

francophones in these particular sports over the last seventy years. Turning to other groups one can observe (not surprisingly) that Germans and Scandinavian backgrounds are prominent in nordic skiing. Thus, it seems clear that athletes from various sections of the Canadian "mosaic" find themselves in nearly all sports but, at the same time, it is noticeable that some groups appear to cluster around particular types of activities.

EXPLAINING THE DIFFERENCES

The data on Canada Games athletes indicate noticeable differences in condition between athletes' families and those of Canadian families generally. More important is that the differences are not randomly distributed, reflecting differences of *individual* abilities, but appear to be affected both by class position and (somewhat more equivocally) status group association. Such findings hardly corroborate an image of Canadian sport which features patterns of mass participation and universal access. Yet, the question might still be legitimately raised as to whether the differences in social condition presented above are simply the result of different choices or differential ambition and effort which is being rewarded in a classless and generally meritocratic system, or whether they represent crystallized social structural barriers which limit both the rate and quality of participation in preferred activities. Such questions easily transcend the limited explanatory power of the descriptive findings of the Canada Games study and an attempt to respond to them in even a conjectural fashion demands some reference to the broader sociological literature on sport, social inequality, and the changing character of Canadian society.

Central to this problem is the nature of the relationship between differences in social condition and the existence of a true equality of opportunity to surpass these differences. To argue that the democratization of sport in Canada has yet to transcend the effects of class position and status-group association is to argue that differences in social condition continue to remain structured in such a way as to put significant limits on the degree of equality of opportunity that can ever be achieved. By contrast, the idealized vision of liberal democracy features the decomposition of structured differences in social condition (like social class) to the point where they eventually become mere quantitative differences between strata and no longer pose any problems for free movement in the reward structure. As an explanation of inequality, a belief in the limited democratization of our institutions (sport included) emphasizes

the continuance of at least some forms of overt discrimination and unconscious structural barriers to the equality of access and achievement. By
contrast, the image of a largely democratized mass society emphasizes
sub-cultural differences in socialization which affect attitudes to achievement, success and preferred activities.

Undoubtedly, both cultural and structural influences have effects on
involvement and achievement in sporting activities of different kinds but
the question of the manner in which they are related to one another is
largely dependent upon the degree to which one concludes that class
and status no longer exert an ascriptive effect. I would like to reempha-
size at this point, that the image of a thoroughly democratized, if not a
completely "mass society" has dominated much of recent sociology (especially in the United States) and for many has become a crucial "domain assumption"[34] in the literature on the sociology of sport. Attendant
to this, has been the elevation of *cultural explanations* of differential involvement and achievement to the apparent level of conventional wisdom. While there are a wide range of specific details believed to be most
significant for understanding differential sport preferences and levels
of aspiration, the majority of cultural explanations are organized around
some combination of three variants.

The first variant emphasizes differences in skills and information in
conjunction with the lifestyles of disadvantaged individuals. A corollary
to this is the assertion that the socialization patterns of the poor, or of
minority status-groups, are not adequate to sufficiently affirm the positive values of such things as fitness, physical recreation and competitive
athletics. Thus, some have argued (see Kraus, 1965) that the poor not
only lack a "constructive concept of leisure" but they also reject sporting
possibilities in favour of more pathological pursuits.

The second variant to cultural explanations of under-representation
is derived from the work of John Roberts, Brian Sutton-Smith and their
co-researchers, (see for example Roberts and Sutton-Smith, 1969; Sutton-
Smith et al., 1969) and develops the argument that sport and game preferences are a reflection of cultural differences in child-rearing. As institutionalized games (Loy, 1969), sports might well provide expressive
models which provide settings wherein the conflicts engendered in child-
rearing are assuaged. Through the buffered learning that different game
and sport forms provide, children ostensibly make enculturative step-by-
step progress toward adult behaviour. Sutton-Smith et al. (1969) argue
that because higher status occupational groups emphasize values of
achievement in child-rearing their children tend to become pre-disposed
toward games of physical skill or combinations of skill and strategy. Alternatively, lower status occupational groups who emphasize responsibility

training predispose their children to prefer activities where the chance element is high (e.g. boxing where, as Weinberg and Arond (1969) have noted, the prospect of a lucky punch exists).

The third and final variant of cultural explanations focusses on the broader milieux of different classes (seen as socioeconomic categories) and status groups and is specifically concerned with the issues of atmosphere and ambition—atmosphere, because it is commonly believed that part of the subculture of lower class life is a concern for toughness and physical dominance which tends to involve the children from these families in sports emphasizing muscular and combative elements; ambition, because it is argued that the values supporting success in sport, school or career are not being appropriately developed. Here the argument is that the kinds of values associated with high performance in any aspect of life in the western industrial societies—individualism, competitiveness and a willingness to delay immediate gratification in order to insure future goals—are more characteristic of middle class rather than lower class culture, of Protestantism rather than Catholicism, and in Canada, of anglophones rather than francophones.

All of these assertions may have some basis in fact but they become problematic when, given a belief in an expanded opportunity structure, they are treated as *independent* or *primary* causes. How independent or primary are they in reality? Consider first, the variant of cultural explanations noted above where it is suggested that lower class and status groups simply reject available opportunities for sports participation or are unaware of their existence. This argument assumes that facilities and programs actually are available and are not limited in any way by geographical and social structural conditions. It is not the fault of the society that lower class groups do not participate heavily in organized sports and recreation, the argument runs; rather the problems lie with the attitudes, abilities and values of the lower classes themselves. Of course, the prerequisite for taking such an argument seriously is the factual demonstration that the opportunities in question actually do exist and that people's perceptions of them have not been substantially influenced by the long-term effects of marginality and subordinate class status. Establishing this prerequisite would have to be done not just by examining the proximity of sports facilities and programs to lower class communities or by distributing attitude surveys to the members of the communities. Consideration would have to be given to the overall costs of sports involvement, the sizes of people's disposable incomes, the nature of their work schedules and work conditions and to the possible ways in which their systems of values have been shaped by the broader structure of advantages and disadvantages that can be identified in the society at large.

Attention to these concerns raises issues that are related to the second variant of cultural explanations of differential involvement in sports —the problem of cultural emphases in child-rearing and their relationships to the game and sport preferences of different classes and status groups. On this issue it should be noted that there does appear to be support (Davis, 1951; Davis and Havighurst, 1946; and Erickson, 1947) for some of the assumptions being made about class differences in child-rearing, but the assignment of sport and game activities to rigid taxonomic categories (skill, strategy and chance) is highly arbitrary and may show little resemblance to the phenomenological meaning that certain activities have for the participants. Moreover, Roberts and Sutton-Smith and their co-researchers emphasize cultural differences between strata without attempting to discuss the mutually interactive role between them and the class structure. The socialization practices that children undergo in specific games and sports are related to their class experiences and in this way they may actually have the consequence of helping to reproduce class relations themselves.

The final variant of cultural explanations of different involvement in sports and games that was mentioned above must also be viewed in its relationships to social structural conditions. For example, the notion of class differences in milieu which finds its broadest base of support in the well known writings of Herbert Hyman (1953) tends to overstate the case for different levels of ambition. As John Porter (1968) has noted, the complete acceptance of the idea of different attitudes to achievements based on class is based on "questionable" assumptions. The disadvantaged classes and status groups may place a lower emphasis on "success" defined in conventional terms, but this may be because they are aware of and have a fatalistic view of existing structures of inequality (cf. Scanzoni, 1967). Parkin (1972:67) for example, notes that "ambition does not flourish in an atmosphere thick with warning against the danger of getting big ideas." Yet, the question of ambition, as Turner (1964) suggests, may really be more related to where one "starts" in the reward structure and the nature of the structural impediments which must be overcome (see Keller and Zavaloni, 1964). The amount of ambition required by an underclass child to reach the same goal as a child from a middle or upper class family must be greater because they have a relatively greater distance to go to attain it. Given problems of cost, access and coaching *it may take more ambition* for a child from a poor family to aspire to a regional championship than it does a middle class child who aspires to be a Canada Games medalist or a national champion. Correspondingly, the involvement of the poor and of certain status groups in sports like boxing or weightlifting must surely be a partial function of their comparatively low costs and even that they are "left" as less preferred activities by the middle classes.

My point in all of this is simply to emphasize that one should be aware of the limitations of cultural explanations of differences in social condition whereby the culture and life styles of the underclasses and minority status groups are seen as the prime contributor to their disadvantaged positions. These explanations may in fact explain little unless they are viewed in the context of the structured nature of inequality that appears to remain a fact of life in the western industrial societies. Structural factors intrude on the culture and life styles of different groups in a variety of ways which may significantly contour both the objective opportunity for, and the subjective attitudes to, participation and achievement. Consider for example, the obvious prevalence of economic barriers. True, more sporting equipment, facilities and programs exist now than any time in Canada past, but this is not to say that the proportional participation of Canadians in sporting activities is any higher than it was 75 years ago or that all have access to these facilities and programs. In fact it is clear that for most Canadians, sporting activities continue to be subordinated to the realities of everyday economic life. According to the 1969 *Senate Committee Report on Poverty* and the *Economic Council of Canada*, anywhere from 25 to 30% of Canadians live at or below conditions that can only be described as impoverished. Moreover, census figures (see *Perspective Canada,* 1974) and longitudinal studies of economic change indicate not only that economic differences between groups are failing to dissolve, but that the gap between the upper and the lower levels of the Canadian income range is increasing rather than decreasing. Leo Johnson[35] (1974:7) for example, outlines how over the last 25 years the highest two deciles of Canadian income earners received about half of all new income, whereas the bottom half of the income range only increased their percentage by 20.

Concurrent with such changes it seems to have been necessary for more members of Canadian families to obtain additional employment in order to cling tenaciously to the economic position presently in hand. This fact, in the context of the effects of additional family responsibilities, the necessity of providing further income, and the possibility of missing opportunities after school because of employment, necessarily precludes regular involvement in organized programs by large numbers of young Canadians. For, while evidence suggests that it is the family environment which represents the *first influence* directing children into

sport and specific types of sporting activity, it is likely the school environment where children get their greatest exposure to low cost recreational, athletic and coaching programs.

Under present conditions, however, the school itself may be less an
agency of democratization than a factor which serves to further crystal-
lize existing differences. While discussing the role of education in fostering occupational mobility and related life chances, Rocher (1975) and
Pike (1975) have pointed out how Canada's educational systems have
tended to legitimate existing class and status differences rather than
working toward the demise of invidious comparisons based on commonly shared social characteristics. Upper and middle class children are
usually more involved and successful in most aspects of school life and
tend to be more attuned to the values which guide educational expectations and goals (Pike, 1975:7). By contrast, underclass children often
suffer by a poorer academic performance and a lack of understanding and
reverence for the school's demands. This lack of understanding and distance from the *formal* dimensions of education itself is also reflected in
the *informal* ones as well. Moreover, the necessity for, and the perceived
possibility of, immediate gratifications in the work world combine with
this distance from educational objectives to terminate many educational
careers, prematurely turning them, as Pike argues (1975:8), into poorly
paid low status employment. As individuals leave an environment where
the cost and availability of sports facilities and programs are partially
controlled for, it seems reasonable to assume that their active participation is largely curtailed and generally transformed into more passive forms
of sports consumption. All of this is not to suggest that the educational
system and achievement in its curricular and extra-curricular programs
is impervious to the ambitions and abilities of underclass children who
come to understand the school's demands and the formal system of rewards and statuses in it; it only suggests that the image of the school as
a necessary guarantor of democratization in any form is perhaps rather
facile.

In summary, the implications of the related character of unequal condition and unequal opportunity in Canada clearly intrude on the question of sport's democratization—both as an aspect of individual life
chances and as a related dimension of social mobility. If we concentrate
on changes in social condition that appear to have characterized Canadian society, we might well argue that the aristocratic standard for participation has been democratized. But to interpret this as any index of
classlessness in Canadian sporting activities would be misleading. In both
leisure-sport, as Curtis and Milton (1976) have pointed out, and high

level competitive sport involvement, as I have attempted to show here, it seems that the effects of sport's democratization have been largely limited to the middle class and at best to those skilled manual workers who may use the middle class as a reference group. Presumably there might be somewhat different patterns in the case of recruitment into professional sport (Kidd and MacFarlane [1972] for example, arguably claim that "Hockey is everyone's sport no matter what their class") and if viewed in a purely cognitive sense, sport may be truly mass-like. But, if one focusses on most forms of amateur sport the following conclusion may be warranted. Until the situation occurs when well-placed families are no longer in a position to confer differential advantages and a broader range of life chances to their children, a high degree of social self-recruitment into preferred activities will continue freely from one generation to the next, broadly based athletic recruitment will be an improbability, and the equality of opportunity to participate and achieve in organized recreational and competitive programs will be higher within classes than between them.

NOTES

1. This paper was originally written in 1975 and has been slightly edited and revised for inclusion in this volume. Since writing the paper I have become less concerned with the distribution of opportunities in sport than with the role that sport plays in the reproduction of the structures of domination inherent in the capitalist mode of production. For an analysis that situates the kind of socioeconomic study presented here in the context of the broader requirements of class analysis see Gruneau (1980).

2. A "meritocracy" is a system where the distribution of rewards is based exclusively on an individual's abilities. In recent years there has been a great debate among social scientists and philosophers over the degree to which social justice in modern life should be based exclusively on meritocratic principles. Some (cf. Davis and Moore, 1945) argue that a system of unequal rewards based on meritocratic standards is necessary to insure quality in leadership and performance in modern life as long as there is open and unrestricted competition, or opportunity, for the highest positions. Others (Spitz, 1974) argue that: (a) as long as a system of highly unequal rewards persists, those who achieve in it will always be in a position to pass on at least some of the advantages associated with their achievements to children or personal associates thereby vitiating true equality of opportunity in future competition; (b) standards set by the meritocratic "elite" at any time may be subconsciously (or even consciously) discriminating; (c) the existence of a meritocracy does not substantially affect the problem of *inequality* itself. In this latter case, it is argued that, while specific individuals may ascend to elite positions, a great percentage of the population will remain substantially neglected or underprivileged. Consider, for example, the full application of meritocratic standards to sport. To emphasize these to their logical limits would imply that programs be designed only for those

who showed the most ability—progressively culling out those who could not compete. This then would be a programme designed in principle and in theory, to develop an athletic elite. On the other hand, consider an *egalitarian* programme designed to meet the play-urges and recreational needs of human beings regardless of their abilities. This would be a programme designed for all individuals. In the former programme, rewards would be based on achievement; in the latter they would be based on participation. The obvious dilemma here is how to balance the moral recognition that all men and women have equal rights and social needs with a desire to develop outstanding performances by the creation of structural systems which guarantee inequalities in result. This dilemma stands at the core of contemporary political philosophy, and as suggested, it also manifests itself in the world of sport. For a more in-depth discussion of these issues as they relate to sport see Gruneau (1975). A broader analysis of the egalitarian-meritocracy debate can be found in Bell (1972), Schaar (1967), Spitz (1974), Jencks et al. (1972) and Simon (1974). An entertaining satire of structured meritocracy can be found in Young (1961).

3. See, for example, Betts (1974), Metcalfe (1976), Dunning (1976) on socioeconomic differences in nineteeth century sport in Britain, Canada and the United States. For an historical review of racial discrimination in sport see McPherson (1974). Material on gender-based discrimination in American sport is provided in Gerber et al. (1974).

4. Elite sports refer to such activities in history as manorial hunting, early tennis and organized equestrian events ("the hounds" or polo). (This list is hardly exhaustive.) Folk sports refer to wrestling, some early forms of ball games (of the inflated bladder variety), cockfighting (and other "blood" sports) and footracing. A discussion of such activities in Elizabethan England can be found in Brailsford (1969).

5. Throughout this paper I use the terms "equality of condition" and "equality of opportunity." Differences in condition refer to variations in factors like income, education, occupation, exposure to health care services, amount of leisure time, and overall quality of life, all of which are contained within the general organizing framework of a society and often manifest themselves as dimensions of structured social ranking (cf. Clement, 1974:3-4, Gilbert and McRoberts, 1975). Conversely the issue of opportunity focuses at the individual rather than the social structural level and is concerned with the degree of freedom that persons have in moving within the restrictions frequently imposed by the reward structure. The main thrust of my concluding argument in this paper is based on a recognition that inequalities in conditions are "ordered" in such a way that they put continuing limits on opportunity (Clement, 1974).

6. Typical of this perspective is Kaplan's (1960) comment that in "no area of American life more than its leisure activity is the outdated concept of class made apparent." Hodges (1964:167) is more guarded when he suggests that class differences in sports and leisure are still often of "transcendent" consequence, but he concludes by suggesting that the barriers are "diminishing in importance as we become an ever more homogeneous people." (Note that Hodges is referring to American society here.)

7. While "mass sport" implies democratization, both Stone (1973) and Kando (1975) argue that the price has been high. Each depicts an increasing tendency for "mass spectacle" and the debasement of many of sport's "nobler" elements as adjuncts to massification. In fact, Kando goes as far as to compare the current state of American sport to that period of decadent Roman history where the colliseum and gladitorial combat were elevated to a moral equivalent of life in the society. Additionally there have been numerous criticisms of "mass

leisure," usually in the context of polemics against the supposed decline of the work ethic, or in the case of neo-Marxists, against the substitution of "trivialized leisure" for a lack of meaningful work (cf., Aronowitz, 1973 and Rinehart, 1975).

8. There is a substantial amount of literature supporting this point but for an excellent overview of the main issues see Westergaard (1972).

9. An example of these correlates would be age, sex, educational level, income level and occupation. For a review of some of the different impacts of such variables on "leisure sport" participation, see Curtis and Milton (1976).

10. We might note here that this finding is even more significant when the differences in sample groups are compared. For example, Collins' (1972) data are based on Olympic athletes, Luschen's (1969) are from a sample of members of German sports clubs and Webb's (1969) and Loy's (1969) data involve athletes from two prominent American universities.

11. For socio-economic data on a limited population of Japanese athletes, see Sugawara (1972). Some tentative findings on class and sport in Australia are detailed in Pavia (1973; 1974).

12. Betts (1974) takes this position when he argues that the relationship of sport to capitalism has been "productive" by virtue of its role in facilitating the proliferation of athletic facilities and the growth of mass sport.

13. As personal relationships become contractually based in the labour market, Marx saw a growing tendency for individuals to be seen less as ends in themselves and more as means—through their labour power—to particular ends (notably production). The contours of the relationships then could be seen as ones which featured an exchange. The labourer was paid for work but at a rate which was not commensurate to the real value of the labour congealed in the productive process. The surplus value remaining then manifested itself as profits for the entrepreneur.

14. While the term rationalization can have a variety of meanings (cf. Mannheim, 1960; Gerth and Mills, 1958), my usage of it throughout this paper has primarily been influenced by the interpretations of its meaning and significance that can be found in the writings of Max Weber. In a general sense, "rationality" refers simply to a "disenchantment" or demystification of the world. Logic and reason other than ideational factors, underlie its development. In an applied economic sense, it becomes the driving force of utilitarian productive process and, in a bureaucratic sense, it refers particularly to "rational efficiency, continuity of operation, speed, precision, and calculation of results" (Gerth and Mills, 1958:49).

15. For a general discussion of the process of "bourgeoisification" in capitalist societies see Miliband (1969).

16. "Bourgeoisie" is a broadly based term referring to the dominant class in the western industrial societies. Moreover as a conception of the occupational order it encompasses a large number of the positions associated with the productive process. Generally, the "bourgeoisie" can best be thought of as "stratified" into two groups. The higher group includes those who largely own or control the process of production itself through shares and board memberships and the lower group is categorized by a range of "middle class" occupations surrounding independent commodity production, professional activities, and the commercial world of business and its administration.

17. For example, as Mallea (1975) notes, early rules of the British A.A.U. included the fact that anyone who was "by trade or employment for wages a mechanic, artisan or labourer" was ineligible to enter its competitions. Also, in Canada, as late as the late 1920's, Blacks were not allowed to compete in some major Canadian boxing events. In 1913 the Canadian Amateur Athletic Union an-

nounced that "no coloured boxer will be allowed to compete in the Canadian championships . . . competition of whites and coloured men is not working out to the increased growth of the sport" (cited in Wise and Fisher, 1974:129).

18. See Jobling (1976) for a brief discussion of urbanization and technology. Various articles detailing other influences on the development of sport can be found in selected issues of the *Canadian Journal of History of Sport and Physical Education*.

19. These values, as Page (1973:27) notes, are particularly emphasized by the "professionalization" of sports wherein ascriptive barriers to recruitment have been "weakened by the rational calculation of big business." For a broader discussion of such themes see Gruneau (1975) and Ingham (1975).

20. Commenting on Canadian sports policy in 1974, Health Minister Marc Lalonde stated that: "We have a double purpose: We want to help the best Canadian athletes in their pursuit of excellence, but at the same time we are equally concerned with the general fitness and recreation of Canadians" (*Toronto Star*, Wednesday, January 2, 1974). Yet such programs as *Participaction* notwithstanding, funding seems overwhelmingly directed to sporting associations, the majority of which are especially concerned with the production of quality athletes. For example, in 1972-73 according to a pamphlet detailing the membership and functions of the "Canadian Sports Federation" *Sport Canada* was to receive 6.5 million in grants and *Recreation Canada* 2.3 million. Most of Sport Canada's money was earmarked for sporting associations and for such agencies as the "Canadian Olympic Association" and "Canadian Coaching Association." Moreover, given that the period from 1970 to the present has involved a major push for Olympic success—*production* has clearly superceded participation as the major goal for sports policy.

21. See Mills' distinction between "personal troubles" and "public issues" in *The Sociological Imagination* (1970:14-16).

22. A broader discussion of the sample and methods of the Canada Games project can be found in Gruneau (1972).

23. In *The Canadian Class Structure*, Forcese (1975) lists Parkin as an author who disagrees with the use of occupations as the proper focus for class analysis. This is certainly an error, since Parkin specifically goes to some lengths to praise Max Weber's recognition that market position rather than property ownership is the major distributive characteristic of class stratification.

24. "Position" however does not imply that the occupational order is a continuum having no "breaks." Parkin (1972:25) notes for instance, that despite a measure of affluence on the part of some skilled labourers, the line of cleavage between "classes" still falls between manual and non-manual occupational categories. The latter group lack comparable long term advantages and fringe benefits, whereas the former's advantages include: "better promotion and career opportunities, greater long-term economic security and, for many, guaranteed annual salary increases on an incremental scale: a cleaner, less noisy, less dangerous, and generally more comfortable work environment; greater freedom of movement, and less supervision. . . ."

25. Examples of occupations classified by Blishen's categories include:
    Category 1 (index number 70:00-79.99); chemical engineers, professors and teachers, selected business owners and managers.
    Category 2 (60.00-69.99); accountants, auditors, owners and managers, health services.
    Category 3 (50.00-59.99); security salesmen and brokers, technicians.

Category 4 (40.00-49.99); real estate salesmen, technicians, telephone operators, foremen in selected industries.

Category 5 (30.00-39.99); postmasters, typists, foreman, plumbers, millmen.

Category 6 (below 30.00); labourers, textile occupations, lumbermen.

The "break" between manual and non-manual work primarily occurs in the fourth and fifth categories. Solid upper-middle class occupations fall in categories 1, 2 ad 3; category 4 and some occupations in 5 include lower-middle class white and sometimes blue collar occupations. The remainder of categories 5 and 6 reflect occupations generally held by lower class individuals. In the analysis at hand, I have made breaks between categories 1, 2, 3 and category 4 and between 4 and categories 5 and 6.

26. See *Perspective Canada*, 1974, a compendium of social statistics released by the Ministry of Industry, Trade and Commerce.

27. Measuring association here, gamma for education correlated with occupation was .786; gamma for income and occupation was .732.

28. However, this table does mask gender differences that may change rankings somewhat. For example, male and female table tennis players came from much different family backgrounds and this fact cannot be observed in Table VI as it now stands. Male and female data are not presented separately because of small subsample sizes. I felt that sport-group differences could best be presented without controlling for gender. It should be recognized that this variable is likely affecting the rankings somewhat. Rankings of participation by sport where gender is controlled for can be found in Gruneau (1972). A modification of Table VI which uses slightly different occupational breakdowns, but which controls for gender, can be found in Gruneau (1975:164).

29. Upper status blue collar occupations might include such things as foremen in craft industries or highly-skilled labourers. See Mackenzie's *The Aristocracy of Labour* (1973).

30. It is somewhat revealing that this theme "Unity Through Sport" was chosen to symbolize the "Games." The "Games" followed barely three months after the events of October, 1970 and the accompanying controversy over the War Measures Act. Thus the theme undoubtedly carries distinct political overtones.

31. Witness Prime Minister Trudeau's comment that in Canada "there is no official culture, nor does any ethnic group take precedence over any other" (cited in Pike, 1975:2).

32. As Porter has suggested, (1966:101-102) Protestantism in Canada (the numerically superior British charter group is mostly Protestant and Anglican) is certainly more associated with higher socio-economic status than Catholicism. However, it is suggested that this relationship is "attributed to historical and social causes rather than to doctrinal differences in religious orientations to the world" (Porter, 1966:100). Thus, the argument is that Weber's thesis regarding the doctrinal incompatibility of Catholicism with a fully developed industrial order is not necessarily being supported by data such as those referred to above. S. D. Clark claims that "essentially the religious influence exerted through Protestantism in Canada has been no more favourable to the promotion of economic enterprise than the religious influence exerted through Roman Catholicism. . . . Where the Protestant religious organization has been strong the Protestant population has tended to be as economically unprogressive as the Roman Catholic population" (Clark, 1968:175).

33. However, this rather neat relationship does not hold beyond these two sports. While much of the Canadian upper-middle class is made up of people with British-Isles family histories, not all British-Isles immigrants have necessarily been located at this level. This seems to have been especially true for Irish Catholics for example. The point is, that while a British-Isles family history has frequently been a characteristic of those with advantaged status in Canadian society, ethnicity in itself has not always been a guarantor of class position.

34. Simply stated, "domain assumptions" refer to underlying beliefs about particular patterns of relationships that structure inquiry and explanation in a specific manner. See Gouldner's description in *The Coming Crisis of Western Sociology* (1970). It is frequently the "domain assumptions" that writers have which comprise the ideological and normative dimensions of their theories.

35. See also Johnson's essay on "The development of class in Canada" in G. Teeple ed., *Capitalism and the National Question in Canada* (1972).

REFERENCES

Aronowitz, Stanley
    1973   *False Promises*. New York: McGraw Hill.

Baltzell, E. Digby
    1958   *Philadelphia Gentlemen*. New York: Free Press.

Barber, Bernard
    1957   *Social Stratification: A Comparative Analysis of Structure and Process*. New York: Harcourt Brace and World.

Bell, Daniel
    1972   "On Meritocracy and Equality." *The Public Interest*, 29, Fall.

Betts, John R.
    1974   *America's Sporting Heritage 1850-1950*. Reading: Addison-Wesley.

Blishen, Bernard
    1958   "The Construction and Use of an Occupational Class Scale." *Canadian Journal of Economics and Political Science*, XXIV, November.
    1971   "A Socio-Economic Index for Occupations." In Bernard Blishen, Frank Jones, Kaspar Naegele, John Porter, (eds.), *Canadian Society: Sociological Perspectives*. Toronto: Macmillan.

Boileau, Roger, F. Landry and Yves Trempe
    1976   "Les Canadiens Francais et les Grands Jeux Internationaux (1908-1974)." In Richard S. Gruneau and J. G. Albinson (eds.), *Canadian Sport: Sociological Perspectives*. Toronto: Addison-Wesley.

Boston, R.
    1968   "What Leisure?." *New Society*, 26, December.

Bottomore, T. B.
    1966   *Classes in Modern Society*. New York: Vintage Books.

Brailsford, Dennis
    1969   *Sport and Society: Elizabeth to Anne*. Toronto: University of Toronto Press.

Burdge, Rable J.
  1974   "Levels of Occupational Prestige and Leisure Activity." In George H. Sage (ed.), *Sport and American Society*. Reading: Addison-Wesley.
Clarke, A. C.
  1956   "The Use of Leisure and its Relation to Levels of Occupational Prestige." *American Sociological Review*, 21, June.
Clark, S. D.
  1968   *The Developing Canadian Community*. Toronto: University of Toronto Press.
Clement, Wallace
  1975   *The Canadian Elite*. Toronto: McClelland and Stewart.
Collins, L. J.
  1972   "Social Class and the Olympic Athlete." *British Journal of Physical Education* 3(4), (4).
Cuneo, Carl and James Curtis
  1975   "Social Ascription in the Educational and Occupational Status Attainment of Urban Canadians." *Canadian Review of Sociology and Anthropology*, 12(1).
Curtis, James and Brian Milton
  1976   "Social Status and the 'Active Society': National Data on Correlates of Leisure-Time Physical and Sport Activities." In R. S. Gruneau and J. G. Albinson (eds.), *Canadian Sport: Sociological Perspectives*. Toronto: Addison-Wesley.
Davis, Alison
  1951   *Social Class Influences Upon Learning*. Cambridge: Harvard University Press,
Davis, Alison and R. J. Havighurst
  1946   "Social Class and Color Differences in Childrearing." *American Sociological Review*, 11, December.
Davis, Kingsley and Wilbert Moore
  1945   "Some Principles of Stratification." *American Sociological Review*, 10, April.
Dofney, Jacques and Marcel Rioux
  1964   "Social Class in French Canada." In Marcel Rioux and Yves Martin (eds.), *French Canadian Society*. Toronto: McClelland and Stewart.
Dunning, Eric
  1976   "Industrialization and the Incipient Modernization of Football." *Stadion* (1), 1.
Du Wors, Richard E. and Richard S. Gruneau
  1972   "Facts Toward a Foundation for Canadian Programmes in Amateur Sports." Research Report presented to the Canadian Fitness and Amateur Sport Directorate, Ottawa.
Emmett, Isabel
  1971   *Youth and Leisure in an Urban Sprawl*. Manchester: Manchester University Press.
Erickson, M. C.
  1947   "Social Status and Child-Rearing Practices." In T. Newcomb and E. L. Hartley, *Readings in Social Psychology*. New York: Holt, Rinehart and Winston.

Forcese, Dennis
    1975   *The Canadian Class Structure.* Toronto: McGraw-Hill Ryerson.
Gerber, Ellen, et al.
    1974   *The American Woman in Sport.* Reading: Addison-Wesley.
Gerth, H. H. and C. Wright Mills
    1958   *From Max Weber, Essays in Sociology.* New York: Oxford University.
Giddens, Anthony
    1973   *The Class Structure of the Advanced Societies.* London: Hutchinson.
Gilbert, Sid and Hugh McRoberts
    1975   "Differentiation and Stratification: The Issue of Inequality." In Dennis Forcese and Stephen Richer (eds.), *Issues in Canadian Society.* Toronto: Prentice-Hall.
Gouldner, Alvin
    1970   *The Coming Crisis of Western Sociology.* New York: Basic Books.
Gruneau, Richard S.
    1972   "A Socio-economic Analysis of the Competitors at the 1971 Canada Winter Games." Unpublished Master's thesis, Department of Sociology, University of Calgary, Alberta.
    1975   "Sport, Social Differentiation and Social Inequality." In D. Ball and John W. Loy (eds.), *Sport and Social Order,* Reading: Addison-Wesley.
    1980   "Power and Play in Canadian Society." In R. J. Ossenberg (ed.), *Power and Change in Canada.* Toronto: McClelland and Stewart.
Hodges, H. M.
    1964   *Social Stratification.* Cambridge, Mass.: Schenkman.
Hobart, Charles
    1974   "Active Sports Participation Among the Young, The Middle-Aged and the Elderly." Paper presented at the C.S.A.A. meeting, Toronto.
Hyman, Herbert
    1953   "The Value Systems of Different Classes." In R. Bendix and S. M. Lipset (eds.), *Class, Status and Power.* Glencoe, Illinois: The Free Press.
Ingham, Alan G.
    1975   "Occupational Subcultures in the Work World of Sport." In D. Ball and J. W. Loy (eds.), *Sport and Social Order.* Reading: Addison-Wesley.
Jencks, Christopher, et al.
    1972   *Inequality: A Reassessment of the Effect of Family and Schooling in America.* New York: Basic Books.
Johnson, Leo
    1972   "The Development of Class in Canada" in G. Teeple (ed.), *Capitalism and the National Question in Canada.* Toronto: University of Toronto Press.
    1974   *Poverty in Wealth.* Toronto: New Hogtown Press.
Jobling, Ian
    1976   "Urbanization and Sport in Canada, 1867-1900." In Richard S. Gruneau and J. G. Albinson (eds.), *Canadian Sport: Sociological Pespectives.* Toronto: Addison-Wesley.

Kando, Thomas
    1975   *Leisure and Popular Culture in Transition*. St. Louis: C. V. Mosby.
Kaplan, Max
    1960   *Leisure in America*. New York: John Wiley.
Keller, Suzanne and Marisa Zavalloni
    1964   "Ambition and Social Class: A Respectification." *Social Forces, 43,*
            October.
Kelner, Merijoy
    1973   "Ethnic Penetration into Toronto's Elite Structure." In James E.
            Curtis and William G. Scott (eds.), *Social Stratification: Canada*.
            Toronto: Prentice-Hall.
Kenyon, Gerald S. and Barry McPherson
    1973   "Becoming Involved in Physical Activity and Sport: A Process of
            Socialization." In G. Lawrence Rarick (ed.), *Physical Activity:
            Human Growth and Development*. New York: Academic Press.
Kidd, Bruce and John MacFarlane
    1972   *The Death of Hockey*. Toronto: New Press.
Kraus, Richard
    1971   *Recreation and Leisure in Modern Society*. New York: Appleton-
            Century Crofts.
    1965   "Recreation for the Rich and Poor: A Contrast." *Quest,* 5.
Lindsay, Peter
    1969   "A History of Sport in Canada: 1807-1867." Unpublished doc-
            toral dissertation. University of Alberta.
Loy, John
    1969   "The Study of Sport and Social Mobility." In G. Kenyon (ed.),
            Aspects of Contemporary Sport Sociology. Chicago: The Athletic
            Institute.
Lüschen, Gunther
    1969   "Social Stratification and Social Mobility Among Young Sports-
            men." In J. W. Loy and Gerald Kenyon (eds.), *Sport, Culture and
            Society*. Toronto: Macmillan.
    1972   "The Interdependence of Sport and Culture." In Marie Hart (ed.),
            Sport in the Sociocultural Process. Dubuque: William C. Brown
            Co. Publishers.
Mackenzie, Gavin
    1973   *The Aristocracy of Labour*. London: Cambridge University Press.
Mallea, John
    1975   "The Victorian Sporting Legacy." *McGill Journal of Education,*
            10(2).
Mannheim, Karl
    1960   "Types of Rationality and Organized Insecurity." In C. Wright
            Mills (ed.), *Images of Man*. New York: George Braziller.
Marchak, Patricia
    1975   *Ideological Perspectives on Canada*. Toronto: McGraw-Hill.
Marshall, T. H.
    1950   *Citizenship and Social Class*. Cambridge University Press.
McPherson, Barry D.
    1974   "Minority Group Involvement in Sport: The Black Athlete." In J.
            Wilmore (ed.), *Exercise and Sport Sciences Review, Volume II*.
            New York: Academic Press.

Metcalfe, Alan
    1972   "Sport and Class Concepts in Nineteenth Century Canada." Paper presented at the Annual Meeting of the American Sociological Association, New Orleans.
    1976   "Organized Sport and Social Stratification in Montreal: 1840-1901." In Richard S. Gruneau and J. G. Albinson (eds.), *Canadian Sport: Sociological Perspectives*. Toronto: Addison-Wesley.

Miliband, Ralph
    1969   *The State in Capitalist Society*. London: Quartet Books.

Page, Charles H.
    1973   "The World of Sport and its Study." In John Talamini and Charles H. Page (eds.), *Sport and Society*. Boston: Little, Brown.

Parker, Richard
    1972   *The Myth of the Middle Class*. New York: Harper Colophon.

Parkin, Frank
    1972   *Class Inequality and Political Order*. London: Paladin.

Pavia, Grant
    1974   "An Investigation into the Sociological Background of Successful South Australian Footballers." *The Australian Journal of Physical Education*, 63, March.
    1973   "An Analysis of the Social Class of the 1972 Olympic Team." *The Australian Journal of Physical Education*, 61, September.

Pike, Robert
    1975   "Introduction and Overview." In Robert Pike and Elia Zureik (eds.) *Socialization and Values in Canadian Society, Vol. II*. Toronto: McClelland and Stewart.

Porter, John
    1966   *The Vertical Mosaic*. Toronto: University of Toronto Press.
    1968   "The Future of Upward Mobility." *American Sociological Review*, 33, (1).

Report of the Special Senate Committee on Poverty
    1971   *Poverty in Canada*. Ottawa: Information Canada.

Rinehart, James
    1975   *The Tyranny of Work*. Toronto: Longmans.

Roberts, John M. and Brian Sutton-Smith
    1969   "Child Training and Game Involvement." In J. W. Loy and Gerald J. Kenyon (eds.), *Sport, Culture and Society*. Toronto: Macmillan.

Rocher, Guy
    1975   "Formal Education: The Issue of Opportunity." In Dennis Forcese and Stephen Richer (eds.), *Issues in Canadian Society*. Toronto: Prentice-Hall.

Scanzoni, J.
    1967   "Socialization, Achievement, and Achievement Values." *American Sociological Review*, 32(3).

Schaar, John
    1967   "Equality of Opportunity and Beyond." In *Nomos IX: Equality*. New York: Atherton Press.

Simon, Robert
    1974   "Equality, Merit and the Determination of our Gifts." *Social Research*, 41(3).
Spitz, David
    1974   "A Grammar of Equality." *Dissent*, Winter.
Stone, Gregory P.
    1957   "Some Meanings of American Sport." Proceedings of the 60th Annual College Physical Education Association Meetings, Columbus, Ohio.
    1973   "American Sport: Play and Display." In John Talamini and Charles H. Page (eds.), *Sport and Society*. Boston: Little, Brown.
Sugawara, Ray
    1972   "The Study of Top Sportsmen in Japan." *International Review of Sport Sociology*.
Sutton-Smith, Brian, John Roberts and Robert M. Kozelka
    1969   "Game Involvement in Adults." In J. W. Loy and Gerald S. Kenyon (eds.), *Sport, Culture and Society*. Toronto: Macmillan.
Turner, Ralph
    1964   *The Social Context of Ambition*. San Francisco: Chandler.
Vallee, Frank G.
    1975   "Multi-Ethnic Societies: The Issues of Identity and Inequality." In Dennis Forcese and Stephen Richer (eds.), *Issues in Canadian Society*. Toronto: Prentice-Hall.
Veblen, Thorstein
    1953   *The Theory of the Leisure Class*. New York: Mentor.
Webb, Harry
    1969   "Reaction to Loy's Paper." In Gerald S. Kenyon (ed.), *Aspects of Contemporary Sport Sociology*. Chicago: The Athletic Institute.
Weber, Max
    1958   Class, Status, Party." In H. H. Gerth and C. W. Mills, *From Max Weber: Essays in Sociology*. New York: Oxford University Press.
Weinberg, S. Kirkson and Henry Arond
    1969   "The Occupational Culture of the Boxer." In J. W. Loy and Gerald S. Kenyon (eds.), *Sport, Culture and Society*. Toronto: Macmillan.
Westergaard, J. H.
    1972   "The Withering Away of Class: A Contemporary Myth." In Paul Blumberg (ed.), *The Impact of Social Class*. New York: Thomas Crowell.
White, T. H.
    1975   "The Relative Importance of Education and Income as Predictors in Outdoor Recreation Participation." *Journal of Leisure Research*, 7(3).
Wise, S. F. and Douglas Fisher
    1974   *Canada's Sporting Heroes*. Toronto: General Publishing.
Young, Michael
    1961   *The Rise of the Meritocracy*. London: Penguin.

"Legitimate Deviance" and Social Class: Bar Behaviour During Grey Cup Week

Alan Listiak

Studies of deviant behaviour have focused on many forms of rule-breaking behaviour, from "major" violations such as crime, drug addiction, mental illness, sexual deviations, suicide, alcoholism and excessive drinking, etc., to "minor" breaches such as pool hustling (Polsky, 1967) swearing (Hartogs, 1967; Sagarin, 1962), smelling bad (Largey and Watson, 1972), being obese (Cahnman, 1969), and work-related infractions (Bensman and Gerver, 1963; Harper and Emmert, 1963; Stoddard, 1968). These works are predicated on the assumption that deviant behaviour is misbehaviour which is not socially sanctioned or highly tolerated especially if it is widespread. Yet, it is commonly known that there are times when and places where widespread deviant behaviour is socially sanctioned and highly tolerated, when, it may be said, deviant behaviour is legitimate.

During periods of legitimate deviance a "Time Out" is "called" from the demands of accountability and conformity, social control is relaxed, and almost anything goes. Such Time Outs are often called by ceremonial arrangement and take the form of ritualistic festivals, fiestas, celebrations, parties, and the like.[2] For example, MacAndrew and Edgerton (1969) summarize a great deal of anthropological research illustrating the universality and frequency of the ceremonial Time Out among Indians and other native peoples. These Time Outs are characterized by a great amount of aggression, violence, debauchery, generally wild behaviour, and, in many cases, extreme drunkenness—behavior which is not tolerated in everyday life.[3]

The ceremonial Time Outs are not restricted to "primitive" societies. Modern, urbanized, so-called developed societies also have a multitude of such rituals. There are countless thousands of festivals, celebrations, and

From *Sociological Focus*, Summer 1974, Vol. 7 (3): 13-44. Reprinted by permission of the author and publisher.

spectacles at the community and other levels in North America and Western Europe. Among the best known of these are the Oktober-Fest in Germany, the Mardi-Gras in New Orleans, the Winter Carnivals in St. Paul and Quebec, the Calgary Stampede in Alberta, the Grey Cup, etc. These urban festivals are characterized by a state of loosened social control which permits and even encourages, within-limits, boisterous and aggressive behaviour, property destruction, illicit sexual behaviour, excessive drinking and drunkenness, frenzied commercial activity, etc. Unfortunately, these rituals have received scant scrutiny from social scientists.

This lack of attention is especially strange in light of the imputed importance of these Time Out rituals in maintaining order and stability in society. Periods of legitimate deviance are believed to function in much the same manner as "deviant" deviance, i.e., as "safety-valves," to maintain system equilibrium, to contribute to solidarity and integration, to demark normative boundaries. (On the functions of "deviant" deviance, see, e.g., Coser, 1967; Davis, 1966; Dentler and Erickson, 1959; Erickson, 1964, 1966.) For example, the liberated atmosphere of these periods allows the expression of "tension release" behaviours which derive from the strain and frustration of living within the confines of the social norms.

> . . . societies have provided traditional, conventional situations in which people could to some degree "let themselves go," abandoning themselves to relatively unrestricted following of impulses that are ordinarily inhibited and limited in expression. . . .

> Such occasions provide a satisfying, yet legitimate, escape from the restrictions of the usual social norms. Particularly in modern society, the maintenance of reserve and dignity is inculcated in the person as an important value from childhood. It is not easy for the individual to drop this decorous posture and most of the time, the norms do not permit him to do so. At times, the norms of propriety may seem confining and frustrating (Turner and Killian, 1957:153-154).

If people save the expression of their frustrations and tensions for "occasions that fall under the purview of one or another form of sanctioned Time Out, not only are the adverse repercussions that would normally ensue either eliminated or significantly reduced, so too is the likelihood that such disruptions will occur at other times" (MacAndrew and Edgerton, 1969:169). By allowing such deviance to occur legitimately during the safety-valve of a "controlled" setting, the society supposedly drains off tensions and strains which could accumulate and eventually "explode" into more "destructive" forms of deviance with a minimum of adverse consequences.

Periods of legitimate deviance also perform an integrative function through their role "in facilitating the resolution of cultural conflict" (Turner and Killian, 1957:155) and thus restoring temporarily community integration and solidarity. This may be accomplished by the symbolic reaffirmation of the basic moral values of the system, as, for example, in the English Coronation (Shils and Young, 1953:67, 72), drawing upon Drukheim, argue that "The Coronation is a ceremony in which the society reaffirms the moral values which constitute it as a society and renews its devotion to those values by an act of communion. . . . The fact that the experience is communal means that one of the values, the virtue of social unity or solidarity, is acknowledged and strengthened in the very act of communion."

The integrative function may also be accomplished by allowing the expression of values which are normally suppressed, implicit, unofficial, or illegal. Turner and Killian (1957:155-157) and Smith (1968) discuss how certain values such as "keeping the Negro in his place," "showing a horse thief no mercy," etc. "cannot always be attained through due process," and thus find expression in a conventionalized pattern of crowd behaviour such as lynching. The contribution to solidarity is noted by Turner and Killian (1957:161): "Even when lynchings were relatively frequent in the South it was observed by the Southern Commission for the Study of Lynchings that a lynching often seemed to give a community a period of immunity from the repetition of such behaviour."

An underlying assumption of both the safety-valve and integrative functions is that social norms and their related institutional goals are uniformly distributed and valued throughout the society. From this it follows that the lower-class by virtue of its structural position has the least access to the legitimate means of realizing the norms and goals of the society. As such, it suffers the greatest strain and frustration from conformity.[4] Consequently, it would benefit the most from such rituals wherein social control is relaxed, and therefore would be expected to have a high rate of participation in them.

The hypothesis of high lower-class participation, generalized as full community participation, has been incorporated into sociological writings with little or no empirical support for either the hypothesis itself or the underlying assumptions. A typical example of such incorporation is the following statement by Quinn (1955:23):

> Generally, the institutions found within the city become functionally integrated in such a manner that most residents obtain locally the satisfactions of their basic needs. Citizens also participate in carrying on local governments and schools; they read the same newspapers,

patronize the same local recreational facilities, and enjoy the same celebrations. Together they share a common social life that reflects much of the general social-cultural complex of the larger society. (Emphasis added.)

It may be true that community life "reflects much of the general social-cultural complex of the larger society." However, some would disagree with the functionalist perceptions of this larger complex and, consequently, disagree with the functionalist portrait of community life and participation. Birnbaum (1953) addressed himself to these issues as they are contained in Shils and Young's (1953) interpretation of the meaning of the Coronation. He notes that the ritual had little effect on the working classes other than the provision of a holiday. He (1953:13) argues that "to speak of the assimilation of the working class into the consensus of British society is to define that consensus by exclusive reference to middle and upperclass groups. . . . The national moral community is defined in terms of the propertied classes and their servitors." Birnbaum (1953:18) goes on to counter Shils and Young's "claim that the family was the social unit 'recognized' as the most appropriate for entry into the Coronation celebration. Since most people were home from work, it is difficult to see what other units they could have formed. But the note on the family contradicts the claim that the Coronation atmosphere overcame the 'customary barriers' between people. The customary barriers of social distance are strongest, by general agreement, where the boundaries of the family begin." Shils and Young claim that the ritual of the Coronation and participation in it *decreases* the social distance between the classes. Birnbaum argues that the ritual serves as an *affirmation* of social distance and is even fundamentally divisive.

The one study presently available of a conventionalized urban Time Out ritual indicates that Birnbaum's critique is well taken. Ossenberg (1969) investigated bar behaviour in a sample of upper-middle-class, middle-class, and lower-class public drinking establishments in Calgary, Alberta during the Calgary Stampede. The Stampede is well-known for its wild and free-for-all Time Out atmosphere. Ossenberg found that participation in the Stampede as indexed by bar behaviour was limited mainly to the middle-class, the lower-class and upper-middle-class choosing to remain outside the festivities. He (1969:34) concluded that the Stampede was "a middle-class binge, suggesting that even socially approved deviant behaviour is endogamous." These results do not support the functionalist hypothesis of high lower-class participation in community sponsored conventionalized Time Out periods of legitimate deviance.

To make sense of such a contradictory finding, one is driven to re-examine the assumption from which the high participation hypothesis is drawn. It is found that the assumption of an inverse relationship be-tween frustration (status-type) and social class is questioned by (1) the many studies which reveal little or no relationship between devi-ance (especially crime and delinquency) and class (see, e.g., Akers, 1964, 1968; Empey and Erickson, 1966; Hirschi, 1969; Mizruchi, 1967, Spiller, 1965; Vaz, 1967; Voss, 1966; Winslow, 1968); (2) the studies which show that the lower-class is characterized by lower success aspira-tions and success pressures than the middle and upper-classes (see, e.g., Empey, 1956; Hyman, 1953; Spiller, 1965; Wilson, 1959; the refer-ences cited in Roach and Gursslin, 1965); (3) the contradictory findings of class differentials in perceived opportunities (Elliot, 1963; Hyman, 1953). Short, Rivera and Tennyson (1965) find that lower-class youth perceive their opportunities to be lower than middle and upper-class youth, whereas Mizruchi (1964) and Winslow (1968) find that lower-class youth perceive equal opportunities or anticipate future opportu-nities on a par with middle-class and upper-class youth; (4) the nonsocial conditions of lower-class life, especially the economic deprivation and lack of satisfaction of physical needs (Roach and Gursslin, 1965, 1967; Roach, 1965, 1967).

The assumption that norms and values and goals are evenly distrib-uted and held in society is also questioned by a good deal of research. These studies indicate that the various social classes are distinguished by different interests, values, life-style, child-rearing and socialization patterns, etc. (see, e.g., Berger, 1960; Gans, 1962; Green, 1946; Kohn, 1969; Miller, 1958, 1959; Rainwater, 1960; Roach, 1965, 1967; Sewell, 1961; Shostak, 1969; Shostak and Gomberg, 1964; Spiller, 1965). The chief differentiating factors between social classes for the purposes of this discussion are the presence of values and actions associated with the material conditions of affluence and the Protestant Ethic in the middle-class and their absence in the lower-class. The middle-class is classically characterized as so future oriented that the present is almost an obses-sion, i.e., in order to assure the "good life" in the future, the daily round must be productive in terms of status enhancement and the attainment of success. Thus, there is great concern for conformity and meeting the expectations of others; deviant and aggressive behaviour are strongly prohibited. Those in the lower-class, in contrast, are noted for their lack of inhibition and their hedonistic propensity for immediate gratification, especially with respect to physical and sexual impulses. Violative be-haviour, inhibition release, and aggression and violence are the keynotes of the lower-class.

Given these considerations, it seems reasonable to hypothesize, as Ossenberg (1969:30) did, that if the middle-class "is more sensitive to legal and other restrictive norms," then it may also be "more responsive to the relaxation of social controls represented by the relatively lax enforcement of those norms during community festivals." Consequently, it would be expected that the middle-class would be the main exhibitor of legitimate deviant behaviour during conventionalized urban Time Out rituals (if, in conjunction, the class structure in the community is relatively "open" and formal social control is not heavily used to prevent the other classes from expressing their frustrations).

To further test these hypotheses and to assess the functionality of the conventionalized Time Out ritual (and in the process generate needed knowledge of both the ritual and the nature of legitimate deviant behaviour expressed during such rituals), a replication of Ossenberg's (1969) study of bar behaviour during the Calgary Stampede was performed during Grey Cup Week 1972 in Hamilton, Ontario, November 27-December 3, 1972. It was hypothesized that during Grey Cup Week 1972 in Hamilton, a high level of legitimate deviant behaviour in the form of festival-related aggressive expressive behaviour would be found in middle-class drinking places and a lower level of such behaviour would be found in lower-class drinking places.[5]

THE GREY CUP

The Grey Cup is emblematic of the Canadian Football League championship. Each year the Western and Eastern Conference winners meet in the final game of the season to determine the league champion. Each year this final game alternates between various cities in Eastern and Western Canada. The Cup itself was donated to the league in 1909 by Earl Grey, then the presiding Governor-General of Canada. Around this game has grown up an urban Time Out festival of clamorous proportions known as Grey Cup Week, which is (obviously) a week long in duration and culminates in the Grey Cup Game itself. (On the history and development of the Grey Cup, see Cosentino, 1969; Currie, 1968; Sullivan, 1970). Grey Cup Week is traditionally associated with forms of legitimate deviant behavior otherwise known as merriment and hoopla, and many observers feel it has become a Canadian nativistic ritual. Fans of the representative teams and interested observers from all across Canada descend upon the particular city chosen that year for a week of unrestrained festivity and celebration. The host city, in conjunction with the Grey Cup Committee, gears itself for the role by putting on all types of activities, (for example, dinners, dances, ceremonies, beauty pageants, special shows, revues, parades, concerts, parties, gigantic sales, etc.), thereby creating an atmosphere of spontaneity and gaiety. This atmosphere is further enhanced by various businesses which decorate themselves in Grey Cup related themes, erect elaborate displays in their windows, and put up signs welcoming visitors and cheering on the respective teams. Obviously, the role of host is most profitable for the city (or at least certain segments of it) in terms of business and publicity. Hotels and motels are booked to capacity, often for miles around the city, and the main business section does a booming business.

The local and national media, especially newspapers and television, give detailed coverage of the week's events, reporting daily highlights and devoting full coverage to both the Grey Cup Parade and the Grey Cup Game—the 1972 Game reached a Canadian television audience of approximately 6 million.

As in most ceremonial Time Outs, alcohol plays an important part in the proceedings: copious quantities of alcohol are such an integral aspect of Grey Cup Week that it is often referred to as "The Grand National Drunk." Many events are marked by a high degree of drunken and boisterous behaviour, often erupting into fights and brawls. Excessive drinking, illegal drinking, fighting, sexual looseness, and generally impulsive behaviour are among the forms of deviance which are legitimated by the attitude of tolerance and constraint shown by the police and other social control agencies. Yet, behaviour during Grey Cup Week cannot be said to be totally uninhibited—there are limits beyond which the type and degree of legitimate deviant behaviour rarely go. The only time these limits were seriously transgressed was in the 1966 festivities in Vancouver, when the ritual became a riot:

> The police haul was 689 persons in four hours of rioting. They broke store windows, ripped street decorations, lit fires in ornamental trash cans, indulged in a wild bottle-throwing melee, engaged in beer bottle attacks. When order was restored the count was 159 charged with unlawful assembly, another 115 were in jail charged with drunkenness and malicious damage and hundreds others were booked on a variety of counts (Sullivan, 1970:167).

The Grey Cup is said to be an integrating device on two levels. At the national level it is said to operate to unite Canada as a nation and to develop Canadian identity. For example, Sam Berger, the owner of the Montreal Alouettes of the C.F.L., has said, "The Grey Cup and the League are Canadian institutions that make us conscious of staying a nation." Donald McNaughton, president of Schenley's (the liquor company which sponsors the annual awards to outstanding players in the League) notes, ". . . Football is . . .the one thing that gets us thinking east-to-west in this country instead of north-to-south. When I travel across Canada during Grey Cup Week that thinking hits a terrific peak. It keeps us conscious of being Canadians" (both cited in Batten, 1972:90).

At the community level, the Grey Cup is said to operate to promote civic pride in the inhabitants both by the favourable publicity of the city generated and the process of "showing the visitors a good time." Hamilton's Mayor, Mr. Vic Copps, said that the Grey Cup "has been a great unifying force for the city," and that the Grey Cup "has made us a first class big city" and would attract business and hotels to the city (*Hamilton Spectator*, December 4, 1972, p. 7). Jack MacDonald, Chairman of the Grey Cup Committee, and a local businessman, found "people saying now that they are proud to be Hamiltonians." Columnist Stan McNeil, the day after the game wrote, "It was impossible to watch yesterday's show . . . not just the game itself, but the whole package . . . without a sudden feeling of pride in being a part of Hamilton" (*Hamilton Spectator*, December 4, 1972, p. 63).

The Grey Cup is said also to operate to promote peace and order within the community by the generalized participation of the inhabitants in legitimate deviance or "tension-release" behaviours. The safety-valve function is noted in an editorial from the *Ottawa Journal* reprinted in the *Hamilton Spectator* on December 5, 1972. "In a climatic national sports contest, such as the Grey Cup, with attendent socializing, parades and fun, we can get that oft needed release from everyday cares."

It was fortunate, for the purposes of this study, that Grey Cup Week 1972 took place in Hamilton, Ontario. Hamilton is a traditional "hotbed" of football enthusiasm, despite being financially overshadowed by its large neighbor, Toronto. Hamilton has always maintained its own football teams in top level leagues (both professional and amateur), and has hosted the Grey Cup seven times before 1972 (the years being 1910, 1912, 1913, 1928, 1935, 1944. For a history of Hamilton's involvement with football, see *Hamilton Spectator*, Grey Cup Edition, November 28, 1972). It was fortunate also in that the hometown Tiger-Cats were scheduled to play in the big game against the Western representative, the Saskatchewan Roughriders. These two facts resulted in a high degree of interest and participation in Grey Cup Week in Hamilton.

Indeed the week's activities certainly lived up to the finest Grey Cup tradition. Legitimate deviant behaviour abounded as social control was relaxed and tensions were released. King Street, Hamilton's main street, was filled to overflowing by thousands of people who danced, drank, cheered, sang, rang cowbells, and fought their way up and down the main business section of the street until at least 4 a.m. on each of the last three nights of the festivities. While people flowed in all directions on both sides of the street, the hard-core revellers moved continuously up and down King Street within a 6-block limit, moving west up King on the north side, crossing over and returning east down King on the south side, crossing over and starting the trip again.

Just as the throngs of people on foot moved up and down King Street whooping it up, so the traffic, jammed up for over half a mile, circled the downtown area to contribute its share to the intensity of the merriment already taking place in the main business section. As the jam moved along, honking all the way, drivers and passengers would jump out of their cars to dance, shout, pass drinks among each other, etc. Several pedestrians were moving in and out of the traffic passing out drinks to the motorists. Cars were painted in Tiger-Cat and Roughrider colours; people were hanging over the outside of the vehicles, and also on the hood, roof, and trunk. Convertibles had their tops down and were filled with people; pick-up trucks were similarly loaded up with celebrants. When traffic moved ahead a few feet, the revellers would hang their heads out of the windows and renew their shouting and cheering.

The legitimacy of most deviance was respected by the police. For example, one obviously inebriated Westerner, resplendent in Saskatchewan colours, was passing out cans of beer from a loaded case tucked under his arm to appreciative passers-by, in full view of nearby police officers. In another instance, several young men standing in a doorway passing a bottle of whiskey among themselves received only a warning from a policeman to "keep the bar moving." The limits of legitimacy were tested on occasion: celebrations in the massive (1,500 seat) Junior Chamber of Commerce hospitality tent got so out of hand that the bar had to be closed before 9:30 P.M. on the night before the game. The Reception Centre at Jackson Square, a favorite meeting place of teenagers, closed shortly thereafter because of a large brawl in which several temporary walls were knocked down. Yet relatively few persons were arrested either that night or during the entire week of the festival.

METHOD

The method employed to measure participation in Grey Cup festivities and exhibition of legitimate deviant behaviour is a participant observation of behaviour in a sample of public drinking establishments in the festival area. The utilization of bar behaviour as the index of participation and exhibition is justified for the following reasons:

1. As indicated earlier, drinking and drinking-related behaviour is an integral aspect of the Grey Cup. Yet, excessive drinking is a taboo in normal life (Jessor, et al., 1968). As such, "excessive drinking represents a form of deviant behaviour which becomes 'normal' and even goal-directed" during the festival (Ossenberg, 1969:31); that is, it becomes a form of legitimate deviance as well as a rationale for explaining away other acts of deviance engaged in (on this point see MacAndrew and Edgerton, 1969).

2. Thus, bars are an important "arena" of Grey Cup action (see Fisher, 1972 for an elaboration of this concept).

3. Bars present a much more stable picture of the situation and are more amenable to participant observation than the street with its fast flowing pace or various activities of relatively short duration.

4. "It is reasonable to assume that inhibitions concerning cross-class interaction are more easily dissolved with the aid of alcoholic beverages" (Ossenberg, 1969:30).

5. "Bars are an effective informal index of the social structure in which they exist" (Ossenberg, 1969:30; Clinard, 1962, 1965; Hunter, 1969).

6. Cavan's (1966) study revealed little difference in the degree of "social licentiousness" in middle-class and lower-class bars, even though behaviour in middle-class bars was expected to be more constrained and respectful than in lower-class bars. If it is reasonable to hypothesize that this finding is applicable to the Hamilton drinking scene, and limited observation indicates that it is, then any differences in licentiousness which are found become that much more significant.[6] However, a difference does exist in the event of physical aggressiveness in lower and middle-class bars. Fights and verbal violence are more common to the lower-class bar. Thus, there are some aspects in which behaviour in middle-class bars is more restrained than lower-class bars, and any observed deviation from this pattern is significant.

7. Like Professor Ossenberg, and maybe even more so, we enjoy drinking beer.

For the study sample, eleven beer parlours and lounges were selected, all of which were within or very close to the core area of the festival site (downtown Hamilton). Of the eleven, six establishments were classified as middle-class and five as lower or working class. In Hamilton, beer parlours are licensed to serve only beer, while lounges are able to serve beer, wine and liquor. As in most Canadian cities, beer parlours traditionally cater to the lower-class (blue-collar workers, Canadian Forces personnel, the unemployed, welfare recipients, old age pensioners, Indians, and other ethnic and immigrant groups). Lounges are usually identified with a middle-class clientele (general office and white-collar workers, middle-level professional and executive types and university and senior high school students, especially since the legal age was lowered to 18).

Upper or upper-middle-class bars are omitted from the sample simply because there were none to be found in Hamilton's core area. This is most likely a reflection of (1) the close proximity to Toronto, (2) the relative lack of "first class" accommodation, and (3) the basic class structure of the city—Hamilton is basically an industrial city and is often called a "lunch bucket" town; in fact, one of the symbols of the city (in great evidence during Grey Cup Week) is a construction worker's hard hat.[7]

Unlike Professor Ossenberg, the present researchers had little prior knowledge of the drinking scene in Hamilton. Bars were included in the sample on the basis of advice from long-term residents. Subsequently, the eleven bars in question were returned to several times in order to gauge behaviour in them on more normal evenings.

Each drinking place was visited on two evenings at the end of Grey Cup Week—a Friday and Saturday. It is reasonable to assume that these two evenings would have the most intense "search for collective gratification" by virtue of their being the last two evenings before the *raison d'etre* of the festival, the Grey Cup itself, as well as being the end of the normal work week.

Within the bars the same aspects were observed as in Ossenberg's (1969:31) research, namely:

1. "The apparent social class comparison of patrons."
2. The wearing of costumes and/or paraphernalia indicative of team support.
3. "The noise level (including the spontaneity and intent of expressive vocalization); and
4. "Physical and social interaction, including evidences of aggression and general themes of conversation." (These last two aspects were observed as to their conformity or deviation from the usual standing patterns of behaviour found in the particular bars).

FINDINGS

Middle-Class Drinking Places

A complicating factor in this study is the fact that the legal drinking age in Ontario was recently lowered from 21 to 18 years of age. This has enlarged the entire drinking population considerably, especially the middle-class drinking population: so much so that line-ups are very common on normal weekends and often on weeknights at many middle-class drinking places. During Grey Cup Week long line-ups were the order of the day at all of the middle-class establishments in the sample. At several lounges, people waited as long as 2 hours to gain entrance. However, because many bars had to be investigated, time could not be wasted standing in line-ups. Therefore, certain forms of circumvention were employed, such as utilizing some prior knowledge of the bouncer (for example, "Bill sent me"), the wearing of Saskatchewan buttons and ribbons as a means of facilitating "hospitable" response,[8] cutting into the line close to the front, and sneaking past the bouncer at the door.

Five of the six middle-class drinking places in the sample were lounges. The sixth was a youth-oriented beer parlour. All of the places had entertainment in the form of various types of live musical presentation: trios, folk groups, rock bands, etc. Observation of those in the line-ups and in the places themselves revealed that the middle-class composition of the patrons was somewhat higher than on more normal days, when a small number of blue-collar and working-class types could usually be found. It was to these places that most of the out-of-towners came, as evidenced by the many patrons wearing Saskatchewan colours. Moreover, when advice was sought from locals as to "where the action was," the answers were to frequent middle-class bars (some of which were in the sample).

Approximately three-fourths of the patrons wore some type of Grey Cup paraphernalia, ranging from team-buttons, ribbons, festive hats of many types (especially stetsons and hard-hats), to full costumes of various types (for example, green and white cowboy suits for Saskatchewan fans and tiger outfits for Hamilton fans). In five out of the six places, the bar personnel were also attired in Grey Cup costumes.

In the middle-class drinking places the "standing patterns of behaviour" were somewhat upset, especially with respect to the range of "permissible behaviour" and "normal trouble."[9] The atmosphere of these establishments was supercharged with a high degree of gregarious behaviour and boisterous conduct, and the level of this legitimate deviance continued to rise as the evening and the drinks flowed on. Spontaneous shouts and yells and horn-blowing emanated from various parts of the bar, competing with each other in terms of volume and also in terms of Eastern Canada versus Western Canada. For example, one group of Westerners would shout, "Yeah Saskatchewan!" or would go through the ritual, "Gimme an 'S,' gimme an 'A,'" etc. In reply, a group of Easterners would attempt to drown out this call with a louder "Yeah, Hamilton!" or "Gimme an 'H,' gimme an 'A,'" etc. Every two or three minutes the Hamilton Tiger-Cat fight song would ring through the entire place:

> Oskee wee wee
> Whiskey wa wa
> Holy Mackinaw
> Tigers,
> Eat 'em raw!

Football was a main topic of conversation, with animated discussions of how the Tiger-Cats would handle the 'Riders, and vice versa. As the evening wore on, the conversations became more expressively pleasure-seeking, turning to themes of how and where to get a sexual partner, where the party was later, retaliation to some "son-of-a-bitch" for a perceived put-down of self, and so forth.

The supercharged effect was not only verbal but physical as well. Males engaged in spirited camaraderie and backslapping types of behaviour. Sporadically, spirited fights would break out, upon which the special football-player-type bouncers (hired for the occasion) would eventually descend to "clean up" the premises. Ladies did not engage in such activities. However, they did involve themselves with males in such practices as indiscriminate necking and sexually charged dancing. In one instance, a young women was sitting on the lap of a male partner surrounded by other men. She was the center of attraction and was obviously enjoying the attention she was receiving in the form of four pairs of hands roaming all over her body.

One establishment, as a measure of economy and precaution, served drinks only in cheap plastic cups. Such a move proved to be a wise one. Several other lounges which served beer in bottles and liquor in glasses, found these objects being used as missiles which were hurled at the walls, at other patrons, and even at the entertainers. It did not take long for the floors of these places to resemble a veritable sea of broken glass. However, the plastic cups were also put to good use. One group of 10 or 12 people, who it seemed all worked in the same office, were sitting at one long table. They began to build a huge pyramid of cups, the base as long as the table, the height up to the ceiling. After a number of futile attempts, which were downed both by missiles thrown at the pyramid and/or the instability of the pyramid itself (much to the chagrin of the builders and the amusement of everyone else), the deed was finally accomplished and rewarded with a great cheer from all—and the demolition received an even greater cheer.

The effect of the prolonged fast and heavy drinking began to take its effects as early as suppertime. In one bar, shortly after 5 P.M., one young gentleman evidently had moved his chair into an area between several tables so as not to disturb his friends, and quietly passed out. Sometime later he awoke, joined his friends, and picked up his drinking where he left off. When his friends decided to leave to get something to eat, he joined our table, introduced himself and bought a round for the table, telling us that he had been going at it for 3 straight days and nights.

The buying of rounds was a common means of facilitating and sustaining interaction between visitors and Hamiltonians, and also between males and females.[10] Westerners were spotted by locals and invited to join their table. Upon entering a lounge, a local gentleman saw us and shouted, "Hey, Saskatchewan!" and offered us a round of beer. He asked about the Saskatchewan football team. Interwoven in the football talk was an exchange of descriptions of life in the West and the East and the spinning of biographies.[11]

Although the majority of patrons were grouped in terms of friendship circles and office-affiliations, table-hopping was common, especially on the part of males "moving in" on females, with round-buying the entrance ticket. In fact, sexual availability was a keynote of the middle-class drinking place, especially once the entertainment and the dancing began.[12] However, unlike Ossenberg's (1969) study, few prostitute of any type were observed. This is most likely because there were few of them in these establishments; the presence of a large number of young eligible women who were willing to "give it away," and, in fact, who often sought out sexual contacts, most likely obviated the demand for a prostitute's services. Young women, recently liberated by both ideology and law, travelled the pub circuit in groups of two, three or more, usually splitting up when suitable partners were "found." In some cases, to make a "find," these ladies were not averse to initiating the contact themselves by starting up a conversation, by requesting a dance, or by buying a drink for the potential partner (thereby establishing the same mutual obligations and potential relationship as when the male treats the female; Cavan, 1966:112-132, 184-186).

Lower Class Drinking Places

The sample of lower-class drinking places consisted of four beer parlours and one lounge. The lounge and two of the beer parlours provided live entertainment, the other two beer parlours had only juke boxes. The lounge and three of the beer parlours had provisions for dancing.

Line-ups at the lower-class bars were conspicuous by their absence. Closely related to this was the absence of the "youth" or student trade. Relatively few university types were to be found in these bars, nor were the groups of young single women found making the rounds of the middle-class bars present. The young people who were present were working types: construction or industrial workers, truck drivers, waitresses, hairdressers, and so forth, who were normally present in these bars.

In fact, most of those who regularly patronized these bars were present along with the usual smattering of drifters. The whole lower-class bar scene could be described as "business as usual." In most cases the premises were just over three-quarters full.

Also conspicuous by their absence were the "Oskee wee wee's" and competing yells which characterized the middle-class bars. The standing patterns of behaviour were as usual; Grey Cup related expressive behaviour was at a minimum. Only about one in ten customers wore any Grey Cup paraphernalia, and this was limited mostly to stetson, or hard-hats, ribbons and buttons; very few patrons were "fully" costumed. Those who were identified in some manner with the Grey Cup sat in groups of three or four or more, and if there was more than one group, they were scattered throughout the place. They did not interact with the other patrons in any meaningful way; it would be fair to say that the regular customers basically ignored them, except in several instances, when one of the regulars took a dislike to one of the Cuppers and started a fight with them. They did not exhibit the same degree of legitimate deviant behaviour as those in middle-class bars. They were very subdued by comparison, sitting quietly drinking their beer, talking about the game and its players, the problems of locating easy sex (if not accompanied by female companions), checking over their financial resources, where to go next, etc. On the whole the Grey Cuppers did not stay much over two or three beers before moving on.

The regular patrons behaved in their normal fashion. While there was some interest in the Grey Cup Game on the part of these patrons (mainly the younger men), it did not dominate conversations and was soon dropped as the beer kept coming. Topics shifted to problems associated with work and family, the fight with "the old lady," the great "lay" of last night, drinking exploits, the virtues, power and speed of their cars and of other makes, etc. Two of the beer parlours were distinguished by the sexual segregation of "ladies and escorts" and "men only" beverage rooms. The only apparent effects of this distinction were the "toning down" of sexually-oriented conversations and the limitation of hustling by both males and females to the ladies' side.

The animation of the conversations and the noise level also rose as the beer poured on until the dull roar was shattered every so often by the sound of breaking glasses, upturning tables, cries of "You cocksucker!" and fists striking jaws. Fights broke out every hour or so, over a number of things, and often over nothing at all. In one case, four gentlemen were sitting arguing over whose turn it was to buy the round when suddenly one of them threw a roundhouse right which landed on another's face. As the second gentleman went over backward in his chair, he took the table and the beer on it with him, to the dismay of the others.

It was not possible to gauge, in concrete terms, the number of prostitutes working these bars, even though a higher proportion of women than usual was present. Certainly they were present, often making no pretensions as to their business. However, even with follow-up visits, no conclusions can be drawn regarding Ossenberg's observations that more hookers may be found in lower-class bars during a festival.

As the evening wore on and the music and dancing started, hustling became a prime activity on the ladies side. Women, on the whole, were older and less aggressive than in the middle-class bars, but just as available, often giving the old "come on" (i.e., big eyes but shy, stare and look away, smile coyly), especially if they were hookers (whereupon if accepted they would leave with the "john" and return within the hour).

SUMMARY AND CONCLUSIONS

Despite the continued debate over the definition of deviance (e.g., Akers, 1968; DeLamater, 1968; Gibbons and Jones, 1971; Gibbs, 1966), there appears to be agreement on some aspects. Among them are the assumptions that deviant behaviour is negatively sanctioned in some manner and not highly tolerated, especially if it is widespread. Yet, there are times when certain forms of deviance receive social sanction and are highly tolerated even though they are widespread; that is, when deviant behaviour is legitimate. These periods of legitimate deviance are manifested in conventionalized Time Out rituals such as urban festivals.

It is believed that members from all classes and status groups participate in these Time Outs. Moreover, the legitimate deviant behaviour expressed during these periods is said to function to restore community solidarity and integration and also as a community safety-valve. The results of a participant observation of bar behaviour in a sample of public drinking places during Grey Cup Week 1972 in Hamilton, Ontario support the hypothesis that more legitimate deviant behaviour would be exhibited by the middle-class than the lower-class. Middle-class patrons were found to exhibit a much higher level of festival-related aggressive expressive behaviour than lower-class patrons. The spontaneity of the middle-class was contrasted with the disinterest of the lower-class in Grey Cup festivities. On this basis, it would appear that Grey Cup Week is more "functional" for members of the middle-class; that is, it is the middle-class which takes advantage of the temporary relaxation of social control to achieve "release from everyday cares" and in the process becomes more unified and integrated. The main forms of deviant behaviour which were legitimated during this period were excessive drinking and drunkenness, sexual immoralities, minor forms of violence and aggression, and loud and boisterous conduct.

These findings suggest that important differences exist in the nature and degree of the tension and frustration suffered by the social classes and/or in the paths by which they vent these frustrations.

Grey Cup Week, like other conventionalized urban Time Out periods of legitimate deviant behaviour, is said to contribute to the solidarity and integration of the host city by involving its citizens in various promotional and recreational activities and by attracting favorable attention to the city. Grey Cup Week is also said to be a safety-valve in that participation in legitimate deviance provides the citizens with the chance to escape the pressures and tensions of everyday life.

It is true that the methodology employed is somewhat subjective and limited (inherent problems in participant observations, especially of large crowds, but not damaging; see Fisher, 1972). It is also true that the definitions of social class employed are broad and unrefined. However, it cannot be denied that despite the physical proximity of the festivities taking place on the street and at various near-by locations, the lower-class was reluctant to become involved in such activities, preferring to remain enclosed in its habitat. In conjunction, the middle-class seldom entered into that habitat; people preferred to stand in line for long periods of time in order to get into middle-class bars rather than go around the corner to a lower-class bar where they would be seated immediately, and where they could conceivably create their own atmosphere of gaiety by simply "taking over" the place.

It is hard to imagine how such behaviour functions to restore community integration and solidarity. Social distance cannot be said to have decreased significantly during Grey Cup Week 1972 in Hamilton, except within the middle-class. If anything was solidified, it was the existing social distance between the classes. The classes remained pretty well endogamous in their behaviour, the middle-class engaging in celebrations and legitimate deviant behaviour, developing feelings of solidarity among themselves as well as feelings of civic pride; the lower-class simply going about its normal routine. Moreover, it was only middle-class business establishments in the downtown business core which involved themselves in "putting on a show" by dressing up windows in Grey Cup themes, putting up signs such as "Welcome Visitors," "Go Tigers Go," etc., and by selling Grey Cup souvenirs and paraphernalia.

In reality, Grey Cup Week 1972 was found to be basically a middle-class "binge" sponsored, promoted, and profited from mostly by businessmen and politicians. As such, Grey Cup Week 1972 functioned both as an integrative device and a safety-valve for the middle-class. It functioned to provide a shot-in-the-arm in terms of immediate economic gain for middle-class businesses by stimulating local consumers and attracting eager tourists. It functioned to promote an image of the city's administration (many of whom are local businessmen) as effective, efficient, and working towards the city's best interests. And it functioned to reinforce the major class boundary existing in the city.[13]

The existence of important class differences and the functional reality of Grey Cup Week are obscured by the somewhat misguided and idealistic functionalist formulations and assumptions. Obviously, a more realistic and penetrating theoretical framework is necessary to handle the reality of Grey Cup festivities and other Time Out periods of legitimate deviance. The findings of this study may be added to the plethora of others which reveal the great gap which exists between theory and research and the in-operation of the dialectic between the theoretical and the observable so necessary to the development of adequate scientific sociological theory (Lachenmeyer, 1971; Listiak, 1971). This lack of empirical content in sociological theory has long been known and criticized (Blumer, 1954; Mills, 1959; Filstead, 1970), and is thought by some to stem from the fact that such theory is ultimately unfalsifiable and untestable in terms of the criteria of scientific logico-deductive models (e.g., Homans, 1964; Douglas, 1970; Park, 1969; Stinchcombe, 1968; Willer, 1967; Zetterberg, 1965; Lachenmeyer, 1971). While this seems to be a plausible explanation of why research showing the existence of class differences in interests, material conditions, values, life-styles, etc., has not been incorporated into theoretical formulations, it seems likely that the problem goes deeper than this.

The growing documentation of the real problems of lower-class work and life (e.g., Romano, 1970; Christoffel, *et al.*, 1970; Beneson and Lessinger, 1970) and the evidence that no substantial structural change or redistribution of wealth or power has taken place in North American society despite the many liberal reform efforts and claims to the contrary (Kolko, 1962; Nossiter, 1964; Christoffel, *et al.*, 1970), does not sit well with the liberal ideology with which sociological functionalism has aligned itself. This ideological commitment together with the static, ahistorical, idealistic, quasiholistic nature of this version of functionalism (e.g., Frank, 1966, 1967; Listiak, 1971) leads to the promotion of a consensus image of society through its attempt to incorporate the lower classes into the mainstream of social life, as defined by middle-class standards, regardless of the reality of the situation. According to Smith (1971), functionalists have identified with the middle class and view its vast growth as the achievement of an efficient and benevolent society. For example, Lipset (1963:440) argues that in such a society "the fundamental political problems of the industrial revolution have been solved; the workers have achieved industrial and political citizenship." As such, lower-class and working people are viewed as typical Canadians with the only difference between them and other Canadians being the social situation in which they happen to live.

In such a view, problems like widespread inequalities in social condition *are not indicative of fundamental contradictions in society,* but are *minor operating problems* which can be resolved on a non-ideological basis by providing more and better opportunities for citizens to participate fully in society. There is no need totally to dismantle or reorganize the society; there is no reason to stop participating. To believe, or do so, is not only illegitimate but an indication that one's grasp of reality is "disturbed." Thus, sociologists who study those who rebel or attack the existing structure of social and political arrangements, or do not participate "fully" in the mainstream of "middle-class" life, show a great deal of concern for the "irrationality" of such actions. Sociological studies of the lower class for example, focus on misanthropy, authoritarianism, anomie, frustrated desires, etc. Lower-class culture is depicted as authoritarian, unsophisticated, anti-intellectual, undemocratic, intolerant, less stable, etc. (Lipset, 1963:114, 113, 121, 91, 94, 110, 108); it is a culture based on stretched or shadow values—values derived from and subordinate to those upheld in the common (read dominant) culture. The unfortunate (read oppressive) socio-cultural conditions in which the lower-class live, engender an inability to live up to the internalized values of the common culture. To cope with these failures and the guilt thus produced, surface rationalizations are developed, but on a *post hoc* and independent basis. Such reactive values have little or no validity in themselves (since they do not reflect how lower-class people really feel) and obviously cannot form a distinct and autonomous culture. Consequently, the lower-class has little it can call its own culturally, and nothing to contribute to the common culture: the lower-class is "culturally deprived" (Hodges, 1970) and should be aided in entering the Great Cultural Mainstream.

However, it is a gross distortion to argue that lower-class culture is not operative and self-sustaining. Even a shadow culture, once created, has a life of its own. Moreover, a culture does not have to be strong and well developed, i.e., effective in determining behavior, to serve as a source of identity and support which could have important social consequences at future dates. It is also a distortion to argue that lower-class culture has few, if any, useful and distinctive values, survival techniques, rituals, etc., of its own.[14] Further, the confinement of attention to socio-cultural factors ignores the significance of the nonsocial environment, in particular, the material conditions in which the social class lives. In the lower-class, economic and material deprivation or the threat of it leads to a preoccupation with physical needs which often are insufficiently satisfied. This deprivation can and does have important effects upon behaviour and culture (e.g., Roach, 1965; Kohn, 1969, 1972).

The expression of legitimate deviant behaviour during a conventionalized Time Out ritual like Grey Cup Week cannot be understood by ignoring such considerations. Nor can the functions of Time Out periods such as Grey Cup Week be understood in terms of the still-life photography of an ideologically blinded functionalism. A proper analysis must investigate the meanings of legitimate deviant behaviour during Time Out periods to various classes and groups as determined by their respective material cultural conditions in conjunction with an holistic consideration of the historical and structural context within which the Time Out has developed and operates. Moreover, this analysis must be developed with continual reference to the reality it represents.

At this stage, only several hypotheses as to the beginning of such an analysis of legitimate deviant behaviour and the functions of Grey Cup Week can be presented.

1. The origin and development of Grey Cup Week in the late 1940's and early 1950's may be depicted as stemming from the monopoly capitalistic nature of Canadian society. Specifically, it appears to have originated from the hinterland-metropolis nature of West-East

relations, the reflection of this relation in the development of Canadian professional football, and the political and personal motives of a Western politician in 1948. Grey Cup Week developed through the expansion and commercialization of the pre-game activities by the Toronto Junior Board of Trade and then by other business and political interests. (Note: Toronto was the host city of every Grey Cup from 1941 to 1957 except two, and of every Grey Cup from 1941 to 1965 except five).

Grey Cup Week functions to provide immediate economic gain and to reduce the effects of competition for business interests. It effectively performs these functions by virtue of the expression of legitimate deviant behaviour allowed by its festival atmosphere and relaxation of social control which attracts many visitors and locals and reduces their "practical" inhibitions. Thus, Grey Cup Week functions at once as both a generator and an absorber of surplus value and is an important aspect of the capitalistic sales effort.

2. a. The continued growth of Grey Cup Week (and the continued growth of commercialized professional football in Canada) is a product of the continued growth of monopoly capitalism in Canada. The legitimate deviant behaviour expressed during Grey Cup Week functions as an outlet for the expression of aggressive and sexual frustrations which stem from the oppressive aspects of urban life and the alienated and oppressive nature of work, leisure and sex in Canadian society. The commercial and sensate consumptive aspects of Grey Cup Week also function to satisfy these needs.

However, the degree of oppression in society varies by class. Those in the middle of the social structure are unable to express openly their aggression and sexuality and find satisfaction in a short-lived period of commercialized, impersonal, aggressive, and overindulgent legitimate deviant behaviour.

Those in the bottom of the social structure are relatively more oppressed, have a lower ability to consume and have a different history than those above them. Hence, they tend to utilize structures more suited to the satisfaction of their needs, e.g., mental disorders, relatively unconstrained physical and sexual expression, consumption of flagrantly "violent" and "sexual" sports (like wrestling, boxing, certain forms of automobile racing, etc.).

b. Grey Cup Week as a Time Out Within-limits allows participants to engage legitimately in "tension-release" behaviour which, while deviant, neither exceeds certain culturally determined limits, nor challenges the basic values of the society, in effect reinforcing capitalistic values (sexism, sensate consumption, etc.). As such, it also functions to promote a degree of solidarity among those who participate in it.

c. As a fragmented conglomerate of parades, contests, special events, special sales, parties, visiting politicians, legitimate deviance, etc., Grey Cup Week is a spectacle which functions to mystify the nature of Canadian society; that is, to present an image of society as so complex and overwhelming that it is impossible to understand, change, or escape.

d. Grey Cup Week thus functions as a mechanism of social control over a limited but important segment of the population. Those who are found not to participate in Grey Cup Week will either have functional equivalents more suited to their needs or will be unimportant to the maintenance of the system (except by virtue of their structural position, i.e., poverty is functional.)

These considerations are, of course, only a preliminary outline of what an adequate analysis must entail. They are certainly not a complete outline, but must be added to and more fully developed in the light of the theoretical framework from which they are drawn. They must be subjected to empirical test at every level by whatever and as many methods as are appropriate.

This empirical verification would involve:

1. Historical analysis of the development of the festival with particular attention to the class interests operative (also to be determined historically).

2. Quantitative analysis (longitudinal if possible) of the absorption and generation of surplus value by examining the increase in business spending on sales efforts, the consumer response, the total amount of resources absorbed, etc.

3. Investigation into the nature of alienation and oppression and its varying degrees by class; into the mechanisms utilized by the classes to relieve themselves; into the place of Grey Cup Week in the total class structure. Participant observation, ethnomethodological and survey investigation into the meanings attached to both the festival and the legitimate deviance expressed during it, and how and why one participates in it or does not participate in it.

4. Participant observations of behaviours indicative of feelings of solidarity (e.g., extending friendship, cross-class interaction, manifestations of civic pride, etc.). Pre- and post-festival surveys as to the degree of solidarity felt by participants as compared to nonparticipants

before, during, and after Grey Cup Week, and also to determine if
any significant differences exist in the background characteristics, perceptions of society, feelings of alienation, frustration, etc. between
those who participate and those who do not.

NOTES

1. Mr. John Woodard assisted in the research for this paper and made useful comments on it. His contribution and support are deeply appreciated.
2. Ceremonial arrangement is not the only way by which Time Outs may be called.
   MacAndrew and Edgerton (1969:168) note that people may call a Time Out
   "by temporarily assuming one or another alternation in their social positions.
   (In the New Guinea highlands, for example, one can escape burdensome economic responsibilities by exhibiting 'wild man' behaviour [Newman, 1964], and
   in Hindu India this escape can be accomplished by donning the orange robes
   of the *sanyasi* [Dumont, 1960].) In other societies, conduct can come under
   the heading of Time Out by virtue either of the willful action of another (as
   in the case, for example, of witchcraft, sorcery, and the like) or by the action
   of a supernatural agent who might briefly take possession of one's will for alien
   purposes . . . in many societies persons have available to them the option of
   calling Time Out by producing an altered state of consciousness in themselves."
3. The deviant behaviour legitimated during Time Outs is not totally uninhibited
   in its expression but almost always stays within certain culturally determined
   limits. See MacAndrew and Edgerton, 1969:Ch. 4.

   Moreover, alcohol is not necessarily an ingredient of Time Outs. In those
   societies where alcohol is believed to produce an altered state of consciousness
   rendering one unresponsible for one's actions, drunkenness is considered as a
   Time Out. However, in North American society excessive drinking and drunkenness are themselves forms of deviant behaviour (Jessor, *et al.,* 1969). Thus,
   during ceremonially arranged Time Outs like urban festivals, the state of drunkenness not only serves to legitimate one's deviance, but itself becomes a form
   of legitimate deviance.
4. This strain and frustration is primarily of the "status" type—the only type theoretically possible because man is conceived as *homo sociologicus* in sociological
   theory. That is to say, sociological theory is built on an image of man who is a
   role player, whose existence is determined entirely by social norms and institutions; man is a social actor whose behaviour is normatively regulated and
   "oriented to anticipated states of affairs such as goals, ends or objectives" (Roach,
   1965:70; Dahrendorf, 1961; Hornosty, 1970; Rich, 1966; Wrong, 1961).

   Thus, within the confines of sociological theory it is virtually impossible to
   deal with frustrations and strains which arise from nonsocial sources, such as
   overcrowding, malnutrition, etc.
5. The concept of "lower-class" as used in this discussion shall encompass both
   the lower-lower-class (those below the poverty level) and the upper-lower-class
   (or working class). It is understood that there are important differences between these two classes, especially with regard to the influence of economic
   and material conditions and to the relative strength of their respective cultural
   elements (Gans, 1962; Roach, 1965, 1967; Roach and Gursslin, 1965, 1967).
   However, the focus of this discussion is upon certain behavioural aspects common to both sub-classes.

   The lower-class in this discussion is defined in terms of the patrons of public drinking places which are frequented by blue collar and construction workers, Canadian Forces personnel, the unemployed, welfare recipients, old-age pensioners, Canadian Indians and other ethnic and immigrant groups.

   Similarly, the concept of "middle-class" used in this discussion shall include both the lower-middle-class and the upper-middle-class (and/or the "old" and the "new" middle classes, depending upon definition: see Mills, 1951; Kahl, 1957; Nelson, 1968; Boskoff, 1970), as it is only certain behavioural characteristics shared by both subclasses which are under scrutiny here.

   The middle-class in this discussion is defined in terms of the patrons of public drinking places which are frequented by general office and white-collar workers, middle-level professional and executive types, and university and senior high school students.

6. Licentious behaviour refers to behaviour which, by usual puritanical middle-class mores, would be regarded as sexually loose or unrestrained, such as overt sexual gestures in public, indiscriminate fondling and necking, connotations which denote sexual availability, etc. This is the normal meaning of the concept and this is the way Cavan (1966) uses it.

7. One particular lounge, located in the city's oldest and poshest hotel, was normally characterized by an upper-middle-class clientele. For the Grey Cup, however, the hotel was the "festival headquarters," thus attracting great crowds to its facilities, and thus diversifying the usual class composition of the lounge.

8. The wearing of Saskatchewan colours was not adopted totally out of devious designs, for the researchers were from the West (Manitoba and Saskatchewan) and were hoping the Roughriders would defeat the Tiger-Cats. Unfortunately, our hopes were not realized. The Tiger-Cats won the game on a last second field-goal.

9. These concepts are taken from Sherri Cavan's classic ethnography of bar behaviour, *Liquor License*. Standing patterns of behaviour "define for the actor what activity can take place as a matter of course and without question, and for what conduct those present will be held accountable. They may further delimit who is or is not eligible to enter a given setting, the ways the routine tasks are to be distributed, the varieties of reputations that can be accorded to those entering, the kinds of fates that can be alloted to those present and the like" (Cavan, 1966:3).

   Her study illustrates that public drinking places, even though they have a Time Out atmosphere, have standing patterns of behaviour which are "both routinely expected within the setting and treated as fitting and proper for the time and place" (Cavan, 1966:7). Because such establishments are Time Out settings in which the usual formality and repression of social life is somewhat relaxed, the range of permissible behaviour and "normal trouble" (that is, "improper activities which are frequent enough to be simply shrugged off or ignored" Cavan, 1966:18) is of greater latitude than in other public settings. The concepts of normal trouble and permissible behaviour are equivalent to our concept of legitimate deviance. The deviance legitimated in bars is not of the same magnitude as during conventionalized Time Out rituals.

10. Cavan (1966:112-113) refers to round-buying as "treating," and elaborates a number of functions to this ritual. Those functions relevant to this discussion at this point are the "binding together temporarily patrons in an ongoing encounter by establishing a set of mutual obligations between them," and "Formalizing the change in relationship between two patrons from interactants to ephemeral acquaintances" (1966: 113, see also pp. 184-186).

11. Because of the openness of patrons and the limited nature of encounters in bar settings, it is possible for an individual to pass himself off to others as almost anything he wants with little fear of exposure either in the present or in the future. See Cavan, (1966: 79-87.)

12. In those places which had no provision for dancing, that is, which had no dance floor, patrons danced in the aisles and between tables, and sometimes on the tables.

13. Although it was not possible to test the functions of the Grey Cup on the national level, it is possible to say a few things. The Grey Cup is said to unite Canada by making Canadians think in terms of East-West and to stir up nationalistic cultural sentiments. To some extent it does do this via the great media exposure and the people travelling to the host city. However, it is a strange nationalism that is fostered, for it is based on a game that is English in origin and American in development and commercialization, and whose stars and heroes and coaches are imported from the United States. Top players are continually playing out the option clause in their contract in order to move "up" to the American professional leagues. Even the commitment of the Canadian Football League itself to Canada is questionable considering the recent debate over expansion into the United States and the relative lack of programs to develop Canadian talent.

14. Those who recognize the existence of an operative cultural system in the lower-class use it as an explanatory device, e.g., the "culture of poverty" group (e.g., Harrington, 1962; Riessman, 1962; Will and Vatter, 1965) and the subcultural delinquency school (e.g. Cohen, 1955; Cloward and Ohlin, 1960). However, they deal only with the upper-lower or working-class and ignore the differences between the working-class and the lower-lower class. The lower-lower-class is characterized by physical frustrations rather than status frustration and a weak normative system which is determined by the harsh economic and material conditions in which it exists (Roach and Gursslin, 1965, 1967).

The working-class, because of its relatively less oppressive economic and material conditions, is able to develop more status concern, to focus more of its frustration, and thus, to develop a stronger cultural system through interaction in subcultures. Yet, to treat working-class culture as reactive or as a shadow or as value-stretched is also a distortion which ignores the physical conditions of the working-class and the fact that the culture itself has been interpreted as a traditional cultural system with a unique set of values developed over many generations (e.g., Miller, 1958, 1959).

REFERENCES

Akers, Ronald L.
   1964   "Socio-economic status and delinquent behaviour: A retest." *Journal of Research on Crime and Delinquency,* 1 (January).
   1968   "Problems in the sociology of deviance: Social definitions and behaviour." *Social Forces,* 46, (June).
Batten, Jack
   1972   "Will the Canadian Football League survive?" *Maclean's,* 86 (October).

Beneson, Harold and Eric Lessinger
1970   "Are workers becoming middle-class?" In Tom Christoffel, *et al.* (eds.), *Up Against the American Myth.* New York: Holt, Rinehart, Winston.

Bensman, Joseph and Israel Gerver
1963   "Crime and punishment in the factory: The function of deviance in maintaining the social system." *American Sociological Review,* 28 (August).

Berger, Bennett
1960   *Working Class Suburb: A Study of Auto Workers in Suburbia.* Berkeley: University of California Press.

Birnbaum, Norman
1955   "Monarchs and sociologists." *Sociological Review,* 3:5-23.

Blumer, Herbert
1954   "What is wrong with social theory?" *American Sociological Review,* 19 (February).

Boskoff, Alvin
1970   *The Sociology of Urban Regions.* 2nd ed. New York: Appleton-Century-Crofts.

Cahnman, Werner
1969   "The stigma of obesity." *Sociological Quarterly,* 9 (Summer).

Cavan, Sherri
1966   *Liquor License: An Ethnography of Bar Behaviour.* Chicago: Aldine.

Christoffel Tom, David Finkelhor, and Dan Gilbarg (eds.)
1970   *Up Against the American Myth.* New York: Holt, Rinehart, Winton.

Clinard, Marshall B.
1962   "The public drinking house in society." In D. J. Pitman and C. R. Synder (eds.), *Alcohol, Culture and Drinking Patterns.* New York: John Wiley.

1965   *The Sociology of Deviant Behaviour.* New York: Holt, Rinehart, Winston.

Cloward, Richard A. and Lloyd L. Ohlin
1960   *Delinquency and Opportunity.* New York: Free Press.

Cohen, Albert K.
1955   *Delinquent Boys.* New York: Free Press.

Cosentino, Frank
1969   *Canadian Football: The Grey Cup Years.* Toronto: Musson.

Coser, Lewis A.
1967   "Some functions of deviant behaviour and normative flexibility." In Lewis A. Coser. *Continuities in the Study of Social Conflict.* New York: Free Press.

Currie, Gordon
1968   *100 Years of Canadian Football.* Toronto: Pagurian Press.

Dahrendorf, Ralf
1961   "Democracy without liberty." In Seymour M. Lipset and Leo Lowenthal (eds.), *Culture and Social Character: The Work of David Riesman Revisited.* New York: Free Press.

Davis, Kingsley
  1966 "Sexual behaviour." In Robert K. Merton and Robert A. Nisbet (eds.), *Contemporary Social Problems.* New York: Harcourt, Brace & World.
DeLamater, John
  1968 "On the nature of deviance." *Social Forces,* 46 (June).
Dentler, Robert A. and Kai T. Erickson
  1959 "The functions of deviance in groups." *Social Problems,* 7 (Fall).
Douglas, Jack D.
  1970 "Deviance and order in a pluralistic society." In John C. McKinney and Edward A. Tiryakian (eds.), *Theoretical Sociology: Perspectives and Developments.* New York: Appleton-Century-Crofts.
Dumont, L.
  1960 "World renunciations in Indian religions." *Contributions to Indian Sociology,* 4.
Elliot, Delbert S.
  1962 "Delinquency and perceived opportunity." *Sociological Inquiry,* 32 (Spring).
Empey, LaMar T.
  1956 "Social class and occupational aspiration: A comparison of absolute and relative measurement." *American Sociological Review,* 21 (December).
Empey, LaMar T. and Maynard L. Erickson
  1966 "Hidden delinquency and social status." *Social Forces,* 44 (June).
Erickson, Kai T.
  1964 "Notes on the sociology of deviance." In Howard S. Becker (ed.), *The Other Side: Perspectives on Deviance.* New York: Free Press.
  1966 *Wayward Puritans.* New York: John Wiley.
Filstead, William (ed.).
  1970 *Qualitative Methodolgy: Firsthand Involvement with the Social World.* Chicago: Markham.
Fisher, Charles S.
  1972 "Observing a crowd: The structure and description of protest demonstrations." In Jack D. Douglas (ed.), *Research on Deviance.* New York: Random House.
Frank, Andre Gunder
  1966 "Functionalism, dialects and synthesis." *Science and Society,* 30 (Spring).
  1967 "Sociology of development and the underdevelopment of sociology." *Catalyst,* 3 (Summer).
Gans, Herbert J.
  1962 *The Urban Villagers.* New York: Free Press.
Gibbons, Don C. and Joseph F. Jones
  1971 "Some critical notes on current definitions of deviance." *Pacific Sociological Review,* 14 (January).
Gibbs, Jack
  1966 "Conceptions of deviant behaviour: the old and the new." *Pacific Sociological Review,* 9 (Spring).
Green, Arnold W.
  1946 "The middle-class male child and neurosis." *American Sociological Review,* 11.

Harper, Dean and Frederick Emmert
  1963   "Work behaviour in a service industry." *Social Forces*, 42 (December).
Harrington, Michael
  1962   *The Other America*. New York: Macmillan.
Hartogs, Renatus with Hans Fantel
  1967   *Four-Letter Word Games: The Psychology of Obscenity*. New York: Dell.
Hirschi, Travis
  1969   *Causes of Delinquency*. Berkeley: University of California Press.
Hodges, Harold M. Jr.
  1970   "Peninsula people: Social stratification in a metropolitan complex." In Robert Gutman and David Popenoe (eds.), *Neighborhood, City, and Metropolis*. New York: Random House.
Homans, George D.
  1964   "Contemporary theory in sociology." In Robert E. L. Faris (ed.), *Handbook in Modern Sociology*. Chicago: Rand McNally.
Horonosty, Roy W.
  1970   "The development of sociological theory and the delinquencies of man." Paper presented at the sixth annual meetings of the Canadian Sociology and Anthropology Association, Winnipeg, Manitoba.
Hunter, V. Dianne
  1969   "The Semi-Legal Drinking Place: Its Characteristics and Functions as a Reflection of the Social Structure." Unpublished M.A. thesis, University of Calgary, Calgary.
Hyman, Herbert H.
  1953   "The value system of different classes: A social psychological contribution to the analysis of stratification." In Reinhard Bendix and Seymour M. Lipset (eds.), *Class, Status and Power*. New York: Free Press.
Jessor, Richard, Theodore D. Graves, Robert C. Hanson, and Shirley L. Jessor
  1968   *Society, Personality and Deviant Behaviour*. New York: Holt, Rinehart, Winston.
Kahl, Joseph A.
  1957   *The American Class Structure*. New York: Holt, Rinehart, Winston.
Kohn, Melvin L.
  1969   *Class and Conformity: A Study in Values*. Homewood, Ill.: Dorsey Press.
  1972   "Class, family, and schizophrenia: A reformulation." *Social Forces*, 50 (March).
Kolko, Gabriel
  1962   *Wealth and Power in America: An Analysis of Social Class and Income Distribution*. New York: Praeger.
Lachenmeyer, Charles
  1971   *The Language of Sociology*. New York: Columbia University Press.

Largey, Gale Peter and David Rodney Watson
    1972   "The sociology of odors." *American Journal of Sociology*, 77 (May).

Lipset, Seymour M.
    1963   *Political Man.* Garden City, N.Y.: Doubleday.

Listiak, Alan
    1971   "A Alienation: The failure of a concept and the failure of positivistic sociology." Paper presented at the thirteenth annual meetings of the Western Association of Sociology and Anthropology, Calgary, Alberta.

MacAndrew, Craig and Robert B. Edgerton
    1969   *Drunken Comportment: A Social Explanation.* Don Mills, Ont.: Thomas Nelson.

Miller, Walter B.
    1958   "Lower-class culture as a generating milieu of gang delinquency." *Journal of Social Issues*, 14.
    1959   "Implications of urban lower-class culture for social work." *Social Service Review*, 33(September).

Mills, C. Wright
    1951   *White Collar.* New York: Oxford University Press.
    1959   *The Sociological Imagination.* New York: Oxford University Press.

Mizruchi, Ephraim Harold
    1964   *Success and Opportunity.* New York: Free Press.
    1967   "Aspiration and poverty: A neglected aspect of Merton's anomie." *Sociological Quarterly*, 8(Autumn).

Nelson, Joel I.
    1968   "Anomie: Comparisons between the old and new middle-class." *American Journal of Sociology*, 74 (September).

Newman, P. L.
    1964   "Wild man behaviour in a New Guinea highlands community." *American Anthropologist*, 66.

Nossiter, Bernard D.
    1964   *The Mythmakers.* New York: Houghton Mifflin.

Ossenberg, Richard J.
    1969   "Social class and bar behaviour during an urban festival." *Human Organization*, 28 (Spring). pp. 29-34.

Park, Peter
    1969   *Sociology Tomorrow.* New York: Pegasus.

Polsky, Ned
    1967   *Hustlers, Beats and Others.* Chicago: Aldine.

Quinn, James A.
    1955   *Urban Sociology.* New York: American Book Co.

Rainwater, Lee
    1960   *And the Poor Get Children.* Chicago: Quadrangle Books.

Reissman, Frank
    1962   *The Culturally Deprived Child.* New York: Harper & Bros.

Rich, Harvey
    1966   "Homo Sociologic and personality theory." *Canadian Review of Sociology and Anthropology*, 3 (August).

Roach, Jack L.
1965   "Sociological analysis and poverty." *American Journal of Sociology,*
        71 (July).
1967   "Toward a theory of lower-class culture." In Llewellyn Gross (ed.),
        Sociological Theory: Inquiries and Paradigms. New York Harper
        and Row.
Roach, Jack L. and Orville R. Gursslin
1965   "The lower-class, status frustration, and social disorganization."
        Social Forces, 43 (May).
1967   "An evaluation of the concept culture of poverty." *Social Forces,*
        45 (March).
Romano, Paul
1970   "Life on the job." In Tom Christoffel, *et al.* (eds.), *Up Against
        the American Myth.* New York: Holt Rinehart, Winston.
Sagarin, Edward
1962   *The Anatomy of Dirty Words.* New York: Lyle Stuart.
Sewell, William H.
1961   "Social class and childhood personality." *Sociometry,* 24 (De-
        cember).
Shils, Edward and Michael Young
1953   "The meaning of the coronation." *Sociological Review,* 1 (Decem-
        ber).
Short, James F., Jr., Ramon Rivera, and Ray A. Tennyson
1965   "Perceived opportunities, gang membership and delinquency."
        American Sociological Review, 30 (February).
Shostak, Arthur B.
1969   *Blue-Collar Life.* New York: Random House.
Shostak, Arthur B. and William Gomberg (eds.).
1964   *Blue-Collar World.* Englewood Cliffs, N. J.: Prentice-Hall.
Smith, Dusky Lee
1971   "The Sunshine Boys: toward a sociology of happiness." In J. David
        Colfax and Jack L. Roach (eds.), *Radical Sociology,* New York:
        Basic Books.
Smith, Thomas S.
1968   "Conventionalization and control: An examination of adolescent
        crowds." *American Journal of Sociology,* 74 (September).
Spiller, Bertram
1965   "Delinquency and middle-class goals." *Journal of Criminal Law,
        Criminology and Police Science,* 56.
Stinchcombe, Arthur L.
1968   *Constructing Social Theories.* New York: Harcourt, Brace & World.
Stoddard, Ellwyn R.
1968   "The 'informal code' of police deviance: A group approach to 'blue-
        coat crime'." *Journal of Criminal Law, Criminology and Police
        Science,* 59 (June).
Sullivan, Jack
1970   *The Grey Cup Story.* Toronto: Pagurian Press.
Turner, Ralph H. and Lewis M. Killian
1957   *Collective Behaviour.* Englewood Cliffs, N.J.: Prentice-Hall.
Vaz, Edmund W. (ed.)
1967   *Middle-Class Juvenile Delinquency.* New York: Harper and Row.

Voss, Harwin L.
    1966   "Socio-economic status and reported delinquent behaviour." *Social Problems*, 13 (Winter).
Will, Robert E. and Harold G. Vatter (eds.)
    1965   *Poverty in Affluence*. New York: Harcourt, Brace & World.
Willer, David
    1967   *Scientific Sociology*. Englewood Cliffs, N. J.: Prentice-Hall.
Wilson, Alan B.
    1959   "Residential segregation of social classes and aspirations of high school boys." *American Sociological Review*, 24 (December).
Winslow, Robert W.
    1968   "Anomie and its alternatives: A self-report study of delinquency." *Sociological Quarterly*, (Fall).
Wrong, Dennis
    1961   "The oversocialized conception of man in modern sociology." *American Sociological Review*, 26 (April).
Zetterberg, Hans L.
    1965   *On Theory and Verification in Sociology*. Totowa, N.J.: Bedminster Press.

Section D

Subcultures, Countercultures and Sport

When a group forms an identity based upon a set of beliefs, norms, and values distinctive from or in conflict with those of the mainstream of society, a subculture has formed. The study of subcultures is a fascinating one for while it focuses attention upon groups which are often colorful, often rebellious, and usually outsiders, it throws light as well upon the take-for granted values of everyday life.

Sport relates to subcultures in two ways. First, already existing subcultures may be drawn to certain sports which they adopt as their own. Whyte shows how the gang in *Street Corner Society* bowled together, the results serving to reinforce their allegiance to the leadership structure.[1] McIntosh notes that its association with the British public schools in the late 19th century invested British football with the values of a "gentlemanly," i.e., upper-class, subculture.[2] And Polsky argues that the demise of the bachelor subculture foretold the doom of the pool hall.[3] Thus certain sports may provide particular appeal for certain subcultural groups.

The other manner in which sport and subcultures can be related occurs when a sport becomes the focal point for subcultural formation. Examples of this phenomenon include the subcultures of ski bums, suffers, and mountain climbers.

Membership in a subculture can be a highly significant aspect of an individual's life, often serving as the activity around which his or her life is focused and upon which a significant proportion of his or her identity is based. From this perspective a subculture can be particularly important when the values an individual endorses are at odds with those of the dominant social group. Subcultural membership then

1. William H. Whyte. *Street Corner Society* (Chicago: University of Chicago Press) 1943.
2. Peter McIntosh. "An Historical View of Sport and Social Control," *International Review of Sport Sociology*, 6:5-16, 1971.
3. Ned Polsky. "Of Pool Playing and Poolrooms," *Hustlers, Beats and others*. (Garden City, N.Y.: Anchor Books) 1969.

serves a doubly important purpose in providing a reference group with which such "deviants" can identify and a social mileau in which they are free to express their own value system.

Focusing upon this theme, Donnelly offers a comprehensive introduction to the study of subcultures. He identifies and discusses seven characteristics of subcultures, then applies his framework to an analysis of the subculture of climbers.

Birrell and Turowetz were searching for the key theme for understanding two very diverse sport subcultures: the world of the collegiate gymnast and the world of the professional wrestler. They discuss several significant aspects of identity construction and focus upon the concept of character. In these two disparate subcultures, they argue, and perhaps in many others, interaction can be understood as an attempt to demonstrate to other members of the subculture that the individual is worthy of respect: that he or she is mindful of the qualities valued by those in their world, possesses such qualities, and will display them in appropriate and even difficult situations. For the gymnast, that quality is poise or composure; for the wrestler, it is the ability to create color (dramatic realism) and heat (genuine audience response).

In the final selection, attention is focused upon the use of sport made by a particular adolescent subculture. Marsh and Harré report their findings from a study of football hooligans in Britain. They present persuasive evidence that, unpredictable as their behavior appears to outsiders, the group is in fact highly structured, orderly, and mindful of a strong set of subcultural norms.

Toward a Definition of Sport Subcultures

Peter Donnelly

INTRODUCTION

Perhaps the most central question in sociology is, "How is society possible?" How and why do people develop the sets of norms, values and sanctions that are manifested as socially acceptable behavior and, for the most part, conform to them? In examining smaller units of society—their social order, social organization and cultural themes—sociologists usually have two aims. They are interested in the units for their own sake as social phenomena; and they believe that the units may provide clues into the overall organization of society.

Among these smaller units of society are subcultures or subsocieties.[1] Subcultures are cultural units sharing much in common with the larger parent cultures, but also possessing identifiable cultural elements of their own. For example, one may conceive in a general sense of American culture, Canadian culture, or even Western culture, but within and between these larger cultures are numerous subcultural units. Subcultures, which may be based on either ascribed or achieved characteristics, are much more amenable to study than total cultures.

For the purposes of sport sociology, those subcultures based on achieved characteristics are of most interest. While not referring specifically to achieved characteristics Loy *et al.* (1978) have noted that three major types of (achieved) subculture are the occupational, the avocational and the deviant. Avocational subcultures include all of the sport and leisure subcultures, but interface with occupational subcultures at the professional level and with deviant subcultures in areas such as gambling and hustling.

The various case studies of sport subcultures are beginning to provide the basis for an understanding of the culture of sport, including the

Prepared for this volume.

cultural evolution of sports, and the similarities and differences between various sports.[2] In addition, several authorities have employed the sports and pastimes of people as a 'culture clue' (e.g., Huizinga, 1955; Caillois, 1961; and Roberts and Sutton-Smith, 1962). The study of sport subcultures may provide insights into the development of culture and the relationships between various aspects of culture.

This article is concerned with providing a working definition of the term 'subculture,' providing a review of some of the case studies of sport subcultures, and presenting several examples from a study of a specific sport subculture.

DEFINITION

Donnelly (1979) and Fine and Kleinman (1979) have reviewed a number of problems associated with the study of subcultures. The problems generally appear to result from the lack of an adequate definition of the concept. Researchers and theorists have not determined the types of groups that may be considered as subcultures, or the characteristics of subcultures. Many investigators have opted for Gordon's original, extremely broad definition[3] of the concept and applied it to the group of their choice. Others have created definitions, and even theories, to meet their own specific needs without regard to broader application. Clarke (1974), noting some of these difficulties, suggested that the term would probably have been rejected as being useless to sociologists if it had not become a part of everyday language.

Ascribed and Achieved Subcultures

The major deterrent to providing a useful definition of subculture has been the attempt to incorporate both ascribed and achieved characteristics into a single definition. When the two are considered separately the problems of definition and analysis become relatively straightforward. Figure 1 represents an attempt to differentiate the two major types of subculture with subdivisions for achieved subcultures.

Ascribed subcultures may be considered as social categories to which people belong because of particulars of birthplace, birthright, age or other forms of sociological typing. Achieved subcultures are those subcultures to which people consciously attain membership. All individuals will belong to four or more of the ascribed subcultures. Even with Gordon's (1964) refinement of 'ethclass'[4] there is a great deal of overlapping between the various subcultural categories and consequent problems in analysis. It is extremely difficult to determine boundaries, specific life

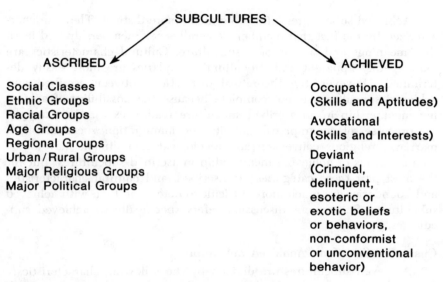

Figure 1. Ascribed and achieved subcultures

styles, or any broadly based cultural characteristics for any of the ascribed subcultures.

The fact that a person has a certain income, occupational index score and/or education does not guarantee that his or her life style or cultural characteristics will be similar to others with a similar income, occupational index score and/or education. The fact that a person belongs to a certain age group, whether it be adolescence, youth, middle age or elderly, does not mean that that person consistently shares any common cultural characteristics with others in the same age group. There may be as wide a variety of individuals in one age group as there are in the entire culture. Elkin and Westley (1955) provide supporting evidence for this point by noting that adolescent or youth culture among the middle class individuals that they studied "has a somewhat mythical character" (p. 684). While some cultural elements were found, they tended to be less prevalent than other patterns.

A similar lack of definition appears to exist in all of the ascribed subcultures. The lack of clearly defined cultural elements specific to ascribed subcultures, together with the confusion associated with overlapping membership and the lack of clearly defined subcultural boundaries, lead to enormous problems of definition and analysis. The situation becomes even more confusing when it is considered that the members of ascribed subcultures may also belong to one or more achieved subcultures.

Achieved subcultures tend to be much more distinct. They are characterized by the fact that members generally seek membership and learn the "meanings and ways"[5] of a subculture. Cultural characteristics are more readily apparent and subcultural boundaries are more easily determined. However, the theoretical distinction between ascribed and achieved subcultures is not complete because the possibility of achieving membership in an ascribed subculture readily exists. For example, the processes of geographical mobility and immigration, social mobility, marriage, religious conversion and ideological commitment may all be seen as means of achieving membership in ascribed subcultures. But for the most part these categories are ascribed, and cultural characteristics and boundaries are much more difficult to determine than with achieved subcultures. Subsequent discussion refers specifically to achieved subcultures.

Characteristics of an Achieved Subculture

Achieved subcultures are defined by the following characteristics:
1. *Identifiable groups:* Subcultures are identifiable groups within a culture or across cultures.
2. *Composition:* Subcultures are collectivities of small groups and individuals.
3. *Cultural characteristics:* Their members employ similar artifacts and symbols, engage in similar types of behavior, and adhere to a set of norms and values specific to the subculture.
4. *Distinctive nature:* These cultural elements have a distinctive nature and are somewhat different from those of the culture(s) in which they exist.
5. *Life style and resources:* Achieved subcultures represent a major element in the life style and allocation of resources of their members.
6. *Scope and potential:* Achieved subcultures are formed around beliefs and behaviors that have scope and potential.
7. *Fulfillment of individual needs:* Subcultures are actively created and maintained by their members as long as they meet the needs of their members.
8. *Interaction and communication:* Subcultures are created and maintained by face-to-face interaction and other forms of communication between their members.

Each of these characteristics is discussed in more detail.

1. Identifiable Groups

While a truly secret society may have all of the characteristics of a subculture, subcultures and their members for the most part tend to become identifiable from without. It is unlikely that a large number of people who are drawn together on the basis of some quality, belief or behavior, who become an ongoing entity, and who manifest similar customs, behaviors, shared understandings and artifacts that are somewhat different from the total culture, would pass unnoticed. In fact, the process of becoming a member of a subculture involves the acquisition of an identity. Since some commitment is involved in achieving membership and the related identity, it is only to be expected that an individual will wish to proclaim that identity. Such declarations serve not only to indicate to other members of the subculture that one is now a member, but also to inform non-members of one's new identity.

Gordon's (1947) original definition of subculture stated that a subculture was "a subdivision of a national culture," but it is apparent that many subcultures extend beyond the bounds of a specific nation and may be considered as international. Because of the vastly improved communications in the 'global village,' national cultures are becoming less distinct and subcultures, particularly those associated with sports and occupations, clearly extend beyond the bounds of a particular nation. This is most apparent in countries that share the same language, such as Britain, the United States, Canada and other Commonwealth countries, but even language need not be a barrier to the internationalization of a subculture. The subculture of skiers provides an ideal example of an identifiable and international subculture.

2. Composition

A subculture usually originates with a particular small group of individuals who are in face-to-face interaction, but cannot be considered as a subculture until the cultural characteristics of that small group have spread beyond its confines to other small groups and individuals. In order to distinguish between the culture of small groups and subcultures Lee (1954) and Gordon (1964) employed the term 'groupculture'. "The distinction allows us to isolate and distinguish from each other phenomena of different scope and import" (Gordon, 1964:40).

Both Wolfgang and Ferracuti (1969) and Phillips and Schafer (1976) have noted the distinction between social groups and subcultures:

> Subcultural values and norms are shared among members of groups, but those who share in a subculture need not interact with one another as a group any more than those who share in the Japanese, Spanish or any other 'parent' culture. Indeed, those who share in many subcultures—hippies, for example—are widely dispersed and could not possibly interact as a group (Phillips and Schafer, 1976: 130).

Thus, subculture boundaries and the boundaries of face-to-face interaction are quite distinct (Lerman, 1967), but the potential for and possibility of face-to-face interaction between all members of a subculture exists.

A subculture may be seen as a collectivity of groups and individuals who possess common cultural characteristics and who interact with each other, or who have the potential and the ability to interact with each other either directly or symbolically (i.e., through such media as magazines and newsletters). In this sense, membership of the various affiliates of a subculture is interchangeable, and while local differences clearly exist there are no real barriers to the exchange of members. When a set of cultural characteristics is confined to a small group linked by informal means of communication, the term 'groupculture' is applicable. Once the set of cultural characteristics spreads to other groups and a (yet to be determined) critical mass is attained, the various groups may devise more formal means of communication in order to propagate the cultural characteristics and the term subculture may be applied.

3. Cultural Characteristics

Tylor's classic definition of culture refers to "that complex whole which includes knowledge, belief, art, morals, law, custom, and any other capabilities and habits acquired by man as a member of society" (Tylor 1871:1). These elements of culture are constantly being created and undergoing change as a result of interaction between people. Similarly, the customs, behaviors, shared understandings and artifacts of subsocieties are constantly evolving and changing.

The study of subcultures involves the analysis of the cultural characteristics of subsocieties, usually employing participant observation methods. But many of the descriptive case studies of subcultures involve an analysis at one point in time without regard for the processes of cultural change. Changes in the 'parent' culture and cultural elements borrowed from other subcultures insure constantly changing cultural patterns in subcultures, and Irwin (1965), Donnelly (1979) and Fine and Kleinman (1979) have all suggested that subcultures should be analyzed historically in order to determine patterns of subcultural change:

> Subcultural systems are undergoing constant changes due to internal processes of growth and change, and due to varying circumstances of the greater cultural-social setting of the subculture. Therefore, certain behavior at one point in time does not have the same meaning, and relationship to the subculture as it has at another time. All considerations of cause must be made with this relationship in mind (Irwin, 1965: 112).

Historical analysis of the set of cultural elements that characterizes a specific subculture may not only shed light on the patterns of evolution of subcultures, but also provide insights into the relationships between subcultures and the relationship of the subculture to the 'parent' culture.

4. Distinctive Nature

While the set of cultural elements that characterize a specific subculture are somewhat different from the culture(s) in which it exists, "no subculture can be totally different from or totally in conflict with the society of which it is a part" (Wolfgang and Ferracuti, 1969:158). However, subcultures do appear to have varying degrees of exclusivity based upon the difficulty involved in attaining membership, or on the levels of commitment required of members. "As a general principle, the more the subculture has special meanings, symbols, dress, values, norms, beliefs, attitudes, language, rituals, etc., for those involved, the greater the spiritual or physical distance from outsiders" (Loy, et al., 1978:181-182).

The idea of exclusivity is supported by Irwin who suggested that "there must be *distinct qualities* in the activities or interests of the group" (1965:112), and by Arnold (1970) and Pearson (1976) who both discuss normative behavior in subcultures and the degree of difference from the 'parent' culture in terms of a continuum. The more removed a subcultural norm is from the cultural norm, the more exclusive and more deviant the subculture becomes.

The degree of exclusivity also appears to be the basis for Toffler's maxim that "the larger the subcult, the higher the odds that it will fragment and diversify" (1971:294). Members of a rapidly growing subculture may feel that the element of exclusivity to which they were originally attracted is disappearing, and they may split away to form the basis of a new subculture by re-creating exclusivity. The exodus of many downhill skiers to the previously more exclusive ranks of free-style and cross country skiers is an example of this process.

5. Life Style and Resources

A subculture may be pictured as a series of concentric circles, each representing one of five levels of membership. The model is based on the relationship between subculture and life style, and on the premise that total membership in a subculture may be seen as the dominant aspect of an individual's life style. Two additional variables are also relevant—commitment and information.

At the Primary level of membership, the core of the concentric circles, are found the principal members of a subculture. These are the individuals for whom the subculture is *the* dominant aspect of their life style; the individuals for whom the subculture represents a major commitment in terms of time, energy, money, friendships, information and other resources; and the individuals who are in possession of the most information regarding the meanings and ways of the subculture. Information is the basic currency of subcultures and core members are those individuals who create and modify the characteristics of a subculture. As such, they are often the best known members of the subculture.

Boundaries between the various levels of membership are usually diffuse, and at the Secondary level of membership are also found members for whom the subculture is the dominant aspect of their life style. Secondary or "auxiliary" level membership includes individuals who aspire to the Primary level, individuals who are fading from the Primary level, and a number of relatively static members. Auxiliary members commit a significant proportion of their resources to membership in the subculture, and are in possession of a great deal of the information that is peculiar to the subculture, but they rarely innovate, modify or create any aspect of the subculture.

At the Third level of membership are found what may be termed 'associate members' for whom the subculture is an important but not dominant aspect of their life style. They commit a certain proportion of their resources to membership and possess enough of the subcultural information to be clearly recognized as members. But they adapt more slowly to new language, dress, techniques or other aspects of the meanings and ways of the subculture than Primary and Secondary level members because their information is more limited. And, as with the Secondary and Fourth levels of membership, the Third level will contain members who are moving toward or away from the core as well as static members.

Fourth level members may be termed 'marginal members' since the subculture represents a relatively minor aspect of their life style. Membership at this level will largely be made up of novices who are just beginning to learn the meanings and ways of the subculture, and retiring members whose knowledge of the meanings and ways is out-of-date. There is a low level of commitment and only partial recognition of Fourth level members as members by those belonging to the first three levels of membership.

Finally, at the Fifth level, are those individuals for whom the subculture cannot be considered as an aspect of their life style. They may be occasional participants with some knowledge of the subcultural meanings and ways, but they are not recognized by subculture members as members and they commit very little of their resources to the subculture. An example of Fifth level membership in occupational subcultures would be a student employed in a summer job.

The number of levels of membership is somewhat arbitrary and may be increased or decreased depending on the level of analysis. In addition, in highly institutionalized subcultures where membership is extremely clear-cut (e.g., certain occupations and professional sports) it may be possible to identify only two or three levels of membership. However, subcultures are clearly stratified in terms of the amount and type of information in possession of the various members, the level of commitment to the subculture in terms of the allocation of resources, and the degree to which the subculture is a dominant aspect of the life style of its members. Certain of these variables should prove to be quantifiable, particularly the allocation of time and money and friendship patterns as indicators of commitment, and should prove to be invaluable in constructing models of the structure of subcultures and the relationships between subcultures.[6]

6. Scope and Potential

The two major themes that emerge from theoretical work on subculture formation may be termed 'environmental response' and 'differential interaction.' The first theme views the emergence of subcultures as a problem-solving response by individuals with similar difficulties or concerns. The second theme views subcultural emergence as a result of the proximity of similar individuals or individuals with similar concerns, and the inevitable interaction of these individuals. A third approach combines the two themes and there is some indication of a temporal sequence with environmental response leading to differential interaction.

Pearson's (1976, 1977) recent theoretical formulations go beyond an account of the conditions leading to the emergence of groups with the potential to form subcultures and attempt to account for the emergence and development of subcultures. Individuals in a similar social situation (e.g., with similar interests) begin to promote differential interaction and to form a group. The group begins to emphasize certain cultural characteristics relevant to the interests of the group, and to reduce the importance of certain aspects of the 'parent' culture. The attitudes, beliefs and behavior of the individual group members are in turn affected and the group forms the basis of a new subculture. This process is outlined in the cycle from 'b' to 'c' to 'd' in Figure 2, and Pearson (1976) notes that the more this cycle is repeated, the more likely the cultural characteristics are to spread to other individuals and groups thereby causing the emergence and growth of a new subculture.

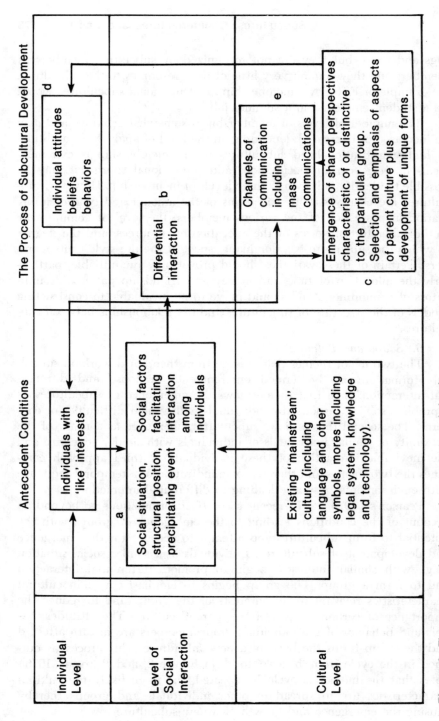

Figure 2. The process of subcultural emergence and development. (Adapted from Pearson, 1976)

The Process of Subcultural Development

Antecedent Conditions

Individual Level

Individuals with "like" interests

a

Individual attitudes beliefs behaviors

d

Level of Social Interaction

Social situation, structural position, precipitating event

Social factors facilitating interaction among individuals

Differential interaction

b

Cultural Level

Existing "mainstream" culture (including language and other symbols, mores including legal system, knowledge and technology).

Channels of communication including mass communications

e

Emergence of shared perspectives characteristic of or distinctive to the particular group. Selection and emphasis of aspects of parent culture plus development of unique forms.

c

However, Pearson's model does not address the question of why some activities, interests or beliefs result in the emergence of subcultures while others do not. The answer appears to lie in the scope and potential of the activity, interest or belief. A subculture is a relatively stable and enduring group and cannot be based on a fad or craze. Thus, the basis for a subculture should be unlimited in scope, have the potential to continue developing, and have the potential to acquire additional characteristics that will become significant aspects of an individual's life style.

For example, the hula hoop became a widespread fad throughout the Western world, but its scope and potential were limited. Beyond establishing a number of endurance records and developing circus acts employing multiple hoops there was little else that could be done. On the other hand, the modern skateboard with polyurethane wheels has a much broader scope and potential. It takes a great deal of skill and nerve to become a highly competent performer, competitive activities have been developed, and skateboarding has been promoted and has undergone a certain amount of institutionalization. Individuals are able to develop a life style around skateboarding and there has been a consequent development of the subculture of skateboarders. Similarly, a number of dance crazes during the 1960's lacked the scope and potential necessary for subculture development, but the more recent disco movement in music, dancing and fashion has proved to be much more enduring. Individuals are able to develop a life style around the music and dancing, a life style well-documented in the film "Saturday Night Fever." The scope and potential of disco have resulted in the formation of a subculture.

7. Fulfillment of Individual Needs

Of equal importance to scope and potential in the formation and maintenance of a subculture is the manner in which its creation meets the needs of the participants. In order for a subculture to develop there must be some benefit to the individual members—they must act to create the subculture, and they are unlikely to act in such a manner if the creation and maintenance of a subculture were not rewarding. Three types of rewards may be identified: psychic, social and material.

The principal psychic reward of subcultures is that they provide their members with an identity (cf., Klapp, 1969; Toffler, 1971). An individual member of a subculture is able to state, for example, "I am a birder (bird-watcher)" or "I am a hang glider." A subcultural identity that is recognized by other members of the subculture, and by non-members, is extremely valuable in combating alienation in modern society; moreover, the more exclusive or unique the subculture, the higher the pay-off is likely to be in terms of identity because the individual member is more able to feel different from the "average" person. In addition, subcultures provide a type of alternative status for their members beyond the traditional means of attaining status. For example, a birder is unlikely to achieve power, fame or wealth for observing an extremely rare bird, but he is likely to achieve a great deal of status among his peers in the subculture of birders.

While status may be seen as both a psychic and a social reward, there are other purely social rewards that accrue from subculture membership. Involvement in a group, feeling of community, and the establishing of long-term friendships or even partnerships with individuals with similar interests are all potential benefits from membership in a subculture.

Material rewards may take a number of forms, but since information is the basic currency of subcultures, and since subcultures are formed primarily as a medium for the exchange of information, those members with the most information may be considered to be the 'richest' individuals in a subculture. In activity-based subcultures the information may take a number of forms, and includes technical information related to the activity, gossip about other members, record keeping, and incidental information. With the expansion of a subculture other types of material reward may become available—turning professional, becoming an instructor, manufacturing and selling equipment, formalizing the dissemination of information by publishing or writing for a magazine or writing books, and allied occupations such as equipment testing and sponsorship, or photography. Even in occupational subcultures a similar reward structure is likely to exist, although the actual material rewards (excluding information) are structured into, and not incidental to, the activity.

The proposition that subcultures are actively created and maintained by their members as long as they meet the needs of their members may be tested by examining a number of activities that have not led to the formation of subcultures. These include deviant or semi-deviant activities (e.g., shoplifting, frequenting peep-shows and pornographic film theaters, or going with prostitutes), and while they may possess the scope and potential for subculture formation this has not occurred. The difference appears to lie in the need for information, and the need to share information for mutual benefit. Whereas prostitutes, drug addicts and homosexuals appear to form subcultures because of the need for information, that same need is not apparent in the activities that do not lead to subculture formation, and there is less inclination for the participants to adopt cultural characteristics.[8]

8. Interaction and Communication

In order to maintain subcultural integrity it is necessary to insure that members of a subculture share similar information. Subcultures result from differential interaction and the formation of a small group where face-to-face interaction is possible, but do not become subcultures until the cultural characteristics of the original small group have spread well beyond its boundaries. Most interaction in subcultures occurs in small face-to-face groups, but these groups do not develop markedly different cultural characteristics because of the various means of communication that serve to link them into a subcultural whole.

The most obvious organs of communication are the various newsletters, magazines and journals that disseminate information of interest to the members of the subculture. They assure a certain amount of conformity in terms of information and cultural characteristics, and allow members of a subculture in widespread areas to remain in contact. They also tend to disseminate unintended information that assists in maintaining conformity. For example, the use of certain expressions by editors and contributors to journals, or the publication of photographs of members of the subculture wearing a certain item of clothing, may cause consequent and widespread changes in the language and dress of the subculture.

However, the various small groups that comprise a subculture tend to function as an informal network for communicating the meanings and ways of the subculture. Group 'A' may be in contact with groups 'B,' 'C' and 'D' either directly, or indirectly if certain members of the groups are acquaintances. Groups 'B,' 'C' and 'D' may in turn be in contact with groups 'E,' 'F' and 'G.' 'H,' 'I' and 'J,' and 'K,' 'L' and 'M' respectively. Networks of this type may continue indefinitely, eventually encompassing all of the members of the subculture. In addition, travel and formal and informal meetings of members of a subculture each assist in subcultural communication. These various forms of communication are essential to the maintenance of a subculture. Without them, subcultures would not evolve, and breakdowns in communication may lead to the formation of separate groups and new subcultures.

SPORT SUBCULTURES

In an attempt to develop case studies of subcultures in order to provide data to be used in constructing a theory of subcultures, Arnold noted that:

> I finally decided to look at sport and hobby subcultures. As I began to do so I came to realize that their importance goes beyond merely providing convenient cases for a sociology of subcultures, and that they have a sociological importance in and of themselves (Arnold, 1972: 1).

Their importance lies in the decline of social classes and the increasing importance of leisure activities which "have come to replace work as the prime *raison-d'etre* for millions of Americans" (Arnold, 1972:2). While there are now a number of case studies in existence, many have adopted different emphases, been carried out in order to contribute to the body of knowledge in an area other than subcultures, or have only dealt with a minor aspect of subcultures such as language.

It is interesting to note that many of the better case studies of sport subcultures tend to reflect the larger sociological over-emphasis on deviant subcultures in their concern with deviance in sport. Polsky (1969) and Steele (1976) were concerned with hustling in pool and bowling respectively. Scott (1968) noted the various forms of deception at the race track. Bryant (1971) studied the illegal sport of cockfighting. Sheard and Dunning (1973) and Thomson (1976) dealt with the non-sport deviant behavior of rugby players, and Faulkner (1971) focused on violence in ice hockey. In addition, there have been a number of studies of high risk sport subcultures, three of which represent the only attempts to apply the data from sport subcultures toward a theory of subcultures. These are Irwin (1965), Pearson (1977) and Donnelly (1979), the first two being studies of the subculture of surfers in California and Australia respectively, and the latter being a study of the subculture of climbers.

While there are obvious difficulties in studying deviant and high risk sport subcultures by participant observation methods, a number of the researchers avoided such difficulties because they were already members of the subcultures concerned. Perhaps the major reason for the number of studies on this type of subculture is that they are so readily identifiable as subcultures. Their cultural characteristics are quite distinct and they clearly dominate the life style and allocation of resources of their members. Also, because their norms are quite different from those of the 'parent' culture they are more exclusive and more recognizable. Unlike the subcultures of baseball and football, for example, where the cultural characteristics have become much more diffuse because of widespread publicity, the deviant and high risk sport subcultures are more self-contained and reward the efforts necessary to become involved as a participant observer.

The theoretical perspectives presented in this article were developed during a study of the subculture of climbers, but owe much to the previous theoretical work employing a sport setting conducted by Irwin and Pearson. The following section presents a brief example of how such theoretical perspectives may be integrated with data to provide a picture of subcultural emergence and development.

THE SUBCULTURE OF CLIMBERS

The subculture of climbers meets all of the criteria for being considered as a legitimate (achieved) subculture. Climbers are an identifiable sub-group of a number of national cultures who, at the first four levels of membership, identify strongly with their subculture. Members are able to identify each other by means of observation or the 'credentialing' process (Donnelly, 1978) and maintain a level of subcultural integrity by employing these processes to distinguish members from non-members or 'pseudo-members.' The processes are also employed to determine mutual status within the subculture because, unlike the more institutionalized sports, climbing does not have a structured status system.

While members of the subculture learn accurately to identify other members during their period of socialization into the subculture, identification of climbers by non-climbers is likely to be much less precise. They are frequently deceived by novices and pseudo-climbers (i.e., non-climbers posing as climbers) because they are not in possession of the requisite information necessary to interpret cues. Novice climbers often rely on these miscues in their willingness to carry equipment, and particularly the rope, for more experienced climbers. They are aware that non-climbers are likely to identify them as the more experienced climber or the leader because they have the equipment, and they wish to be identified as such. But despite such mistakes in identification, it is important that non-climbers believe that the subculture exists, and that they are able to identify the members.

Formation of the Subculture

The subculture of climbers originated in the Alps during the first half of the Nineteenth Century. At that time it was possible for scientists and tourists to hire local guides to take them to the summits of certain mountains. While climbing remained in the province of science and tourism, no subculture was possible since it is unlikely that a subculture would be based on scientific experiments requiring altitude or on a unique tourist experience. Similarly, to give a modern example, tourists who have visited the top of the Empire State Building are unlikely to form a subculture. The subculture began to emerge as a change in attitude occurred —as some of the scientists and tourists began to enjoy the experience of climbing, began to repeat the experience purely for pleasure, and began to make a commitment to the activity. The preconditions for subculture development were established, but because the individuals involved were uncertain of public reaction to any suggestion that they were climbing purely for pleasure, they maintained the guise of science and tourism for a time.

Eventually the need occurred for individuals who were climbing for pleasure to begin to interact. Differential interaction resulted from a need to share experiences and information with a wider circle of individuals than those immediately involved in a specific climb, and to share them with individuals of a similar background (i.e., other British upper and upper-middle class individuals, as opposed to the guides who were peasants from Alpine villages). Differential interaction occurs in two different ways. The first is recruitment—socializing friends and acquaintances into climbing in order to share the experience with individuals with whom one enjoys interacting. The second is to make contact with other climbers beyond one's immediate circle of friends in order to share information and experiences, and to meet new climbing partners. Differential interaction also provided mutual affirmation and support for what was, at the time, a radically new and different type of behavior.

The need to interact in order to share experiences and information and to provide mutual affirmation, encouragement and support, provides the key to subculture formation. If the need to interact did not exist (as among tourists who have visited the top of the Empire State Building), no subculture would be formed because subcultures are actively created and maintained by their members as long as they meet the needs of their members. There appear to be three distinct phases of subculture development which McDougall (1979) has termed "informal affiliations," "incipient institutions," and "advanced institutional development." During the early stage of development subcultures expand only by direct recruitment of new members. This stage lasts while informal means of communication (word of mouth and letter) are feasible.

Once a critical mass is attained, the point at which informal means of communication cease to be efficient, the subculture will move into the second stage of development. While smaller groups continue to interact and recruit on a face-to-face basis, communication in the form of books, articles, newsletters and journals appears to link the various groups and keep them informed. In addition, the publications begin to reach a wider audience, thereby creating new recruits who seek contact with a member of the subculture.[9] A third stage of development occurs when the means of recruitment, socialization, and advancement within the subculture become formalized or institutionalized. The subculture of climbers has largely resisted this third stage, preferring the informality and individuality of the second stage. But there are signs that the subculture is moving into the third stage of development.

In order for the cycle of subculture development to occur the activity must be perceived to have scope and potential. While the object of climbing was to attain the summits of the major peaks in the Alps, its scope and potential was limited and it could have faded out as a fad or a craze once those summits were all attained. A change in emphasis after 1865 (when the Matterhorn—the last major summit in the Alps— was climbed) led to the development of the 'search for difficulty' and ensured the future of the subculture. The search for difficulty involved climbing major peaks in other important mountain ranges, seeking alternative routes to the summits of major peaks in the Alps, climbing minor peaks in the Alps, and developing rock climbing and snow and ice climbing in minor mountain areas as practice for the summer season in the Alps. The change was aided by the fairly strong subcultural foundations that had been laid in that the participants were not prepared to let the activity die out, and the search for difficulty vastly increased the scope and potential of climbing. Despite the fact that each generation of climbers until the present one has felt that it has achieved the ultimate in what was possible (thereby marking the end of the subculture because of the lack of future scope and potential), each subsequent generation has proved them wrong.

Characteristics of the Subculture

The cultural characteristics of a subculture develop at two levels. At the primary level are the beliefs and behavior directly associated with the subculture. In activity-based subcultures such as the subculture of climbers, the behavior exists before the development of the subculture, but once the subculture begins to form, the act of climbing and the knowledge associated with climbing become the unique possession of the subculture. The acts of recruitment and socializing new members into the subculture lead to a certain amount of standardization in teaching climbing skills and the knowledge necessary in order to climb safely. These become the primary level of cultural characteristics.

Ancillary knowledge and behavior not directly concerned with the act of climbing develop as a secondary level of cultural characteristics. A number of the secondary characteristics eventually become primary characteristics. For example, the development of new techniques, equipment and ethics (informal rules of climbing) initially appears at the secondary level. Individuals, usually at the core of the subculture, begin to experiment with new equipment, techniques and limitations on climbing. If these are considered to be advantageous or necessary to the development of climbing they become accepted by the whole subculture and thus become primary characteristics. Present-day novices are taught different techniques from their predecessors and learn a different code of ethics.

Secondary level characteristics that are not directly associated with the act of climbing, include the following: dress and language specific to the subculture (these characteristics tend to undergo frequent changes); status concerns—the development of stratification within the subculture and associated with the grading (difficulty) of climbs, the recording of ascents, lore concerning the difficulty of certain climbs and the ability of certain climbers, and the development of subcultural heroes; other concerns, including environmental and ethical concerns, access problems, the response to accidents and fatalities, and concern over external controls and growing institutionalization; and the social characteristics associated with non-climbing behavior. The latter category includes not only knowledge of social meeting places such as equipment stores, camp sites and bars, but also the ability to interact correctly with other climbers. The code of interaction involves not bragging, and downplaying one's achievements, not asking outright how good another climber is, not overtly displaying the fact that one is a climber (e.g., sitting in a bar with a climbing rope slung across one's shoulders can gain one a reputation as a 'poseur'), and by deferring to better climbers in route selection.

The combination of primary and secondary characteristics constitutes the normative domain of a subculture, and the exclusivity of a subculture is related to the distance of cultural norms from the subcultural norm. The normative behavior of, for example, tennis players may be extremely close to the cultural norm. Tennis is readily accessible, within the normative experience of a great many people, and widely understood because of widespread media coverage. Exclusivity exists only near the core of the subculture of tennis players among the highly skilled professionals and top class amateurs. The normative behavior of climbers appears to be more removed from the cultural norm. Climbing is not readily accessible (although it is becoming more so), not within the adult normative experience of many people (although many will have enjoyed scrambling on rocks and small cliffs as children), and not readily understood because of the lack of media coverage (another aspect that is beginning to change rapidly). Therefore, the subculture of climbers may be considered to be more exclusive than the subculture of tennis players, and many other more conventional sport subcultures, and the exclusivity has greater pay-offs in terms of identity.

The subculture of climbers is unique among sport subcultures. It may be considered as the first of the high risk sport subcultures, but it has resisted the conventional pattern of development and institutionalization. Climbing is a sport without rules. There are no ruling bodies and no officials to govern behavior within the sport. However, there are self-imposed limitations on climbers that take the form of a socially constructed and socially sanctioned code of ethics. The ethics developed because modern equipment and techniques have made the ascent of any mountain or cliff possible by almost any route. Ethics are created in order to maintain the sporting element in climbing and to insure the possibility of failure. They set limitations on the type of equipment and techniques that may be employed on different types of climbs.

Climbing may now be considered to have reached the borderline between the second and third stages of subcultural development, and resistance to the third stage is apparent. Even the subculture of hang gliders, which shares many characteristics with the subculture of climbers as another high risk activity, has reached the third stage of development although it has been in existence for less than fifteen years. There is certification and formal assessment of skill levels, and there are ruling bodies and formal competitive meets. The lack of overt, rule-based, competition and disregard of negative publicity has been characteristic of climbers in non-Communist countries who have had neither the need nor the desire to institutionalize their activity. If one observation supercedes all others it is that climbers enjoy the mystique and the informality associated with climbing. It is an unconventional activity that appeals to individuals who wish to avoid the badges, certificates, rankings, rules and formality associated with other more conventional activities.

CONCLUSIONS

In the formal definition of subcultures presented in this article a number of theoretical propositions have been made regarding the nature of subcultures. Further research is necessary before these cultural units are clearly understood. There are now a number of case studies of sport subcultures in existence, and the type of integration of theory with data presented here should prove to be invaluable. While the propositions appear to apply to a number of sport subcultures they need to be tested over a wider variety of subcultures, particularly those associated with conventional sports in an advanced stage of institutional development.

Once methods are devised to assess the allocation of resources by members of subcultures, it should be possible to create accurate models of the structure of subcultures and the relationships between subcultures. In addition, more work is needed in order to determine individual and group needs, and the scope and potential of attributes and behaviors that lead to subculture formation. A complete theory of subcultures should be able to predict which types of attributes and behavior are likely to lead to subculture formation.

Finally, following the model adopted in research on occupational subcultures, it is possible to examine membership in a sport subculture as a career with analyses of socialization into and desocialization from a sport subculture, and career contingencies. Such analyses should provide important insights into the culture and evolution of sports and the relationships between sports.

NOTES

1. While some investigators have attempted to distinguish between subcultures and subsocieties, and to consider subcultures as abstractions consisting of sets of norms and values, it is proposed here to reify the concept of subculture for the purposes of analysis and to treat subcultures and subsocieties as synonymous units of society. The term employed should indicate the level of analysis, although the term subculture has attained a great deal more popularity than subsociety. Reification is justified because it:

    . . . involves an attitude that things necessarily are as they are, that the humanly created world of objects is a world of *real* objects with unvarying essences. When people speak of their careers, their obligations, the groups to which they belong, or the society of which they are members, they are indicating and acting toward objects. Many of these are more or less abstract objects, to be sure, but they tend to be treated as if they were concrete things that exist and must be taken into account (Hewitt, 1976: 230).

    Both members and non-members believe in the existence of subcultures and are usually able to identify members and non-members. The theoretical reification of subcultures is functional because it broadens the possibilities for analysis.
2. Recent research by Birrell and Turowetz (1979) has identified a number of surprising cultural similarities between the subcultures of male professional wrestlers and female gymnasts.
3. Gordon first defined a subculture as "a subdivision of a national culture, composed of a combination of factorable social situations such as class status, ethnic background, regional and rural or urban residence, and religious affiliation, but *forming in their combination a functioning unity which has an integrated impact on the participating individual*" (Gordon, 1947: 40, original emphasis).
4. 'Ethclass' involves a combination of ethnicity and social class, as in Irish American-Upper Class or Greek American-Middle Class. If taken to their logical conclusions such combinations of ascribed subcultures could reach ridiculous extremes, as in the subculture of Mid-Western, Urban, German American, Middle Class, Catholic Republicans.
5. The term 'meanings and ways' is employed to indicate "what is involved in 'subculture'. It includes normative guides to social behavior, the overarching values such guidelines reflect and the various symbols and modes of operation which represent and convey meaning" (Pearson, 1976: 2n).
6. With reference to the boundaries between subcultures, Arnold has asked:

    Are subcultures discrete or overlapping? Are their boundaries clear or fuzzy? Do individuals belong to just one? Or many? Or can someone not belong to any at all? (Arnold, 1970: 82).

While a preliminary attempt has been made to answer these questions (Donnelly, 1979), more in-depth and quantified analysis of subculture should provide a clearer picture of the structure of and relationships between subcultures.

7. Arnold (1970) has provided a detailed analysis of these theoretical approaches to the study of subcultures. The "environmental response" approach views subcultures as resulting from specific environmental conditions or problems, with the subculture emerging as a response to the situation. Gans, writing with reference to urban ethnic subcultures such as the Italian community in West Boston, summarized the approach by noting that, "The subcultures which I have described are *responses* that people make to the *opportunities* and *deprivations* that they encounter" (Gans, 1962: 249). Shibutani explicitly denied "environmental response" theory and presented the "differential interaction" approach. "Variations in outlook arise through differential contact and association; the maintenance of social distance—through segregation, conflict, or simply the reading of different literature—leads to the formation of distinct cultures" (Shibutani, 1955: 565). In addition, we tend to interact to a greater degree with individuals who have similar interests and concerns. A number of investigators have combined both approaches, and Cohen makes an extremely strong statement to this effect: "The crucial condition for the emergence of new cultural forms is the existence, *in effective interaction with one another, of a number of actors with similar problems of adjustment*" (Cohen, 1955: 59). An example of group formation (Lindesmith and Strauss, 1956) indicates that there may even be a temporal sequence to "environmental response" and "differential interaction." A shortage of insulin in Hong Kong during the Second World War became a common environmental problem for diabetics. In response, the diabetics began to interact in order to pool their resources to obtain insulin. While the example does not refer to subculture formation because it is concerned with a relatively small number of individuals in a limited geographical area who had a short term problem, it does give some indication of the manner in which subcultures may emerge.

8. The concept of "hiding" is also relevant here since individuals involved in deviant activities are often obliged to attempt to hide their involvement. Individuals may hide "alone" or "together," and those who hide alone are unlikely to form subcultures. They may not need mutually beneficial information or reinforcement, they may be ashamed of their behavior, and their environmental problems may not be solved by differential interaction. Those who hide together tend to form subcultures because of the benefits to be gained.

9. Modern media, particularly television, also create new recruits.

REFERENCES

Arnold, D. O., (ed.), *Subcultures.* Berkeley: The Glendessary Press, 1970.

Arnold, D. O., "The Social Organization of Sky Diving: A Study in Vertical Mobility." Paper presented at the Annual Meeting of the Pacific Sociological Association, Portland, Oregon, April, 1972.

Birrell, S. and A. Turowetz, "Character Work-Up and Display: Collegiate Gymnastics and Professional Wrestling." *Urban Life,* 8 (1979):219-246.

Bryant, C. D., "Feathers, Spurs and Blood: Cockfighting as a Deviant Leisure Activity." Paper presented at the Annual Meeting of the Southern Sociological Society, May, 1971.

Caillois, R., Man, *Play and Games.* New York: Free Press, 1961.

Clarke, M., "On the Concept of Subculture." *British Journal of Sociology*, 25 (1974):428-441.

Cohen, A. K., *Delinquent Boys*. New York: Free Press, 1955.

Donnelly, P., "On Determining Another's Skill." Paper presented at the Annual Meeting of the Canadian Sociology and Anthropology Association, London, Ontario, May, 1978.

———., *The Subculture and Public Image of Climbers*. Unpublished doctoral dissertation, University of Massachusetts, Amherst, 1979.

Elkin, F. and W. A. Westley, "The Myth of Adolescent Culture." *American Sociological Review*, 20(1955): 680-684.

Faulkner, R. E., "Violence, Camaraderie, and Occupational Character in Hockey." Paper presented at the Conference on Sport and Social Deviancy, Brockport, N.Y., December, 1971.

Fine, G. A. and S. Kleinman, "Rethinking Subculture: An Interactionist Analysis." *American Journal of Sociology*, 85(1979): 1-20.

Gans, H. J., *The Urban Villagers*. New York: Free Press, 1962.

Gordon, M. M., "The Concept of Subculture and Its Application." *Social Forces*, 26(October, 1947): 40-42.

Hewitt, J. P., *Self and Society: A Symbolic Interactionist Social Psychology*. Boston: Allyn and Bacon, 1976.

Huizinga, J., *Homo Ludens: A Study of the Play Element in Culture*. Boston: Beacon Press, 1955.

Irwin, J., *Surfers: A Study of the Growth of a Deviant Subculture*. Unpublished Master's thesis, University of California, Berkeley, 1965.

Klapp, O. E., *Collective Search for Identity*. New York: Holt, Rinehart and Winston, 1969.

Lee, A. M., "Attitudinal Multivalence in Relation to Culture and Personality." *American Journal of Sociology*. (November, 1954): 294-299.

Lerman, P., "Gangs, Networks and Subcultural Delinquency." *American Journal of Sociology*, 73(1967): 63-72.

Lindesmith, A. R. and A. L. Strauss, *Social Psychology*. New York: Holt, Rinehart and Winston, 1956.

Loy, J. W., B. D. McPherson and G. Kenyon, *Sport and Social Systems*. Reading: Addison-Wesley, 1978.

McDougall, A. A., *The Subculture of Hang Gliders: Social Organizations of a High Risk Sport*. Unpublished Master's thesis, University of Western Ontario, 1979.

Pearson, K., "Subcultures, Drug Use and Physical Activity." Paper presented at the International Congress of Physical Activity Sciences. Quebec City, July, 1976.

———., *Surfing Subcultures: A Comparative Analysis of Surf Life Saving and Surf Board Riding in Australia and New Zealand*. Unpublished doctoral dissertation, University of Queensland, Australia, 1977.

Phillips, J. and W. Schafer, "Subcultures in Sport: A Conceptual and Methodological Approach." In, A. Yiannakis, *et al.* (eds.), *Sport Sociology: Contemporary Themes*. Dubuque, Iowa: Kendall/Hunt, 1976. 129-134.

Polsky, N., *Hustlers, Beats, and Others*. New York: Anchor Books, 1969.

Roberts, J. and B. Sutton-Smith, "Child Training and Game Involvement." *Ethnology*, 1(1962): 166-185.

Scott, M. B., *The Racing Game*. Chicago: Aldine, 1968.

Sheard, K. G. and E. Dunning, "The Rugby Football Club as a Type of Male Preserve: Some Sociological Notes." *International Review of Sport Sociology*, 8(1973): 5-24.

Shibutani, T., "Reference Groups and Perspectives." *American Journal of Sociology*, (May, 1955): 562-569.

Steele, P. D., "The Bowling Hustler: A Study of Deviance in Sport." In, D. M. Landers (ed.), *Social Problems in Athletics*. Urbana: University of Illinois Press, 1976, 86-92.

Thomson, R., *Sport and Deviance: A Subcultural Analysis*. Unpublished doctoral dissertation, University of Alberta, 1976.

Toffler, A., *Future Shock*. New York: Bantam, 1971.

Tylor, E. B., *Primitive Culture*. London: John Murray, 1871.

Wolfgang, M. and F. Ferracuti, *The Subculture of Violence*. London: Tavistock, 1969.

Character Work-Up and Display: Collegiate Gymnastics and Professional Wrestling

Susan Birrell and Allan Turowetz

Much attention has been paid to the manner in which individuals interact with one another to construct and preserve consensual definitions of situations and supportable situational identities. Goffman (1959, 1967) has argued that each individual's identity is the result of social consensus: Each individual presents a face he feels appropriate to the situation while accepting and supporting the presentations of others. Through this mutual face work, the particular situation or encounter is preserved, and the existence of interactions is reaffirmed. Berger asserts a similar perspective when he reports that "human dignity is a matter of social permission" (1963:103): An individual's identity is tightly circumscribed by what others will allow him to be.

Identity, then, is socially constructed and situationally influenced. Each individual has a collection of identities or a repertoire of acceptable and tested roles from which to select the situationally appropriate face. One of the many faces an individual is likely to have within his repertoire of life roles is his work identity, and the significance of that particular role has been noted by many. For example, when he urged sociologists to explore the "social drama of work," Hughes argued:

> A man's work is one of the more important parts of his social identity. . . . Work experience is so important and fateful a part of every man's life that we cannot make much headway as students of society and social psychology without using work as one of our main social laboratories (1958: 43).

Reprinted from *Urban Life* Vol. 8 No. 2, July 1979, © 1979, pp. 219-246, by permission of the Publisher, SAGE Publications, Inc. Beverly Hills, London.
Authors' note: We would like to thank Robert Faulkner for his assistance in earlier stages of this project and Michael Rosenberg for his coauthorship with Turowetz on other wrestling articles from which excerpts appear in this paper.

This paper is concerned with work identities and the means by which a competent work identity is created, maintained, and displayed.

A major difference exists between Goffman's general perspective of self-presentation and the presentation of self in the specific setting of the occupational world. Goffman sees identity construction as a socially cooperative and supportive interaction; the presentation of a valid occupational face, however, is often of a competitive nature, and the worker/actor must extricate whatever positive definition he is capable of assuming from a stingy environment.

Moreover, the work identity an individual is allowed by his coworkers to assume is delineated by his task performance; he cannot claim for himself qualities related to task performance which he does not possess. Since the efficient production of quality products is a matter of the highest organizational concern, an individual's occupational worth has traditionally been assessed in terms of his ability to perform specific tasks or by the quality of the product he produces. An interesting situation arises when the occupational setting requires that the worker's performance becomes the product. Such a situation is typical of the sport world, where the competitive aspects of task performance create a highly visible, easily observed situation.

The worlds of the high level collegiate woman gymnast and professional wrestler offer an interesting opportunity to discover relationships between individuals and their work environment which have general significance across a wide range of occupational settings. The problematic placement of the gymnast's world within the larger context of the sociology of occupations permits an examination of such diverse kinds of social activity. For, indeed, not all work takes place within an occupational structure although that is where sociologists tend to look for it. When divergent situations can be handled within the same theoretical framework, sociologists have taken a step forward toward meaningful comparative analysis and the "common themes" of human activity become more evident.

METHODS AND SETTINGS

The data for this paper initially were collected and analyzed independently by the two authors. A growing recognition that a comparative analysis between the two worlds would enhance the observations of each led to this joint endeavor.

The data on the gymnastics world were gathered by Birrell during the competitive season 1974-1975. The group selected for observation was a woman's collegiate gymnastics team which had ranked as one of the top three teams in the United States for the previous three years.

Nonparticipant observation of the group began two months before the competitive season and continued throughout the regular dual-meet season and the regional championships. Observation settings included daily and auxiliary practices, intrasquad practice meets, dual meets, and the regional meet.

Focused interviews were conducted during the entire observation period and included seven interviews with gymnasts and three follow-up interviews; two interviews with an ex-gymnast who continued her association with the team by providing choreographic aid to them; two interviews with the coach; and an interview with a gymnastics judge. Much information was also gathered through informal conversations with the coach, gymnasts, and other members of the previous year's team.

The data collected on the wrestling world was the outcome of three and a half years of participant observation in a Montreal wrestling circuit. The participation did not take the form of wrestling; Turowetz became a wrestling reporter covering the Montreal circuit for a major wrestling magazine. This role provided access to the wrestling world and a definite function to fulfill in that world: one of benefit not only to the research but also to the journal and the community. Only in this way was much of the extensive information control exercised by the wrestling community overcome. It was this kind of information control which had hampered previous research in this world.

Structured and unstructured interviews were carried out with the promoter, wrestlers, and public relations director. These interviews were conducted at the wrestling office, private homes, restaurants, and the Montreal Forum on Mondays and Fridays—those days on which wrestlers do not travel. Special appointments were made when the interviews were not held at the wrestling office. The role of reporter facilitated the use of a tape-recorder for most of the structured interviews. In the months that followed, the taped interviews were typed and maintained in a field note catalogue.

THE WRESTLER AND THE GYMNAST

The obvious difference between professional wrestling and college gymnastics is, of course, legitimacy.[1] By legitimacy is meant that interactions are what they appear to be. Interaction in wrestling and in gymnastics appears to be of a competitive nature. But in professional wrestling, that appearance is structured to deceive. While collegiate gymnasts are competing for points and championships decided by their own physical skill, the outcome of professional wrestling matches is determined in advance by promoters. Although the illegitimacy of the wrestling contest is never acknowledged overtly, all performers and many, if not all, of the audience are aware of the deception. For the professional wrestler, what is problematic is not the outcome but the quality of the dramatic display.

The sociologist's concern with legitimacy is not centered upon the moral issue (cf., Hughes 1971:316), however, but upon the constraints that legitimacy or illegitimacy place upon the process of work. The work script for actors in these worlds varies in terms of actions, outcomes, and most important, character work. Whereas the script for the wrestler is finalized in private backstage areas, the gymnastics script is flexible and public. Wrestling is an activity of determinate outcomes and determinate identities; in gymnastics the outcomes and identities are indeterminate, or problematic.

Regardless of the moral issues, or perhaps because they present such a striking contrast, a comparison of these two worlds has much to offer the sociologist, for, in fact, the work worlds of the wrestler and the gymnast are more similar than dissimilar. Legitimate or illegitimate, both share a concern over the maintenance of a valid occupational character.

CHARACTER

In his excellent essay "Where the Action Is," Goffman (1967) is concerned with situations in which individuals willfully take practical gambles. Although they perceive that the activities in which they engage are both problematic and consequential, they undertake such risky situations for their own sake. Within this framework of "action" situations, an individual's character is revealed. Of character, Goffman says "these capacities (or lack of them) for standing correct and steady in the face of sudden pressures are crucial; they do not specify the activity of the individual, but how he will manage himself in this activity" (1967:217). Few situations provide a clearer opportunity for observing character than does sport.

In many situations, as in sport, assessment of character focuses upon the one characteristic most highly valued by that particular setting. Some attention has been paid to the manner in which athletes work up an acceptable self-definition by means of self-expressive responses to commonly perceived tests of occupational character (Faulkner, 1974). It is not unusual for a work world to value some particular aspect of task performance most highly. In sport, this valued aspect often serves as the basic resource for the negotiation of occupational character.

Faulkner (1974) has shown that ice hockey players use violence as a "presentational resource" for the display of honorable, respectable occupational behavior. A similar pattern has been noted by Weinberg and Arond in their study of the occupational culture of the boxer:

> There is . . . a cult of a kind of persevering courage, called a "fighting heart" which means "never admitting defeat." The fighter learns early that his exhibited courage—his ability, if necessary, to go down fighting—characterizes the respected, audience-pleasing boxer (1969: 444).

Based on his observations of the racetrack, Scott (1968) concluded that

> attributes of moral character are established only in risk-taking situations: before we are ready to impute to a person the quality of strong character, he must be seen as voluntarily putting something on the line.

> At the racetrack, we find a sphere of life where men are out to establish character, demonstrate virtue, and achieve honor. . . . The jockey is one of the few survivals of the traditional concept of "the man of honor" (1968: 25).

Scott goes on to state that while gallantry and integrity are important aspects of the jockey's character,

> above all, the jockey with strong character possesses the perceived virtue of coolness in risky situations (1968: 26).

And Polsky's study of the pool-hall revealed that

> the hustler must have "heart." The *sine qua non* is that he is a good "money player," can play his best when heavy action is riding on the game. Also, he is not supposed to let a bad break or distractions in the audience upset him. Nor should the quality of his game deteriorate, when, whether by miscalculation on his part or otherwise, he finds himself much further behind than he would like to be (1967: 45).

For the gymnast, character hinges upon poise—the ability to display composure in stressful situations. Cool competence is the mark of the superior gymnast and is displayed through face work and through body work. The face must remain serene, confident, and pleasant; the body must not shake or show signs of strain or nervousness. The effort which must be expended to mask the effort of performing the routine is considerable: There is a certain amount of irony in testing oneself to the very limit of one's ability while maintaining by face and posture the impression that one is coasting effortlessly and gracefully through a simple routine.

When the professional wrestler performs in front of an audience, his competence is also assessed by the degree to which he succeeds in creating the desired impression for the audience. For the wrestler, character is focused upon two highly related characteristics: color and heat.

Color refers to the ability of the wrestler to dramatize and make "real" to the audience the manufactured image relegated to him by the promoter. Dramatic image is set up on the basis of good and evil. In the native language of the promotional office, the roles of good and evil are referred to as "babyface" and "heel." The babyface is considered a "clean" wrestler in that he follows what are supposed to be, and what are perceived by audiences as, the rules. The heel is the wrestler who breaks these supposed rules in order to gain what the audience should consider an unfair advantage. For example, he will surreptitiously use "brass knuckles," which he conceals in his wrestling trunks (Turowetz and Rosenberg, 1977).

The wrestler who is successful in his presentation, that is, the wrestler with color, is able to generate audience response, or what wrestlers refer to as "heat." The promoter aids the process by matching two colorful opponents, generally a babyface and a heel. To maximize heat, ethnic or moral characteristics of the two will usually be emphasized. Regardless of his assigned image, a wrestler without color, like a gymnast without poise, has little chance of remaining where the action is for long. In order to earn the right to display their character claims in public, both must win the respect of the preliminary gate-keepers in the back regions: the coach in the case of the gymnast and the promotor in the wrestler's case. The components of work identity to which these significant others are attuned are physical skills and presentational skills.

CHARACTER WORK-UP

Goffman has provided social analysts with a neat way to differentiate between two important areas in which identity work takes place. Aside from a *front region* where an identity is publicly presented, or performed, for a generally appreciative "audience" of interactants, Goffman identifies a *backstage* or *back region* in which identities are tried out and practiced in private. The backstage is not necessarily an area; it may be differentiated from on-stage actions by secrecy among team members: a whisper between confederates, a glance, a conspiratorial chuckle at the excluded audience's expense.

In some realms of everyday life, however, front and back regions are conveniently separate spaces, and such a geographical division allows the observer an opportunity to see a model situation. In sport, the observer is afforded an opportunity equaled only by the theatre itself, for sport is handily separated into a performance area—the arena, field, or gym—and backstage areas designated as the practice gym and the locker-room. All sport worlds, legitimate or illegitimate, share this structure.

In the practice gym, physical skills are learned and polished, and in the locker-room, players change into their game uniforms and "mentally" prepare themselves for the competition. But of course, much more takes place in these backstage areas, and physical skills, uniforms, and psych-up jobs are only the visible portions of the work that goes on. More important is the work that goes into the creation and management of valid and acceptable work identities. In both wrestling and gymnastics this process may be referred to as identity work-up.

Physical Skill

Because wrestling and gymnastics are perceived to be sports by their audiences, the basic component of each is demonstration of physical skill. Without a display of basic physical skill, neither the wrestler nor the gymnast can maintain his or her credibility. This is more obvious perhaps in a legitimate work world such as gymnastics.

The high level collegiate gymnast spends upwards of 500 hours a season in the practice gym, in close contact with her coaches and teammates, learning and practicing her physical skill. The gymnast who cannot perform basic physical skills will never progress to a level of serious contention within the gymnastics world.

The unit of physical skill in the gymnastics world is the "trick." Some tricks are applicable to any event—walk-overs, handsprings, aerials, somersaults; some are specifically suited to certain pieces of equipment—beating the bar, hip circles, sole circles. Display of minimal competence in learning and performing such tricks with skill is mandatory: It is impossible to negotiate with the judges over skill one does not possess.

Learning entails practice, repetition, and considerable amounts of pain. "Beating the bar" is a required move in uneven parallel bar routines and entails hanging from the top bar and hitting the bottom bar with one's hips, using the force of the impact to rebound one's body into another move. One gymnast nicely understated the effects of this process:

> You get tremendous bruises along here (the hips) and like I have blood blisters there and stuff like red and blue and underground eggs like little lumps because it's not really that natural of a thing to be doing. . . . It hurts you but you do it. You don't think about it.

Tricks are interspersed with connective "moves" and the entire series of tricks and moves are finally assembled as the finished product, the "routine."

In wrestling, the unit of physical skill is the "hold," such as basic leg holds, arm-locks, head-locks. As in gymnastics, connective moves are used to join the action into a meaningful whole. Trip-ups and rope work are examples, and they are assembled to form a "match."

A wrestler goes through a long training period, generally between two and three years. During his apprenticeship, the wrestler is evaluated by his trainers and promoters almost entirely in terms of his physical skills. One essential element of skill for which the trainer is searching is balance.

> Balance is the most important thing that he should know about. There are some guys who have been working for twenty years and never got the balance. They don't know about it at all. In that way, they work three times as hard as a wrestler who has the balance. If they know how to distribute their weight, they do not have to exert that much force to keep the other guy down. It's like the guy on the tightrope. It's only a question of balance, and that is all that counts in the long run.

Staging of the physical skills is an important aspect of the wrestler's world. The audience must be led to believe, however willingly, that the series of holds, moves, falls are not rehearsed. This contingency requires added levels of learning physical skill. Not only must the wrestler possess a degree of "real" physical skill, he must possess enough physical skill to provide the audience with a believable parody of legitimate wrestling.

For a performance to be convincing it must be a detailed and accurate rendition of both wrestling and a contest. The progress of every match must proceed as if each sequence of holds were being applied full force, and each hold must be accompanied by its appropriate escape. Overt and clumsy fakery is too easy for the audience to recognize.

> The people in the crowd let you know how good you are. Let's use Claude as an example. Now don't get me wrong because I like him a lot. But he just does not have it and the people don't care to watch him. They laugh at him and boo him all of the time; it's not because he is a heel but because he is a crappy wrestler. When I walk into the ring you can see the difference. They want to kill me. They pray that the other guy will destroy me. That is the difference.

Wrestlers rate one another in terms of physical skill and not, as the audience tends to, in terms of color. Some exhibit pride in their special accomplishments:

> My expertise was with my legs. I knew that if I could hook the other guy that within 15 seconds the bout would be mine. That shows you that I had a style that suited me. Many lose their balance after they have taken the leg hold and end up underneath the pile. It's a question of style and experience.

Others display anger and frustration when the promoter schedules them to lose to a physically inferior opponent.

> Shit man. This really bugs me. I'm U.S. champion. The promoter calls me in for a one-night stand and I blow it to that fat little Jap. He's real shit. He can't wrestle to save his life. Why do I have to take all this. I'm in my prime and one of the best in North America. This kind of thing hurts my pride.

Clearly, the possession and display of adequate physical skills are a major concern of both worlds.

Presentational Skills

Presentation includes the display of physical skill. The most important component, however, is the totality of the image the gymnast or wrestler displays. For that reason, the work backstage is not devoted solely to learning physical skills; identities are worked-up.

Central to the idea of identity work-up is the matter of style. Style should accentuate the actor's ability to fulfill role expectations: to perform with poise in the gymnast's case or with color in the wrestler's. An interesting contrast between the two roles focuses on the question of style. As gymnasts are quick to explain, "The object of gymnastics is to make something very difficult look very easy." But for the professional wrestler, style does not require minimizing the appearance of effort but rather exaggerating it, or making things seem more difficult than they are.

All gymnasts must display poise and all wrestlers must have color. But the means for working-up these appearances depend to some extent upon the particular style of the actor. In gymnastics, a woman may be roughly categorized as a "dancer" or a "tumbler," an indication that style is often circumscribed by physical capabilities. Style may determine which events a woman enters (floor exercise rather than uneven parallel bars) and it will certainly determine the content of her routines. But even within such a gross generalization, gymnasts believe that each gymnast has her own style which dictates aspects of her routine and which should be capitalized upon in a meet situation. The gymnast must learn to minimize her limitations and maximize her strong points.

> If you don't have that many stunts you try to space them in between really good poses . . . you have to learn what looks really good on you. If you have a short neck like myself, you have to really see that all my poses sort of accentuate a nice long line.

Throughout practice, gymnasts can be observed working alone in front of mirrors, trying out moves and poses and finding out for themselves what looks good on them.

Deference paid to another's style often conditions the nature of help available to the gymnast. One ex-gymnast who was helping create routines for several gymnasts commented:

> It's really hard for me to adapt my style to fit most of the kids in the gym. Things that feel good to me have to be toned down or toned up somehow, shaped up to fit the person's style I'm working with. It's double the work.

In this sort of helping relationship, the creative partner often visualizes moves that must be discarded because they do not fit the performer's style.

In much the same way, the wrestler must learn to identify his strengths and then develop the presentational skills that will enable him to capitalize on them. When the wrestler first begins to develop an individual style, he is usually free to choose the dramatic image with which he is most comfortable. This is not always the case, however, as the promoter will often interfere if he feels that the wrestler has a "natural touch" for some image. The two general roles available to the wrestler are the "babyface" or the "heel," but within those choices are a range of available identities, generally based around the idea of ethnicity.

Color is the wrestler's responsibility. Because of his concern with style, the wrestler never ceases to train. He is always engaged in perfecting his technique and exploring new possibilities. The wrestler experiments with many styles during training and preliminary matches and chooses the one with which he feels most comfortable. Thus, while the trainer is concerned with physical ability and the promoter is concerned with dramatic ability, the wrestler views the training process as one which will result in the development of his own personal style.

Unlike the gymnast, the successful wrestler's career is not limited in time. Because of his relatively long career, the wrestler may have to face two problems of image maintenance that gymnasts do not. As he becomes older, for example, he will have to change his style to fit his changed abilities.

You peak at about forty, but then you can keep on going. As you get older, you develop a style all your own and this tends to make things much easier. I used to wrestle with strength all the way through, but what happens now is that you have to be able to shift your weight in an effort to make use of the other guy's size.

Socialization into a new image must then take place backstage so that the audience never witnesses the change. Promotors must always have some means available for regenerating heat. If necessary the promotor will tamper with the wrestler's style. As the wrestler well knows, he must go along or face, as one promoter put it, "unemployment." While the wrestler may become angry, he will usually obey. When a new image is assigned, it is the responsibility of the wrestler to master the presentational skills of his new image equally well.

FRAMING BEHAVIOR

Not all character work is displayed in the wrestling ring or on the gymnastics apparatus. Framing behavior, such as entrances and exits, is an integral feature of both worlds, and appropriate behavior must be learned. Time must be spent backstage working up this portion of one's identity; judges and audiences evaluate the totality of the work situation, and even actions which appear to be "backstage" or peripheral are being monitored in this intermediary phase for clues to character.

The wrestler must emerge from the dressing-room not only in full costume, but in full work identity as well, as this example from a match illustrates:

> The Shiek's ring entrance in full costume (Arabic robe, head-dress, sandals and prayer rug) provoked an emphatic audience response of boos, hisses and thrown objects. Pedro Morales was carried in from the dressing-room on the shoulders of four fans to the screaming and Puerto Rican flag-waving of the audience. Responding to the audience, Morales began to wave two miniature flags, a Puerto Rican and an American, which had previously been concealed in his robe. After the introduction of the combatants, the Shiek re-emphasized his ethnic "otherness" from the flag-waving Morales, by enacting a Moslem prayer.

The entire process, of course, serves to generate heat.

A similar situation occurs in gymnastics. Although a judge's evaluation of performance formally begins when the gymnast touches the apparatus and ceases when she breaks contact with the apparatus, gymnasts believe, and with good reason, that all their behavior in the gym is being monitored unofficially by the judges. Therefore, the gymnast's behavior immediately before and after her performance is carefully controlled.

The most ritualized of these behaviors are salutations to the head judge. According to the gymnast, the salutation is "a salute of recognition or tribute the competitor gives to the judge." Again and again throughout the competitive season, the same patterns are observed.

In the vault, for example, the gymnast waits at attention for recognition from the head judge. When the judges are ready, they settle themselves in an attentive attitude. The gymnast raises her hand to salute the head judge. The better gymnast makes this a slow, full, dramatic gesture which concentrates attention on herself; she makes a point of trying to establish eye contact with the judge as well. The judge responds by raising a green flag. The gymnast then noticeably draws herself inward, fixes a determined look on her face, runs down the runway, and executes the vault. As she lands, she raises both hands above her head to round off the performance and signal completion. She then turns to the head judge and once more addresses her by standing at respectful attention, once again making eye contact, if possible. This behavior is coached, just as other significant performance details are. Time after time during practice, a gymnast who had neglected to "finish" the routine with arms extended was called back to do so. And during the practice meet judged by the coach, points were deducted for failure to salute before and after the routine or vault.

The vault is judged from the time the gymnast hits the springboard until she lands on the mat on the other side of the horse. Theoretically addressing the judge and approaching the springboard are not parts of the routine. In actuality, however, gymnasts attend to this display.

> I try to start off slow and build up speed so that when I hit the board I'm going at the fastest speed. I've seen that influence the crowd. They see somebody speeding up and that builds excitement so it makes the vault look more impressive.

A similar pattern occurs in other events as well. In the floor routine, for example, the gymnast salutes the judge, then walks onto the mat, takes a position, and awaits the beginning of her music. At the completion of her routine, she addresses the judge once more. Walking onto the mat is part of the performance and movements must be controlled, posture erect, toes pointed. Exit from the mat is not part of the performance but should be accomplished with a graceful run which indicates untapped reservoirs of energy "even if you're dead."

Entrances and exits are learned behavior, practiced in backstage areas and displayed during formal presentations as part of the total image of the competent worker.

CHARACTER DISPLAY

As the previous section has shown, the working-up of work identities and routines is similar in both gymnastics and professional wrestling. The other side of the work world for both is the performance stage where identities and routines are displayed and evaluated. Although the underlying difference in the legitimacy or illegitimacy of the two worlds makes it appear that the performance stages are vastly different, in fact they are fundamentally the same. Performances are concerned with how identity-defining action gets handled, and the processes are similar for those engaged in the legitimate performance of the gymnast and the illegitimate performance of the professional wrestler. To understand these processes further, one might focus attention upon four important aspects of the performance: character work, teamwork, mistakes and recoveries, and evaluation.

Character Work

Performances are oriented toward the displaying of character. Since character in these worlds revolves around either poise or heat, presentation of these qualities serves as the general theme of the performance. Others important to the gymnastic and wrestling worlds—audiences, teammates, coaches, judges—attend critically to the display of poise or the creation of heat. An observer at a gymnastics meet, for example, might form a general impression of the gymnast. The judge does the same but in a more formal manner. "General impression" is the most critical category of the gymnast's score. It is worth one full point out of the total of ten: a substantial portion of the score, particularly in a highly competitive meet. Moreover, this is the one portion of the score which the judge is free to award or deduct as she sees fit. She may take points off for failure to salute before an event; she may deduct if the gymnast rearranges her clothing, pulls down her leotard, or fixes her hair while about to perform. But she is not bound by the rules of judging to do so. She is bound only by her own norms as to the true nature of character.

A gymnast knows that loss of points in this category can ruin her score and thus the public announcement of herself as a qualified gymnast. The wise gymnast makes full use of all resources available to her for impression management in order to negotiate with the judge for this assessment of her character.

Although the character of the gymnast is revealed to the audience during the course of the routine, an experienced wrestling fan need not wait for a match to begin in order to determine whether a given wrestler is a "heel" or a "babyface." Wrestlers exhibit their dramatic image in their appearance and behavior, calling on character-expressive attributes which might be called the attributes of conventional decency. The babyface is expected to be clean-shaven, serious but polite, good-looking, and articulate. The heel is expected to be violent and uncontrolled, to possess some peculiarity which sets him apart, such as being unkempt or overimmaculate, being scarred, or having a nervous twitch, and he is expected to be practically inarticulate. The purpose of such appearance and behavior is not simply to make the wrestler recognizably good or evil but, by exaggerating those qualities, to produce a strong audience response (Rosenberg and Turowetz, 1976).

The wrestler's business, then, is to generate heat and stimulate audience participation to a level one step below rioting. The gymnast's business, on the other hand, is to remain as cool as possible and to separate herself as performer from the audience. Asked about the audience, one gymnast replied:

> I'm not paying very much attention to them. . . . Once I mount, there's nothing more but me and the apparatus and sometimes I can go through a whole routine and not remember doing it. I don't even pay attention to people because I figure I'm the one that's going to get the personal satisfaction out of it. They're going to enjoy watching me no matter if I hit or miss because I'm exciting to watch.

Despite the differences, however, there is common to both worlds one way in which audience excitement is generated. In wrestling, it is the "card" or arrangement of matches so that all matches add to the mounting excitement until the finale. In gymnastics, it is the "line-up" or the arrangement of routines so that the best gymnast appears last. Yet, whereas wrestling promotors may manipulate the card to generate more heat, the gymnastics coaches may use manipulation of the line-up as a strategy to garner more points from the judge.

> If I did well it would not only psych out the other team—I mean when you look at a third beam routine and you see an 8.95—you know that's pretty hard because none of their kids can score that high on beam. And knowing that [our best gymnast] is still going up and knowing that there are two other kids—it mentally worked.

For the team, then, rather than the audience, the strategy was an important one.

Teamwork

Performances often entail teamwork, and sport performances, even in individual sports such as gymnastics and wrestling, are particularly apt to have teamwork as a basic component of the work setting. Teams can be defined in terms of accessibility of information: between team-mates, the distribution of work-relevant information must be symmetrical; between teams in competition, information distribution is asymmetrical.

Although the gymnast always performs solo, gymnastics is a team sport. In fact, at any dual gymnastics meet, four teams are in attendance. Each set of gymnasts and coaches is a team, the judges are a third team, and the audiences a fourth. The teams are arranged in terms of exclusion from performance information. Through the course of the meet, routines and scores are finally revealed to all.

Professional wrestling provides an interesting parody of legitimate teamwork. Wrestlers appear to be competitors, yet they are in fact team members: all have access to information concerning the outcome and sequence of holds. Furthermore, the team is even larger than that. Train-ers, promotors, and referees are also privy to the performance informa-tion. Finally, since the audience is so willingly deceived, they too might be considered as part of the team.

It is, of course, naive to view professional wrestling as solely deter-mined by the manipulation of audience response, for much of what goes on in wrestling is generated in concert with that audience. Imagine how ridiculous a professional wrestling match would be if it were played to *no* audience. A gymnast's routine can provide her with some sense of accomplishment independent of any audience. Yet professional wrestling makes sense only in the context of an audience (Rosenberg and Turo-wetz, 1976). Those that seek to be manipulated are constrained by the ability or the desire of the audience to understand the dimensions through which they are being manipulated. Stone (1971: 301) reports overhear-ing the following invective from an avid fan: "I don't give a damn if it is a fake!! Kill the son-of-a-bitch!"

Teamwork in wrestling, regardless of how extensive the information network is, is the result of collusion, and collusion is one of the constraints an illegitimate script places on action.

Mistakes and Recoveries

"Fateful mistakes," as Hughes (1971) would have it, are occurrences that disrupt the flow of work. Moreover, given the nature of sport as an action situation in which one is often laying one's character on the line, fateful mistakes in sport can often result not merely in embarrassment but in failure. Furthermore, as Ball (1976) has observed, failure can reduce the individual to nonpersonage status and limit, if not prohibit, meaningful interaction in the future. To reduce this possibility, ways must be found to handle fateful mistakes.

Fateful mistakes in the worlds of gymnasts and wrestlers are those which undermine the impression upon which a competent performance is based. When a gymnast's poise or a wrestler's color are in danger of being lost or discredited, embarrassment occurs: The validity of work identity, focused around that one work-relevant quality, is imperiled. Like all workers, gymnasts and wrestlers must have ways to handle such embarrassing contingencies. To avoid being perceived and labeled as incompetent—a phony wrestler, a shaky gymnast—remedial identity work must be accessible and routinized, and one may depend upon one's teammates to help with that remedial work. In general, remedial work gets handled through preventative action and recovering moves.

The most fateful mistake in wrestling is the miscue, generally attributable to a breakdown in information distribution. To prevent errors, wrestlers use a universal cue system which serves to keep such mistakes at a minimum. This is important not only to prevent physical injury but because even simple mistakes can subvert the impression of contest, destroying the heat. This is neatly expressed in the following statement:

> There is a universal code of wrestling cues in the profession. Certain moves are the same and they are used in all parts of the country. Most of the good performers usually carry the poorer fighters in the ring. They figure that if their opponent looks bad in the match so will they. If someone misses a cue, everyone is in trouble—here's a guy pulling a handful of nothing across the ring. Some wrestlers actually talk you through and tell you what to do move by move. Other times the referee does it for you. Before a step-over-toe hold the opponent will tap you in the leg which he wants to grab. To get you in a head-lock, the guy will tap you on the neck.

Miscues do occur, however, and such errors can be catastrophic. While examples are legion, one notorious incident is the losing of an ear by "Yukon" Eric Humbolt in a match with Wladek "Killer" Kowalski more than a decade ago.

In gymnastics, a fateful mistake is called a "major break." A major break is an interruption of the momentum of the routine and is symbolic of breaking with the ideal, of not continually maintaining an assurance of physical and mental control. Such things as scraping the floor or losing momentum on the bars, stumbling after the vault, or falling off the beam or during the floor routine are flaws to a smooth and continuous routine. Shaky muscles, signs of fatigue or strain are likewise character flaws. The judge deducts points for minor flaws as she sees fit, but major breaks carry automatic deductions of a half to one full point.

To minimize the possibility of mistakes, wrestlers will sometimes "talk through" a series of holds or even an entire match so no miscues will occur. Gymnasts, too, talk about "talking through" a routine. For them, however, it is an individual effort, an attempt to concentrate and thus avoid major breaks.

> I think about what I'm doing through the whole thing. I think about every move I make. Sometimes, when I get to the end though I can't remember thinking about the move but I know I talk myself through the routine quite a few times.

Because mistakes do occur, however, actors must have a routinized means of handling them. To cover mistakes, gymnasts and wrestlers may make changes in their ongoing work. A gymnast may eliminate some difficult tricks in her routine if she has trouble with them earlier in the routine; wrestlers may redo a weak move to demonstrate proficiency.

Recovering from recognizable mistakes is a true test of character. Recovery entails more than physically bouncing back and is symbolic of saving face, restoring image, and reestablishing imperiled character. Wrestlers must regenerate heat as quickly as possible. Gymnasts must remain cool and unruffled.

However, while both wrestlers and gymnasts seek to recover their composure after a fateful mistake, the form of that recovery varies. The difference hinges on the extent of damage a recognizable miscue can cause. In gymnastics a mistake discredits the individual performer, but in wrestling a mistake discredits not only the actor but the entire work world. For that reason wrestlers deal with miscues as nonevents. By refusing to recognize the fact that a mistake has occurred, the wrestlers free themselves and their audience from the necessity of having to deal with an imperfect world.

In contrast, gymnasts deal with their mistakes explicitly. Indeed mistakes are a natural part of their work, and handling mistakes is not only a recognized contingency, but a coached behavior.

Falling from the gymnastics beam is one of the more common major breaks. Remounting the beam after a fall is therefore an important move and all gymnasts practice remounts so that, if necessary, they can be smoothly incorporated into the routine. Coaches furnish explicit instructions to gymnasts not to boost their seats onto the beam and then swing their legs up. Such a posture is unworthy of a gymnast. Instead, mounting moves similar to the ones used to begin the routine are used.

Often the gymnast must recover from situations she has not created. Bows which fall from the hair, a lost slipper, even completely disarranged hairdos must be totally ignored and never touched. Such behavior would apparently indicate the acknowledgement of a character break. The extreme example of this is drawn from an incident concerning a nationally acclaimed gymnast which was recounted by another gymnast.

Because of an injury, she had an ace bandage wrapped around her knee. In the middle of her beam routine, the bandage became unwound

> and she finished the rest of the routine trailing the bandage. Even her dismount, which was a front somersault, she did with it flyng through the air.

To have touched the bandage would have permitted the judges the opportunity to deduct points under "general impression." Continuance of the routine, on the other hand, was actually quite dangerous, sparking an incredulous response from the informant "that the sport cannot make accommodations for things like that." By continuing her performance, the gymnast demonstrated to all observing that she was a competent performer, able to maintain her composure in the face of the most unsettling challenges. Occupational character thus has to do with keeping one's entire competitive self in order and under complete control at all times.

Evaluating Work

Evaluation of work identities is the focal point of the performance for gymnasts and wrestlers, and for both performers two sets of evaluations are rendered. Evaluation concentrates upon the competence of the presentation for both but an interesting inversion of judgments exists between the two.

For both worlds, there are judges and audiences. However, they differ in the importance of the feedback of these two types of reactors.

The gymnastics judge is the gatekeeper of the work world. Evaluation is presented in the form of a score based on a possible perfect ten points. The gymnasts and judges negotiate this score between themselves—the gymnast performing tricks of "superior" difficulty to build up her credit; the judges deducting for a variety of faults, ranging from major breaks to lack of creativity to shakes and other indications of loss of composure.

The audience input into this process is minimal. Though gymnasts will sometimes acknowledge attempts to manipulate scores through capturing the audience's fancy, judges are bound by scoring conventions to discount audience reaction.

The evaluations that count to the gymnast are those of the judge and the coach. Based upon the gymnast's score for a routine, the coach will move a gymnast up or down in the line-up in an attempt to get the fairest and most dramatic combination.

The wrestling referee is also the gatekeeper of that work world— but not in his formal capacity as referee. The outcome, of course, has been determined backstage, and the referee, as team member, has access to the outcome and the script of the entire match. The declaration of a winner is merely a formality.

But the referee is also responsible to the promoter, and it is the promotor who defines who and what the wrestler is. In the last analysis, the wrestling culture is the promoter's culture. The criteria used by the promoter in assessing the wrestler will include dramatic ability as well as physical ability (Rosenberg and Turowetz, 1976). By far the most important criterion for the promoter is audience response. Unlike gymnastics, wrestling requires an audience. Therefore, it is the paying audience member who maintains the wrestling world and it is professional wrestling as entertainment which supports wrestling as a business and a career. Therefore, the promoter evaluates the wrestler in terms of the heat his performance has generated. Audience input is not disregarded as in gymnastics but furnishes an important element of information about the course of the match. Thus, the wrestling audience may be dealt with once again as part of the team. Without their feedback, the information is incomplete.

The gymnastics coach uses the judges' score to evaluate her gymnasts, and that score is, in a large part, a reflection of the poise the gymnast has displayed. The wrestling promoter uses the heat of the audience to evaluate his wrestlers and that heat is a reflection of the color the wrestlers have created.

CONCLUSION

Focusing on the worlds of the gymnast and the professional wrestler, this article has examined the ways in which competent work identities are created, maintained, and displayed. Motivated by Hughes's (1958) suggestion that one look for commonalities and uniformities among all occupations, this comparative analysis has uncovered some important similarities drawn from two apparently different social worlds. By describing the processes of character work-up and character display for both activities, this project has seriously attended to Hughes's request.

It is important to note that Hughes was not concerned solely with the development of typologies and categories for understanding large banks of ethnographic data. He advanced analyses of occupations in order to sensitize sociologists of work and social psychologists to the fact that all work is governed by practical routine everyday life activity. He recognized that while structural relations and contexts come to differ by occupational arrangement, interpersonal relations in many work worlds tend to be appropriated, announced, and managed in much the same way. Persons act and interact, work up identities, make mistakes, experience successes and failures, and are routinely called upon to do their share of "dirty work."

As has been shown in this paper, gymnasts and wrestlers engage in precisely these kinds of activity. What is strikingly different about this comparative analysis, however, is that one of the work activities does not take place within an occupational structure. This would suggest that an examination of divergent "work" situations such as these may provide sociologists with an interesting forum for future research in the sociology of occupations.

NOTE

1. Throughout this paper the terms "wrestler" and "wrestling" refer to the *professional* form of that sport. Collegiate and amateur wrestling are, of course, far different.

REFERENCES

Ball, D. (1976) "Failure in sport." American Sociological Review: 41 (Aug.): 726-739.

Berger, P. L. (1963) Invitation to Sociology. Garden City, N.Y.: Anchor.

Birrell, S. (1974) "Negotiations for occupational character." Department of Sports Studies, University of Massachusetts, unpublished.

Faulkner, R. (1974) "Making violence by doing work." Sociology of Work and Occupations 1 (Aug.):288-304.

Glaser, B. and A. Strausss (1967) The Discovery of Grounded Theory. Chicago: Aldine.

Goffman, E. (1961) Interaction Ritual. Garden City, N.Y.: Anchor.

——— (1959) The Presentation of Self in Everyday Life. Garden City, N.Y.: Anchor.

Hughes, E. C. (1971) The Sociological Eye: Book Two. Chicago: Aldine.
——— (1958) Men and Their Work: Chicago: Aldine.
Polsky, N. (1969) Hustlers, Beats and Others. Garden City, N.Y.: Anchor.
Rosenberg, M. and A. Turowetz (1976) "Exaggerations and inversions of reality: the case of professional wrestling." Unpublished.
Scott, M. (1968) The Racing Game. Chicago: Aldine.
Stone, G. P. (1971) "Wrestling: the great American passion play," pp. 301-335 in E. Dunning (ed.) The Sociology of Sport. London: Frank Cass.
Turowetz, A. (1974) An Ethnography of Professional Wrestling. M. A. thesis, McGill University.
——— and M. Rosenberg (1977) "Exaggerating everyday life: the case of professional wrestling," in J. Haas and B. Shaffer (eds.) Identities in Canadian Society. Englewood Cliffs, N.J.: Prentice-Hall.
Weinberg, S. K. and H. Arond (1968) "The occupational culture of the boxer," pp. 439-452 in J. W. Loy and G. S. Kenyon (eds.) Sport, Culture and Society. New York: Macmillan.

The World of Football Hooligans

Peter Marsh and Rom Harré

There is widespread belief in Britain that certain soccer fields are scenes of chaos, random violence, and bloody fights that make them only barely distinguishable from battlefields. A sample of headlines from the daily papers reflects this view:

SOCCER HOOLIGANS RUN RIOT
FENCE THEM IN
SMASH THESE THUGS
CLOBBER BOYS ON THE RAMPAGE

The rhetoric is typically British, but the mixed images of anarchy, mindlessness, and complete opposition to public order are as likely to appear in Europe, South America, or the United States. So is the pervasive tone of fear and moral outrage—as if the famous juvenile delinquents of the 1950s were about to explode into violent characters out of *A Clockwork Orange,* or more likely into sheer savagery.

This is not the place to speculate on the ultimate historical significance or moral value of soccer riots. But the prevalent view that they are chaotic, irrational, and extremely dangerous is wrong in every respect.

Young people have reasons for what they are doing. They interpret what is happening around them, and the events that we view as disordered and irrational have a very different meaning for those involved. Our work has revealed a social orderliness of a remarkable kind. Among these supposedly wild adolescents, we have found clear directions for the attainment of ambitions and personal worth that they feel are impossible to realize within official institutions. These youths, in short, follow rules; and to say so is neither to approve nor to sentimentalize their behavior. The rules are simply there to be discovered.

The complex society of aggressive young soccer (called football in Britain) fans is mostly made up of adolescents for whom the weekday world of school, and sometimes of work, provides no opportunities for the development of a sense of worth, dignity, and personal value. Thus school and football "hooliganism" can be seen as closely related. Young working-class students often find themselves written off as uneducable by the age of 12. To a great extent their state schools, like many ghetto schools in the United States, becomes mere warehouses.

To most of the fans we talked with, school seemed to be a waste of time—an institution imposed on them from above. Too often, teachers and school officials impressed these students (all on a nonacademic, working-class track) as being soft, arrogant, contemptuous, cowardly, unfair, incompetent, or indifferent. And so the students "mess about" in school, lock their teachers in closets, and generally raise hell. These classroom disorders are also more orderly than critics commonly assume, but the rules are not quite the same as those we have studied among "football hooligans."

What happens when these adolescents get together away from an institution like school, which was made *for* them, and find a place where they can construct institutions for themselves? That is the fascination of the football terraces; for on the terraced concrete grandstands overlooking soccer fields there flourishes a complex society of the adolescents' making, and one in which teachers (good, bad, or indifferent) hold no power. Here boys—never girls—see the chance of becoming men and of carving out careers in which they stand some chance of success and prestige.

"Ends"—the spectators' stands behind the goals—may look quite unremarkable to outsiders. But to the dedicated adolescent males we are describing, these terraces are sacred territories to which only they, as members of larger fan groups, are admitted access. It is on these slabs of concrete, which are now surrounded throughout much of Britain by fences, moats, and policemen, that collections of hooligans have created their microsocieties.

Fans who eventually become what we shall call Rowdies enter the soccer-terrace culture as Novices, or what older fans call "little kids," when they are as young as nine or ten. Attracted by the noisy spectacle, excitement, and possible danger, they congregate on the edges of the main body of fans. They are there to learn what being a Rowdy is all about, and they spend most of their time watching the activities of their elders instead of the game. Their models are easily identified by a style of dress, synchronized chanting and hand clapping, and from time to time, various forms of ritualized aggression. These older lads are known collectively in the outside world as hooligans. But since the word hooligan is used somewhat differently by insiders, we have preferred to call them Rowdies, a term that they themselves use.

Becoming Rowdy is the first upward step in the terrace structure, because until a boy has gained acceptance in this group, there are no status positions of any kind available. Fortunately for the aspiring Novice, there are no initiation rites and no painful tests to pass. He has simply to demonstrate knowledge of the appropriate songs and chants, to wear appropriate gear, to support the right team, and to be "one of the lads." The gear, for those who have never watched a British football game, changes with the fashions. But while we were studying the society of the terraces, gear included such items as denim jackets and blue jeans, baggy white trousers, heavy boots, thin shirts even in the depths of winter, and colorful silk scarves tied around the neck or to the wrists. As we will see later, various subtleties of dress, which are well understood by the Rowdies themselves, make it clear that we are dealing with a small society and not just a bunch of deranged individuals.

It is sometimes possible to join the Rowdies without passing through the Novice stage. For example, a lad of 13 or 14 who is already known to the older boys may, after a short apprenticeship, stand on the terrace with his mates. After that, the potential for an ambitious Rowdy is great. Among the roles available to him (all of which afford a special kind of personal value) are those of Chant Leader, Aggro Leader, Organizer, and Hooligan. There is even the chance of recognition as a Nutter.

Aggro Leaders are Rowdies who have established a reputation for being constantly involved in battle with the fans of the opposing team. A 17-year-old boy named Phil had this to say about his role as an Aggro Leader:

"Lots of the smaller kids really look up to you. . . . They look up to you and think you're a good fighter."

"And are you a good fighter?"

"Yes—well . . . used to be quite a bit. If people start some trouble or something like that, then I'll be in there. If you live up on the Leys [a fairly rough housing development] then you have to fight or else people piss you about and think you're a bit soft or something. . . . So I'm in there making them run—that's what you're trying to do—and make them feel small. So we're round outside after the game and down the road after them. But I don't go around thumping people all the time. You don't have to. People know who you are."

Phil was known as a "hard man" on the terraces and he later ended up in jail for cashing fraudulent checks. A hard Aggro Leader, however, is not to be confused with a good fighter, Aggro (the word comes from "aggravation," not "aggression," but the coincidence is convenient) has more to do with ritual displays of aggression than with acts of physical violence. There is a lot of show and verbal abuse, accompanied by gestures of hostility and defiance. Occasions on which rival fans actually come to blows are, despite widespread opinion to the contrary, rare. The Aggro Leader might never have to fight anybody in his whole career. To be accepted in his role, though, he must convince his peers that if a fight arose, he would be man enough to win it. He must be seen to stand his ground when rivals threaten to invade his territory. And when visiting fans are forced to retreat to their buses at the end of a match, he must be in the vanguard. In general, an Aggro Leader has to show a distinct sense of fearlessness. He has to be a kind of "hard case." But his lack of fear must not be too great; for total, unreasonable fearlessness is the prerogative of the Nutter.

Fans are in no doubt as to where bravery ends and sheer lunacy begins, and Nutters are individuals whose actions are seen by other fans to fall outside the boundaries of acceptable conduct. They "go crazy" and do "nutty" things like attempting to beat some poor rival fan to a pulp. If given free rein, they can inflict serious injury on themselves and others. Because the social order to which virtually all Rowdies subscribe requires the restraint of such injuries, Nutters are held back, for instance, in their almost suicidal attempts to take on, single-handed, large groups of rivals. The Nutters confirm the existence of a certain social order among the fans. If all were anarchy and chaos on the terraces, Nutters would be unremarkable and unidentified. But in fact they are deviants within the terrace culture, and like their counterparts in other social worlds, they confirm the majority's notions of what is proper and prescribed.

To call a fan a Nutter is not to use a term of abuse. It is simply to make a comment on his style of doing things. Blackpool fans even have a chant that runs: "We are the Nutters—we come from the sea." The implication is that rivals had better watch out because Rowdies from Blackpool might not be restricted by normal conventions. The chant "There's gonna be a Nasty Accident" expresses a similar sentiment. Fortunately, the implied devastation is never fully realized.

A Chant Leader has a straightforward role. His task is to initiate songs, chants, and patterns of hand clapping at appropriate times. If the rival club is chanting its team's name—for example, "Chelsea! Chelsea!"—

the Chant Leader may try to sabotage that chant by interposing some four-letter word between each "Chelsea." A simple ploy, but upsetting to Chelsea. The lear must be familiar with the entire repertoire.

The task has its hazards. A Chant Leader can get the timing wrong. And to sing out the starting line of a chant and find that nobody follows means a loss of dignity and prestige. One needs confidence as well as competence and a degree of social skill that takes some time to acquire. (Being tall and having a loud voice are also helpful.)

The successful Chant Leader becomes a kind of conductor of terrace rituals—a focus for collective and unifying activity. As such, he figures strongly as a central character in the informal football hierarchy. He is also much in evidence on the buses that are hired to transport fans to away matches. On these, the repertoire of ritual insults and chants aimed at instilling fear in the opposition is refined and rehearsed. Good Chant Leaders are expected to come up with new variations of old themes and to turn items of topical interest into witty songs.

Of course the wit is pretty rough. Like the insults used in the fans' everyday lives, the chants rely heavily on scatology and the implication that the enemy is unmanly, effeminate, or actually female. Goalkeepers have to suffer the accusation that they are homosexuals. Forwards all seem to have cerebral palsy. Masturbation is an almost universal theme: "Swindon Boys, Wank, Wank, Wank" is typical of chants among the fans of Oxford United. Naturally the Oxford fans characterize their own players as tough guys:

Oxford boys, we are here,
Shag your women and drink your beer.

A recent self-serving chant refers to one's own players as "bionic." And sometimes the insults of the opposition are class conscious rather than sexual. One Rowdy song goes:

In their slums,
In their Nottingham slums,
They look in the dustbin for something to eat,
They find a dead cat and they think it's a treat,
In their Nottingham slums.

The responsibility of arranging buses for away games falls on the shoulders of Organisers. Not all football terraces have such figures, but those that have them benefit considerably. Organisers arrange the hire of transport, collect the money for it, and enlist others to help in limiting damage and vandalism. The need for such a role is most pressing when the official fan clubs refuse to allow anybody under the age of 18 to join or to use their travel facilities. Thus the Rowdies, most of whom are under 18, have to look after themselves. Organisers may also be called on to arrange petitions or to lead protests against club officials. These protests are almost always ineffectual, but they help to confirm a sense of collective identity on the terraces.

The last major role, that of Hooligan, may be the most interesting. The word hooligan comes from an antisocial family named Houlihan that lived in East London during the 19th Century. (For years press dispatches out of the Soviet Union have mentioned Russians arrested for hooliganism, as if it were some sort of catch-all antisocial crime.) But it was not until about 1970 that young people in Britain began being called hooligans by journalists and magistrates. Before that, some football fans might have been labeled ruffians or tearaways. The increased use of "hooligan" marks a distinct stage in a process of media amplification and goes hand in hand with horror stories of "carnage," "mob rule," and "animal savagery."

Terms that begin as labels of abuse or disapproval often become used by the targets of censure to mean something quite different. Thus football Rowdies have incorporated "hooligan" into their own vocabulary and use it to refer to boys who commit acts worthy of special praise within the terrace microculture. Such acts might involve minor damage to property or disruption of certain routine social events. The main characteristic, however, is not the act itself but the manner in which it is carried out. In particular, it has to be funny. Hooligans are actors of wit and style; they are entertainers. Anybody, for example, can steal the billboards or wastepaper baskets outside a newsstand. But not everybody can do an elaborate waltz with them up and down the street before returning them—and without getting caught by the infuriated owner.

Hooligans gain honor from such escapades. For a season at Oxford United a 16-year-old named Geoff was famous for his "wicked acts." One day a rival fan threw a lump of dog feces at him. In retaliation Geoff climbed up onto a terrace overlooking the offender and his friends, who were drinking tea, and urinated on them—onto their "heads and into their tea and all over," according to one of Geoff's comrades, "and it's raining a bit as well so they don't notice. Me and some others, we run down and were watching this and we're killing ourselves. But Geoff, he don't shout out or anything—he just waits for a bit till they finish their tea and then he shouts out 'Enjoy your tea then,' and as they look up he pisses a bit more and they go barmy."

An unedifying scene, perhaps. And yet around these roles is woven a network of well-defined social relationships. Beyond these roles, moreover, are the unwritten but cogent rules of being a football Rowdy.

These rules fall into two categories: interpretive and prescriptive. First, certain regular events must be given specific kinds of meaning. What constitutes a challenge to fight? What are "bundles," "riots," and acts of "provocation" on the part of the police, and when is a piece of territory "violated" by the "illegitimate" entry of rival Rowdies? These matters have to be quickly resolved by reference to a set of guidelines; for only when fans can decide the question "What is happening?" can the second, prescriptive question "What should be done?" be answered. Having used rules to define the situation, Rowdies call on rules for action to maintain the peculiar order of their collective behavior.

These prescriptive rules play a vital role because their major function is to keep social action within distinct boundaries. They stop fans from going too far in fights and attacks on rivals. In listening to the accounts of fans and through closely observing their actions, we have found that those who flout the rules or "go over the top" are subject to severe moral sanctions and social control. Their activities will be declared "out of order" or they will be viewed as Nutters and subsequently will be kept well in check by their peers. Throughout the accounts we have collected are references to actions that are "not right," "going too far," "not on," "out of order," "not playing the game," and "breaking the code." Even references to unwritten rules crop up in the Rowdies' everyday talk.

The mapping of these sets of rules is a task that is amenable to the interactive principles of a social psychology that regards as largely the result of self-monitoring and self-direction instead of as the outcome of environmental pressures. With this approach it is possible to develop a reasonably systematic discovery procedure that has been shown to be applicable to a variety of other settings. The first stage of such a procedure can begin before any accounts have been obtained from the participants, as long as the activities in question are easily visible. The use of film and video recordings can be of considerable value in these cases.

If you look at a disruption or a fight on the terraces, it is easy to imagine that something very bloody and dangerous is happening. One sees fists and boots flying and a surging mass of fans pouring over fences and barriers. It looks like mayhem and is described as such whenever television crews capture the incidents. But if you look very closely at films of these events, some remarkable things appear. Time after time the actual motor patterns of fighting seem to be tailor-made to cause only minimal injury. Straight punches or kicks to sensitive areas of the body are much rarer than are bent-arm blows to nonsensitive areas and kicks that connect with nothing at all. We have films of Rowdies who are lying on the ground, apparently being kicked senseless by five or six rivals—and at the end of such attacks the victim has picked himself up, dusted himself off, and walked away with only a few bruises.

The fact that there are rules against murderous assaults can be established in other ways than by examining films. More important, we have interviewed a great many Rowdies at length. Once one penetrates their vocabulary and understands how much exaggeration it contains, the rules against excessive violence become clear. In fact, we have not accepted anything as a real rule unless we found complete consensus on the matter among Rowdies. The following exchange is typical:

Questioner: What do you do when you put the boot in?

Fan A: You kicks em in the head don't you? . . . Strong boots with metal toecaps on and that.

Questioner: And what happens then?

(Quizzical look from Fan A)

Questioner: Well what happens to the guy you've kicked?

Fan A: He's dead.

Fan B: Nah—he's all right—usually anyway.

Here is another revealing interview:

Questioner: Do you think that when people are going into fights or "getting mad" that they aren't deliberately trying to hurt other people very much?

Mike: Oh Yes.

Questioner: Do you mean they are actually setting out to hurt them?

Mike: Yes—well you're just swinging around and when it's packed out and everybody's pushing to get at the same people—you can't really take any swings at anybody—it's, well, just feeble efforts really.

When pressed, Rowdies usually become realistic. Exaggeration, of course, is one of the rules of the game. And underlying these exaggerations are other rules. Even when a thousand fans are chanting, "You're gonna get your fucking head kicked in," physical violence may not follow—although that chant does convey a grave message of rising hostility. (Usually the chant follows a goal by the rival team—a warning that if the rival team wins the game, a fight will be justified.)

Aside from the rules implicit in fights between rivals and in the roles of Aggro Leader, Hooligan, Nutter, and so on, we found other rules governing: the level of challenge implicit in various insults, the goals of fighting, the termination of fights, and much more. To call someone a "cunt," for example, is much more provocative than to call him a "wanker." The goals of a fight include much more than the infliction of physical pain; if the enemy flees, the fight is won, and that is a sign to end it. In a one-on-one confrontation, certain displays of submission are usually enough to end hostilities. And this orderliness pervades a good deal of the lives of Rowdies on football day. For instance, virtually everyone we interviewed would follow an invariable sequence each Saturday when a game was scheduled: dressing in his special aggro gear (after getting up late); hanging around and "doing nothing" until about 1:30 in the afternoon; arriving at the soccer grounds between 1:30 and 2:00; achieving the critical Rowdy density on the terraces between 2:15 and 2:30; "seeing off" the visiting Rowdies after the game, between about 4:40 and 5:30; and then proceeding on to discos, pubs, and more hanging around.

One other way in which we established the existence of rules, limits, and other shared interpretations of behavior was by experiment. One of these experiments involved the meanings of the clothes Rowdies wear. We commissioned a series of 21 watercolor paintings depicting a single fan dressed in various combinations of the typical aggro gear we had found in a careful study of our films. Then we showed these paintings to a group of Rowdies and asked them what kinds of people the paintings depicted and how they were likely to behave. Their interpretations were not entirely consistent, but among experienced Rowdies (as distinguished from Novices) certain statistical patterns emerged from a computerized analysis.

Denim jackets made the models look "harder" than those without denim jackets. Club scarves, naturally, were a sign of "loyalty." (These terms are the Rowdies,' not ours.) Scarves on the wrist rather than around the neck indicated exceptional loyalty *and* hardness. Fans wearing such combinations as scarf, flag, T-shirt, and white baggy pants struck many boys as "right Hooligans," but they did not seem as hard as most of the other models. Jeans, boots, and denim jacket *without* a scarf pointed to hardness without loyalty, while models without scarves and who were otherwise dressed rather conventionally in casual jacket, trousers, and shoes seemed both hard and loyal. Why the latter interpretation? Because in the context of Rowdies, these more conventionally dressed fans looked like recent graduates of the Rowdy subculture, a type of fan called Town Boys, whose toughness and loyalty have already been proven.

Another experiment points up certain tacit rules not only of interpretation but of action. We took a true and typical story of a minor confrontation between two rival Rowdies and then changed some of its elements. After that we told the story and its variants to a series of Rowdies to see if they found anything wrong with it. Most of them agreed with what was right, what was wrong, and why.

The true story was simple. An Oxford Rowdy taunts a Sheffield Wednesday Rowdy. A fight ensues. Then a Town Boy intervenes and breaks it up. Everyone we told this story to found it commonplace and hardly worth talking about. But when we gave the story a new denouement—in which the Sheffield Wednesday fan calls over some of his mates, who then give the Oxford Rowdy a kicking—the boys objected. One commented: "You don't get your mates into it like that—well, only when there's too many of them or something and you're going to get kicked about or something like that. He could have just stood up or something and maybe they'd have had a go at each other. But nothing would have come of it 'cos the police are always around there [near the half-time tea stall where the incident was said to have taken place] and they'd soon move in. He's from Sheffield—I don't know—but he shouldn't get his mates in just for that—Oxford would get mad for that." This is a fairly subtle series of interpretations, and it was shared by others.

We changed the story again so that it ended with the Sheffield Wednesday fan simply walking away from his confrontation with the taunting Oxford Rowdy. A fan commented: "You can't just walk off like that. He ought to have done something. . . . If I was in there I'd just—well I'd just turn round and maybe have a bit of a go or something. . . . You shouldn't walk off like that so that he can think he's big like."

Our Rowdies generally agreed in their interpretations of these stories. If life on the terraces was truly disordered—anarchic, anomic, savage, unpredictable—the Rowdies would see nothing surprising however the story ended.

We must say again that even if social order, rather than anarchy, is the rule of the football terraces, there may still be something wrong with the whole phenomenon. A minisociety that looks coherent from the inside—and in fact is coherent hardly guarantees that all is well. From time to time people are hurt and property is damaged.

But given the fact that over half a million people are at football games every Saturday, it would be remarkable if this were not so. Rules on the terraces, like rules in any other area of society, do get broken. Moreover, since we can gain satisfaction and prestige at some relatively peaceful combination of work and play, there is no need for us to seek some alternative like the life of a football Rowdy, with its exaggerations, its machismo, and its frequent lack of a future. And yet to look at the terrace life from the inside is to see it much more clearly than outsiders commonly see it, and by looking at it from the inside we can understand its larger social functions and its value to those who participate in that life. It seems obvious to us, for one thing, that the Rowdies gain glory and excitement on the terraces that they cannot gain in the drab weekday world of home, school, work, and welfare. The normal society is not truly theirs, nor does it supply them with the satisfactions that orderly society is famous for. And so they have invented their own order. It may strike some people as barbaric, but it serves the Rowdies' purposes.

The outraged public often contrasts the orderly world of well-behaved spectators with the supposedly anarchic world of the Rowdies. They would do better to contrast the dull world of working-class youths headed for an even duller adulthood with the much more interesting world of the terraces. They would do well, too, to compare that terrace world with their own. Both societies include hierarchies, rules, standards, roles, careers, communities, and chances of achieving prestige. Both societies are similar in that they differ from collections of people in which all these rituals and institutions are absent and in which rules are arbitrary or nonexistent—and in which people are truly dehumanized, as they are by certain modern forms of war and propaganda. Although Rowdies and other subcultures of the young do not represent a problem of that order, they do indicate that some adolescents are abandoning the general social order in favor of another. And that should give us pause.

RELATED LITERATURE

Harre, Rom, and Paul F. Secord. *The Explanation of Social Behaviour.* Littlefield, Adams and Co., 1973.

Marsh, Peter. *Aggro: The Illusion of Violence.* J. M. Dent and Sons, 1978.

Marsh, Peter, Elizabeth Rosser, and Rom Harré. *The Rules of Disorder.* Routledge and Kegan Paul, 1978.

Willis, Paul. *Profane Culture.* Routledge and Kegan Paul, 1978.

Part IV

Sport in Cross-Cultural Context

Section A

Contrasting Styles of Sport Involvement

Few topics have captured the imagination of sport analysts as much as the notions that "sport is a mirror of society" and that "sport reflects national character." The topic is such a complex one that no studies have yet been designed that approach it in a systematic manner. Nevertheless, observational data and reasoned arguments provide us with some fascinating starting points for discussion.

In this section we shift our attention from dominant institutions (Part II) and divergent subgroups and subcultures (Part III) in order to focus upon the larger unit of analysis, the society or nation. By comparing the sports which occupy the highest profile, which capture the imagination of the nation, or which traditionally have been the acknowledged symbol of the nation's sporting interest—the national sport—we can move toward a deeper appreciation of the powerful relationship between sport and other expressive elements of a culture.

Geertz provides an insightful reminder that sport is often a significant cultural clue: a system which, once understood, unlocks the door to understanding many other profound aspects of the culture. During a field study in Bali, Geertz discovered that an important key to understanding the Balinese character was to understand the central position the cockfight held in their social experience. By understanding the concept of "deep play," Geertz was able to see a pattern to previously incomprehensible behavior.

Zurcher and Meadow confront most directly the topic of sport as a reflection of national character. They compare the family and sport systems in Mexico and the United States, hypothesizing that the structure of the family in these two countries is reproduced symbolically in the "national sport" of each. Specifically, Zurcher and Meadow hypothesize that sport provides a socially acceptable means through which to relieve the hostilities engendered by the authority structure of the family. Their analysis of the Mexican bullfight and American baseball provides a fascinating test of their hypothesis.

623

Deep Play: Notes on the Balinese Cockfight

Clifford Geertz

OF COCKS AND MEN

Bali, mainly because it is Bali, is a well-studied place. Its mythology, art, ritual, social organization, patterns of child rearing, forms of law, even style of trance, have all been microscopically examined for traces of that elusive substance Jane Belo called "The Balinese Temper."[1] But, aside from a few passing remarks, the cockfight has barely been noticed, although as a popular obsession of consuming power it is at least as important a revelation of what being a Balinese "is really like" as these more celebrated phenomena.[2] As much of America surfaces in a ball park, on a golf links, at a race track, or around a poker table, much of Bali surfaces in a cock ring. For it is only apparently cocks that are fighting there. Actually, it is men.

To anyone who has been in Bali any length of time, the deep psychological identification of Balinese men with their cocks is unmistakable. The double entendre here is deliberate. It works in exactly the same way in Balinese as it does in English, even to producing the same tired jokes, strained puns, and uninventive obscenities. Bateson and Mead have even suggested that, in line with the Balinese conception of the body as a set of separately animated parts, cocks are viewed as detachable, self-operating penises, ambulant genitals with a life of their own.[3] And while I do not have the kind of unconscious material either to confirm or disconfirm this intriguing notion, the fact that they are masculine symbols *par excellence* is about as indubitable, and to the Balinese about as evident, as the fact that water runs downhill.

The language of everyday moralism is shot through, on the male side of it, with roosterish imagery. *Sabung*, the word for cock (and one which appears in inscriptions as early as A.D. 922), is used metaphorically to

This is slightly abridged from "Deep Play: Notes on the Balinese Cockfight" by Clifford Geertz, Daedalus, 1972, pp. 1-37. Reprinted by permission of the publisher.

mean "hero," "warrior," "champion," "man of parts," "political candidate," "bachelor," "dandy," "lady-killer," or "tough guy." A pompous man whose behavior presumes above his station is compared to a tailless cock who struts about as though he had a large, spectacular one. A desperate man who makes a last, irrational effort to extricate himself from an impossible situation is likened to a dying cock who makes one final lunge at his tormentor to drag him along to a common destruction. A stingy man, who promises much, gives little, and begrudges that is compared to a cock which, held by the tail, leaps at another without in fact engaging him. A marriageable young man still shy with the opposite sex or someone in a new job anxious to make a good impression is called "a fighting cock caged for the first time.[4] Court trials, wars, political contests, inheritance disputes, and street arguments are all compared to cockfights.[5] Even the very island itself is perceived from its shape as a small, proud cock, poised, neck extended, back taut, tail raised, in eternal challenge to large, feckless, shapeless Java.[6]

But the intimacy of men with their cocks is more than metaphorical. Balinese men, or anyway a large majority of Balinese men, spend an enormous amount of time with their favorites, grooming them, feeding them, discussing them, trying them out against one another, or just gazing at them with a mixture of rapt admiration and dreamy self-absorbtion. Whenever you see a group of Balinese men squatting idly in the council shed or along the road in their hips down, shoulders forward, knees up fashion, half or more of them will have a rooster in his hands, holding it between his thighs, bouncing it gently up and down to strengthen its legs, ruffling its feathers with abstract sensuality, pushing it out against a neighbor's rooster to rouse its spirit, withdrawing it toward his loins to calm it again. Now and then, to get a feel for another bird, a man will fiddle this way with someone else's cock for a while, but usually by moving around to squat in place behind it, rather than just having it passed across to him as though it were merely an animal.

In the houseyard, the high-walled enclosures where the people live, fighting cocks are kept in wicker cages, moved frequently about so as to maintain the optimum balance of sun and shade. They are fed a special diet, which varies somewhat according to individual theories but which is mostly maize, sifted for impurities with far more care than it is when mere humans are going to eat it and offered to the animal kernel by kernel. Red pepper is stuffed down their beaks and up their anuses to give them spirit. They are bathed in the same ceremonial preparation of tepid water, medicinal herbs, flowers, and onions in which infants are bathed, and for a prize cock just about as often. Their combs are cropped, their plum-

.age dressed, their spurs trimmed, their legs massaged, and they are inspected for flaws with the squinted concentration of a diamond merchant. A man who has a passion for cocks, an enthusiast in the literal sense of the term, can spend most of his life with them, and even those, the overwhelming majority, whose passion though intense has not entirely run away with them, can and do spend what seems not only to outsider, but also to themselves, an inordinate amount of time with them. "I am cock crazy," my landlord, a quite ordinary *afficionado* by Balinese standards, used to moan as he went to move another cage, give another bath, or conduct another feeding. "We're all cock crazy."

The madness has some less visible dimensions, however, because although it is true that cocks are symbolic expressions or magnifications of their owner's self, the narcissistic male ego writ out in Aesopian terms, they are also expressions—and rather more immediate ones—of what the Balinese regard as the direct inversion, aesthetically, morally, and metaphysically, of human status: animality.

The Balinese revulsion against any behavior regarded as animal-like can hardly be overstressed. Babies are not allowed to crawl for that reason. Incest, though hardly approved, is a much less horrifying crime than bestiality. (The appropriate punishment for the second is death by drowning, for the first being forced to live like an animal.)[7] Most demons are represented—in sculpture, dance, ritual, myth—in some real or fantastic animal form. The main puberty rites consists in filing the child's teeth so they will not look like animal fangs. Not only defecation but eating is regarded as a disgusting, almost obscene activity, to be conducted hurriedly and privately, because of its association with animality. Even falling down or any form of clumsiness is considered to be bad for these reasons. Aside from cocks and a few domestic animals—oxen, ducks—of no emotional significance, the Balinese are aversive to animals and treat their large number of dogs not merely callously but with a phobic cruelty. In identifying with his cock, the Balinese man is identifying not just with his ideal self, or even his penis, but also, and at the same time, with what he fears, hates, and ambivalence being what it is, is fascinated by—The Powers of Darkness.

The connection of cocks and cockfighting with such Powers, with the animalistic demons that threaten constantly to invade the small, cleared off space in which the Balinese have so carefully built their lives and devour its inhabitants, is quite explicit. A cockfight, any cockfight, is in the first instance a blood sacrifice offered, with the appropriate chants and oblations, to the demons in order to pacify their ravenous, cannibal hunger. No temple festival should be conducted until one is made. (If it is omitted someone will inevitably fall into a trance and command with the voice of an angered spirit that the oversight be immediately corrected.) Collective responses to natural evils—illness, crop failure, volcanic eruptions —almost always involve them. And that famous holiday in Bali, The Day of Silence (*Njepi*), when everyone sits silent and immobile all day long in order to avoid contact with a sudden influx of demons chased momentarily out of hell, is preceded the previous day by large-scale cockfights (in this case legal) in almost every village on the island.

In the cockfight, man and beast, good and evil, ego and id, the creative power of aroused masculinity and the destructive power of loosened animality fuse in a bloody drama of hatred, cruelty, violence, and death. It is little wonder that when, as is the invariable rule, the owner of the winning cock takes the carcass of the loser—often torn limb from limb by its enraged owner—home to eat, he does so with a mixture of social embarrassment, moral satisfaction, aesthetic disgust, and cannibal joy. Or that a man who has lost an important fight is sometimes driven to wreck his family shrines and curse the gods, an act of metaphysical (and social) suicide. Or that in seeking earthly analogues for heaven and hell the Balinese compare the former to the mood of a man whose cock has just won, the latter to that of a man whose cock has just lost.

THE FIGHT

Cockfights (*tetadjen; sabungan*) are held in a ring about fifty feet square. Usually they begin toward late afternoon and run three or four hours until sunset. About nine or ten separate matches (*sehet*) comprise a program. Each match is precisely like the others in general pattern: there is no main match, no connection between individual matches, no variation in their format, and each is arranged on a completely ad hoc basis. After a fight has ended and the emotional debris is cleaned away— the bets paid, the curses cursed, the carcasses possessed—seven, eight, perhaps even a dozen men slip negligently into the ring with a cock and seek to find there a logical opponent for it. This process, which rarely takes less than ten minutes, and often a good deal longer, is conducted in a very subdued, oblique even dissembling manner. Those not immediately involved give it at best but disguised, sidelong attention; those who, embarrassedly, are, attempt to pretend somehow that the whole thing is not really happening.

A match made, the other hopefuls retire with the same deliberate indifference, and the selected cocks have their spurs (*tadji*) affixed— razor sharp, pointed steel swords, four or five inches long. This is a delicate job which only a small proportion of men, a half-dozen or so in most villages, know how to do properly. The man who attaches the spurs also provides them, and if the rooster he assists wins its owner awards him the spur-leg of the victim. The spurs are affixed by winding a long length of string around the foot of the spur and the leg of the cock. For reasons I shall come to presently, it is done somewhat differently from case to case, and is an obsessively deliberate affair. The lore about spurs is extensive—they are sharpened only at eclipses and the dark of the moon, should be kept out of the sight of women, and so forth. And they are handled, both in use and out, with the same curious combination of fussiness and sensuality the Balinese direct toward ritual objects generally.

The spurs affixed, the two cocks are placed by their handlers (who may or may not be their owners) facing one another in the center of the ring.[8] A coconut pierced with a small hole is placed in a pail of water, in which it takes about twenty-one seconds to sink, a period known as a *tjeng* and marked at beginning and end by the beating of a slit gong. During these twenty-one seconds the handlers (*pengangkeb*) are not permitted to touch their roosters. If, as sometimes happens, the animals have not fought during this time, they are picked up, fluffed, pulled, prodded, and otherwise insulted, and put back in the center of the ring and the process begins again. Sometimes they refuse to fight at all, or one keeps running away, in which case they are imprisoned together under a wicker cage, which usually gets them engaged.

Most of the time, in any case, the cocks fly almost immediately at one another in a wing-beating, head-thrusting, leg-kicking explosion of animal fury so pure, so absolute, and in its own way so beautiful, as to be almost abstract, a Platonic concept of hate. Within moments one or the other drives home a solid blow with his spur. The handler whose cock has delivered the blow immediately picks it up so that it will not get a return blow, for if he does not the match is likely to end in a mutually mortal tie as the two birds wildly hack each other to pieces. This is particularly true if, as often happens, the spur sticks in its victim's body, for then the aggressor is at the mercy of his wounded foe.

With the birds again in the hands of their handlers, the coconut is now sunk three times after which the cock which has landed the blow must be set down to show that he is firm, a fact he demonstrates by wandering idly around the rink for a coconut sink. The coconut is then sunk twice more and the fight must recommence.

During this interval, slightly over two minutes, the handler of the wounded cock has been working frantically over it, like a trainer patching a mauled boxer between rounds, to get it in shape for a last, desperate try for victory. He blows in its mouth, putting the whole chicken head in his mouth and sucking and blowing, fluffs it, stuffs its wounds with various sorts of medicines, and generally tries anything he can think of to arouse the last ounce of spirit which may be hidden somewhere within it. By the time he is forced to put it back down he is usually drenched in chicken blood, but, as in prize fighting, a good handler is worth his weight in gold. Some of them can virtually make the dead walk, at least long enough for the second and final round.

In the climactic battle (if there is one; sometimes the wounded cock simply expires in the handler's hands or immediately as it is placed down again), the cock who landed the first blow usually proceeds to finish off his weakened opponent. But this is far from an inevitable outcome, for if a cock can walk he can fight, and if he can fight, he can kill, and what counts is which cock expires first. If the wounded one can get a stab in and stagger on until the other drops, he is the official winner, even if he himself topples over an instant later.

Surrounding all this melodrama—which the crowd packed tight around the ring follows in near silence, moving their bodies in kinesthetic sympathy with the movement of the animals, cheering their champions on with wordless hand motions, shifting of the shoulders, turnings of the head, falling back *en masse* as the cock with the murderous spurs careens toward one side of the ring (it is said that spectators sometimes lose eyes and fingers from being too attentive), surging forward again as they glance off toward another—is a vast body of extraordinarily elaborate and precisely detailed rules.

These rules, together with the developed lore of cocks and cockfighting which accompanies them, are written down in palm leaf manuscripts (*lontar; rontal*) passed on from generation to generation as part of the general legal and cultural tradition of the villages. At at fight, the umpire (*saja komong; djuru kembar*)—the man who manages the coconut—is in charge of their application and his authority is absolute. I have never seen an umpire's judgment questioned on any subject, even by the more despondent losers, nor have I ever heard, even in private, a charge of unfairness directed against one, or, for that matter, complaints about umpires in general. Only exceptionally well-trusted, solid, and, given the complexity of the code, knowledgeable citizens perform this job, and in fact men will bring their cocks only to fights presided over by such men. It is also the umpire to whom accusations of cheating, which, though rare in the extreme, occasionally arise, are referred; and it is he who in the not infrequent cases where the cocks expire virtually together decides which (if either, for, though the Balinese do not care for such an outcome, there can be ties) went first. Likened to a judge, a king, a priest, and a policeman, he is all of these, and under his assured direction and animal passion of the fight proceeds within the civic certainty of the law. In the dozens of cockfights I saw in Bali, I never once saw an altercation about rules. Indeed, I never saw an open altercation, other than those between cocks, at all.

This crosswise doubleness of an event which, taken as a fact of nature, is rage untrammeled and, taken as a fact of culture, is form perfected, defines the cockfight as a sociological entity. A cockfight is what, searching for a name for something not vertebrate enough to be called a group and not structureless enough to be called a crowd, Erving Goffman has called a "focused gathering"—a set of persons engrossed in a common flow of activity and relating to one another in terms of that flow.[9] Such gatherings meet and disperse; the participants in them fluctuate; the activity that focuses them is discreet—a particulate process that reoccurs rather than a continuous one that endures. They take their form from the situation that evokes them, the floor on which they are placed, as Goffman puts it; but it is a form, and an articulate one, nonetheless. For the situation, the floor is itself created, in jury deliberations, surgical operations, block meetings, sit-ins, cockfights, by the cultural preoccupations—here, as we shall see, the celebration of status rivalry—which not only specify the focus but, assembling actors and arranging scenery, bring it actually into being.

In classical times (that is to say, prior to the Dutch invasion of 1908), when there were no bureaucrats around to improve popular morality, the staging of a cockfight was an explicitly societal matter. Bringing a cock to an important fight was, for an adult male, a compulsory duty of citizenship; taxation of fights, which were usually held on market day, was a major source of public revenue; patronage of the art was a stated responsibility of princes; and the cock ring, or *wantilan*, stood in the center of the village near those other monuments of Balinese civility—the council house, the origin temple, the marketplace, the signal tower, and the banyan tree. Today, a few special occasions aside, the new rectitude makes so open a statement of the connection between the excitements of collective life and those of blood sport impossible, but, less directly expressed, the connection itself intimate and intact. To expose it, however, it is necessary to turn to the aspect of cockfighting around which all the others pivot, and through which they exercise their force, an aspect I have thus far studiously ignored. I mean, of course, the gambling.

ODDS AND EVEN MONEY

The Balinese never do anything in a simple way that they can contrive to do in a complicated one, and to this generalization cockfight wagering is no exception.

In the first place, there are two sorts of bets, or *toh*.[10] There is the single axial bet in the center between the principals (*toh ketengah*), and there is the cloud of peripheral ones around the ring between members of the audience (*toh kesasi*). The first is typically large; the second typically small. The first is collective, involving coalitions of bettors clustering around the owner; the second is individual, man to man. The first is a matter of deliberate, very quiet, almost furtive arrangement by the coalition members and the umpire huddled like conspirators in the center of the ring; the second is a matter of impulsive shouting, public offers, and public acceptances by the excited throng around its edges. And most curiously, and as we shall see most revealingly, *where the first is always, without exception, even money, the second, equally without exception, is never such.* What is a fair coin in the center is a biased one on the side.

The center bet is the official one, hedged in again with a webwork of rules, and is made between the two cock owners, with the umpire as overseer and public witness.[11] This bet, which, as I say, is always relatively and sometimes very large, is never raised simply by the owner in whose name it is made, but by him together with four or five, sometimes seven or eight, allies—kin, village mates, neighbors, close friends. He may, if he is not especially well-to-do, not even be the major contributor, though, if only to show that he is not involved in any chicanery, he must be a significant one.

Of the fifty-seven matches for which I have exact and reliable data on the center bet, the range is from fifteen ringgits to five hundred, with a mean at eighty-five and with the distribution being rather noticeably trimodal: small fights (15 ringgits either side of 35) accounting for about 45 per cent of the total number; medium ones (20 riggits either side of 70) for about 25 percent; and large (75 ringgits either side of 175) for about 20 per cent, with a few very small and very large ones out at the extremes. In a society where the normal daily wage of a manual laborer—a brickmaker, an ordinary farmworker, a market porter—was about three ringgits a day, and considering the fact that fights were held on the average about every two-and-a-half days in the immediate area I studied, this is clearly serious gambling, even if the bets are pooled rather than individual efforts.

The side bets are, however, something else altogether. Rather than the solemn, legalistic pactmaking of the center, wagering takes place rather in the fashion in which the stock exchange used to work when it was out on the curb. There is a fixed and known odds paradigm which runs in a continuous series from ten-to-nine at the short end to two-to-two at the long: 10-9, 9-8, 8-7, 7-6, 6-5, 5-4, 4-3, 3-2, 2-1. The man who wishes to back the *underdog cock* (leaving aside how favorites, *kebut*, and underdogs, *ngai*, are established for the moment) shouts the short-side number indicating the odds he wants *to be given*. That is, if he shouts *gasal*, "five," he wants the underdog at five-to-four (or, for him, four-to-five); if he shouts "four," he wants it at four-to-three (again, he putting up the "three"), if "nine," at nine-to-eight, and so on. A man backing the favorite, and thus considering giving odds if he can get them short enough, indicates the fact by crying out the color-type of that cock—"brown," "speckled," or whatever.[12]

As odds-takers (backers of the underdog) and odds-givers (backers of the favorite) sweep the crowd with their shouts, they begin to focus in on one another as potential betting pairs, often from far across the ring. The taker tries to shout the giver into longer odds, the giver to shout the taker into shorter ones.[13] The taker, who is the wooer in this situation, will signal how large a bet he wishes to make at the odds he is shouting by holding a number of fingers up in front of his face and vigorously waving them. If the giver, the wooed, replies in kind, the bet is made; if he does not, they unlock gazes and the search goes on.

The side betting, which takes place after the center bet has been made and its size announced, consists then in a rising crescendo of shouts as backers of the underdog offer their propositions to anyone who will accept them, while those who are backing the favorite but do not like the price being offered, shout equally frenetically the color of the cock to show they too are desperate to bet but want shorter odds.

Almost always odds-calling, which tends to be very consensual in that at any one time almost all callers are calling the same thing, starts off toward the long end of the range—five-to-four or four-to-three—and then moves, also consensually, toward the short end with greater or less speed and to a greater or lesser degree. Men crying "five" and finding themselves answered only with cries of "brown" start crying "six," either drawing the other callers fairly quickly with them or retiring from the scene as their too-generous offers are snapped up. If the change is made and partners are still scarce, the procedure is repeated in a move to "seven," and so on, only rarely, and in the very largest fights, reaching the ultimate "nine" or "ten" levels. Occasionally, if the cocks are clearly mismatched, there may be no upward movement at all, or even a movement down the scale to four-to-three, three-to-two, very, very rarely two-to-one, a shift which is accompanied by a declining number of bets as a shift upward is accompanied by an increasing number. But the general pattern is for the betting to move a shorter or longer distance up the scale toward the, for sidebets, nonexistent pole of even money, with the overwhelming majority of bets falling in the four-to-three to eight-to-seven range.[14]

As the moment for the release of the cocks by the handlers approaches, the screaming, at least in a match where the center bet is large, reaches almost frenzied proportions as the remaining unfulfilled bettors try desperately to find a last minute partner at a price they can live with. (Where the center bet is small, the opposite tends to occur: betting dies off, trailing into silence, as odds lengthen and people lose interest.) In a large-bet, well-made match—the kind of match the Balinese regard as "real cockfighting"—the mob scene quality, the sense that sheer chaos is about to break loose, with all those waving, shouting, pushing, clambering men is quite strong, an effect which is only heightened by the intense stillness that falls with instant suddenness, rather as if someone had turned off the current, when the slit gong sounds, the cocks are put down, and the battle begins.

When it ends, anywhere from fifteen seconds to five minutes later, *all bets are immediately paid.* There are absolutely no IOU's, at least to a betting opponent. One may, of course, borrow from a friend before offering or accepting a wager, but to offer or accept it you must have the money already in hand and, if you lose, you must pay it on the spot, before the next match begins. This is an iron rule, and as I have never heard of a disputed umpire's decision (though doubtless there must sometimes be some), I have also never heard of a welshed bet, perhaps because in a worked-up cockfight crowd the consequences might be, as they are reported to be sometimes for cheaters, drastic and immediate.

It is, in any case, this formal assymetry between balanced center bets and unbalanced side ones that poses the critical analytical problem for a theory which sees cockfight wagering as the link connecting the fight to the wider world of Balinese culture. It also suggests the way to go about solving it and demonstrating the link.

The first point that needs to be made in this connection is that the higher the center bet, the more likely the match will in actual fact be an even one. Simple considerations of rationality suggest that. If you are betting fifteen ringgits on a cock, you might be willing to go along with even money even if you feel your animal somewhat the less promising. But if you are betting five hundred you are very, very likely to be loathe to do so. Thus, in large-bet fights, which of course involve the better animals, tremendous care is taken to see that the cocks are about as evenly matched as to size, general condition, pugnacity, and so on as is humanly possible. The different ways of adjusting the spurs of the animals are often employed to secure this. If one cock seems stronger, an agreement will be made to position his spur at a slightly less advantageous angle— a kind of handicapping, at which spur affixers are, so it is said, extremely skilled. More care will be taken, too, to employ skillful handlers and to match them exactly as to abilities.

In short, in a large-bet fight the pressure to make the match a genu- inely fifty-fifty proposition is enormous, and is consciously felt as such. For medium fights the pressure is somewhat less, and for small ones less yet, though there is always an effort to make things at least approximately equal, for even at fifteen ringgits (five days work) no one wants to make an even money bet in a clearly unfavorable situation. And, again, what statistics I have tend to bear this out. In my fifty-seven matches, the fav- orite won thirty-three times over-all, the underdog twenty-four, a 1.4 to 1 ratio. But if one splits the figures at sixty ringgits center bets, the ratios turn out to be 1.1 to 1 (twelve favorites, eleven underdogs) for those above this line, and 1.6 to 1 (twenty-one and thirteen) for those below it. Or, if you take the extremes, for very large fights, those with center bets over a hundred ringgits the ratio is 1 to 1 (seven and seven); for very small fights, those under forty ringgits, it is 1.9 to 1 (nineteen and ten).[15]

Now, from this proposition—that the higher the center bet the more exactly a fifty-fifty proposition the cockfight is—two things more or less immediately follow: (1) the higher the center bet, the greater is the pull on the side betting toward the short-odds end of the wagering spectrum and vice versa; (2) the higher the center bet, the greater the volume of side betting and vice versa.

The logic is similar in both cases. The closer the fight is in fact to even money, the less attractive the long end of the odds will appear and, there- fore, the shorter it must be if there are to be takers. That this is the case is apparent from mere inspection, from the Balinese's own analysis of the matter, and from what more systematic observations I was able to col- lect. Given the difficulty of making precise and complete recordings of side betting, this argument is hard to cast in numerical form, but in all my cases the odds-giver, odds-taker consensual point, a quite pronounced minimax saddle where the bulk (at a guess, two thirds to three-quarters in most cases) of the bets are actually made, was three or four points further along the scale toward the shorter end for the large-center-bet fights than for the small ones, with medium ones generally in between.

In detail, the fit is not, of course, exact, but the general pattern is quite consistent: the power of the center bet to pull the side bets toward its own even-money pattern is directly proportional to its size, because its size is directly proportional to the degree to which the cocks are in fact evenly matched. As for the volume question, total wagering is greater in large-center-bet fights because such fights are considered more "interesting," not only in the sense that they are less predictable, but, more crucially, that more is at stake in them—in terms of money, in terms of the quality of the cocks, and consequently, as we shall see, in terms of social prestige.[16]

The paradox of fair coin in the middle, biased coin on the outside is thus a merely apparent one. The two betting systems, though formally incongruent, are not really contradictory to one another, but part of a single larger system in which the center bet is, so to speak, the "center of gravity," drawing, the larger it is the more so, the outside bets toward the short-odds end of the scale. The center bet thus "makes the game," or perhaps better, defines it, signals what, following a notion of Jeremy Bentham's, I am going to call its "depth."

The Balinese attempt to create an interesting, if you will, "deep," match by making the center bet as large as possible so that the cocks matched will be as equal and as fine as possible, and the outcome, thus, as unpredictable as possible. They do not always succeed. Nearly half the matches are relatively trivial, relatively uninteresting—in my borrowed terminology, "shallow"—affairs. But that fact no more argues against my interpretation than the fact that most painters, poets, and playwrights are mediocre argues against the view that artistic effort is directed toward profundity and, with a certain frequency, approximates it. The image of artistic technique is indeed exact: the center bet is a means, a device, for creating "interesting," "deep" matches, *not* the reason, or at least not the main reason, *why* they are interesting, the source of their depth. The question why such matches are interesting—indeed, for the Balinese, exquisitely absorbing—takes us out of the realm of formal concerns into more broadly sociological and social-psychological ones, and to a less purely economic idea of what "depth" in gaming amounts to.[17]

PLAYING WITH FIRE

Bentham's concept of "deep play" is found in his *The Theory of Legislation*.[18] By it he means play in which the stakes are so high that it is, from his utilitarian standpoint, irrational for men to engage in it at all. If a man whose fortune is a thousand pounds (or ringgits) wages five hundred of it on an even bet, the marginal utility of the pound he stands to win is clearly less than the marginal disutility of the one he stands to lose. In genuine deep play, this is the case for both parties. They are both in over their heads. Having come together in search of pleasure they have entered into a relationship which will bring the participants, considered collectively, net pain rather than net pleasure. Bentham's conclusion was, therefore, that deep play was immoral from first principles and, a typical step for him, should be prevented legally.

But more interesting than the ethical problem, at least for our concerns here, is that despite the logical force of Bentham's analysis men do engage in such play, both passionately and often, and even in the face of law's revenge. For Bentham and those who think as he does (nowdays mainly lawyers, economists, and a few psychiatrists), the explanation is, as I have said, that such men are irrational—addicts, fetishists, children, fools, savages, who need only to be protected against themselves. But for the Balinese, though naturally they do not formulate it in so many words, the explanation lies in the fact that in such play money is less a measure of utility, had or expected, than it is a symbol of moral import, perceived or imposed.

It is, in fact, in shallow games, ones in which smaller amounts of money are involved, that increments and decrements of cash are more nearly synonyms for utility and disutility, in the ordinary, unexpanded sense—for pleasure and pain, happiness and unhappiness. In deep ones, where the amounts of money are great, much more is at stake than material gain: namely, esteem, honor, dignity, respect—in a word, though in Bali a profoundly freighted word, status.[19] It is at stake symbolically, for (a few cases of ruined addict gamblers aside) no one's status is actually altered by the outcome of a cockfight; it is only, and that momentarily, affirmed or insulted. But for the Balinese, for whom nothing is more pleasurable than an affront obliquely delivered or more painful than one obliquely received—particularly when mutual acquaintances, undeceived by surfaces, are watching—such appraisive drama is deep indeed.

This, I must stress immediately, is *not* to say that the money does not matter, or that the Balinese is no more concerned about losing five hundred ringgits than fifteen. Such a conclusion would be absurd. It is because money *does*, in this hardly unmaterialistic society, matter and matter very much that the more of it one risks the more of a lot of other things, such as one's pride, one's poise, one's dispassion, one's masculinity, one also risks, again only momentarily but again very publicly as well. In deep cockfights an owner and his collaborators, and, as we shall see, to a lesser but still quite real extent also their backers on the outside, put their money where their status is.

It is in large part *because* the marginal disutility of loss is so great at the higher levels of betting that to engage in such betting is to lay one's public self, allusively and metaphorically, through the medium of one's cock, on the line. And though to a Benthamite this might seem merely to increase the irrationality of the enterprise that much further, to the Balinese what it mainly increases is the meaningfulness of it all. And as (to follow Weber rather than Bentham) the imposition of meaning on life is the major end and primary condition of human existence, that access of significance more than compensates for the economic costs involved.[20] Actually, given the even-money quality of the larger matches, important changes in material fortune among those who regularly participate in them seem virtually nonexistent, because matters more or less even out over the long run. It is, actually, in the smaller, shallow fights, where one finds the handful of more pure, addict-type gamblers involved —those who *are* in it mainly for the money—that "real" changes in social position, largely downward, are affected. Men of this sort, plungers, are highly dispraised by "true cockfighters" as fools who do not understand what the sport is all about, vulgarians who simply miss the point of it all. They are, these addicts, regarded as fair game for the genuine enthusiasts, those who do understand, to take a little money away from, something that is easy enough to do by luring them, through the force of their greed, into irrational bets on mismatched cocks. Most of them do indeed manage to ruin themselves in a remarkably short time, but there always seems to be one or two of them around, pawning their land and selling their clothes in order to bet, at any particular time.[21]

This graduated correlation of "status gambling" with deeper fights and, inversely, "money gambling" with shallower ones is in fact quite general. Bettors themselves form a sociomoral hierarchy in these terms. As noted earlier, at most cockfights there are, around the very edges of the cockfight area, a large number of mindless, sheer-chance type gambling games (roulette, dice throw, coin-spin, pea-under-the-shell) operated by concessionaires. Only women, children, adolescents, and various other sorts of people who do not (or not yet) fight cocks—the extremely poor, the socially despised, the personally idiosyncratic—play at these games, at, of course, penny ante levels. Cockfighting men would be ashamed to go anywhere near them. Slightly above these people in standing are those who, though they do not themselves fight cocks, bet on the smaller matches around the edges. Next, there are those who fight cocks in small, or occasionally medium matches, but have not the status to join in the large ones, though they may bet from time to time on the side in those. And finally, there are those, the really substantial members of the community, the solid citizenry around whom local life revolves, who fight in the larger fights and bet on them around the side. The focusing element in these focused gatherings, these men generally dominate and define the sport as they dominate and define the society. When a Balinese male talks, in that almost venerative way, about "the true cockfighter," the *bebatoh* ("bettor") or *djuru kurung* ("cage keeper"), it is this sort of person, not those who bring the mentality of the pea-and-shell game into the quite different, inappropriate context of the cockfight, the driven gambler (*potét,* a word which has the secondary meaning of thief or reprobate), and the wistful hanger-on, that they mean. For such a man, what is really going on in a match is something rather closer to an *affaire d'honneur* (though, with the Balinese talent for practical fantasy, the blood that is spilled is only figuratively human) than to the stupid, mechanical crank of a slot machine.

What makes Balinese cockfighting deep is thus not money in itself, but what, the more of it that is involved the more so, money causes to happen: the migration of the Balinese status hierarchy into the body of the cockfight. Psychologically an Aesopian representation of the ideal/demonic, rather narcissistic, male self, sociologically it is an equally Aesopian representation of the complex fields of tension set up by the controlled, muted, ceremonial, but for all that deeply felt, interaction of those selves in the context of everyday life. The cocks may be surrogates for their owners' personalities, animal mirrors of psychic form, but cockfight is—or more exactly, deliberately is made to be—a simulation of the social matrix, the involved system of crosscutting, overlapping, highly corporate groups—villages, kingroups, irrigation societies, temple congregations, "castes"—in which its devotees live.[22] And as prestige, the necessity to affirm it, defend it, celebrate it, justify it, and just plain bask in it (but not, given the strongly ascriptive character of Balinese stratification, to seek it), is perhaps the central driving force in the society, so also—ambulant penises, blood sacrifices, and monetary exchanges aside—is it of the cockfight. This apparent amusement and seeming sport is, to take another phrase from Erving Goffman, "a status bloodbath."[23]

The easiest way to make this clear, and at least to some degree to demonstrate it, is to invoke the village whose cockfighting activities I observed the closest—the one in which the raid occurred and from which my statistical data are taken.

As all Balinese villages, this one—Tihingan, in the Klungkung region of southeast Bali—is intricately organized, a labyrinth of alliances and oppositions. But, unlike many, two sorts of corporate groups, which are also status groups, particularly stand out, and we may concentrate on them, in a part-for-whole way, without undue distortion.

First, the village is dominated by four large, patrilineal, partly endo-gamous descent groups which are constantly vying with one another and form the major factions in the village. Sometimes they group two and two, or rather the two larger ones versus the two smaller ones plus all the unaffiliated people; sometimes they operate independently. There are also subfactions within them, subfactions within the subfactions, and so on to rather fine levels of distinction. And second, there is the village itself, almost entirely endogamous, which is opposed to all the other vil-lages round about in its cockfight circuit (which, as explained, is the market region), but which also forms alliances with certain of these neigh-bors against certain others in various supra-village political and social contexts. The exact situation is thus, as everywhere in Bali, quite distinc-tive; but the general pattern of a tiered hierarchy of status rivalries be-tween highly corporate but various based groupings (and, thus, between the members of them) is entirely general.

Consider, then as support of the general thesis that the cockfight, and especially the deep cockfight, is fundamentally a dramatization of status concerns, the following facts, which to avoid extended ethnographic de-scription I will simply pronounce to be facts—though the concrete evi-dence-examples, statements, and numbers that could be brought to bear in support of them is both extensive and unmistakable:

1. A man virtually never bets against a cock owned by a member of his own kingroup. Usually he will feel obliged to bet for it, the more so the closer the kin tie and the deeper the fight. If he is certain in his mind that it will not win, he may just not bet at all, particularly if it is only a second cousin's bird or if the fight is a shallow one. But as a rule he will feel he must support it and, in deep games, nearly always does. Thus the great majority of the people calling "five" or "speckled" so demonstratively are expressing their allegiance to their kinsman, not their evaluation of his bird, their understanding of prob-ability theory, or even their hopes of unearned income.

2. This principle is extended logically. If your kingroup is not involved you will support an allied kingroup against an unallied one in the same way, and so on through the very involved networks of alli-ances which, as I say, make up this, as any other, Balinese village.

3. So, too, for the village as a whole. If an outsider cock is fighting any cock from your village you will tend to support the local one. If, what is rarer circumstance but occurs every now and then, a cock from outside your cockfight circuit is fighting one inside it you will also tend to support the "home bird."

4. Cocks which come from any distance are almost always favorites, for the theory is the man would not have dared to bring it if it was not a good cock, the more so the further he has come. His followers are, of course, obliged to support him, and when the more grand-scale legal cockfights are held (on holidays, and so on) the people of the village take what they regard to be the best cocks in the village, regardless of ownership, and go off to support them, although they will almost certainly have to give odds on them and to make large bets to show that they are not a cheapskate village. Actually, such "away games," though infrequent, tend to mend the ruptures between village members that the constantly occurring "home games," where village factions are opposed rather than united, exacerbate.

5. Almost all matches are sociologically relevant. You seldom get two outsider cocks fighting, or two cocks with no particular group backing, or with group backing which is mutually unrelated in any clear way. When you do get them, the game is very shallow, betting very slow, and the whole thing very dull, with no one save the immediate principals and an addict gambler or two at all interested.

6. By the same token, you rarely get two cocks from the same group, even more rarely from the same subfaction, and virtually never from the same sub-subfaction (which would be in most cases one extended family) fighting. Similarly, in outside village fights two members of the village will rarely fight against one another, even though, as bitter rivals, they would do so with enthusiasm on their home grounds.

7. On the individual level, people involved in an institutionalized hostility relationship, called *puik*, in which they do not speak or otherwise have anything to do with each other (the causes of this formal breaking of relations are many: wife-capture, inheritance arguments, political differences) will bet very heavily, sometimes almost maniacally, against one another in what is a frank and direct attack on the very masculinity, the ultimate ground of his status, of the opponent.

8. The center bet coalition is, in all but the shallowest games, *always* made up by structural allies—no "outside money" is involved. What is "outside" depends upon the context, of course, but given it, no outside money is mixed in with the main bet; if the principals cannot raise it, it is not made. The center bet, again especially in deeper games, is thus the most direct and open expression of social opposition, which is one of the reasons why both it and match making are surrounded by such an air of unease, furtiveness, embarrassment, and so on.

9. The rule about borrowing money—that you may borrow *for* a bet but not *in* one—stems (and the Balinese are quite conscious of this) from similar considerations: you are never at the *economic* mercy of your enemy that way. Gambling debts, which can get quite large on a rather short-term basis, are always to friends, never to enemies, structurally speaking.

10. When two cocks are structurally irrelevant or neutral so far as *you* are concerned (though, as mentioned, they almost never are to each other) you do not even ask a relative or a friend whom he is betting on, because if you know how he is betting and he knows you know, and you go the other way, it will lead to strain. This rule is explicit and rigid; fairly elaborate, even rather artificial precautions are taken to avoid breaking it. At the very least you must pretend not to notice what he is doing, and he what you are doing.

11. There is a special word for betting against the grain, which is also the word for "pardon me" (*mpura*). It is considered a bad thing to do, though if the center bet is small it is sometimes all right as long as you do not do it too often. But the larger the bet and the more frequently you do it, the more the "pardon me" tack will lead to social disruption.

12. In fact, the institutionalized hostility relation, *puik*, is often formally initiated (though its causes always lie elsewhere) by such a "pardon me" bet in a deep fight, putting the symbolic fat in the fire. Similarly, the end of such a relationship and resumption of normal social intercourse is often signalized (but, again, not actually brought about) by one or the other of the enemies supporting the other's bird.

13. In sticky, cross-loyalty situations, of which in this extraordinarily complex social system there are of course many, where a man is caught between two or more or less equally balanced loyalties, he tends to wander off for a cup of coffee or something to avoid having to bet, a form of behavior reminiscent of that of American voters in similar situations.[24]

14. The people involved in the center bet are, especially in deep fight, virtually always leading members of their group—kinship, village, or whatever. Further, those who bet on the side (including these people) are, as I have already remarked, the more established members of the village—the solid citizens. Cockfighting is for those who are involved in the everyday politics of prestige as well, not for youth, women, subordinates, and so forth.

15. So far as money is concerned, the explicitly expressed attitude toward it is that it is a secondary matter. It is not, as I have said, of no

importance; Balinese are no happier to lose several weeks' income than anyone else. But they mainly look on the monetary aspects of the cockfight as self-balancing, a matter of just moving money around, circulating it among a fairly well-defined group of serious cockfighters. The really important wins and losses are seen mostly in other terms, and the general attitude toward wagering is not any hope of cleaning up, of making a killing (addict gamblers again excepted), but that of the horseplayer's prayer: "Oh, God, please let me break even." In prestige terms, however, you do not want to break even, but, in a momentary, punctuate sort of way, win utterly. The talk (which goes on all the time) is about fights against such-and-such a cock of So-and-So which your cock demolished, not on how much you won, a fact people, even for large bets, rarely remember for any length of time, though they will remember the day they did in Pan Loh's finest cock for years.

16. You must bet on cocks of your own group aside from mere loyalty considerations, for if you do not people generally will say, "What! Is he too proud for the likes of us? Does he have to go to Java or Den Pasar [the capital town] to bet, he is such an important man?" Thus there is a general pressure to bet not only to show that you are important locally, but that you are not so important that you look down on everyone else as unfit even to be rivals. Similarly, home team people must bet against outside cocks or the outsiders will accuse it—a serious charge—of just collecting entry fees and not really being interested in cockfighting, as well as again being arrogant and insulting.

17. Finally, the Balinese peasants themselves are quite aware of all this and can and, at least to an ethnographer, do state most of it in approximately the same terms as I have. Fighting cocks, almost every Balinese I have ever discussed the subject with has said, is like playing with fire only not getting burned. You activate village and kin-group rivalries and hostilities, but in "play" form, coming dangerously and entrancingly close to the expression of open and direct interpersonal and intergroup aggression (something which, again, almost never happens in the normal course of ordinary life), but not quite, because, after all, it is "only a cockfight."

More observations of this sort could be advanced, but perhaps the general point is, if not made, at least well-delineated, and the whole argument thus far can be usefully summarized in a formal paradigm:

THE MORE A MATCH IS . . .

1. Between near status equals (and/or personal enemies)
2. Between high status individuals

THE DEEPER THE MATCH.

THE DEEPER THE MATCH . . .

1. The closer the identification of cock and man (or: more properly, the deeper the match the more the man will advance his best, most closely-identified-with cock).
2. The finer the cocks involved and the more exactly they will be matched.
3. The greater the emotion that will be involved and the more the general absorbtion in the match.
4. The higher the individual bets center and outside, the shorter the outside bet odds will tend to be, and the more betting there will be overall.
5. The less an "economic" and the more a "status" view of gaming will be involved, and the "solider" the citizens who will be gaming.[25]

Inverse arguments hold for the shallower the fight, culminating, in a reversed-signs sense, in the coin-spinning and dice-throwing amusements. For deep fights there are no absolute upper limits, though there are of course practical ones, and there are a great many legend-like tales of great Duel-in-the-Sun combats between lords and princes in classical times (for cockfighting has always been as much an elite concern as a popular one), far deeper than anything anyone, even aristocrats, could produce today anywhere in Bali.

Indeed, one of the great culture heroes of Bali is a prince, called after his passion for the sport, "The Cockfighter," who happened to be away at a very deep cockfight with a neighboring prince when the whole of his family—father, brothers, wives, sisters—were assassinated by commoner usurpers. Thus spared, he returned to dispatch the upstarts, regain the throne, reconstitute the Balinese high tradition, and build its most powerful, glorious, and prosperous state. Along with everything else that the Balinese see in fighting cocks—themselves, their social order, abstract hatred, masculinity, demonic power—they also see the archetype of status virtue, the arrogant, resolute, honor-mad player with real fire, the ksatria prince.[26]

FEATHERS. BLOOD, CROWDS, AND MONEY

"Poetry makes nothing happen, "Auden says in his elegy of Yeats, "it survives in the valley of its saying . . . a way of happening, a mouth." The cockfight too, in this colloquial sense, makes nothing happen. Men go on allegorically humiliating one another and being allegorically humiliated by one another, day after day, glorying quietly in the experience if they have triumphed, crushed only slightly more openly by it if they have not. *But no one's status really changes.* You cannot ascend the status ladder by winning cockfights; you cannot, as an individual, really ascend it at all. Nor can you descend it that way.[27] All you can do is enjoy and savor, or suffer and withstand, the concocted sensation of drastic and momentary movement along an aesthetic semblance of that ladder, a kind of behind-the-mirror status jump which has the look of mobility without its actuality.

As any art form—for that, finally, is what we are dealing with—the cockfight renders ordinary, everyday experience comprehensible by presenting it in terms of acts and objects which have had their practical consequences removed and been reduced (or, if you prefer, raised) to the level of sheer appearances, where their meaning can be more powerfully articulated and more exactly perceived. The cockfight is "really real" only to the cocks—it does not kill anyone, castrate anyone, reduce anyone to animal status, alter the hierarchical relations among people, nor refashion the hierarchy; it does not even redistribute income in any significant way. What it does is what, for other peoples with other temperaments and other conventions, *Lear* and *Crime and Punishment* do; it catches up these themes—death, masculinity, rage, pride, loss, beneficence, chance—and, ordering them into an encompassing structure, presents them in such a way as to throw into relief a particular view of their essential nature. It puts a construction on them, makes them, to those historically positioned to appreciate the construction, meaningful—visible, tangible, graspable—"real," in an ideational sense. An image, fiction, a model, a metaphor, the cockfight is a means of expression; its function is neither to assuage social passions nor to heighten them (though, in its play-with-fire way, it does a bit of both), but, in a medium of feathers, blood, crowds, and money, to display them.

The question of how it is that we perceive qualities in things—paintings, books, melodies, plays—that we do not feel we can assert literally to be there has come, in recent years, into the very center of aesthetic theory.[28] Neither the sentiments of the artist, which remain his, nor those of the audience, which remain theirs, can account for the agitation of one painting or the serenity of another. We attribute grandeur, wit, despair, exuberance to strings of sounds; lightness, energy, violence, fluidity to blocks of stone. Novels are said to have strength, buildings eloquence, plays momentum, ballets repose. In this realm of eccentric predicates, to say that the cockfight, in its perfected cases at least, is "disquietful" does not seem at all unnatural, merely, as I have just denied it practical consequence, somewhat puzzling.

The disquietfulness arises, "somehow," out of a conjunction of three attributes of the fight: its immediate dramatic shape; its metaphoric content; and its social context. A cultural figure against a social ground, the fight is at once a convulsive surge of animal hatred, a mock war of symbolical selves, and a formal simulation of status tensions, and its aesthetic power derives from its capacity to force together these diverse realities. The reason it is disquietful is not that it has material effects (it has some, but they are minor); the reason that it is disquietful is that, joining pride to selfhood, selfhood to cocks, and cocks to destruction, it brings to imaginative realization a dimension of Balinese experience normally well-obscured from view. The transfer of a sense of gravity into what is in itself a rather blank and unvarious spectacle, a commotion of beating wings and throbbing legs, is effected by interpreting it as expressive of something unsettling in the way its authors and audience live, or, even more ominously, what they are.

As a dramatic shape, the fight displays a characteristic that does not seem so remarkable until one realizes that it does not have to be there: a radically atomistical structure.[29] Each match is a world unto itself, a particulate burst of form. There is the match making, there is the betting, there is the fight, there is the result—utter triumph and utter defeat—and there is the hurried, embarrassed passing of money. The loser is not consoled. People drift away from him, look through him, leave him to assimilate his momentary descent into nonbeing, reset his face, and return, scarless an intact, to the fray. Nor are winners congratulated, or events rehashed; once a match is ended the crowd's attention turns totally to the next, with no looking back. A shadow of the experience no doubt remains with the principals, perhaps even with some of the witnesses, of a deep fight, as it remains with us when we leave the theater after seeing a powerful play well-performed; but it quite soon fades to become at most a schematic memory—a diffuse glow or an abstract shudder —and usually not even that. Any expressive form lives only in its own present—the one it itself creates. But, here, that present is severed into a string of flashes, some more bright than others, but all of them disconnected, aesthetic quanta. Whatever the cockfight says, it says in spurts.

But, as I have argued lengthily elsewhere, the Balinese live in spurts.[30] Their life, as they arrange it and perceive it, is less a flow, a directional movement out of the past, through the present, toward the future than an on-off pulsation of meaning and vacuity, an arhythmic alternation of short periods when "something" (that is, something significant) is happening and equally short ones where "nothing" (that is, nothing much) is—between what they themselves call "full" and "empty" times, or, in another idiom, "junctures" and "holes." In focusing activity down to a burning-glass dot, the cockfight is merely being Balinese in the same way in which everything from the monadic encounters of everyday life, through the clanging pointillism of *gamelan* music, to the visiting-day-of-the-gods temple celebrations are. It is not an imitation of the punctuateness of Balinese social life, nor a depiction of it, nor even an expression of it; it is an example of it, carefully prepared.[31]

If one dimension of the cockfight's structure, its lack of temporal directionality, makes it seem a typical segment of the general social life, however, the other, its flat-out, head-to-head (or spur-to-spur) aggressiveness, makes it seem a contradiction, a reversal, even a subversion of it. In the normal course of things, the Balinese are shy to the point of obsessiveness of open conflict. Oblique, cautious, subdued, controlled, masters of indirection and dissimulation—what they call *alus,* "polished," "smooth,"—they rarely face what they can turn away from, rarely resist what they can evade. But here they portray themselves as wild and murderous, manic explosions of instinctual cruelty. A powerful rendering of life as the Balinese most deeply do not want it (to adapt a phrase Frye has used of Gloucester's blinding) is set in the context of a sample of it as they do in fact have it.[32] And, because the context suggests that the rendering, if less than a straightforward description is nonetheless more than an idle fancy, it is here that the disquietfulness—the disquietfulness of the *fight,* not (or, anyway, not necessarily) its patrons, who seem in fact rather thoroughly to enjoy it—emerges. The slaughter in the cock ring is not a deception of how things literally are among men, but, what is almost worse, of how, from a particular angle, they imaginatively are.[33]

The angle, of course, is stratificatory. What, as we have already seen, the cockfight talks most forcibly about is status relationships, and what it says about them is that they are matters of life and death. That prestige is a profoundly serious business is apparent everywhere one looks in Bali—in the village, the family, the economy, the state. A peculiar fusion of Polynesian title ranks and Hindu castes, the hierarchy of pride is the moral backbone of the society. But only in the cockfight are the sentiments upon which that hierarchy rests revealed in their natural colors.

Enveloped elsewhere in a haze of etiquette, a thick cloud of euphemism and ceremony, gesture and allusion, they are here expressed in only the thinnest disguise of an animal mask, a mask which in fact demonstrates them far more effectively than it conceals them. Jealousy is as much a part of Bali as poise, envy as grace, brutality as charm; but without the cockfight the Balinese would have a much less certain understanding of them, which is, presumably, why they value it so highly.

Any expressive form works (when it works) by disarranging semantic contexts in such a way that properties conventionally ascribed to certain things are unconventionally ascribed to others, which are then seen actually to possess them. To call the wind a cripple, as Stevens does, to fix tone and manipulate timbre, as Schoenberg does, or, closer to our case, to picture an art critic as a dissolute bear, as Hogarth does, is to cross conceptual wires; the established conjunctions between objects and their qualities are altered and phenomena—fall weather, melodic shape, or cultural journalism—are clothed in signifiers which normally point to other referents.[34] Similarly, to connect—and connect, and connect—the collision of roosters with the devisiveness of status is to invite a transfer of perceptions from the former to the latter, a transfer which is at once a description and a judgment. (Logically, the transfer could, of course, as well go the other way; but, like most of the rest of us, the Balinese are a great deal more interested in understanding men than they are in understanding cocks.)

What sets the cockfight apart from the ordinary course of life, lifts it from the realm of everyday practical affairs, and surrounds it with an aura of enlarged importance is not, as functionalist sociology would have it, that it reinforces status discriminations (such reinforcement is hardly necessary in a society where every act proclaims them), but that it provides a metasocial commentary upon the whole matter of assorting human beings into fixed hierarchical ranks and then organizing the major part of collective existence around that assortment. Its function, if you want to call it that, is interpretive: it is a Balinese reading of Balinese experience; a story they tell themselves about themselves.

Notes

1. Jane Belo, "The Balinese Temper," in Jane Belo, ed., *Traditional Balinese Culture* (New York: Columbia University Press, 1970; originally published in 1935), pp. 85-110.
2. The best discussion of cockfighting is again Bateson and Mead's (*Balinese Character*, pp. 24-25, 140), but it, too, is general and abbreviated.

3. *Ibid.*, pp. 25-26. The cockfight is unusual within Balinese culture in being a single-sex public activity from which the other sex is totally and expressly excluded. Sexual differentiation is culturally extremely played down in Bali and most activities, formal and informal, involve the participation of men and women on equal ground, commonly as linked couples. From religion, to politics, to economics, to kinship, to dress, Bali is a rather "uni-sex" society, a fact both its customs and its symbolism clearly express. Even in contexts where women do not in fact play much of a role—music, painting, certain agricultural activities—their absence, which is only relative in any case, is more a mere matter of fact than socially enforced. To this general pattern, the cockfight, entirely of, by, and for men (women—at least *Balinese* women—do not even watch), is the most striking exception.

4. Christian Hooykaas, *The Lay of the Jaya Prana* (London, 1958), p. 39. The lay has a stanza (no. 17) with the reluctant bridegroom use. Jaya Prana, the subject of a Balinese Uriah myth, responds to the lord who has offered him the loveliest of six hundred servant girls: "Godly King, my Lord and Master/I beg you, give me leave to go/such things are not yet in my mind;/like a fighting cock encaged/indeed I am on my mettle/I am alone/as yet the flame has not been fanned."

5. For these, see V. E. Korn, *Het Adatrecht van Bali*, 2d ed. ('S-Gravenhage: G. Naeff, 1932), index under *toh*.

6. There is indeed a legend to the effect that the separation of Java and Bali is due to the action of a powerful Javanese religious figure who wished to protect himself against a Balinese culture hero (the ancestor of two Ksatria castes) who was a passionate cockfighting gambler. See Christiaan Hooykaas, *Agama Tirtha* (Amsterdam: Noord-Hollandsche, 1964), p. 184.

7. An incestuous couple is forced to wear pig yokes over their necks and crawl to a pig trough and eat with their mouths there. On this, see Jane Belo, "Customs Pertaining to Twins in Bali," in Belo, ed., *Traditional Balinese Culture*, p. 49; on the abhorence of animality generally, Bateson and Mead, *Balinese Character*, p. 22.

8. Except for unimportant, small-bet fights (on the question of fight "importance," see below) spur affixing is usually done by someone other than the owner. Whether the owner handles his own cock or not more or less depends on how skilled he is at it, a consideration whose importance is again relative to the importance of the fight. When spur affixers and cock handlers are someone other than the owner, they are almost always a quite close relative—a brother or cousin—or a very intimate friend of his. They are thus almost extensions of his personality, as the fact that all three will refer to the cock as "mine," say "I" fought So-and-So, and so on, demonstrates. Also, owner-handler-affixer triads tend to be fairly fixed, though individuals may participate in several and often exchange roles within a given one.

9. Erving Goffman, *Encounters: Two Studies in the Sociology of Interaction* (Indianapolis: Bobbs-Merrill, 1961), pp. 9-10.

10. This word, which literally means an indelible stain or mark, as in a birthmark or a vein in a stone, is used as well for a deposit in a court case, for a pawn, for security offered in a loan, for a stand-in for someone else in a legal or ceremonial context, for an earnest advanced in a business deal, for a sign placed in a field to indicate its ownership is in dispute, and for the status of an unfaithful wife from whose lover her husband must gain satisfaction or surrender her to him. See Korn, *Het Adatrecht van Bali*; Theodoor Pigeaud, *Javaans-Nederlands Handwoordenboek* (Groningen: Wolters, 1938); H. H. Juynboll, *Oudjavaansche-Nederlandsche Woordenlijst* (Leiden: Brill, 1923).

11. The center bet must be advanced in cash by both parties prior to the actual fight. The umpire holds the stakes until the decision is rendered and then awards them to the winner, avoiding, among other things, the intense embarrassment both winner and loser would feel if the latter had to pay off personally following his defeat. About 10 per cent of the winner's receipts are subtracted for the umpire's share and that of the fight sponsors.

12. Actually, the typing of cocks, which is extremely elaborate (I have collected more than twenty classes, certainly not a complete list), is not based on color alone, but on a series of independent, interacting, dimensions, which include, beside color, size, bone thickness, plumage, and temperament. (But *not* pedigree. The Balinese do not breed cocks to any significant extent, nor, so far as I have been able to discover, have they ever done so. The *asil*, or jungle cock, which is the basic fighting strain everywhere the sport is found, is native to southern Asia, and one can buy a good example in the chicken section of almost any Balinese market for anywhere from four or five ringgits up to fifty or more.) The color element is merely the one normally used as the type name, except when the two cocks of different types—as on principle they must be—have the same color, in which case a secondary indication from one of the other dimensions ("large speckled" v. "small speckled," etc.) is added. The types are coordinated with various cosmological ideas which help shape the making of matches, so that, for example, you fight a small, headstrong, speckled brown-on-white cock with flat-lying feathers and thin legs from the east side of the ring on a certain day of the complex Balinese calendar, and a large, cautious, all-black cock with tufted feathers and stubby legs from the north side on another day, and so on. All this is again recorded in palm-leaf manuscripts and endlessly discussed by the Balinese (who do not all have identical systems), and full-scale componential-cum-symbolic analysis of cock classifications would be extremely valuable both as an adjunct to the description of the cockfight and in itself. But my data on the subject, though extensive and varied, do not seem to be complete and systematic enough to attempt such an analysis here. For Balinese cosmological ideas more generally see Belo, ed., *Traditional Balinese Culture,* and J. L. Swellengrebel, ed., *Bali: Studies in Life, Thought, and Ritual* (The Hague: W. van Hoeve, 1960); for calendrical ones, Clifford Geertz, *Person, Time, and Conduct in Bali: An Essay in Cultural Analysis* (New Haven: Southeast Asia Studies, Yale University, 1966), pp. 45-53.

13. For purposes of ethnographic completeness, it should be noted that it is possible for the man backing the favorite—the odds-giver—to make a bet in which he wins if his cock wins or there is a tie, a slight shortening of the odds (I do not have enough cases to be exact, but ties seem to occur about once every fifteen or twenty matches). He indicates his wish to do this by shouting *sapih* ("tie") rather than the cock-type, but such bets are in fact infrequent.

14. The precise dynamics of the movement of the betting is one of the most intriguing, most complicated, and, given the hectic conditions under which it occurs, most difficult to study, aspects of the fight. Motion picture recording plus multiple observers would probably be necessary to deal with it effectively. Even impressionistically—the only approach open to a lone ethnographer caught in the middle of all this—it is clear that certain men lead both in determining the favorite (that is, making the opening cock-type calls which always initiate the process) and in directing the movement of the odds, these "opinion leaders" being the more accomplished cockfighters-cum-solid-citizens to be discussed below. If these men begin to change their calls, others follow; if they begin to make bets, so do others and—though there is always a large number of frustrated bettors crying for shorter or longer odds to the end—the movement more or less ceases. But a detailed understanding of the whole process awaits .what,

alas, it is not very likely ever to get: a decision theorist armed with precise observations of individual behavior.

15. Assuming only binomial variability, the departure from a fifty-fifty expectation in the sixty ringgits and below case is 1.38 standard deviations, or (in a one direction test) an eight in one hundred possibility by chance alone; for the below forty ringgits case it is 1.65 standard deviations, or about five in one hundred. The fact that these departures though real are not extreme merely indicates, again, that even in the smaller fights the tendency to match cocks at least reasonably evenly persists. It is a matter of relative relaxation of the pressures toward equalization, not their elimination. The tendency for high-bet contests to be coin-flip propositions is, of course, even more striking, and suggests the Balinese know quite well what they are about.

16. The reduction in wagering in smaller fights (which, of course, feeds on itself; one of the reasons people find small fights uninteresting is that there is less wagering in them, and contrariwise for large ones) takes place in three mutually reinforcing ways. First, there is a simple withdrawal of interest as people wander off to have a cup of coffee or chat with a friend. Second, the Balinese do not mathematically reduce odds, but bet directly in terms of stated odds as such. Thus, for a nine-to-eight bet, one man wagers nine ringgits, the other eight; for five-to-four, one wagers five, the other four. For any given currency unit, like the ringgit, therefore, 6.3 times as much money is involved in a ten-to-nine bet as in a two-to-one bet, for example, and, as noted, in small fights betting settles toward the longer end. Finally, the bets which are made tend to be one- rather than two-, three-, or in some of the very largest fights, four- or five-finger ones. (The fingers indicate the *multiples* of the stated bet odds at issue, not absolute figures. Two fingers in a six-to-five situation means a man wants to wager ten ringgits on the underdog against twelve, three in an eight-to-seven situation, twenty-one against twenty-four, and so on.)

17. Besides wagering there are other economic aspects of the cockfight, especially its very close connection with the local market system which, though secondary both to its motivation and to its function, are not without importance. Cockfights are open events to which anyone who wishes may come, sometimes from quite distant areas, but well over 90 per cent, probably over 95, are very local affairs, and the locality concerned is defined not by the village, nor even by the administrative district, but by the rural market system. Bali has a three-day market week with the familiar "solar-system" type rotation. Though the markets themselves have never been very highly developed, small morning affairs in a village square, it is the micro-region such rotation rather generally marks out— ten or twenty square miles, seven or eight neighboring villages (which in contemporary Bali is usually going to mean anywhere from five to ten or eleven thousand people) from which the core of any cockfight audience, indeed virtually all of it, will come. Most of the fights are in fact organized and sponsored by small combines of petty rural merchants under the general premise, very strongly held by them and indeed by all Balinese, that cockfights are good for trade because "they get money out of the house, they make it circulate." Stalls selling various sorts of things as well as assorted sheer-chance gambling games (see below) are set up around the edge of the area so that this even takes on the quality of a small fair. This connection of cockfighting with markets and market sellers is very old, as, among other things, their conjunction in inscriptions (Roelof Goris, *Prasasti Bali*, 2 vols. [Bandung: N. V. Masa Baru, 1954]) indicates. Trade has followed the cock for centuries in rural Bali and the sport has been one of the main agencies of the island's monetization.

18. The phrase is found in the Hildreth translation, International Library of Psychology, 1931, note to p. 106; see L. L. Fuller, *The Morality of Law* (New Haven: Yale University Press, 1964), pp. 6ff.

19. Of course, even in Bentham, utility is not normally confined as a concept to monetary losses and gains, and my argument here might be more carefully put in terms of a denial that for the Balinese, as for any people, utility (pleasure, happiness . . .) is merely identifiable with wealth. But such terminological problems are in any case secondary to the essential point: the cockfight is not roulette.

20. Max Weber, *The Sociology of Religion* (Boston: Beacon Press, 1963). There is nothing specifically Balinese, of course, about deepening significance with money, as Whyte's description of corner boys in a working-class district of Boston demonstrates: "Gambling plays an important role in the lives of Cornerville people. Whatever game the corner boys play, they nearly always bet on the outcome. When there is nothing at stake, the game is not considered a real contest. This does not mean that the financial element is all-important. I have frequently heard men say that the honor of winning was much more important than the money at stake. The corner boys consider playing for money the real test of skill and, unless a man performs well when money is at stake, he is not considered a good competitor." W. F. Whyte, *Street Corner Society*, 2d ed. (Chicago: University of Chicago Press, 1955), p. 140.

21. The extremes to which this madness is conceived on occasion to go—and the fact that it is considered madness—is demonstrated by the Balinese folktale *I Tuhung Kuning*. A gambler becomes so deranged by his passion that, leaving on a trip, he orders his pregnant wife to take care of the prospective newborn if it is a boy but to feed it as meat to his fighting cocks if it is a girl. The mother gives birth to a girl, but rather than giving the child to the cocks she gives them a large rat and conceals the girl with her own mother. When the husband returns the cocks, crowing a jingle, inform him of the deception and, furious, he sets out to kill the child. A goddess descends from heaven and takes the girl up to the skies with her. The cocks die from the food given them, the owner's sanity is restored, the goddess brings the girl back to the father who reunites him with his wife. The story is given as "Geel Komkommertje" in Jacoba Hooykaas-van Leeuwen Boomkamp, *Sprookjes en Verhalen van Bali* ('S-Gravenhage: Van Hoeve, 1956), pp. 19-25.

22. For a fuller description of Balinese rural social structure, see Clifford Geertz, "Form and Variation in Balinese Village Structure," *American Anthropologist*, 61 (1959), 94-108; "Tihingan, A Balinese Village," in R. M. Koentjaraningrat, *Villages in Indonesia* (Ithaca: Cornell University Press, 1967), pp. 210-243; and, though it is a bit off the norm as Balinese villages go, V. E. Korn, *De Dorpsrepubliek tnganan Pagringsingan* (Santpoort [Netherlands]: C. A. Mees, 1933).

23. Goffman, *Encounters*, p. 78.

24. B. R. Berelson, P. F. Lazersfeld, and W. N. McPhee, *Voting: A Study of Opinion Formation in a Presidential Campaign* (Chicago: University of Chicago Press, 1954).

25. As this is a formal paradigm, it is intended to display the logical, not the causal, structure of cockfighting. Just which of these considerations leads to which, in what order, and by what mechanisms, is another matter—one I have attempted to shed some light on in the general discussion.

26. In another of Hooykaas-van Leeuwen Boomkamp's folk tales ("De Gast," *Sprookies en Verhalen van Bali*, pp. 172-180), a low caste *Sudra*, a generous, pious, and carefree man who is also an accomplished cock fighter, loses, despite his accomplishment, fight after fight until he is not only out of money but down to his last cock. He does not despair, however—"I bet," he says, "upon the Unseen World."

His wife, a good and hard-working woman, knowing how much he enjoys cockfighting, gives him her last "rainy day" money to go and bet. But, filled with misgivings due to his run of ill luck, he leaves his own cock at home and bets merely on the side. He soon loses all but a coin or two and repairs to a food stand for a snack, where he meets a decrepit, odorous, and generally unappetizing old beggar leaning on a staff. The old man asks for food, and the hero spends his last coins to buy him some. The old man then asks to pass the night with the hero, which the hero gladly invites him to do. As there is no food in the house, however, the hero tells his wife to kill the last cock for dinner. When the old man discovers this fact, he tells the hero he has three cocks in his own mountain hut and says the hero may have one of them for fighting. He also asks for the hero's son to accompany him as a servant, and, after the son agrees, this is done.

The old man turns out to be Siva and, thus, to live in a great palace in the sky, though the hero does not know this. In time, the hero decides to visit his son and collect the promised cock. Lifted up into Siva's presence, he is given the choice of three cocks. The first crows: "I have beaten fifteen opponents." The second crows, "I have beaten twenty-five opponents." The third crows, "I have beaten the King." "That one, the third, is my choice," says the hero, and returns with it to earth.

When he arrives at the cockfight, he is asked for an entry fee and replies, "I have no money; I will pay after my cock has won." As he is known never to win, he is let in because the king, who is there fighting, dislikes him and hopes to enslave him when he loses and cannot pay off. In order to insure that this happens, the king matches his finest cock against the hero's. When the cocks are placed down, the hero's flees, and the crowd, led by the arrogant king, hoots in laughter. The hero's cock then flies at the king himself, killing him with a spur stab in the throat. The hero flees. His house is encircled by the king's men. The cock changes into a Garuda, the great mythic bird of Indic legend, and carries the hero and his wife to safety in the heavens.

When the people see this, they make the hero king and his wife queen and they return as such to earth. Later their son, released by Siva, also returns and the hero-king announces his intention to enter a hermitage. ("I will fight no more cockfights. I have bet on the Unseen and won.") He enters the hermitage and his son becomes king.

27. Addict gamblers are really less declassed (for their status is, as everyone else's, inherited) than merely impoverished and personally disgraced. The most prominent addict gambler in my cockfight circuit was actually a very high caste *satria* who sold off most of his considerable lands to support his habit. Though everyone privately regarded him as a fool and worse (some, more charitable, regarded him as sick), he was publicly treated with the elaborate deference and politeness due his rank. On the independence of personal reputation and public status in Bali, see Geertz, *Person, Time, and Conduct,* pp. 28-35.

28. For four, somewhat variant, treatments, see Susanne Langer, *Feeling and Form* (New York: Scribners, 1953); Richard Wollheim, *Art and Its Objects* (New York: Harper and Row, 1968); Nelson Goodman, *Language of Art* (Indianapolis: Bobbs-Merrill, 1968); Maurice Merleau-Ponty, "The Eye and the Mind," in his, *The Primacy of Perception* (Evanston: Northwestern University Press, 1964), pp. 159-190.

29. British cockfights (the sport was banned there in 1840) indeed seem to have lacked it, and to have generated, therefore, a quite different family of shapes. Most British fights were "mains," in which a preagreed number of cocks were aligned into two teams and fought serially. Score was kept and wagering took place both on the individual matches and on the main as a whole. There were also "battle Royales," both in England and on the Continent, in which a large number of cocks were let loose at once with the one left standing at the end

the victor. And in Wales, the so-called "Welsh main" followed an elimination pattern, along the lines of a present-day tennis tournament, winners proceeding to the next round. As a genre, the cockfight has perhaps less compositional flexibility than, say, Latin comedy, but it is not entirely without any. On cockfighting more generally, see Arch Ruport, *The Art of Cockfighting* (New York: Devin-Adair, 1949); G. R. Scott, *History of Cockfighting* (1957); and Lawrence Fitz-Barnard, *Fighting Sports* (London: Odhams Press, 1921).

30. *Person, Time, and Conduct,* esp. pp. 42ff. I am, however, not the first person to have argued it: see G. Bateson, "Bali, the Value System of a Steady State," and "An Old Temple and a New Myth," in Belo, ed., *Traditional Balinese Culture,* pp. 384-402 and 111-136.

31. For the necessity of distinguishing among "description," "representation," "exemplification," and "expression" (and the irrelevance of "imitation" to all of them) as modes of symbolic reference, see Goodman, *Languages of Art,* pp. 6-10, 45-91, 225-241.

32. Northrop Frye, *The Educated Imagination* (Bloomington: University of Indiana Press, 1964), p. 99.

33. There are two other Balinese values and disvalues which, connected with punctuate temporarily on the one hand and unbridled aggressiveness on the other, reinforce the sense that the cockfight is at once continuous with ordinary social life and a direct negation of it: what the Balinese call *ramé,* and what they call *paling. Ramé* means crowded, noisy, and active, and is a highly sought after social state: crowded markets, mass festivals, busy streets are all *ramé,* as, of course, is, in the extreme, a cockfight. *Ramé* is what happens in the "full" times (its opposite, *sepi,* "quiet," is what happens in the "empty" ones). *Paling* is social vertigo, the dizzy, disoriented, lost, turned around feeling one gets when one's place in the coordinates of social space is not clear, and it is a tremendously disfavored, immensely anxiety-producing state. Balinese regard the exact maintenance of spatial orientation ("not to know where north is" is to be crazy), balance, decorum, status relationships, and so forth, as fundamental to ordered life (*krama*) and *paling,* the sort of whirling confusion of position the scrambling cocks exemplify as its profoundest enemy and contradiction. On *rame,* see Bateson and Mead, *Balinese Character,* pp. 3, 64; on *paling, ibid.,* p. 11, and Belo, ed., *Traditional Balinese Culture,* pp. 90ff.

34. The Stevens reference is to his "The Motive for Metaphor," ("You like it under the trees in autumn,/Because everything is half dead./The wind moves like a cripple among the leaves/And repeats words without meaning"); the Schoenberg reference is to the third of his *Five Orchestral Pieces* (Opus 16), and is borrowed from H. H. Drager, "The Concept of 'Tonal Body,'" in Susanne Langer, ed., *Reflections on Art* (New York: Oxford University Press, 1961), p. 174. On Hogarth, and on this whole problem—there called "multiple matrix matching"—see E. H. Gombrich, "The Use of Art for the Study of Symbols," in James Hogg, ed., *Psychology and the Visual Arts* (Baltimore: Penguin Brooks, 1969), pp. 149-170. The more usual term for this sort of semantic alchemy is "metaphorical transfer," and good technical discussions of it can be found in M. Black, *Models and Metaphors* (Ithaca: Cornell University Press, 1962), pp. 25ff; Goodman, *Language as Art,* pp. 44ff; and W. Percy, "Metaphor as Mistake," *Sewanee Review,* 66 (1958), 78-99.

On Bullfights and Baseball: An Example of Interaction of Social Institutions

Louis A. Zurcher, Jr. and Arnold Meadow

A "social institution," typically considered, is "a comparatively stable, permanent and intricately organized system of behavior formally enforced within a given society and serving social objectives regarded as essential for the survival of the group." Four major social institutions are found very widely in human society: 1) economic, 2) familial, 3) political, and 4) religious. Through these the society strives to achieve material well-being, an adequate population, organization, and some feeling of control over the unknown or unexpected. As a society becomes more urbanized, more "highly developed," it may evolve additional institutions, such as the recreational, the educational and the aesthetic, which take over functions no longer adequately performed by the basic four.

Since individuals have overlapping roles in a number of the society's institutions, and since each institution is a functional segment of the total, ongoing society, the interaction of institutions presents itself as a fruitful area for study. This interaction is a key variable in the process of social change and highlights cultural themes running through the structures of a society.

The central institution of a society and its primary agent of socialization is the family—which interacts in various degrees with other institutions. Whiting and Child, for example, have described the impact of values learned in the family upon behavior in other social institutions (1953). Kardiner has written of the ways in which the religious institution is shaped by family patterns (1939). Tumin has described the interaction between the family and the economic institution (1956).

From *International Journal of Comparative Sociology*, 1967, Vol. 8:99-117. Copyright 1967 by E. J. Brill, Publisher. Reprinted by permission of the publisher.

In this paper the authors will focus their attention on some aspects of the interaction between two social institutions: 1) the family and 2) the institutionalized recreation form known as the "national sport." It is hypothesized that the national sport symbolizes in its structure and function the processes in the modal family that both engender and restrict hostility toward authority, and that it also exemplifies a socially legitimized means for the expression of that hostility.

As Dollard has described it, the socialization process itself engenders hostility toward authority. The demands of socialization, which of course have their focal point in the family, conflict in many instances with the child's own behavioral choices. The child is thus frustrated and desires to move against the restrictive figure but does not do so because he fears punishment. This fear acts as a catalyst, inciting further aggressive feelings toward the frustrating agent. Repression of this aggression is not complete and the individual seeks sources for its legitimized expression (1938).

Hostility toward authority is especially generated in the authoritarian family milieu, or when some characteristics of the parents create for the child an uncertainty of or rejection of his or the parent's familial role. Situations such as this not only arouse keen hostility but are also usually unyieldingly restrictive and harshly punitive of any demonstration of that hostility.

From another view, it is quite possible that hostility toward authority is a lesson of, as well as a reaction to, socialization. That is the characteristics of the society may be such that a general distrust for or hatred of authority has become part of the cultural value system. This is particularly the case in those societies which have undergone long periods of manipulation and oppression under a tyrannical or exploitative power structure.

Since every society depends, from the family up, on authority to maintain relative consistency of behavior, and since not all the members of the society will take well to that restrictive authority, it follows that the society must provide as a further means of control some outlet for the resultant hostility toward authority—not only that incited in the family situation or learned in socialization, but also the generalized forms of hostility that are re-awakened and intensified by the demands of interpersonal relations. The provisions for such expression, as well as the degree to which it is controlled, vary from society to society. As Dollard points out, "Each society standardizes its own permissive patterns, and differs from the next in the degree to which hostility may be expressed" (1938).

In the terminology of modern dynamic psychiatry, it can be said that the defense processes which societies employ to channel hostility differ from culture to culture. These defense processes will be differentially manifested not only in the families of different societies, but also, as we hypothesize, in their "national sports," since both are institutions of these societies.

Play has been considered by a number of social scientists to be of major importance in the socialization and personality formation of the individual. Other writers have seen the various forms of play as reflecting the particular traits, values, expectations, and the degree of social control in a given culture. In addition to the foregoing functions, play is a "permissive pattern," a "channel" serving as a legitimized means for the symbolic demonstration of hostility toward authority figures.

There is a hierarchy of play extending from seemingly purposeless, repetitive movements in the crib, through games (with competition, an "ethic" of some sort, elaborate rules and regulations, mutual player expectations, and an ostensible purpose), up to the highest level of complexity, the "organized sport" (with schedules, painstaking record keeping, large audiences, governing bodies supplying officials and dispensing rules, "seasons," recruiting, training, and if professional, the paying of participants). The "national sport" is an organized sport that has been adopted by a nation as its own special "home-owned" variety. When, for example, the "American Way" is alluded to, it implies, among other things, apple pie, hot-dogs, mothers, Disneyland and *baseball*.

It is hypothesized, then, that the national sport, as the epitome of institutionalized recreation, maximally reflects that aspect of the "social character" of a society which establishes the degree of tolerance for the expression of hostility toward authority. Furthermore, it is hypothesized that the national sport replicates, on the playing field or in the arena, the family processes which engender, exacerbate or restrict that hostility, and will manifest the "societal ideal" for its expression.

Baseball is the national sport of the United States of America. Its counterpart in the United States of Mexico is the *corrida de toros*, the bullfight. It should be mentioned here that the *aficionado* (dedicated fan) would object to the association of the bullfight with the term "sport," and there are good arguments in support of his opinion. For the sake of parsimony, however, and since the bullfight approaches the criteria established in this paper, it will be considered, for analysis, the equivalent of a national sport. An analysis of baseball and the bullfight, and of the modal family patterns in their respective societies, should reveal, especially with regard to the dynamic of hostility toward authority, a facet of the interaction between the social institutions of family and recreation. In addition to the formation and legitimized expression of hostility, the analysis should reveal, as they appear in both the family and the sport, some of the characteristic defense mechanisms, values and social relationships shared by members in each of the two societies.

ANALYSIS OF FAMILY PATTERNS

The Mexican family typically is described as a proving ground for the dominance needs of the father. Though the family structure is essentially mother centered, the father compulsively strives to maintain his *macho* (manly) role and to prove that he has *huevos largos* (large "eggs"), *muy cojones* (abundant testicles) or "hair on his chest" by playing the role of the emotionally detached but severely authoritarian head of the household. He overtly disparages the achievements of, violently disapproves of any show of independence in, and physically punishes any demonstration of hostility by his wife or children. Often the children are punished by their father for sins (especially sexual) projected upon them from his own guilt-ridden repertoire. Drunkeness, promiscuity and abandonment, as components of *machismo*, further compound the overpowering image of father. This pattern of behavior has been detailed in the literature by Lewis (1961), Gillin (1961), Meadow et al. and Diaz-Guerrero (1961).

The question then arises, how do the children, especially the males, handle the hostility that they cannot direct against the mitigated feudalism of such an unyielding socialization figure as the Mexican father? It appears that the son attempts to recoup his identity by emulating the father's example, but he does so in other quarters (dominating his younger sisters and brothers, fighting, being sexually promiscuous). The wife and daughters seem to develop a solidly female "mutual protection society," adopt a passively controlling "martyr" role and wait patiently to seize control whenever the father's dominance falters. Thus exists a climate which fosters over-compensating sons, with ambivalence (passive-aggressive) toward the father, and daughters who, because of hostility toward a punishing father, distrust all men.

A safe but indirect manner for the Mexican male to express hostility against his father, then, seems to be one of "showing the old boy that I am as much, or more, man than he is." This, however, cannot be done in direct confrontation. Rather it is done in spheres away from the father's bailiwick—away from his watchful eye. As Jesus Sanchez puts it, "to grow up away from your parents helps you to become mature." (Lewis, 1961). The son can't compete with the father directly, so he acts out his hostility guided by his father's examples, but on his own terms in his own battle field.

The family is, of course, a reflection of and the basis for culture. Mexican culture is, as is the family, authoritarian and hierarchial in structure. Though Mexican citizens have a general distrust of and disregard for the "officials" in government, church and other large-scale organizations, they are most hesitant to directly or overtly criticize them. This passiveness in the face of authority has, as the passiveness to the father, an aggressive counterpart. As a matter of fact, Meadow et al., in depth studies of Mexican psychopathology, cite different degrees of passive-aggressiveness as a central feature of the modal personality of the Mexican. Does this aggressive component demonstrate itself in a socially acceptable manner in a Mexican institution? The premise here is that the bullfight will relive aspects of the frustration engendering conflict and provide an outlet for the resultant aggression. It would be expected, from observations of the Mexican family and from examination of the symptom-formation in Mexican psychopathology, that the legitimized expression would be of a type allowing "acting out" of hostility. But first, before considering the bullfight itself, let us examine by contrast the situation in the Anglo-American family.

If the Anglo-American father were to attempt to follow the dominance pattern of his Mexican counterpart, he would posthaste be imprisoned, divorced with the condemnation of the court, or at best, socially ostracized.

In the Anglo nuclear family, as in the Anglo culture, the ideological byword is equality. Mother, father, son and daughter are "members of the group" and have a *right* to be heard, to voice their opinion and to register their vote around the family conference table. Everyone "shares the responsibility" and "pulls his weight" in the "togetherness" of the family.

The Anglo ethic, loaded as it is with the popular meaning of "democracy," encourages an unrealistic muting of authority as it exists in the society. Fathers and mothers are not supposed to be authority figures but "pals," "buddies," "good heads" and "regular guys." They are still, however, expected to be the prime socialization agents of Anglo society, and as such, must impress upon the child an awareness of behavior which is accepted and expected by that society. This cannot be done without the exertion of authority. Socialization makes demands that often are contrary to the child's own preferences. Thus, the frustration-aggression cycle is manifested. But how can the child demonstrate overt hostility to a "pal," a "buddy" or an equal. Furthermore, the vagueness of the parental role in the Anglo family presents the child with a mercurial identification model. Should he be dependent upon or independent of his parents—and when? Mother preaches togetherness, but usually agrees with the television and movie stereotype of the well-meaning, bungling father who needs her subtle domination.

Authoritarianism from people who are not supposed to be authoritarian, vagueness of or conflict in role expectations, obscure role models, plus the restrictions of socialization, set the stage for hostility toward authority in the Anglo family. Typically, however, this hostility, and in fact most familial conflict, is intellectualized and abstracted into elaborate displacements and double-bind communications.

The Mexican child seems to have clear reason for hostility, but can't reveal it to the father because he may be beaten. He can't be hostile to the mother because she was a "saint." The Anglo child has difficulty showing overt hostility in his family because, first, he has a hard time tracing the basis for his frustration, and second, he can't be aggressive to two "buddies." But the hostility from socialization and role conflict is still there and needs expression.

The Mexican is forced to be passive to the frustrating agent, but along with this passiveness rides an aggressive component. If the Mexican has been shaped into a passive-aggressive, then it seems feasible to posit as a central feature of the Anglo modal personality the defense mechanism of intellectualization. The Anglo child learns from his parents to intellectualize conflict, to abstract hostility, to disengage it from painful affect, and to deal with it in a symbolic, ritualistic fashion. Whereas the Mexican acts out his hostility, the Anglo rationalizes it and elaborately disguises it with verbal repartee. Manual Sanchez observed "life in the United States is too abstract, too mechanical. The people are like precision machines" (Lewis, 1961).

As does the Mexican family in the Mexican culture, the Anglo family reflects and maintains the Anglo culture. Anglo society has been characterized by a plethora of writers as being abstract, universalistic, materialistic, impersonal, unemotional and bureaucratic. One would expect, then, the ideal legitimized outlets for hostility to be similarly complex, elaborately diffuse, and intellectualized, impersonalized and de-affected after a bureaucratic fashion. The national sport of the United States, baseball, we have hypothesized, should fully reflect this pattern.

THE BULLFIGHT

Aficionados who are of a mind to describe the essence of the bull-fight do so in terms that parallel the *corrida* with a Greek drama. Robinson writes that the theme of the bullfight lies "somewhere between the themes of fate and death" (1964). Allen proclaims the bullfight to be "the last drama of our times that has death as an immediate object" (1953). In *The Brave Bulls*, two of Lea's Mexican characters discuss the *fiesta brava* as follows:

> ". . . It is a form of drama as certainly as the works of Sophocles. But what a difference between the happenings on a stage or in a poem, and the happening in a plaza!"

> ". . . The festival of bulls is the only art form in which violence, bloodshed, and death are palpable and unfeigned. It is the only art in which the artist deals actual death and risks actual death that gives the art its particular power. . . ." (Lea, 1949).

Who, then, do the principals in this drama represent? Who is killing, and who is being killed? We have hypothesized that the events in the bullfight will provide a socially legitimized symbolic vehicle for the aggression toward authority which has been developed mainly in and by the Mexican family situation.

Since the reader may be unfamiliar with the structure of the bullfight, we shall undertake here a brief description before proceeding to the analysis.

Prior to the appearance of any of the principals in the *corrida*, the *alguacil*, a mounted bailiff, rides across the bull ring and, with a bow and a flourish, renders his respect to the Presidente (a national, state or local official), who is in charge of the conduct of the bullfight. The *alguacil* will thereafter be the courier for the *Presidente*, and will transmit orders from him to the principals in the *corrida*. Thus is the hierarchial nature of Mexican society represented in the bullfight. No major shift in action, no new sequence is attempted without first gaining the nod of the *Presidente*. It is he who will pass final judgment upon the performance of the *matador*. He, and only he can decide that the bull shall live (on rare occasions), or die. In essence he has the power of life and death. It is interesting to note that, though disapproval in the highly emotional framework of the *corrida* may incite the crowd eloquently and thoroughly to curse and insult the *matador*, his assistants, his mother, father, *compadres*, lovers, children and future children, there is seldom a harsh word directed toward the sacrosanct *Presidente*. This respect remains, ironically, while symbolically authority is about to be murdered in the ring!

Upon receiving the nod from the *Presidente,* the *alguacil* rides out of the ring to lead back the *paseo,* or parade, which consists of in splendid order the *matadors,* their *banderilleros* (assistants), the *picadors,* the ring attendants and the harnessed team whose task it will be to remove the dead bull from the ring. The *matadors* halt directly beneath the *Presidente* and bow their respect. Following this, all the principals, usually with the exception of a *banderillero,* leave the ring. The *Presidente* gives permission for the bull to be released, and the assistant receives the bull.

The bullfight itself consists of three major parts (*Los Tres Tercios de la Lidia*). In the first, the *banderilleros* work the bull with the cape, thus allowing the *matador* to observe the toro's idiosyncracies (direction of hook, favored eye and straightness of charge). Then the *picadors* pic the bull, this to demonstrate the bull's courage (by his charge to the horse) and to lower his head. Following this, the ring is cleared—the bull remains, having "conquered," for a moment, all his antagonists. The *banderilleros* (sometimes the *matador*), in the second major part, place the *banderillas* (barbed sticks), these to correct for the bull's tendency to hook in one or the other direction. The third part consists of *brindis,* or formal dedication of the bull to the *Presidente* (then to anyone else in the crowd the matador chooses), the work with the *muleta* (small red cloth), and, finally, the sword.

Since there are two bulls for each *matador,* and two or three *matadors* in each bullfight, these three segments are repeated from four to six times in an afternoon.

Such is the bare structure of the bullfight. This tells nothing of the key to, the vitality of, the drama in the ring, the feeling in the crowd or the symbolic expression of hostility.

Perhaps a discussion of this can best be introduced by quoting the *matador* protagonist in Ramsey's *Fiesta* as he describes, when facing the bull, "a fear that never quite left him, and that encompassed others too indefinite for him to understand or even name, a fear of authority, of the powerful, the patron. . . ." (Ramsey, 1955) of the *father!* Freedom from this authority is granted, he contends, in those rare moments when fear is combated and overcome.

Characteristically, the Mexican son profoundly fears his father. Manuel Sanchez testifies that in order to become a man, the individual must escape his father. Yet it was not until he, himself, was twenty-nine years old that he smoked in his father's presence. At that time, Manuel, though fearful, felt himself to be acting most bravely by showing his father that he was a man—*at twenty-nine years of age!*

This need for "manhood" (courage, domination, sexual prowess) which we have mentioned many times above is crucial enough in the Mexican culture to claim a syndrome entity all its own—the *machismo*. *Macho* connotes maleness—demonstrable and blatant maleness. The individual who is *macho* is *muy hombre* (much man), abundantly endowed with sexual organs, and fears nothing. The most grave and threatening insult to the Mexican male is one that challenges his masculinity.

What more natural pre-occupation could one expect from a son who has been subject to an emasculating father—to a father whose own fear of male competition has led him to use his physical size to dominate his son? We have mentioned that one way the son can compensate for his subordinate role is to emulate his father in another sphere, and later in his own home with his own wife and children. But through the bullfight another compensation is offered. As a spectator (or better, a principal) he can compensate symbolically, uninhibitedly, with all the hate, insult, and invective that he can muster. What clearer representative of the father than the bull with his flagrant masculinity, awesome power and potential to maim and kill? What clearer representative of the son than the delicate, almost fragile, *matador* whose protection obviously cannot be strength but must be courage? See how the bull charges the *banderilleros!* See how he hurls himself against the pic and the horse! How can the *matador* stand up to the bull? How can the son stand up to the father? Aha; *Toro!* Aha!

The *matador* provides the spectator with an amazingly flexible psychological figure. He can identify with the *matador's* courage, with his expertise, with his kill, and yet he can project upon the *matador*, especially in a bad performance, accusations of cowardice and powerlessness he has experienced himself in the constantly losing battle with his father. It is interesting that many bullfighters take nicknames with diminutive denotations—Joselito, Armillita *Chico*, Amoros *Chico*, Gallito, Machaquito, etc. Similarly, well over three hundred *matadors* whose names have been entered in the records have somewhere in their nickname the word *nino* (child)—El Nino de la Palma, etc. Thus is emphasized their smallness, their fragility vis-a-vis the bull. Thus is emphasized symbolically the helplessness of the child vis-a-vis the father. Strength is not nearly so valued an attribute of the *matador* as is demonstrable courage. The great *matadors* are not remembered for their muscle but for their *macho*. Belmonte was sickly, Maera had wrists so fragile that he often dislocated them in a *faena* (series of passes), Manolete was painfully thin. In fact, size and strength may be a disadvantage. Joselito, a tall, athletic and graceful man, often complained that he had to take more chances with the bull than the physically struggling Belmonte in order to make his *faenas* appear as difficult. When asked how he developed strength for the *corrida,* Gallo is said to have replied, "I smoke Havana cigars," adding that one cannot possibly match the bull for strength, but he can for courage. The *matador* must, then, appear finite when facing the awesome power of the bull. A sign of fear is acceptable even desirable, if the *faena* is good. Thus is highlighted the fact that the *matador* has in spite of his fears faced, dominated and killed the bull. A too calm, too nonchalant, too perfect *matador,* without the emotion of fear (and pride in controlling that fear), who cannot convey to the crowd that his is in fact a struggle in which he has faced, averred and administered death to an over-powering force, may be viewed as a *matador* without *salsa*—without "sauce." The fact of the matter is that the Mexican father is threatening, does physically hurt and *does* strike fear in the heart of his sons. To dominate and destroy him *would* be a remarkable feat. If the bullfight is to provide symbolically a resolution of this one-sided affair then it must be representative of its acts, events and especially of its emotions.

We have mentioned earlier that the passive role forced upon the Mexican child brings with it an aggressive component—a dynamic seen again and again in the Mexican personality structure. This interaction is beautifully manifested in the three commandments for the *matador's* conduct in the bullfight—Parar! Templar! Mandar! (Keep the feet quiet! Move the cape and *muleta* slowly! Dominate and control the bull!) The central feature is, in the modern bullfight, the domination of the bull. But domination is expressed in the *bonita corrida* with a studied parsimony of movement, with a deliberately slow tempo. Boyd writes that "the *matador* gains mastery by his cunning awareness of the power of the absence of movement." (1956). The most valued placing of the *banderillas* and the most honored kill both consist of the *matador* performing these tasks while passively standing his ground and receiving the charge of the bull. The *matador's* knees may knock together with fright, and the crowd will understand—as long as he continues to *parar.*

Kluckhohn sees this passive element in another Mexican institution, religion. She describes the Mexican's dependence upon the Saints and submissive and accepting attitude toward the supernatural (1961). Since the basic cultural values run through all of a society's institutions, it is not surprising to find this same passivity modifying the legitimized expression of hostility toward authority in the bullfight.

The *matador* demands submissive behavior from his own assistants. Traditionally, the latter have not been allowed to eat at the same table with the *matador,* must obey his orders immediately and without question and, regardless of the amount of the *matador's* income, are paid very poorly. Hemingway writes ". . . a *matador* feels that the less he pays his subordinates the more man he is and in the same way the nearer he can bring his subordinates to slaves the more man he feels he is." Thus, out of the ring as well as in, the *matador* perpetuates the *machismo*. This is also observed in the sexual exploits of *matadors*, and highlighted especially by their blatant disregard for and high incidence of syphilis. "You cannot expect," Hemingway says, "a *matador* who has triumphed in the afternoon by taking chances not to take them in the night" (1945).

Often the *matador* will single out a woman in the crowd and dedicate the kill to her, expecting, of course, some token of appreciation in return. One of the authors witnessed a *matador* leaving the *Plaza de Toros* after a successful corrida survey a bevy of adoring females, make his selection with a toss of the head and beckoning gesture with his blood-stained arm, and walk off hand-in-hand with the amazed and grateful girl to her car.

It would seem from the *matador's* point of view that the crowd is symbolically female. The *matador* (son) looks for approval to the crowd (mother) when he demonstrates his domination, his superiority over, the bull (father). The crowd continually calls on the *matador* to work closer to the bull. It *demands* that he take chances and promises in return to give him manifestations of approval. In his study of Mexican psychopathology, Meadow has observed that the Mexican mother subtly encourages the son to compete with the father, thus providing her an added element of control. It is not surprising, then, to see this dynamic represented in the *corrida*. The crowd (mother) calls for the *matador* (son) to challenge, to dominate, the bull (father), and offers love as a reward. *Matadors* who have been gored when responding to the crowd's urges have been reported to turn to the crowd, blaming it, shouting, for example, "See what you have done to me! See what your demands have done!" It may well be that the females in the crowd would enjoy seeing both the *matador* and the bull destroyed, thus expressing the generalized hostility that Mexican women have toward men. For the Mexican female, the *corrida* may be a legitimized way of acting out aggression towards dominating husbands, fathers and lovers.

A famous breeder of *toros* writes that ". . . certain of their (the fighting bulls) number will stay home to take care of the cows and carry on the breed with those formidable sacs that swing between their legs. But not our fighters to the death. They are virgins. It is a curious thing, our festival." (Lea, 1949). The bull has not experienced mating, and never will, because the *matador* will kill him. Perhaps the son will have dominated and killed that symbolic father before he can mate with the mother (the matador prays before each fight to the Virgin Mother).

In *capeas,* or informal street bullfights, the bull may be slaughtered by many people (if the town can afford the loss) and often the testicles will be cut off, roasted, and devoured. At one time it was customary in the *corrida* to remove the testicles (criadillas) of the first killed bull of the afternoon and serve them as a prepared meal to the Presidente during the killing of the fifth bull. Thus with one symbolic move were expressed and satisfied two needs—to dominate and render forever impotent the father and to incorporate the "source" of his strength. In the same vein, small children are often seen flooding the ring after the last kill, dipping their fingers in the fallen bull's blood and licking their fingers of this fluid of courage. If the *matador* has performed well and is acclaimed by the crowd the *Presidente* may award him the bull's ear, two ears, or two ears and a tail, in that ascending order of honor.

Thus through the *corrida* does the Mexican spectator, identifying with the matador and re-enacting the family situation, not only symbolically dominate and destroy the unyielding and hated authority figure, but he captures some of that figure's awesome power.

The bullfight itself has undergone considerable change. What exists now, as "modern bullfighting," began with Belmonte in the early 1930's, and according to the *aficionado,* is considerably different from its earlier stages. Hemingway writes,

> As the *corrida* has developed and decayed, there has been less emphasis on the form of the killing, which was once the whole thing, and more on the cape work, the placing of the *banderillas,* and the work with the *muleta.* The cape, the *banderillas,* and the *muleta* have all become ends in themselves rather than means to an end. . . ."
>
> "A bullfighter is now judged, and paid much more on the basis of his ability as a swordsman. The increasing importance and demand for the style of cape work and work with the *muleta,* that was invented or perfected by Juan Belmonte; the expectation and demand that each *matador* pass the bull, giving a complete performance with cape, in the *quites;* and the pardoning of deficiency in killing of a *matador* who is an artist with the cape and *muleta,* are the main changes in modern bullfighting (Hemingway, 1945).

Pre-Belmonte, then, the "kill" was the focal point of the bullfight. The *matador* who could kill with lust and enjoyment was admired and loved. The earlier phases of the *corrida* were to demonstrate the bull's courage and power and to prepare him for the kill. The essence of the bullfight was the final sword thrust, the actual encounter between man and bull where for an interminable moment they became one figure and was called the "Moment of Truth." Now, to accommodate the emphasis on the cape and *muleta* work, the bulls are smaller and killing is barely a "third of the fight" and anticlimactic to the cloth work (Hemingway, 1945). As Boyd points out, the "Moment of Truth" is now at the highlight of domination with the cape and *muleta*, not at the kill (1956). Hemingway agrees, writing that the emphasis in the modern *corrida* is upon dominance rather than killing and that this has gone hand-in-glove with the padding of the horses, the smaller bulls and the changing of the *picador's* function for lowering the bull's head and showing his courage to weakening him (Hemingway, 1945). There are, say the older *aficionados,* no longer *matadors,* but now only toreadors (Hemingway, 1945).

Mexico has been gradually evolving from the feudal social structure and caste system imposed by the Conquistadors toward urbanization and industrialization. The reference group emulated in this transition is, of course, the "advanced" Western world, especially the United States. The trend toward urbanization brings with it more emotionally restrictive patterns of socialization and more abstract channels for the expression of hostility. The position of father in the Mexican family has, with urbanization, also begun to shift toward the "advanced" western model. It might be said that as the father figure becomes less fearsome, less overpowering, there is less need to "kill" him symbolically—domination alone is an adequate expression of hostility. Western Europeans and Anglo-Americans are usually "shocked," for example, by the "brutality" of the bullfight and tend to dub cultures of which it is a part as "primitive." The more urbanized cultures do not, however, deny the need for legitimized expression of hostility. Kemp, a leading opponent of the bullfight, writes: "One of the functions of civilization is to direct the expression of one's desires by early training and social pressures so that, ideally, we will receive the minimum harm and maximum value from that expression" (1954). He admits to the need for satisfaction of the appetite for violence in all members of society but thinks that they must be satisfied less grossly than in the bullfight.

The general disapproval of Western Europe and the United States concerning the "barbarism" of the bullfight certainly must have had considerable influence on its conduct. (The padding of the horses was instigated by the English-born wife of a King of Spain, following promptings from her own country.) Since the institutions of a society reflect its culture, since the culture is influenced by the demands of other more powerful societies, and since urbanization itself accounts in part for change in cultural patterns, we would expect to see corresponding changes in all of the subject society's institutions, including the bullfight. Thus is seen the shift in emphasis from the "primitive" killing of the bull to the more abstract, more aesthetic, and certainly more "acceptable" domination with the cape and *muleta*. Thus is seen the complete elimination of the kill in Portugal and Switzerland, and in Spain and Mexico, its secondary, almost apologetic status.

Urbanization not only demands more intellectualized dealing with hostility but also brings with it a need for task specialization. This too is reflected in the modern *corrida*. The well rounded "generalist" *matador* is rare. Most are specialists—cape men, *muleta* men, and a few who are known for their work with the *banderillas*.

The shift in emphasis in the bullfight (some say, the emasculation of the bullfight) has not affected the average American spectator's reaction of being revolted, disgusted, even sickened by the *corrida*. In sounding the reactions of some American college students to their first (and usually last) attendance at a bullfight, the authors have noted the recurring theme: "It's too much," "too blatant," "overpowering." Robinson writes "the bullfight allows the American, protected from reality all his life by the palliation of modern American society, to face up to the real thing" (1964). And the "real thing" is "too much."

No doubt the highly "civilized" Anglo-American is threatened by such a direct acting out of hostility and violence as is manifest in the bullfight. But in addition to this he is very likely frightened by such a direct confrontation with death. Americans tend to deny death, even avoiding it in their speech (he "passed away," was "laid to rest," etc.). In Mexico, according to Robinson, "the bullfight spectacle is only one of the forms through which Mexicans make their obeisance to death" (1964). Brenner noted that concern for death is "an organic part of Mexican thought" (1929). The possibility of early or violent death is much greater for the average Mexican than for the average Anglo. To see death averted by the matador is pleasing to the Mexican, giving him some feeling of control over an event that he witnesses, not atypically, taking place in the streets. To the American the drama is a grim reminder of the inevitability of an event he seldom sees and chooses to deny. Hemingway writes, "We, in games, are not fascinated by death, its nearness and avoidance. We are fascinated by victory and we replace the avoidance of death by the avoidance of defeat" (1945). The symbolic "victory" over another team is certainly at a higher level of emotional abstraction than the symbolism of the domination of and bloody killing of a bull.

Anglo-Americans, the authors have observed, tend to "root" for the bull during a *corrida*. The picadors are soundly hooted (Mexicans only demonstrate disapproval if the bull is "ruined") and a tremendous barrage of invective pummels the *matador* if it takes him more than one sword to make a kill (even if all his swords are perfectly "over the horns").

This may be the result of the proclivity of the American to identify with the underdog, or the revulsion at seeing an animal (who, in the American ethic, is also a "buddy") killed. This seemingly irrational preference to see the man rather than the bull killed may also be influenced by a degree of prejudice in the ethnocentric Anglo toward the Mexican *matador*. It may also be that the *corrida* does not present to the Anglo a perception of two "evenly matched" antagonists. The opponents are not "equal"— few *matadors* are killed, but the bull rarely lives. This may run counter to the "fair play" ethic of the Anglo.

If the bullfight's overt display of hostility with its over-riding components of inevitable death, animal suffering and inequality, is not acceptable as a suitable means for the expression of aggression to the Anglo, what does he prefer? As mentioned earlier, the Anglo, too, is subject to socialization, and he, too, experiences conflict situations which engender hostility toward parents and parent surrogates. How, then, as reflected in the Anglo national sport of baseball, is the expression of hostility toward authority legitimized?

BASEBALL

It was presented above that the Anglo child is prevented from directly manifesting hostility toward parents by their representation as "good guys" and "pal." Verbal aggression, elaborately intellectualized, is usually the most overt form of hostility allowed to the child. Whereas the Mexican seems painfully aware of conflict, hates his father and acts out his hostility (displaces, projects), the Anglo appears hopelessly ambivalent toward the vague "buddy" father and represses the fact that conflict exists. A good part of his psychic life is spent sustaining this repression compulsively and obsessively. In general, the legitimized means of expressing hostility are just as subtle as is the subtlety of the hostility generating conflict situation—this mutedness is manifest as we shall see in the national sport.

The matador's servile bow to the *Presidente* is an obvious and undisguised move of deference. In the prelude to a baseball game, however, the players line up, facing the flag, and stand quietly during the playing of the National Anthem. Tribute to authority here certainly is less direct than in the bull ring. A flag is a considerably more abstract and less threatening symbol than the pompous gentlemen in the privileged box. The government official who, as *Presidente*, attends the *corrida*, controls its conduct and can directly interfere in the performance. Government officials who attend baseball games are in no way able to interfere with play—at most, they throw in the first ball.

While the observer need only take a quick glance at the "barbaric" *corrida* to see a dramatically overt display of violence and aggression, he is hard pressed, after considerable observation, to see any marked degree of hostility in the structure of the "good clean sport" of baseball. He looks out over the field and sees two teams (composed of an equal number of similarly uniformed men), patiently and systematically taking an equal number of turns (innings) in the attempt to score. The field is elaborately chalked, demarcating those areas of "fair" from "foul" play, and an elaborate system of rules dictates when a player can get a "hit," take or advance a base, score a run, be "safe" or "out." The observer becomes aware of the game's dramatic emphasis on numbers (the most abstract of symbols)—the scoreboard, the batting averages, the earned-run averages, the team win percentages, and even the players, who are granted relative impersonality by the numbers on their backs.

Unlike the *matador,* who constantly communicates with the crowd, the baseball players are seen to remain distinctly aloof from them. The player's allegiance is to the team, and he who performs ostentatiously for the crowd is ostracized as a "grandstander." Contrast, for example, the baseball player's downcast eye and turf-kicking toe after an outstanding move with the *matador's* haughty glance and proud posture following a good series of passes. Contrast the convertible or television set given ritualistically by the crowd to the ball player on "his day" with the immediate, spontaneous and extremely emotional reaction of the crowd following an appreciated *corrida*—they clamor for the *Presidente* to give him awards, throw him wine flasks, sombreros and often rush into the ring to carry him about on their shoulders. It might be said that in baseball, the crowd is expected to observe, in a relatively detached way, the spectacle being performed for them on the field. At the bullfight, however, the crowd is expected to be one with the *matador,* to participate, fully, in the emotions of the fight.

There is, by contrast to the *corrida,* a noticeable lack of heterosexuality in the game of baseball. While the *matador* often dedicates his bull or tosses an ear to a senorita, the baseball player, on the field anyway, limits his interaction to male teammates, chattering to them, shaking their hands in success, slapping their buttocks in encouragement, and mobbing and hugging them for superlative feats of play.

There is, of course, competition taking place in the game—but nothing that can parallel the direct, individual confrontation of the *matador* with the bull. In baseball, two "teams" meet and the more evenly matched they are, the better the "contest" is. There are fans for both sides, each rooting for his team, hoping that it will win the "contest." After the game is over there will be a winner and a "good loser." It is interesting that the participants in baseball are called "players." The matador is not "playing" at the *corrida*—it is a *fight*. The aggressive component that one would expect in competition is muted by the rules governing the conduct of play and by the expectations of the crowd. There are occasional emotional outbreaks between rival players, between players and umpires and between managers and umpires, but these "rhubarbs" are ephemeral and seem somehow distant and artificial. The shouts and jeers of the crowd, with an occasional "murder the bum," lack the emotional punch and especially the personal reference of the venomous insults hurled by the displeased Mexican *aficionado*.

Some psychoanalytically oriented behavioral scientists have written vividly of the symbolic castration represented in the baseball games. Stokes, for example, calls baseball "a manifest exercise in phallic deftness" (1956). Petty sees the contest as a safe re-creation of the battle between father and son for the sexual favors of the mother (1963).

However, if hostility generated in a father-son competition is manifested here, how safe, how muted, is its expression? Its release is legitimized only under the restrictions of elaborate rules, omnipresent umpires, and with the insistence that each team systematically take turns playing one role or the other. It is diffused throughout a "team," no one man taking full responsibility and is submerged in a morass of batting and pitching rituals and superstitions that are unsurpassed by the most extreme of religion and the military. Batters will use only certain bats, stand a certain way, pound home plate a certain number of times, spit, rub dust, rub resin (or all three) on their hands, pull their clothing into a certain position before batting, wear lucky numbers, lucky charms, lucky hats, lucky sox or use a lucky bat. Many pitchers have elaborate series of movements before delivering the ball—touch cap, rub ball, grab resin bag, scuff dirt, adjust glove, re-touch hat, re-rub ball. . . . Professional pitcher Lew Burdette has taken as long as a full minute to complete a series of irrelevant gestures, ticks, clutches, and tugs before throwing the ball. Similarly, an observer would be hard pressed to find a baseball player who doesn't ritualistically chew gum.

Furthermore, the conduct of the game, and therefore any expression of hostility, is closely scrutinized by at least three umpires. Interestingly enough, the word umpire is derived from the Latin, meaning not equal. Thus, on a playing field where equality is a central ethic, the umpires are unique. They are the only personnel on the field who even during inning intermissions cannot sit down or relax. Like the "super ego" theirs is an unrelenting vigilance. Their word is law, and disrespect for them can bring an ousting from the game. But how different is the player-umpire relationship from that of the *matador-Presidente*. The *Presidente* is treated with deference, and the interaction between authority and *matador* is seen to be personal and direct. As in the Mexican society at large, the authority figure, though he may be hated, is shown the utmost respect. Mexican patients have described their fathers as drunkards, brutes, etc., but always add that they "respect" them. Ruscon, Arizona school teachers often report that the behavior of the Mexican-American students vis-a-vis the teacher is exemplary, though their dropout and absentee records indicate a low value for education.

The umpire on the other hand, is an impersonal figure. How many "fans" know the names of big league umpires? So abstract is the black-suited authority that "kill the umpire" can be vociferously and safely shouted. How nonthreatening is the typical reaction of the umpire to the complaints, admonishments, and verbal aggressions of the players and managers—he turns his back and slowly walks away. Authority is challenged—and with impurity! There is, however, a carefully defined limit to the amount of abuse the umpire is expected to endure. Physical violence and certain profanities bring not only a removal from the game but severe fines to the offender. Since there are fixed fines for specific obscenities, angry players will often turn to the umpire and, escaping the fine by ascending a rung on the abstraction ladder, declare, "You're that five hundred dollar word!"

Another phenomenon, certainly cultural in nature, is the ritual hypochondriasis of baseball players. *Matadors* traditionally disregard wounds (the *macho* does not fear, avoid or show disability because of pain) and have even fought with assistants who tried to carry them out of the ring after a serious goring. Baseball players leave the field for a simple pulled muscle. Yards of tape, gallons of ointment, heat treatments, vitamin pills, "isometrics," "training rules," arm warmers, whirlpool baths and rubdowns pamper the ball player. Pitchers are carefully protected from the wind, rain, and cold "dugout" seats, and can ask to be relieved if they are feeling tired.

As the conduct of the bullfight has changed with the increasing urbanization in Mexico, so also has the conduct of baseball changed with the increasing bureaucratization in the United States. In the early 20th Century, fines for insulting (or even striking) the umpire were non-existent. The crowd very often displayed displeasures by throwing bottles and cushions at specific individuals in the field. In general, the level of expression of hostility was more direct and involved somewhat more acting out. The farm club system, its scouting ties with organized collegiate athletics and the bureaucratic "front office" were far less expansive. Rules and regulations were less restricting, and the tobacco chewing, swearing, sweating player was typical as contrasted with the "gentleman players" who grace our fields and television commercials today. Nine innings then took about two-thirds the time they do now, the ball was "dead" and the number of players on the team's roster was smaller. There were fewer substitutes, and pitchers as a rule stayed in for the entire game.

In the present situation even the abstract "team" concept has been made obsolete by increasing bureaucratization. The authors witnessed members of the winning (1963) Los Angeles Dodgers speaking proudly of the "Dodger Organization," and the good job the "front office" had done.

In a television interview, Bill Veeck, an ex-professional manager, expressed dismay with the unnecessary "dragging out" of the game by prolonged warm-up pitches, drawn-out sessions of verbal haranguing, "long" walks to the dugout and summit meetings of the pitcher, catcher and manager. He complained about the time-wasting rituals of motion indulged in by both pitcher and batter. Veeck thus testifies to the increasing obsessive quality in the game, as its emphasis shifts to more and more diffuse, indirect and disguised means for expressing hostility.

One wonders, in fact, if the restrictions in baseball are too many, if the fans aren't growing dissatisfied. The increasing public attendance at professional football games, reaching a point where some sports analysts predict that it will replace baseball as the National sport, may be an indication of the demand for a less abstract expression of hostility in spectator sports. Nevertheless, from the point of view of social control, baseball masterfully mutes aggression behind its reciprocity, rules, records and rituals. It duplicates the vagueness and intellectualization of the conflict situation in the American family and provides a markedly abstract and controlled expression of hostility toward authority. Macoby, et al., write that baseball represents the *ideal* of American society (1964). It remains to be seen whether or not this ideal can, in the face of a need for a clearer expression of hostility, remain intact.

SUMMARY

The passive-aggressive component of the Mexican modal personality can be traced to the dominant and harshly punitive role of the father and to the general authoritarian nature of the Mexican culture. This passive-aggressiveness is perpetuated in the *macho* pattern of the Mexican male and in the "martyr" pattern of the Mexican female. Any acting out of the resultant hostility to authority must be carried out in spheres safely distant from that authority's immediate control.

The bullfight is seen to depict, symbolically, the power of the father, the subtle demands of the mother and the fear of the child. Unlike the family situation, the awesome authority does not prevail, but rather is dominated and destroyed through the courage and daring of the *matador*. He, however, acting for the spectator, must accomplish this hostile act in a framework of "respect" for authority, and with a studied passiveness in and control of movement.

By contrast, the "intellectualization" component of the Anglo modal personality can be traced to the superficial ethic of "equality" among family members and to the general intellectualized nature of highly urbanized societies. The attempt to mute authority by a pseudo-philosophy of togetherness, when authority is in fact assumed by the father, the mother and by the society, engenders a vagueness in role definitions, confusion in behavioral expectations and an intellectualization of the resultant conflict. Hostility toward this intangible yet frustrating authority figure is expressed by the individual in a manner as abstract and as ritualized as its causative factors.

The national sport of baseball is set in a framework of equality. Hostility toward authority takes the symbolic form of competition and desire to win, and is smothered under a covering of rules, regulations and player rituals. Guided by the authority of umpires (who are sufficiently impersonal to be challenged with relative impunity), and protected in the safety of numbers as a member of a team, the players systematically alternate roles, allowing each to have an equal opportunity to "be aggressive."

Spectators of the baseball game view two similarly uniformed teams consisting of the same number of players vying for an abstract "victory." The spectators' emotional participation in the game is distant and safe— "murder the bum" or "kill the umpire" does not have enough of a personal referent to arouse guilt or anxiety. They can take sides in occasional and severely regulated conflicts on the field, because such conflicts have "meaning" only in the game, and are forgotten when the game is over.

Since 1920, the bullfight has gradually been modified to accentuate domination rather than the kill. Paralleling this, the position of the father in the Mexican family has, with gradual urbanization, come more closely in line with that of the "advanced" Western model. He is less threatening, less fearsome, and can be dominated to a degree sufficient to reduce the importance of his symbolic destruction.

Baseball, since 1920, has similarly undergone significant changes. With the increasing bureaucratization of Anglo society, and with the increasing emphasis upon "equality" and impersonality in the family have come the more complex bureaucratization and the more elaborate ritualization of baseball.

The family, and the institutionalized recreation form known as the national sport, mutually reflect, as they appear in Mexico, the cultural centrality of death, dominance, "personal" relationships, respect for and fear and hatred of authority and the defense systems of the passive-aggressive character structure.

In the Anglo culture, these two institutions mutually reflect the cultural importance of equality, impersonality, and the defense mechanism of intellectualization.

Both national sports provide a socially acceptable channel for the expression of hostility toward authority. This channel is modified by other cultural values and expectations, and is framed in an activity which duplicates, symbolically, aspects of the hostility generating familial situation.

RELATED LITERATURE

Allen, J. H. *Southwest*. New York, 1953.
Boyd, G. On bullfight. Wright, M. ed. *The Field of Vision*. New York, 1956: 100-111.
Brenner, A. *Idols Behind Altars*. New York, 1929.
Diaz-Guerrero, R. *Estidios de Psichologia del Mexicano*. Mexico, 1961.
———. Socio-cultural premises, attitudes, and cross-cultural research. *Cross-Cultural Studies of Attitude Structure and Search*. Proceedings of 17th International Congress of Psychology. Washington, D. C., 1963.
Dollard, J. Hostility and fear in social life. *Social Forces*. 42, 1938: 15-25.
Gillin, J. P. Ethos and cultural aspects of personality. Y. A. Cohen, ed. *Social Structure and Personality*. New York, 1961: 288-300.
Hemingway, E. *Death in the Afternoon*. New York, 1945.
Kardiner, A. *The Individual and His Society*. New York, 1939.
Kemp, L. *The Only Beast*. New York, 1954.
Kluckhohn, F. and Strodbeck, F. L. *Variations in Value Orientation*. New York, 1961.
Lea, T. *The Brave Bulls*. Boston, 1949.
Lewis, O. *Children of Sanchez*. New York, 1961.
Lundberg, G. A., Schrag, L. C., and Larsen, O. N. *Sociology*. New York, 1958.
Macoby, M., Modiano, N., and Lander, P. Games and social character in a Mexican village. *Psychiatry*. 1964: 50-61.
Meadow, A., Zurcher, L., and Stoker, D. Sex role and schizophrenia in Mexican culture. *International Journal of Social Psychiatry* (forthcoming).

Meadow, A., and Stoker, D. Symptomatic behaviour of Mexican-American and Anglo-American child guidance patients. Unpub. paper, University of Arizona.

Ramsey, R. *Fiesta*. New York, 1955.

Robinson, C. *With the ears of strangers*. The Mexican in American Literature. Tucson, Ariz., 1964.

Stokes, A. Psychoanalytic reflections on the development of ball games. *International Journal of Psycho-Analysis*. 37, 1956:185-192.

Tumin, M. M. Some disfunctions of institutional imbalance. *Behavioral Science*. 1, 1956: 218-223.

Whiting, J. W. and Child, I. L. *Child Training and Personality: A Cross-Cultural Study*. New Haven, Conn., 1953.

Section B

Diffusion of Sport Styles:
Acceptance and Resistance

One of the most remarkable features of sport is the variety of forms it takes throughout the world. The geographical diffusion of sport forms can be partly understood in terms of culture contact, the process through which aspects of cultural life are transmitted from one group to another as the result of sustained interaction. Taken to an extreme, culture contact could result in the homogenization of culture and a world in which cultural differences no longer existed. But the process is usually not so automatic or complete. For example, many new cultural forms, such as sports, are introduced to groups, but not all are equally accepted. Research has yet to discover why some new sports are consciously resisted or rejected categorically while others catch the fancy of their new clientele who embrace them with total enthusiasm or, more commonly, modify them so that they develop a distinctive form or style that better suits their national taste. The key to understanding adoption or rejection apparently lies in some element of appeal which has yet to be identified by sociologists. Varying degrees of resistance and acceptance to new sports are discussed in the articles in this section.

Reisman and Denney discuss the diffusion of sport with reference to football in America. In their classic article they explain how American impatience with the ambiguity of the British football (soccer) rules led to rule changes that were significantly to change the form of football in America.

Finlay extends Reisman and Denney's analysis by comparing the forms of football presently popular in the United States, Canada, and Britain. Finlay isolates three factors that he feels epitomize the differences between the games, and he relates them to other cultural differences among the three nations.

Kidd documents a case of self-conscious resistance to the encroaching involvement of one country on the sport forms of another. Kidd's article reflects the growing concern among many Canadians that their national identity is being obscured by American domination. Such domination extends to control of important message systems in Canadian life: television, movies, books, and sport. Kidd traces the involvement of American interest in Canadian sport and expresses the danger many feel exists when the symbolic systems of a nation are effectively controlled by outsiders.

Football in America:
A Study in Cultural Diffusion

David Riesman and Reuel Denney

I

On October 9, 1951, Assistant Attorney General Graham Morrison instituted an anti-trust action against a number of universities on account of their efforts to limit TV broadcasts of their games—efforts dictated by the terrible burdens of what we might speak of as "industrialized football." This action occurred only a few weeks after the scandal of the West Point student firings, which, along with the William and Mary palace revolution, indicated that fooball was indeed reaching another crisis in its adaptation to the ever-changing American environment. Small colleges such as Milligan—a church-supported school in the mountains of Eastern Tennessee—were discovering that football was now so mechanized that they could no longer afford the necessary entry fee for machinery and personnel. Last year, Milligan spent $17,000, or two-thirds of its whole athletic budget—and did not get it all back in the box-office net. Football had come to resemble other industries or mechanized farms, into which a new firm could not move by relying on an institutional lifetime of patient saving and plowing back of profits, but only by large corporate investment. The production of a team involves the heavy overhead and staff personnel characteristic of high-capital, functionally rationalized industries, as the result of successive changes in the game since its post-Civil-War diffusion from England.[1]

It would be wrong, however, to assert that football has become an impersonal market phenomenon. Rather, its rationalization as a sport and as a spectacle has served to bring out more openly the part it plays

From *American Quarterly*, 3, 309-319. Copyright 1951 by The Trustees of University of Pennsylvania, Philadelphia, Pa. Reprinted by permission of the authors and publisher.

in the ethnic, class, and characterological struggles of our time—meaning, by "characterological struggle," the conflict between different styles of life. The ethnic significance of football is immediately suggested by the shift in the typical origins of player-names on the All-American Football Teams since 1889. In 1889, all but one of the names (Heffelfinger) suggested Anglo-Saxon origins. The first name after that of Heffelfinger to suggest non-Anglo-Saxon recruitment was that of Murphy, at Yale, in 1895. After 1895, it was a rare All-American team that did not include at least one Irishman (Daly, Hogan, Rafferty, Shevlin); and the years before the turn of the century saw entrance of the Jew. On the 1904 team appeared Pierkarski, of Pennsylvania. By 1927, names like Casey, Kipke, Oosterbaan, Koppisch, Garbisch, and Friedman were appearing on the All-American lists with as much frequency as names like Channing, Adams, and Ames in the 1890's.

While such a tally does little more than document a shift that most observers have already recognized in American football, it raises questions that are probably not answerable merely in terms of ethnic origins of players. There is an element of class identification running through Amercian football since its earliest days, and the ethnic origins of players contain ample invitations to the making of theory about the class dimensions of football. Most observers would be inclined to agree that the arrival of names like Kelley and Kipke on the annual All-American list was taken by the Flanagans and the Webers as the achievement of a lower-class aspiration to be among the best at an upper-class sport. The question remains: what did the achievement mean? What did it mean at different stages in the development of the game? Hasn't the meaning worn off in the fifty-odd years, the roughly two generations since Heffelfinger and Murphy made the grade?

There are many ways to begin an answer to such questions, and here we can open only a few lines of investigation. Our method is to study the interrelations between changes in the rules of the game (since the first intercollegiate contest: Rutgers, 6 goals—Princeton, 4 goals, in 1869) and to analyze the parallel changes in football strategy and ethos. All these developments are to be seen as part of a configuration that includes changes in coaching, in the training of players, and in the no less essential training of the mass audience.

Since football is a cultural inheritance from England, such an analysis may be made in the perspective of other studies in cultural diffusion and variation. Just as the French have transformed American telephone etiquette while retaining some of its recognizable physical features, so Americans have transformed the games of Europe even when, as in track or tennis, the formalities appear to be unaltered. Even within the Western industrial culture, there are great varieties on a class and national basis, in the games, rules, strategy, etiquette, and audience structures of sport. In the case of college football—we shall leave aside the symbolically less important professional game—the documentation of sportswriters (themselves a potent factor in change) allows us to trace the stages of development.

II

A study of Anatolian peasants now under way at the Bureau of Applied Social Research indicates that these highly tradition-bound people cannot grasp the abstractness of modern sports. They lack the enterprise, in their fatalistic village cultures, to see why people want to knock themselves out for sportsmanship's remote ideals; they cannot link such rituals, even by remote analogy, with their own. These peasants are similarly unable to be caught up in modern politics, or to find anything meaningful in the Voice of America. Nevertheless, football itself, like so many other games with balls and goals, originated in a peasant culture.

Football, in its earliest English form, was called the Dane's Head and it was played in the tenth and eleventh centuries as a contest in kicking a ball between towns. The legend is that the first ball was a skull, and only later a cow's bladder. In some cases, the goals were the towns themselves, so that a team entering a village might have pushed the ball several miles en route. King Henry II (1154-89) proscribed the game, on the ground that it interferred with archery practice. Played in Dublin even after the ban, football did not become respectable or legal until an edict of James I reinstated it. The reason was perhaps less ideological than practical: firearms had made the art of bowmanship obsolete.

During the following century, football as played by British schoolboys became formalized, but did not change its fundamental pattern of forceful kicking. In 1823, Ellis of Rugby made the mistake of picking up the ball and running with it towards the goal. All concerned thought it a mistake: Ellis was sheepish, his captain apologetic. The mistake turned into innovation when it was decided that a running rule might make for an interesting game. The localism, pluralism, and studied casualness of English sports made it possible to try it out without securing universal assent—three or four purely local variants of football, football-hazing and "wall games" are still played in various English schools. Rugby adopted "Rugby" in 1841, several years after Cambridge had helped to popularize it.[2]

This establishment of the running or Rugby game, as contrasted with the earlier, kicking game, had several important results. One was that the old-style players banded themselves together for the defense of their game, and formed the London Football Association (1863). This name, abbreviated to "Assoc," appears to have been the starting point for the neologism, "Soccer," the name that the kicking game now goes by in many parts of the English-speaking world. A second result was that the English, having found a new game, continued to play it without tight rules until the Rugby Union of 1871. As we shall see, this had its effects on the American game. The third and most important result of Ellis' "mistake," of course, was that he laid the foundations for everything fundamental about the American game between about 1869 and the introduction of the forward pass. (The forward pass is still illegal in Rugby and closely related football games.)

III

In the Colonial period and right down to the Civil War, Americans played variants on the kicking football game on their town greens and schoolyards. After the war, Yale and Harvard served as the culturally receptive importers of the English game. Harvard, meeting McGill in a game of Rugby football in 1874, brought the sport to the attention of collegiate circles and the press—two identifications important for the whole future development of the game. But if Harvard was an opinion leader, Yale was a technological one. A Yale student who had studied at Rugby was instrumental in persuading Yale men to play the Rugby game and was, therefore, responsible for some of Yale's early leadership in the sport.

It happened in the following way, according to Walter Camp and Lorin F. Deland.[3] The faculty in 1860, for reasons unknown, put a stop to interclass matches of the pre-Rugby variety. "During the following years, until 1870, football was practically dead at Yale. The class of '72, however, was very fond of athletic sports, and participated especially in long hare and hound runs. The revival of football was due in a large measure to Mr. D. S. Schaft, formerly of Rugby School, who entered the class of '73 and succeeded in making the sport popular among his classmates, and eventually formed an association which sent challenges to the other classes."

Soon after the period described by Camp, it became clear that American players, having tasted the "running" game, were willing to give up the soccer form. It became equally clear that they either did not want to, or could not, play Rugby according to the British rules. "The American players found in this code [English Rugby Rules] many uncertain and knotty points which caused much trouble in their game, especially as they had no traditions, or older and more experienced players, to whom they could turn for the necessary explanations," says Camp. An example of such a problem was English rule number nine:

"A touchdown is when a player, putting his hand on the ball in touch or in goal, stops it so that it remains dead, or fairly so."

The ambiguity of the phrase "fairly so" was increased by the statement in rule number eight that the ball is dead "when it rests absolutely motionless on the ground."

Camp's description of these early difficulties is intensely interesting to the student of cultural diffusion not only because of what Camp observed about the situation, but also because of what he neglected to observe. Consider the fact that the development of Rugby rules in England was accomplished by admitting into the rules something that we could call a legal fiction. While an offensive runner was permitted to carry the ball, the condition of his doing so was that he should *happen* to be standing behind the swaying "scrum" (the tangled players) at the moment the ball popped back out to him. An intentional "heel out" of the ball was not permitted; and the British rules of the mid-nineteenth century appear to take it for granted that the difference between an intentional and an unintentional heel-out would be clear to everyone. Ellis' mistake became institutionalized—but still as a mistake. This aspect of Rugby rule-making had important implications for the American game.

British players, according to tradition as well as according to rules, could be expected to tolerate such ambiguity as that of the heel-out rule just as they tolerated the ambiguity of the "dead" ball. They could be expected to tolerate it not only because of their personal part in developing new rules but also (a point we shall return to) because they had an audience with specific knowledge of the traditions to assist them. In America it was quite another matter to solve such problems. No Muzafer Sherif was present[4] to solidify the perceptions of "nearly so," and the emotional tone for resolving such questions without recurrent dispute could not be improvised. Rather, however, than dropping the Rugby game at that point, because of intolerance for the ambiguities involved, an effort was undertaken, at once systematic and gradual, to fill in by formal procedures the vacuum of etiquette and, in general, to adapt the game to its new cultural home.

The upshot of American procedure was to assign players to the legalized task of picking up and tossing back out of scrimmage. This in turn created the role of the center, and the centering operation. This in turn led to a variety of problems in defining the situation as one of "scrimmage" or "non-scrimmage," and the whole question of the legality of passing the ball back to intended runners. American football never really solved these problems until it turned its attention, in 1880, to a definition of the scrimmage itself. The unpredictable English "scrum" or scramble for a free ball was abandoned, and a crude line of scrimmage was constructed across the field. Play was set in motion by snapping the ball. Meanwhile Americans became impatient with long retention of the ball by one side. It was possible for a team that was ahead in score to adopt tactics that would insure its retention of the ball until the end of the period. By the introduction of a minimum yardage-gain rule in 1882, the rulemakers assured the frequent interchange of the ball between sides.

The effect of this change was to dramatize the offensive-defensive symmetry of the scrimmage line, to locate it sharply in time ("downs"), and to focus attention not only on the snapping of the ball, but also on the problem of "offside" players. In the English game, with no spatially and temporally delimited "line of scrimmage," the offside player was penalized only by making him neutral in action until he could move to a position back of the position of the ball. In the American game, the new focus on centering, on a scrimmage line, and on yardage and downs, created the need for a better offside rule. From that need developed offside rules that even in the early years resembled the rules of today. American rulemakers were logically extending a native development when they decided to draw an imaginary line through the ball before it had been centered, to call this the "line of scrimmage," and to make this line, rather than the moving ball itself, the offside limit in the goalward motion of offensive players. At first, lined-up players of the two sides were allowed to stand and wrestle with each other while waiting for the ball to be centered; only later was a neutral zone introduced between the opposing lines.

Even with such a brief summary of the rule changes, we are in a position to see the operation of certain recurrent modes or patterns of adaptation. The adaptation begins with the acceptance of a single pivotal innovation (running with the ball). The problems of adaptation begin with the realization that this single innovation has been uprooted from a rich context of meaningful rules and traditions, and does not work well in their absence. Still more complex problems of adaptation develop when it is realized that the incompleteness of the adaptation will not be solved by a reference to the pristine rules. In the first place, the rules are not pristine (the English rules were in the process of development themselves). In the second place, the tradition of interpreting them is not present in experienced players. In the third place, even if it were, it might not be adaptable to the social character and mood of the adapters.

Let us put it this way. The Americans, in order to solve the heelout problem, set in motion a redesign of the game that led ultimately to timed centering from a temporarily fixed line of scrimmage. Emphasis completely shifted from the kicking game; it also shifted away from the combined kicking and running possible under Rugby rules; it shifted almost entirely in the direction of an emphasis on ballcarrying. Meanwhile, to achieve this emphasis, the game made itself vulnerable to slow-downs caused by one team's retention of the ball. It not only lost the fluidity of the original game, but ran up against a pronounced American taste for action in sports, visible action. There is evidence that even if players had not objected to such slowdowns, the spectators would have raised a shout. The yardage rule was the way this crisis was met. This, in turn, led to an emphasis on mass play, and helped to create the early twentieth-century problems of football. But before we consider this step in the game's development we must turn to examine certain factors in the sport's audience reception.

IV

A problem posed for the student of cultural diffusion at this point can be stated as follows: What factor or factors appear to have been most influential in creating an American game possessing not only nationally distinct rules, but also rules having a specific flavor of intense legality about many a point of procedure left more or less up in the air by the British game?

We can now go beyond the rule-making aspect of the game and assert that the chief factor was the importance of the need to standardize rules to supply an ever-widening collegiate field of competition, along with the audience this implied. The English rulemakers, it appears, dealt with a situation in which amateur play was restricted to a fairly limited number of collegians and institutions. The power of localism was such that many an informality was tolerated, and intended to be tolerated, in the rules and their interpretation. American football appeared on the American campus at the beginning of a long period in which intercollegiate and interclass sportsmanship was a problem of ever-widening social participation and concern. Football etiquette itself was in the making. Thus, it appears that when early American teams met, differences of opinion could not be resolved between captains in rapid-fire agreement or penny-tossing as was the case in Britain. American teams did not delegate to their captains the role of powerful comrade-in-antagonism with opposing captains, or, if they did, they felt that such responsibilities were too grave.[5]

Into just such situations football players thrust all of the force of their democratic social ideologies, all their prejudice in favor of equalitarian and codified inter-player attitudes. Undoubtedly, similar considerations also influenced the audience. Mark Benney, a British sociologist who is familiar with the games played on both sides of the Atlantic, points out that, whereas the American game was developed in and for a student group, the English game was played before quite large crowds who, from a class standpoint, were less homogeneous than the players themselves, though they were as well informed as the latter in the "law of the game." Rugby football was seldom played by the proletariat; it was simply enjoyed as a spectacle.

Held by the critical fascination the British upper strata had for the lower strata, the audience was often hardly more interested in the result of the game than in judging the players as "gentlemen in action." "The players," Mr. Benney writes, "had to demonstrate that they were sportsmen, that they could 'take it'; and above all they had to inculcate the (politically important) ideology that legality was more important than power." The audience was, then, analogous to the skilled English jury at law, ready to be impressed by obedience to traditional legal ritual and form, and intolerant of "bad form" in their "betters." The early Yale games, played before a tiny, nonpaying audience, lacked any equivalent incentive to agree on a class-based ritual of "good form," and when the audience came later on, their attitude towards upper-class sportsmanship was much more ambivalent—they had played the game too, and they were unwilling to subordinate themselves to a collegiate aristocracy who would thereby have been held to norms of correctness. The apparent legalism of many American arguments over the rules would strike British observers as simply a verbal power-play.

Such differences in the relation of the game to the audience, on this side of the Atlantic, undoubtedly speeded the development of the specifically American variant. Native, too, are the visual and temporal properties of the game as it developed even before 1900: its choreography could be enjoyed, if not always understood, by nonexperts, and its atomistic pattern in time and space could seem natural to audiences accustomed to such patterns in other foci of the national life. The midfield dramatization of line against line, the recurrent starting and stopping of field action around the timed snapping of a ball, the trend to a formalized division of labor between backfield and line, above all, perhaps, the increasingly precise synchronization of men in motion—these developments make it seem plausible to suggest that the whole procedural rationalization of the game which we have described was not unwelcome to Americans, and that it fitted in with other aspects of their industrial folkways.

Spurred by interest in the analysis of the athletic motions of men and animals, Eadweard Muybridge was setting out his movie-like action shorts of the body motion (more preoccupied even than Vesalius or da Vinci with the detailed anatomy of movement)[6] at about the same time that Coach Woodruff at Pennsylvania (1894) was exploring the possibilities for momentum play: linemen swinging into motion before the ball is snapped, with the offensive team, forming a wedge, charging toward an opposition held waiting by the offside rule. In Philadelphia, the painter Eakins, self-consciously following the tenets of Naturalism and his own literal American tradition, was painting the oarsmen of the Schuylkill. Nearby, at the Midvale plant of the American Steel Company, efficiency expert Frederick Winslow Taylor was experimenting with motion study and incentive pay geared to small measurable changes in output—pay that would spur but never soften the workman.[7]

Since we do not believe in historical inevitability, nor in the necessary homogeneity of a culture, we do not suggest that the American game of football developed as it did out of cultural compulsion and could not have gone off in quite different directions. Indeed, the very effectiveness of momentum play, as a mode of bulldozing the defense, led eventually to the rule that the line must refrain from motion before the ball is snapped. For the bulldozing led, or was thought to lead, to a great increase in injuries. And while these were first coped with by Walter Camp's training table (his men had their choice of beefsteak or mutton for dinner, to be washed down with milk, ale, or sherry), the public outcry soon forced further rule changes designed to soften the game. After a particular bloody battle between Pennsylvania and Swarthmore in 1905, President Roosevelt himself took a hand and insisted on reform.[8]

Camp's colleague at Yale, William Graham Sumner, may well have smiled wryly at this. Sumner was exhorting his students to "get capital," and cautioning them against the vices of sympathy and reformism—a theme which has given innumerable American academes a good living since—while Camp was exhorting his to harden themselves, to be stern and unafraid. In spite of them both, the reformers won out; but the end of momentum play was not the end of momentum. Rather, with an in-genuity that still dazzles, the game was gentled and at the same time speeded by a new rule favoring the forward pass. But before going on to see what changes this introduced, let us note the differences between the subjects of Sumner's and Camp's exhortations on the one hand, and Taylor's on the other.

Frederick Taylor, as his writings show, was already coming up against a work force increasingly drawn from non-Protestant lands, and seeking to engender in them a YMCA-morality, whereas Camp was inculcating the same morality into young men of undiluted Anglo-Saxon stock and middle- to upper-class origins. Not for another fifty years would the sons of Midvale prove harder, though fed on kale or spaghetti, and only in-termittently, than the sons of Yale. Meanwhile, the sons of Yale had learned to spend summers as tracklayers or wheat harvesters in an effort to enlarge their stamina, moral toughness, and cross-class adventures.

Nevertheless, certain basic resemblances between the purposes of Taylor and those of Sumner and Camp are clearly present. In contrast with the British, the Americans demonstrated a high degree of interest in winning games and winning one's way to high production goals. The Americans, as in so many other matters, were clearly concerned with the competitive spirit that new rules might provoke and control. (British sports, like British industry, seemed to take it more for granted that com-petition will exist even if one does not set up an ideology for it.) Much of this seems to rest in the paradoxical belief of Americans that compe-tition is natural—but only if it is constantly recreated by artificial systems of social rules that direct energies into it.

Back of the attitudes expressed in Taylor, Sumner, and Camp we can feel the pressure not only of a theory of competition, but also a the-ory of the emttional tones that ought to go along with competition. It is apparent from the brutality scandals of 1905 that President Roosevelt reacted against roughhouse not so much because it was physical violence, but for two related reasons. The first and openly implied reason was that it was connected with an unsportsmanlike attitude. The second, unacknowledged, reason was that Americans fear and enjoy their ag-gression at the same time, and thus have difficulty in pinning down the inner meanings of external violence. The game of Rugby as now played in England is probably as physically injurious as American football was at the turn of the century. By contrast, American attitudes toward foot-ball demonstrates a forceful need to define, limit, and conventionalize the symbolism of violence in sports.

If we look back now at England, we see a game in which shouted signals and silent counting of timed movements are unknown—a game that seems to Americans to wander in an amorphous and disorderly roughhouse. Rugby, in the very home of the industrial revolution, seems pre-industrial, seems like one of the many feudal survivals that urbanization and industrialization have altered but not destroyed. The English game, moreover, seems not to have developed anyone like Camp, the Judge Gary of football (as Rockne was to be its Henry Ford): Camp was a sparkplug in efforts to codify inter-collegiate rules; he was often the head of the important committees. His training table, furthermore, was one of the signs of the slow rise in "overhead" expense—a rise which, rather like the water in United States Steel Stock, assumed that abunddance was forthcoming and bailing out probable, as against the British need for parsimony. But at the same time the rise in costs undoubtedly made American football more vulnerable than ever to public-relations considerations: the "gate" could not be damned.

V

This public relations issue in the game first appears in the actions of the rules committee of 1906—the introduction of the legalized forward pass in order to open up the game and reduce brutal power play. Between 1906 and 1913 the issue was generally treated as a problem centered about players and their coaches, and thus took the form of an appeal to principles rather than to audiences. However, the development of the high audience appeal that we shall show unfolding after 1913 was not autonomous and unheralded. If public relations became a dominant factor by 1915, when the University of Pittsburgh introduced numbers for players in order to spur the sale of programs, it had its roots in the 1905-13 period. The rules committee of 1906, by its defensive action on roughhouse rules had already implicity acknowledged a broad public vested interest in the ethos of the game. Let us turn to look at the speed with which football was soon permeated by broad social meanings unanticipated by the founders of the sport.

By 1913, the eve of the First World War, innovation in American industry had ceased to be the prerogative of Baptist, Calvinist, and North of Ireland tycoons. Giannini was starting his Bank of America; the Jews were entering the movies and the garment hegemonies. Yet there were exceptions, and the second generation of immigrants, taught in America to be dissatisfied with the manual work their fathers did, were seldom finding the easy paths of ascent promised in success literature. Where, for one thing, were they to go to college? If they sought to enter the

older eastern institutions, would they face a social struggle? Such anxie-
ties probably contributed to the fact that the game of boyish and spirited
brawn played at the eastern centers of intellect and cultivation was to
be overthrown by the new game of craft and field maneuver that got its
first rehearsal at the hands of two second-generation poor boys attending little-known Notre Dame.

The more significant of the two boys, Knute Rockne, was, to be sure,
of Danish Protestant descent and only later became a Catholic.[9] During
their summer vacation jobs as lifeguards on Lake Michigan, Rockne and
Gus Dorais decided to work as a passing team. Playing West Point early
in the season of 1913, they put on the first demonstration of the spiral
pass that makes scientific use of the difference in shape between the
round ball used in the kicking game and the oval that gradually replaced
it when ball-carrying began. As the first players to exploit the legal pass,
they rolled up a surprise victory over Army. One of the effects of the
national change in rules was to bring the second-generation boys of the
early twentieth century to the front, with a craft innovation that added
new elements of surprise, "system" and skull-session to a game that had
once revolved about an ethos of brawn plus character-building.

With the ethnic shift, appears to have come a shift in type of hero.
The work-minded glamor of an all-'round craftsman like Jim Thorpe
gave way to the people-minded glamor of backfield generals organizing
deceptive forays into enemy territory—of course, the older martial virtues are not so much ruled out as partially incorported in the new image.
In saying this, it must not be forgotten, as sports columnist Red Smith
has pointed out, that the fictional Yale hero, Dick Merriwell, is openly
and shamelessly represented as a dirty player in the first chapters of his
career. But the difference is that his deviation from standard sportsmanship consisted largely of slugging, not of premeditated wiliness. In fact,
the Yale Era, even into Camp's reign, was characterized by a game played
youthfully, with little attention to the players' prestige outside college
circles. Again, the second-generationers mark a change. A variety of
sources, including letters to the sports page, indicate that a Notre Dame
victory became representational in a way a Yale or Harvard victory never
was, and no Irish or Polish boy on the team could escape the symbolism.
And by the self-confirming process, the Yale or Harvard showing became
symbolic in turn, and the game could never be returned, short of intra-
muralization, to the players themselves and their earlier age of innocent
dirtiness.[10] The heterogeneity of America which had made it impossible
to play the Rugby game at Yale had finally had its effect in transforming the meaning of the game to a point where Arnold of Rugby might

have difficulty in drawing the right moral or any moral from it. Its "ideal types" had undergone a deep and widespread characterological change.

For the second-generation boy, with his father's muscles but not his father's motives, football soon became a means to career ascent. So was racketeering, but football gave acceptance, too—acceptance into the democratic fraternity of the entertainment world where performance counts and ethnic origin is hardly a handicap. Moreover, Americans as onlookers welcomed the anti-traditional innovations of a Rockne, and admired the trick that worked, whatever the opposing team and alumni may have thought about the effort involved. One wonders whether Rockne and Dorais may not have forgotten a particular pleasure from their craftiness by thinking of it as a counter-image to the stereotype of muscle-men applied to their fathers.

It was in 1915, at about the same time that the newcomers perfected their passing game, that the recruitment of players began in earnest. Without such recruitment, the game could not have served as a career route for many of the second generation who would not have had the cash or impetus to make the class jump that college involved.[11]

The development of the open and rationalized game has led step by step not only to the T formation, but also to the two-platoon system. These innovations call for a very different relationship among the players than was the case under the older star system. For the game is now a coöperative enterprise in which mistakes are too costly—to the head coach, the budget, even the college itself—to be left to individual initiative. At least at one institution, an anthropologist has been called in to study the morale problems of the home team, and to help in the scouting of opposing teams. To the learning of Taylor, there has been added that of Mayo, and coaches are conscious of the need to be group-dynamics leaders rather than old-line straw bosses.

Today, the semi-professionalized player, fully conscious of how many people's living depends on him, cannot be exhorted by Frank Merriwell appeals, but needs to be "handled." And the signals are no longer the barks of the first Camp-trained quarterback—hardly more differentiated than a folkdance caller's—but are cues of great subtlety and mathematical precision for situations planned in advance with camera shots and character fill-ins of the opposing team. James Worthy and other advocates of a span of control beyond the usual half-dozen of the older military and executive manuals might find support for their views in the way an eleven is managed. Industrial, military, and football teamwork have all a common cultural frame.

Yet it would be too simple to say that football has ceased to be a game for its players, and has become an industry, or a training for industry. In the American culture as a whole, no sharp line exists between work and play, and in some respects the more work-like an activity becomes, the more it can successfully conceal elements of playfulness.[12] Just because the sophisticated "amateur" of today does *not* have his manhood at stake in the antique do-or-die fashion (though his manhood may be involved, in very ambivalent ways, in his more generalized role as athlete and teammate), there can be a relaxation of certain older demands and a more detached enjoyment of perfection of play irrespective of partisanship.

The role of football tutor to the audience has been pushed heavily onto radio and TV announcers (some of whom will doubtless be mobile into the higher-status role of commentators on politics or symphony broadcasts). The managerial coalescence of local betting pools into several big oceans has also contributed to the audience stake in the game. Yet all that has so far been said does not wholly explain alumnus and subway-alumnus loyalties. It may be that we have to read into this interest of the older age groups a much more general aspect of American behavior: the pious and near-compulsory devotion of the older folks to whatever the younger folks are alleged to find important. The tension between the generations doubtless contributes to the hysterical note of solemnity in the efforts of some older age groups to control the ethics of the game, partly perhaps as a displacement of their efforts to control youthful sexuality.

And this problem in turn leads to questions about the high percentage of women in the American football audience, compared with that of any other country, and the high salience of women in football as compared with baseball imagery (in recent American football films, girls have been singled out as the most influential section of the spectators). The presence of these women heightens the sexual impact of everything in and around the game, from shoulderpads to the star system, as the popular folklore of the game recognizes. Although women are not expected to attend baseball games, when they do attend they are expected to understand them and to acquire, if not a "male" attitude, at least something approaching companionship on a basis of equality with their male escorts.[13]

For all its involvement with such elemental themes in American life, it may be that football has reached the apex of its audience appeal. With bigness comes vulnerability: "inter-industry" competition is invited, and so are rising costs—the players, though not yet unionized, learn early in high school of their market value and, like Jim in Huckleberry Finn, take pride in it.[14] The educators' counter-reformation cannot be laughed off. With the lack of ethnic worlds to conquer, we may soon find the now-decorous Irish of the Midwest embarrassed by Notre Dame's unbroken victories. Perhaps the period of innovation which began in 1823 at Rugby has about come to an end in the United States, with large changes likely to result only if the game is used as a device for acculturation to America, not by the vanishing stream of immigrants to that country, but by the rest of the world that will seek the secret of American victories on the playing fields of South Bend.

NOTES

1. The growing scale of college football is indicated by its dollar place in the American leisure economy. In 1929, out of $4.3 billion recreation expenditures by Americans, the college football gate accounted for $22 million. In 1950, out of $11.2 billion in such expenditures, it accounted for $103 million. While something less than 1% of the total United States recreation account, college football had ten times the gross income of professional football. The 1950 gate of $103 million suggests that a total capital of perhaps $250 million is invested in the college football industry. The revenue figures, above, of course, do not include the invisible subsidization of football, nor do they hint at the place that football pools occupy in the American betting economy.

2. A commemorative stone at Rugby reads as follows:

THIS STONE
COMMEMORATES THE EXPLOIT OF
WILLIAM WEBB ELLIS
WHO WITH A FINE DISREGARD FOR THE RULES OF
FOOTBALL, AS PLAYED IN HIS TIME,
FIRST TOOK THE BALL IN HIS ARMS AND RAN WITH IT,
THUS ORIGINATING THE DISTINCTIVE FEATURES OF
THE RUGBY GAME
A. D. 1823

3. Walter Camp and Lorin F. Deland, *Football*.

4. Cf. his *An Outline of Social Psychology*, pp. 93-182.

5. "Fifty years ago arguments followed almost every decision the referee made. The whole team took part, so that half the time the officials scarcely knew who was captain. The player who was a good linguist was always a priceless asset." John W. Heisman, who played for both Brown and Penn in the 1890's, quoted in Frank G. Menke, *Encyclopedia of Sports*, p. 293.

6. Sigfried Giedion, *Mechanization Takes Command*, pp. 21-27.

7. In view of the prejudice against "Taylorism" today, shared by men and management as well as the intellectuals, let us record our admiration for Taylor's achievement, our belief that he was less insensitive to psychological factors than is often claimed, and more "humane" in many ways than his no less manipulative, self-consciously psychological successors.

8. "In a 1905 game between Pennsylvania and Swarthmore, the Pennsy slogan was 'Stop Bob Maxwell,' one of the greatest linesmen of all time. He was a mighty man, with the amazing ability to roll back enemy plunges. The Penn players, realizing that Maxwell was a menace to their chances of victory, took 'dead aim' at him throughout the furious play.

   "Maxwell stuck it out, but when he tottered off the field, his face was a bloody wreck. Some photographer snapped him, and the photo of the mangled Maxwell, appearing in a newspaper, caught the attention of the then President Roosevelt. It so angered him, that he issued an ultimatum that if rough play in football was not immediately ruled out, he would abolish it by executive edict." Frank G. Menke, *Encyclopedia of Sports*.

   Notice here the influence of two historical factors on football development: one, the occupancy of the White House in 1905 by the first President of the United States who was a self-conscious patron of youth, sport, and the arts; two, the relative newness in 1905 of photographic sports coverage. Widespread increased photographic coverage of popular culture was the direct result of the newspaper policies of William Randolph Hearst, beginning about 1895.

9. "After the church, football is the best thing we have," Rockne.

10. One of us, while a Harvard undergraduate, sought with several friends to heal the breach between Harvard and Princeton—a breach whose bitterness could hardly be credited today. The Harvards believed Princeton played dirty—it certainly won handily in those years of the 20s—while Princetonians believed themselves snubbed by Harvard as crude parvenus trying to make a trio out of the Harvard-Yale duo. The diplomatic problems involved in seeking to repair these status slights and scars were a microcosm of the Congress of Westphalia or Vienna—whether the Harvard or Princeton athletic directors should enter the room first was an issue. A leak to the Hearst press destroyed our efforts, as alumni pressure forced denials of any attempt to resume relations, but the compromise formulas worked out were eventually accepted, about the time that the University of Chicago "solved" the problem of the intellectual school by withdrawing from the game altogether.

11. See George Saxon, "Immigrant Culture in a Stratified Society," *Modern Review*, II, No. 2, February 1948.

12. Compare the discussion of Freud's playful work, pp. 331-333, below.

13. Anthropologist Ray Birdwhistell convincingly argues that football players play with an eye to their prestige among teammates, other football players, and other men.

14. Their pride varies to some extent with their place on the team. Linemen, with the exception of ends, have lower status than backfield men. Many players believe that backfields are consciously and unconsciously recruited from higher social strata than linemen.

Homo Ludens (Americanus)

John L. Finlay

In the last two decades North America has witnessed a startling rise in the popularity of football, so that this game and not baseball is now *the* American game. An explanation of this development has been offered by Marshall McLuhan, who writes that

> the T.V. image . . . spells for a while, at least, the doom of baseball. For baseball is a game of one-thing-at-time, fixed positions and visibly delegated specialist jobs such as belonged to the now passing mechanical age. . . . In contrast, American football is non-positional, and any or all of the players can switch to any role during play. It is, therefore, a game which is supplanting baseball in general acceptance. It agrees very well with the new needs of decentralised team play in the electric age.[1]

Implicit in this analysis is the claim that American football's continued popularity is virtually assured. Indeed, McLuhan recognizes that his explanation raises problems, in that sports-conscious Russia has taken to soccer and ice hockey, "two very individualist forms of game which seem little suited to the psychic needs of a collectivist society."[2] While he can explain away this deviation, McLuhan yet suggests that in time American-style football should prove more congenial to Russian society.

The sociology of sport is in its infancy. Yet there does exist a fine article by Riesman and Denney on American football.[3] Interestingly, these writers come to the opposite conclusion and wonder whether football has a future. Clearly there is room for further speculation in this area.

❖   ❖   ❖

In order to isolate the elements of American football which are prized, it will not be sufficient to compare it with baseball—that would be much like comparing apples and pears. Rather it will be necessary to examine

From *Queen's Quarterly* 78: 353-364, 1971. Copyright according to provisions of an Act of Parliament of Canada, 1907. Reprinted by permission of the author.

not merely the American game, but other brands of football, too. Such an approach is facilitated by the fact that these games are not independent; until about the middle of the nineteeth century there was but an ill-defined ur-football. It was from this that the individual varieties crystallized out, and in doing so they seized upon and developed certain aspects of the game which appealed to the host society; these aspects will presumably be the characteristics which give the game its tremendous popularity in any particular setting.

An important dimension to be considered is that which may be called the "limits" of a sport. Ur-football was weakly structured, but any game which is to become a professional mass spectacle must impose limits upon itself. But if all modern forms are limited, there is still room for different conceptions of limitation.

To begin with, there is the question of officiating, which in the early stages of development was quite ineffectual. Rather than by whistle, the game was controlled by the waving of a flag, a technique which favoured a Nelsonian response; early officials were often more akin to umpires who arbitrated appeals than to referees who decreed—and cricket, which is an older form than football, has retained this outlook. Such weaknesses had to go. But whereas soccer and rugby (of both league and union varieties) manage with three officials, the North American codes demand many more. Indeed, the difference is even greater than it seems, for the non-American referee has powers which quite dwarf those of his assistants, the linesmen, whose duties are restricted, in effect, to deciding when the ball is out of play and to giving advice—when there is a question of offside—again by raising a flag. The American and Canadian games demand no less than six officials, and although there is a head judge, the gap between him and the others is not nearly so wide as in the non-American games. This autonomy of the lesser officials can be seen in the ability of all judges to note an infraction by the throwing of a flag onto the field at the point of illegality. Such action has about it an assertiveness which completely eclipses any mere waving by the linesman. Futher to build up the North American notion of powerful officialdom is the presence of the two minions whose task it is to carry the yardsticks which, in disputed gains, decide whether sufficient forward progress has been made. Finally, one should note that the timekeeper becomes an autonomous figure in the American code, and one, moreover, who dramatizes his presence by showing the one-minute warning flag before the conclusion of each period of play. In North America the idea that the game is minutely limited is driven home at all costs.

Time is another aspect of limitation to be considered. In soccer and rugby the referee is the sole judge of time. Given his other duties, it is recognized that his timing of a game must be rather hit-and-miss. The division of the games is similarly rudimentary; in order to equalize the advantage of sun, slope, and so on, the game is simply divided into halves. How differently is time managed in North America. Not only is its measurement taken out of the hands of the referee and lodged in those of a specialist, but the element of "guessing" is removed. The game and the clock are stopped between actions, and time begins to elapse only when the referee whistles for play to resume. It is also to be noted that in North America there is a more sophisticated ordering of the game. There are two halves, but each half is further divided into two, which helps to equalize opportunity more successfully. One further point should be grasped in connection with time. In soccer and rugby it is very easy to waste time; rugby union runs the risk of boring the onlooker by allowing constant kicking for touch. (Rugby league, on the other hand, has managed to get round this trouble; of all the European games of football it is the one which most closely resembles the American pattern, a fact which will be alluded to later on.) But in North America time wasting is impossible; here, time is not only precise, it is precious.

The ability to penalize time-wasting is facilitated by the significant fact that in North American football time is space—the penalty for time-wasting is the loss of territory. Here is another aspect of limitation, the way in which space is conceived and handled. It is to be noted that the European games are most cavalier when it comes to fixing the playing area; in both soccer and rugby maximum/minimum dimensions are given. Moreover, these boundary lines are the only ones which matter; they serve to mark off a neutral, equal space. A glance at a soccer field, or better still at a diagram of one, will make this perfectly clear. The only serious irruption into the emptiness of the pitch is the penalty area about the goal, a magical exception designed to protect the taboo-figure of the goalkeeper, the one player permitted to handle the ball, the one player dressed deviantly. Rugby is somewhat more space-conscious. Although overall dimension is equally fluid, the dividing up of the field is more apparent, and lines are needed ten yards from the centre stripe and twenty-five from the goal-line; in addition, a dead-ball line and one five yards in from touch are also necessary.

Such thinking is foreign to the North American pattern. To begin with, the dimensions of the playing area are rigidly prescribed and deviation is not permitted. The entire area becomes a gridiron, since the game's characteristic, the making of ten yards' progress in a given number of attempts, calls for the marking of each yard on the field. (In fact only each tenth yard is run right across the field, but the others do exist.) And, as in rugby, there are lines in from touch, though in this case much more than five yards. In all this it is crucial to grasp that no point of the field is of more value than any other. While soccer players know that the relatively small goal is all-important, and that an infraction inside the magic territory guarding it results in a penalty which is an almost automatic goal, the North American player refuses to acknowledge any point as of more importance than another—forward movement at any point of the field is what counts. In this, rugby is more akin to the American style than is soccer. But even so, it must be pointed out that rugby's estimation of the goal is greater than the American's; in rugby a dropped goal, equal to a try, is still a feature of the game, and a conversion is worth two-thirds of a try. In North America the dropped goal has been assimilated to the field goal and is worth but half of a touchdown, while a conversion counts only one-sixth of a touchdown; indeed, in the college game the option exists of running the ball into the end zone after a touchdown, and this is worth twice a kicked conversion.

It is at this point that the deeper significance of space and its handling begins to emerge, a significance which goes to the root of the philosophies of the various codes. Soccer sees its field, other than the goal area, as a neutral space within which the action is allowed to build up. The objective is the goal, and the field exists merely to allow the team to group itself, mount an attack, and move in on that goal. Rugby, while not so pure in this respect, is essentially very similar. On the other hand, for the North American player each piece of the field is, in a sense, the goal line. Whereas the soccer player scores explosively, apocalyptically, the North American must score on the installment plan.

The basic divergence here under discussion may be illustrated by way of a comparison of penalties. In European games the method of compensating for infraction is a kick or scrum taken at the point of infraction, the ball being handed over to the team offended against. This amounts to little more than giving this team a chance of better position, and in many cases the advantage gained is little more than an opportunity to restructure the field-player relationship. Only in the case of a soccer penalty or some rugby penalties is the gain clear-cut, and this, as hinted at earlier in the example of soccer, is punishment for a taboo-infraction. But in North America an infraction usually means the loss of a certain number of yards, so that the team offended against creeps another installment nearer. So sophisticated, in fact, is the American understanding of space that it enables penalties to run on into the future, as it were. What this means can be seen by comparing the results which flow from an infraction which attempts but fails to prevent a score; in Europe no notice is taken of it (that is, at a team level; evidently the offending individual may suffer), the goal itself being penalty enough; but in America the infraction would be remembered, and when play resumed the offending team would find itself closer to its own goal line than would otherwise have been the case. Crime and punishment is a much more inexorable matter in North American sport than elsewhere.

From what has been said of the dimension of limits, it will be seen that the North American game is much more precise, standardized, indeed efficient than the European. In short, it approaches the scientific criteria of control and replication as closely as any sport can without forfeiting that element of unpredictability which must always be there. The clinching point here is the use of statistics. The American sports fan is avid for figures and more figures which will make possible "true" comparisons and facilitate that favourite North American pastime, the composition of "dream teams." While not totally unknown in Europe, such attitudes are exceptional. Nor is it enough to counter by saying that North American sports lend themselves to this approach whereas European ones do not; the development of North American games was governed precisely by this urge to quantify. This can be proved by setting the European practice of a Canadian game against the original product. Recently on the air, reference was made to a Canadian hockey exile who was at the top of the British league; the commentator wished to give his Canadian audience some idea of this player's prowess but was obliged to confess that he was unable to prove since British officials do not keep the detailed statistics that Canadians take for granted.

The next dimension to be looked at is the way in which the participant is perceived, that is, the way in which he is viewed *vis à vis* the other members of the team and *vis à vis* his opposition—this term is employed to include the opposing team and the ball, for both are elements which must be controlled and manipulated.

Until recently European games have restricted a team to the actual number allowed by the rules to be in play at any one time. These and no others took part, and should one player be so injured as to have to withdraw, no substitute was allowed, and the side had to struggle along short-handed. This situation has been modified of late, and limited substituting is now permitted. In North America, however, the practice of substitution has had a long history, and players are continually being taken off and sent in. Alongside this distinction is another akin to it. The North American coach never relinquishes control of his team, and he and his roof-top spotter are constantly analyzing the game and adjusting the team strategy accordingly; the captain on the field has but limited powers of interpreting the game and shaping it as it unfolds. With the decline of the captain goes the fragmenting of his office; at the Super Bowl no less than six "captains" were busy shaking hands before the kick-off. Indeed, so institutionalized is coach-dominated football that sides are permitted to take so many "time-outs" per game, occasions when the clock is stopped and quarterback and coach huddle to discuss the situation. (Time-outs are not allowed in the Canadian game, which in this and other respects exhibits its greater dependence on European patterns.) Of course, the episodic character of football, which allows for huddles on the field between each play, aids this bench control at all times, for plays may be sent in with the substituted player.

These two points taken together lead to the conclusion that in North America the player is devalued—the players are not so much playing as being played. And when unsatisfactory, whether because of injury or because of an off-day or because changed opposition tactics demand countering changes, the player is removed. The team, in a way, overshadows the individuals who compose it and to it they are from time to time sacrificed. This impression is confirmed by noting the American practice of specialization, and here McLuhan is quite wrong in his characterization. Rather than the game being one of interchanging players able "to switch to any role during play," football is a most restricted form, much more specialized than outward appearance would suggest. For long the game has been played by two squads, one for offense and one for defence, and a total change-over accompanies a change in ball possession. But specialization goes further than this; even on the offence there are players who are held to be ineligible receivers, and should they by chance be downfield to receive a forward pass they would be penalized. Clubs keep on the roster players whose sole function it is to kick the ball, and specialized formations such as the punt-return formation are referred to. The climax, one imagines, of this trend was recently established by a team in a minor American league; its specialized field-goal kicker is able to perform adequately only with a specialized ball holder, his wife, and she dons full uniform and trots out by his side whenever such goals are to be kicked! It is interesting to note that in European games the trend has been the other way. In older forms of soccer a distinction was made between the heavier backs and the lighter forwards, the former guarding the goal and feeding the latter. But the logic of the game, especially as developed by the Latins, destroyed this nascent specialization, and now all must be potential attackers, all possible defenders. The same has been true of modern rugby, with the French, especially, showing how even forwards can be taught to handle like backs.

The difference between the American and European games in respect of the player-opposition relationship is striking, too. In soccer, and in a different way in rugby, the player must attempt to control a refractory ball. In the former game all but the goalkeeper have given up the "natural" use of hands and have limited themselves to the use of feet. This means that when it comes to beating an opponent, it is not merely a two-way interaction of attacker *versus* defender; rather it is a three-way interaction of two players and the ball. This outlook which gives so much importance to the ball is well seen in the case of scoring. It is not enough in soccer to pass a certain point; the ball must go into a relatively small, guarded goal, and so ball-control remains crucial even when the attacker has broken through into the clear. Thus it is that in soccer the varying playing surfaces are not seen necessarily as flaws, but as opportunities for the gifted player to show himself superior to, say, a clinging pitch. One is tempted to go so far as to claim that the absence of covered pitches in Europe is due not so much to technological backwardness as to a different philosophy of sport.

Rugby has moved some way from this approach: for instance, the goal line rather than the goal is the aim. Yet kicking which demands allowance for ground conditions (grub-kicking) and dribbling are still a part of the game, and dropped goals may even now decide a match. Above all, the shape of the ball, together with the fact that the rules demand that on occasion it shall bounce (set-scrums), and the fact that in the course of a game the ball very frequently does bounce, means that the ball and ball-control must remain vital.

This is no longer so in the American game. Any manoeuvre which exposes the ball to the vagaries of the turf or of its own shape is suppressed. Thus, heeling the ball to the quarterback has given way to the snap-back; kicking on the run has all but disappeared, as has the lateral pass. Passing and receiving have become once and for all exercises, one is either in the right spot to catch the ball or one is not, and if the ball is caught, as often as not that ends that particular play and its interest. One could say, in fact, that in the American codes the ball serves merely to "legitimate" a particular player. For instance, to score in rugby the ball must be firmly grounded behind the goal line, but in football this stipulation does not apply. More, there is no need for the ball to cross the line; it is enough for the ball carrier to get into the end zone. What has happened, in effect, is that the European three-way interaction has been reduced, *for those in touch with the ball,* to a two-way interaction.

The italics are crucial. In the American game there are three-way inter-actions, the triangle being completed by a player who normally does not touch the ball and indeed hardly expects to. At first sight it would appear that a triangle of two animate elements and one inanimate has been re-placed by one in which all the elements are animate. This, however, would be a false reading of the situation. In the American game one of the three is a blocker, a player whose job it is to take the opposing tackle out of the play and so spring his team-mate into the clear. Evidently, such a blocker must see his own body less as an end than as a means, an instru-ment in the service of the player for whom he is blocking. The triangle, in fact, is still one with an inanimate element, one player having been reduced in stature. It is for this reason that American football may be considered violent, not simply because of the savage body contact, but rather because the contact is virtually an end in itself. At times one sus-pects that Americans recognize this fact and are ashamed of it. Sports writers and commentators overcompensate and go out of their way to speak of the *ball* game; but who ever heard hockey referred to as the *puck* game?

After looking at this second dimension—that of the way in which the player is perceived—two points can be made. First, the feeling that foot-ball is a more precise game has been strengthened, for it is a game which pits specialized teams composed of interchangeable parts against each other, with the complicating factors such as ball and personality reduced to a minimum. Secondly, it emphasizes another aspect of the managed, production-line aspect of the American game, the dehumanization of the worker/player and his subordination to the system. The use of totally disguising uniforms is but another indication of this.

The insights gained so far may be summarized and more light thrown, perhaps, upon the distinctiveness of American football by considering a third dimension. The varieties of football form a spectrum running from fluid to static. Clearly soccer would be at the fluid end, and North Amer-ican at the static; but which kind of North American? Knowing the stronger European heritage of Canada, and bearing in mind Canada's refusal to become as thrusting as America, one would predict that the Canadian would have to yield pride of place at the static end to the Amer-ican variety. This is precisely what one finds. The wider Canadian field encourages sweeps and lateral passing, whereas the American demands a greater concentration on up-the-middle running. The deeper end zones in Canada encourage passing for touchdowns and lessen the emphasis upon powering over the goal lines. The American game allows four downs in which to make the ten yards, the Canadian but three, with the result that the Canadian game sees more changes of possession—lessening the notion of an inexorable progress which is to be interrupted only by some "fault"—and sees more kicking, which always makes for a more fluid situation. This advantage is off-set by the fact that Canadian linemen have to be a yard apart and the fact that the entire backfield may be in motion, two rules which give the offence an edge—but one gained by increasing mobility and fluidity. The gap between Canadian football and soccer would be filled by rugby, with the union variety standing towards the static, the league towards the fluid end; in the former, frequent set-pieces, such as scrums and lineouts, are encountered, while in the latter these elements are played down or abolished. The order, then, would be American—Canadian—Union—League—Soccer, an order beginning with the most and ending with the least "computerable." Has no one yet written a comparison of Vietnam and Malaya, the former a football, the latter a soccer war?

A term which has been lurking behind the discussion must now be brought forward openly. The three dimensions all illustrate what may be termed the "rationality" of American football. This Weberian term at once raises the question of whether it is supremely the game of the Protestant-Capitalist mind. To answer the question adequately would demand a very full study. Although Riesman and Denney do make mention in passing of the Protestant dimension, they do not probe the link and seem to make it mean little more than WASP establishment. (Also mentioned but not developed is the idea of "feudal" rugby.) It may be remarked that the Canadian scene tends to bear out this tentative Protestant identification. It has long been recognized that French Canada is under-represented in Canadian football, and the absurd explanation is frequently offered that French Canadians are not tough enough. The absurdity lies in the equally well recognized fact that French Canadians are over-represented in ice hockey, an equally tough sport. Now, at the risk of infuriating hockey enthusiasts, it may be pointed out that hockey is nothing but soccer on ice, even down to the fact that the rink's dimensions are of the maximum/minimum type. Hockey, a game without genuine specialization (defenceman Bobby Orr is a leading goal scorer), a game in which changes in the direction of attack are bewilderingly frequent, is a game with instinctive appeal to the Catholic mind and is essentially foreign to the Protestant. It is, of course, ridiculous to counter that Notre Dame has always been a leading football college. In America, as Glock and Stark have noted in another context,[4] there is, sociologically speaking, Catholic community.

One must conclude from all this, then, that McLuhan was wrong in claiming that football was not "a game of one thing at a time, fixed positions and visibly delegated specialist jobs." Far from football's belonging to the electronic age, it belongs to a way of life now superseded. If any sport is suited to the electronic age, that sport is soccer; and if its failure to "take" in the U.S.A. turns out to be permanent, then the rise of basketball may fulfill the requirements.

*   *   *

But if football belongs to the mechanical age, the problem still remains of why it is rising and baseball declining. Does this suggest that McLuhan was wrong here also, that baseball is not a game of the mechanical age? Again the way to test this suggestion is to set baseball against its alternatives, see which are its essential characteristics, and so establish if this signifies a move towards or away from "rationality."

A slight problem arises in that baseball is, in effect, *sui generis;* there are no relations to form a family as in the case of football. But would it be impossible to set it alongside cricket? After all, there are great similarities.[5] Both are summer games, played on a field within a field, that is, a diamond/wicket of precise dimensions and well-defined elements set in a much more vaguely structured outfield. Both are contests between throwers and hitters, the one aiming to dismiss his opponent, the other attempting to score by running between the bases/wickets. Moreover, while all are expected to be hitters, only the specialists are called upon to be throwers. Those who are not throwers have other specialized tasks in the field, a state of affairs best seen in the catcher/wicketkeeper. The hitting side has one man actually engaged in hitting, but "subordinates" are on the field at the same time who have just been engaged in hitting or hope to be just about to do so. In both games the teams alternate innings. Certainly Harry Wright showed that there was not too great a divergence; Wright was the Yorkshire cricketer lured to Cincinnati in 1865 to be the professional to that city's cricket club, and who within two years had gone over to baseball.[6]

But, as in the case of football, the differences are crucial. A study of the two kinds of playing area immediately suggests that in these games, too, the divergence of American-English thinking is going to be along the same lines. The baseball diamond and the outfielder are linked in a "directional" sense; the hitter must direct the ball in front of him into an outfield which is an extension of the diamond. In cricket the playing surface, a circle, totally surrounds the wicket. Play behind the wicket is possible, and indeed calls for some of the most highly prized and difficult strokes. Hitting in baseball is direct, the bat being a club pure and simple, but a cricket bat is quaint and its use stylized. Pitching is equally direct, but the bowler is restricted in not being allowed to bend the elbow. The bowler must not only beat the bat, he must also hit the wicket and dislodge the bail. The pitcher, on the other hand, aims at a square of space. A score is made in cricket when the batsmen cross, having gone nowhere in particular, but in baseball a score is a round trip. This point gains in strength when it is remembered how early baseball knew two variants which did not feature this "circular" pattern. But the two kinds in which completion was at a distance from the batter's plate quickly faded away. Cricket matches are measured in days, baseball's in innings, and so decisions are more easily reached in the latter game; indeed, cricket is negative in that a batsman's glory may lie in merely remaining, scoring having become a secondary consideration. (It is noteworthy that just as rugby league, which approaches more closely to football than does rugby union, is found in the working-class industrial north of England, so too is league cricket, a game which differs from its parent in having a much more rational approach to time limits, scoring rates, and so on. There decisions are the important consideration.)

It seems clear, then, that baseball represents a shift towards the rationality demanded by a mechanical society, and that McLuhan was correct in his characterization of it. It is, after all, extremely telling that baseball only began to supplant cricket after the Civil War.

*   *   *

Is it to be concluded from this that baseball and football are not essentially different and that if one is sinking and one is rising it is accidental? Such a conclusion would make nonsense of the foregoing analysis, of course. In fact, there is one ground on which the two sports diverge radically and which will account for the difference in fortunes.

Baseball has about it elements which have to be described as unfair. Although a home run, the only score, may be made up in installments, these installments in themselves cannot be translated into scores. Thus it may well happen that one team loads far more bases than its opposition does, but fails adequately to capitalize upon these beginnings and so allows the other team to outscore it where it counts, in home runs. This sort of thing may happen in football, too, but its effects are masked and it does not have the salience that it has in baseball. The same truth may be seen in a slightly different way. Whereas in football each yard gained is identical, in baseball one hit is not the same as another. For example, a team may load three bases by successively having its hitters gain a base at a time, which, since the game's glory is the home run, may be looked upon as relative failures. At this point the big hitter may unleash a home run, so counting four for his side. Had the same hit been made at the start of an inning, only one run would have resulted. It is true that the way would be open for the bases to be loaded again and for the big hitter to make another appearance, indeed this process could go on indefinitely. The point is that this possibility is not real to the spectators. (Cricket has something of this "accidental" quality, for a ball which just crosses the boundary will score four, that which just fails to do so may count but one.) Another way of illustrating this point is to contrast the episodic nature of baseball with the continuous narrative of football. (Clearly, "episodic" is being used here in a sense different from that when it was applied to football.) In baseball the innings ends any advantage; for instance, three loaded bases count for nothing. But consider the analogous situation in football when there are two evenly-matched teams unable to make first downs and obliged to kick. Eventually the superior team will approach the opponent's goal line, if only by the difference between the two punts, and in this way it is possible for any interim advantage to be transformed into a score.

Then again, there is the very meaning of the home run. There is something apocalyptic about such an explosion of power which, once it has connected with the ball, makes a formality of the hitter's tour of the bases. There is nothing comparable in football. The nearest is the long pass, but there is nothing so clear-cut about this—either in definition, or in execution—and there is nothing in the statistics to set beside the home run. The favourite football statistics are averages, either ground gains or completed passes, and averages are decidely non-apocalyptic.

The implication is that if both baseball and football are similarly attuned to a rational capitalist environment, baseball is the game of an early, football of a mature capitalism. The early capitalist period, above all in the U.S.A., was a time when the rational, calculating approach was yet shot through with a gambling, piratical residue—the robber-baron era, in fact. Baseball is a robber-baron game. But when capitalism matures and moves into the stage of staid corporateness which prefers safety to spectacle, certain small gains to risky windfalls, its sports style must similarly shift. It is interesting to note that football is America's patriotic game. The staging of the game and the atmosphere which surrounds it are exercises in high seriousness; compare this with baseball, which is light-hearted and even irreverent, incapable of carrying a nationalistic charge. And that this is not simply a distinction of winter/summer crowds is indicated by comparing soccer and cricket atmospheres and indeed the games themselves; in this dichotomy it is cricket which represents capitalist planning, patience, and application to detail; Newbolt's "There's a deathly hush in the close tonight" has no parallel in soccer and cannot have.[7]

It is instructive, also, to see how Japan reacted to the American occupation. That country, engaged in industrialization itself and still in the early, heroic stages of capitalism, has avidly taken to baseball but not to football. It is not a question of Japanese physique serving as a determinant, for rugby, which might also be thought to favour large players, has long had a following in Asia. Rather, it is another illustration of the Japanese craving for gambling, as seen in their addiction to *pachinko*. It may be predicted, then, that when baseball has been fully internalized by the Japanese, and when their capitalism has moved into a higher stage, they will move on to football.

NOTES

1. Marshall McLuhan, *Understanding Media: The Extensions of Man* (New York: Signet Books, 1966), p. 212.
2. Ibid.
3. D. Riesman and R. Denney, "Football in America: a Study in Cultural Diffusion," *American Quarterly*, 1951.
4. C. Y. Glock and R. Stark, *Christian Beliefs and Anti-Semitism* (New York: Harper & Row, 1966).
5. There is a school of thought which derives baseball from cricket rather than from rounders. See F. G. Menke, ed., *The Encyclopedia of Sport*, 4th edition, 1969.
6. Philip Goodhart and Christopher Chattaway, *War without Weapons* (London: W. H. Allen, 1968), p. 38.
7. Sir Henry Newbolt, "Vitai Lampada" in *Poems New and Old*, 2nd ed. (London: John Murray, 1919). In this poem the stress is upon "hanging on," it reflects a dour approach to life, and yet another indication of why cricket was not suitable for the post-Civil War American scene.

Sport, Dependency and the Canadian State

Bruce Kidd

"To achieve higher levels of participation and fitness, and excellence in sport, will be of great value both for the image we have of ourselves and for our national spirit."

—Iona Campagnolo, Green Paper on Sport, Oct. 1977.

"Once again, Americans have taught us what it means to be a Canadian."

—Fred Mooney, *The Toronto Clarion*, Oct. 3, 1979, à propos of the excitement generated by the Montreal Expos' drive to the pennant.

Despite the idealist's hope that forms of sport are separate, and represent a "respite" from everyday reality, each of these cultural forms carries within it the typing or "genetic stamp" of the mode of production and particularly the social relations of the society or societies in which it is created and played. Whatever the extent forms of sport become reified and take on a semi-autonomous existence, we must never forget that they were created, and then elaborated, redesigned and streamlined by groups of humans in specific human societies: these innovators and players—the George Beers, Bobby Orrs, and Al Eaglesons—could not dream up or improvise their contests, rules, norms, favorite "plays" and associated mythologies on any other basis than from their own experience. Thus we can see in the amateur code, which continues to have force even today in sports like track and field, the vestiges of an attempt a century ago by the largely aristocratic and bourgeois ruling groups in sport to limit working class participation, an attempt which both reinforced and drew inspiration from similar confrontations in virtually every sphere

From *Proceedings of the Queen's Symposium on Sport, Culture and the Modern State.* Reprinted with permission of the author and the Sport Studies Research Group, Queen's University.

of economic, political and cultural life. We can see in the nineteenth-century prohibitions against Indian athletes in Canada, in part, a specific statement of the widespread belief that the native peoples were innately different from "civilized" whites and therefore had to be banished to reservations in marginal areas.[1] It is for this reason that forms of sport can play such a significantly ideological role, despite their seeming innocence: they invariably contain within them statements about social relations, which in turn serve to reinforce or, as the case may be, contest the dominant social relations or arrangements of power. These statements tend to encourage some kinds of behavior and discourage others. Thus the amateur code, with its eloquent affirmation of participation for participation's sake, has not only served to exclude many talented working class athletes, but also to discourage its many adherents from questioning the ethical basis of wage labour under capitalism and from even demanding full remuneration from the sports entrepreneurs or governments for whom they toil.[2] To the extent that beliefs acquired and elaborated through sport are transferred by participants to their other activities, the entire interconnected system of social relations, including under capitalism, wage labour, political beliefs, and even the teaching of the social sciences in universities, is reinforced, further developed, or contested.

Others have discussed the inter-relationships between sport, the state, class and the logic of production in advanced state monopoly capitalism.[3] In this paper, I would like to explore the ideological role of sport, as it is affected by the state, in connection with the question of nationalism or independence. Specifically, I will consider the role that forms of sport have played in the disintegration of English-speaking Canada as a distinct national community. Although "nation" can never be separated from "class," it will be instructive to study sport as ideology from this perspective.

Let us briefly consider the interrelationships between forms of sport and national communities. By "nation," I mean an ethnic community with certain specific characteristics: a common language, territory and economic life; a common culture and sense of identity. It is not necessarily synonymous with a nation-state.[4] Those familiar with Canadian history and political affairs will readily recognize this terminology. Both Quebec and the Dene are "nations," although neither have formed their own nation-states. English-speaking Canada is also a "nation" in this sense, although it's becoming more difficult to define its unique characteristics. Perhaps this distinction is clearest in the present referendum debate in Quebec—both René Lévesque and Claude Ryan are in agreement that Quebec is a "nation"; they differ on what is its best relationship to the present Canadian state.

In the capitalist era, forms of sport have often strengthened or accelerated the development of national communities, especially those which become nation-states. This is a well argued thesis. Roland Barthes, to take one example, contends in his National Film Board essay, *Of Sport and Men*, that many games not only express national characteristics, but do so in a way that enables people to discover and articulate these characteristics for themselves. Hockey captures both the passion, and the struggle of life in the Canadian winter; La Tour de France is a catechism of the geographical and cultural majesty of France.[5] Although many of these sports are now played—and refashioned—by other national communities, distinctive styles are still very much in evidence, as Soviet hockey, Brazilian samba soccer, and West Indian cricket dramatically attest. In some cases, forms of sport served to express and solidify the idea of a national community well before it enjoyed common political boundaries. The Turner movement which grew out of the gymnastics curriculum of Friedrich Ludwig Jahn after the Prussian defeat by Napoleon in 1799, consciously articulated the aspirations of pan-German unity, even during 23 years of state prohibition. Although this movement would later be appropriated by both the left and the right—the workers' sports movement and the Nazis—in many of the feudal German principalities in the nineteenth century, it was simultaneously an expression of the liberal bourgeoisie. In 1848, when the Prussian Emperor invaded Hesse to put down the provisional government declared by the Frankfurt Assembly, it was the Turners who first sprang—unsuccessfully, it turned out—to the defense of the fledgling republic.

Forms of sport have contributed to the development of national culture in at least one other significant way: by providing a format—international competition—in which the national community can be symbolically represented. Pierre de Coubertin was right: the prospect of national victories in sport has proven to be a powerful stimulus, to which the survival of the modern Olympics, despite many problems, is striking testimony. To the extent that these performances developed and reinforced beliefs in the national community, they served to strengthen and buttress a whole range of economic and social policies and behaviors, from protective tariffs, selective purchasing and hiring to the explicit concern with autonomy.

In Canada, long before its respective national communities could win complete autonomy in political affairs, the English-speaking community, and particularly the professional classes of Montreal and the manufacturing centres in southern Ontario, avidly sought to articulate a national interest in the growing accomplishments of Canadian athletes. In the 1880s, Ned Hanlan won a string of sculling races that, in the approving words of the Toronto *Globe*, "carried the name of Canada around the world." Hanlan was better known than Prime Minister Macdonald and his victories were widely perceived to be an example of the growing strength of the young Dominion.[6] The career of Tom Longboat, the Onondaga marathoner who was the most famous athlete in the land in the decade prior to World War I, is also instructive. Throughout his life, Longboat would be smeared by the charge that he never trained, that he exhibited—in the words of the *Globe*—"all the waywardness and lack of responsibility of his race."[7] But when he won against runners from other countries, he would be toasted as an example of Canadian courage and determination. "This man Longboat has done more to help the Commissioner of Industries than any other Canadian," a Toronto City Controller told the press the day after Longboat's victory in the 1907 Boston marathon.[8] Increasingly, the state has been active in fostering sport as a symbol of the national community. The first such attempts came during WW1 when the army staged a number of exhibitions and competitions in an effort to stimulate recruiting and arouse the patriotism of Canadian soldiers.[9] In recent years, the most prevalent form of state intervention has been direct and indirect subsidization of national teams.[10]

Many people today, on both the left and the right, regard nationalism as a restrictively conservative, if not a reactionary force,[11] and to the extent to which the slow-to-change forms of sport reinforce it, particularly in cases of hegemonic national communities, they regard sport as inherently reactionary as well.[12] But we should not conclude that forms of sport are necessarily conservative, that they can never serve as an outlet or part crucible for progressive ideas, or what Gruneau calls the "transformative power of play."[13] According to C. L. R. James' account of cricket in the West Indies, *Beyond a Boundary*, the black players' struggle for full recogition on representative teams selected and dominated by white colonial administrators ebbed and flowed in counterpoint harmony with the larger struggle for independence until in Trinidad it finally broke out in riot in early 1960 and gave the independence movement the final push to remove all remaining forms of colonial rule.[14] Forms of sport are much less suited to the expression of conflict, as Hargreaves[15] and Beamish[16] have argued, but they have and can express progressive ideas as well as conservative ones.

Like other ideological forms, forms of sport not only reinforce certain categries in the mode of production, but also challenge or question them. In each of the examples already cited, the ideas about national community spread through sport gradually supplanted ideas that reinforced kinship, feudal and regional practices and institutions. What can be described in approving terms as articulation, development and reinforcement, and subversion. Although the native peoples of Canada once enjoyed a wide variety of highly developed games, they gradually altered —and in many cases, eventually abandoned—these games and the beliefs which accompanied them in the face of the pressure and encouragement to do so from the more numerous and economically advanced white invaders. At the international level, the two faces of this single process are imperialism and disintegration.[17]

Few generations in English-speaking Canadian history have not puzzled over the distinct nature of their national identity: apart from our now challenged ability to subjugate Quebec, what is it that we share that defines us as a nation? Whatever the disagreement about the national characteristics, there is now little debate that many common economic patterns, political institutions, and cultural forms are rapidly disintegrating with the advance of American and other forms of state monopoly capital, with the result that in each of these spheres, groups of Canadians are losing control over the forces shaping their lives. The examples are well known. What is so terrifying is that the details indicate further deterioration every day.

The economy has never emerged from its reliance upon staple exports as the leading sector, leaving it vulnerable not only to the boom and bust cycles necessitated by the size of investment in staple extraction, but the fluctuating prices characteristic of international commodity markets. Foreign control of the strategic, non-renewable oil and gas resource, and the political influence associated with that control, has exacerbated inter-regional tensions and has militated against a two-tier price system for Canadian products that could stimulate Canadian manufacturing. (U.S. producers and consumers get Canadian oil from $6 to $9 per barrel below the world price.) On the eve of this conference, the Governor of the Bank of Canada told a House of Commons committee he had no choice but to raise interest rates—now a record 14 per cent—in step with an earlier increase by U.S. banks. Culturally, U.S. books, periodicals, films, television sit-coms and musical entertainers so dominate Canadian stores, libraries, radio and television stations, and theatres that many Canadians recognize U.S. authors and entertainers more readily than our own. At last year's hearings on the renewal of the CBC's radio and television license, a commissioner of the CRTC, the national regulating agency, asked CBC President Al Johnson: "Do you really believe, Mr. Johnson, that the average citizen in this country really wants to be a Canadian?" Johnson, to his credit, answered in the affirmative,[18] but the question illustrates the extent to which "English-Canadian" has become a minority culture. Politically, the federal Liberals were long able to govern Canada by adroitly mediating between popular and nationally articulated needs and aspirations and American state monopoly capital,[19] but as that task has become increasingly difficult, if not impossible, they were defeated in May. The Clark government threatens to dismantle even more of the institutions which Canadians have tried to manage for their benefit as a national community.

In sport, the styles of play, norms of behavior and team loyalties which once combined to enunciate a national sense of identity have now become coopted by the very forces that seek to undermine it. Consider the case of hockey, the game Al Purdy once called "the Canadian specific" and Ralph Allen, "the national religion." In 1926, Conn Smythe purchased the Toronto St. Pats from a syndicate of mining entrepreneurs headed by J. P. Bickell. Smythe had heard that Bickell's group was planning to sell the team to a partnership in Philadelphia for $200,000. He raised $160,000 and approached Bickell. "How can you, a group of loyal Canadians, sell the team to the United States?" he is alleged to have asked Bickell. Smythe got the team for $160,000. Renamed the Toronto Maple Leafs, the team quickly became a highly visible symbol for English-speaking Canada. During the 1930s, its games—against Quebec's national team, Les Canadiens, and representative teams from several U.S. cities—were broadcast live on the growing national radio network, and as a result of this, shrewd public relations, and the ruthless buying and selling of players, the Leafs gradually replaced prominent local and regional teams in the loyalties of English-speaking Canadians. During one playoff game against Detroit, Hockey Night in Canada is said to have drawn more than 6 million listeners, almost three quarters of the entire English-speaking population.

But the Leafs not only created new national loyalties, particularly in the estranged prairie provinces, the team also encouraged beliefs which would ultimately undo the sense of national identity it had created. The commodity market in players, which it visibly engaged in and celebrated during the radio intermissions on the Hot Stove Lounge, seriously compromised the community loyalty that could be developed by representative teams. Athletes and spectators were still expected to go all out for "their" team, but if its composition could be arbitrarily changed and local players replaced by players from another region—or today, from another continent—it suggested that the community didn't really have much to boast or care about. If the majority of players could only find playing jobs across the border—with the result that local fans transferred their loyalties to New York, Chicago, Detroit and Boston—the national symbolism expressed by hockey was further divided. Leaf operations undercut the sense of national community in further ways. Its hockey broadcasts were sponsored by Imperial Oil—one of the most successful early attempts to give imperialism a Canadian face—and the mass audiences they created provided markets for a string of American radio shows, from the racist Amos and Andy to the progressive Mercury Theatre of Orson Welles. The state played a not unimportant role in this process—the creation of the CBC and the abdication of editorial control of Hockey Night in Canada to McLaren's Advertising gave the national radio network to commercial hockey in the 1930s. During World War II the exemptions it provided individual hockey players and teams travelling across the border kept the NHL in operation while its competitors in the Canadian Amateur Hockey Association (CAHA) were forced to fold. By the war's end, with its influence and economic power, the NHL was able to reduce the CAHA to what Gordon Juckes called the "Gold Coast slave farm of hockey," with the control of rules, revenues, style of play, player development, and even the national team entered in international tournaments firmly in its hands.[20]

Two aspects of this process warrant emphasis. In his ideology history of advertising in the 1920s, *Captains of Consciousness*, Stuart Ewan shows how young people were systematically singled out as advertising targets in the attempt to transform them into models—teachers—for the new patterns of consumption. For those who believe the ruling class doesn't have an explicit strategy for social control, the book provides powerful evidence to the contrary.[21] The extent to which the NHL had a consciously ideological marketing strategy still must be determined, but the player cards, team sweaters, special bank accounts and other widely advertised souvenirs all contributed to the weakening of a national sense in hockey-playing youth. Long before multi-national brand logos became a popular decoration on clothes—another indication of the extent to which western peoples have internalized their role as commodities—generations of Canadian boys grew up wearing (and never taking off) sweaters celebrating the cities of another country, while living in ignorance of their own. Secondly, while these processes were shaped in step with similar changes—the continuing penetration of U.S. capital and the concomitant shift in exports from east-west to north-south—they did not simply mirror or reflect these other changes, they interacted with them with a force of their own. They reinforced each other, *together* accelerating the disintegration of the beliefs and practices which had once supported and nurtured autonomous Canadian institutions.

Of course, explanation lies neither in U.S. expansion nor national betrayal, but in the dynamics of capital. Once sport became a sphere of commodity production, a process supported from the very beginning by the state, then it was almost inevitable that the best Canadian hockey would be controlled by the richest and most powerful aggregates of capital and sold in the richer and more populous markets of the U.S. The disappearance of community control over Canadian hockey strengthened a much larger process—the centralization of all popular forms of culture.

The case of Canadian football is distinctly different, but the ultimate impact very similar. Its early development—the articulation and continuous amendment of rules, the design and redesign of strategies and plays, equipment—was largely in the hands of the southern Ontario and English-speaking Montreal professional classes, centered around the universities and private clubs. But when its adherents tried to transform it into a national game with uniform rules from coast to coast, it became the object of long and bitter intersectional disputes, in the course of which the western representatives, always aided by one or two eastern mavericks, were successful in streamlining the rules in ways which encouraged teams to bring in Americans who had played under similar rules.[22] The first athletic director and director of the School of Physical and Health Education at the University of Toronto, for example, came to Toronto after one such rule change permitted the forward pass. In the warmup of his first home game, Stevens threw the first forward pass ever seen in Toronto. The crowd gave him a standing ovation and when he retired his fame was such he was immediately hired by the university. When postwar incomes permitted the full professionalization of the game and rational-instrumental norms replaced community ties, the Americanization became explicit: seasoned U.S. pros, whose only advantage over their Canadian counterparts was that they had previously played on a full-time basis, were hired in increasing numbers. When team management became almost universally American a decade later, the belief developed and spread that Canadians were naturally inferior. When Russ Jackson retired, the Roughriders announced they would have to look for a replacement in the States, despite the fact that Jackson played his college football at one of the weakest teams in Canada. The CFL now has a rule—not challenged in the recent Jamie Bone appeal before the Ontario Human Rights Commission—which penalizes a team with a Canadian quarterback. The so-called national championship Grey Cup is proudly proclaimed by its sponsors as a vehicle for Canadian unity, but the claim is vitiated by the lowly status of Canadian players,[23] and its dependence upon and subordination to U.S. commercial football.[24] There has never been a truly national English-Canadian game of football, played on the same basis from coast to coast, directed and controlled by Canadians.[25] Although the Canadian Amateur Football Aassociation has begun to fight for greater autonomy—it no longer uses the CFL rulebook, for instance—financially, and ideologically, the commercial league effectively controls the game. In every way, it undermines the belief in Canadian independence.

During the last decade, U.S. dominated commercial sport has expanded further into Canada, assisted increasingly by the state. Liquor interests in Montreal and Toronto have brought U.S. baseball franchises to their respective cities, greatly encouraged by federal tax laws, heavily subsidized municipal stadia, and CBC broadcasts. The entrepreneurs enjoy the free advertising from the spillover of the U.S. media, and they also benefit from the development of another symbol for their beverages which can circumvent provincial restrictions on alcohol advertising. In 1974, the federal government did step in to stop the expansion of the now defunct World Football League into Toronto—"We know what 'world' means," Toronto Alderman Karl Jaffary said at the time—but the bill in question (which died after second reading when the election was called) neither changed the structure of the CFL, despite the promise to lower entry requirements for teams in other Canadian cities, nor prevented dumping of NFL telecasts by the CBC.[26]

But while the Canadian state has unwittingly assisted the process of cultural disintegration in those sports which have been heavily commercialized, it has attempted to foster the Olympic sports as a symbol for national unity, defined by and equated to the pan-Canadian state. Although the federal government began making financial contributions to national teams in 1920, Mackenzie King told the House of Commons in 1936 that Canadian athletic teams should not be considered as representative of government.[27] This was during the all-too-brief period when Canadian political institutions were not subordinate in any significant way to those of the United Kingdom or the U.S. At the same time, dominated international hockey with ridiculous ease, enjoying what seemed almost to be an advantage of natural selection (in the same way the Finns dominated distance running and javelin throwing during this period, the English, soccer.) But Canadian international hockey supremacy came to an end in 1954, the result of Soviet sport science and the depletions of senior hockey by the war and the NHL. In sports like track and field and swimming, where Canadians had competed successfully in the interwar years, they were now falling further and further behind. The war and its sovereignty-ending defense production agreement with the U.S., the spread of American television and the invasion of a new wave of U.S.

branch plants all contributed to another crisis of Canadian identity. In sport, the Diefenbaker Government's Fitness and Amateur Sport Act was in part a response.

But the Conservatives' FAS Directorate not only provided a new source of funds for the national teams fielded by the volunteer amateur sports governing bodies, it also attempted to stimulate local sport participation and non-competitive fitness and recreation, through a program of shared-cost provincial grants. It continued to leave the responsibility for the success of national teams in the hands of the sports governing bodies. It was only with the return of the Liberals and the ascension of Pierre Trudeau in 1968 that international success in sport—as an explicit means of strengthening national unity—became stated state policy. With John Munro at the helm, provincial programs were terminated, non-competitive programs sharply curtailed, and the level of spending for what came to be known as "elite" sport dramatically increased. Although Ottawa did not intend that Montreal should stage the Olympic Games, after the award was announced it made a significant contribution to both operating and construction costs and stepped up its assistance to national teams. The sports governing bodies were nominally still in charge, but Sport Canada increasingly assumed direction and control, to the point that on the eve of the 1978 Commonwealth Games, the responsible minister, Iona Campagnolo, announced detailed medal quotas for Canadian athletes.[28] Few steps were omitted that would enhance performance, or the desired image of national success. Last year, Sport Canada subsidized the salaries of at least two journalists to file regular reports to the Canadian media on Canadian performances abroad.[29] The latest scheme, an official told a Toronto conference last spring, is to subsidize the efforts of the national associations in those sports where success depends upon subjective judging to pack technical committees and lobby for favorable judges.[30] The success of these measures was demonstrated by Canadian successes at the Edmonton Games, several of which were accompanied by ardent flag-waving and nationalist cheering of a type never seen before among members of a Canadian team.

It is my contention that the state's assumption of the direction of these national teams can best be explained in relation to the crisis of legitimacy which has faced it, the federal Liberal party and the loose alliance of indigenous and multi-national capital which supported it, since the mid-1960s. The Quiet Revolution in Quebec had unleashed a nationalist sentiment so powerful that a political party would subsequently be formed, committed—not to a restructuring of the pan-Canadian state along the lines of *deux nations*—but to a distinct Quebec state. In English-speaking

Canada, the expansion of American imperialism into even more areas of human existence, the simultaneous erosion of Canadian autonomy, the stimulus of Quebec nationalism and the youth radicalization of the 1960s all gave impetus to a new surge of English-speaking Canadian nationalism. This movement was divided in several key ways, but it served to pressure the federal state in both economic and cultural policy areas. Finally, the growing industrialization, unemployment, and regional disparity of the 1970s, all in large part the result of the vulnerability of the Canadian economy to the multi-nationals, aggravated class tensions.

In this situation, the Liberals adopted as one solution a long-standing proposal by many in the sports community: greater state assistance for national teams. Other factors contributed, to be sure. The support of national teams was also linked to the staging of international games—the Pan Ams in Winnipeg in 1967, the Olympics in 1976, the Commonwealth Games in 1978—facility construction for which provided an important means of capital accumulation for the construction industry, some short-term employment for construction workers. In fact, the prospects for capital accumulation and corporate legitimacy were so great at the Olympic Games that major multi-nations like GM and Esso, as well as the large Canadian-controlled companies, "contributed" in one way or the other to the Games. When a group of Canadian athletes threatened to boycott the Games if their demands for increased living allowances were not met, the Canadian Olympic Association paid the requested grants, not, in the opinion of the program administrator, because national pride was at stake, but because the adverse publicity was hurting Olympic-related sales.[31] In 1978, the COA, now financed by a trust representing both foreign and domestic capital—proposed that donations to national teams be given tax exemptions at a rate of 125 per cent.[32]

But the success of the Liberals' attempt to solve national, economic, political and cultural discontents by accentuating the role of sport as a symbol of "One Canada" was comprised by the same forces that led it to do so in the first place. The success at events like the Edmonton Games was more than matched by their repeated failure, in the face of continuous NHL opposition, to develop an adequate national hockey team. In the 1960s, the CAHA had tried to develop such a team, but after mixed results, Fitness and Amateur Sport joined with the NHL to kill it. Future national teams became the property of the state-NHL partnership, Hockey Canada. It was only Paul Henderson's last-minute goal which saved Pierre Trudeau from the ignominy of the "goat's" role in the first Canada-Soviet series. Trudeau had been powerless to stop the NHL from banning four WHA players, including Bob Hull, from Team Canada.

The effort to make sport a symbol of national vitality has also been compromised by the use of publicly funded Games facilities for U.S.-dominated commercial sport (and not local athletes), its increasing reliance upon multi-national sponsors like Imperial Oil, its inability to fund fully those athletes who are now competing at the International level (so that the Edmonton successes will not be repeated in Moscow), and its outright refusal to redress any of the great inequalities of income and opportunity that divide the Canadian sport "community." With the election of a new government, the future of Sport Canada is up in the air. If further cutbacks are imposed, perhaps in the name of reducing elitism, even this short-lived attempt to provide a focal point for Canadian identity will disappear.

There is much to add to what I have sketched in here. The mechanisms of cultural disintegration in sport must be studied in greater detail. Take the U.S. athletic scholarship: Why do some athletes head south unquestioningly, while others pay their way to study in Canada? What backgrounds do they come from? What considerations are foremost in their minds? What is the result of this experience on their subsequent behavior? If they return to Canada, do they lobby for similar opportunities in Canada, or do they become part of the conduit for Canadian athletes to U.S. colleges? Answers to these and similar questions would enrich our understanding of the process.

It would also be useful to consider the interactions between forms of sport and other categories at key moments in Canadian history. Rick Salutin, in his award-winning play *Les Canadiens,* has suggested that the hockey team sustained the hopes and combativeness of Quebec nationalism during many long and hopeless periods, only to evaporate as a cultural symbol the night *le Parti québécois* won the election. Nick auf der Maur has often said that the Québécois press coverage of the Canada-Soviet hockey series differs markedly from that published in the English-language press. These suggestions merit more careful study and similar questions should be investigated for English-speaking Canada. What role have forms of sport played in strengthening English-Canadian hegemony over Quebec?

The programatic response is difficult. In the first place, nationalism can be a reactionary force, even in a dependent country, if, as in the Liberals' version, it encourages the continued denial of the rights of self-determination to subordinate national minorities, and masks the systematic underdevelopment of local sports organizations. There is "no way" a team of foreign players like the Expos can represent a sports community like that in Montreal, especially when the public funds poured into the stadium in which they play could have been used much more effectively by local athletes. Secondly, although nationalists of all stripes have looked to the Canadian state for assistance—and with some success, I might add—that path is fraught with booby traps. As a life-long lobbyist for increased state funds for sport, I am embarrassed to see the extent to which Canadian teams have manipulated to carry the message of "One-Canada," and to which athletes, now underpaid state workers, are less and less the subjects of their own activity, but increasingly the raw material for a vast scientific cadre of coaches, doctors, psychologists and bureaucrats.

The problem is that strategies for the democratic control of Canadian sport cannot be posed solely in terms of nationalism, for classes as well as peoples are oppressed, and increasingly the state plays an active role in the process. Strategies for change must therefore address all of these contradictions, not just one of them. It means that the struggle for the Canadianization of the NHL must be linked with the struggle for social ownership of the game and a measure of player control. Struggles in sport must be linked to other struggles in the community (as several athletes in the pre-Olympic period linked their demands for improved opportunities to specific struggles in the city of Montreal and a more generalized campaign for better public fitness and recreation programs everywhere[33]). The task of defining a strategy of this complexity is difficult, but not impossible. All of these concerns are linked by a common desire for individual and collective autonomy or self-control.

NOTES

1. In the years immediately following Confederation, when the idea of the Indian as "noble savage" still held many adherents, the native athlete faced two contradictory forms of racism: either he was considered a "natural" and therefore provided unfair competition or he was "inferior" and not worthy to play with whites. Both ideas led to his exclusion. Bruce Kidd, *Tom Longboat* (Toronto: Fitzhenry and Whiteside, 1980.)

2. "I know it's crazy, but I felt guilty during the five weeks of intensive training I took, even though it helped me immensely," national discus champion Carol Martin told this writer a year before the 1976 Olympics. "Amateurism Dies Hard," *Weekend*, July 19, 1975.

3. See the *Proceedings of the Queen's Symposium on Sport, Culture and the Modern State*, Kingston, Ont.: The Sport Studies Research Group, Queen's University, forthcoming 1980.

4. Stanley B. Ryerson, *Unequal Union* (New York: International Publishers, 1968), p. 23.

5. This brilliant film is no longer in distribution, but a copy of Barthes' commentary, dated September 8, 1961, is available from the NFB.

6. Frank Cosentino, "Ned Hanlan—A Case Study in 19th Century Professionalism: *Canadian Journal of History of Sport and Physical Education,* V (2), 1974.

7. *The Globe,* Jan. 22, 1909.

8. *Toronto Daily Star,* April 20, 1907. Prior to the 1908 Olympics, the secretary of the Amateur Athletic Federation of Canada, one of the rival sports federations, travelled to London to support the American AAU's charge that Longboat was a professional and therefore ineligible to compete. This "treasonous" action angered so many of its own supporters that it soon was forced to disband, leaving the Amateur Athletic Union of Canada as the sole multi-sport governing body.

9. Kevin Jones, "The Effects of the First World War on Canadian Sport," *Proceedings* of the Second World Symposium on the History of Sport and Physical Education, Banff, May 31-June 3, 1971.

10. For the best summary of state assistance to sport, see Eric Broom and Richard Baka, *Canadian Governments and Sport* (Calgary: CAHPER, 1979.)

11. E.g., Harry G. Johnson, *The Canadian Quandry* (Toronto: McClelland and Stewart, 1977); Eric Hobsbawn, "On 'The Break-up of Britain'", *New Left Review,* 105, 1977.

12. E.g., Alex Natan, "Politics and Sport" in Natan (ed.), *Sport and Society* (London: Bowes and Bowes, 1958). Jean-Marie Brohm, *Sport: A Prison of Measured Time* (London: Ink Links, 1978).

13. Richard S. Gruneau, "Power and Play in Canadian Social Development," *Working Papers in the Sociological Study of Sports and Leisure,* vol. 2, no. 1, Kingston, Ont.: The Sport Studies Research Group, Queen's University, 1979.

14. C. L. R. James, *Beyond a Boundary* (Kingston, Jamaica: Hutchinson, 1963).

15. John Hargreaves, "Sport and Hegemony," *Proceedings of the Queen's Symposium on Sport, Culture and the Modern State,* Kingston, Ont.: The Sport Research Group, Queen's University, forthcoming 1980.

16. Robert Beamish, "Sport and the Logic of Capitalism," *Proceedings of the Queen's Symposium on Sport, Culture and the Modern State,* Kingston, Ont.: The Sport Studies Research Group, Queen's University, forthcoming 1980.

17. In Canada, the process has variously been described as "continentalization," "colonization," "Americanization" and "disintegration." Although each of these terms contains a measure of accuracy, I much prefer the latter. "Continentalization" obscures the unequal power relations that have developed, while "colonization" seems to ignore the fact that the Canadian state retains at least the form of independent political institutions. "Americanization" obscures the essential role that capital has played in the process.

18. Joyce Nelson, "The Global Pillage," *This Magazine* 13 (2), 1979, p. 32.

19. James Laxer and Robert Laxer, *The Liberal Idea of Canada* (Toronto: Lorimer, 1977).

20. Bruce Kidd and John Macfarlane, *The Death of Hockey* (Toronto: New Press, 1972).

21. Stuart Ewen, *Captains of Consciousness* (New York: McGraw-Hill, 1976).

22. Frank Cosentino, *Canadian Football* (Toronto: Musson, 1969).

23. Donald W. Ball, "Ascription and Position: A Comparison of 'Stacking' in Professional Football," in Gruneau and Albinson, *Canadian Sport: Sociological Perspectives* (Don Mills: Addison Wesley, 1976).

24. Bruce Kidd, "The Continentalization of Canadian Sport: Football," *Canadian Dimension* 6 (2), 1969.

25. Even in the host city, significant class differences in "Grey Cup behavior" have been observed. See Alan Lystiak, " 'Legitimate Deviance' and Social Class: Bar Behavior During Grey Cup Week," in Gruneau and Albinson, *op. cit.*

26. Both public and private media have played a key role in educating Canadians about the relative importance of U.S. sport and the insignificance of Canadian sport, as a glance at any newspaper or sports telecast will show. The prevalence of this kind of coverage is best explained by the active ideological and financial partnership between the media and commercial sport. See Bruce Kidd, *The Political Economy of Sport* (Calgary: CAPHER, 1979), pp. 32 and 40-49.

27. Canada, House of Commons *Debates,* Feb. 13, 1936.

28. *The Globe and Mail,* Aug. 5, 1978.

29. Personal communication from Abby Hoffman.

30. Marion Lay, "The Role of Sport in International Relations," presentation to the International Studies Association, Toronto, March 21, 1979.

31. Personal communication from Abby Hoffman.

32. Canadian Olympic Association, *Toward a national policy on amateur sport* (Montreal: COA, 1978).

33. Bruce Kidd, "Canadian athletes should support the Olympic Games and help defeat Jean Drapeau," *Canadian Dimension* 9 (4), 1973 and "Olympics '76," *Canadian Dimension,* 11 (5), 1976.